IB DIPLOMA PROGRAM

History of Europe and the Middle East

COURSE COMPANION

Mariam Habibi

Peyman Jafari

Richard Jones-Nerzic

David Keys

David Smith

OXFORD

OXFORD
UNIVERSITY PRESS

Great Clarendon Street, Oxford OX2 6DP

Oxford University Press is a department of the University of Oxford.
It furthers the University's objective of excellence in research, scholarship,
and education by publishing worldwide in

Oxford   New York

Auckland   Cape Town   Dar es Salaam   Hong Kong   Karachi
Kuala Lumpur   Madrid   Melbourne   Mexico City   Nairobi
New Delhi   Shanghai   Taipei   Toronto

With offices in

Argentina   Austria   Brazil   Chile   Czech Republic   France   Greece
Guatemala   Hungary   Italy   Japan   South Korea   Poland   Portugal
Singapore   Switzerland   Thailand   Turkey   Ukraine   Vietnam

Oxford is a registered trade mark of Oxford University Press
in the UK and in certain other countries

British Library Cataloguing in Publication Data

Data available

ISBN 9780199180776

10 9 8 7 6 5 4 3 2 1

Printed in Great Britain by Bell and Bain Ltd., Glasgow

Paper used in the production of this book is a natural, recyclable product
made from wood grown in sustainable forests. The manufacturing process
conforms to the environmental regulations of the country of origin.

Acknowledgements

The publisher would like to thank the following for permission to repro-
duce photographs

P4: Kean Collection/Getty Images; **P6**: The Bridgeman Art Library/
Photolibrary; **P12t**: MPI/Getty Images; **P12m**: Apic/Getty Images; **P17**:
The Print Collector/Photolibrary; **P19bl**: Marek Slusarczyk/Dreamstime.
com; **P19br**: Walter G Allgower/Photolibrary; **P20**: Bettmann/Corbis; **P26**:
Classic Image/Alamy; **P27**: Getty Images; **P28**: Bettmann/Corbis; **P29t**: Apic/
Getty Images; **P29b**: Hulton Archive/Getty Images; **P31**: The Bridgeman
Art Library/Photolibrary; **P32**: Hulton Archive/Getty Images; **P36**: General
Bonaparte in Egypt, from 'A Collection of Works of Jean-Leon Gerome in
100 Photogravures', 1881 (photogravure) (see also 183490), Gerome, Jean
Leon (1824-1904) (after) / © Dahesh Museum of Art, New York, USA / The
Bridgeman Art Library; **P37**: Hulton Archive/Getty Images; **P38**: Hulton
Archive/Getty Images; **P53t**: And there's no help for it, plate 15 of 'The
Disasters of War', 1810-14, pub. 1863 (etching), Goya y Lucientes, Francisco
Jose de (1746-1828) / Private Collection / Index / The Bridgeman Art Library;
p53b: 193-0082186 And they are like wild beasts, plate 5 of 'The Disasters
of War', 1810-14, pub. 1863 (etching), Goya y Lucientes, Francisco Jose de
(1746-1828) / Private Collection / Index / The Bridgeman Art Library; **P54
& 69**: North Wind Picture Archives/Alamy; **P73**: akg-images/ullstein bild;
P79: Imagno/Hulton Archive/Getty Images; **P82**: Imagno/Hulton Archive/
Getty Images; **P83m**: Disderi/Corbis; **P83b**: John Sartain/Bettmann/Corbis;
P90: The Print Collector/Photolibrary; **P92**: akg images; **p97**: Classic Im-
age/Alamy; **P100, 103, 105, 110, 112**: akg images; **P113t**: Wagner als
Generalissimus / Karik.1870/akg-images; **p113b**: akg-images; **P122**: akg-
images; **P125 & 126**: Time & Life Pictures/Getty Images; **P139 & 140**:
akg-images; **P144**: Nadar/Hulton Archive/Getty Images; P145: Apic/Hulton
Archive/Getty Images; **P146**: akg-images; **P151**: Hulton Archive/Getty
Images; **P154**: akg/North Wind Picture Archives; **P164m**: Mary Evans Pic-
ture Library/Photolibrary; **P164b**: Cartoonstock.com; **P166**: London
Stereoscopic Company/Getty Images; **P167**: Liverpool Record Office; **P168**:
Topical Press Agency/Hulton Archive/Getty Images; **P169**: akg images;
P179: © The British Library Board. Add. 41178, f.3; **P182**: Armenian
National Institute; **P184**: Hulton Archive/Getty Images; **P191**: OUP to pro-
vide; **P198**: Bettmann/Corbis; **P199**: Imagno/Hulton Archive/Getty Images;
P203ml: United Kingdom Government; **P203mr**: United Kingdom Govern-
ment; **P203bl**: United Kingdom Government; **P203br**: Tobias Zywietz;
P204: Bettmann/Corbis; **P205**: The Irgun; **P206**: Henryk Thomasz Kaiser/
Photolibrary; **P212**: James Pringle/AP Photo; **P214bl**: Hulton-Deutsch
Collection/Corbis; **P214br**: AFP; **P217**: Central Press/Getty Images; **P220**:
Hulton Archive/Getty Images; **P226**: akg-images; **P227**: Evening Standard/
British Cartoon Archive, University of Kent; **P230**: Bettmann/Corbis; **P239**:
General Photographic Agency/Hulton Archive/Getty Images; **P249**: Mary
Evans Picture Library; **P251**: Time Life Pictures/US Army/Getty Images;
P256: Jose Fuste Raga/Photolibrary; **P261**: Hulton-Deutsch Collection/
Corbis; **P265**: Pictorial Parade/Hulton Archive/Getty Images; **P269**: Time
Life Pictures/US Army/Getty Images; **P274**: The Audiovisual Library of the
European Commission; **P280**: Bettmann/Corbis; **P281t**: Randall Bytwerk;
P281b: Mary Evans Picture Library; **P283**: Jose Luis Saenz de Heredia for
Chapalo Films; **P285**: Real Madrid/Getty Images; **P288**: Bettmann/Corbis;
P294: Sahm Doherty/Time Life Pictures/Getty Images; **P295**: Keystone/
Getty Images; **P296**: Kurt Rohwedder/BPK; **P299**: Picture-Alliance/Ber-
liner_Kurier!; **P302**: Carlos Alvarez/Getty Images; **P303**: Jacques Pavlovsky/
Sygma/Corbis; **P305**: Manuel P. Barriopedro/EPA; **P307**: STR New/Reuters;
P309: PixAchi/Shutterstock; **P317**: Henri Bureau/Sygma/Corbis; **P320**:
Intercontinentale/AFP; **P324**: Time & Life Pictures/Getty Images; **P326**:
Getty Images; **P327**: Selwyn Tait/Corbis; **P332**: UPI Pool/AP Photo; **P333**:
Peter Turnley/Corbis; **P349**: Muhammed Muheisen/AP Photo; **P352**: AFP;
P353: AP Photo; **P354**: Saif Dahlah/AFP; **P360l**: AFP/Getty Images; **P360r**:
Bridgit folman film gang/Les films d'ici /Album/akg-images; **P374**: Gabriel
Duval/AFP; **P382**: George Grantham Bain collection/Library of Congress;
P383: David Montgomery/Hulton Archive/Getty Images; **P393**: Brian Rasic/
Rex Features; **P396**: Michel Euler/AP Photo; **P397**: Trinity Mirror/Mirrorpix/
Alamy; **P401**: Martin Jenkinson/Alamy; **P407**: Henri Bureau/Sygma/Corbis;
P410: Shepard Sherbell/Corbis SABA; **P414**: Dave Bartruff/Corbis; **P417**:
Dan Tuffs/Getty Images; **P418**: Getty Images; **P425**: Kaveh Kazemi/Hulton
Archive/Getty Images; **P451t**: Ronald Grant Archive; **P451m**: Christine
Spengler/Sygma/Corbis; **P451b**: Gareth Cattermole/Getty Images.

Course Companion definition

The IB Diploma Programme Course Companions are resource materials designed to provide students with extra support through their two-year course of study. These books will help students gain an understanding of what is expected from the study of an IB Diploma Programme subject.

The Course Companions reflect the philosophy and approach of the IB Diploma Programme and present content in a way that illustrates the purpose and aims of the IB. They encourage a deep understanding of each subject by making connections to wider issues and providing opportunities for critical thinking.

These Course Companions, therefore, may or may not contain all of the curriculum content required in each IB Diploma Programme subject, and so are not designed to be complete and prescriptive textbooks. Each book will try to ensure that areas of curriculum that are unique to the IB or to a new course revision are thoroughly covered. These books mirror the IB philosophy of viewing the curriculum in terms of a whole-course approach; the use of a wide range of resources; international-mindedness; the IB learner profile and the IB Diploma Programme core requirements; theory of knowledge; the extended essay; and creativity, action, service (CAS).

In addition, the Course Companions provide advice and guidance on the specific course assessment requirements and also on academic honesty protocol.

The Course Companions are not designed to be:

- study/revision guides or a one-stop solution for students to pass the subjects
- prescriptive or essential subject textbooks.

IB mission statement

The International Baccalaureate aims to develop inquiring, knowledgable and caring young people who help to create a better and more peaceful world through intercultural understanding and respect.

To this end the IB works with schools, governments and international organizations to develop challenging programmes of international education and rigorous assessment.

These programmes encourage students across the world to become active, compassionate, and lifelong learners who understand that other people, with their differences, can also be right.

The IB learner profile

The aim of all IB programmes is to develop internationally minded people who, recognizing their common humanity and shared guardianship of the planet, help to create a better and more peaceful world. IB learners strive to be:

Inquirers They develop their natural curiosity. They acquire the skills necessary to conduct inquiry and research and show independence in learning. They actively enjoy learning and this love of learning will be sustained throughout their lives.

Knowledgable They explore concepts, ideas, and issues that have local and global significance. In so doing, they acquire in-depth knowledge and develop understanding across a broad and balanced range of disciplines.

Thinkers They exercise initiative in applying thinking skills critically and creatively to recognize and approach complex problems, and make reasoned, ethical decisions.

Communicators They understand and express ideas and information confidently and creatively in more than one language and in a variety of modes of communication. They work effectively and willingly in collaboration with others.

Principled They act with integrity and honesty, with a strong sense of fairness, justice, and respect for the dignity of the individual, groups, and communities. They take responsibility for their own actions and the consequences that accompany them.

Open-minded They understand and appreciate their own cultures and personal histories, and are open to the perspectives, values, and traditions of other individuals and communities. They are accustomed to seeking and evaluating a range of points of view, and are willing to grow from the experience.

Caring They show empathy, compassion, and respect towards the needs and feelings of others. They have a personal commitment to service, and act to make a positive difference to the lives of others and to the environment.

Risk-takers They approach unfamiliar situations and uncertainty with courage and forethought, and have the independence of spirit to explore new roles, ideas, and strategies. They are brave and articulate in defending their beliefs.

Balanced They understand the importance of intellectual, physical, and emotional balance to achieve personal well-being for themselves and others.

Reflective They give thoughtful consideration to their own learning and experience. They are able to assess and understand their strengths and limitations in order to support their learning and personal development.

A note on academic honesty

It is of vital importance to acknowledge and appropriately credit the owners of information when that information is used in your work. After all, owners of ideas (intellectual property) have property rights. To have an authentic piece of work, it must be based on your individual and original ideas with the work of others fully acknowledged. Therefore, all assignments, written or oral, completed for assessment must use your own language and expression. Where sources are used or referred to, whether in the form of direct quotation or paraphrase, such sources must be appropriately acknowledged.

How do I acknowledge the work of others?

The way that you acknowledge that you have used the ideas of other people is through the use of footnotes and bibliographies.

Footnotes (placed at the bottom of a page) or endnotes (placed at the end of a document) are to be provided when you quote or paraphrase from another document, or closely summarize the information provided in another document. You do not need to provide a footnote for information that is part of a "body of knowledge". That is, definitions do not need to be footnoted as they are part of the assumed knowledge.

Bibliographies should include a formal list of the resources that you used in your work. "Formal" means that you should use one of the several accepted forms of presentation. This usually involves separating the resources that you use into different categories (e.g. books, magazines, newspaper articles, Internet-based resources, CDs and works of art) and providing full information as to how a reader or viewer of your work can find the same information. A bibliography is compulsory in the extended essay.

What constitutes malpractice?

Malpractice is behaviour that results in, or may result in, you or any student gaining an unfair advantage in one or more assessment component. Malpractice includes plagiarism and collusion.

Plagiarism is defined as the representation of the ideas or work of another person as your own. The following are some of the ways to avoid plagiarism:

- Words and ideas of another person used to support one's arguments must be acknowledged.
- Passages that are quoted verbatim must be enclosed within quotation marks and acknowledged.
- CD-ROMs, email messages, web sites on the Internet, and any other electronic media must be treated in the same way as books and journals.
- The sources of all photographs, maps, illustrations, computer programs, data, graphs, audio-visual, and similar material must be acknowledged if they are not your own work.
- Works of art, whether music, film, dance, theatre arts, or visual arts, and where the creative use of a part of a work takes place, must be acknowledged.

Collusion is defined as supporting malpractice by another student. This includes:

- allowing your work to be copied or submitted for assessment by another student
- duplicating work for different assessment components and/or diploma requirements.

Other forms of malpractice include any action that gives you an unfair advantage or affects the results of another student. Examples include, taking unauthorized material into an examination room, misconduct during an examination, and falsifying a CAS record.

Contents

Authors

Mariam Habibi is Assistant Professor with the American Graduate School of International Relations and Diplomacy, based in Paris. She is a workshop leader for InThinking, IB Teacher Workshops.

Peyman Jafari is a researcher at the International Institute of Social History in Amsterdam, and is currently a Phd candidate in the University of Amsterdam, Faculty of Social and Behavioural Science.

Richard Jones-Nerzic teaches History at the European School Brussels and runs the website www.internationalschoolhistory.net. He previously taught IB History in France and Slovakia. He is co-ordinator of the European History e-Learning Project (e-Help).

David Keys teaches IB History at the British International School, Bratislava, Slovakia. He has taught History and English in Turkey, Saudi Arabia and the UK and is a translator and writer.

David Smith teaches at the Ecole Lindsay Thurber Comprehensive High School in Alberta, Canada. He is a workshop leader for IB Americas, an examiner, application reader and a faculty member for the Online Curriculum Centre.

Introduction

This book is designed to be a companion to the study of the history of Europe and the Middle East. It follows the International Baccalaureate Diploma Programme history course for first examination in 2010. This volume covers route 2: Higher Level option 5 on aspects of the history of Europe and the Middle East. Written by experienced IB history teachers and examiners, and independent researchers, it contains a wealth of teaching and learning ideas, as well as providing historical background and analysis of the syllabus content.

History is an exploratory subject that encompasses many academic and social disciplines. It encourages an understanding of the present through critical reflection upon the past. The IB Diploma Programme course provides both structure and flexibility, fostering an understanding of major historical events in a global context. It requires you to make comparisons between similar and dissimilar solutions to common human situations, based on political, economic and social circumstances and the interpretation of events as they unfold. Through the study of history you can develop a strong international mindedness recognizing common humanities and you will have a better understanding of the world and of our responsibilities to society.

As Karl Marx wrote in a pamphlet published in 1852 on the events leading up to Louis Bonaparte's *coup d'état* of 2 December 1851, "Men make their own history, but not of their own free will; not under circumstances they themselves have chosen but under given and inherited circumstances with which they are directly confronted." It is these circumstances and the men, women and children who continue to be affected by them that make the study of history both so compelling and so necessary.

The authors of this title hope that this Course Companion will assist students to become effective historians, social analysts and critical thinkers through providing the necessary background to many of the ongoing conflicts, tensions, and critical new developments in today's globalized world. By working through the core subject areas, topics and focus countries covered by this title, students will develop not only a closer understanding of the specific regions and periods in question, but also a greater understanding of historical methodology and models for analysis. In support of this, the Course Companion provides a number of special features:

TOK Links History is an area of knowledge that is an integral part of the IB Diploma Programme Theory of Knowledge (TOK) course. Different areas of knowledge and ways of knowing are examined through selected case studies.

Glossary terms Definitions for key historical concepts and terms are placed in the margins to encourage students to identify and understand any new terminology.

Biographies To give more background detail on selected individuals of relevance to the period being discussed, sample biographies are provided. Students are encouraged to do broader research on the key figures of interest to them.

Activities All chapters contain a wide range of classroom and individual activities to encourage active learning and participation. These activities include class debates, source analysis questions and methodologies, data presentation and statistical analysis, approaches to essay-writing and research.

Discussion points There are many discussion points throughout the text, intended to sum up the main points being covered in each section, and encourage active class discussion. They provide a forum for debate and further research, as well as a means for making connections to broader global issues of interest to students.

Source analysis There is a strong emphasis placed on primary and secondary sources. This underlines the principle that history is not only a study of the past but also the process of interpreting, recording and understanding a topic through analysing its sources to validate knowledge claims.

Exam practice Each chapter contains sample examination questions that are modelled on the type of questions set for examinations.

Recommended further reading Each chapter concludes with suggestions for further reading. This is to encourage a deeper understanding of the topics covered through the latest available research and key texts on the subject area. Students are also encouraged to pursue the many source details provided in the chapters themselves and online archives.

Guidelines for study

Paper 3: Europe and the Middle East

Students and teachers should identify three sections of this option as detailed in the History Guide for in-depth study. The bullet points in the guide indicate topics on which examination questions may be set. In each examination paper two questions will be set from each section. It is therefore important to study material relating to ALL the bullet points in each section. If this is not done, candidates may have a limited choice of questions.

During your course and especially near the examinations make sure you study past examination questions. This will improve your ability to understand the focus of each question and make sure your essays answer the question set.

Identify command terms and typical issues relating to particular historical topics. For example, the administrative reforms of Napoleon Bonaparte are a frequent topic but focus of questions may vary – such as why they happened or how successful they were.

Use the facts to support your argument but make sure you have an argument. Make sure the evidence you select is relevant to the question don't just write down everything you know about the topic. If the question is about the reasons why the Central Powers lost the First World War don't write about the causes.

Examination essays should be a balance of factual knowledge and analytical comment related to the focus of the question. For example if there is a question on Bismarck's foreign policy aims you should identify the aims and then indicate how each foreign policy decision contributes to the achievement of those aims.

Study the mark bands that examiners have to use and you will see that essays which consist of relevant factual material only (however detailed and accurate) will only reach a middle range mark. This is also true for essays which show an understanding of the question and focus on issues but which are not supported by evidence.

When you get your question paper in the examination, use the reading time to do two things:

1 Identify the questions, which relate to the sections of the guide you have studied.
2 Read the questions carefully to make sure you understand what the question is asking you to do. If the question has two parts then make sure you know enough about both parts to write a full answer before attempting to answer it. This is particularly important for "cause and consequence" type questions or for a request to "compare and contrast".

When writing your answers make sure your analysis is referring back to the question. Have a separate paragraph for each issue you wish to consider–a BRIEF plan or a list of buzzwords may help here. Your concluding paragraph should sum up your argument and reach a judgement. Don't be afraid to challenge the question as long as you have presented evidence which supports your views.

Watch the clock. Time yourself so that all three essays have an equal amount of time spent on them. If you begin to run out of time write brief notes to demonstrate your knowledge of the evidence and the conclusions you have reached.

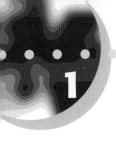

1 The French Revolution and Napoleon

By the beginning of the 21st century, the word **revolution** is used to connote all manner of events, movements, and products. There are revolutions in music, athletics, painting, technology, and literature. Running shoes, computer games, television shows and guitarists can be revolutionary. In light of such wide and varied usage we need to come to a common understanding of the definition so that we can better analyse the events of the two decades that straddled the turn of the 19th century. We will talk of revolution as a process of relatively rapid change—change in political structure, social organization. Many revolutions revolve around competing ideologies or world views. Vital to this is the notion of revolution as a process rather than an event. By looking at the French Revolution as a process, we can identify characteristics common to socio-political revolution that will then help us analyse and understand other revolutions.

While we examine the complex developments that swept over Europe in the period from the mid-18th century to 1815 we will keep a weather eye to the great historic processes of concern to all historians—continuity and change; and cause and effect.

> **Revolution** A process of relatively rapid societal change.

By the end of this chapter, students should be able to:

- understand the political, social, and economic causes of the French Revolution
- demonstrate an understanding of the progress of the Revolution through this period
- evaluate the international impact of the Revolution and Napoleonic period
- analyse the rise of Napoleon
- assess both the foreign and domestic policy of Napoleonic France
- explain the political, social, and economic effects of the French Revolution and Napoleonic Empire.

Origins: challenges posed and unmet

Intellectual challenges

"I saw that everything depended fundamentally on politics, and that, no people could ever be anything but what the nature of its government made it." Lynn Hunt, quoting Jean Jacques Rousseau, used these words in the opening to her study on the French Revolution to describe the novelty of the situation of France in the mid-18th century. When Rousseau wrote them, he was suggesting what would go on to become a central tenet of the French

Revolution, that there was a very direct relationship between a government and the people it ruled—that politics was central to the everyday life of all citizens.

Hobbes and Locke

Rousseau was one of a number of important thinkers that were turning their considerable intellects to what they saw as a central question of the 18th century—who should rule? A century before the *Bastille* fell in Paris, however, two English philosophers were grappling with this very question, arriving at two very different conclusions. Thomas Hobbes and John Locke shared a conviction that the **legitimacy** of any form of government had to be justified through rational thought and not, as it had in the past, by resort to theology or tradition. It was not enough for a government to claim that its right to rule rested on the will of God or the simple fact that it had always been thus. The proper form of government could be reasoned, according to Hobbes and Locke, and this very reasoning was the foundation of the right to rule.

In the study of history, as in much of life, context is vital to understanding cause and effect. Hobbes developed much of his political thinking during the English Civil War of the 1640s. This period of destruction and instability had a profound effect on Hobbes's view of human nature and consequently what he believed the proper form of government should be. His rather low opinion of human beings and what he saw as a constant competitive struggle for survival in nature led him to the conclusion that a strong absolutist form of government was the best defence against the great beast of civil unrest. In this conception, humans would give up their individual rights to the absolute ruler in return for the stability provided by this ruler. This transaction, according to Hobbes, was a one-time affair. Once people gave up their rights, their fate, for good or ill, was in the hands of the ruler. In practical terms, this meant that citizens had no right to rebel regardless of the actions of the government. For Hobbes, absolutism was not the end in itself, but rather a means to an end—and this end was civil peace and concord.

John Locke, starting from an alternative view of human nature, arrived at a very different conclusion as to the nature of government. While Hobbes believed that humans in a **state of nature** were in a state of perpetual conflict, Locke saw humans as reasonable and peaceful, naturally inclined to co-operate in the best interests of society. According to Locke, humans in this state of nature had certain **inalienable rights** by virtue of the fact that they were human. As a keen proponent of the human capacity to learn, Locke trusted that humans had the capacity for self-government, the primary duty of which was to protect the life, liberty, and property of the governed. The relationship between the government and the governed was one of mutual obligation and responsibility. What would happen should the government fail in this duty? Locke advocated that citizens had the right to change this government, peacefully or otherwise, should it fail to protect their life, liberty or property. They had the right to rebel.

Legitimacy is the characteristic of government that has the support of those whom it rules. It is the belief, by the ruled, that the government is the rightful ruler.

A **state of nature** is the theoretical state of humans in the absence of organized society. This is the starting point from which many Enlightenment thinkers tried to determine the ideal form of government. It is closely related to "human nature".

Inalienable rights are those personal rights that accrue to people by virtue of the fact that they are alive. These are rights conferred by nature and cannot be taken away. Exactly what these rights are is a matter for debate.

Because of the different conclusions that they each reached, the ideas of Hobbes and Locke were seized upon by opposing sides in a number of political conflicts during their lifetimes and in the years after they died. The language and visions of Locke pervade the founding documents of the United States. The logic, if not the deeper motives and principles, of Hobbes has been invoked to rationalize state power into the 20th and 21st centuries.

While they embarked on their enquiry from different premises which, in turn, led them to different conclusions, what they had in common was perhaps more important. Both were convinced that the proper application of human reason could lead to the best form of government without recourse to archaic tradition or arcane theology. Perhaps more importantly, they both conceived of the relationship between the ruler and the ruled as a **social contract**. This **contract theory** approach to political philosophy would dominate discussion in the coffee houses and **salons** of Europe for the century leading up to the French Revolution and help structure the essential debates within the Revolution itself.

Voltaire

Four years after Locke published his seminal work of political philosophy and democratic ideals, *Two Treatises of Government*, in 1689, François-Marie Arouet, known to history by his pen name, Voltaire, was born. Throughout his life, Voltaire would use his pen to mock and skewer ideas and people he believed contemptible and laud and praise those who espoused and lived his ideas of personal freedom. In many ways, Voltaire was a combination of Hobbes and Locke. He believed, as did Locke, in the human ability to learn and the idea that reason should guide all decisions of state. He shared with Hobbes a very low opinion of humans in their natural state, and their inability in this natural state to govern themselves. It was this lack of faith in the uneducated masses, which confirmed Voltaire as a fervent opponent of indiscriminate democracy. Who should rule, but the educated and able, according to Voltaire. So long as they ruled according to Enlightenment principles—progress, freedom of religion, freedom of speech, freedom of thought, organized and rational policy—Voltaire did not care how much power they had. It is in his emphasis on reason and freedom wherein Voltaire's political legacy lay. Institutions such as the Church and the Monarchy whose control, according to Voltaire, was based on superstition, tradition, and force, rather than reason, were archaic and deserved to be swept away or at the very least ridiculed. Voltaire wrote volumes criticizing these institutions. Satire, novels, drama, essays, histories were all tools that Voltaire employed in his assault on the enemies of reason.

> ## Discussion point: The state of nature
>
> *The state of nature has a law of nature to govern it, which obliges every one: and reason, which is that law, teaches all mankind, who will but consult it, that being all equal and independent, no one ought to harm another in his life, health, liberty, or possessions.*
> John Locke, *Second Treatise of Government*, 1690
>
> *During the time men live without a common power to keep them all in awe, they are in that conditions called war; and such a war, as if of every man, against every man.*
> Thomas Hobbes, *Leviathan*, 1651
>
> Both Locke and Hobbes began their inquiry with the state of nature, but their views of human nature were somewhat different.
>
> **Who do you think was more accurate in his estimation of the state of nature? Why?**

A **social contract** is a voluntary agreement by individuals to co-operate in the organization of society.

Contract theory is the theory in political science that organized society rests on an agreement between those who rule and those who are ruled. Accordingly, both ruled and rulers have rights and responsibilities.

Salons were gatherings of individuals in the 17th century in which the current events, ideas, literature, and science were discussed. They were often organized by prominent women and were important forums for the dissemination of new ideas.

Voltaire (1694–1778)

Voltaire was the pen name of François-Marie Arouet a French writer of satire, political treatises, drama, history, philosophies, and novels. He became one of the most important and influential of the Enlightenment thinkers. His fame was such that he was able to live on the proceeds of his writing and the pensions that his reputation garnered him. In terms of his philosophy, he was a champion of personal freedom. This often took the form of satirical works lampooning the Catholic Church and calling for religious freedom. No advocate for democracy, which he believed to be little better than mob rule, Voltaire instead favoured the rule of the able—the Enlightened despot, guided by reason and unencumbered by religious superstition. Frederick the Great of Prussia, with whom he corresponded and resided for a number of years, was as close a model to that despot as Voltaire could find in 18th-century Europe.

Rousseau

If Voltaire was the intellect of the Revolution, Jean Jacques Rousseau was its heart, and like many matters of the heart his contribution was ambiguous, contradictory and fraught with double meaning. He shared a number of ideas regarding the relationship of the individual to the state with Voltaire and John Locke. He believed that humans, by virtue of being human, were imbued with certain inalienable rights. His later writings were based on contract theory. For Rousseau society was based on a social contract among all citizens. But whereas Locke and Hobbes saw this contract as an agreement between the rulers and the ruled, Rousseau saw it as an agreement between the citizens themselves. This civil society was to be ruled not by kings or governments or bureaucracies but rather by an amorphous concept he called the **General Will**. The General Will was the embodiment of the wishes of the people. While this may seem straightforward, the difficulty came in determining what that general will actually was. While a majority vote may be useful, Rousseau did not think it could be the only, or even the main, gauge. The General Will was more the collective good of the whole society—the common interests that united the people. These community interests were to take precedence over individual interests. This vague conceptualization, though popular among many before the Revolution, was to prove fractious and even deadly as the Revolution moved forward. The prime stumbling block was how exactly to determine the General Will, or, more precisely, who spoke for or knew the General Will. Revolutionaries of all political stripes claimed to understand the General Will more completely than their opponents. This ambiguity has helped Rousseau's ideas live long into the 20th century. While 20th century democrats have claimed the system of majority voting in a modern liberal democracy is the most efficient method of determining the General Will, dictators throughout the century have claimed a special knowledge of the General Will, which uniquely positions them to lead the state.

TOK Link

Ways of Knowing— Reason

The watchword for the Enlightenment and many of the developments that flowed from it such as the French Revolution was "Reason". Enlightenment thinkers believed that through the careful application of reason, as opposed to superstition, tradition, bigotry, and intolerance, a more ordered and "natural" society would emerge. This elevation of reason reached its peak in 1793 when radical French Republicans, bent on the de-Christianization of French society, formalized this "reason worship" in the Cult of Reason, complete with festivals and ritual.

What are the strengths and weaknesses of using reason as the sole organizing principle of society? How could other ways of knowing be used to guide society?

The **General Will** was Rousseau's notion of what was good or desirable for a society as determined by the population as a whole and not just individual interests.

Beyond the General Will, Rousseau's spectre floats through the entire revolutionary period. In commenting on the nationalistic aspirations of the Poles, Rousseau presaged the nationalistic aspirations of the French republic. His words would echo in the speeches of major revolutionaries of all parties. Marie Antoinette was an admirer. Rousseau's philosophies shaped Robespierre's thinking. His tomb was an important pilgrimage. His imprecise political conceptions could be seized upon by any number of very different ideologies precisely because they were imprecise. As historians such as Simon Schama and Lynn Hunt have illustrated, perhaps Rousseau's most important contribution to the French Revolution was that he helped provide a language that all the participants of the Revolution could use to express new ideas and programmes.

Social challenges

Every society or group has a structure, an understood organization of society, which places the participants in roles and assigns expectations, influence and power. In some cases this structure is formalized in rules or laws, while in other circumstances it develops on its own. Ranks in the military are officially prescribed while social positions that develop in schools are not officially sanctioned though are no less real for it. Occasionally this phenomenon can lead to two or more competing social structures within one group. In one sense this was the case with pre-revolutionary France. On the one hand there was an official social structure prescribed by law that had existed for centuries. On the other hand, over the first decades of the 18th century the reality of everyday life in France had evolved into a new social order that was in many cases quite different to what it was supposed to be "on paper".

The *ancien régime* in theory and law

The official social structure of France, laid down in law and observed for centuries, was based on a system of feudal obligations. Officially every subject of the French King belonged to one of three official classes, called estates. At the top of this pyramidal social structure was the person and institution of the monarch—the "first gentleman of the realm". On paper the French King was absolute; his will was law. This principle was best illustrated in the practice of *lettre de cachet*—a document signed by the King, which authorized his arbitrary power. This arbitrary power could mean the imprisonment or banishment of a subject—noble or otherwise—the suspension of assemblies, or the registration of new taxes. To its detractors, *lettres de cachet* were the embodiment of despotism, ruling by whim. To proponents of traditional absolutism, they were an earthly expression of **divine right**.

The first estate consisted of the clergy, from the most powerful cardinal or bishop, to the poorest of the parish priests and made up about one per cent of the population. At the top of this estate were the cardinals, bishops and abbots who possessed or controlled most of the churches' wealth. Many of the clergy came from aristocratic families who saw the clergy as an acceptable outlet for sons in excess of what the family fortune could support. As an institution, the Catholic Church controlled or owned up to a tenth of the land in

Discussion point:

Although they may not call it the General Will, throughout the 20th century both democratic and non-democratic governments have claimed to act in the interests of the General Will.

How did the following regimes claim to know the General Will?

- France, 1958
- Germany, 1933
- USSR, 1936

Divine right This is the short form of Divine Right of Kings, the political theory that a monarch's right to rule, his or her legitimacy, is conferred by God. The monarch's will, therefore, becomes closely associated with the will of God.

France. It had powers of taxation, specifically the tithe, a Church tax on agricultural products that could either be collected by individual clergy or by one of the many powerful Church "corporations" such as monasteries. The First Estate enjoyed influence at the highest political level. High-ranking officers of the Church had been appointed to top government positions for centuries. One such example in the years leading up to the Revolution, was the appointment of the Archbishop of Toulouse, Loménie de Brienne as chief minister to Louis XVI.

The roughly 300,000 to 400,000 French subjects who were officially members of the Noble or Second Estate were marked by the official privilege they enjoyed. Indeed, it was "privilege" which was the essential element of the concept of "nobility" in France of the 18th century. Nobles drew their position from their feudal role as the warriors of the realm, *noblesse d'épée*—**Nobility of the Sword**. To these nobles were added, sometime later, a second class of nobility, aristocrats whose nobility derived from promotion to royal administrative positions. These were *la noblesse de robe*—the **Nobility of the Robe**. The privileges they enjoyed were many, from ceremonial distinction in terms of dress and emblems to the very practical exemption from the onerous direct tax called the *taille*. They had a virtual monopoly of high office in the government, army, navy and Church and controlled the provincial assemblies and *parlements*. To these privileges, the French nobility, specifically the rural nobility, could add myriad rights and dues from hunting rights to *banalités*—fees for milling, pressing wine and any number of other agrarian services. They were tried in separate courts and had the right to imprison members of the Third Estate on a whim.

About 98 per cent of the population of France officially belonged to the Third Estate. This included rural peasants, urban wage earners, bankers, lawyers, bureaucrats, and journalists. Officially the main tax burden, the *taille*, fell on the Third Estate. They were also subject to the *tithe*, the *capitation* tax, property tax if they owned property, the *vingtième*, the *banalités*, military service, and any number of indirect taxes on goods such as salt (the *gabelle*).

The *ancien régime* in reality

By the 1780s, however, this social structure though preserved in tradition and even law, looked very different. In practice there were two levels of clergy. The upper clergy in many cases saw the priesthood as but one of a number of sources of income and influence. Talleyrand would hold several lucrative Church positions before he was even ordained to the priesthood. Many of the upper clergy were absentees from their parishes, delegating or even selling the less glamorous local administration of their Church properties. They collected taxes and enjoyed great influence in government and even some at court.

> **Nobility of the Sword** This is the more ancient category of nobility in France and dates from the feudal period when elevation to the aristocracy was through military service.

> **Nobility of the Robe** This category of nobility in France was relatively new and rewarded those who performed administrative service to the crown. Because it did not depend on military service or heredity, it was the category that was open to more Frenchmen and was therefore growing in size.

A FAUT ESPERER Q'EU SE JEU LA FINIRA BENTOT

Il faut esperer que ce jeu finira bientôt (we must hope that things will soon sort themselves out). A popular depiction of French social structure in the period leading up to 1789 was that of the Third Estate supporting the First and Second Estate. To what degree is this an accurate depiction? How might a member of the Second Estate depict the social structure of France under the *ancien régime*?

The lower clergy enjoyed few such privileges. While they ministered to their flock, their position in local society had been diminished by the **secularization** of the Enlightenment. Likewise their income suffered during this period. The tithe had been altered in many parts of France such that it would barely support the local clergy. In these cases the value of the tithe had been transferred to larger Church corporations such as monasteries or bishoprics or even in some cases to non-church interests that would then pay a fixed portion to the local clergy—the *portion congrue*. It was then up to the local clergy to collect the tax from their parishioners. The fixed nature of the *congrue* meant that as the cost of living increased, the material position of the local clergy decreased. The position of parish clergy had deteriorated to such an extent by the 1770s that groups of disaffected priests began to gather in groups to voice their anger. The despotic authority of the upper clergy quickly outlawed such assemblies. In short, power, influence and wealth was unevenly distributed in the state-within-a-state that was the French Catholic Church and, too many, unfairly so.

> **Secularization** The growing emphasis on non-religious ideas in a society.

The reality of the Second Estate during the second half of the 18th century was likewise far more complex than its legal status might suggest. Foremost was the fact that the boundaries between the Estates were permeable. Nobility and the privilege that accompanied it was available to those who could afford it. A number of **venal offices** carried with them the status of nobility and in many cases hereditary nobility. As demand for these offices increased so did the price, limiting all but the wealthiest members of the Third Estate from taking this route to nobility. Another strategy for ennoblement was to ask the Crown to convert the office already held by the aspiring noble into one that conferred nobility. This, of course took money, but was not uncommon in the 18th century. Service to the government was another avenue into the Second Estate. The King would regularly grant **letters patent** to those who had distinguished themselves in the service of France or the person of the King. A number of engineers, writers, scientists, and artists were ennobled in this fashion. In total, historian William Doyle estimates that wealthy members of the Third Estate were making their way into the ranks of nobility at an average rate of two people per day throughout the 18th century. Including their families this adds up to about 45,000 new nobles.

> **Venal offices** were administrative positions within the French government that could be purchased. The purchase of a venal office was one avenue to nobility for those who could afford it.

> **Letters patent** were documents signed by the King that conferred some exclusive right such as a pension or trading monopoly.

The terms Nobility of the Robe and Nobility of the Sword no longer encompassed the vast array of occupations from which the French nobility drew income. A great many nobles participated in commerce from owning mining interests to banking and mercantile trade. Nobles, as a social class, participated in most aspects of the 18th century French economy. They owned land, loaned money, invested in shipping ventures and served in government. In fact, the political influence of the nobility had grown steadily since the death of Louis XIV, who had devoted a great deal of his reign and his country's resources to controlling the nobility. Throughout the reign of Louis XV and Louis XVI, French aristocrats had succeeded in gaining most of this back with interest. The political influence of the nobility came from their basic monopoly of high office, specifically control of the regional *parlements*. *Parlements* were the legal nexus of the realm,

> **Discussion point:**
>
> The French King could recognize distinguished citizens by ennobling them. How are such citizens recognized in your country?

where royal will met the population. As France's highest courts they were an important link in the legislative chain, registering all laws proclaimed by the King. The *parlements* and the 1,200 to 2,200 judges and officials that administered them were alternately seen as champions of the will of the people against autocratic rule or the instrument of that rule. Regardless, from the time of Louis XV the nobility and the *parlements* had been gaining power.

Astounding wealth was not the whole story of the nobility of Louis XVI. In fact, by some estimates, it was not the story for over half of the noble families of France in this period. Many nobles were of only moderate means, and some reduced to utter poverty. Some owned small estates. Others earned a living farming small plots of land. In lifestyle they were little different from their peasant neighbors and in some cases worse off. In many ways, all these nobles had was the theoretical privilege that birth granted them and as such they were determined to protect it.

The reality of the Third Estate also bore little resemblance to the traditional feudal order. As mentioned previously, the boundary between the Second and Third Estate was very permeable. The wealthiest of the Third Estate ennobled themselves by purchasing venal offices or marrying into noble families. Tax exemptions, a great mark of privilege, were freely bought and sold. **Bourgeois** families purchased huge country estates, luxuriating in the physical and social comfort that accompanied them. More and more of the land in France, perhaps a quarter by the Revolution, was owned by the bourgeoisie. The money for this social mobility came from the rapidly expanding commercial revolution of the 18th century. Trading opportunities presented themselves from all over the world. The products and profit from these ventures in turn fed a growing industrial complex. Professional and financial enterprises, such as banking and legal services, grew to meet the demands of these commercial and industrial concerns. The result was a bourgeois class that was growing in number, influence and wealth.

At the other extreme of the Third Estate were the poor, and by all accounts there were many in 18th-century France. By some estimates the poor could number up to one third of the population of the country, perhaps even higher in bad times. A growing population and a rising cost of living, which over the course of the 18th century had outstripped the increase in wages by a factor of 3:1, compounded this problem. The vast majority of the French population were peasants, upwards of 80 per cent, and they owned and worked as small farms about 20 per cent of the land in France. France was a country of small farmers. This agrarian system was therefore susceptible to the vagaries of the small farm —rising input prices and bad weather. Most of these farm families were forced to supplement their income with wage earning propositions at various times during the year. Many of these opportunities were in local towns and cities. Skilled trades in these cities and towns were very difficult to enter, controlled as they were by powerful guilds. The Third Estate itself, then, was a pyramidal shape itself, with the wealthy bourgeoisie at the top slipping into the Second Estate once they had amassed enough wealth and the vast majority of the rural farming poor at the bottom.

> **Discussion point:**
>
> The day-to-day administration of France was an incredibly complex enterprise, requiring the work of countless officials and institutions.
>
> To what extent was Louis XVI an absolute monarch?

The **bourgeoisie** was the social/economic class in French society that was technically part of the Third Estate, but whose members earned their living through business ownership as in merchants and bankers, or a professional occupation such as lawyers. As such they tended to be the wealthiest of the Third Estate.

The truth of the **ancien régime**, then, was considerably different than it looked in law and tradition. It was not as stagnant as it looked. Social mobility, especially between the Third and Second Estate, was well established. Nor were there, simply, three estates. All three estates were subdivided by wealth, power, and influence. The wealthy landowning bourgeois had far more in common with the middling nobility that they did with the peasant farmers of the realm. The lifestyle of indigent nobility resembled the rural poor far more than it did the powerful noble families of Paris. Even the First Estate was a stratified hierarchy not only of formalized rank, but also of power and wealth. The historian R.R. Palmer has thus characterized the social causes of the French Revolution as a collision of two moving objects—a rising aristocracy and a rising bourgeoisie. But we also see a lesser nobility bent on defending the last vestiges of noble privilege and a rural population that was one bad harvest away from rebellion, which made this volatile situation unstable. In any case, the legal social structures of the *ancien régime* no longer corresponded to the reality of power, wealth, and influence distribution in France.

> The **ancien régime** is the term that refers to the structure of French society and its government before the Revolution.

Activity:
Social structure

The social structure has often been visually represented by a triangle depicting the relative size and power of the three estates.

On a large piece of poster board create a diagram that depicts the social structure of your school. The diagram can be any shape and should identify the major social groups within the school, their membership and the relative power they have to each other. Be sure to include the staff and administration of your school. Once you have completed the diagram, present it to the class and explain why you chose the physical representation that you did. How might your depiction differ from how the administration would depict the social structure of the school?

Create a second illustration, this time depict the social structure of your country. What similarities and differences are there between the social structure of the *ancien régime* and your country? The basis for social power within the *ancien régime* was land and hereditary title. What is the basis of social power in your country?

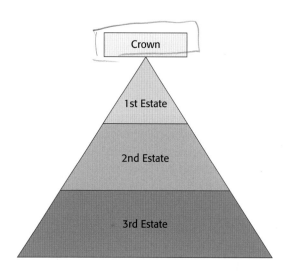

Political challenges

Very simply defined, politics is the process by which groups of people make decisions. In the France of Louis XVI, however, there was nothing simple about it. While in theory, Louis was absolute, his will was law, in reality he depended on a complex system of assemblies, courts, and bureaucracies to translate this will, not only into law, but more crucially into obedience. This is the central issue for all governments, be they democracies, autocracies, theocracies, or oligarchies. How do you cause the ruled to obey the law? Generally, citizens obey for a combination of two motivations—a fear of sanction and a belief in the legitimacy of either the law or the law-making institution. In the years leading up to the Revolution these two elements were achieved through the combination of a belief in the right of the King to rule tempered by the courts, **parlements**, and assemblies, augmented by a fear of arbitrary arrest, the mass enforcement of the army and the more selective enforcement of the constabulary or *Maréchausseé*. Although there had always been varying degrees of tension within this complex system of compliance, it came to a head in the years immediately preceding the Revolution.

The key tool of opposition to the absolute power of the monarchy was the system of *parlements*—the highest courts in the realm. These thirteen *parlements* were located in provincial centres and manned by noble judges. Apart from administering justice and performing any number of bureaucratic tasks necessary for local commerce to function, it was their duty to register all laws proclaimed by the monarch and, more importantly, to issue remonstrances pointing out any errors in the laws. In this way the *parlements* could delay legislation, thereby acting as a check on the sovereign will of the King. Depending on the legislation and how it might affect the relative position of the nobility to the monarch, it was a check that they did not hesitate to use, especially the powerful *parlement* of Paris. For his part the King could resort to *lettres de cachet* to coerce the *parlements* to acquiesce to his will. Such conflicts grew more heated in the decades leading up to the Revolution. Louis XV clashed frequently with the *parlements* during his reign. Perhaps the most divisive came near the end of his reign in 1766 when his chief minister, René Nicolas de Maupeou, tried to implement legislation without the consent of the noble justices. They were exiled and their venal offices abolished. It was not until Louis XVI ascended to the throne, in a more conciliatory mood at the beginning of his reign than his grandfather had been at the end of his, that the pre-Maupeou *parlements* were restored. Throughout these battles, the *parlement* would consistently paint themselves as the guardians of the freedoms of the people and the nation against the unrestricted tyranny of the monarchy. They would not always be seen as such. By the spring of 1789 both the monarchy and the *parlements* had lost, in the eyes of many of the people of France, the legitimacy upon which obedience partially depended. In the absence of this legitimacy, the government would have to rely on their monopoly of force, but this would prove to be a short-sighted recourse. It was this kind of obstruction that Charles-Alexandre de Calonne encountered when he attempted to reform the French financial system.

Parlements were French courts of the *ancien régime* whose role was to carry out and interpret the administrative laws as set out by the Royal Government. It was also their traditional role to challenge these laws when they were believed to overstep the traditional power of the monarch.

The financial crisis

It has become a cliché to speak of the long-term and immediate causes of the French Revolution in terms of powder kegs and sparks. Nevertheless, the factors that we have so far discussed had been brewing for a number of years and even decades. What brought matters to a head in 1789 was a financial crisis that bordered on collapse. It was not a matter of absolute numbers, however. France's debt did not nearly equal that of the British. Great Britain spent roughly the same proportion of its budget on debt and defence. Instead, the crisis revolved around the simple financial fact that what the French government took in as revenue came nowhere near to servicing the nation's long-term obligations.

Extravagance of foreign wars

Much of these long-term obligations were the result of half a century of ambitious and not always successful foreign policy. The **Seven Years War** was nothing short of a struggle for global supremacy between France and Britain—much was at stake. Fighting ranged from Continental Europe to the subcontinent of India to North America. In the end, it was British naval power that decided the outcome. From Quebec to India, if it was not the Royal Navy that won the battles, it certainly secured and consolidated these victories. For as successful as British arms had been during this global war, having won victories in all theatres and maintaining her command of the seas, the peace was far from disastrous for the French. They gave up largely unprofitable land in North America to the British and the Spanish, but maintained their interests in the far more profitable Caribbean. In India, the French also maintained commercial interests. The Seven Years War did not significantly interrupt French trade with any part of the world.

Strategically and emotionally, however, the effects of the Seven Years War on the French were far more ambiguous. The military, social and political influence of France had been humbled around the globe. In the time of Louis XIV, the French army had been the standard to which modern armies aspired. By 1763 the world looked to Prussia for a model modern army and to the British for an exemplar of naval power. The war itself had been massively expensive. By 1764, servicing the French debt took 60 per cent of the annual budget; three times what it had been a decade earlier. Although Schama has pointed out that these numbers were in line and in some cases less than other European powers, they were still a significant concern for the financiers of France. Part of the problem lay in the fact that the combination of a bruised national pride and a global trading network that remained intact led French foreign ministers to conclude that they would need to rebuild and maintain a massive peacetime army and navy. While re-establishing this global presence, they would also pursue France's traditional foreign policy of maintaining a balance of power on the European Continent. The upshot of this ambitious strategy was that once the prospect of revenge against the British rose among the disgruntled citizens of the Thirteen Colonies of America in the 1770s, military spending accelerated again, especially for the navy.

When the American colonists declared their independence in 1776, the French Foreign Minister Charles Gravier, Count de Vergennes saw an opportunity to strike a blow both for French prestige and against British global hegemony. The problem was how to finance it. The King's finance minister, Anne Robert Jacques Turgot cautioned against anything as extravagant as a foreign war. As this was not what the King or his other ministers wanted to hear, Turgot found himself replaced by the more accommodating Swiss

> The **Seven Years War** was a struggle between the powers of Europe in the years 1756–63. The primary antagonists were France and Great Britain. Through the terms of the Treaty of Paris, Britain strengthened her colonial empire while French colonial holdings shrank.

 How did the fact that the Seven Years War was a global war affect France in the years following 1763?

Protestant financier Jacques Necker. Necker believed that if French finances could be rationalized, a popular Enlightenment notion, confidence in its financial system would be bolstered, allowing the American war to be financed with loans rather than taxes. As all loans, as well as taxes, had to be registered by the *parlements*, this was a politically astute plan. Taxes are always less politically palatable than loans. And, in the short term, it was successful. Necker was able to raise over 500 million *livres* between 1777 and 1781. But by the time the Americans had definitively won their independence this would only amount to about half the overall cost of the war for the French. All told, the French debt in 1787 came to about 4 billion *livres*, the service of which accounted for about half of the government budget. Yet this was in-line with many European states, including Great Britain. Wherein then, lay the financial crisis that gripped Louis XVI's government at the end of the 1780s?

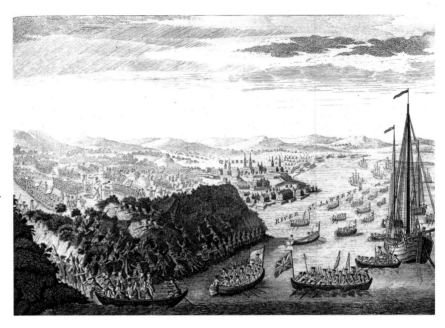

The Seven Years War was a truly global conflict with the French and British fighting in North America, Europe, India and on the high seas.

Jacques Necker (1732–1804)

Necker was a Protestant of Swiss birth who made a fortune as an investor and banker in Paris. By 1777 he had risen to the post of Director General of Finance in Louis XVI's government. His Protestantism and reformism alienated members of the royal family and Catholic members of Louis's cabinet. This enmity saw him dismissed in 1781. He was recalled in 1788 when Calonne and Brienne could not save the French financial system. He was integral in calling the Estates General and determining its composition. His dismissal in 1789 precipitated the storming of the Bastille.

Accessing the wealth of France

Like most things in history, the answer is far from simple. In basic terms, however, France as a country had more than enough money. The nobility and the bourgeoisie were piloting a relatively dynamic economy that was producing wealth. The problem was that the government could not access this wealth for various structural reasons, foremost was the complicated taxation system with its myriad exemptions. Wealthy bourgeoisie ennobled themselves, dodging taxation. The Church, prosperous though it was, avoided taxation altogether. This problem was compounded by government policies and decisions, such as participation in the American Revolutionary War and the sale of offices. It was the abortive attempts by ministers of the Crown, specifically Calonne, the chief financial minister from 1783 to 1787, to solve this predicament that turned a financial crisis into a political crisis.

Calonne's solution to the problem involved dismantling the system of privilege that insulated the government from the wealth of the

Activity:
Who Pays?

In groups, brainstorm possible solutions to France's financial crisis. List the strengths and weaknesses for each solution. What group in France would be the most affected by each solution?

country at the same time as setting up a methodical tax regime. Calonne proposed that the current system of temporary loans and taxations be replaced by a permanent tax on property from which there would be no exemptions. Provincial assemblies of representative landowners would administer this tax scheme. Not content to simply remodel the tax system, Calonne also sought to increase the overall wealth of the country by embracing the economic philosophies of the **physiocrats** and this meant abandoning the complex system of economic regulation set in motion by the **mercantilist** policies of Jean Baptiste Colbert a hundred years earlier and moving toward free trade, both within the kingdom and with its neighbors. As economically sensible as this ambitious plan may have seemed on paper, it struck at several central tenets of France's political reality. By abolishing tax exemptions, the scheme attacked the noble judges of the *parlements* as well as the entire Second Estate. By proposing representative assemblies, Calonne would subvert the power of the *parlements* themselves. In that these assemblies would essentially collect taxes, they would be a rival to the position of the Farmers-General, a powerful association of men who advanced the crown money in exchange for the right to collect all manner of taxes. If he succeeded in deregulating the economy, the regulating power of the *parlements* would likewise be jeopardized. There were few men of influence and power in 1786 France who would not have been alarmed at what Calonne was proposing.

The **physiocrats** were a group of philosophers in the 18th century who focused on what is now known as economics. In general the *physiocrats* argued for a smaller role for government in the economy and an emphasis on the wealth produced from agriculture as opposed to trade. As such they were opposed to mercantilism and favoured unfettered individualism in economic matters.

Mercantilism is an economic theory that there is only a fixed amount of wealth, as expressed in gold and silver, in the world. Therefore, in an effort to stop gold and silver from flowing out of a country, exports must be maximized and imports minimized. As part of such a strategy, mercantilist countries established colonial empires that could supply the mother country with raw materials.

Discussion point:

When should national debt be avoided?

In principle, national budgets are not that different from household budgets, enumerating obligations and income. In both instances, deficits need to be addressed either by cutting spending, or finding new sources of income (which includes loans).

What do the French Royal budgets of the 1770s and 1790s tell us about government priorities? Examine the budget of your own country. On what is your government spending money?

What are the long-term consequences of financing deficits with credit? Under what circumstances might it be advisable to incur national debt? Why?

How then to avoid the inevitable opposition? If Calonne could somehow find a consensus for change in the nation as a whole he could, quite rightly, claim a degree of legitimacy. There was a body that was capable of such a consensus, the Estates General. An imposing assembly of representatives from all three estates, the Estates General was a body that had not been called for 175 years. Monarchs were loathe to summon it as once called it could prove to be unmanageable. It was, regardless of absolutist theory, a measure of power sharing and as such anathema to the absolutist kings of

France. The monarchy had little control over it once it was called. The members of the estates themselves chose representatives. In 1787, this would have meant a powerful bourgeois delegation bent on concessions from the nobles. There we as also a growing number of nobles who wanted a change in the system of government. As we have seen, nobles were involved in all manner of bourgeois concerns, from manufacturing to finance and trade. As Schama has pointed out, a formidable number of these nobles wanted change as well. Bringing these volatile elements together could mean trouble, not only for Calonne's reforms, but also perhaps for the monarchy as a whole.

There was an alternative to the unpredictable Estates General. The monarch had, in the past, called together an Assembly of Notables the members of which were nominated by the crown. This assembly would give the illusion of consultation and the associated legitimacy but in fact, would be easily manipulated by Calonne. In January 1787, 144 notables assembled at Versailles and quickly proved themselves anything but easy to manipulate. Some historians have contended that the notables' hostility had its roots in personal and political antagonism to Calonne himself and the self-interest of the notables themselves, while others believe it to be in the fact that Calonne's reforms were not radical enough. Depending which view one takes, Calonne's Assembly of Notables was either one of the last vestiges of the *ancien régime* or one of the first revolutionary steps. Regardless of the view, by March the notables proclaimed that there was no consensus and this would eventually lead to Calonne's downfall. His replacement, Brienne, fared no better and by May, some of the notables were calling for a more representative body to be called—the **Estates General**.

> The **Estates General** was a representative assembly of the three estates of the *ancien régime*. The Estates General was called together infrequently to advise and aid the monarch in ruling France. Procedurally, each estate had one vote.

Brienne was not that desperate, yet. He instead decided to press on with the reforms without the consent of the notables. But that would mean acquiescence of the *parlements* who had to register all new taxes. When it became evident that Brienne had merely traded the obstinance of the notables for the obstinance of the *parlement* of Paris, which refused to register the new taxes, the King exiled the *parlement* in August 1787. As news spread of the *parlement's* stand against unfettered absolutism, supportive crowds gathered in the capital. Its legitimacy slipping away, the Crown resorted to increased censorship, a crackdown on political clubs and the presence of royal troops in the streets in an attempt to restore order and obedience to the Crown. As the tension escalated, so too did calls for the Estates General.

The immediate resort to this ancient yet radical option was almost forestalled by a budding compromise between the Crown and the *parlement*. The Crown for its part would cancel the exile imposed on the *parlements* and remove all new taxes. The *parlement* of Paris would respond by registering the continuation of old taxes. But when, at the end of the session introducing the plan, the King ordered the *parlement* to register the law because it was his will that it be so, the fine balance between royal authority and representative rights was smashed and the *parlement* once again refused. The *parlementary* rebellion spread to *parlements* throughout Louis's realm. Nevertheless, short-term financing was secured. In May of 1788, the *parlement* of Paris made clear its constitutional position in regards to the calling of the Estates General as the only body legally capable of authorizing the kind of long-term financing that the crisis required thereby incurring the wrath of the Crown and once again being disbanded. Predictably, *parlements* around the country protested, this time the political protests were joined by popular disturbances throughout France.

By the summer of 1788, the treasury was almost bare, putting the crown's ability to meet its military payroll, among other obligations, in jeopardy. Without the support of the army, and with the *parlements* in open rebellion and the money and stock markets in paralysis, Louis and his government were threatened with the loss of both their monopoly of force and their legitimacy. In a last attempt to inject confidence into the market and the nation, Brienne set a date for the convening of the Estates General and persuaded the King to recall the popular finance minister, Jacques Necker. The Estates General would meet for the first time in 175 years in the spring of 1789.

Far from solving problems or soothing the nation, the call for the Estates General created a whole new set of controversies. As constituted in 1614, the voting procedures of the Estates general reflected the relative privilege of the orders. Each of the three estates would vote as a block. There were, therefore, only three votes in the Estates General. Necker, in the spirit of renewal, released imprisoned journalists and relaxed censorship, with the predictable result—an outpouring of broadsheets and pamphlets attacking the proposed voting system and those who defended it. Ironically it was the *parlements* that bore the brunt of this criticism, the same body that had been popular heroes in their call for the Estates General. Even when the King announced, in December 1788, that the representation of delegates from the Third Estate would be doubled, it did not soothe the masses, for he would not concede to a one delegate, one vote process. So while the calling of the Estates General seemed to mark the regime as amenable to the possibility of change, in reality it had only postponed the question that was central to that change. Would the delegates, and by extension the people they represented, be thought of as individuals or as a group.

The Estates General

In order to help guide the deliberations of the Estates General, the King ordered that the representatives of each estate in each of the representative districts should compile lists of grievances and proposals for change. These **cahiers** on one hand were as varied as the localities that produced them, but certain patterns do emerge in this rich historical record. The Clerical *cahiers* reflected the disenchantment of the impoverished parish priests. The nobility, especially those from urban areas, were actually quite enlightened in their *cahiers* and in fact many members of the Second Estate argued that the Estates General should sit permanently, to speak for the nation, though they still balked at the thought of voting by head. Whereas the nobility saw the Estates General as a method of curtailing the power of the monarchy, the *cahiers* of the Third Estate reveal that the mass of the population looked to Louis as a protector of their traditional rights *vis a vis* the nobility. The *cahiers* reveal a King who still enjoyed a great deal of popular support.

The **cahiers** were compilations of grievances generated by each of the three estates throughout France. They were intended to guide the discussions in the Estates General.

Activity:

Interpreting *Cahiers*
Cahiers of the Nobility of Blois

Art. I. *In order to assure the exercise of this first and most sacred of the rights of man, we ask that no citizen may be exiled, arrested or held prisoner except in cases contemplated by the law and in accordance with a decree originating in the regular courts of justice.*

That in case the States General determine that provisional detention may be necessary at times, it ought to be ordained that every person so arrested shall be delivered, within twenty-four hours into the hand of appropriate judges, to be judged with the least possible delay, in conformity with the laws of the kingdom; that evocations be abolished, and that no extraordinary commission be established in any instance; finally that no person be deprived of his position, civil or military, without judgment in due form.

From the right of personal liberty arises the right to write, to think, to print and to publish, with the names of authors and publishers, all kinds of complaints and reflections upon public and private affairs, limited by the right of every citizen to seek in the established courts legal redress against author or publisher, in case of defamation or injury; limited also by all restrictions which the States General may see fit to impose in that which concerns morals and religion.

We indicate further a number of instances in which natural liberty is abridged:

1. *The abuse of police regulations, which every year, in an arbitrary manner and without regular process, thrusts a number of artisans and useful citizens into prisons, work-houses and places of detention, often for trivial faults and even upon simple suspicion;*

2. *The abuse of exclusive privileges which fetter industry;*

3. *The guilds and corporations which deprive citizens of the right of using their faculties;*

4. *The regulations governing manufactures, the rights of inspection and marque, which impose restrictions that have lost their usefulness, and which burden industry with a tax that yields no profit to the treasury.*

Cahiers of The Third Estate of Dourdon

The order of the third estate of the City, Bailliage, and County of Dourdan, imbued with gratitude prompted by the paternal kindness of the King, who deigns to restore its former rights and its former constitution, forgets at this moment its misfortunes and impotence, to harken only to its foremost duty, that of sacrificing everything to the glory of the Patrie and the service of His Majesty. It supplicates him to accept the grievances, complaints, and remonstrances which it is permitted to bring to the foot of the throne, and to see therein only the expression of its zeal and the homage of its obedience.

It wishes:

1. *That his subjects of the third estate, equal by such status to all other citizens, present themselves before the common father without other distinction which might degrade them.*

2. *That all the orders, already united by duty and a common desire to contribute equally to the needs of the State, also deliberate in common concerning its needs.*

3. *That no citizen lose his liberty except according to law; that, consequently, no one be arrested by virtue of special orders, or, if imperative circumstances necessitate such orders, that the prisoner be handed over to the regular courts of justice within forty-eight hours at the latest.*

4. *That no letters or writings intercepted in the post [mails] be the cause of the detention of any citizen, or be produced in court against him, except in case of conspiracy or undertaking against the State.*

5. *That the property of all citizens be inviolable, and that no one be required to make sacrifice thereof for the public welfare, except upon assurance of indemnification based upon the statement of freely selected appraisers. …*

15. *That every personal tax be abolished; that thus the capitation and the taille and its accessories be merged with the vingtiemes in a tax on land and real or nominal property.*

16. *That such tax be borne equally, without distinction, by all classes of citizens and by all kinds of property, even feudal and contingent rights.*

17. *That the tax substituted for the corvee be borne by all classes of citizens equally and without distinction. That said tax, at present beyond the capacity of those who pay it and the needs to which it is destined, be reduced by at least one-half. …*

Source: http://www.historyguide.org.

Source-based questions

1. What evidence is there in these documents that the nobility drew income from non-traditional sources?

2. Compare and contrast the views of the monarchy as expressed in these two documents.

3. Using these documents and other resources, discuss the relationship between the grievances of the Second and Third Estate and the principles of the Enlightenment.

As the *cahiers* were prepared and elections were held throughout the winter of 1789, the social composition of the coming Estates General came into sharper focus. The realm was divided into 234 electoral districts, electing two representatives for each of the first and second estates and the Third Estate electing four. From the end of April they gathered in Paris for the opening ceremonies to be held on 5 May at Versailles.

Once these ceremonies had concluded, voting rights remained a key issue. The first two estates immediately declared that they were committed to voting by order. The Third Estate took a little more time to solidify their position, but emerged by the end of the first week as dedicated to voting by head. While there was some effort to achieve a compromise it was short-lived. Leadership at this point was not forthcoming from the King and the Estates General seemed moribund shortly after its birth.

The meeting of the Estates General was a grand affair accompanied by much ritual and ceremony. Many of these ceremonies, the clothing, and even the seating in the Estates General were designed to reinforce the social structure that the National Assembly would eventually overthrow.

? How can ruling elites use ritual and costume as a form of propaganda?

It took three poor priests from the provinces to quicken it. They sat with the Third Estate on the morning of June 13. By the end of the week nearly 100 priests who had decided to make common cause with the Third Estate had joined these three. When these priests were added to the nobles who had stood for election from the Third Estate rather than the first, men such as the Comte de Mirabeau, this group could rightly claim to have representatives from all the orders of France, that they in fact represented the nation as a whole. As such they named the body the **National Assembly**. As significant as that was, in the next motion they declared that all taxes were invalidated unless approved by the National Assembly—in essence declaring themselves to be the legitimate government of France.

Activity:

The Estates General

The reality of France's social composition was far more complex than the division into three estates would suggest. Research the Estates General and its composition:

- What social groups represented each estate?

- To what extent did the social composition of the representatives of each estate exclude elements in French society? What significance might this have for the future of the Revolution?

National Assembly This was the first revolutionary government in France. It was originally formed out of representatives of each of the three estates in June 1789. This would be the form of government until it was overthrown in August 1792.

The King and his government faced the age-old issue confronting all governments—how to make their subjects obey. Unable in the short term and at least partially unwilling to resort to force, Louis decided to rely on the legitimacy of his position. He would insist on a compromise and rely on the force of this insistence to carry the day. When the delegates of the National Assembly found themselves locked out of their meeting chamber, ostensibly because of preparations for the royal pronouncement, they repaired to a

Activity:

The opening of the Estates General

Political ceremonies and ritual are generally designed for a specific purpose. Research paintings and accounts of the opening of the Estates General in 1789.

- Describe the seating and ceremony at the opening.
- What was the political and social significance of the seating and ritual at the opening?
- Why do you think the ceremony and seating was designed in this way?

Research the following political rituals. Analyse the purpose of each ritual and how it reflected the goals and principles of the regime that designed it.

- The coronation of Napoleon I
- The proclamation of the German Empire, 1871
- The State Opening of the UK Parliament, November 2009
- The Nuremburg Rally, 1936

tennis court a few blocks away. Before the gathering of representatives on the tennis court, the deputies took an oath, known as the Tennis Court Oath, to continue to meet until a written constitution had been approved by a majority of their members. At this point nothing the King could have said short of declaring the National Assembly a sovereign body could have assuaged the deputies or the growing mobs in the streets of Versailles and Paris.

So, following a profound lack of leadership on the part of Louis XVI, a series of half-steps failed to please either side and served to alienate the National Assembly even further. The King adopted a contradictory approach that at the very least confused those upon whom he might have counted for support. Although he did, on Necker's advice, propose a set of sound solutions to the issues facing the nation, he also summoned 20,000 troops to Versailles—a clear threat to the National Assembly and its supporters in the streets. Nevertheless he still allowed the National Assembly to meet without explicitly siding with the nobility in the dispute. If this confusing stance was frustrating to the deputies of the National Assembly, it was even more disturbing to the growing crowds in the streets. It was to the King that they looked to safeguard them against the nobility. In fact, the French monarchy had a long history of confronting the nobility. When Louis summoned troops to Paris and did not support the National Assembly against the Second Estate, many felt betrayed and driven to more radical positions. They saw the King becoming a puppet of the nobility and as such hostile to the principles for which the fledgling National Assembly stood. These principles hinged on the notion that France was more than the property of the King, that it belonged to all those who called themselves French. It belonged to the **nation**.

To the Bastille

Louis XVI's inaction bought time for the deputies of the National Assembly. They spent it attempting to fulfill the terms of the Tennis Court Oath, writing a constitution. While the Assembly got down to business, popular disturbances continued to plague both the capital and the countryside. Mobs vandalized shops, and local police forces such as they were, were powerless to control them. These disturbances were not simply statements of political outrage and fear. They were, in many ways, extensions of the bread riots

Discussion point:

Legitimacy and force continue to be important elements in the ability of a government to rule.

How does your government establish legitimacy? To what extent does it use force to govern?

Nation/Nationalism A nation is a group people who share a number of commonalities that generally include language, culture, historical development, and land or territory. Nationalism is an emotional attachment to this group of people and its desire for political independence.

that had been disrupting French life since the spring. Prices had been increasing throughout the country and, as they had done for centuries, the French peasantry, to whom the price of bread was a matter of great importance, took to the streets to show their hunger, to intimidate bakers and in extreme cases, take what they could not afford to buy. In an effort to protect themselves from unruly elements real and imagined, towns, cities and individual citizens began arming themselves. They were not the only ones arming themselves, the number of troops, both French and foreign, massing around the capital and Versailles were increasing drastically. It was becoming clear to observers, both in the assembly and in the streets that these troops were being summoned as a means for the monarchy to regain control and disband the National Assembly.

These suspicions gained credence when, on 11 July, on the advice of conservative noble elements including his wife and brother, the King dismissed Necker whom they blamed for unleashing this tempest by means of his reforms. As news of Necker's dismissal spread and unrest began to increase in size and intensity, some of the foreign troops were called into the capital to restore order, accelerating the fear in the streets. On 12–13 July the unrest gained direction and strength attacking a number of locations of royal authority, real and symbolic, looking for arms and ammunition. On 14 July the search led them to the **Invalides** were they found weapons. Eventually a crowd gathered at the **Bastille**, the great symbol of royal authority in Paris. After a tense stand off in which shots were exchanged, the governor of the Bastille understood the hopelessness of his situation and surrendered the fortress, having his head paraded around on a pike for his troubles.

On learning of the popular affront to his authority, Louis made ready to use the forces he had been gathering in anticipation of just such an occasion. His military commanders, however, were unsure that their troops could be trusted to obey orders to attack the Parisians, especially in light of the performance of the soldiers in front of the

> **Invalides** A military hospital and armoury built by Louis XIV.

> **The Bastille** A fortress and prison in Paris. Before the Revolution it had gained a reputation, only partially true, for harsh treatment and torture. In the *ancien régime* the king and nobility could have a member of the Third Estate imprisoned without trial. As such the Bastille came to symbolize the absolute power of the king.

Discussion point: Peaceful protest

The photographs above are from the same protest that involved peaceful and violent episodes. While protest is a key element to modern democratic activity most governments agree that the right to

gather in protest has its limits. What do you think these limits should be?

 Is the government ever justified in using force on protestors? If so, when and why?

Bastille. Louis had now lost the second vital element in the ability of any government to rule. Having already lost a good deal of his legitimacy to the National Assembly, it now appeared that he had lost his monopoly of force to the mob of Paris.

Activity:

Storming the Bastille

The following is an account written by Thomas Jefferson, an American diplomat in Paris, describing early accounts of the storming of the Bastille.

De Corney advised the people then to retire, retired himself, and the people took possession of the arms. It was remarkable that not only the Invalids themselves made no opposition, but that a body of 5,000 foreign troops, encamped within 400 yards, never stirred.

Monsieur de Corny and five others were then sent to ask arms of Monsieur de Launai, Governor of the Bastille. They found a great collection of people already before the place, and they immediately planted a flag of truce, which was answered by a like flag hoisted on the parapet. The deputation prevailed on the people to fall back a little, advanced themselves to make their demand of the Governor, and in that instant a discharge from the Bastille killed four people of those nearest to the deputies. The deputies retired, the people rushed against the place, and almost in an instant were in possession of a fortification, defended by 100 men, of infinite strength, which in other times had stood several regular sieges and had never been taken. How they got in,

has as yet been impossible to discover. Those, who pretend to have been of the party tell so many different stories as to destroy the credit of them all.

Source: Thomas Jefferson, quoted in Boyd, Julian. (ed.) 1958. *The Papers of Thomas Jefferson*, vol.15. Princeton University Press. Also available at "The Beginning of the French Revolution, 1789". http:// www.eyewitnesstohistory.com.

Research other primary and secondary source accounts of the storming of the Bastille. Compare and contrast their accounts of:

● The number of participants

● The social class of the participants

● The level of violence

● The goals of the Parisians

● The aftermath of the storming.

Write a newspaper article based on your research.

With the citizens of Paris in the ascendance, the forces of conservatism in France began to flee. This included members of the royal household all the way down to the newly ennobled, all fearful of their fortunes, privilege and lives. These well-heeled refugees became known as the *émigrés* and would spread their fear to the nobles of neighbouring countries. As events in France accelerated throughout the spring and early summer of 1789, other European powers paid closer attention. Foreign reaction to these early stages of the Revolution was varied.

The days immediately following the storming of the Bastille were a whirlwind of activity. The King announced that he would order the troops surrounding the capital to disperse. By 17 July he had come to the capital to address the newly formed city council with its newly elected mayor, a position that had not hitherto existed in Paris. A citizens' guard had been formed with the Marquis de Lafayette, the self-promoting noble who had gained fame in the American Revolution, at its head.

Gilbert du Motier, Marquis de Lafayette (1757–1834)

Lafayette was a reform-minded aristocrat who had fought in the American Revolution and been deeply influenced by its principles. He was a member of the Assembly of Notables and later the National Assembly. After the storming of the Bastille he was appointed to the command of the National Guard. As the Revolution radicalized, he ran foul of both the Royalists and the radicals. His heavy handed attempts to maintain order and secure a place for the monarchy alienated many in Paris and he was widely held to be complicit in the massacre at the Champ de Mars in 1790 especially by his enemies in the Jacobin Club. Lafayette fled France and was captured by the Austrians and held in prison until his release in 1797.

Many moderate reformers, hoped that this was the Revolution begun and ended. The King's absolute authority had been replaced by a body representing the nation. A citizens' army, one born out of civic obligation and duty rather than royal whim and mercenary needs, was in its infancy. The Assembly was hard at work on a written constitution that would formalize all these gains. But, as with most legislation, the devil is in the details. There would emerge in the days and weeks following deeply divided opinion on the form that this new state would take. These difficulties were compounded by the fact that the problems that in large part gave rise to the riots culminating in the storming of the *Bastille* were unsolved. Bread prices were still high and many of the deputies of the Assembly ideologically favoured a deregulated grain trade, which would allow prices to fluctuate with the market, a measure that would certainly push bread prices higher. The King's concessions did not immediately restore order in the capital or the rest of the country. Roaming mobs, and occasionally units of the new National Guard took retribution on those whom they thought were not sufficiently supportive of their goals.
As elusive as public order was in the capital, the situation in the provinces was worse, compounded as it was by distance from the new government in Paris. Wild rumours of plots and counterplots fuelled a situation made all the more volatile by the breakdown of regular law and order. What had started as a reaction to spreading bread riots now bordered on panic that what gains that had been made in Paris would now be undone—**The Great Fear**. The National Assembly had an enormous task. It had to re-establish governmental authority in the country without any clear idea of what that authority would look like while at the same time seeing to the day- to-day mechanics of running a vast state of 30 million people.

While they wrestled with the banal aspects of governance such as feeding the population and keeping public order, the deputies of the National Assembly sought the root cause of these issues. Most would have agreed that in one form or another it was the system of privilege that bound the *ancien régime*. On 4 August nobles and clergy alike began relinquishing feudal privileges. This lead to an orgy of renunciation, with deputies trying to outdo each other in their self-sacrifice, while making certain that the sacrifice was not theirs alone. Noble dues and church taxes were swept away. Venal offices and privileges were eliminated. The net result was the abolition of feudalism in France, but not in the sweeping manner that many in the streets and countryside had expected and indeed wanted.
As mentioned, the deputies in the National Assembly were drawn from the nobility, the clergy and most numerously from the bourgeoisie, a social class that in general had a respect for the sanctity of property. Venal offices, hunting rights, feudal dues were all seen as some form of property and by the time this altruism had made its way into a decree, all of this relinquished property was to be compensated by the state.

The Great Fear A period in the early Revolution during which, in the absence of a strong central authority, towns and villages armed themselves to guard their property and grain supplies against roaming mobs. The rumour about counter-revolution also increased tension throughout the country.

The King to Paris

Louis was in a strange limbo as to his own authority and power. While the events of July seemed to place authority in the hands of the National Assembly, the country still hung on how Louis would receive the August decrees and more importantly the Declaration of the Rights of Man and Citizen. The Declaration of the Rights of Man and Citizen was the principles of the Revolution drafted into the form of a constitution. It was designed to set out the general principles that would guide the drafting of the more comprehensive constitution. The general principles embodied in this document were:

- equality before the law
- freedom of religion
- freedom of the press
- rights of *habeus corpus*
- equality of taxation
- law as an activity of the nation, not the King
- accountability for public officials.

The Declaration was necessarily broad in its wording. The precise nature of the new state, the actual constitution, was yet to be decided. Vital to these questions were debates in the Assembly as to what the power of the monarch was to be in the new France. Should he have anything but symbolic power? Should he have a veto that allowed him to delay laws, but not strike them down, or should he have a complete veto? While these debates were going on, Louis acted as though there had been no change in his status. He accepted some of the reforms of August, though not all, and he vacillated on accepting the Declaration of Rights. As would become more and more common, those who thought they were in charge were overtaken by events as they erupted in the streets.

Activity:

Are all declarations created equal?

The struggle of Britain's thirteen North American colonies for independence had a profound effect on the causes, personalities, and principles of the French Revolution. The founding documents of both the United States of America and the French Revolution were styled as declarations. Review the extracts below.

Declaration of Independence

We hold these truths to be self-evident, that all men are created equal, that they are endowed by their Creator with certain unalienable rights, that among these are life, liberty and the pursuit of happiness. That to secure these rights, governments are instituted among men, deriving their just powers from the consent of the governed. That whenever any form of government becomes destructive to these ends, it is the right of the people to alter or to abolish it, and to institute new government, laying its foundation on such principles and organizing its powers in such form, as to them shall seem most likely to effect their safety and happiness … The history of the present King of Great Britain is a history of repeated injuries and usurpations, all having in direct object the establishment of an absolute tyranny over these states. To prove this, let facts be submitted to a candid world. …

He has refused to pass other laws for the accommodation of large districts of people, unless those people would relinquish the right of representation in the legislature, a right inestimable to them and formidable to tyrants only. …

He has dissolved representative houses repeatedly, for opposing with manly firmness his invasions on the rights of the people. …

He has obstructed the administration of justice, by refusing his assent to laws for establishing judiciary powers. He has made judges dependent on his will alone, for the tenure of their offices, and the amount and payment of their salaries.

He has erected a multitude of new offices, and sent hither swarms of officers to harass our people, and eat out their substance. …

He has affected to render the military independent of and superior to civil power. …

For quartering large bodies of armed troops among us: …

For cutting off our trade with all parts of the world:

For imposing taxes on us without our consent:

For depriving us in many cases, of the benefits of trial by jury: …

The Declaration of the Rights of Man and Citizen

Approved by the National Assembly of France, August 26, 1789.

The representatives of the French people, organized as a National Assembly, believing that the ignorance, neglect, or contempt of the rights of man are the sole cause of public calamities and of the corruption of governments, have determined to set forth in a solemn declaration the natural, unalienable, and sacred rights of man, ... Therefore the National Assembly recognizes and proclaims, in the presence and under the auspices of the Supreme Being, the following rights of man and of the citizen, Articles:

1 *Men are born and remain free and equal in rights. Social distinctions may be founded only upon the general good.*

2 *The aim of all political association is the preservation of the natural and imprescriptible rights of man. These rights are liberty, property, security, and resistance to oppression.*

3 *The principle of all sovereignty resides essentially in the nation. No body nor individual may exercise any authority which does not proceed directly from the nation.*

4 *Liberty consists in the freedom to do everything which injures no one else; hence the exercise of the natural rights of each man has no limits except those which assure to the other members of the society the enjoyment of the same rights. These limits can only be determined by law. ...*

6 *Law is the expression of the general will. Every citizen has a right to participate personally, or through his representative, in its foundation. It must be the same for all, whether it protects or punishes. All citizens, being equal in the eyes of the law, are equally eligible to all dignities and to all public positions and occupations, according to their abilities, and without distinction except that of their virtues and talents.*

7 *No person shall be accused, arrested, or imprisoned except in the cases and according to the forms prescribed by law. ...*

9 *As all persons are held innocent until they shall have been declared guilty ...*

10 *No one shall be disquieted on account of his opinions, including his religious views, provided their manifestation does not disturb the public order established by law.*

11 *The free communication of ideas and opinions is one of the most precious of the rights of man. Every citizen may, accordingly, speak, write, and print with freedom, but shall be responsible for such abuses of this freedom as shall be defined by law. ...*

12 *A common contribution [tax] is essential for the maintenance of the public forces and for the cost of administration. This should be equitably distributed among all the citizens in proportion to their means.*

13 *All the citizens have a right to decide, either personally or by their representatives, as to the necessity of the public contribution [tax]; to grant this freely; to know to what uses it is put; and to fix the proportion, the mode of assessment and of collection and the duration of the taxes.*

14 *Society has the right to require of every public agent an account of his administration. ...*

15 *Since property is an inviolable and sacred right, no one shall be deprived thereof except where public necessity, legally determined, shall clearly demand it, and then only on condition that the owner shall have been previously and equitably indemnified.*

Source-based questions

1 Compare and contrast the two declarations according to the following areas:
   - Rights
   - Responsibilities
   - Over-all tone

2 What evidence is there that the documents were influenced by Enlightenment principles?

3 With reference to their origin and purpose, discuss the values and of these documents to historians studying principles guiding the French Revolution.

Grandiose proclamations, promulgations, and protestations had done nothing to bring down the price of bread and this age-old issue brought unrest to the streets of the country as it always had done. The women of Paris were the face of that unrest. Their role as keepers of the household and its finances meant that they confronted the price of bread on a daily basis. As an autumn of want seemed to presage a winter of famine, some 6,000 women of Paris rose on 5 October 1789 and rampaged through the capital before setting off for Versailles to express their concern to both the National Assembly and the king himself. The events of October 1789, after a good deal of high drama, culminated in the royal household and the National Assembly being forcibly relocated to the capital (in essence making it a true national capital). Again, all this begged the question as to who or what exactly was in charge of France.

Declaration of Rights and other constitutions, 1789–91

As bread prices settled down, the National Assembly continued its work in turning the principles of the Declaration of Rights into a detailed document that would provide a workable theory of governance. The comprehensiveness of these changes is often overshadowed by the radicalism of those that followed, but the changes wrought by the National Assembly would touch all aspects of French life. The administration of religious life was to be no exception.

It is important to remember that the clergy, especially members of the lower clerical orders, had been involved in all aspects of the Revolution. They had broken ranks with their estate to sit as individuals in the National Assembly. They had been the first to renounce their privileges on the night of 4 August. They had been instrumental in drafting the Declaration of Rights. When the National Assembly turned its attention to the official role of the Church in the new French state many clergy who had been leaders in the new order would find themselves fighting rear-guard actions to protect the Catholic Church in France.

The Civil Constitution of the Clergy was designed to bring the principles of the Revolution to matters of faith. To that end the size of the clergy was reduced to only those who actually administered to parishioners, eliminating friars, monks, nuns and the like who did not have direct contact with church goers. The land that belonged to these convents and monasteries was to be forfeited to the state. The state would accept the responsibility of paying the clergy to ensure principles of equality were observed and the church would cease to be an avenue of enrichment. The Pope would retain all authority on matters spiritual, but not administrative. The Assembly considered, however, the appointment of clergy to be an administrative task and sought to apply the principle of popular election to this office as it had all other offices of state. When this was coupled with the idea of equality it meant that non-practising Catholics, Protestants and Jews would have a say in choosing the clergy. Even the more reform-minded of the clergy began to balk at this provision. Likewise, it became a rallying point for the most radical of the members of the National Assembly, representing a litmus test for the sovereignty of the Assembly. They had determined that they would not be dictated to by their own monarch, but how could they bow to the will, or even acknowledge the authority of a foreign power—the Pope? These deputies and eventually a majority of the members of the Assembly decided that devotion to the new order had to be explicit and devised an oath to test that devotion.

The Civil Constitution of the Clergy
This was a document which brought the Catholic Church in France under the authority of the National Assembly. Among other things it confiscated church property and appointed priests by popular vote. The Civil Constitution of the Clergy essentially replaced the Pope with the National Assembly as the head of the Church.

Pope Pius VI for his part advised the faithful of the French clergy that to take the oath meant to forsake the true church. In any event, the oath and the Civil Constitution of the Clergy divided the Revolution. It was deeply unpopular among the majority of the Third Estate. It served to drive Catholic worship underground, thereby creating an enforcement headache for the Assembly.

In theory the Civil Constitution of the Clergy would help solve another root cause of the Revolution—the financial crisis, which did not evaporate with the Declaration of the Rights of Man. Confiscated Church land would be used to back a new form of paper currency called **assignats**, that could then be used to pay of government debt. The problem became evident when hard currency such as gold and silver became increasingly scarce—many hoarding it as a hedge against even more unstable times ahead or a life in exile. The result was that the government had to print more and more assignats with predictable inflationary results.

As the Tennis Court Oath had stipulated, the primary duty of the National Assembly was to draft a constitution, a duty that took the better part of two years. Debates raged over the position of the monarchy, the relative merits of bicameral and unicameral structures, separation of powers, and voting qualifications. As the deliberations went on, the shape of the new state began to emerge. Decentralization was the central theme. The deputies wished to create a system in which no one person or even one group of people could become too powerful. There would be strict separation of powers. The King as the head of the executive branch of government could appoint ministers, but these ministers could be removed by the legislative branch. The king could use his veto to delay legislation for a maximum of three years. The Legislative Assembly was to be chosen through a system of indirect elections, in which the ultimate office holder had to pay significant taxes, and the participants in the decision-making process— the basic voter as an "active citizen"—could be far less wealthy. Citizens would also elect all local office holders and administrative positions. The administrative map of the country was also overhauled. France was divided into 83 roughly equal departments each self-governing through a complex system of subdivisions and elections.

Political clubs

Political life in France during the years 1789 to 1791 was increasingly dominated by the presence of a dizzying array of what have become known as political clubs—the Jacobin Club, the Cordelliers Club, the Feuillants Club and many others. These were groups of citizens who gathered to discuss the form and substance of the newly emerging France. These clubs were essentially local groups though as the Revolution moved forward they also debated national issues. As their interests diversified, they also began affiliating into wider bodies. The most famous, and increasingly the most powerful, was the Jacobin Club, so named for the abandoned Paris monastery where it had initially met. By 1790, the Jacobin Club had roughly 1,200 members in the capital and affiliated clubs throughout the country, its deliberations keenly watched and reported. The Jacobin Club became an important

> **Assignats** Paper money issued by the National Assembly. There value was backed by confiscated Church lands. However, they were continually devalued as the Assembly and later the Convention printed more and more *assignats* as their financial needs increased.

Discussion point:

To what extent is it possible for governments to dictate belief? Is there a difference between dictating religious practice and religious belief?

Activity:
Political clubs

Research one of the following revolutionary clubs/factions. Produce a political pamphlet to promote it.

● The Mountain

● The Plain

● Cordelier Club

● The Jacobin Club

● The Girondins

● The Feuillant Club

shaper of public opinion and a place where the politically ambitious could gain a national stage. Over time, the Jacobin Club itself would be fragmented into other political groupings with more conservative elements by turns breaking off, forming other clubs such as the *Feuillants*, leaving a radical core. Radical revolutionary leaders such as Maximilien Robespierre, Georges Danton, Camille Desmoulins, Jacques-Pierre Brissot and Jean-Paul Marat were all members of the Jacobin Club at some point and became important leaders during the Terror.

The Jacobin Club was one of the most radical of a number of political clubs that developed prior to and during the Revolution. "Jacobinism" became an imprecise term used throughout Europe during and after the Revolution to label radical, often republican political views.

The flight to Varennes, 1791

The sovereignty of Louis XVI essentially ended when the women of Paris compelled him and his family to return with them to Paris. After his return to Paris, he publicly acquiesced to proposals presented by the National Assembly and played the role that the Assembly cast for him. Privately, however, he wanted no part of the Revolution and although he was astute enough to actively and sincerely dissuade his brother, the Comte d'Artois, from launching a counter-revolution from abroad, he became increasingly sceptical of his future role in the new France. For example, his acceptance of the Civil Constitution of the Clergy was for public consumption as he still practised Catholicism with priests who had not taken the oath. When incidents such as this were reported, as they inevitably were, they served to reinforce the public's perception that there were many conspiratorial dealings to which the king and his Austrian wife were party. When Louis and his family tried to leave Paris to spend time at their chateau in Saint-Cloud, the Parisian mob physically stopped them and they had to return to the Tuileries Palace in Paris. It was becoming evident to Louis that he and his family were prisoners of the Revolution and he began to formulate a plan of escape. On 20 June 1791 Louis and his family slipped out of Paris in disguise. The plan depended on the help of a number of co-conspirators including the Swede Count Axel von Fersen and the French nobleman, Louis Auguste le Tonnelier de Breteuil. The royals' identity and plot were discovered soon enough and they were stopped in the town of Varennes. The flight to Varennes was an important event in the radicalization of the Revolution. Even though Louis did not realize it, until June 1791 he enjoyed a degree of public support. His private actions including the private religious practice and an ill-informed military banquet in which the King and Queen were reported to have participated in denigrating the Revolution and its leaders, squandered what public support the King still had.

The Flight to Varennes presented a very serious problem for the National Assembly. The deputies had spent two years crafting a constitution in which the King played a significant role. It was now evident that he could not be trusted and that he held all this work in

 Can you find specific instances when the terms "Jacobin" was used outside of France?

contempt, a contempt that the Flight to Varennes had now made embarrassingly public. In a feeble effort to preserve the new constitution, the Assembly endorsed a fiction in which the King and his family had been kidnapped by counter-revolutionary forces from whom the vigilant citizens of Varennes had rescued them. The reality, lost on no one, was that the King was no friend of the Revolution. From June 1791, Louis XVI would have no hand in shaping the Revolution. This also put the new constitution itself in grave danger even before it had been formally adopted.

War, 1792

The reaction of the rest of Europe to the developments in France was anything but predictable and opinion was varied. Early in the Revolution British sentiment seemed to side with the revolutionaries who appeared on their way to a French version of the Glorious Revolution. The Hapsburg Emperor Joseph, though concerned for the fate of his sister, the French Queen, and lobbied by the growing numbers of *émigré* nobility, was not overly troubled to see unrest in France weaken his rival strategically. The same sentiment seemed to be shared by the other European rulers. To the nationalist movements in Poland and Belgium the weakened France could offer little more than an example.

Nevertheless the events in France soon began to cause concern among European rulers. The confinement of the royal family in Paris and the aborted flight to Varennes seemed to suggest the King was a prisoner of his subjects and this was a concern to all monarchs. The Civil Constitution of the Clergy alienated the Pope and the Catholic monarchs. As pamphlets and other revolutionary literature that poured out of France became more radical, the spectre of republicanism began to haunt intellectual discourse. The flow of *émigrés* continued unabated, and in fact increased. These *émigrés* brought with them warnings of the consequences of constitutionalism run amok.

By July of 1791, Joseph's successor, Leopold, decided to act, albeit tentatively. He called on his fellow monarchs to join him on a crusade to restore the French monarchy.

This image depicts the arrest of the royal family in Varennes. Despite its ultimate failure, the flight could have worked. The vast majority of the French population had never laid eyes on their monarch and thus it was entirely plausible that he could have passed undetected through France to the border.

 How was the flight to Varennes a turning point in the Revolution?

Activity:

Foreign reaction: going deeper

Both popular and official sentiment regarding the Revolution was divided in the other major European powers, especially early in the Revolution. For each of the following major powers develop arguments for and against intervening to save the monarchy in France.

Power	Arguments for intervention	Arguments against intervention
United Kingdom		
Prussia		
Russia		
Austria		

Only the King of Prussia responded to the call, and that was only by way of agreeing to a meeting at Pilnitz at the end of the summer. The Declaration of Pilnitz was no more solid. It proclaimed concern for what was going on in France and issued vague threats that neither Austria no Prussia could really carry out.

> ### Jacques–Pierre Brissot (1754–1793)
>
> Brissot was a moderate revolutionary who was elected to both the National Assembly and the Convention. As a member of the Jacobin Club he argued for war with Austria and shortly thereafter Great Britain, but later decried the associated radical violence that erupted within France. He became a leading figure in the Gironde faction and was eventually expelled from the Jacobin Club. After the Gironde was defeated by the Mountain faction, Brissot was arrested, tried and executed.

The emptiness of these threats, however, was lost on many revolutionaries within France. There grew among some of them, notably Brissot and a new faction within the Jacobin movement known as the Girondins, an obsession with visions of *émigré* armies returning to wreak vengeance on the revolutionaries. The issue of war split the Jacobin Party with a number of prominent members such as Robespierre arguing against war.

There seemed a willingness to go to war on the part of Louis and the royalists as well. Throughout the rest of 1791 and the beginning of 1792, the voices advocating caution were overrun by a combination of patriotic fervour and fear of foreign invaders. In April 1792, the King announced to the National Assembly that France was at war with Austria. Prussia soon joined her Austrian ally.

From a constitutional monarchy to a republic, 1792

The flight to Varennes brought into the light of day those revolutionaries who had previously kept republican aspirations to themselves, among them Danton, Desmoulins and Robespierre. When they put these ideas into writing and called for a mass demonstration on the Champs de Mars on 17 July 1791 it was met with the musket fire of the National Guard scattering the champions of republicanism and silencing them for a time. Throughout the autumn and winter of 1791–2, the Assembly increasingly turned to elements of martial law to keep control in the streets, rife as they were with rumours of plots and counter plots and the growing pressure of rising bread prices.

The declaration of war in April 1792 again radicalized the population. War frequently puts pressure on prices. When this was combined with the already precarious state of the poorest French citizens and the near collapse of the *assignats*, unrest flowed through the streets of Paris and other urban centres. By the summer it was clear that the war was not going well for France. The Duke of Brunswick, the Prussian commander issued what became known as the **Brunswick Manifesto** proclaiming a terrible fate for the entire French capital should anything happen to the royal family. This resulted in a patriotic swell that identified the King and Queen as a key threat to the survival of the Revolution. Republican sentiments, expressed in tracts, speeches, and posters, escalated dramatically during the summer of 1792.

> **Discussion point:**
>
> Robespierre opposed the war on a number of grounds. He declared that he believed the proposed war to be counter-revolutionary. What do you think he meant by this?
>
> What were the arguments for and against war in 1792?

> **Brunswick Manifesto** Proclamation of the Duke of Brunswick, the commander of the Prussian forces attacking France in 1792, that if the revolutionaries did not restore the King and his family to their previous position of authority and freedom, the Prussian forces would raze the city of Paris.

On 10 August 1792, mobs in Paris, egged on by Marat, Danton, and other Jacobins, attacked the palace in which the royal family was housed. At the same time revolutionaries stormed the meeting place of the municipal Parisian government and abolished it, setting up a Revolutionary Commune which immediately abolished the National Assembly and proclaimed a new national government called the National Convention to be elected by universal male suffrage. In many ways the radical Jacobins, men such as Danton, Robespierre, Marat, and Hébert, used their influence with the Commune to pressure the more representative, and on the whole less radical, National Assembly and later National Convention to radicalize the Revolution. Though the Convention repeatedly resisted such moves, it nevertheless highlights the precarious nature of the new government.

> **Jean Paul Marat (1744–1793)**
>
> Trained as a doctor, Marat earned his reputation as an early revolutionary radical through his fiery speeches and journalism. A member of both the Cordeliers and Jacobin Clubs, his oratory could whip the population into a fury as it did in the period leading up to the September Massacres. Essentially a populist, Marat was inflexible in his calls for the death of the king, the danger of the *émigrés* and the use of terror. He was elected to the Convention, but was put on trial when his extremism alarmed the Girondins when they held sway. His acquittal was a sign that the Revolution was radicalizing. Marat was assassinated by Charlotte Corday as he sat in a bath.

The insurrection of 10 August 1792 was not enough to assuage the fear of Paris citizens, especially those who now collectively referred to themselves as *sans culottes* (literally "without breeches"), the tradesmen, artisans, and urban working poor who wished to distinguish themselves from the bourgeoisie and aristocracy (who wore knee breeches). As the Prussian army advanced on Paris and with the Brunswick Manifesto still ringing in their ears, mobs of frightened Parisians, again encouraged by radicals, particularly Marat, stormed the overflowing prisons of the capital and butchered the priests, nobles and their associates imprisoned there. In the end some 1,300 prisoners were murdered. These September Massacres posed an important question for the new government: who was in charge? If a functioning, stable government needs legitimacy and a monopoly of force to govern, the September Massacres exposed a dangerous weakness in the Convention and Commune. These bodies may have enjoyed a high degree of legitimacy, especially in Paris, but if mobs continued to take the law into their own hands, how could they claim to possess a monopoly of force? Over the next few months the National Convention would establish such a monopoly and build for itself the apparatus of massacre.

The newly formed National Convention in one of its first acts abolished the French monarchy,

> **Georges Danton (1759–1794)**
>
> Danton was a Parisian lawyer who became active in local politics after the Revolution broke out. He was active in both the Cordelliers Club, of which he was a founding member, and increasingly in the Jacobin Club. He played a role in the overthrow of the monarchy in August 1792. He would serve as the Republic's first Minister of Justice, a deputy to the National Convention, and as the first chairman of the Committee of Public Safety. During this time Danton feuded bitterly with Brissot and the Girondin faction. As Robespierre spurred on revolutionary terror, Danton sought to curb it and was eventually branded a moderate. He was arrested in March 1794 and his trial was a public sensation, but, despite rallying the gathered throngs, he was dutifully found guilty and executed.

inaugurating the first French Republic. The Convention duly drafted a new Republican constitution, but immediately suspended it in October 1793 at the urging of the Mountain, a radical Jacobin faction, so named for their habit of sitting in the highest seats in the Convention until the war was won. It did not take long for the radicals to call for Louis XVI to be put on trial for treason against the French people. While the ensuing trial and verdict may have been a foregone conclusion, the sentence was not. It was no small matter to kill a king. Nevertheless, by the slimmest of majorities and amid the protests of the Girondins, the Convention voted that the former King of France should die on the **guillotine**, and on 21 January 1793 he did. This radicalization of the Revolution meant that the Girondin faction of the Jacobin Club, the faction that led France into the war and with much of its support in departments outside of Paris, was eclipsed by the more radical Mountain faction, with its support in the Paris mob. The pendulum of Revolution now dictated that the previously radical Girondins were now the moderates, a moniker that would soon become very dangerous.

The **guillotine** was a device designed to decapitate those condemned to death. Adopted by the National Assembly in 1791, it was seen as a humane form of execution that helped realize the principle of equality before the law. Previously only aristocrats had the "privilege" of decapitation if condemned; peasants were hanged.

Revolutionary culture

With the radicalization of the Revolution came a keen desire by many revolutionaries, most notably Robespierre, to completely overhaul French society. For these men, this was not just politics. They saw in the proclamation of the Republic an opportunity to transform society to its core. One of the most startling efforts was the creation of an entirely new revolutionary calendar. From September 1793, the years would be renumbered starting with Year I. Each year consisted of 12 months, each month had three ten-day weeks, and each day had ten hours which lasted 100 minutes. The days leftover at the end of the year were reserved for Republican festivities. The months were renamed to better reflect the weather—the summer month Thermidor was taken from the Greek word for summer heat, and days were named after tools, animals or food. To the enlightened thinkers of the Revolution the use of a base ten was a very rational and ordered concept, mirroring the use of base ten measures—the adoption of a metric system. With the metric system, the whole country was brought under one rational system of measurement. Streets and cities were renamed. Titles were abolished and the blanket egalitarian form of address "citizen" was used for all— emphasizing the indivisibility of person from nation.

The new revolutionary republic that was taking shape if not in the streets then at least in Robespierre's mind came to be called the Republic of Virtue. Virtue had a fairly specific connotation in terms of the Republic. Robespierre sought to replace the Christian basis for the state with Virtue—that which the state needed to survive. In some ways it was a kind of civic mindedness raised to the level of quasi religion complete with festivals, ritual, icons and music. By June 1794 this quasi-religion was formalized into the Cult of the Supreme Being, designed to give an amorphous form to the idea of Virtue that would be acceptable to Christians resistant to the secularization of the

Discussion point:

What role does ritual and pageantry play in society? Why did Robespierre feel the need to dress up his idea of Virtue with public celebrations?

state while not disagreeable to those who had embraced the Cult of Reason earlier in the Revolution. The painter Jacques-Louis David was the main propagandist of this Republic of Virtue, at once purging the images, songs and rituals of the Christian monarchy and replacing them with Republican imagery, music, and festivals—lady liberty, reason, the tricolour of the Revolution, *les Marseilles*. Because of the increasing centralization of control, these cultural developments carried with them the force of law and this meant enforcement by the Committee of Public Safety, the main instrument of the Terror.

Maximilien Robespierre (1758–1794)

Robespierre was a lawyer from the north of France who came to prominence in the National Assembly as a member of the Jacobin Club and later as a public accuser in Paris. He was instrumental in the machinations that brought the National Convention into existence. As a delegate to the Convention and member of the Jacobin Club he argued strenuously against war with Austria and for the execution of the king both of which brought him into conflict with the Girondin faction of the Jacobin Club. He was elected to the Committee of Public Safety in July 1793, soon dominating that body and using his position to root out those he believed too moderate in revolutionary fervour such as Brissot and Danton and those whom he feared politically such as Hebert. Although he was widely thought to be "incorruptible" his increasing fanaticism alienated the population and eventually the Convention and even the Committee of Public Safety. He was arrested in July, 1794 and executed.

The Terror, 1793–94

By 1793 the National Convention was faced with a number of very serious problems. On the home front it had to deal with a riotous population in Paris, and series of regional revolts in places such as the **Vendée**, soaring prices made worse by war-time shortages, and an invading enemy that was now bolstered by the finances and naval power of Great Britain. The approach adopted by the Convention, now dominated by the radical Jacobin faction known as the Mountain, was one of centralized economic control, uniformity of opinion, and violent, state-sponsored repression—The Terror.

The Terror was a programme by which the Convention hoped to gain control of the country and win the war. The Committee of Public Safety, a committee of the Convention, was entrusted with the management of this programme. This group of twelve, each of whom had to stand for re-election by the Convention each month, began to function very much like an executive, with broad power to pursue the war, which in fact gave it broad powers to co-ordinate the economy, dictate military strategy, round up and try suspected counter-revolutionaries, and manage the apparatus of censorship. Eventually this Committee even drafted the new republican constitution.

The Committee of Public Safety's plan for winning the war centred on mobilizing the whole nation:

- *levée en masse*—conscription of men and material
- wage controls—law of maximum
- price controls—law of maximum
- seizure of gold
- ban on the export of gold
- ban on hoarding
- centralization of scientific and industrial innovation.

The **Vendée** is a region in west central France that rose in open rebellion against the Republican Convention in the spring of 1793. Grievances revolved around the Civil Constitution of the Clergy, conscription and centralization. The civil war in the Vendée raged until 1796.

At the heart of the work of the Committee of Public Safety was the suppression of counter-revolutionaries. To this end the Committee was assisted by a number of laws, which biased the proceedings in the Committee's favour. The Law of Suspect, passed on 17 September 1794, empowered Revolutionary Tribunals and local revolutionary committees to round up and try anyone who through their actions or words had not shown sufficient devotion to the Revolution. Later in the Terror this incredibly sweeping law was augmented by the Law of 22 Prairial through which the accused was deprived of defence counsel and the Tribunals limited to a sentence of death in the case of a guilty verdict. Without a clear definition of what constituted counter-revolutionary activity, the Terror was an instrument of political vengeance as much as revolutionary zeal. Even before the Terror officially began in September of 1793, leading Girondins had been dragged from the Convention to face charges of counter-revolution and eventual execution at the hands of an extremist faction of the Jacobins led by Jacques René Hébert. In turn, throughout the Terror, Hébert and his followers were sent to the guillotine as were Georges Danton and his followers. Hébert and his followers, the *enragés*, were calling for ever more radical suppression of suspected counter-revolutionaries. Danton and his followers, the *indulgents*, on the other hand called for an end to the Terror. Both of these factions were Jacobins, but their ideas were a threat to the work of the Committee of Public Safety and its chairman, Robespierre.

? What are the risks involved in using force to eliminate political rivals?

A fiery orator, Danton was a controversial revolutionary leader. Initially a radical he eventually was the acknowledged leader of the *indulgents*, a faction that called for an end to the reign of Terror. His last words typified his personality, "Show my head to the people. It is worth seeing." Although Robespierre eliminated most of his rivals, both the *indulgents* and the *enragés*, still others rose in opposition.

Throughout the course of 1793–4, the Terror saw to the arrest of over 300,000 people, 17,000 of whom were executed although some estimates are much higher. This does not include those who died in prison, nor does it include those killed in combat in provinces that were in open revolt against the Convention such as the Vendée and Britanny. One might think that what was left of the aristocracy or **refractory clergy** made up the majority of those deemed to be counter-revolutionaries. This was not the case. The majority of the Terror's victims were members of the Third Estate. The Terror was not a monolithic structure. It operated differently at different times and in different places. While uttering pro-royalist (or Dantonist or Hébertist) musings could get you brought before a Tribunal, so could any number of other less political actions. The **reverse onus** implied by the Law of Suspect and the Law of 22 *Prairial* meant that the Terror could be, and was, used to settle all manner of political, economic, business or

Refractory clergy Clergy who refused to take the oath of allegiance to the French government as head of the Church.

Reverse onus is the legal practice of requiring the accused in an action to prove their innocence. In terms of Terror, the accused had to prove that were not counter-revolutionary. Reverse onus places a great deal of power in the hands of accusers.

personal matters. An accusation was often all it took to get arrested and brought before a Tribunal and ultimately to the guillotine. The public ritual of execution became an important aspect of the Terror. The condemned rode through the streets in carts to the central square where the guillotine was set up on a platform. This applied to all the condemned, from the former Queen, Marie Antoinette executed in October 1793, to countless condemned peasants. The executions were a common pastime for many citizens and were often witnessed by large crowds, especially early in the Terror. The public nature of the executions had it purpose. It demonstrated the coercive power of the state and was therefore seen as a deterrent to counter-revolutionaries. It was also an act of the nation and as such should be witnessed by the nation—an example of civic participation.

Outside of Paris the example of the Vendée spread to other areas and cities of France. At times Bordeaux, Toulouse, Lyons, and Marseilles were in revolt against the central government in Paris. The Convention labelled these rebellions Federalism, adherence to which then became an example of counter-revolutionary activity and subject to the Terror. Representatives from the Convention were sent "on mission" to various departments of the country to ensure obedience to the dictates of the Convention and the Committee of Public Safety and to apply the Terror when they were not obeyed.

By the summer of 1794, however, the popularity of the Committee was at a low ebb. The war was now going well for France and the public could see little reason for the continuation

TOK Link
Ways of Knowing—Language

Robespierre defended the Terror in a speech to the National Convention on 5 February 1794. In it he explained the relationship of Terror to Virtue:

If the spring of popular government in time of peace is virtue, the springs of popular government in revolution are at once virtue and terror: virtue, without which terror is fatal; terror, without which virtue is powerless. Terror is nothing other than justice, prompt, severe, inflexible; it is therefore an emanation of virtue; it is not so much a special principle as it is a consequence of the general principle of democracy applied to our country's most urgent needs.

Maximilien Robespierre. "Justification of the Use of Terror", Speech to the National Convention, 5 February 1794. *Modern History Sourcebook*, http://www.fordham.edu/halsall/mod/robespierre-terror.html.

Any terrorist attack is an act of cowardice. It is an act of murder. It is a barbaric act that violates the fundamental principles of human decency.

Kevin Rudd, Prime Minister of Australia, responding to the bombing of a Jakarta hotel, 2009.

 How does Robespierre's use of the word "Terror" differ from Prime Minister Rudd's usage? What do you think are the reasons for this difference? What are the knowledge issues associated with each of these statements?

Discussion point:

A number of modern constitutions expressly state that those accused of crimes have the right to the presumption of innocence.

 Why do some people believe the idea of reverse onus in criminal law to be dangerous? When else in history has the concept of reverse onus been used by governments?

Activity:
Robespierre

Maximilian Robespierre is a complex historic figure with his principles and actions often seemingly at odds with each other. Research, analyse and evaluate the career of Robespierre from the 1780s through to his execution in July of 1794 using the following topics as a guide.

● Philosophical influences and principles

● Early career

● Role in the National Assembly

● Role in the National Convention

● Role on the Committee of Public Safety

● Ideas of Virtue and the implementation of the Republic of Virtue

● Conflict with the *enragés* and the *indulgent*

of the draconian policies of the Committee of Public Safety. Much of this animosity was directed against the chairman of the Committee and virtual dictator of the country, Robespierre. As the rate of executions rose during the late spring of 1794, public dissatisfaction turned into political dissatisfaction. The Convention took action against Robespierre and his followers in July 1794 (*Thermidor* in the new revolutionary calendar). After a brief struggle in which the army sided with the Convention, Robespierre and his followers, having lost both their legitimacy and monopoly of force, were captured and put to the guillotine the next day.

The Directory, 1795–99

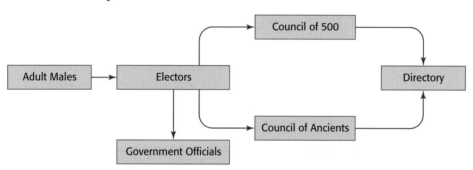

With the fall of Robespierre and the **Thermidorian Reaction** that followed, the revolutionary pendulum began to swing back. After a short, sharp period of reactionary popular and official violence against Terrorists called the White Terror, the Convention set about constructing yet another system of government in hopes of realizing the principles of the Revolution. The result was to be a return of the bourgeoisie as the dominant political class in the new government, called the Directory for the executive branch of government.

This new government was to be indirectly elected by universal adult male suffrage. These voters would choose electors, generally wealthy and propertied, who would then choose local and national officials as well as the members of the bicameral legislative assembly. By the time the first free elections were held under the new constitution in 1797, royalist politicians dominated the results, a fact that did not bode well for members of the Convention who had played roles in the trial and execution of the King or the Terror. Without any significant legitimacy, as the elections proved, these ex-Conventionists would have to rely on establishing a monopoly of force to govern, and this would mean the complicity of at least part of the army. The general to whom they turned was Napoleon Bonaparte.

The **Thermidorian reaction** refers to the removal of Robespierre, Louis de Saint-Just and their followers from power in the summer of 1794 (Thermidor in the new calendar). The Thermidoreans quickly moved to dismantle the instruments of the Terror including the Committee of Public Safety, but not before it executed Robespierre, Saint-Just and other "Terrorists".

Discussion point:

… the Revolution, like Saturn, devouring successively all her children, will produce at last a despotism with the calamities that accompany it …

This quote is from a speech by the Girondin Pierre Vergniaud on 13 March 1793. Examine the events from 1789 to 1794. To what extent is his characterization of the French Revolution devouring its children accurate in this period? To what extent did his prediction of tyranny come to pass?

Activity:

Source analysis

Was there a revolutionary Class?

Source A

The following is an excerpt from *The German Ideology* written by Karl Marx in 1845–46.

> *When the French bourgeoisie overthrew the rule of the aristocracy, it thereby made it possible for many proletarians to raise themselves above the proletariat, but only insofar as they became bourgeois.*

Source: Karl Marx quoted in Furet, F. (ed.). 1986. *Marx and the French Revolution*. Chicago, USA. University of Chicago Press. p. 146.

Source B

The following is an excerpt written by the historian William Doyle in 2001.

> *… few fortunes were made in the professions. The lot—and often indeed the aim—of most professional bourgeoisie was to vegetate in modest, undemanding, but comfortable circumstances….*

Source: Doyle, William. 2002. *The Oxford History of the French Revolution*. Oxford, UK. Oxford University Press. p. 25.

Source C

The following is an excerpt written by the historian Simon Schama in 1992.

> *One of the prevailing clichés of old-régime history is that privilege was inimical to commercial enterprise. But even a cursory examination of the eighteenth-century French economy … reveals the nobility deeply involved in finance, business and industry … Less well known, however, is the extent to which they were important participants in banking, maritime trade … and in industrial enterprise of the most innovative kind. At the very heart of the French elite, then,*

is a capitalist nobility of immense significance to the future of the national economy.

Source: Schama, Simon. 1992. *Citizens: A Chronicle of the French Revolution*. New York, USA. Alfred Knopf. p. 18.

Source D

The following is an excerpt from the pamphlet "What is the Third Estate?" written by the revolutionary Emmanuel-Joseph Sieyès in 1789.

> *It is not sufficient to show that privileged persons, far from being useful to the nation, cannot but enfeeble and injure it; it is necessary to prove further that the noble order does not enter at all into the social organization; that it may indeed be a burden upon the nation, but that it cannot of itself constitute a nation.*

Source: Whitcomb, M. (ed.). 1899. *Translations and Reprints from the Original Sources of European History*. vol. 6. Philadelphia, USA. University of Pennsylvania History Department. pp. 32–35.

Questions

1 **a** What does Schama mean when he writes "One of the prevailing clichés of old-régime history is that privilege was inimical to commercial enterprise?" [Source C]

b What were "the professions?" [Source B]

2 Compare and contrast the views of the nobility in Source C and Source D.

3 With reference to their origin and purpose, evaluate the value and limitations of Source A and Source B to historians studying the *ancien régime*.

4 Using the sources and further research, evaluate the extent to which the social structure of the *ancien régime* was a major cause of the French Revolution.

Bonaparte's Rise

By 1796 the French Republic had been at war for four years, and had finally managed to take the fight beyond its borders. Bonaparte took command of French forces fighting the Austrians in northern Italy. This Italian campaign and surrounding events were to prove pivotal in the development of Bonaparte not only as a military leader but as a civil administrator as well. Operating far from a weak central government meant that Napoleon had a great deal of freedom. His soldiers were paid because of him, not the Directory. His defeated enemies negotiated with him, not the Directory. It was he who administered his conquered territory, not the Directory. In essence, he fulfilled the duties of a central government in northern Italy, all the while gaining important experience.

Bonaparte's influence became evident when it was to him that the government turned when the royalists won the elections of 1797. In September of that same year, under the watchful eye of

Bonaparte's troops, the Directory invalidated the elections and purged sympathetic directors and officials, thereby repudiating what legitimacy it did enjoy. This was the coup d'état of Fructidor. In the absence of any meaningful legitimacy after 1797, the Directory had to rely on its monopoly of force, which included a return to many of the tactics of the Committee of Public Safety and most importantly a dependence on the army and this meant a reliance on Napoleon.

France's most significant and constant enemy since 1792 had been Great Britain. It had been the British fleet that had occupied the port of Toulon and British funds that had sustained Austrian forces since 1792. The political and financial burdens of its anti-revolutionary foreign policy had significantly weakened Britain's ability to press the fight. The British treasury was haemorrhaging gold to support its allies. Poor harvests threatened its food supply. Even the vaunted Royal Navy was in crisis. In 1797 ships of the Channel Fleet at Spithead and Nore mutinied against poor wages and living conditions. The principles of the French Revolution provided much of the intellectual structure to these mutinies. The net result of these developments was that peace with France was an attractive prospect for the British Prime Minister William Pitt.

 How might the IB Learner Profile relate to the recovery and study of antiquities?

After five years of war and all the difficulties that accompanied it, peace would also seem appealing to the Directory. Not necessarily. Much of the dictatorial powers that the Directory claimed and exercised were justified by the necessities of war. If peace broke out, the calls for free elections, the end of censorship, arbitrary arrest, the purging of opposition and the like would be hard to ignore. Likewise, the problem for Bonaparte was that, as a soldier, his career advancement required war.

After the coup d'état of Fructidor and Napoleon's role in it, the prospect of peace with Britain evaporated and the French government began plotting an invasion of Great Britain, an expedition to be commanded by Napoleon. Despite Britain's tribulations, the prospect for the success of such an invasion was dubious and Napoleon knew it. How then to threaten Britain while at the same time advancing his career? The unlikely answer was Egypt.

As unfeasible as an expedition to Egypt may seem in hindsight, at the time it was infinitely preferable to an invasion of the British Isles. From Egypt, theoretically, France could threaten Britain's rich eastern

Napoleon conceived of the expedition to Egypt as more than a military mission. He took academics, scientists, and historians to study the ancient Egyptian culture and uncovered and studied treasures such as the Rosetta Stone. Much of the treasure that the French discovered returned with them to Europe. The ownership of these articles has been disputed ever since.

trade. The expedition suited Napoleon's growing estimation of himself. Had not Alexander's fame been cemented in Egypt? The intellectual treasures of Egypt appealed to Bonaparte's Enlightenment pedigree. For the Directory, an expedition to Egypt would keep the ambitious and increasingly popular Napoleon away from Parisian intrigues while maintaining the need for war-time measures. The **Mamelukes** who administered Egypt for their Ottoman overlords, though fierce warriors, should pose little problem for Bonaparte's veterans of the Italian campaign. It would certainly be easier to elude the Royal Navy in the vast Mediterranean than in the narrow English Channel. In 1798, Napoleon and an army of 40,000 embarked at Marseilles, evaded a British Royal Navy squadron in the Mediterranean and landed in Egypt.

From Directory to Consulate

As we will see, Napoleon's Egyptian escapade did not last long. In his absence the Directory grew even weaker, the population grew weary of yet another repressive regime, high prices and rumours of corruption. Foreign armies were again moving against France and there appeared to be no relief in the immediate future. The Directory, indeed, had little faith in itself, with men like the Abbe Sieyès, Talleyrand, and Roger Ducos musing that France needed a form of government with a stronger executive branch. Again, however, in the absence of any popular legitimacy, these conspiratorial directors needed a monopoly of force to achieve the change they sought. Getting wind of this plot and seeing opportunity in it, Napoleon abandoned his army in Egypt and returned to France to once again lend muscle to a seizure of power. He remained popular despite being stranded in Egypt, but he was not strong enough to assume power alone. In November 1799, he called together the Council of 500 and demanded that it change the constitution to reflect the views of Sieyès and the other conspirators. To the General's shock the 500 refused and began to hurl abuse at him. At this point, troops were called in to accomplish with muskets what Bonaparte could not with words and so completed Napoleon's second coup d'état—the coup d'état of 18 Brumaire. The Directory was thus abolished and yet another governmental system was established, the fourth since the Revolution had begun ten years earlier.

The Consulate was a sort of triumvirate, where three Consuls shared power, though not equally. The Consuls were guided by three bodies. The Council of State drafted proposed laws. The Tribunate could debate these laws, but had no decision-making power. The Legislative Assembly could pass or reject legislation without discussion. Theoretically, members

The **Mamelukes** were a caste of soldiers and administrators who defended and oversaw parts of the Ottoman Empire such as Egypt in the name of the Sultan.

Activity:
Napoleon and Egypt

Divide the class into three groups:

- Group A: Supporters of Napoleon
- Group B: Opponents of Napoleon
- Group C: Directors

Group A will make a presentation arguing in favour of the expedition to Egypt in 1798. Group B will argue against this expedition. Group C will question both groups and vote on whether or not to authorize the expedition.

Emmanuel-Joseph Sieyès, abbé (1748–1836)

Very influential in the early stages of the Revolution having a hand in the drafting of both the Tennis Court Oath and the Declaration of the Rights of Man, Sieyès had long been a vocal opponent of vested privilege. He sat in the Estates General, National Convention, The Council of 500, and eventually became a Director. He even served a short term on the Committee of Public Safety after the fall of Robespierre. Convinced that democracy run amok had caused the worst excesses of the Revolution, Sieyès argued for the strengthening of the executive branch of the government at the expense of the legislative branch and as such was instrumental in the coup that brought Napoleon and the Consulate to power in 1799.

of these bodies were elected by universal male suffrage. Citizens voted candidates to lists of Notables. It was from these lists that the Council of State would appoint all the officials of the regime, including the members of the three parliamentary bodies. It was not difficult to discern that real decision-making rested with the Council of State and within this body primarily with the First Consul. Napoleon was the First Consul. Nevertheless, Napoleon felt the need for some expression of popular legitimacy for this new regime and so submitted this scheme to the people of France. In an overwhelming show of support of questionable legality and validity, the French accepted the Consulate in a referendum held in November 1800. They were not to be meaningfully consulted again.

Charles Maurice de Talleyrand-Périgord (1754–1838)

Talleyrand was a ubiquitous politician and diplomat throughout the Revolutionary, Napoleonic, and Restoration period. Born into the Second Estate, Talleyrand later joined the clergy and grew even wealthier from church appointments. He was elected to represent the First Estate in the Estates General of 1789. A skilled orator and negotiator, Talleyrand was instrumental in the drafting of the Civil Constitution of the Clergy. As the Revolution radicalized, Talleyrand escaped to London and later to the United States. After the Thermidorian Reaction he returned to France and in 1797 was named Foreign Minister. Seeing the rise of Napoleon as an opportunity for his own advancement, Talleyrand drew close to the future Emperor after 1797 becoming the Consulate's Foreign Minister and later Foreign Minister in the Empire until 1807. He distanced himself from Napoleon after 1807. Having spent the time after 1807 ingratiating himself to those who would eventually defeat Napoleon, he was France's representative at the Congress of Vienna, his skill largely responsible for the favorable terms France received from the victors. Talleyrand would once again emerge as an important figure in the reign of King Louis-Philippe as France's ambassador to Great Britain.

Why did France accept this sham democracy, this thinly veiled dictatorship? The answer is more complex than it might at first seem. In short, Napoleon gave many French citizens what they had been looking for after ten years of revolutionary upheaval—stability. Stability, however, meant different things for different people. For the majority of working people it meant economic stability in the form of stable prices. For businessmen it meant stable currency and an ordered economic system. For aristocrats and royalists it meant a legally stable system that would protect them as much as it would protect the revolutionaries. For terrorists and regicides it likewise meant a legally stable system that would protect them from those that would take revenge for their past deeds while at the same time protect the gains that had been made in human equality. For manufacturers it meant a stable demand for their wares. For Catholics it meant a stable religious system that permitted them to worship in public. For all citizens of France it meant social and administrative stability and an end to outbursts of mob justice. For French nationalists it meant a stable and united France, purged of regional revolt. Stability was thus Napoleon's goal, not ideological or philosophical principle. As a master of military logistics, it was practicality that he valued. If enlightenment principles brought stability, so be it. If he needed to resort to elements of the *ancien régime* then he would. Liberalism and conservatism were meaningless labels to him. He would reward those who could and would help him, regardless of political background. Amnesty was granted to *émigrés* who returned and pledged their loyalty to him. He valued competence and loyalty and received it in good measure. Through his embrace of pragmatism, Napoleon found ways to achieve either the stability that each group desired or at least the illusion of that stability.

France under Napoleon

The Concordat of 1801

One of the most deeply divisive policies of the Revolution was the National Assembly's imposition of the Civil Constitution of the Clergy. The legislation of religion is tricky. Organized religion, like any other human behaviour, can be controlled through legislation. Governments can and do restrict public worship, the training of clergy, the publication and distribution of sacred texts, and the display of religious articles. The problem, however, is that organized religion is but the formalized manifestation of belief, and belief is far more difficult to control by law. Outlawing public worship and closing Catholic seminaries, confiscating church lands and denying the sovereignty of the Pope, did not stop the French from believing in the tenets of Catholicism. It only served to embitter the moderately devout and drive the seriously devout underground. It alienated Catholics that had been sympathetic to the goals of the Revolution and created a rallying point for the enemies of the Revolution. The rebellion of the Vendée had been in large part a response to the restrictions placed on the Catholic religion by the Civil Constitution of the Clergy.

This was patently obvious to Napoleon, himself deeply ambivalent to religion in general. He simply recognized that the Civil Constitution of the Clergy was causing dissatisfaction within France to no advantage. In mid 1800, Napoleon indicated that he was interested in a rapprochement with the Pope and his church. After nine months of negotiation an agreement was reached that was acceptable to both Napoleon and Pope Pius VII. The Concordat of 1801 re-established the Catholic Church in France under the following conditions:

- Church lands that had been confiscated under the Civil Constitution would not be returned.
- The clergy would continue to be appointed by the French government, but had to be confirmed by the Pope.
- The French government would pay the French clergy a reasonable salary.
- Napoleon pledged that the majority of the French people would be Catholic.
- Clergy were placed under the authority of the Pope.
- Catholic public worship was allowed.
- Catholic seminaries in France were reopened.
- By signing the Concordat, the Pope recognized the legitimacy of the French Republic.

Enlightenment notions like the separation of church and state and the idea that the church, as part of national society should be subject to the same central authority as other aspects of the national body politic, were cleverly preserved in the Concordat. Napoleon agreed that the majority of French citizens would be Catholic, a fact that was true then and is, indeed, true today. Napoleon did not promise that all French citizens would be Catholic and so as long as 50 percent plus one was Catholic, the remainder could be whatever religion they chose or none at all. He even extended the salary that had been promised to the Catholic clergy to the Protestant clergy. Religious belief, be it Catholic, Protestant or even atheist, was removed as a barrier to or requirement for full French citizenship as defined by Napoleon. In reality Napoleon gave up very little to regain the recognition of the Vatican and the legitimacy that came with it. Religious stability had been cheaply bought, but to some degree short-lived—Napoleon was excommunicated in 1809 after his relations with the Vatican again soured.

The Code Napoleon

One of the by-products of the personal rule of the *ancien régime* had been the accumulation over centuries of scores of legal ordinances, traditions, customs, laws and regulations. The foundation of law in the south of France was Roman law while a different set of customs were used as the basis of law in the north of the country. The Church also exercised a great deal of legal authority throughout the *ancien régime*. The regulations that governed business in the south of France may never have even been heard of in the north. The administration of justice in Arras differed from the administration of justice in Marseilles. To this exceedingly complex system was added ten years of chaotic revolutionary rule. By the time Napoleon took control, in the form of the Consulate in 1799, the legal framework of France was confused and confusing. Napoleon took issue with this state of affairs on two levels. In practical terms it was an affront to Napoleon the soldier. It was an incredibly inefficient structure in which there was great opportunity for corruption and waste. Where this corruption and waste extended into the financial realm, it bred a dangerous lack of confidence both within France and across Europe, making financing the regime and its wars increasingly difficult. The Revolution had destroyed many of the traditional sources of legal authority such as the *parlements* and the Church. The soldier in him understood that an effective organization could not long operate on such a foundation or lack of one. The soldier in him saw a strong central authority as the natural solution to this problem. On the other hand, the current state of affairs offended Napoleon the enlightenment thinker. The codification of laws had been a common theme amongst the enlightened despots of the 18th century from Catherine the Great of Russia to Maria Theresa of Austria. Enlightenment thought held that just as the natural world was governed by natural laws, standardized and predictable laws should likewise govern the social, political and economic world. Such was the dual motivation for Napoleon's drastic reorganization of the civil administration of France.

Napoleon assembled a commission of jurists to carry out this massive project. By 1804 the Civil Code was ready to be published. It would be followed by a code of civil procedure, a code of criminal procedure, a commercial code, and a penal code over the course of the following five years.

Economics

The failure of the previous revolutionary regimes, and indeed the *ancien régime,* can be attributed, in large measure, to their inability to find a lasting solution to France's financial problems. Napoleon also understood that if he were to realize his Imperial ambitions it would require war and war was expensive. He needed a sound financial system through which he could finance his wars. The key to establishing such a system was confidence. Only when there was widespread confidence in the French financial system could he raise the money he would need to rule France and conquer Europe. To this end, he established the Bank of France.

The Bank was at first quite independent of the government. It was a private stock company that had the sole right to issue bank notes at first in the Paris region and later in the whole country. The initial capitalization of 30,000,000 francs was divided into 30,000 shares, some of which were purchased by Napoleon and his associates. Its initial independence from the government was in part an attempt to disassociate it from the poor performance of previous governments in managing the French economy. By 1806, the Bank was experiencing difficulties and Napoleon took more direct control of its operations. Confidence in the Bank grew and its notes became increasingly accepted largely because of the fact that they were convertible to gold coins on demand, yet they were not to become **legal tender** until 1848. Nevertheless, Napoleon, through the Bank of France, established France's first sound paper currency.

> **Legal tender** A term that denotes currency that, by law, must be accepted as payment.

The Napoleonic Code also set out the rights, or rather lack thereof, for French workers. The Code banned organized labour unions and restricted the movement of workers. Workers were required to carry passbooks and were forbidden from taking legal action against their employers, presumably to ensure an adequate workforce in areas that needed it. Aware of the danger posed by high bread prices, Napoleon took pains to control food prices. As his wars dragged on, he began restricting the export of grain, as part of a broader protectionist trade policy.

Taxation too was regularized. Tax exemptions were abolished, removing any lingering social stigma associated with paying them. The collection of taxes was bureaucratized and made more efficient and the system closely supervised for waste and corruption. These tax reforms finally realized the goals of successive revolutionary governments and they allowed the Napoleon's regime to establish predictable financial plans. Government expenditures and accounting were regularized by Napoleon's growing bureaucracy and this too bred increased confidence in the system.

> **Discussion point:**
>
> What role does confidence play in an economic system? Why is it important?

Social policy

As we have mentioned, a guiding principle for Napoleon's administration was that government and military careers were open to those who had talent. No longer was social standing, political connection, or wealth a guarantee of position. Increasingly, education was seen as a path to a career and if Napoleon wanted the best and the brightest that France had to offer, it made sense to him that education had to be more widely accessible and geared towards practical matters. To this end he developed a system of state-run secondary schools to train young men for government and military careers. The regime established scholarships to encourage those with ability. This movement continued throughout Europe during the 19th century as the privileges of aristocratic government were assailed and cries for democracy and equality grew louder. Education was increasingly seen as the great equalizer and the mechanism by which a more democratic society could be achieved. In higher education, Napoleon's tastes also ran to practical subjects. He patronized the sciences across France while at the same time ignoring and indeed suppressing much of the liberal arts.

Women did not fare well in any of the social reforms that Napoleon initiated. The codes established that the husband controlled all rights to property, including the children of a marriage. Even if the property was owned by the wife, she needed her husband's consent to sell it or to leverage it for a loan. Although Napoleon established the legality of civil marriage and divorce, a wife's ability to bring divorce proceedings against her husband was severely limited.

Napoleon largely succeeded in establishing domestic stability in France by means of rationalization and centralization and at the cost of civil liberties and open discourse. His state police, directed by Joseph Fouché, ensured that any dissent was within the parameters set out by Napoleon and these were generally narrow. While he encouraged scientific inquiry, Napoleon's regime suppressed expressions of the liberal arts, especially when they targeted his policies. The domestic stability he achieved was in many ways a means to his foreign policy ends, which in turn, served to undo much of that same domestic stability.

Activity:

The progress of the Revolution

Use points from the timeline on page 57–8 to plot the course of the Revolution with the calling of the Estates General as your point of origin. Using specific evidence to support your position, explain why the Revolution took the course it did.

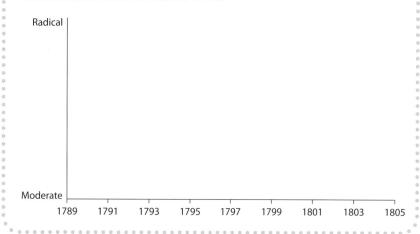

The Napoleonic Wars

For the purposes of study, we have divided Napoleon's domestic policy from his foreign policy, but this is by and large an artificial partition. As in most countries, domestic policy and foreign policy flow from each other and are circumscribed by the domestic and foreign context at any given time. For example, war, one of the primary tools of foreign policy, requires money, often obtained from taxation, which is a key component of domestic policy. Napoleon's aggressive foreign policy and the compulsion to Empire originated from a number of impulses including the legacy of the Revolution, the traditional French desire to achieve what were considered to be the country's natural boundaries, the prevailing economic circumstances, Napoleon's considerable ego, and Europe's response to these impulses.

Revolutionary warfare

The French Revolution changed the concept of nation in France, and also throughout Europe over time. With this change in the nature of the state came a resultant transformation in all the enterprises of state, from gathering taxes, to choosing leaders. One of the most profound changes came in the theory and practice of war. No longer was war the purview of aristocratic officers commanding professional soldiers in the name of a monarch. The revolutionary armies of France, at least initially, were citizen armies. If war was a national action and the people were the nation, then military service became a national duty. The flight of the *émigrés* had essentially decapitated the army, the nobility composing as they had the officer corps in the Royal army. This opened the officer ranks to men of talent in a very practical way even as the Declaration of Rights of Man had done in a theoretical way. Many of Bonaparte's generals and later marshals had come through the ranks in a way that had been impossible in the army of Louis XVI. This new conception of "nation" also allowed for a mass mobilization of men and material on a scale that had not been seen before as the *levée en masse* of 1793 illustrated. The quality of these material resources was also improving, allowing for more and larger artillery, greater mobility and improved communication. Military organization was also changing by the time of the Revolution. Military theorists, many of them French, began to advocate a so-called divisional structure in which armies were divided into independent divisions each containing all the elements it needed to fight on its own—cavalry, artillery, infantry and signals. This allowed for greater mobility and flexibility in deploying forces. Bonaparte would later improve on this system by bringing several of these divisions together into a corps, which increased the offensive power of the division while maintaining the flexibility and unifying its command. So it appears, then, that Napoleon inherited a military Revolution as much as he created one. Perhaps his great organizational genius was the ability to take each of these innovations in pursuit of a unified vision— Napoleon's own Imperial vision.

Warfare as characterized by the Napoleonic Wars was unlike the continuous conflict inherent in modern total war. Wars, as such, were more a series of campaigns in which commanders spent weeks, even months, manoeuvering their forces into position for a large pitched battle that might last one or two days. Mobility and the provisioning of armies was therefore the key to success, immortalized in one of Napoleon's many aphorisms, "An army marches on its stomach". It is also why all of Europe was subject to the hardship of massive armies roaming the Continent feeding themselves on what they could forage from the countryside.

Napoleon's opponents: the coalitions

Napoleon seldom faced individual countries as opponents. Such was the alarm he and an expansionary France engendered in the other European powers. The contagion of revolutionary ideals also frightened the established regimes of Europe. When this alarm was combined with the national aspirations of these same powers, they were able, at least for short periods of time, to put aside differences and make common cause against Bonaparte. It is important to remember that each power's foreign policy did not revolve solely around defeating Napoleon and restoring the **status quo ante bellum**. Each power had a definite interest in checking Napoleonic domination, but each also had its own ambitions and these interests were not always complimentary and indeed engendered a measure of distrust between the allies.

> **status quo ante bellum** This is a Latin phrase referring to the state of affairs before the start of any given war.

Great Britain

When the Revolution broke out it was greeted by a divided public opinion in Great Britain and as such it initially drove the government of William Pitt to the middle. He was worried about the implications of the Revolution for British interests in Ireland and looked upon radical politics with disdain, but he was also committed to reforming Britain's finances and could hardly afford any Continental adventures. Nevertheless, by the time Europe lined up against France in 1792, Pitt was eying the Continent with increasing concern. Should France take the Channel ports, it would pose a direct threat to the national interests of Great Britain. By the end of 1792, the combination of the September Massacres, the establishment of the Convention, the invasion of the Low Countries and the trial of the King of France impelled Pitt to take a more direct role in Continental developments. From 1792 until Napoleon's final defeat at Waterloo in 1815, Britain played a central role in either fighting the French or financing those countries that were fighting the French. In many ways the Third Coalition was cemented together as much by British sterling as it was by any fear of Napoleonic expansion. After Spanish and Portuguese citizens rose against French occupiers in 1808, Britain committed a sizable force to their support sparking the Peninsular War that would drag on for five years. To these various military, diplomatic and financial manoeuvres was added the age-old British strategy of naval blockade.

Austria

Geography helped dictate the traditional rivalry between the Austrian Hapsburgs and France. A foreign policy goal since the reign of Louis XIV, France's aspiration to reach its natural boundaries, would have to be at the expense of Austrian holdings, particularly in the Netherlands and among its client states on the Rhine. The Revolution did nothing to change this situation and in fact aggravated it. Marie Antoinette was the sister of the Hapsburg Emperor Leopold II and aunt to his successor Francis II. The Convention's attempts to curtail the rights of German princes in the Rhine region, particularly in Alsace, also threatened Austrian interests. Austria joined with Prussia in war against France in 1792 and would wage this war intermittently until 1815, first against Revolutionary France and later against Napoleonic France. Napoleon's reorganization of Central Europe and his domination of the Italian states ensured this. At times the Austrians did well against the French armies, particularly at the beginning of the War of the Second Coalition, 1799–1803. Several decisive defeats at the hands of Napoleon and his marshals forced Austria to make peace with the French on Napoleon's terms at Campo Formio (1797), Lunéville (1801), and Pressburg (1805). In 1809, the Austrians would again rise against Napoleon, notably in what was characterized as a war of national liberation, calling on concepts such as liberty and nationalism, concepts born out of the French Revolution. Clearly, military dominance was not enough to control Austria and so Napoleon turned to an equally old diplomatic tool, marriage. The Emperor married the Austrian princess Marie Louis, daughter to the Austrian Emperor, in 1801 in an effort both to sire a son and bind the Austrians to him by more than just military defeat. This had the awkward consequences, however, of making Napoleon the nephew by marriage of the executed Louis XVI and bringing another "Austrian woman" to the throne of France.

Prussia

Although she was drawn into a war with France in 1792, Prussia was more interested in developments on her eastern frontier. The status and partition of Poland, so thought Frederick William II, was more important to the future of Prussia. The combined menace of Russia and Austria in the east, both also deeply interested in the partition of Poland, impelled Prussia to keep the bulk of her forces in the east during the War of the First Coalition. As such, Prussia never wholeheartedly pursued the war against Revolutionary France and abandoned the First Coalition in 1795 after signing the Peace of Basel. Napoleon would rouse Prussia ten years later with his reorganization of the German states. Electing to stay out of the Third Coalition, Frederick William III found himself alone and isolated after the Austro-Russian armies were routed at Ulm and Austerlitz. It was then the turn of the vaunted Prussian army to be humbled by Napoleon and his *grande armée*. This combination of indecision, delay and defeat meant that Prussia would suffer greatly in the period 1807–12, but she would return to prominence in the final defeat of Napoleonic France in 1815.

Russia

Russia has always had a complicated relationship with Western Europe. At times it has pursued an almost isolationist stance, preferring to look either inward or to Asia and Asia Minor as a focus of its energies. At other times it has become deeply involved in the affairs of Western Europe. Such was the case during the revolutionary period. From the enlightened pretensions and western expansion of Catherine the Great to the would-be peacemaker Alexander I, Russia played a direct role in the efforts to check Napoleonic ambition in Europe. Initially Catherine saw the instability in France along with Austria's and Prussia's admittedly half-hearted interest in crusading against the Revolution, as demonstrated by the contingent wording in the Declaration of Pillnitz, as a chance to acquire portions of Poland. Only after Prussia objected did she propose to share Poland with Frederick William in order to avoid a war. Polish nationalism engendered by the partition and fanned as it was from Paris, kept Catherine's gaze focused on Poland throughout the war of the First Coalition. When Tsar Paul I ascended to the throne in 1796, his deep suspicion of the ideals of the Revolution led him into the Second Coalition and Russia's armies into Western Europe. Russia's ambitions, especially in the Mediterranean and south-central Asia, often collided with British interests and this made co-operation between the two powers difficult if not impossible at times. This clash caused Russia to withdraw from the Second Coalition in 1799. After Alexander I, who was more deeply and genuinely influenced by the Enlightenment than his grandmother Catherine, came to the throne in 1802, he increasingly saw Napoleonic expansion as a threat to any rational and enlightened system of European diplomacy. It was this enlightened self-interest mixed with Alexander's sizable ego that impelled Russia to wade again into the affairs of Western Europe in the War of the Third Coalition. Alexander's desire for more economic independence increasingly alienated Russia from the strictures of the Continental system eventually provoking the folly of Napoleon's 1812 invasion. Alexander I would play a key role in the occupation of France and the deliberations at the Congress of Vienna.

Activity:

Coalition partners

In groups, take the role of one of the following.

- British representatives
- Prussian representatives
- Russian representatives
- Austrian representatives
- Reporters

Representatives: Research and analyse your country's decision to join (or not join in the case of Prussia) the second coalition against France.

Reporters: Prepare questions for a news conference with the representatives. Your goal is to discover the various reasons for each country's position and its role in the coalition.

News conference: The representatives present a brief statement on their country's position. The reporters ask questions of the representatives and then write a newspaper article to report their findings.

Napoleon's opponents: the coalitions

Coalition	Members	Events	Results

First Coalition, 1793–97	Austria
	Prussia
	Britain
	Spain
	Sardinia
		● National Assembly declares war on the Austrian Empire, April 20, 1792
		● Prussia joins with Austria against France
		● Allied armies invade France and take Verdun and Longwy
		● France stops Prussians at Valmy, September 20, 1792
		● French forces under Dumouriez invade Austrian Netherlands and defeat Austrians at Jemappes
		● France occupies Nice, Mainz and Frankfurt, October 1792
		● Britain joins war in February 1793
		● France invades Dutch Republic
		● Spain joins Coalition, March 1793
		● French army defeated at Neerwinden
		● French General Dumouriez defects to Austrians, April 1793
		● Toulon occupied by British, August 1793
		● Austrian retreat from France after Battle of Fleurus in June 1794
		● France reoccupies Rhineland and Belgium
		● France occupies Netherlands and establishes Batavian Republic as a client state
		● By the Peace of Basel, Spain and Prussia withdraw from the War, 1795
		● French Armies invade German states across Rhine—eventually pushed back
		● Napoleon invades Italy and defeats Austrians and Sardinians – Sardinia withdrew from war
			Peace of Basel, May 1795
			● Between France, Spain, and Prussia
			● Prussia withdrew from the war
			● Prussia ceded Rhineland to France
			● France recognized Prussian dominance in Northern Germany
			● France obtained resources from the rich territory
			● Spain withdrew from the war
			Treaty with Dutch Republic, May 1795
			● Set up Batavian Republic
			● Dutch forced to paid a war indemnity to France
			● Dutch forced to loan money to France at favourable interest
			● Southern Dutch territories ceded to France
			● Dutch forced to pay for French occupying forces
			Peace with Sardinia, May 1796
			● Nice and Savoy permanently transferred to France
			   Napoleon sets up Cisalpine Republic
			   Venice partitioned between France and Austria
			   Treaty of Campo Formio, October 1797
			● Between France and Austria
			● Austria quits war
			● Austria recognized French possession of Belgium and Rhineland and control of Italian states
			Britain remained at war
			Napoleon gains valuable experience as a civil administrator and diplomat while his reputation in France soared.

Second Coalition, 1799–1802	Britain Russia Austria Portugal Ottoman Empire	● Napoleon leads French expedition to Egypt ● British Royal Navy destroys French fleet at Battle of Nile, 1798 ● Coalition forms in 1799 ● Austrians under Archduke Charles drove French back across Rhine ● Russian General Suvarov commanding a Austro-Russian army drove French from most of Italian holdings ● Suvarov invaded Helvetic Republic (Switzerland) ● British army fight French to a standstill in the Netherlands ● French forces defeat Russians in Switzerland – Russians withdraw from Coalition ● The French under Napoleon defeat Austrians at Battle of Marengo, June 1800 forcing Austrians to negotiate ● Ottomans invade Egypt ● Royal Navy under Nelson destroys Danish fleet at Battle of Copenhagen	France briefly holds Egypt, but its army withdraws after Ottoman invasion in 1801 Russian forces withdraw to Central and Eastern Europe France maintained control of Italy and Switzerland Peace of Lunéville, 1801 ● Between France and Austria ● French holding in Italy were enlarged ● France claimed left bank of Rhine ● Belgium absorbed into France ● Tuscany to become independent state ● Papal States to be controlled by the Pope ● Austria left Second Coalition Austria lost influence among the German states Peace of Amiens, March 1802 ● Between Britain and France ● British to return Cape Colony to Batavian Republic ● Trinidad, Tobago and Ceylon to Britain ● France withdraw troops form Papal States ● Malta to be neutral ● Island of Minorca to Spain The end of the War of the Second Coalition led to a brief period of peace from 1802 to 1803.

Third and Fourth Coalitions, 1805–1807	Britain Austria Russia Sweden	<ul><li>Britain and France go to war in 1803</li><li>Angered by Napoleon's reorganization of Central Europe, Francis II of Austria joins Britain in the Third Coalition, 1805</li><li>Russia under Alexander I joins coalition in return for British subsidies</li><li>Napoleon prepares to invade Britain</li><li>Napoleon moves troops to Central Europe to face Austro-Russian forces</li><li>Napoleon defeats Austrians at Ulm, October 1805</li><li>The Royal Navy defeats Franco-Spanish fleet at Trafalgar, October 1805</li><li>Napoleon defeats Austro-Russian army at Austerlitz December 1805—Austria withdraws from Coalition</li><li>Russian armies withdraw behind her borders</li><li>Napoleon defeats Prussians at Jena and Auerstädt, October 1806</li><li>Napoleon fights Russian armies to a standstill at Eylau in February 1807 and defeats them at Friedland in June 1807.</li><li>Russia and France make peace with Treaty of Tilsit, July 1807</li></ul>	**Treaty of Pressburg, December 1805**<ul><li>Austria to pay indemnity to France</li><li>Austria to give land to Napoleon's German allies</li><li>Venice given to Kingdom of Italy</li><li>Austrian withdrew from Third Coalition</li></ul>Trafalgar cemented British control of the seas from the rest of the 19th century and secured Britain from invasion Russian armies retreat to Russia Prussia, threatened by Napoleon's reorganization of German states, forced to act alone against France after she did not join the Coalition. **Treaty of Tilsit, July 1807**<ul><li>Between France, Russia and Prussia</li><li>France would aid Russia against Ottomans</li><li>Russia would join the Continental System</li><li>Prussia lost land to Kingdom of Westphalia and the Grand Duchy of Warsaw</li><li>France occupied Berlin</li></ul>
Fifth Coalition, 1809	Britain Austria	<ul><li>Austria rose again against Napoleon in 1809</li><li>The French were victorious in the battles of Landshut and Eckmühl</li><li>After suffering a major defeat at Wagram, the Austrians again sued for peace</li></ul>	**Treaty of Schönbrunn, October 1809**<ul><li>Austria gave up Carinthia, Carniola, and ports on the Adriatic</li><li>Poles received Galicia</li><li>Bavarians received part of the Tyrol</li><li>Austria paid indemnity</li><li>Austria joined Continental System</li></ul>Napoleon would eventually marry the Austrian Princess Marie Louis
Sixth Coalition, 1812–1814	Britain Austria Russia Sweden German states	<ul><li>After the catastrophic Russia Campaign, Napoleon rebuilt his forces and won the battles of Lützen, Bautzen and Dresden</li><li>Napoleon was defeated at the battle of Nations in October 1813</li><li>Napoleon's forces were driven from Germany and Spain</li></ul>	Napoleon surrenders, abdicates and is sent into exile on the island of Elba

The impulse to Empire

It is common to see the French Revolution as having ended in 1799 when Napoleon assumed the position of First Consul. While this is by and large true, it is important to remember that the ideals of the Revolution—ideas like democracy, nationalism, liberty, constitutionalism—did not end in 1799. These ideas had spread across Europe as much on the winds of populism as on the tips of French bayonets. It is a deep historic irony that while these ideals spread across Europe, Napoleon had transformed France into a stable dictatorship all with the appearance of a legitimacy garnered from plebiscites and popular demonstrations. By 1804, France had

Discussion point:

What advantages does a dictatorship have over democracy?

Under what circumstances might people give up democratic rights to a dictator?

all the trappings of an autocracy. Napoleon had himself confirmed as First Consul for life in 1803 and in 1804 he sought to extend that beyond his own life by making himself Emperor of the French and imbuing that office with hereditary legitimacy—all confirmed by popular vote. And so, 11 years after having executed their King, the French found themselves ruled by an Emperor—citizens of an Empire.

France had largely achieved her natural borders by the time of the War of the Second Coalition, although, as the Coalition's expedition in the Netherlands had demonstrated, this was not stable and certainly not recognized by the rest of Europe. Therefore much of Napoleon's campaigning in the years after his return from Egypt can be seen as trying to achieve this stability. Yet there can also be little doubt that his ambitions ran beyond these borders. He had indicated as much when he reorganized the Italian states in 1797. Likewise he took the opportunity afforded by the dissolution of the Second Coalition and the brief Peace of Amiens in 1802 to expand what would become the French Empire. For its part, Great Britain needed the peace to regroup and deal with pressing domestic concerns such as inflation, poor harvests and a change in government. Neither country seriously considered Amiens to be anything other than a respite before hostilities resumed.

While conflict with Great Britain seemed a historic inevitability, the conflict on the Continent hinged on Napoleon's ambitious vision of French, and therefore personal, **hegemony**. Continental peace was within Napoleon's grasp had he been more conciliatory, particularly toward Austria. But this was not in his nature. His efforts during the brief interlude of peace in 1802–3 illustrate this. He formed the Italian Republic out of the ruins of the Cisalpine Republic. He created the Confederation of Switzerland out of his older creation the Helvetic Republic. Each of these recreated states was to be led by Napoleon. He watched and encouraged the German princes to fight again each other for the scraps left after France had annexed the west bank of the Rhine, leaving the remaining German states further dependent on France. All of these geo-political manoeuvres were direct affronts to Austria's sphere of influence in Central Europe.

> **Hegemony** refers to an overarching dominance and influence of one person or group over others. In this case it refers to French domination and control of the European Continent.

As the Third Coalition went the way of the previous two, Napoleon once again added to his Empire at the expense of Austria and Prussia. He swept away the shell of the Holy Roman Empire and replaced it with the Confederation of the Rhine with himself as protector. The Italian Republic became the Kingdom of Italy with the addition of Venice. Polish nationalists saw their hopes rekindled when Napoleon created the Duchy of Warsaw from Prussian spoils.

The administration of this Empire was a complex task. Napoleon used three basic structures to do so. By 1807, the states of Europe fell into three basic categories:

- Those that had been annexed to France
- Those that were protectorates of France
- Those that had signed treaties with France

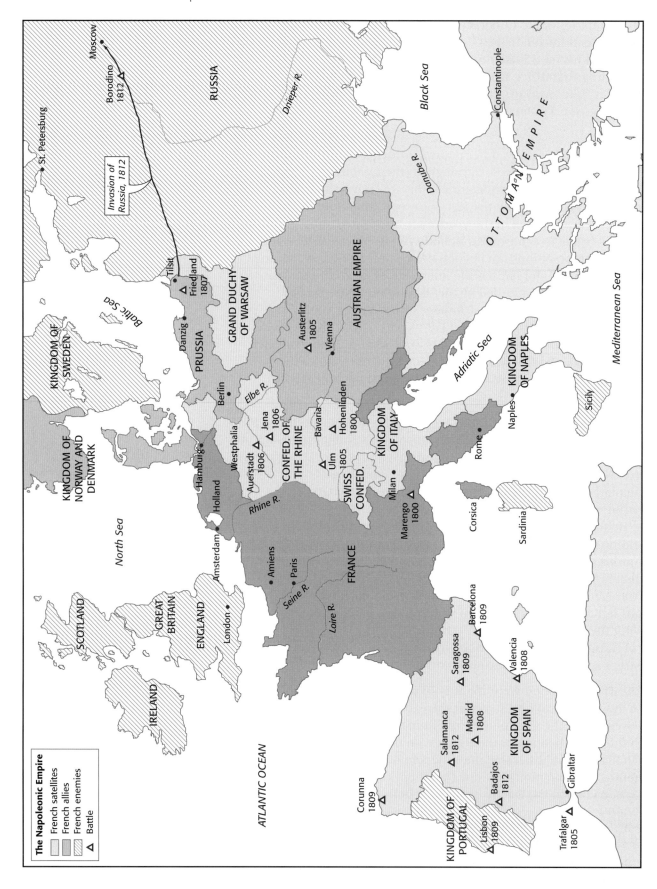

The Napoleonic Empire
△ French satellites
△ French allies
△ French enemies
△ Battle

Moscow
Borodino 1812
Invasion of Russia, 1812
St. Petersburg
RUSSIA
Dnieper R.
Black Sea
Constantinople
OTTOMAN EMPIRE
Tilsit
Friedland 1807
Danzig
PRUSSIA
GRAND DUCHY OF WARSAW
AUSTRIAN EMPIRE
Danube R.
Baltic Sea
KINGDOM OF SWEDEN
Austerlitz 1805
Vienna
Berlin
Elbe R.
Jena 1806
Hohenlinden 1800
Bavaria
Adriatic Sea
KINGDOM OF NAPLES
Westphalia
Auerstadt 1806
CONFED. OF THE RHINE
Ulm 1805
KINGDOM OF ITALY
Naples
Sicily
KINGDOM OF NORWAY AND DENMARK
Hamburg
Holland
Rhine R.
SWISS CONFED.
Milan
Marengo 1800
Rome
North Sea
Amsterdam
Amiens
Paris
Seine R.
FRANCE
Loire R.
Corsica
Sardinia
Mediterranean Sea
SCOTLAND
GREAT BRITAIN
ENGLAND
London
Barcelona 1809
Valencia 1808
IRELAND
Saragossa 1809
Madrid 1808
Salamanca 1812
KINGDOM OF SPAIN
ATLANTIC OCEAN
Corunna 1809
Badajos 1812
Lisbon 1809
KINGDOM OF PORTUGAL
Gibraltar
Trafalgar 1805

France had achieved her natural borders by annexing Belgium, the Netherlands and the Rhineland, which had thus become departments of France and administered as such. As the Continental System required more direct control over maritime trade, Napoleon annexed more and more coastal territory to France. Napoleonic and revolutionary innovations such as the Code Napoleon, regularized taxation, and balanced budgets were incorporated into these territories often with the support of the population. These populations also became subject to mandatory French military service, a less popular innovation, one that, however, helped maintain the size of Napoleon's massive army. Almost one quarter of the French Imperial army came from conquered territory.

The territories immediately beyond France's natural borders became vassal states, nominally independent, but in reality controlled as puppets by Paris. Napoleon was the Mediator of the Swiss Confederation, the Protector of the Confederation of the Rhine, President of the Italian Republic and then King of Italy when he transformed that territory into a Kingdom after the Treaty of Pressburg. The Grand Duchy of Warsaw, the Papal States, and various smaller states also fell into this category. These states had no independence of action, owed men and money to France and were forced to incorporate Napoleonic policies as directed from Paris. Again, many of these changes were welcomed by local populations, which often collaborated with the French. Over time, however, these same populations bridled under French control and, taking the lessons of the French Revolution to heart, sought to throw off their French overlords.

The longer Napoleon ruled, the more he took on the trappings of an hereditary monarch. This included placing his confidants and family members on the thrones of Europe. His brother Jerome was made King of Westphalia. His brother Joseph was first the King of Naples and later the King of Spain. When his brother was sent to Spain, the crown of Naples was given to a marshal, Joachim Murat, who was married to Napoleon's sister.

The Great Powers of Europe that Napoleon continually defeated in battle between 1800 and 1808 formed the third component of Napoleon's Empire. These states were bound by the terms of various treaties to the French Empire. These terms could include the payment of war indemnities and loss of territory as with Prussia, or merely an agreement to cease hostilities and co-operate in future endeavors such as the Continental System, as with Russia. Beyond the terms of the treaties, these states were independent.

Discussion point:

Napoleon controlled his Empire in a number of different ways. Some states he annexed to France and ruled directly. Other territories were formed into client states, nominally autonomous, but in reality dependent on France. Still other states he controlled through agreements and treaties, enforced by the threat of French arms.

 What are the advantages and disadvantages of each of Napoleon's three methods of controlling his vast Empire?

Activity:

Nationalism and the Napoleonic Empire

By the time Napoleon had established his Empire, nationalist movements were rising against French control. Research the nationalist movements that grew up against French control in the following countries:

● Spain

● Prussia

● Austria

● The German states

Questions

1 What did these movements have in common? In what ways were they different?

2 What role did the national government play in each movement?

3 To what degree was each movement successful in achieving its goals?

4 How did the French respond to each movement?

5 Evaluate the role each played in the downfall of the Napoleonic Empire.

The Continental System

By 1807 Napoleon had beaten the powers of Continental Europe into a reluctant submission, and yet Britain persisted in her resistance to a European order in which France held sway. As long as Britain held out the hope of financial aid to Continental allies willing to resist Napoleonic control, his Empire could not be secure. Yet to best Britain required a fleet and Napoleon's had been smashed by Nelson at Trafalgar in 1805. His answer was a scheme of economic warfare known as the Continental System.

The Continental System was essentially a reverse blockade. Napoleon forbade any of the territories under his control from trading with Great Britain. The idea was not new. The Convention, Directory and Consulate had all tried some form embargo before. The difference in Napoleon's attempt was that he was in a position to force compliance on close to the whole of Europe, something out of the reach of the previous French governments. Also, the previous attempts had been more about boosting French commerce than it was about hurting British commerce. Napoleon hoped to destroy the revenue Britain received from trade and thus bring it if not to its knees than at least to the negotiation table.

The **Berlin Decrees** of November 1806 brought the System into effect, but only after the Treaty of Tilsit ensured Russia's participation did the system begin to wound British commerce, slashing her exports by up to 20 per cent. In terms of British imports, much of the timber, tar and hemp for the British Royal Navy came from the Baltic, now shut off from British trade. Napoleon strengthened the terms of the Decrees by demanding a certificate of place of origin for all goods. Any ships visiting a British port were subject to confiscation along with their cargo. When that, too, failed to bring the results Napoleon desired, he declared that any ship from a neutral country searched by the Royal Navy on the high seas was also subject to seizure. For its part a British "order in council" of 1807 declared that neutral shipping could enter a Continental port only after it had passed through a British port.

> The **Berlin Decrees, 1806** These were the Decrees that prohibited countries under Napoleonic control from trading with Great Britain or her dependents, inaugurating the Continental System. It also provided for the confiscation of neutral ships that had stopped in British ports.

Predictably, the Continental System hurt Continental commerce as much as it did British commerce, provoking a deep bitterness amongst all participants. Smuggling was rampant and because the French were the only ones really committed to enforcing the System, it sapped their manpower while at the same time rendering the embargo very inefficient. To this was added the hardship of the British blockade, which bit deeply into not only overseas trade but also coastal trade within Europe. Napoleon was forced to take ever more drastic measures to enforce compliance including the invasion of Portugal, Spain and most disastrously Russia.

Discussion point: The Mahan thesis

Alfred Mahan was a 19th-century American naval officer and strategist. After studying the Anglo-French wars of the 18th century he developed what became known as the Mahan Thesis. His thesis posited that in these conflicts it was naval power that determined the outcome. Without control of the sea, no colonial power can win a protracted conflict with a state that does control the sea. Mahan's ideas were very influential in the arms race that led up to the First World War.

In looking at the revolutionary and Napoleonic wars, what evidence can you find that supports Mahan's Thesis? What evidence contradicts it? Does Mahan's thesis hold true for conflicts in the 19th and 20th centuries?

Iberian adventures and Russian winters

Portugal had long had a close relationship with Great Britain, dating back to the Middle Ages. Through much of the Revolutionary and Napoleonic Wars it had managed to remain neutral. Neutrals fared well under the Continental System, but when Napoleon insisted that Portugal adhere to the embargo, Portugal resisted and in 1807 Napoleon invaded, through Spain. The French quickly occupied Portugal and then turned their attention to her reluctant Spanish ally. Napoleon sent a large army under Murat to take control of Spain in 1808, placing his brother Joseph on the throne and incurring the wrath of patriotic Spaniards. This started the Peninsular War.

TOK Link
What is evidence?

When Napoleon's troops invaded Spain it sparked a brutal guerrilla war that sapped the energy of the Napoleonic Empire and spread suffering throughout the Iberian Peninsula. Spanish artist Francisco Goya depicted the horrors of this conflict in a number of major paintings and the print portfolio known as "The Disasters of War" produced in 1810–14. Study the prints below and answer the questions that follow.

Source-based questions

1 What are the value and limitations of using these prints as historical evidence?

2 What role does emotion play in them? How does this affect their use as evidence?

3 What do they reveal about Goya's opinions of war in general and specifically the Peninsular War? What leads you to these conclusions?

4 Of what propaganda value might these images have been for the Spanish nationalist resistance?

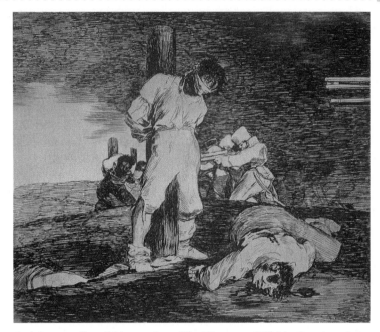

And they are like wild beasts, from "The Disasters of War" by Francisco Goya.

And there's no help for it, from the "The Disasters of War" by Francisco Goya.

The Peninsular War was a new kind of war in a number of ways. First, it cast Napoleon and the French not as the liberators, but as the oppressors. The nationalism popularized by the French Revolution now took root in Spain against the French. This resistance took an innovative form—guerilla war. From the very beginning of the French occupation, anti-French riots had broken out in Madrid. Citizens banded together in irregular units and attacked French forces. In some areas full-scale revolts erupted. Each act of resistance was met with savage repression, which in turn provoked equally savage reprisals against French forces and officials. Although the Spanish regular army had only 100,000 troops, Spanish nationalism and the guerilla concept multiplied that many times over. Soon the British took advantage and in August 1808 landed troops under Arthur Wellesley, the future Duke of Wellington, in Portugal. Wellesley commanded a small army with skill and determination. With the co-operation of the Spanish citizens, he drove the French from Portugal. Over the course of the next six years, the stagnant Peninsular War would sap Napoleon's energy, finances and manpower.

The example of Spanish resistance and its own growing sense of nationalism swept through Europe. But this nationalism was far from monolithic. It could be liberal or conservative, secular or clerical. It could be bourgeois or aristocratic, republican or monarchical. It manifested itself in the Austrian War of Liberation, but also in the Polish nationalists' support for Napoleon. Regardless, the majority of this burgeoning nationalism increased resistance to Napoleonic rule. By the end of 1810, resistance became more entrenched and threatening when Tsar Alexander I formally withdrew Russia from the Continental System.

The Continental System had been damaging to Russian interests in a number of ways. Economically it had cut into Russian exports to Britain and not fully replaced them with Continental trade. The promises of Russian dominance in Asia Minor and south central Asia held out by Napoleon at Tilsit were never realized and the French support for these endeavors never materialized, specifically the partition of the Ottoman Empire. Personally, Alexander I, himself a man of considerable ego, became embittered at his role of understudy to Napoleon's starring role in the affairs of Europe. To Alexander it fitted neither his own stature nor that of the Russian Empire. He had had his own ambitions. For his part, Napoleon rationalized the need to woo the Tsar in practical terms. If the Continental System was to work, Russia must participate. A Russian defeat would remove the possibility of an Anglo-Russian alliance and keep the British isolated.

Napoleon seemed to welcome the impending clash and, while making overtures to solve the impasse diplomatically, he began military preparations in earnest. Military

Marshal Ney was one of a number of talented marshals who commanded Napoleon's armies. Davout, Soult, Lannes, and Murat were young men who benefited from the opening of the higher ranks to men of talent rather than birth.

 What role did these men play in Napoleon's victories in battles such as Austerlitz, Jena, Wagram, and Ulm? What does this tell us about Napoleon's leadership style?

IN THE MUSEUM OF VERSAILLES   MARSHAL NEY SUSTAINING THE REAR-GUARD OF THE GRAND ARMY   ENGRAVED BY HENRY WOLF

Marshal Ney bringing Napoleon's French rear guard out of Russia with heavy losses, 1812.

solutions had always suited Napoleon, he was more sure-footed while commanding armies than he was in negotiation, diplomacy requiring tact and nuance. Spain notwithstanding, this approach had always worked for the Emperor, and he duly thought this campaign would proceed as his others had—a few weeks of manoeuvre followed by one or two decisive battles after which he would bring the Tsar to heel by way of a treaty. Alexander and his generals had a different war in mind.

Napoleon massed an enormous force for his invasion of Russia—a truly Imperial Army of close to 700,000 soldiers. These soldiers came from all over the Empire. Only some 300,000 were French with roughly the same number raised from the Emperor's German holdings. Beyond this there were Italians, Portuguese, Swiss, Poles, and Dutch. The Austrians were forced to provide 30,000 troops and the Prussians 20,000 troops. Subtracting those on supply and garrison duty, Napoleon had more than 400,000 men to subdue the Russians. This mammoth force lumbered into Russia in June 1812.

The Russians did not offer battle in the early part of the campaign. This was partially by design—Russian forces were being recalled from south-western Europe—and partially due to poor co-ordination and slow deployment. As the Russian army retreated, they left little for the enemy to forage, creating a supply problem for the French that was compounded by poor logistics and increasingly precarious supply lines. Throughout the summer, harassing tactics by the Russians and disease bit into Napoleon's forces. By early September it seemed that the Emperor would get his wish. 120,000 Russians under General Kutusov met the French on the march to Moscow at Borodino. Napoleon's 150,000 troops technically won the day, but both armies were badly mauled in the process. Moscow was now open to Napoleon and he occupied the largely abandoned city on 14 September. Within days, the remaining citizens of Moscow set fire to their city.

Robbed of the satisfaction of a Russian surrender, the comfort of billets, necessary provisions, and apparently his legendary military acumen, Napoleon reluctantly ordered retreat on October 17. Since the invasion in June his forces had shrunk continually while his enemy's had increased. The supply problems that had plagued him from the beginning of the invasion now grew into a crisis. And to all this was added the looming Russian winter. As the *grande armée* retreated, Kutusov began a series of attacks that the French were ill-equipped to repel. By the time his remaining marshals dragged what was left of the *grande armée* out of Russia in December 1812—Napoleon had already returned to Paris to quell a *coup d'état*—battle, capture, starvation, desertion, disease, and exposure had reduced it to less than 100,000, only a fraction of which were capable of fighting.

His enemies, quick to recognize Napoleon's predicament, were ready to pounce once the opportunity presented itself. By 1813, Italy was in revolt. Wellington swept the French from Spain. Prussia, Austria, Sweden quickly joined with Russia in another coalition and smashed a hastily raised French army at the Battle of Leipzig in October 1813. Deposed by his senate in March 1814, Napoleon abdicated on April 4 and awaited terms from the allies.

Activity: ● ● ● ● ● ● ● ● ● ●

The Russian Campaign

Analyse the role played by each of the following elements in the French defeat in Russia.

- Strategy
- Tactics
- Supply
- Troops
- Leadership
- Geography
- Climate

As with many such partnerships, the allies had little trouble agreeing on what they were fighting against, Napoleonic hegemony. Problems, however, arose when they tried to articulate, much less agree on, what they were fighting for. What would replace the Napoleonic Empire? While the United Kingdom wanted Napoleon gone and Belgium independent, Austria simply wanted a France dependent on her, regardless of who was in charge, and had no real interest in who controlled Belgium. The Austrian Foreign Minister, Prince Metternich formally offered as much to Napoleon. His Frankfurt Proposals offered control of a greatly reduced France to Napoleon, who declined the offer. Interestingly enough, one of the first things that the allies agreed upon was a mechanism to enforce the as yet undetermined peace settlement. This mechanism was to be the Quadruple Alliance, formed in 1813 and renewed two years later at the Congress of Vienna. Austria, Prussia, Russia, and the United Kingdom pledged 150,000 troops each to ensure their demands were met and kept. Clearly they could not leave a power vacuum in Paris, and they quickly decided that the least objectionable immediate solution was to restore the Bourbon dynasty in the person of Louis XVIII to the French throne while they agreed to meet in September in Vienna to discuss a more comprehensive peace. For his part Louis XVIII was willing to agree to just about anything to regain the throne and this included retaining many of Bonaparte's reforms such as Concordat of 1801 and the Code Napoleon. By so doing he established France as a constitutional monarchy. Now the allies had somebody with whom they could discuss a settlement.

Activity:

Continuity and change in France, 1789–1812

Complete the following chart comparing French society under the *ancien régime* (before 1789), The National Assembly (1789–92), the Convention (1792–5) and Napoleon (1799–1812).

	Ancien Régime before 1789	National Assembly 1789–1792	Convention 1792–5	Napoleon 1799–1812
Legal rights				
Gender rights				
Labour rights				
Social control				
Financial policies				
Religious rights				

Timeline for the French Revolution and Napoleon		
Ancien Régime	1763	France defeated in Seven Years War
	1778	France sends troops and money to fight in American Revolution
	1787	February: Assembly of Notables meets
	1788	August: Necker recalled to government
		November: Assembly of Notables advises on structure of Estates General
	1789	May: Estates General meets at Versailles
National Assembly (moderate stage)		June 17: National Assembly proclaimed
		June 20: Tennis Court Oath
		July 11: Necker is dismissed
		July 14: Storming of the Bastille
		July 16: Necker is recalled
		July–August: Great Fear
		August 4: Feudal privileges abolished
		August 26: Declaration of the Rights of Man and Citizen published
		October 5: Women of Paris march to Versailles
		November: Church property confiscated
	1790	July 12: Civil Constitution of the Clergy published
	1791	June 20: Flight to Varennes
		July 17: Massacre at the Champs de Mars
		August 27: Declaration of Pilnitz
		September 13: Constitution adopted
	1792	April 20: War declared on Austria
		June 13: Prussia declares war
		July 25: Brunswick Manifesto
		August 9: Paris Commune created
National Convention (radical stage)		August 10: Insurrection overthrows government and creates National Convention
		September 2–6: September Massacres
		September 22: French Republic proclaimed
	1793	January 21: Louis XVI executed
		March: Vendée rises in revolt
		April 6: Committee of Public Safety created
		June 2: Girondins expelled from National Convention
		August: Levée en masse
		October: Revolutionary calendar adopted
		October 16: Marie Antoinette executed
		October 31: Girondin leaders executed
	1794	March 24: Hébertists executed
		April 5: Dantonists executed
		July 28: Robespierre overthrown
	1795	October 26: National Convention dissolved

Activity:
Revolutionary perspectives

Choose five of the following people and write a paragraph that explains how he or she might have viewed the French Revolution at that particular time and place. Be sure to justify your answer with historical evidence.

- French peasant, May 1789
- Parisian banker, May 1789
- Parisian bricklayer, July 1789
- Parish priest in the Vendée, July 1791
- Polish lawyer, 1809
- Russian peasant, July 1812
- Italian lawyer in Milan, 1798
- British member of the House of Lords, 1800
- French Protestant, 1802
- French shopkeeper in Amiens, 1795

The Directory	1797	July 8: Establishment of the Cisalpine Republic
		September 4: Coup d'état of Fructidor
		October 17: Treaty of Campo Formio
	1798	July 21: Battle of the Pyramids
		August 1: Battle of the Nile
	1799	October 9: Napoleon returns to France
		November 9: Coup d'état of Brumaire
The Consulate		December 15: Consulate established
	1800	August: Civil Code drafted
	1801	July 15: Concordat signed
	1802	March 25: Treaty of Amiens signed with the United Kingdom
The Empire	1804	May 18: Napoleon proclaimed Emperor
	1805	October 21: Battle of Trafalgar
		December 2: Battle of Austerlitz
	1806	July 12: Confederation of the Rhine formed
		October: Battles of Jéna and Auerstadt
		November 21: Continental system proclaimed
	1807	February 8: Battle of Eylau
		July 7: Treaty of Tilsit
	1809	July 6: Battle of Wagram
	1810	April 2: Napoleon marries Marie Louis
	1812	June 24: French troops invade Russia
		September 7: Battle of Borodino
		September 14: Napoleon enters Moscow
		October 18: Retreat from Russia begins
	1813	October: Battle of Leipzig
	1814	March 13: Allies enter Paris
		April 12: Napoleon abdicates
The 100 Days	1815	February 26: Napoleon escapes to Elba
		March 20: Napoleon returns to Paris
		June 18: Battle of Waterloo
		June 22: Napoleon abdicates
	1821	May 15: Napoleon dies

The Congress of Vienna

Europe had been in flux since 1789, acutely so since 1792: borders shifted; monarchs deposed; empires established; republics emerged and disappeared. Revolutionary terms such as liberty, constitutionalism, equality, and nationalism had spread throughout Europe, and could not be revoked. As such the powers, great and small, which assembled at Vienna in the autumn of 1814 had a mammoth task before them. They sought to stabilize the borders, regimes, commerce and diplomacy of Europe in a way that would satisfy all enough to avoid a future war and prevent another Revolution from threatening the whole of Europe. But this was not before they had once again to defeat Napoleon.

After his abdication, Napoleon was exiled to the Mediterranean island of Elba where he remained until February 1815 when he escaped and returned to France. The force sent to capture him—led by Marshal Ney—joined him. As he marched towards Paris, by a circuitous route through the French Alps, his former soldiers and supporters of the Revolution flocked to his banner, news of which caused Louis XVIII to again flee the capital. Napoleon spent the next 100 days trying to reorganize and administer France while raising yet another army to face the allies—this time in Belgium. It was not to be. Napoleon was defeated by an Anglo-Prussian force under the British Duke of Wellington and the Prussian field marshal Blücher at Waterloo in June 1815. This time Napoleon did not escape his exile on the South Atlantic island of St Helena, where he died in 1821.

After the Hundred Days the proceedings at Vienna resumed with the powers even more determined that no aberration such as Napoleon or the Revolution that gave birth to him could ever again destabilize Europe. To this end, the Congress was guided by four key principles:

Balance of power

It was agreed that the five major powers—the United Kingdom, France, Austria, Prussia and Russia—should remain roughly balanced in land and influence such that each could enjoy independence of action. It also meant that should this independence of action threaten the other powers, a coalition could deter the aggressive action as a form of collective security. Under Napoleon, French power had so outweighed the rest of Europe that coalitions were not effective. Nevertheless, it was never seriously considered that France should be excluded from this balance. France, therefore, was reduced to her 1790 borders.

Legitimacy

Wherever possible or practical, the rulers deposed by revolutionary and Napoleonic expansion were restored, as in the case of the Bourbons in France as well as in places such as Spain, Portugal, Tuscany and Modena.

 Why not execute Napoleon?

Discussion point:

Until 1919, there were few meetings of European leaders that rivalled The Congress of Vienna for the array of powerful luminaries in attendance. Each came with his own agenda of national goals. For any lasting peace to be established, these national, often competing, goals had to be balanced against each other and against the broader desire for peace after 23 years of war.

 To what degree were these goals successfully balanced?

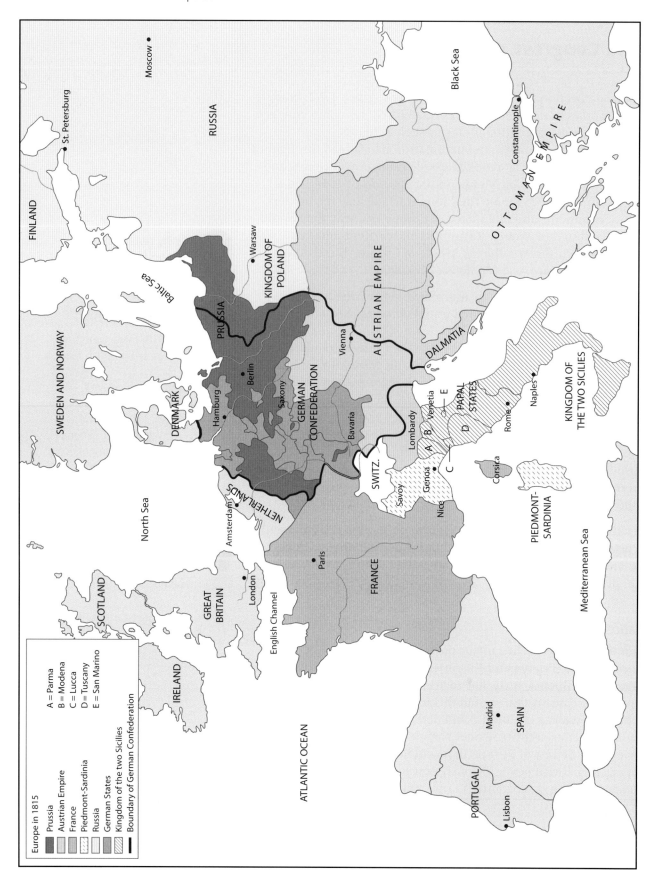

Europe in 1815

Prussia

Austrian Empire

France

Piedmont-Sardinia

Russia

German States

Kingdom of the two Sicilies

Boundary of German Confederation

A = Parma
B = Modena
C = Lucca
D = Tuscany
E = San Marino

Buffer states

Lesser powers were reconstituted, created or enlarged on the orders of France to create a buffer between it and the rest of Europe such as Piedmont–Sardinia, Belgium, the Netherlands and the German Confederation and Prussian acquisitions on the west bank of the Rhine.

Conservatism

No one forgot that the 26 years of upheaval in Europe started with the overthrow of the absolute monarchy of Louis XVI by children of the Enlightenment. Those present at the congress advocated a conservatism that was more than a fear of change. They believed it was a comprehensive foundation for a stable society. Conservatives argued that reason was not a sufficient basis for a society. Established institutions provided the stability by which all members of society could prosper. Many pointed to the chaotic years of the Revolution to support their position. To that end, the members of the Congress pledged to co-operate in the suppression of dangerously radical ideas such as nationalism and liberalism. In the following years this pledge was taken to heart as Prince Metternich issued the Carlsbad Decrees in 1819, suppressing liberal and nationalistic expressions in the German states, and in the United Kingdom (the Peterloo massacre, in Manchester) in that same year.

The diplomats that assembled at Vienna in 1815 redrew the map of Europe to reinforce the principles of legitimacy and balance of power. They also created a number of states designed as buffers to stop any potential French expansion. To what extent were they successful?

 In what ways did the territorial changes agreed to at Vienna support or violate the concept of nationalism as developed throughout the French Revolution?

Activity:

Congress of Vienna

Form groups to represent the following countries at the Congress of Vienna:

- United Kingdom
- France
- Austria
- Prussia
- Russia

Phase 1: Preparation

After a period of research, each group will prepare a negotiation dossier containing:

1 The current political, social, and economic context of the country.

2 A map outlining the geography of Europe as it stood at the beginning of the Congress and the territorial demands that the country is making.

3 A list of demands, in order of priority that the country will make at the Congress with a written rationale for each. Bear in mind the principles of conservatism, legitimacy, and buffer states.

Phase 2: The Congress

Arrange the negotiating delegations in a circle.

1 Each delegation presents its demands in turn.

2 After a 15-minute period of negotiation, in which countries are free to discuss and make deals with any other country or countries, the congress reassembles and with the teacher acting as moderator outlines the situation as it stands after the negotiation. Keep track of the agreements made. A supply of outline maps of Europe at the beginning of the Congress will help delegations with the territorial negotiations.

3 Repeat the period of negotiation until either:

- A settlement gets consensus
- Negotiations are at an impasse

Phase 3: Debrief

As a class, use the following questions to guide a discussion on the activity:

1 Which countries initially had the strongest negotiation positions? Why?

2 Which countries had the most compatible positions? Why?

3 Which countries gained the most from the negotiations? Which countries gained the least?

4 What elements made the negotiations difficult?

5 How well were the principles of conservatism, legitimacy, and buffer states maintained?

The Provisions of the Congress of Vienna, 1814–5		
United Kingdom	**Austria**	**Prussia**
Viscount Castlereagh	Prince Metternich	Karl August von Hardenberg
<ul><li>Retained Cape Colony, Tobago, Malta, and Ceylon</li><li>Received Heligoland, Mauritius and Santa Lucia</li><li>Received Trinidad</li></ul>	<ul><li>Regained Tyrol and Salzburg</li><li>Regained Lombardy and Venetia</li><li>Received part of Dalmatia and the Illyrian Provinces</li><li>Tuscany and Modena returned to House of Hapsburg</li><li>Retained Eastern Galicia</li></ul>	<ul><li>Received part of Saxony</li><li>Received Rhineland</li><li>Received Westphalia</li><li>Received city of Danzig</li><li>Received Pomerania</li></ul>
Russia	**France**	**Other**
Alexander I	Talleyrand	
<ul><li>Received part of Duchy of Warsaw</li><li>Retained Finland</li><li>Received Bessarabia</li></ul>	<ul><li>Continental borders reduced to 1789 borders</li><li>Received Guiana, Martinique, and Guadeloupe</li><li>Had to pay war indemnity to allies</li></ul>	<ul><li>German Confederation created out of Confederation of the Rhine and reduced to 39 states—dominated by Austria</li><li>Kingdom of the Netherlands created (included Belgium)</li><li>Kingdom of Hanover created</li><li>South German states such as Baden, Bavaria, and Württemburg retained gains made under Napoleon</li><li>Papal States were restored</li><li>Sardinia received Genoa</li><li>Swiss neutrality guaranteed by the Great Powers</li><li>Sweden received Norway</li></ul>

Was there a clear winner at Vienna? Not really. All the Great Powers could claim to have achieved at least a portion of their goals. The United Kingdom emerged as the dominant European colonial power and would remain so for the next century. Russia had entered the affairs of Western Europe and would continue to play a role for the next 40 years. She had increased her Polish holdings and secured her northern territories with the retention of Finland. Alexander had won some limited support for his vague notion of a Holy Alliance designed to adhere to Christian principles in the administration of European affairs. Ironically, the Pope did not sign this agreement, nor did the UK or the Sultan of the Ottoman Empire. The architect of much of the Vienna settlement was Prince Metternich, the Austrian Foreign Minister.

Activity:
Political and economic control

Place each of the following revolutionary governments on the grid below according to the extent each balanced economic and political control. Write a paragraph using specific evidence to support your claims.

1 Ancien régime
2 National Assembly
3 National Convention
4 Directory
5 Consulate
6 Empire

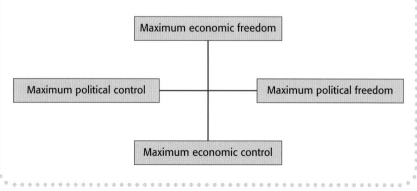

As such he succeeded in securing Austria as the dominant power in Central Europe. He also constructed a system by which the Powers agreed to co-operate in the administration of Europe and ensure that no disaster like the French Revolution and Napoleon could threaten the stability of Europe again. The Powers would meet four times in the seven years following the Congress of Vienna to ensure a conservative order maintained control in Europe. Closely associated with the Congress system is the so-called Metternich system. Generally this refers to the efforts of the Powers over the course of the next 30 years to maintain the shape and principles of the Congress of Vienna. As such it came to be associated with conservative efforts to suppress liberalism and nationalism. This effort was largely successful. At Vienna the Great Powers created a system that would generally hold for much of the next 50 years. In terms of international conflict, the years 1815–54 were largely peaceful. The ideas unleashed by the French Revolution would have their most profound effect within the borders of the states entrenched by the Congress of Vienna.

What order can then be placed on these 26 years of turmoil in Europe? What patterns emerge? The Revolution in France was sparked out of a number of factors:

- intellectual trends emphasizing change and individualism
- a change in the social and economic status of the bourgeoisie with no corresponding change in their political status
- the inability of the royal government to solve a financial crisis by accessing the wealth of the nation
- popular unrest created by food shortages and high bread prices.

It is important to remember that the French Revolution was the culmination of these factors some of which had been developing over the better part of a century. While the Revolution was a dramatic and violent break with the past, this was an acceleration of developments rather than an eruption of entirely unforeseen events. These causal factors came not just from above but also from below, from the streets of Paris and other urban centres as well as from the peasants in the rural areas of France. In fact it was when the revolutionary energy from above and from below met, that some of the most significant changes occurred during the Revolution. This can be seen in the:

- storming of the Bastille
- march of the Parisian Women to Versailles
- September Massacres and insurrection of August 1792
- Thermidorean Reaction and White Terror

In each case, popular unrest, sometimes harnessed and sometimes instigated by leading revolutionaries, helped drive the Revolution into a new phase: from Assembly to Convention; from Convention to Terror; from Terror to Directory. Each progression brought a new revolutionary leadership to power. Once in power these leaders redefined what the Revolution meant and in so doing shifted what it meant to be a moderate or a radical. As the pendulum swung back to its starting point, the autocratic tendencies of Napoleon brought something like a lasting domestic peace to France. In so doing, in many ways he set the personality of France for the next century; dominated by the middle class, it alternated between republican and imperial, legalistic, and occasionally expansionary drives.

Exam practice and further resources

Sample questions

1 How important were social and economic problems as causes of the French Revolution?
2 Analyse the reasons for the radicalization of the Revolution in the years 1789–94.
3 "The weaknesses of the Directory not military glory was the main factor in Napoleon Bonaparte becoming first Consul in 1799." To what extent do you agree with this statement?
4 How successful were the domestic policies of Napoleon 1?
5 Analyse the contribution of military failure to the collapse of Napoleon's regime?
6 How successfully did the Congress of Vienna stabilize Europe?

Recommended further reading

General:

Doyle, William. 1989. *The Oxford History of the French Revolution.* Oxford, UK. Oxford University Press, 1989.

Kennedy, Emmet. 1989. *A Cultural History of the French Revolution.* New Haven, USA. Yale University Press.

Hunt, Lynn. 1984. *Politics, Culture and Class in the French Revolution.* Berkeley, USA. University of California Press.

Ideas:

Baker, Keith Michael. 1990. *Inventing the French Revolution: Essays on French Political Culture in the Eighteenth Century.* Cambridge, UK. Cambridge University Press.

The Terror:

Andress, David. 2006. *The Terror: The Merciless War for Freedom in Revolutionary France.* New York, USA. Farrar, Straus & Giroux.

Scurr, Ruth. 2006. *Fatal Purity: Robespierre and the French Revolution.* New York, USA. Henry Holt and Co.

Gender Issues:

Godineau, Dominique. 1986. *The Women of Paris and Their French Revolution.* Berkeley, USA. University of California Press.

Napoleon:

Dwyer, Phillip. 2008. *Napoleon: The Path to Power.* New Haven, USA. Yale University Press.

Congress of Vienna:

Kissinger, Henry A. 1957. *A World Restored: Metternich, Castlereagh and the Problems of Peace 1812–1822.* Boston, USA. Houghton Mifflin.

2 German and Italian unification

German and Italian unification

The mid-19th century is marked by massive changes in the global geo-political structure. Independence movements swept through South America. The southern states of the United States attempted to secede from their union sparking a bloody civil war that would have ramifications throughout the USA for over a hundred years. The United Kingdom's North American colonies became the Dominion of Canada. Japan embarked on a period of modernization that prompted a challenge for Great Power status by the turn of the century. European empires scrambled to add African territories to their holdings. In Europe, Germans and Italians created their own nation-states, drastically changing the balance of power on the continent. The political map of the world looked very different in 1900 than it had in 1850.

By the end of the chapter, students should be able to:

- define the terms and understand the relationship between nation, nationalism, and nation-state
- analyse the sources of European stability and instability in the years from 1815–48
- assess the impact of the Revolutions of 1848 on subsequent German and Italian unification
- discuss the causes, processes and effects of German and Italian unification
- understand the role of Austria in German and Italian unification
- evaluate the role of Camillo di Cavour and Otto von Bismarck in the unification of Italy and Germany.

Nations, nation-states and nationalism

At its heart a nation is a group of people. From this point, however, it gets far more complex. The people that make up a nation generally share certain commonalities, but not all nations share the same ones. One of the most pervasive of these common characteristics is language. Members of a nation generally speak the same language or at least a common enough language that they can understand each other. Often, members of a nation share a common geographic area, and a common historical development. Religion can be one of the factors that helps bring a nation together, though not always. Culture, itself an amorphous term, is another element that is shared.

If these elements are more or less present in national groups, then what is it that is common to all nations? What is the one element that is fundamental to the concept of "nation"? It must be that the members of the nation see and feel themselves to be part of the nation. The fundamental element is a sense of nation, of belonging, of shared existence.

It is this common feeling that separates similar groups that had existed before the last half of the 18th century, and had arguably always existed, from those that came after the French Revolution. One of the most profound legacies of the French Revolution is the birth of a shared experience of nation that grew among French citizens during the Revolution. They began to see themselves as part of France rather than just people who lived in various different regions of a country called France. When the first French Republic was proclaimed in the autumn of 1792, France literally ceased to be the property of the French monarchs. If not the property of the King, then who did it belong to? France must therefore belong to the French people. It is this connection between the physical, geographical location and all its varied, representative interest groups coming under one banner as an idea that gives birth to the concept of the nation-state.

Outside of France, the United Kingdom, and perhaps the Scandinavian states, the idea of the nation as the dominant organizing concept for a political unit was new in Europe. States were either conglomerates of many nations, such as Russia and Austria, or endlessly divided small territories that were politically independent but nationally the same as those around them, such as the German states. Once the Revolutionary and later Napoleonic armies began to march across Europe they took these ideas of nation, nurtured in the crucible of the Revolution and the early defeats in the war, with them and these ideas soon took root wherever they went. It is one of the great historic ironies that these same ideals, specifically nationalism and liberty, ended up sounding the death knell for the Napoleonic Empire. This is because one of the consequences of a growing sense of nationalism is the idea that a nation should be in charge of its own affairs—that is, that it should be politically independent. It is this desire for national, political independence that drove much of world history throughout the 19th and 20th centuries. Nationalism can also been seen to dominate the domestic affairs of countries as well. If the state is the property of those who identify themselves as a nation, then those people have a say in its actions. This means democracy in some way, shape or form.

Discussion point:

The nation as the principle unit of organization in not the only one that states can use to bring a country together.

**What other principles can states organize around?
What are the strengths and weaknesses of these?**

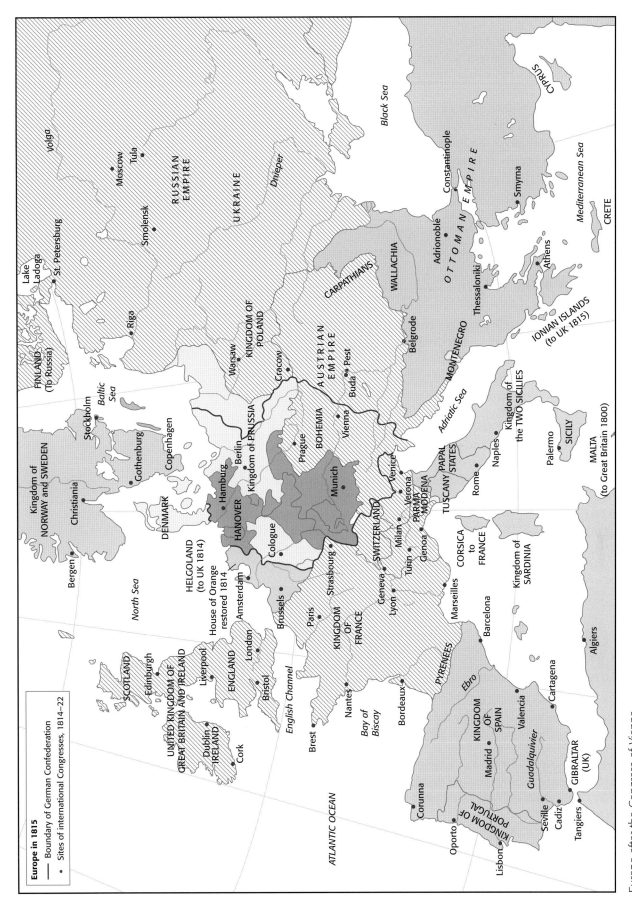

Europe in 1815
— Boundary of German Confederation
• Sites of international Congresses, 1814–22

Europe after the Congress of Vienna.

Nationalism, therefore, is a sense of belonging to and loyalty toward one's nation coupled with a desire for that nation to be politically united and independent—in other words as a nation-state. In this sense, nationalism can be seen in two manifestations. The first is a divisive expression and happens when larger units comprised of more than one nation divide into nation-states. The decolonization movement of the 20th century is one of the most marked examples of this manifestation of nationalism. The other expression of nationalism, more common in the 19th Century, is unifying nationalism, where disparate members of a national group join together in a single, larger independent nation-state. It is two of these great 19th-century nation-building projects that the rest of this chapter will analyse—by focusing on the move towards unification in Germany and Italy.

When the diplomats at the Congress of Vienna redrew the map of Europe in 1815, they tried to maintain a rough balance of power. In terms of geography, how successful were they?

 What geographic evidence is there that the Congress of Vienna ignored nationalism?

Nationalism after 1815

The nationalism that crossed European borders with the French armies did not immediately spark independence and unification movements. Nationalism seemed to first catch the imagination of academics and intellectuals. Throughout Europe, professors and philosophers were examining the essence of their particular culture, history, and geography, laying what would become the intellectual foundation of growing nationalist movements. In Germany, thinkers such as Hegel, Herder, and Goethe began to conceive of a unique German culture and history, indeed a world-view or national character, building on the ideas of 18th-century thinkers such as Hume and Montesquieu. Friedrich List, a German economist argued for a national economic system designed to protect and nurture German trade. Historians such as Friedrich Schlosser wrote national histories. More important, perhaps, than simply identifying such ideas, these theorists saw their particular national character as an intrinsic good—something to be preserved and promoted. The national character should be the core value or chief organizing structure around which a nation-state was built.

TOK Link
History and nationalism

The historian Margaret McMillan has written:

> *History provides much of the fuel for nationalism. It createsthe collective memories that help to bring the nation into being. The shared celebration of the nation's great achievements —and the shared sorrow at its defeats— sustain and foster it. The Further back the history appears to go, the more solid and enduring the nation seems—and the worthier its claims.*

Source: MacMillan, M. 2008. *The Uses and Abuses of History*. Toronto, Canada. Penguin. p. 87.

Research one of the following nationalist movements and explain how history has been used to legitimize its cause.

- Basques
- Quebecoise
- Irish Republicans
- Chechens
- Scots

What knowledge issues are raised by MacMillan's claim? What are the purpose(s) of history? How does the relationship of history to nationalism described by MacMillan fit with these purposes?

 What strengths and weaknesses of history as an area of knowledge does MacMillan's claim expose?

Nationalism and the arts

These intellectual currents closely mirrored developments in the arts. Nationalism flows from a feeling of distinctiveness based on one's national group and an emotional connection to this group. Mozart recognized the relationship of the arts to nationalism in the 18th century. He argued for the validity of German language operas over the prevailing Italian chauvinism in the 18th century. This artistic expression of nationalistic aspirations continued in the 19th century. Poets, composers, and writers began championing a national literature in Italy, Germany, and Poland. Chopin's **Polonaises** were based on Polish dances and were written to extol Polish culture and propagandize the Polish independence movement. Wagner was uncompromising in his Germanic choice of theme and form in his operas. The Brothers Grimm published traditional German folk stories while researching German dialects in the mid-19th century.

In many ways the French Revolution was the ideological spark for 19th-century nationalism, but much of the practical advancements were achieved through the administration of the Napoleonic Empire. Napoleon brought together Italian states for the first time since the Roman Empire, first in the Cisalpine Republic and later in the Italian Republic and the Kingdom of Italy. He reorganized the German states into the Confederation of the Rhine, eliminating the Holy Roman Empire in the process. Catholicism, shared by the Spanish, Irish and Polish alike, had bound the **Holy Roman Empire** together to the exclusion of the Protestant German states. Therefore, Napoleon's reorganization, ignoring as it did religious affiliation, partially reflected something unique to the German states—a sense of being German. Napoleon's motives were far more administrative than nationalistic, yet these geo-political rearrangements helped kindle in the people of these territories a sense of national uniqueness.

> **Polonaise** A slow Polish folk dance for couples made popular by Frederick Chopin's musical renditions.

Activity:

Intellectuals and nationalism

Research the works of the following intellectuals. Compare and contrast their views on nationalism. To what extent were these views evident in the unifications of Germany and Italy?

- Johann Wolfgang von Goethe
- Johann Gottfried von Herder
- Georg Wilhelm Friedrich Hegel
- Friedrich Schlosser
- Friedrich List

> **Holy Roman Empire** A political union of Catholic states in Central Europe led by the Holy Roman Emperor. It existed in some form from 800 until it was disbanded by Napoleon I.

Activity:

Nationalism in art

Artists often depicted important events such as battles, and gave form to the principles and values that motivated nationalism. The arts also appeal to our senses and emotions.

Liberty Leading the People, painted in 1830 by Eugene Delacroix.

American Progress, painted by John Gast in 1872.

Questions

1 Compare and contrast these paintings. How would you interpret their subject matter?

2 What are the values and limitations of using art as historical sources? Use one of these examples as a reference point to analyse the events portrayed.

3 Create a piece of art depicting nationalism in your country. What events/people would you depict? What values and principles would you focus on? How would you represent them?

Austria and the German States, 1815–48

The Congress of Vienna left the German states largely disunited, owing to the will of Prince Metternich, the Austrian Foreign Minister. Keeping the German states divided made them easier to control in the **Diet** of the German Confederation, dominated as it was by Austria. The conservative order that was re-established at Vienna further aggravated German nationalists. The groundswell of national sentiment that had risen under the feet of French overlords, continued in the German states, primarily in universities among students and academics. *Burschenschaften* were student organizations that looked to a Romantic view of a united Germany, replete with **Teutonic** images, literature, and ritual, that spread across German-speaking states. These sentiments were echoed in the popular press and often took the aristocracy as their prime target. This aristocratic order was the prime mechanism by which Metternich wished to control liberal ideas in Europe to ensure that the spectre of Revolution would never again darken Europe's door. This set liberal and nationalistic ideas against what has been called the "Metternich System" that emerged out of the Congress of Vienna.

Metternich was a conservative of the first order, but certainly not a reflexive tyrant. His conservatism was served by a practicality that raises him above the ranks of blind reactionaries. While keeping his eye keenly focused on the goal of a stable European order that was guided by the wisdom of monarchs and their aristocracies, he used whatever means he deemed useful in its pursuit. While this often meant bribery, secret police and military force, it also meant cajoling, persuading, and pandering to the collection of states that made up the German Confederation.

The Congress left a number of Napoleon's Germanic creations and enhancements intact. States such as Baden, Württemberg and Bavaria were inclined to support efforts to contain dangerous ideas that might see their power diminished in any kind of larger German union. Other German princes were likewise jealous of any encroachments on their power and autonomy and thus conservative by nature. It, therefore, wasn't difficult for Metternich to convince them of the danger inherent in the activities of the *Burschenschaften* or the liberal press and to get these princes to endorse the **Carlsbad Decrees** in September 1819. These decrees pledged the member states of the German Confederation to impose a uniform set of press censorship laws, to supervise and control school curriculums and to outlaw the *Burschenschaften*. Unopposed in Italy, controlling as it did the states of the Italian peninsula directly or indirectly, Austria was able to act more

> **Diet** A representative assembly, used in the Holy Roman Empire and later in the German Confederation.

> **Teutonic** Being characteristic of Teutons, an ancient Germanic tribe of north-eastern Europe.

Activity:

Metternich

Research the career of Clemens von Metternich. What were his goals and aims? How did he attempt to achieve these aims? To what extent was he successful?

> **Carlsbad Decrees** A set of laws passed within the German Confederation that controlled education and supressed the press. They were designed to fight growing nationalism.

independently to quell independence movements, keep the forces of liberalism and nationalism at bay, and maintain the *status quo* throughout the 1820s and 1830s.

Within the Austrian Empire, however, Metternich was not so unencumbered. The polyglot empire of the Hapsburgs was the most multi-ethnic European state outside of Russia. Although Germans made up the single largest national group within the Empire, they were scarcely a quarter of its total population. Czechs dominated Bohemia and Magyars dominated Hungarian domains within the Empire. Beyond these groups the multi-ethnic nature of Austria was staggering. The two Hapsburgs to rule the Empire in the first half of the 19th century, Francis I and Ferdinand I, counted Serbs, Romanians, Poles, Italians and Slovenes among their subjects. These domains were not immune to the spread of liberal, nationalistic ideas. But even this would have been straightforward compared to the varying aspirations of these groups. Some wanted independence while others wanted a limited and others a not-so-limited autonomy within the Empire. The Magyars of the Kingdom of Hungary had long harboured nationalistic ambitions and had risen against their rulers in Vienna on several occasions in the two centuries preceding Metternich's ascendancy in Austria's Imperial affairs. During this time they had won for themselves a semi-autonomous assembly— The Hungarian Diet—that had to approve any laws before they could be enforced in Hungary. Such an ethnically complex realm with institutional barriers such as the Hungarian Diet made the kind of centralization that Metternich saw as necessary to the stability of all European states, and even Europe itself, very challenging.

As the age of Metternich waned, and Europe weathered the convulsions of 1830, approaching the nationalistic conflagration of 1848, Austria stumbled into the industrial age. Industrialization had been transforming British society for the better part of a century and had finally begun to take root in Western Europe. Austria, however, was considerably behind its Western rivals in industrialization and by the mid century, increasingly, behind its German rivals—most notably Prussia. Although thriving in certain areas such as cotton textile production, the Austrian Empire was far outstripped by the German states in railroad construction, coal production and iron production. Industrialization in Austria was very localized, leaving vast tracts of the Empire untouched by industrial production. Austria remained a largely agricultural economy bound by serf labour. Even this agricultural base was stagnant. There was nothing approaching the agricultural revolution that had helped create the preconditions for industrialization in the United Kingdom within the Hapsburg's borders. As railroad construction and industrial expansion was spreading along the Rhine, it was beginning to have an impact on its great partner in world affairs—the military. Military strength, or potential strength, was quickly coming to be equated with industrial strength and as such the Hapsburg Empire was falling behind. As a result, on the eve of the great events of the mid 19th century, Austria, that for so long under Metternich's watchful eye had resisted the tide of modern ideas, found itself in danger of being swamped by an economic, diplomatic and nationalistic flood.

Discussion point:

School curriculums have been used to reinforce social and political principles for centuries.

To what extent does your school curriculum reflect your society's principles?

To what extent does it encourage you to challenge those principles?

Activity:

19th-century ideologies

The 19th century was a period of intense ideological innovation. In groups research one of the ideologies below. Use the following headings to guide your research.

Major thinkers

- Main principles/brief history
- Ideas on social reform
- Collectivism vs. individualism
- Attitude to revolution
- Political organization

Ideologies

1 Romanticism
2 Socialism
3 Classical liberalism
4 Marxism
5 Positivism

The revolutions of 1848

The first surge of this rising tide of nationalism came in 1848. There had been stirrings in 1830 that had turned into outright revolution in France, which in turn spread to Belgium, Italy and Poland. In the wake of 1830, Metternich had tightened Vienna's centralized control of the German states and had beaten down the nationalist movement within them. Tsar Nicholas did the same in Poland. These victories were not to last. Despite Metternich's Six Articles, passed in 1832 and the Ten Articles that followed later that same year, both designed to restrict nationalist movements within the German Confederation whether they came in parliamentary or revolutionary form, liberal nationalism continued to smoulder in all the major states of Europe.

Economic problems accelerated across Europe from 1840 through to 1847. Poor harvests, stagnant industrial demand and reduced production spread across Europe from Ireland to Russia in the 1840s. Grain shortages drove food prices up, while this in turn bit into the demand for industrial goods, throwing workers into unemployment. Economic troubles enhanced the appeal of ideologies such as socialism, further threatening those in power, be it economic or political. Socialists in general believed that the wealth generated by the engine of industrial capitalism needed to be more evenly distributed. Socialists like Robert Owen from the UK and Saint-Simon in France were far from violent political revolutionaries. Nevertheless, their ideas represented a desire to change the current state of economic relations and share the decision-making and wealth across a wider constituency. This struck a chord with many liberal nationalists, concerned as they were with changing the basis upon which states were constituted. The economic crisis drove middle-class nationalists, starving peasants, unemployed workers, university intellectuals, and Romantic artists together in 1848 and the result was, of course, revolution; but not one revolution, rather many disparate, unco-ordinated and diverse revolutions.

As might be expected, it started in France in February of 1848. Although by February a number of Italian territories were already embroiled in insurrection, it was the French example that spread across Western and Central Europe. When barricades were thrown up around Paris and the population poured into the streets, Louis-Philippe, the King of France, fled to London. By the end of February, France was a republic once again. Further demonstrations in June, mostly by urban workers in Paris, turned into open warfare in the streets of Paris. In many ways this confusing street battle pitted the emerging socialist movement and its working class "soldiers" against the moderate-middle class republicans and its regular army, supplemented by volunteers from outside of Paris. When the smoke cleared a few days later, the uprising had been crushed with thousands of deaths and arrests. In effect, this was one of the first, unabashedly class-oriented struggles of the 19th century.

How then does this relate to the concept of nationalism? Intellectuals have debated the relationship of class to nation ever since. In many ways it comes down to a debate over what one believes the most important or natural organizing unit of society is. Radical socialists and those influenced by the works of Marx argue that one's class—determined by one's relationship to the dominant **mode of production**—is what structures people's lives and indeed reality. To this way of thinking, workers have more common interest with workers of other countries than they do with the middle-class of their own country. In this conception, the idea of a nation is at best a benign fiction or at worst a dangerous distraction manufactured by the ruling class to divert potentially revolutionary energies and engender loyalty to the existing government. Nationalists, on the other hand, contend that the nation is a natural unit of society, often based as it is on ethnicity, and is therefore the idea around which states should be organized. Of course, as with any intellectual dichotomy, it really exists on a spectrum with myriad positions between the two extremes.

The revolutions of 1848 reflected the concerns of the various groups in Europe at the turn of the century. France, itself already a largely democratic nation-state in the 19th century sense, experienced the convulsions of 1848 primarily as a class event, with limited nationalist or liberal democratic elements. This reflected the dominant domestic concerns of the French population at the end of the economic crisis and the social dislocation of the 1840s—economic welfare and the maintenance of order. When the revolutionary impulse crossed into the German states—made up of the disunited elements of what many German intellectuals saw as a single German nation—the revolutions emerged as the uniting manifestation of nationalism. In the lands controlled by the Hapsburgs in Central Europe and Italy, the revolutions materialized as the divisive manifestation of nationalism, national independence being a dominant concern of these populations at that particular point in time.

In this way it was the idea of revolution as a means of radical change rather than the particular ends of that change that spread from France to the rest of Europe in March of 1848. Riots and demonstrations in Prussia persuaded Friedrich Wilhelm IV to grant a representative assembly, initially dominated by radical liberal democrats.

The initial successes of the German revolutionaries outside of Prussia seemed no less spectacular. In the absence of a strong centralized control to subdue the demonstrations that followed close on the heels of those in France, a self-appointed assembly came

> The **mode of production** is the combination of the elements or factors of production—such as land, labour and capital—and how these are organized and controlled to produce goods.

Discussion point:

The French Revolution took three years and a European war to spread beyond the borders of France.

 Why did the revolutions of 1848 spread so far so quickly?

The Frankfurt Assembly, 1848, from a lithographic print by Gustav May.

together in March. These German nationalists conceived of a permanent assembly representing all German states whose representatives would be elected by universal adult male suffrage in a system of proportional representation. This parliament met in May in Frankfurt.

The pattern held in Austria as well. News of the February revolution in France made its way to Vienna where the population rose up in arms on 13 March and the Hungarian Diet demanded complete autonomy within the Austrian Empire. Metternich, the strong hand who had steered the Austrian ship of state for 30 years, fled. The confused Emperor Ferdinand quickly acquiesced to the creation of a constitutional monarchy in Austria and autonomy for Hungary and Bohemia within a matter of days. Slowly, however, the Austrian government began to reassert its authority. This was made considerably easier by the dysfunction of the revolutionary movements. Again, it was only the method of revolution that came flooding out of France. The substance of the revolutions was incredibly heterogeneous and the diverse ethnicities and class interests within the Austrian Empire exposed these divisions early on. Non-German Austrians wanted varying degrees of independence, but this offended the Germans who saw their territories as integral to Austria. Magyars ignored the interests of non-Magyar Hungarians. Austrian peasants and middle-class business owners had little in common with the urban workers. As the Austrian government regrouped after the flight of Metternich it began exploiting these divisions and by the end of 1848 it had jettisoned the erratic Ferdinand in favour of his nephew Franz Joseph.

Nevertheless, the failures of 1848 were instructive to those who would embark on nationalist projects after 1848. While the theory of nationalism as such was becoming more refined, the Frankfurt Parliament illustrated that there needed to be a practical component to nationalist projects. Taxes needed to be collected. Laws needed to be enforced. Trade had to continue. Future nationalist revolutionaries would have to answer the paradoxical question of how to maintain a degree of stability in the midst of a revolution. The revolutions of 1848 also emphasized for the first time the concerns of the working class. What's more, these urban workers, growing ever more numerous in industrializing Europe, began to act in the collective interests of their class, in some cases in opposition to other economic classes within society. Likewise, as seen in Vienna, middle-class interests could run counter to those of the working class. Any future nationalist movement would need to reconcile these often competing interests in the common cause of the nation.

Another factor emerging was the issue of ethnicity as a key determinant of national identity that would lead to a number of problems. First the term itself was not used consistently and thus could mean a number of different things to different people. In practical terms, the nationalist projects of the 19th century had the creation of some form of nation-state as their ultimate goal that both acknowledged the land and its people. Even if we assume that all the participants are using the same conception of ethnicity, the fact is that on the frontiers between these national

The Frankfurt Parliament found little difficulty passing legislation guaranteeing broad freedoms and good governance. It, however, found the day-to-day management of a state more challenging. Why was this so?

 What is the relationship between principle and practice in governing a state?

groups, one ethnicity will bleed into another through intermarriage and centuries of living together. Where then to draw the borders of these new states? This leads to disputed territory—to competing nationalisms. Any new state has to be able to defend what it claims as its territory, regardless of the national rhetoric that helped create it.

Activity:

The revolutions of 1848: a written debate

Individually, research the revolutions of 1848 and complete the following chart. Once you have completed your research, find a partner to debate the following statement:

"The revolutions of 1848 helped advance the development of nationalism in the 19th century."

One of you will take the positive position and the other will take the negative position. Each of you will write a defence of your position using the research for specific support. Once you have both finished, exchange papers and write a rebuttal to the specific points made by your partner. Once you have completed the rebuttal, take some time to discuss the role of the revolutions of 1848 in the history of 19th-century nationalism.

Revolution	Causes	Revolutionaries	Events	Challenges	Result
France					
Germany					
Austria					
Italian states					

Activity:

Impressions of 1848

Source A

Louis Napoleon's Campaign Manifesto, November 1848. Louis Napoleon was running for election in the wake of the collapse of the 1848 revolution in France.

> If elected president, I shall shrink from no danger, from no sacrifice, in the defense of society, which has been so outrageously assailed. I shall devote myself wholly and without reservation to the consolidation of the republic, so that it may be wise in its laws, honest in its aims, great and strong in its deeds. My greatest honor would be to hand on to my successor, after four years of office, the public power consolidated, its liberties intact, and a genuine progress assured . . .

Source: http://history.hanover.edu/early/fr1848.html

Source B

Friedrich Wilhelm IV, King of Prussia: Proclamation of 1849 issued after he was asked to be the constitutional monarch of the German Confederation.

> I am not able to return a favorable reply to the offer of a crown on the part of the German National Assembly [meeting in Frankfurt], because the Assembly has not the right, without the consent of the German governments, to bestow the crown which they tendered me, and moreover because they offered the crown upon condition that I would accept a constitution which could not be reconciled with the rights of the German states.

Source C

From Le Constitutional, 5 December 1848.

> What we–the moderates, the immense majority of Frenchmen–need is the Republic and order. That is to say, no more [political] clubs that stir up and deprave the people day after day... The Republic with a system of taxes that will not ruin the rich or well-to-do citizens–a ruin detrimental to the poor because it makes it impossible for the rich to employ them–and that will not cause the disappearance from our country, together with all wealth, of our luxury industries which are the staple of our export trade.

Source: Roger Price, ed. 1975. *1848 in France*. Ithaca, USA. Cornell University Press. p. 127.

Source D

Karl Marx, January –October 1850 for the *Neue Rheinische Zeitung*.

> The Provisional Government which emerged from the February barricades necessarily mirrored in its composition the different parties which shared in the victory. It could not be anything but a compromise between the different classes which together had overturned the July throne, but whose interests were mutually antagonistic. The great majority of its members consisted of representatives of the bourgeoisie.

Karl Marx. 1969. *Selected Works*. vol. 1. Moscow. Russia. Progress Publishers. Also at http://www.marxists.org/archive/marx/works/1850/class-struggles-france/index.htm.

Questions

1 **a** What does Friedrich Wilhelm mean when he writes of the "German governments" in Source B?

  b What does Marx mean when he writes of interests that were "mutually antagonistic" in Source D?

2 Compare and contrast the view of European society expressed in Source C and Source D.

3 With reference to their origin and purpose evaluate the value and limitations of Source A and Source C for historians investigating the reasons for the collapse of the 1848 revolutions.

4 Using these documents and further research analyse the reasons that the 1848 revolutions in Germany and France were unsuccessful.

The unification of Italy

Tuscany	Independent states in 1815
────	Northern boundary of Kingdom of Italy, 1866–1919
1859	Joined by plebiscite with Sardinia
1860	Joined by revolution and plebiscite with Sardinia to form Kingdom of Italy, proclaimed in 1861
1856, 1870	Joined with Kingdom of Italy

Italy, 1815–48

In the spirit of restoration, the Congress of Vienna re-established Austrian control of the Italian peninsula in 1815. From the Alps in the north to the shores of Sicily in the south, the Hapsburgs controlled the Italian peninsula in some way, shape or form. The Bourbon dynasty had been restored to the throne of the Two Sicilies or the Kingdom of Naples and was dependent on Austria in all meaningful ways. The duchies of Tuscany, Modena, and Parma were ruled by branches of the Hapsburg family. Austria directly controlled Venetia and Lombardy. The central swathe of the peninsula was occupied by the Papal States. These were territories under the control of the Church of Rome. In the 19th century the Papacy was not merely a religious institution, it had temporal sovereignty in these Italian territories limiting administrative positions to the Catholic clergy. As hundreds of years of Papal history had shown, without a strong military to protect its interests, the Papacy and her states were prey to the imperial and dynastic ambitions of Catholic monarchs across Europe. The **Pope** maintained a small army, but throughout the 19th century depended on the arms and

If the Kingdom of Sardinia emerged as the dominant power in Italian unification, why was the capital situated in Rome after 1870?

? What are the geographic challenges for any central Italian government?

The Pope is the spiritual leader of the Catholic Church worldwide. In the 19th Century the Pope also had temporal control of lands in Central Italy

77

good graces of France and Austria, the two dominant Catholic countries in Europe, to maintain the integrity of its borders. This meant that any attempt to wrest control of these states from the restoration leaders would have to deal with the formidable might of Austria.

The capital of the Papal States was Rome. In fact, Rome represented the heart and soul of the Italian nation. The Roman Empire supplied much of the historical justification and nationalist pride for Italians in the 19th and 20th centuries. As the home of the Vatican, Rome was also the spiritual capital of the world's Catholics and as such had both an international forum as well as international influence. Even during the Renaissance, when the peninsula was divided into numerous city-states with varying degrees of power, Rome as the seat of the papacy had a degree of influence not enjoyed by the other city-states. It was therefore natural for Italian nationalists to imagine Rome as the de facto capital of the Italian nation-state.

In the years after the restoration, Italy slumped back into political and economic stagnation. Economically, Italy was still massively agricultural, almost feudal. Agriculture laboured under sometimes primitive techniques and was always under-capitalized. Tariff barriers cut the peninsula and the states within the peninsula from north to south and east to west, stifling trade and discouraging even moderate gains in economic efficiency or technical innovation. This was exacerbated by the intense localism that gripped Italy. Locales sought to preserve ancient privileges, regulations, and traditions at the expense of economic efficiency. Politically, the states of Italy, under Metternich's guidance, took every opportunity to suppress liberal reform. The Vatican's control of education reinforced this conservatism. Much of the population growth from the turn of the 19th century was in rural areas, placing more pressure on land ownership and rural employment. With the European peace that accompanied the restoration came a drop in demand for agricultural products and an increase in production that sent prices lower.

It is not surprising, then, that there grew in Italy a dynamic and radical reform movement, albeit underground. Secret societies blossomed in the years after the Congress of Vienna in Italy and across Europe. These societies were primarily middle-class organizations that met to discuss liberal, democratic, nationalistic ideas, disseminate banned literature, occasionally plot murders and uprisings. In Italy the **Carbonari** were among the largest, but there were others. Looking to revolts in Spain and in Spanish America for inspiration, a revolt broke out in Sicily in 1820 forcing the Bourbon monarch, Ferdinand, to acquiesce to a constitution. This was crushed the next year by the intervention of the Austrian army acting under the terms of the Congress of Vienna. In 1821 another revolt broke out in Piedmont which was also put down with the assistance of foreign troops. After the success of the 1830 revolts in Paris, insurrection spread across the Italian states. These met the same fate as the risings of the 1820s when the Pope Gregory XVI asked for and received Austrian military assistance. The Carbonari and other secret societies that had supported these unco-ordinated and essentially local insurgencies gave way to more pan-Italian nationalist movements that would lead Italy into the revolutions of 1848.

Carbonari This was a secret societies devoted to Italian nationalism. These societies were general liberal and republican in their outlook.

Activity:

The Carbonari

Research the Carbonari, its goals, methods, successes and failures. Make a presentation to your class of your findings.

In the period from 1830–48 one man was universally associated with the cause of Italian nationalism—Giuseppe Mazzini. Mazzini was a middle-class intellectual from Piedmont who was a confirmed Italian nationalist from an early age. For Mazzini, there were no dividing issues of liberal reform from political independence and unification in the Italian peninsula. Like most Romantic thinkers, Mazzini believed that for the Italians, and indeed all people, to reach their full potential as humans, liberty, both

Giuseppe Mazzini (1805–1872)

A liberal nationalist, Mazzini had been a member of the Carbonari before forming his own movement dedicated to the unification and independence of Italy called Young Italy. Mazzini was a Romantic nationalist in many ways and believed that the unification project was more than just a political exercise, but also had moral, intellectual and spiritual dimensions that would transform Italy and, in turn, the rest of Europe. After failed insurrections in the 1830s, Mazzini went into exile where he would spend the time leading up to the revolts of 1848. He joined Garibaldi during the revolts of 1848 and became leader of the short-lived Roman Republic, the collapse of which sent him again into exile. As a republican, Mazzini was never reconciled to the final form of Italian unification.

personal and national was necessary. It is in this moral component that 19th-century Romanticism had its most profound impact on the nationalist movements. For many Romantics, nationalism was not merely a practical end to a more efficient and modern state. Nor was it simply a matter of cultural pride or ethnic conceit. Rather it was an imperative to the progress of human society. Inherent in this idea was a belief in the pervasive corruption of the existing regimes flouting the will of those whom they governed. Nationalist projects for these Romantic nationalists were part political independence, part moral regeneration. Even though there were as many variants of Romanticism as there were Romantics (the idea of personal interpretation was actually a main tenet of the movement) most Romantics dating back to their great antecedent, Jean Jacques Rousseau, held with the essential equality of all humans, and as such Romantic nationalists like Mazzini were predisposed to republicanism. In terms of method, Romantics seemed to value deed over debate, action over administration. Many believed that it was through violent revolution that these changes were to take root and transform society. Certainly the vigour with which uprisings and revolts were put down in the years 1815–30 gave them no reason to believe otherwise. To these ends Mazzini formed a new movement in the wake of the failures of 1830 that he hoped would supplant the overly localized Carbonari. He called it "Young Italy" (*giovane Italia*) and he wrote and published tirelessly in its interests. Mazzini himself

Activity:

Mazzini: An assessment

The following is an assessment of Mazzini by historian Denis Mack Smith.

> [Mazzini] *had proved impossibly utopian in believing the populace would rise against tyranny on their own initiative and resolve all the problems of national and class selfishness. When they did rise, it was usually for selfish and non-nationalist reasons of their own, and he found them to be far from the progressive force he had hoped. His disillusionment was profound. … Worse still, Mazzini knew that his failure was partly due to his own intractable nature, to his distrust of compromise, and to the temperamental obstinacy which ultimately alienated even his former friend Garibaldi.*

Source: Mack Smith, Denis. 1997. *Italy: A political history*. Ann Arbor, USA. University of Michigan Press. p. 14.

Questions

1 What does Mack Smith mean by "impossibly utopian"?
2 Critically evaluate Mack Smith's assessment. What specific evidence can you find that supports his view? What evidence contradicts it?

spent much of the rest of his life exiled to various states in Europe ending up, as others exiles before and after him, in London. Mazzini and Young Italy never realized their aims, running into the stubborn obstacles to Italian unification—localism, class interests, and the repressive measures of the Hapsburgs and the Vatican. Nevertheless, by 1848, Italian nationalists were ready to make another attempt to overthrow the established order.

Momentum toward 1848 had begun with the elevation in 1846 of Cardinal Giovanni Maria Mastai-Ferretti to the papacy as Pius IX. The new Pope inaugurated his papacy with some limited reforms— amnesty for political prisoners, reform of Rome's municipal government, the creation of a civic guard, and the creation of an advisory council of laity—which were greeted with popular enthusiasm throughout the Papal States and concern in Vienna. He stood up to Metternich when the Austrian Foreign Minister placed a garrison of Austrian troops in Ferrara endearing himself not only to liberals, but also to liberal nationalists. In all, however, Pius IX was far more of a moderate reformer than a confirmed liberal or nationalist as many hoped. Nevertheless, as the urban middle class saw the door to reform open a crack under the new Pope, they grew determined to push it open further. By the dawn of 1848, liberal ideas were openly discussed throughout Pius's domains, especially in Rome, eventually spilling over into the Hapsburg duchies of Tuscany, Modena, and Parma and, eventually, into Piedmont and the Austrian territories of Lombardy and Venetia.

Revolution erupted, not in Rome or even in Piedmont, but rather in Palermo on the island of Sicily in January of 1848. In very short order the revolutionaries had forced a constitution on the Bourbon King of Naples, Ferdinand II. Even this early success, however, was circumscribed by localism. Much of what drove the Sicilians to revolt revolved around the economic hardships faced by the peasants. Those of the revolutionaries who thought beyond material complaints to a broader vision wanted a return to a form of constitutional independence that the island had enjoyed in 1812, not unification with other Italian states. This, then, would seem to be an example of the divisive manifestation of nationalism with an eye more to the past than to the future. This had the potential to set up competing nationalisms within any broader Italian unification project and in fact presaged some of the divisions that would contribute to the failure of the 1848 revolutions in the Austrian Empire and the German states.

In the north, King Charles Albert of Piedmont had begun to follow the reforming example set by Pope Pius IX in late 1847, granting some civil liberties and eventually a constitution to his subjects. Charles Albert also took this opportunity to expand the Piedmontese army, suggesting that he perhaps had ambitions beyond a more liberal Piedmont. A stronger army, on the one hand, would allow him to resist any threats against his liberal reforms from a reactionary Austria. The likelihood that any such threats could actually be carried out is doubtful. Piedmont was one of the buffer states positioned between France and the rest of Europe by the Congress of Vienna. Were Austria to violate this sovereignty, it would call into question

> *"Insurrection by means of guerrilla bands is the true method of warfare for all nations desirous of emancipating themselves from a foreign yoke. It is invincible, indestructible."*
>
> Giuseppe Mazzini

Activity:
Young Italy

Research Mazzini's Young Italy movement, examining the following:

- Origins
- Principles
- Aims
- Successes
- Failures

Once you have completed your research make a presentation to your class analysing the influence of Young Italy on the later unification of Italy.

Discussion point:

The Papal States were unique in that within the territory the Pope exercised not only religious but also temporal authority.

 What challenges did the Popes authority within the Papal States pose for lay politicians in the territory?

What challenges did this create for other states in their diplomatic relationship with the Papal States?

the balance established in 1815 and perhaps provoke reaction from one or more of the major European powers. On the other hand, if Charles Albert saw Piedmont as the anchor state in a unified Italy as some leading middle-class liberals in Piedmont had advocated, it would require a stronger army to defend such a unified state and to wrest other Italian territories from the Austrians. Certainly, there were liberals in Piedmont who were urging the King in this direction. Enthusiasm for Charles Albert's reforms spilled into other regions of Italy, including Lombardy and Venetia. Popular demonstrations against the Hapsburgs forced a constitution in Tuscany. These demonstrations quickly developed into street fighting in Milan, the capital of Lombardy, by 18 March on news of the revolt in Vienna. Within a few days, revolutionary mobs had driven the Austrian garrison of 13,000 troops from Milan. The pattern repeated itself in Venice, which proclaimed itself an independent republic shortly after the withdrawal of the Austrian troops.

With the Austrian troops on the run, Charles Albert saw his chance to take the reigns of the Italian cause. The Piedmontese army invaded Lombardy on 23 March and quickly pushed the relatively small Austrian force to the Venetian frontier. Along the way, volunteers and regular forces from the Papal States and Naples rallied to the Piedmontese banner. Mazzini, who hastened back to Lombardy from exile in Paris, urged all class and ideological divisions be checked until the Austrians had been driven completely out of Italian lands, which put him on the side of the moderates and the Piedmontese as their army represented their best chance of defeating the Austrians. Similar debates raged in Tuscany where moderate liberals, driven by a fear of radical republicanism, sided with the rulers who in turn were only Italian nationalists in so far as it benefited their position. Supporting Piedmont's expansion did not fit this bill. By July the moderate argument had carried the day throughout northern Italy and Venetia, Lombardy, Parma, and Modena voted to join with Piedmont.

Activity:

A debate on Lombardy

In Milan, the revolution against the Hapsburgs sparked a fierce debate between moderate liberals who advocated annexation by Piedmont— also favoured by Charles Albert—and radical republicans who wanted independence and, at most, a federalist model for the emerging Italy.

In groups take the position of one of these groups—moderates and radicals—and prepare an argument. Conduct a class debate on the course that Lombardy should follow.

For discussion

1 Which position had the most chance of succeeding in throwing off Austrian domination? Why?

2 Write a detailed response from Mazzini to both sides in the debate.

3 How would Pope Pius IX have responded to the debate?

4 What does the debate tell us about why the revolution failed?

By the summer, however, the Hapsburg's had begun to recover their nerve and to exploit the weaknesses that were appearing in the revolutionary cause. In southern Italy, Ferdinand led a coalition of moderates and conservatives against the revolutionaries and recovered control of his territory on the mainland. In the north the Austrians decisively defeated the Piedmontese at the Battle of Custozza on 25 July and then proceeded to push the Piedmontese out of Lombardy. Further defeat on the battlefield ended Charles Albert's ambitions and indeed his reign. He **abdicated** in 1849.

> **Abdicate** When a monarch gives up the crown, he or she is said to have abdicated.

In the Papal States, the radicals rose to prominence near the end of 1848. With their accession amid popular demonstrations, the Pope took refuge with the recently emboldened Ferdinand, paving the way for the proclamation of the Roman Republic in November. By spring of 1849 the Roman Republic was invaded by Ferdinand's Neapolitan army, a small contingent of the Spanish Army and the French Army all bound together by the cause of Catholicism. Rome itself was besieged in June and the defenders, led by Mazzini and Giuseppe Garibaldi, held out for month before surrendering the city. When the Pope returned, he re-established conservativism, turning his back on the reforming reputation he had earned at the beginning of his papacy.

How then do these 1848 spasms of Italian nationalism relate to the great unification projects of the coming decades? The participation of established rulers, initially the Pope, Charles Albert, and eventually the reluctant Ferdinand, gave the impression of a true nationalist movement that encompassed all social classes. While this might have been the reality within these states, the relationship between these states meant that one of them would have to dominate which was unacceptable to the others. Even a loose federation was bound to founder on these same rocks of regional interests. The inclusion of all social classes in the revolution was an initial benefit, but ultimately led to serious fractures in the revolutionary cause. Plunging as it did, into a war at the very outset of the revolution, did not allow the various societal interests to negotiate a mutually satisfactory social platform for the "new" states such as Lombardy, Venetia, Tuscany, and Rome. The pressures of war expose cracks in the social foundation of even the most stable societies, let alone those barely a few months old. Also, the doomed Roman Republic showed the extent to which popular and Romantic enthusiasm can carry a cause in the face of large, organized states and the military might that they can muster. Future nationalist efforts, if they were to be successful, would need to wed this enthusiasm with the kind of administrative and military stability of established states such as Piedmont and Prussia.

Giuseppe Garibaldi (1807–1882)

If the nationalism of the mid 19th century sprang from both the political vision of the political elite and the nationalistic enthusiasm of the masses, Garibaldi can be seen as the embodiment of the latter. He joined Mazzini's Young Italy and fled to South America after its abortive insurrection in Genoa in 1834. While in South America he continued to give vent to his nationalistic passions, fighting in the wars of South American independence. On his return to Italy he led the defence of the Roman Republic in 1849 and fled Italy again when it was defeated. He returned to participate in Camillo di Cavour's unification project and led the force that brought Sicily and Naples into the union. Garibaldi was an Italian nationalist first and a republican second and this helps explain his co-operation with Cavour and Victor Emanuel II in the founding of the constitutional monarchy that Italy would become.

The unification of Italy

Piedmont-Sardinia and Camillo di Cavour

As the remainder of Italy was once again under Hapsburg and Papal control, the Kingdom of Piedmont-Sardinia entered a period of economic modernization and moderate reform. Charles Albert's successor, his son Victor Emanuel II, came to the throne of a constitutional monarchy that emerged from the turbulent period of the 1848 revolutions intact and independent. While she was required to pay a war indemnity to Austria, her position as a buffer between the potential rivals of France and Austria ensured her sovereignty. By 1852 Camillo di Cavour came to power as the Prime Minister at the head of a coalition of middle-class politicians and immediately set to work by all means, constitutional and otherwise, to modernize Piedmont-Sardinia.

In many ways his goal was the example set by the United Kingdom. He saw how the growing industrial might of the British had allowed it freedom of action in foreign affairs, dependent on none of the other powers. To Cavour's way of thinking, if Piedmont-Sardinia was to play a leading role in any future Italian nation-state, a position he advocated, on its own terms, the region must first industrialize its economy and modernize its administration. He oversaw the expansion of international trade, concluding agreements with a number of European states. Railway construction increased drastically during his years in power. Textiles industries—silk, cotton and woollens—also thrived. Cavour could rightly take some personal credit for these improvements as many were nurtured through substantial government subsidies. It must be remembered that this economic modernization set Piedmont-Sardinia apart from the rest of the country, though still behind other parts of Europe. It also suffered from a shortage of coal and iron— both essential to an economy the size and shape of Britain's. Nonetheless, this productive capacity and the revenue it generated, supplemented by significant foreign loans,

Victor Emanuel II (1820–78)

Victor Emanuel II came to the throne of Piedmont-Sardinia in 1849 upon his father's abdication in the wake of Piedmont-Sardinia's defeat at Novara. After the appointment of Cavour to the position of Prime Minister, the two men worked together to modernize Piedmont-Sardinia. In the events of unification, Victor Emanuel II and Cavour had an at times tense relationship, with Cavour resigning at one point. When Victor Emanuel's forces marched on the Papal States and eventually joined Garibaldi's forces in the south, he was excommunicated by the Pope. He was proclaimed King of the new Kingdom of Italy in March 1860.

Camillo di Cavour (1810–1864)

Born into Piedmontese nobility, Cavour spent his early life travelling through Western Europe. During that time he came to be a great admirer of British classical liberals and this would come to dominate much of his economic thinking. Before turning to politics, Cavour spent time modernizing his family's business concerns and dabbling in journalism. Once he did embark on his political career in 1848, his rise was meteoric—becoming a minister in 1850 and Prime Minister of Piedmont in 1852. Cavour was a classical liberal by temperament and a skilled practitioner of *Realpolitik* by situation. He was not above parliamentary manipulation, but kept his sights clearly on the establishment of a modern constitutional state on the Italian peninsula.

was enough for Cavour to modernize the Piedmontese army. Cavour worked to limit the role of the Church in society and introduced a measure of efficiency to the financial management of the state.

Cavour, therefore, at first glance, may look the part of a classical liberal of the British mould he so admired. On closer examination, however, he emerges as one of the great pragmatists of the period. While the constitution was fine in principle, Cavour never let it hinder his actions. He used parliament against the Crown and the Crown against parliament. He ruled by executive order when it suited him and often sought permission from parliament for actions already taken. He was no champion of democracy but was never really impeded by Piedmont-Sardinia's limited electorate—around two percent of the population was allowed to vote—and he was thus more than willing to bask in the illusion of the legitimacy it bestowed. While he was in favour of unimpeded free-market capitalism if it moved the economy in the direction that he wanted, he was not above using government subsidies to push it in that direction. British classical liberals generally eschewed military spending, but much of Cavour's domestic policy revolved around the modernization and enlargement of Piedmont-Sardinia's army and navy. A free press may have been a liberal hallmark, but Cavour, himself among many other things a journalist, did not hesitate to close down and otherwise censor radical publications, including Mazzini's. He may have been a classical liberal by inclination, but as he guided his country and the Italian nation through a decade of nation-state building, Camillo di Cavour was a pragmatist above all else.

> "I have discovered the art of deceiving diplomats. I tell them the truth and they never believe me."
>
> Camillo di Cavour

Activity:

The source of nationalism

Read the following excerpt from a speech made by Mazzini in 1857.

> It was not for a material interest that the people of Vienna fought in 1848; in weakening the empire they could only lose power. It was not for an increase of wealth that the people of Lombardy fought in the same year; the Austrian Government had endeavoured in the year preceding to excite the peasants against the landed proprietors, as they had done in Gallicia; but everywhere they had failed. They struggled, they still struggle, as do Poland, Germany, and Hungary, for country and liberty; for a word inscribed upon a banner, proclaiming to the world that they also live, think, love, and labour for the benefit of all. They speak the same language, they bear about them the impress of consanguinity, they kneel beside the same tombs, they glory in the same tradition; and they demand to associate freely, without obstacles, without foreign domination, in order to elaborate and express their idea; to contribute their stone also to the great pyramid of history. It is something moral which they are seeking; and this moral something is in fact, even politically speaking, the most important question in the present state of things. It is the organisation of the European task. It is no longer the savage, hostile, quarrelsome nationality of two hundred years ago which is invoked by these peoples.

> The nationality … founded upon the following principle: Whichever people, by its superiority of strength, and by its geographical position, can do us an injury, is our natural enemy; whichever cannot do us an injury, but can by the amount of its force and by its position injure our enemy, is our natural ally,—is the princely nationality of aristocracies or royal races. The nationality of the peoples has not these dangers; it can only be founded by a common effort and a common movement; sympathy and alliance will be its result. In principle, as in the ideas formerly laid down by the men influencing every national party, nationality ought only to be to humanity that which the division of labour is in a workshop—the recognised symbol of association; the assertion of the individuality of a human group called by its geographical position, its traditions, and its language, to fulfil a special function in the European work of civilisation.

Source: "Giuseppe Mazzini: On Nationality, 1852". Modern History Sourcebook. http://www.fordham.edu/halsall/mod/1852mazzini.html

Write a response

Respond to this speech by writing a letter on behalf of either Cavour or Bismarck. Be sure to highlight points upon which they would agree with Mazzini and those on which they would disagree and the reason for these.

The Crimean War, 1854–56

Five years after the revolutions of 1848 rocked Europe, the Great Powers went to war for the first time since 1815. The Crimean War finally broke the conservative log-jam, the status quo balance of power constructed at the Congress of Vienna and carefully maintained by Metternich. The resulting flux made possible the creation of modern Italy and Germany for it was foreign affairs as much as German and Italian affairs that would determine the shape of these two nation-states.

It is an old truth that politics like nature hates a vacuum. It was just such a vacuum that appeared to be developing in Asia Minor in the mid-19th century. The Ottoman Empire had been in decline for a hundred years. As in any empire, this loss of control was first seen on the frontiers of the Empire, but by the 1820s it had spread closer to the centre and this centre was of vital strategic interest to the powers of Europe. The Ottoman Empire controlled the key maritime route between Central Europe and the Mediterranean— the Dardanelles and the Bosphorus. If Russia had designs on sea access to the west, it would have to control these two straits. As such, disputes over these two bodies of water as well as Turkish control of the Balkans had been the cause of numerous Russo-Turkish wars. As the Sultan's control over his territories eroded, Tsar Nicholas I, anticipating a vacuum, hoped to gain what for generations had eluded the Romanovs—access to the Mediterranean. When Russian forces occupied the Danubian principalities in July of 1853, The Ottoman Empire declared war. France had long had interests in the Middle East and had no desire for Russia to exert more influence in the region. For its part, Britain opposed any access to the Mediterranean for the Russian Black Sea fleet that might challenge Britain's naval supremacy. Thus, for their own reasons, both France and Britain supported the Turks against the Russians, moving their fleets into the Black Sea to protect Ottoman shipping after the Russian's destroyed the Turkish fleet at the Battle of Sinope in November 1853. Shortly thereafter, both France and Britain declared war on Russia. Lacking a common border between belligerents, fighting would eventually erupt on the Crimean peninsula when British and French Troops landed troops there in 1854.

It is in the position of Piedmont-Sardinia and Austria that the Crimean war began to affect the future nation-state of Italy. Austria had traditionally seen herself as the master of Central and Eastern Europe. The confusing diplomacy that resulted in the Crimean War, however, saw two potentialities—both abhorrent to Austria. One was a Russian domination of the Balkans by way of the Danubian principalities to the exclusion of Austria. The other potential outcome was that the United Kingdom and France dictated the outcome according to their interests. Austria, therefore pursued the only course open to it—neutrality. That is, until the Russians evacuated the Danubian principalities, which the Austrians were more than willing to occupy. However, this opportunistic neutrality earned Austria only a limited say in the peace settlement that would follow the war.

Such was not the case for the forward-thinking Cavour. He understood that if Piedmont-Sardinia was to draw other Italian states into a larger union he would need to have the backing of at least some of the major powers. Italian unification, however, was not on the agenda of any of the Great Powers in 1854. Cavour calculated that participation in the Congress that would attend the conclusion of the war was a forum from which he could pitch the case for unification, or at least the right to some moderate spoils for Piedmont's sacrifice. He was wrong. The Piedmont-Sardinian army saw only limited action against the Russians and Cavour saw only limited action at the ensuing Congress of Paris. The thought that Piedmont-Sardinia would be compensated for such a small contribution with territory was wishful thinking. Cavour also hoped that the powers would censure Austria's occupation of Italian lands. It was, however, France, that came to occupy the Papal States. The United Kingdom was in no way interested in becoming embroiled in a dispute in an area that was of little strategic importance. Whether the Italian Peninsula was occupied by a large but weak Austria or a small but weak Piedmont-Sardinia mattered not to the British government.

Military expenditures of the Great Powers in the Crimean War calculated in millions of British pounds (£)					
	1852	**1853**	**1854**	**1855**	**1856**
Russia	15.6	19.9	31.3	39.8	37.9
France	17.2	17.5	30.3	43.8	36.3
United Kingdom	10.1	9.1	76.3	36.5	32.3
Turkey	2.8	?	?	3.0	?
Sardinia	1.4	1.4	1.4	2.2	2.5

Source: Kennedy, P. 1989. *The Rise and Fall of the Great Powers*. London, UK. Fontana. p. 227.

Nevertheless, the Crimean war drastically weakened Austria's position in Europe. It had allowed foreign powers to decide issues on Austria's borders, and shown it to be militarily too weak to intervene against Russia. This situation was salvaged somewhat by the fact that Russia was itself militarily too weak to hold the Danubian principalities. Piedmont-Sardinia had grown in stature and ambition from its small contribution. Although he did not achieve any of his aims at the Congress of Paris, Cavour had been at the table and his modernized army had now been battle tested. Both Cavour and Napoleon III saw an opportunity in this new situation.

The War of 1859

Cavour, ever the pragmatist, understood that if the northern Italian states of Lombardy and Venetia were to be added to a greater Piedmont, it would require the active, support of at least one Great Power. Although the UK seemed willing to offer moral support, France was the best bet for actual military support. Napoleon III wanted to show himself the arbiter of Europe and pushed for a modern Europe against the old conservative version established at Vienna and now defended by the waning powers of Russia and Austria. The nation-building ambitions of Cavour seemed an ideal opportunity. There was also the small matter of Cavour's anti-clerical campaign in Piedmont, for Napoleon also saw himself as the protector of the Papacy, and his troops in the Papal States made this a reality. Again the pragmatic Cavour weighed the anti-clerical sentiments in Piedmont, which he shared with the more radical nationalists, against the necessity of French aid and came to the conclusion that an alliance with Napoleon to oust the Austrians from Northern Italy was more of a priority. At a secret conference at **Plombières** in July 1858 Cavour and Napoleon concluded an alliance as well as a plan for the ensuing war with Austria. The plan was to provoke a war, jointly defeat Austria in battle and construct a federal Italian nation-state. Napoleon would attempt to isolate Austria diplomatically and Cavour would provoke Austria into war. For her efforts, France would receive Savoy and Nice and a marriage of Napoleon's cousin Jerome into the royal House of Savoy. By any account this is a conservative turn for Cavour, but one he was willing to take in the interest of the beginning of a unified Italy. Consequently, Cavour had to distance himself from the more radical republican nationalists in Piedmont, including Mazzini. To this end, press censorship was tightened and the most dangerous of the radicals deported to mollify Napoleon's anxiety over any sort of popular revolution like 1848, which had ironically brought him to power.

> **Plombières** A spa town in eastern France at which Cavour and Napoleon III negotiated the secret Treaty of Plombières by which France and Piedmont-Sardinia would co-operate in a war against Austria.

While Napoleon was successful in getting a vague promise of neutrality from Russia, the British were deeply opposed to the war, which they thought could quite easily escalate into a general European conflict. Nevertheless, short of actually intervening militarily, which they were not willing to do, the British could only offer diplomatic disapproval. Prussia likewise took issue with the war against Austria, but stopped short of pledging military support. As preparation for war became more overt, Russia began to worry lest a general European war erupt, obliging them to get involved, and suggested a European congress to negotiate a settlement without resort to arms. For Austria, this only made it more likely that further concessions would be demanded. If they could come to the congress table in a position of strength, hard earned on the battlefield, it would be harder to wring such concessions from the Hapsburgs. As tension ratcheted up in the spring of 1859, Cavour **mobilized** Piedmont-Sardinia's army in March, which forced Austria to do likewise. In an attempt to make Piedmont look the provocateur, Austria demanded that they demobilize. Just when it appeared that Napoleon was bending to diplomacy—to the British government, and to the menace of Prussia—the Austrians decided to force the situation and crossed the frontier into Piedmont when Cavour refused to demobilize. Napoleon then played the protector and entered the war as per his promise at Plombières.

> **Mobilization** is the immediate military preparation for war. It can include the calling up of reserves, movement of troops to the frontier, requisitioning and transport of supplies, and the stock-piling of ammunition.

The sluggish movement of Austria's 90,000 soldiers was matched by the apathetic mobilization of Piedmont's army, which, though relatively modern, fell far short of the size that Cavour and Victor Emanuel had envisioned. The Austrian delay allowed the French force of 200,000 to reach the front by rail. The Austrians evacuated Lombardy after French victories at Magenta and Solférino in June. The plan seemed to be progressing as Cavour and Napoleon had intended.

Napoleon, however, had other concerns. The Congress of Vienna had given the Rhineland to Prussia and so it remained in 1859. This put Prussian forces essentially on the French border, a fact that made Napoleon anxious. He was specifically concerned that if he and Cavour inflicted a humiliating defeat on the Austrians, Prince William, the Prussian Prince Regent, would have to bow to nationalist pressure and come to the aid of its fellow German state. Napoleon was also becoming apprehensive at the prospect of a stronger Piedmont on his south-eastern frontier. With these concerns in mind, Napoleon III concluded a separate peace with the Austrians at Villafranca on 11 July 1859 and later formalized at Zürich in November. The terms were by no means injurious to Piedmont-Sardinia, but it fell far short of what Cavour had hoped for. Lombardy would be ceded to Piedmont. Venetia would remain in Austrian hands. The Central Duchies of Tuscany, Modena, and Parma would also remain under their traditional leaders—the Hapsburgs. Savoy and Nice would remain with Piedmont. Despite gaining Lombardy, Cavour was forced to resign.

The Central Duchies

Just when it seemed that Italian nation-building had stalled, it was revived, not in Piedmont, but rather in the Central Duchies. When the war of 1859 broke out, the rulers of the duchies fled to Austria and were replaced by nationalist governments. When news that their former rulers were to return and the status quo be reinstated reached the Duchies, they looked to Piedmont for aid. Napoleon had already precluded direct Austrian intervention in the duchies by the agreement signed at Zürich. This also meant that Piedmont could not intervene militarily. Instead, French troops occupied the Duchies to supervise popular **plebiscites** on the issue of annexation to Piedmont. For his trouble, Napoleon received the previously promised Savoy and Nice. After the results of the plebiscites were tallied in March 1860 it surprised no one that the duchies with the added Papal territory of Bologna had voted overwhelmingly to join Piedmont-Sardinia. All of this was stage-managed by Cavour who had returned to power in January 1860. This first phase of Italian unification was a major success for Cavour and his diplomacy. He had only been denied Venetia, but had also unexpectedly won the Central Duchies and a portion of the Papal States. The fact that it did not go according to plan, highlights Cavour's essentially pragmatic and opportunistic approach to foreign affairs. The period from 1858–60 also illustrated the extent to which the nation-building projects of the mid-19th century were just as much European concerns as they were either domestic Italian or German concerns. As such, war remained and would continue to remain a vital tool in the construction of modern Italy and Germany.

Activity:

A separate peace

Write a letter from Cavour to Napoleon III on the occasion of Napoleon's separate peace with Austria explaining the Sardinian position and asking him to reconsider the Peace of Villafranca. Share this letter with a partner. Have your partner reply to the letter as Napoleon.

Plebiscite This is a direct vote by all eligible voters on a question or issue.

Activity:

Preventing war

Since 1815 the Congress System was used to try to maintain the peace of Europe. Could a Congress have stopped the Italian War of 1859?

Form into six groups. Each group will become the diplomatic team representing one of the following countries meeting at a congress to prevent the outbreak of the Italian War of 1859.

- United Kingdom
- Piedmont-Sardinia
- France
- Austria
- Prussia
- Russia

Each group will research and present the position of their country, in reference to their own national situation in 1859, its aims at the congress, and how it plans to achieve them.

After each country has made a presentation, discuss and debate the issues and how a war might be avoided. When the discussion has wound down, write down any consensus that has been reached.

Debrief by discussing the following questions:

1   What positions were irreconcilable? Why?
2   Which countries had the most to gain and lose at the congress?
3   Which countries were in a position to stop the war?
4   To what extent was the war inevitable?

Naples, Southern Italy and the Papal States

After 1860 Cavour's eyes were firmly set on Venetia, but he understood that it would require another war to deliver it. For this he had to remain on good terms with the French. Events, however, overtook him. The island of Sicily rose up once again in rebellion against its Bourbon rulers in April 1860. The revolt was led by radical republicans, hardly the moderate nationalist enterprise favoured by Cavour and certainly not one that Napoleon III looked upon with any kind of sympathy. The issues at play in Sicily were not so much about nationalism as about local class-based concerns. Wary of the radicals taking matters into their own hands in Sicily, Cavour kept his distance. Garibaldi, on the other hand, seeing in these same radicals kindred spirits, raised 1,000 volunteers from the north to join in the insurrection and liberate the island from its Neapolitan overlords.

In many ways this forced Cavour's hand. If he were to keep a hand on the tiller of the unification project, he could not grant Garibaldi a free hand in the south. It might provoke a French or Austrian response that would jeopardize his designs on Venetia. Ever the politician, Cavour also realized that supporting Garibaldi's Sicilian adventure might relieve some domestic pressure that he was feeling in the aftermath of the 1859 war and subsequent plebiscites. Taking a middle course, Cavour did not actively support, nor did he interfere when Garibaldi first captured Palermo and then crossed to the mainland, conquering all of the Kingdom of Naples by September 1860. All that remained was the Papal States with her small army and Rome itself protected by French troops. Cavour was now faced with the very real possibility that it would be Garibaldi who completed the unification or, even worse, drag the as yet unformed nation-state into a disastrous war against France or Austria or both. In a bold move to regain the initiative, Cavour invaded the Papal States of Umbria and the Marches, explaining to Napoleon that it was the only way to restore stability to the situation and to curtail a dangerously out of control Garibaldi. In short order Cavour's army reached the northern border of Naples and prepared to confront Garibaldi's popular army. As he faced the Piedmontese army Garibaldi also faced the ugly prospect of civil war. To avoid such a breech in Italian national unity, Garibaldi turned Naples and the Island of Sicily over to Victor Emanuel the annexation of which was soon confirmed by plebiscite. The modern Kingdom of Italy had been created. There was, however, the vital question of those territories not included in the new Kingdom, *Italia Irredenta* (Unredeemed Italy), most importantly Rome and Venetia.

Activity:

Garibaldi and Cavour

This cartoon from 1862 in the British magazine *Punch* from 1862 depicts Cavour handing out weapons to Garibaldi's Red Shirts.

PUNCH, OR THE LONDON CHARIVARI.—August 24, 1861.

THE REAL ITALIAN BRIGAND CHIEF.

Questions

1 What is the cartoonist saying about Cavour's role in Garibaldi's expedition?

2 Do some research on Garibaldi's expedition to Sicily. What evidence is there to support this contention?

Problems after unification

Before the more dramatic questions could be addressed, the new Kingdom of Italy, proclaimed in March 1861, had to face the more mundane problems associated with administering a new state amid rival visions, factions and significant difficulties. The most pressing difficulty came with the unexpected death of Cavour in 1861. There were no other statesmen of his ability waiting in the wings and the new nation-state experienced a series of administrations over the course of the next five years.

The economies of the individual Italian states had not been strong prior to unification and the stresses of two years of instability and war only worsened the situation. The strongest of the economies, Piedmont, had paid for Cavour's ambitious policies with deficit financing and these loans and bonds needed to be serviced. The debts of the duchies of Lombardy, Naples and Sicily did not evaporate with unification and these too had to be serviced. If Rome and Venice were to be redeemed, the military would have to be strengthened and this too would cost money. Three years of instability had sapped productive capacity and the revenues that came with it. Agriculture, especially in the south, was inefficient and heavily indebted. By 1861 expenses outstripped revenues significantly. If the new state were to modernize the infrastructure across Italy to the extent that Piedmont was modernized, it would take huge infusions of cash. In order to keep the kingdom's finances afloat, the government secured ever more foreign loans, devalued the currency and confiscated Church land. Taxes skyrocketed.

Before he died Cavour had decided on the form that the new state was to take. He believed in the modernizing influence of Piedmont and the fact that the wars and policies that he had pursued over the past decade had been to unify Italy and thus it must be administered as a unified whole, not a collection of semi-independent states—not a federation. In the months before his death he came to see a federal model as a stepping-stone to division and even **secession** with an attendant civil war. Just such a disaster was playing itself out at that very time in the United States.

After Cavour's death Italy adopted a centralized system in which the country was divided into administrative units controlled by prefects reporting to the central government. This imposition ignored the deeply localized nature of Italian society in the 19th century. Language, currency, weights and measures, legal codes, tax and tariff structures all varied from one end of the country to the other. A centralized government would have to harmonize all of these if it were to realize a unified state. Nowhere was this challenge more evident than in the south. The revolutionaries who flocked to Garibaldi's banner fought for some form of autonomy and were now under the impression that they had simply traded Austrian domination for that of the Piedmontese. The aristocracy quickly grew dissatisfied with northern, middle-class rule. New taxes and regulations bore heavily on the peasants of Sicily and Naples. The sorry result was a series of small civil wars fought within Sicily and Naples that sapped Italy's economy and her sense of national-unity.

Italia irredenta could not be solved with parliamentary motions or unilateral Italian military action. With Napoleon's garrison protecting Rome and the Austrian possession of Venetia, redemption of these territories needed to involve one or more of Europe's major powers. An opportunity for just such an involvement presented itself as Prussia and Austria drifted towards war in the period between 1864 and 1866. Where Cavour had turned to France for military help against Austria in 1859, Prime Minister Alfonso Ferrero La Marmora turned, in 1866, to Prussia. Otto von Bismarck, the Minister President, hoped that an alliance with Italy would divert some Austrian troops to the south at the most and at the least it would prevent Italy from siding with Austria—an unlikely eventuality in any case. In exchange for Italy's military support, Prussia would diplomatically support Italy's claim to Venetia, which it was assumed Italian forces would have by then redeemed from the Austrians. The war went poorly for the Italians, suffering defeat on both land and sea. Nevertheless, the Prussian victory over the Austrians was so complete that Venetia was ceded to Italy.

Similarly, the addition of Rome to the Kingdom of Italy was precipitated by an impressive Prussian military victory. When Napoleon's forces were defeated by the Prussians at Sedan in

Secession This is the process by which territories leave a political union.

Discussion point:

What methods can modern states use to ensure that regional interests are respected, while at the same time keeping the state a centralized whole?

September of 1870, the French garrison protecting the Pope was recalled to France. With the agreement of the major Catholic powers of Europe, the Italian army occupied Rome that same month. But physically occupying the territory was only part of the problem. The new kingdom had now to come to an agreement with the Pope. While nominally a secular state, in practice Italy was overwhelmingly Catholic. For the sake of domestic peace the Italian government could not afford to appear vindictive or even overbearing in its relations with the Vatican. The Catholic Church was also the largest international organization of its time and as such commanded respect and influence throughout Europe. Italy as a nascent European power, and a small one at that, could not risk the wrath of Catholic powers such as France and Austria. The Vatican would have to be handled with care.

Pius IX turned against reform in the 22 years since he had become Pope. Successive revolutions and the rise and fall of the radical revolutionaries, the growing tide of secularism in European society, and the dissolution of his temporal lands had turned the once reforming Pope into a stubborn conservative. It would not be until 1929 that the Vatican would recognize the legitimacy of the Italian state. For its part, the Italian government gave the Pope sovereignty over Vatican City and paid him a yearly allowance. The Vatican also maintained its control of education in Italy.

Yet a number of problems persisted in the new Italy. North and south remained divided, politically, socially and economically. The perception in the south that they were second-class residents in an Italy dominated by the north created a great deal of resentment. In the north, where many of the politicians and most of the civil administrators came from, there was a persistent feeling that they had done all of the hard work in the creation of Italy and continued to drive the economy, supporting the inefficient and backward southern provinces. As with all such complaints there was a measure of truth in each of these perceptions. Industry was centred in the north and the south remained reluctant to reform land ownership and agriculture. The north did dominate the political culture of the state to the resentment of southerners. Victor Emanuel II, of the northern House of Savoy, had moved seamlessly to the throne of a united Italy, creating some resentment in other parts of the peninsula.

This lack of a national unity went deeper than north–south resentment. Deeply entrenched localism and regionalism meant that loyalties to this new creation called Italy often ran a distant third or fourth in the case of devout Catholics. Inadequate communication and transportation further exacerbated these divisions. Stress on the state, such as war or economic depression, would only serve to deepen these fractures. Nationalism in Italy had been far more of an idea, mostly of middle-class intellectuals, than it had ever been a feeling deeply held by the majority of the peninsula's population. There still existed important Italian-speaking territories outside the Italian state. Italians made up the majority of the population in the Austrian controlled Trentino and along the Adriatic coast centred in

Garibaldi and Pius IX, from a caricature published in the London-based magazine, *Punch*, in 1860.

Although Garibaldi was a republican and favoured a secular state, he understood the importance of the Pope and King Victor Emanuel to Italian unification.

 Why was Victor Emanuel vital to Italian Unification? What role did Pope Pius IX play in the unification project?

Activity:

The Vatican

The Vatican continues to occupy an interesting international position. Research the Vatican's position in the world today. Use the following topics to guide you your research.

● Territory

● Income

● Wealth

● Diplomacy

● Policing

● Relationship with the Italian state

the cities of Fiume and Trieste. More radical views of *Italia irredenta* also claimed a number of islands in the Adriatic and Mediterranean. In the years following unification, irredentism became an important plank in the platform of Italian nationalist parties.

The ongoing dispute with the Vatican created a further rift in Italian society. It presented an acute dilemma for devout Catholics as citizens of a state, the legitimacy of which their spiritual leader denied. The strained relations between the Italian state and the Vatican would last until 1929.

Economically, Italy lagged far behind the industrial powers of Western Europe whose company it wished to join. Agriculture in the Italian south was stagnant and largely peasant-based. The north, though beginning to industrialize, relied on imported coal and iron, the two great military and industrial ingredients. While this situation had begun change by the turn of the 20th century, Italy remained far behind the other European Powers in terms of industrial output.

Activity:

Italian unification: An assessment

Below are four possible explanations for the course of Italian Unification. After doing some research write an assessment as to the extent which you believe these explanations capture the causes and course of Italian unification. Use specific evidence to support your views.

Explanation 1

Italian Unification was an expression of nationalism that was growing across Europe in the mid 19th century. Unification was the culmination of this growing nationalism.

Explanation 2

Italy was ultimately accomplished as a result of the political machinations of men like Cavour, Victor Emmanuel and Garibaldi. Italian unification was a product of political agendas and rivalries.

Explanation 3

Italian Unification was primarily the result of long-term economic and social factors including growing industrialism and trade. Middle-class elites guided unification to entrench their political and economic position.

Explanation 4

Unification was a result of growing liberalism that had been developing it in the various territories of the Italian peninsula since the early 19th century. A united Italy was one of a number of possible outcomes of this development.

The unification of Germany

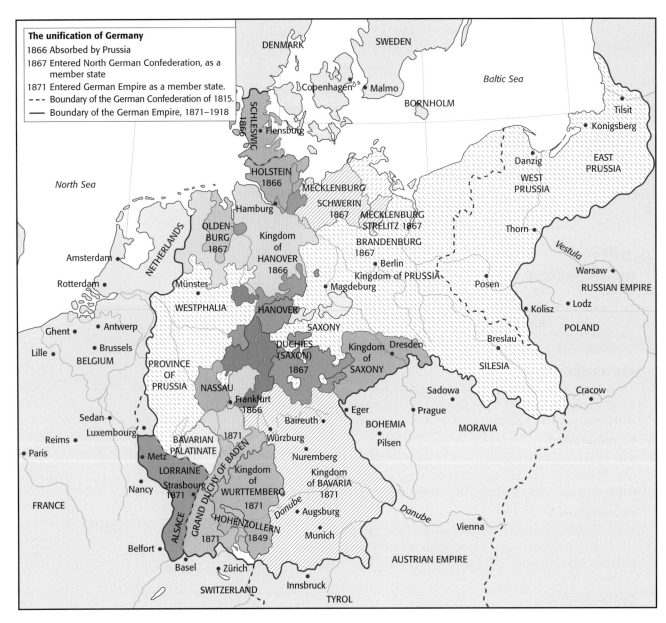

The unification of Germany
1866 Absorbed by Prussia
1867 Entered North German Confederation, as a member state
1871 Entered German Empire as a member state.
--- Boundary of the German Confederation of 1815.
— Boundary of the German Empire, 1871–1918

The German states before unification

The states that made up the German Confederation created in 1815 varied in size, government, economy, religion, influence and even dialect. On the one end of the scale were the two rival powers in the Confederation, Prussia and Austria—both large powerful monarchies with modern militaries—one Protestant, one Catholic. At the other end of the scale were the free cities such as Frankfurt. In between these two ends of the spectrum were all manner of states generally ruled by some form of princely monarchy. The German states were divided by religion, Catholicism predominating in the south and Protestantism in the north. Dynastic rivalries were also woven through

 The early stages of German Unification were dominated by a struggle between Austria and Prussia for leadership of any future unified German state. In terms of geography, which state had an advantage in this struggle? Why?

the fabric of the German Confederation. The aborted reforms of 1848 had left a legacy of weak parliamentary government throughout the German states, perhaps stronger in the south, still manned mostly by the growing middle-class and intelligentsia.

Although the industrialization of the German states had begun earlier, it accelerated rapidly after 1850. As in other industrializing states, the process was driven by an expansion of railways throughout the region. Railways made raw materials such as coal and iron available to industries far from their sources. Products that had once enjoyed limited local markets now found consumers throughout Germany. Between 1850 and 1870 the length of rail in Germany more than tripled. Although the percentage increase was far greater in Austria, the absolute length of track in Germany was also three times what it was in Austria. After 1850, Prussia's coal and iron industry began to expand rapidly.

Economic comparison between Austria and the German Reich of 1871			
		Austria	Germany
Pig-iron production (per 1000 tonnes)	1850	155	210
	1870	279	1,261
Hard coal production (per 1000 tonnes)	1850	665	5,500
	1870	3,759	26,398
Steam engine capacity (per 1000 horse-power)	1850	100	260
	1870	800	2,480
Railways (kilometres)	1850	1,357	5,856
	1870	6,112	18,876
Cotton spindles (per 1000)	1850	1,346	940
	1870	1,500	2,600

Source: Nipperdey, T. (trans. Nolan, D.). 1983. *Germany from Napoleon to Bismarck, 1800–1866*. Princeton, USA. Princeton University Press.

A burgeoning middle class led, and in turn was partially created by, much of this industrialization, especially in the west. Many of the new capitalists came from families that had established themselves in the expansion of trade that had occurred between 1800 and 1850 and these families were looking for new outlets for their trading profits. Depending on local conditions, the landed aristocracy also saw in the new industries opportunities for profit. This was especially true for those who had raw materials on their lands. An exploding population worked in these new factories. The states of the German Confederation experienced a 60 per cent increase in population between 1816 and 1865. In Prussia this increase was over 80 per cent and in Austria close to 50 per cent. Although much of this growth was centred in rural areas, as industrialization gathered speed it began to migrate to the cities. In 1800 there were three German cities with a population over 100,000; by 1870 there were 11. If we define a nation as primarily a group of people, it is clear that the German nation was undergoing significant structural changes in the period preceding the nation-building process of 1854–71.

Politically, Germany consisted of 39 nominally sovereign states. Each of these states was controlled by some form of monarchy. Some of these monarchs were constrained by constitutions, usually weak, while others operated more or less unfettered. Nevertheless, this was not the absolutism of the previous century. The rulers performed important functions of state from foreign policy, to administration of the budget and the military. They complemented the bureaucratization of government that had been increasing throughout Europe since the previous century. These German Princes were part of the state far more than they were the state.

The Congress of Vienna had cobbled these 39 states together into a loose confederation. The sovereignty of the individual states was closely guarded and as such the Confederation accomplished very little in its early years. Sovereignty began to be subordinated to anti-liberal reaction as the central Diet took more of a direct role in maintaining the status quo in the years after 1820. Austria and Prussia formed the dominant centre of the Confederation, though neither had much inclination to see the position of the Confederation strengthened. Austria, in the person of Metternich, saw it as a tool of reaction. Prussia saw it as a tool to restrict the possibility of an over-ambitious Austria. This dualism created a balance in the Confederation that allowed it to avoid either outright Prussian or Austrian domination and allow at least a modicum of sovereignty for the smaller states. When the smaller German states within the Confederation banded together, they could, on occasion, offer a counterbalance to the hegemony of the two powers, though this was infrequent.

The practical merits of unity first emerged less as a result of liberal nationalist sentiment and instead out of the power of free trade. From the early 1820s there had been efforts to tear down the myriad customs and tax regulations that restricted trade across Central Europe. The result had been a number of smaller customs unions, one centered on Prussia, another on the southern states and a third on the central German states among others. From there it seemed a logical step, championed by economists such as Friedrich List, to bring these customs unions together. It was not, however logical to all. Free trade arguments encountered strong opposition, as they always do, from protectionist sentiments, especially from within the Austrian Empire. The end result of this argument was the creation in 1834 of a German customs union called the **Zollverein** that encompassed 28 of the 39 states in the German Confederation by 1842. Austria remained outside the Zollverein while Prussia emerged as the acknowledged leader of the customs union. While the success of the Zollverein upset the hegemonic balance between Prussia and Austria in Prussia's favour, economic union is not synonymous with political union. Indeed there was developing an argument that the Zollverein was delivering the economic benefits of unity while preserving state sovereignty—in the form of state vetoes within the union. Nevertheless, the creation of the Zollverein was an important step toward a united Germany.

The emergence of Prussia: Otto von Bismarck

When Friedrich Wilhelm I came to the Prussian throne in 1860 there were a number of powerful forces on the move in both Germany and Prussia. Demographic and economic changes have been noted. Ideologically there was a resurgence in liberalism during this period. The new industrialists, especially in the west, embraced a liberalism that looked to more of a constitutional basis for Prussian society and a more limited role of for government. This liberalism was being wedded to a renewed German nationalism that had been dormant in the aftermath of 1848. The power balance between Prussia and

Discussion point:

What are the benefits of free trade?

Which social and economic classes would benefit from free trade in Europe in the mid-19th century? Which classes would it harm? How can these developments affect nationalism?

Zollverein The Zollverein was a customs union in Central Germany, in which internal tariffs were abolished and a common trade policy with outside states was developed.

Discussion point:

Other than economic advantages, how might a unified Germany benefit the individual states?

Austria also became strained in the years leading up to the accession of King Wilhelm I. Both Austria and Prussia attempted to reconfigure the German Confederation to their respective advantages in the 1850s. Both plans were wrecked because of the jealously held sovereignty of the German princes. The Zollverein was tipping economic advantage towards Prussia. In response, Austria proposed a broader customs union that included Austria and its non-German lands. This idea too came to nothing. It appeared that neither Prussia nor Austria were strong enough to dominate Germany on their own. For Prussia, this would have meant forcing Austria out of German affairs. For Austria to prevail, she would have to counter Prussia's growing economic power and alleviate the fears of the German princes. While the status quo seemed to have reasserted itself by the end of the 1850s, it would not survive the following decade and the promotion of Otto von Bismarck to the position of Prussian minister president.

> ### Otto von Bismarck (1815–1898)
>
>
>
> Born into a Junker family, he was educated in the law and drifted into political life as a member of the Federal Diet and later as ambassador to Russia and France. When he took the post of minister president in Prussia in 1862 he set about freeing the Prussian executive from the constraints of the assembly and the constitution. Throughout the process of German unification he showed himself to be a sharp political realist as well as a perceptive opportunist. He embarked on the unification of Germany as a means to the great power and glory of Prussia. He had a tumultuous relationship with King Wilhelm I of Prussia, and threatened to resign on numerous occasions. After the three wars of German unification, he sought to avoid a war that could tear apart the German Empire. To that end he designed and maintained a number of complex alliances with the powers of Europe. Within Germany he continually sought to co-opt, limit and repress elements such as the Catholic Church and the socialist movement that he believed to be a threat to the autonomy of the Crown and executive in the German Empire. He resigned after a clash with the young King Wilhelm II.

Bismarck came from East Prussia and was a member of its traditional landowning aristocracy—the **Junkers**. He was university-educated and had served as an elected member of Prussia's assembly as well as in administrative and ambassadorial positions. Bismarck would come to epitomize an approach to politics known as *Realpolitik*. Principles mattered less than outcomes. Ideology mattered less than the exercise of power. Alliances were tools of policy and once they had served their purpose could be abandoned. By inclination, Bismarck was a conservative, but he was no mere reactionary. Even his conservatism was a means to an end. He could play the role of the reforming parliamentarian or German nationalist if he needed to, though he was neither of these things. He had a developed sense of duty and that duty was to Prussia the state. He was clever and quick thinking, quickly grasping the potential in situations. He had no grand scheme for German unification, but rather responded to opportunities to strengthen Prussia. It was this Prussian focus that drew Bismarck to the conclusion that the future of Prussia depended on the exclusion of Austria from German affairs.

Bismarck saw in parliamentary democracy a tool to use or, depending on the situation, an obstacle to be overcome, but never an end in itself. Likewise, war was a tool to be used in the interests of broader goals. He found it an unpredictable and clumsy tool, but Bismarck was no warmonger. Nevertheless, the structure of the German Confederation was such that if Prussia were to dominate the German states at the expense of Austria, it would have to be through military power.

Junkers The Junkers were a class of aristocratic Prussian landowners centred in north-eastern Prussia. As a class, Junkers tended to be conservative and they made up the core of Prussia's military and administrative leadership.

"Anyone who has ever looked into the glazed eyes of a soldier dying on the battlefield will think hard before starting a war."

Otto von Bismarck

Bismarck was not alone in this estimation. The inability of Prussia to play significant role in the Crimean War had illuminated the fact that the once fierce Prussian army, had fallen into neglect. This was to be rectified with the appointment of Helmut von Moltke to the position of army chief of staff in 1857. Moltke instituted a series of military reforms in the early 1860s that were to transform the Prussian military into the model of a modern army.

As Paul Kennedy has pointed out, the Prussian army was far from perfect in practice. Doctrines were ignored and the rail system did not always operate with the efficiency of the war plans. Military advantage is seldom absolute, but rather relative to one's potential enemies. In this sense, the Prussian army reforms of the 1860s had created the pre-eminent military force of its day.

Prussian military reform
Terms of Service Males owed the state three years military service in the regular army, followed by four years of service in the reserve army after which they served in the militia (*Landwehr*)
Organization Moltke created a professional General Staff, which spent the time between conflicts studying strategy and planning situational operation plans.
Transportation The growing Prussian railway system was integrated directly into the operational plans and supervised by military officers. New rail lines were constructed to meet military as well as commercial needs.
Technology The professional officers of the General Staff continually looked for technological advantage and to remedy technological problems as they arose.

Military personnel of the Great Powers, 1816–80				
	1816	1830	1860	1880
United Kingdom	225,000	140,000	347,000	248,000
France	132,000	259,000	608,000	544,000
Russia	800,000	826,000	862,000	909 000
Prussia/Germany	130,000	130,000	201,000	430,000
Habsburg Empire	220,000	273,000	36,000	273,000
United States	16,000	11,000	26,000	36,000

Source: Kennedy, P. 1989. *The Rise and Fall of the Great Powers*. London, UK. Fontana Press. p. 197.

The need for such a military machine was far from obvious and ran into considerable opposition. The source of this opposition was the liberal core that had become an influential political force in the Prussian Assembly (*Landestag*). The crux of their complaint was twofold. First was the expense that would come with the expansion of the army. Taxation was anathema to classical liberal sentiments. Second, the new and powerful military machine that would grow out of the reforms was traditionally under the command of the king, not the assembly, and guided by the Junker class who provided much of the Prussian officer corps. This offended middle-class liberal loyalty to constitutionalism. When the Assembly would not grant the money required for the reforms, a parliamentary deadlock festered for two years. It was this deadlock that brought Otto von Bismarck to the position of minister president in 1862.

Bismarck's solution to the impasse was, on the surface, simple enough. He ignored both the assembly and the constitution. Under his guidance the government passed budgets, collected the taxes and spent the money, all without consulting the elected Assembly. Bismarck was betting that the majority of Prussians considered the Executive, in the form of the King and his appointed ministers, as a more legitimate source of authority than the assembly and its constitution and that when called to obey, they would. He was correct. The funds were raised and Prussia had her military reforms. Nevertheless, the next two years were spent in a running battle between Bismarck and the Assembly, a battle that was undermining Prussia's position within the German Confederation.

The Danish War

Germany was famously unified after a series of three wars. The first of these was the Danish War and it grew out of a complex dynastic crisis that arose when the King of Denmark died without a male heir in November 1863. The complexity revolved around two rival claimants to the throne and the status of the duchies of Schleswig-Holstein in the border lands. Traditionally, the duchies were overseen by the King of Denmark who in turn permitted the territories a good deal of autonomy, a status that had been confirmed by a series of treaties in the 1850s—the **London Protocols**. When the new king, Christian IX, came to the throne, he moved to absorb Schleswig into Denmark by way of a new Danish constitution. While this was met with great approval by Danish nationalists, German nationalists were outraged and the German Confederation voted for armed intervention. A small German force occupied Holstein. The Prussians and the Austrians presented a third position on the emerging crisis. While Bismarck cared little for nationalist sentiment, he could not sit back and watch the smaller states of the German Confederation take action on their own, as it undermined Prussian authority, nor could he allow Austria to assume a leadership role. Military intervention on the side of the Confederation, ignoring as it did the Treaties of 1850, might provoke a Russian or French response. For her part, Austria could not let Prussia act unilaterally and shared Bismarck's disdain for German nationalists. Prussia and Austria, therefore, jointly insisted that the treaties of the 1850s be upheld and the status quo enforced. When the Danes were not accommodating, a joint force of Austrians and Prussians moved into the duchies in early 1864, pre-empting any further military action on the part of the German Confederation.

London Protocols A set of agreements signed in 1852 that followed the First Schleswig War. The Protocols established the status of the Duchies of Schleswig-Holstein.

After eight months of fighting, the Danes capitulated. Christian IX had hoped that foreign intervention—British or French—would save his cause. No such aid was forthcoming. The fighting exposed weaknesses in the new Prussian military machine although, by the final engagements, the Prussians were beginning to reap the rewards of von Moltke's reforms. Militarily, the Austrians acquitted themselves quite well. The resultant treaty ceded the duchies to joint Prussian and Austrian control. The German Confederation, as had been Bismarck's goal, was excluded from the settlement. The administration of the territories was laid out in the **Convention of Gastein**, Schleswig falling under Prussian authority and Holstein under Austrian authority. By appearing to act in the interests of "Germany", Bismarck had begun to reform his image among German nationalists, a development that in turn began to fracture the liberal nationalist movement in Prussia. Many liberals still looked upon him as a dangerous conservative, while those who were primarily German nationalists saw in his assertive foreign policy the road to a more unified Germany. For Bismarck's part, the terms "nationalist" or "liberal" had little meaning, but he did understand that there would soon have to be a reckoning with her German rival—Austria.

Convention of Gastein This was an agreement between Austria and Prussia on the administration of Schleswig-Holstein on the conclusion of the Danish War.

The Austro-Prussian War

In terms of nationalist projects, Germany was unique. The nation as a group of people contained two major European Powers. Both Prussia and Austria were ambitious and jealously guarded their major power status. While this did not preclude co-operation in the settlement of the German Question, as in the Danish War and the Convention of Gastein, the rivalry ran deep. Austria had been fighting a rearguard action against growing nationalism within its borders since 1815. By the 1860s it had seen its European stature rocked first by the Crimean War and later by the chiseling away of some of its Italian holdings and influence. Prussia, on the other hand, had seen its fortunes, both within Germany and within Europe, rise in this period. Economically Prussia's mines and factories were consistently increasing production while the Zollverein increased trade revenues. After 1862 it had at its helm a statesman of ability and determination. Bismarck had as his goal the expansion of Prussian power and authority both within Germany and within Europe as a whole. By 1866, therefore, the German States had one major power in a slow decline and the other in ascendancy. While it was not necessarily inevitable that they would come to blows, the fact that the overall goals of the two powers were mutually exclusive made war likely.

Bismarck saw in the Convention of Gastein the potential to force the question. He had agreed to the Convention because it was on the one hand acceptable in the short term and allowed him time to consider and prepare his next move. While the Danish War did not threaten the European balance of power, and indeed on the surface was fought to preserve it, a war between Austria and Prussia had much broader implications. While Bismarck and von Moltke were confident that Prussia could prevail against Austria alone, the outcome should any other power join with Austria was far from certain. Bismarck therefore needed to make diplomatic preparations before the Prussian military could be unleashed. France posed the most serious threat. A divided Germany had long been a key component of French foreign policy and as such, Napoleon III had no particular objection to watching Prussia and Austria beat themselves bloody in a German war. If, however, the result was a more united Germany under the dominance of one of these powers, this presented a major concern for Napoleon. After a series of meetings with Napoleon in 1865, Bismarck came away convinced that the French would stay out of any future Austro-Prussian conflict, although the sources of that conviction is unclear. Napoleon, playing a complicated and dangerous diplomatic game, also came to an agreement with Austria by May 1866 whereby he would stay neutral in return for potential concessions on the Rhine. The result was that, regardless, France would stay out of the coming war. Seeking to secure his southern flank and divide Austrian forces, Bismarck next concluded a short-term military alliance with the new Kingdom of Italy in which they pledged to support each other in the case of war with Austria. Italy would be compensated with Venetia in the event of an Austrian defeat. As for Russia, her non-participation was secured by ongoing domestic concerns and her alienation from Austria that had developed since the Crimean War.

Discussion point:

How had France attempted in the past to keep Germany either dependent or fractured?

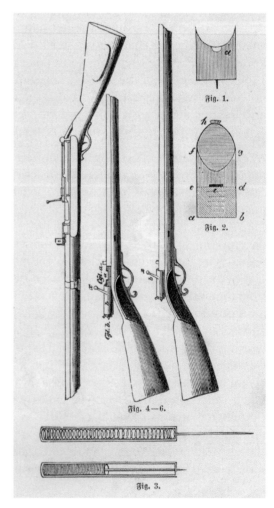

The Needle Gun invented by Nikolaus von Dreyse, and adopted by the Prussian army from 1858. This illustration was reproduced in the Leipzig-based *Illustrierte Zeitung* on 14 July 1866.

Tensions over the administration of Schleswig-Holstein grew through the first months of 1866, both Austria and Prussia accusing the other of violating the Convention of Gastein. In April, Italy began to mobilize its army, triggering a partial Austrian mobilization and a consequent Prussian mobilization. By June Bismarck decided to press the situation and ordered the Prussian army into Austrian-controlled Holstein, which the Austrians abandoned. Austria rallied the smaller German states of the Confederation to her side, frightened as they were of Prussian domination. With the Italian declaration of War on Austria in mid June the stage was set for war.

Most observers predicted a long war. Austria and Prussia were fairly evenly matched in manpower in the main theatre of war. The addition of the northern German states to the list of Prussia's enemies required her to deploy some of her forces in the West. The Italian offensive likewise required that Austria divide its forces. Austria was never able to make concerted use of her German allies, ensuring that the decisive engagements would be fought in Bohemia. The Prussians were able to quickly move smaller bodies of troops to the point of criticality and once there effectively bring them together into a large co-ordinated force. Although the Austrians had an advantage in artillery, the Prussians made wide use of the breech-loading rifle known as the "needle-gun". The Austrians responded by throwing massed troops at the enemy. The rapid fire of the needle-gun mowed down the charging Austrian masses. The combination of effective troop movement and tactical advantage helped the Prussians deliver a crushing defeat on the Austrians at Sadowa on 3 July 1866. Three short weeks later an armistice was concluded that ended the fighting before the other European powers could react.

The treaty that emerged in August 1866 cemented Prussia as the dominant German power and banished Austria from a meaningful role in German politics. By the Treaty of Prague Prussia annexed Hanover, Schleswig-Holstein, Hessen-Kassel, Nassau, and Frankfurt. The German Confederation was dissolved and replaced by a North German Confederation, which consisted of an expanded Prussia and 21 other northern German states. Austria, Bavaria, Baden, Württemburg, and Hesse-Darmstadt were untouched—though all but Austria concluded military alliances with Prussia—but were also excluded from this reorganization. Austria ceded Venetia to the Kingdom of Italy. Germany had in fact been divided into three pieces—a greatly enlarged Prussia, a slightly reduced Austria, and the southern states. In a matter of seven short weeks the balance of power that had stood since the Congress of Vienna had fallen.

Bismarck and the North German Confederation

Bismarck, once despised by liberals as a dictator, was now lauded as a national visionary, political genius, and diplomatic innovator. The Confederation went so far, at his behest to pass an act that pardoned him for his extra-constitutional actions in previous years. Bismarck's relationship with the liberals was complex—insofar as they were willing to support is measures, he would work with them, or in some case use them. Bismarck's relationship with German

Discussion point:

Bismarck was adamant about wanting no Austrian territory and shrank from continuing on to Vienna after the victory at Sadowa.

 Why did Bismarck move to end the war so quickly when the Prussian armies were dominating the Austrians?

The fast, breach-loading Dreyse Needle Gun transformed military tactics as it became more widely used in the Prussian army. This became evident in the Austro-Prussian War during which the Austrian forces were still using muzzle-loading weapons and the Prussians were using the Needle Gun.

 How does this demonstrate the relationship of military technology to tactics? At what other points in history has technological change radically altered accepted military tactics?

Activity:

The North German Confederation: Something for everyone

With the constitution of the North German Confederation Bismarck was able to paint himself as the democrat, appeal to a wide spectrum of political sensibilities and retain a great deal of power within the Federation. Analyse the form of the Confederation and explain why it appealed to each of the following groups:

● German Liberals

● German Conservatives

● German Nationalists

● German Industrialists.

conservatives was much the same. Regardless, Bismarck's power and influence was high with both conservatives and liberals in the wake of the victory over Austria.

It was at this point that Bismarck donned the robes of a constitutional democrat within his newly created North German Confederation. The constitution of this new confederation made it, on the surface, one of the most democratic states in Europe.

- It was bicameral.
- The upper house (*Bundesrat*) was based on representation by state.
- The lower house (*Reichstag*) was based on representation by population, elected by universal adult (25 years old) male suffrage.
- Four-year budgets had to be approved by the lower house.
- Freedom of speech was entrenched.

There were, however, important non-democratic features to this constitution:

- Bismarck as the Chancellor of the Federation and other ministers were responsible to the Crown, not the assembly.
- The government had access to revenue, mostly tariffs, over which the assembly had no control.
- Elected representatives could not introduce legislation.

Just as he sought to play rival powers off against each other in his foreign policy, Bismarck was adept at balancing the various forces within Germany. From 1866 Bismarck recognized another important element in this balance. In a broad sense it was "the German people" and Bismarck's populism can be seen as an attempt to harness its support against other interests within Germany. This attempt can be seen in the democratic components of the constitution. Bismarck also saw in the burgeoning socialist movement both a looming threat and a potential ally. The threat he would deal with later. In the meantime he used the franchise to draw German socialists into a populist "bloc" that could be used as a balance against either conservative landowners or liberal bourgeois interests.

The new German state: unfinished business

The Treaty of Prague left southern Germany in an unstable situation. The states were militarily allied to Prussia and economically part of the *Zollverein*, but politically independent. Public opinion in the southern states largely opposed any unification with the north. German nationalists, however, saw the exclusion of these states from the North German Confederation as an affront to national unity. Bismarck saw in them a potential ally for either France or Austria and as such a threat. On the broader European stage, the rapid and convincing defeat of Austria had robbed Napoleon III of any satisfaction he might have gained as a potential arbiter between the two German powers. He also received no compensation for his neutrality in the war. Now he faced a strong and more or less united Germany on his eastern frontier, something that French foreign policy had worked to avoid for two centuries. Napoleon faced further public criticism over his Mexican adventure and the rise of a new Italy on France's south-eastern frontier. France would have to oppose any further German unification.

TOK Link
Emotion

Nationalism is, in part, an emotional attachment to one's nation. Bismarck, Mazzini, Garibaldi and Cavour all understood and used this to their advantages. Bismarck played on nationalist emotion that was running high after the Austro-Prussian War to create the North German Confederation and get the Reichstag to absolve him of his previous unconstitutional acts. Garibaldi was a master at rallying followers to his cause.

 What are the strengths and weaknesses of emotion as a political tool? Find examples in the media of politicians using emotion to influence the public.

For each news item, identify the knowledge issues involved. Share these with the rest of the class.

Discussion point:

 How do historians gauge public opinion?

What documents can help a historian understand what the general public is thinking?

The first sign of tension came over the status of the Grand Duchy of Luxemburg. Napoleon III had indicated that it should be ceded to France in part for his neutrality in the Austro-Prussian War and even offered to purchase it from the King of the Netherlands in early 1867. The proposition outraged German nationalists, though Bismarck, whose role in the affair is debated, was far more ambivalent. Regardless of his role in shaping it, he felt he could not openly defy this nationalist sentiment. The international conference that decided the fate of Luxemburg as a neutral state advantaged neither Prussia nor France, while increasing the tension between them.

The spark for the war that would complete the German Empire came from an unlikely source—a succession crisis in Spain. After Queen Isabella was deposed by revolution in 1868, the Spanish parliament began to search for a suitable replacement. One such candidate was the Prussian king's cousin, Leopold of **Hohenzollern**. While King Wilhelm was initially opposed to his cousin's candidature, he was eventually persuaded by the persistent Spanish delegates and gave his permission in June 1870. Word of the agreement incited official alarm and public outrage in France. This would put Hohenzollerns on two of her borders. The French demanded that the candidature be renounced and King Wilhelm obliged. Not fully satisfied with this response, the French ambassador sought assurances that no Hohenzollern would ever take the Spanish throne, something to which Wilhelm was not so amenable. The King refused this request, informing Bismarck in a telegram sent from the resort of Bad Ems where he was vacationing.

Bismarck had favoured the candidacy for the same reasons that the French feared it and was disappointed when it was retracted. He saw, however, in the King's telegram, an opportunity to "wave a red rag in front of the Gallic bull". At his manipulative best, Bismarck cleverly edited the telegram to leave the simultaneous impression that German honour had been affronted and French proposals brusquely dismissed. When the "Ems Dispatch" was released to both the German and French press on 13 July 1870, calls for war resounded throughout both countries. By 19 July France had declared war on Prussia.

At the conclusion of the Austro-Prussian War, Bismarck had been content with the situation, looking more to consolidate his successes both within Germany and within Europe. Having largely accomplished this by 1870, he was ready to settle accounts with

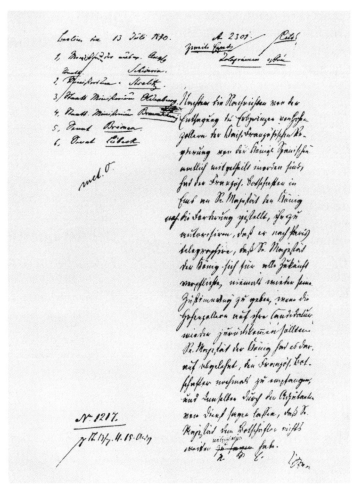

The Ems Dispatch. A telegram, dated 13 July 1870 about the meeting of King Wilhelm IV with the French ambassador, Bennedetti, showing Bismark's comments.

Hohenzollerns The royal family that formed the ruling house of Prussia in the 19th century.

 The Ems Dispatch is one of the classic examples of the doctrine of *Realpolitik*. What does the incident tell us about Bismarck's overall approach to the unification project?

Do you think Bismarck had a detailed plan for achieving unification, or was it more of a broad goal, with no clear idea of how he would bring it about? Justify your answer.

France and readjust the unstable situation of the south German states. He did not plan the Franco-Prussia war, and in fact saw war as a clumsy and unpredictable tool of diplomacy, but he knew his goals would likely require a war with France for the reasons set out above. If, however, such a war were to frighten the south German states into a union with the North, as Bismarck wanted, France would have to strike first. Bismarck was willing to wait for that to happen. The Hohenzollern candidacy and the Ems Dispatch gave him an opportunity to encourage the French to act. Had the French not mobilized, Prussia would probaby not have gone to war at that time.

Activity:
Franco-Prussian War Press Conference

Form into four groups:

● Bismarck and advisors

● Napoleon III and advisors

● The south German states

● The press

Have the first three groups research and present the case for war. The press is there to question and challenge them to justify their position.

Debrief questions

1 Who had more to gain from the Franco-Prussian War—Napoleon or Bismarck?

2 Who had the most to lose from the war?

3 What were the German war aims?

4 What were the French war aims?

5 Was the war necessary?

The Franco-Prussian War, 1870–1

On news of the French mobilization in July 1870, Moltke's military machine wound into action. The Prussian army was enthusiastically supported by troops from the south German states—more from nationalistic fervor than fear of French domination. France, on the other hand would fight alone. The British disapproved of both the French position on the candidacy and its Mexican escapades. Russia's Black Sea ambitions would benefit from a French defeat. Italy saw in the war an opportunity to remove French troops from Rome, and Austria was still smarting from the Austro-Prussian war and implementing a programme of domestic reform. The well-oiled and battle-tested Prussian military machine quickly mobilized over a million soldiers and transported over 400,000 to her western frontier. Mobilizing far more slowly, the French could bring only 250,000 troops to meet them.

Despite the Prussian advantage in numbers, the two sides were more closely matched in equipment. The French had introduced their own breech-loading rifle, which was a match for the "needle-gun". The French had sound artillery and the Prussians had remedied the deficiencies in their own artillery exposed in the Austro-Prussian War. As with most wars, both sides missed opportunities and committed blunders. Nevertheless, when sound Prussian planning and superiority in numbers was compared with the ineptitude of the French, the French were clearly at a disadvantage. Moltke outmanoeuvred one of the main French armies under the command of General McMahon and with Napoleon III in attendance encircled them near the Belgian border. The resultant Battle of Sedan on 1–2 September 1870 ended with

Discussion point:

Why would the French public demand war over such a seemingly trivial slight as presented in the Ems Dispatch? Why would Napoleon III bow to this pressure?

Although the Franco Prussian War would continue for some months after, it was the Battle of Sedan that in large part determined the outcome of the war. It was a massive military disaster for the French that would haunt the French Army until 1914, when they would have fresh military nightmares to haunt them.

 Why did the French lose at Sedan? What role did Napoleon III personally play in the defeat?

Activity:

The conduct of war

The following is an excerpt from a letter written in 1880 by the architect of the Prussian army, General Helmut von Moltke. It was written in response to a letter written by the Swiss international law expert, Johann Kaspar Bluntschli.

> *The greatest good deed in war is the speedy ending of the war, and every means to that end, so long as it is not reprehensible, must remain open. In no way can I declare myself in agreement with the Declaration of St. Petersburg that the sole justifiable measure in war is "the weakening of the enemy's military power." No, all the sources of support for the hostile government must be considered, its finances, railroads, foodstuffs, even its prestige.*

Source: Pross, Harry. ed. 1959. *Die Zerstörung der deutschen Politik: Dokumente 1871–1933*. Frankfurt, Germany. pp. 29–31. Translated by Richard S. Levy at http://hnet.org/~german/gtext/kaiserreich/moltke.html.http://hnet.org/~german/gtext/kaiserreich/moltke.html.

Questions

1 Based on the conduct of the Austro-Prussia War and the Franco-Prussian War, what do you think von Moltke would have believed to be "reprehensible"?.

2 What does von Moltke mean by "even its prestige"?

3 In what ways does this passage by von Moltke presage the concept of Total War?

4 How does von Moltke's notion of the appropriate conduct of war apply to the following wars?

● The Napoleonic Wars

● The First World War

● The Spanish Civil War

● The Korean War

● The Vietnam War

● The Iran Iraq War

the surrender of over 100,000 French soldiers and the Emperor Napoleon III himself. With the capture of the Emperor came the downfall of his government in Paris. A new national government desperately carried on the war for another five months. During that time Paris was besieged and eventually bombarded into surrender by the end of January 1871. Peace talks eventually led to the Treaty of Frankfurt in May.

The Treaty of Frankfurt had two notable clauses. The first was the requirement that France pay an enormous war indemnity of five billion gold francs to the victorious Germans. Units of the Prussian army would occupy France until this amount was paid. The other significant element of the Treaty of Frankfurt was the annexation of the French frontier territories of Alsace and Lorraine by the new German Empire. The German logic behind the annexations was mostly a matter of national security. The two territories would provide a

The Battle of Sedan, 1870.

buffer wherein the Germans could station troops to thwart any future French aggression. From the French point of view the annexation of the territories was a constant reminder of the humiliation of 1871, their reclamation a matter of national honour. It would remain so until 1914 when the outbreak of the First World War gave the French army the opportunity to reclaim this honour with disastrous results.

Activity:

Wars of unification

Complete the following chart.

War	Combatants	Significance
Crimean War, 1854–56	United Kingdom France Russia Ottoman Empire Piedmont-Sardinia	
War of 1859	Piedmont-Sardinia France Austria	
Conquest of Sicily and Naples	Garibaldi's Red Shirts Kingdom of Two Sicilies	
Danish War, 1863	Prussia Austria Denmark	
Austro-Prussian War, 1866	Austria Prussia Italy	
Franco-Prussian War, 1870–71	North German Confederation Prussia France	

Questions

1 Why did the revolution of 1848 have such a limited impact on the German states?

2 Assess the contribution of Cavour to the unification of Italy.

3 "Economic strength was the key factor in the rise of Prussia as a powerful state by 1862." Examine the validity of this statement.

4 Analyse the contribution made by nationalism to the decline of Austria by 1866.

5 Compare and contrast the means by which Italy and Germany were unified by 1870.

6 How successful were Bismarck's domestic policies 1870–90?

The German Empire

Even before Paris succumbed to the weight of German artillery, the German princes had gathered in the Hall of Mirrors at Versailles to proclaim the foundation of the German Empire. From the outbreak of the war, Bismarck had busied himself with the preparation for the absorption of the south German states into a wider German union. While the states enthusiastically honoured their military commitments to Prussia, some, specifically Bavaria and Württemburg, harboured ambitions of independence and these had to be overcome if Bismarck was to have his union. He also faced unlikely resistance to the scheme from his own monarch. Wilhelm I was deeply attached to his hereditary title of King of Prussia. Any new position as head of the German Empire would have to preserve this in some meaningful way without implying that the other states were simply being absorbed into a Greater Prussia. True to his belief in the principle of dynastic legitimacy, he would not accept the Crown if offered by the Reichstag, representing, as it did, the people. To Wilhelm, it was his birthright, not any kind of popular legitimacy. This is why it was important, at least to him, that the assembled princes at Versailles offer him the title of German Emperor.

The objections of Bavaria and Württemburg were overcome by a combination of money and realism. The two states would be no more meaningfully independent outside a strong Germany than they would be inside a strong Germany, perhaps even less so given the overwhelming economic, diplomatic and military power that the new Germany would possess. Popular opinion within both states favoured joining the German union. As further incentive, funds flowed from Prussia to Bavaria to help King Ludwig with financial difficulties. For his part Bismarck was willing to sweeten the pot even further. Both Bavaria and Württemburg were allowed to maintain their own armed forces within the new German Empire that would pass over to Imperial control only in time of war. Both crowns were also maintained within the Empire as was a symbolic independence in foreign affairs. A degree of financial autonomy was also permitted in the form of certain taxation rights.

The German Empire was basically an extension of the North German Confederation. Eighteen states, four kingdoms as well as the free cities of Hamburg, Bremen, and Lübeck were brought together in a federal structure. Alsace-Lorraine would be administered as a separate territory. The executive consisted of the Emperor, the Chancellor and the cabinet. The **Bundesrat** (upper house) was based on state representation, while the Reichstag (lower house) was based on representation by population selected by universal adult male suffrage. The *Reichstag* could debate policy and approve budgets, but would soon dilute this power by approving budgets for several years in advance. The *Bundesrat* could initiate and debate legislation. While on the surface there were a number of democratic features in this constitution, especially by 19th-century standards, the executive retained a great deal of power and was responsible to the Crown rather than to the assembly. Within the executive, the Crown possessed immense power, from commanding the military, to interpreting the constitution. The German Empire was in theory a constitutional monarchy, but that constitution vested the majority of power in the monarch. The federal division of powers gave individual states jurisdiction over many matters concerning the daily lives of their citizens. As we have mentioned, larger states such as Bavaria retained other powers denied to smaller states. Of course, Austria played no role in this structure. Central Europe now had two empires.

Discussion point:

Sovereignty, regardless of belief, principle, or desire, must be backed by practical support. Evaluate the following elements to the exercise of meaningful sovereignty.

● Military

● Currency

● Budget

● Foreign policy

● Trade

These are the two houses of the German parliament. The **Bundesrat** was the upper house where representation was based on geography while the lower house, the **Reichstag**, had representation based on population.

Discussion point:

What are the relative advantages of a unicameral (one house) and a bicameral (two house) parliamentary system?

Unification timeline

Year	Italian unification	German unification
1850	● Cavour becomes Prime Minister of Piedmont-Sardinia	
1854	● Crimean War: Piedmont- Sardinia joins allies against Russia	● Prussia remains out of Crimean War
1859	● Sardinia and France go to war against Austria ● Lombardy joins Piedmont Sardinia	
1860	● Central Duchies join new Kingdom of Italy ● Garibaldi attacks Kingdom of Two Sicilies ● Marche and Umbria vote to join Kingdom of Italy	
1861	● Kingdom of Two Sicilies join Kingdom of Italy ● Cavour dies	● Bismarck appointed minister president of Prussia
1863		● Danish War: Austria and Prussia gain Schleswig-Holstein
1866	● Italy concludes military alliance with Prussia ● Italy acquires Venetia	● Austro-Prussian War ● North German Confederation created
1870	● French troops evacuate Rome ● Rome claimed by Kingdom of Italy	● Franco-Prussian War begins ● French defeated at Sedan
1871	● Rome made capital of Kingdom of Italy	● France capitulates ● German Empire proclaimed

Activity:
Compare and contrast

Complete the following chart comparing and contrasting the unification of Italy and Germany.

Element	Italian unification	German unification
Aims		
Personalities		
Use of force		
Opposition		
Economy		
Foreign intervention		
Problems after unification		

Bismarck's Germany

Domestic policy

Much has been said about the economic powerhouse that Prussia had become from 1850. But rapid economic expansion is always accompanied by a number of potential hazards. To increased industrial production and railway construction was added ballooning economic optimism fuelled by victory in the Franco-Prussian War and the subsequent unification. Much of the five billion gold francs paid by France as a war indemnity found its way into infrastructure projects that further stimulated the economy. This economic and nationalistic enthusiasm loosened capital markets and credit flowed freely, funding a number of overambitious projects that, at least in hindsight, could not have been sustained. By 1873 investment scandals in the railway industry helped trigger a crisis in investor confidence that spread across the entire German economy.

Such were the internal factors that led to the economic depression of the 1870s in Germany. The world economy, however, was increasingly integrated by this time. Credit and goods flowed around the globe. This meant that economic problems could not long remain localized. Price changes in one region influenced prices around the world. Bank failures could have effects in far off countries. At about the same time that German investors were experiencing their crisis of confidence in 1873, a world depression set in that would shrink credit markets around the world for the better part of 20 years and this compounded Germany's economic woes. As often happens in times of economic crisis, political opinion began to polarize. The national consensus that had backed the unity project was now torn between those who continued to advocate the liberal trade policies of the 1860s and early 70s and those who saw in **protectionism** a cure for the depression that was taking hold in Germany. As we have seen, Bismarck was not one to gravitate to doctrine and this practicality continued through the early years of the Empire.

Bismarck did not drift into the conservative protectionist camp right away. In fact he relied on the support of the National Liberal Party until 1878. Throughout the 1870s the National Liberal party was the strongest party in the *Reichstag*. Despite the nationalistic language used in protectionist propaganda, Bismarck recognized this and saw that the future of the Empire rested on the twin strength of the army and capitalist enterprise and that this enterprise flourished most when relatively unimpeded by regulation. So arose a mutual reliance between Bismarck and the liberals during the early 1870s. While such co-operation may seem unlikely, Bismarck and the liberals shared a number of common means if not ends. Both Bismarck and the liberals wanted a more centralized and unified state. For Bismarck such control was an extension of the unity project. If a united Germany was a stronger Germany, as Bismarck believed, then the economic, legal, and political **particularism** that characterized the German Empire in 1871 had to be banished. For the liberals, such centralization and rationalization was the prerequisite for a modern industrial society. It was therefore quite easy for the German liberals and Bismarck to agree on measures such as the establishment of a

Protectionism These are policies that limit the access that foreign goods and services have to a country's domestic market . Protectionism is generally adopted to protect the development of a country's own industries.

Discussion point:

What are the benefits and drawbacks of the increasing globalization of capital markets?

Particularism An exclusive partisanship or attachment to one's own nation, political party, or other affiliated group.

national bank, the adoption of a single currency, and the rationalization of commercial and criminal law across the *Reich*. These were not concessions by either the chancellor or the liberals, but rather mutually beneficial policies that furthered both their agendas.

There was, of course, much upon which Bismarck and the liberals did not agree. Their visions diverged on the liberalization of the state. Bismarck firmly believed that authority in the state must remain with the Crown, the chancellor and the cabinet, a situation that he had enshrined in the constitution. Liberals, on the other hand, would have the *Reichstag* strengthened; something that Bismarck was unwilling to do. To that end liberal legislation was ignored or watered down. By 1878 Bismarck had turned against the parliamentary liberals who had to that point dominated the *Reichstag*. By the end of the 1870s, many of the policies that Bismarck and the liberals could or would agree on were reality, and Bismarck saw that the needs of the *Reich* might better be served by the policies advocated by the political right. Under the weight of the worldwide depression and a flood of American and British goods being dumped into German markets, protectionism had become popular with both Germany's major industrialists and increasingly among the Junker agricultural interests, and these interests formed the backbone of the Conservative and Imperial Party in the *Reichstag*. The Centre Party was also strongly protectionist. By advocating protectionism Bismarck could forge a parliamentary alliance with these parties and break the dominance of the National Liberals. Tariffs would also bring money into the Reich's coffers. The protectionist policies adopted by Russia and France and the increased competition from overseas seemed to demand a nationalist economic response that would theoretically make Germany more self-sufficient. By 1879 new tariffs were introduced and the government moved to create a state monopoly in tobacco production. Bismarck's break with the liberals was complete. Tariffs increased and the National Liberal Party faded from parliamentary dominance.

While certain measures of state centralization suited German liberal sensibilities, they certainly alienated other groups, namely the Catholic Church. The Empire that came together in the wake of the Franco-Prussian War contained a significant Catholic minority, especially in the southern states and this interest group formed the core of the Centre Party that took seats in the *Reichstag* from its inception. Such a political force within the Empire that was, in the opinion of many, especially German liberals, ultimately beholden to a foreign power, the papacy, seemed to fly in the face of the entire unification project, a belief that was strengthened by the generally anti-clerical position of liberals across Europe. Liberals and Churches, both Protestant and Catholic, had clashed on issues of social policy in the United Kingdom, France, and Italy. Any such rival

Bismarck and Pius IX, from a wood engraving by Wilhelm Scholz, published in the Berlin-based satirical journal *Kladderadatsch* in 1875.

authority within Germany was also anathema to Bismarck, another factor that encouraged his greater co-operation with the liberals in the early 1870s. Again we see that Bismarck and the liberals agreed more on means than ends. Liberals were ideologically opposed to any role for the Church, any Church, in affairs of state, infringing as they saw it on natural individual rights. For Bismarck it had nothing to do with individual rights. He believed Catholics within the Reich were Germans first and as such owed primary allegiance to the Crown, not to Rome. When, in 1870, Pope Pius IX introduced the doctrine of **Papal Infallibility**, he seemed to be demanding the opposite from German Catholics and as such posed a direct challenge to the authority of the German state. To meet this challenge, Bismarck declared a legislative war against the Catholic Church in Germany, what liberals called a *Kulturkampf*, a "cultural war" between the Church and the state.

> **Papal Infallibility** This is a doctrine of the Catholic faith formalized by Pope Pius IX in 1870. By this doctrine the Pope is without error when proclaiming official Catholic doctrines.

Discussion point:

Bismarck's *Kulturkampf* was an attempt to subordinate religion to the state through government legislation.

What other attempts have there been to regulate belief in European history? To what degree were these successful?

The *Kulturkampf* was a series of laws that restricted the ability of the Catholic Church to operate in Germany. Schools were brought solely under the authority of the state. The Jesuits as an order, always a target of suspicion, were essentially expelled from Germany. The government prescribed the education of clergy and in some cases could appoint Church officials. Civil marriage was encouraged. When the Vatican responded by forbidding Catholics from observing these laws on the threat of excommunication, the German government outlawed most monastic orders within the Reich, imprisoning and exiling those who chose the authority of Rome over the German state.

The legislation of belief is complicated and seldom successful. Despite the formidable repression exerted by the German government, the Centre Party actually increased its representation in the Reichstag throughout the *Kulturkampf*. The repression was endangering Germany's relations with Catholic foreign powers, notably Austria-Hungary. As Bismarck moved toward severing his ties with the German liberals, his anti-clerical stance was less necessary. As a means to a political end, Bismarck began to question the wisdom of *Kulturkampf*. Initiated as a means of strengthening centralization of authority, it had grown to destabilize the unity achieved in 1871. As this realization dawned on Bismarck in 1878, the *Kulturkampf* was called off. The end of this religious oppression must be understood within the context of Bismarck's broader social and economic realignment with the right.

Discussion point:

The control of education has always been an important instrument for controlling modern states.

Why is this?

What arguments can you think of for and against the idea of private schools?

The liberals were not the only ideological position to the left of Bismarck. The spectre of socialism had been rising across Europe for the better part of the century and Germany was no exception.

German socialism however was modest in its aims and organization. They had a relatively small presence in the Reichstag and support among some of the working class. Nevertheless, Bismarck saw in this socialist spectre a threat not only to Germany, but also the established European order. The Paris Commune raised alarm among many European governments. The republicanism of socialists was repugnant to the chancellor. He distrusted the internationalism of many socialists and feared it might spread more radical socialist thought within Germany. After 1878 the abrupt end to the *Kulturkampf* and subsequent peace with German Catholics allowed Bismarck to focus the repressive power of the state on Germany's socialists. Two failed attempts on the Kaiser Wilhelm's life gave Bismarck the *causa bellum* he needed. Socialist newspapers were banned and meetings outlawed. The anti-socialist laws were renewed regularly until 1890 by which time the growth of the German socialist movement had been well and truly stunted.

"Keeping it down": the socialist devil being pushed back into his box. A caricature referring to the Anti-Socialist Laws instituted in 1878 by Bismarck. This caricature was published in *Punch* magazine on 28 September 1878.

Bismarck did not rely on simple banning and censorship to eliminate socialism from German political and social life—the *Kulturkampf* had shown the folly of such a one-dimensional approach. He had a tool at hand in his war on socialism, however, that he did not have in the war on Catholicism. While he could not use the German state to replace the appeal of Catholicism, he could use it to blunt the appeal of the socialists. The result was a series of paternalistic laws designed to provide a bare social safety net for German workers. This net included a modest state pension plan, medical insurance and insurance against disability caused by industrial accidents. Nevertheless, the Social Democratic Party did not fade into obscurity and actually gained members and seats in the Reichstag by 1890.

Bismarck attacked the socialist directly, but also by co-opting a number of their ideas.

 What elements of Bismarck's domestic policy would be palatable to socialists?

Foreign policy

For Bismarck, the 1860s had been consumed by the disruption of European stability in the cause of a united Germany and strengthened Prussia. After 1871 his diplomacy shifted to focus on the maintenance of the new European order he had in large measure created. He wanted to preserve the German Empire and, to his mind, this meant a diplomacy that preserved a central role for Germany while avoiding conflicts that could drag his new state again to war, a war he believed could undo all the work of the 1860s.

The chancellor was always cognizant of the pervasive French desire to redeem both her reputation and the territories of Alsace and Lorraine after 1871. To discourage any rash action on the part of the French, Bismarck sought to diplomatically isolate them. Leaving France with no continental allies of note was a key motivation behind the Three Emperors League engineered by Bismarck in 1873. In the League, Tsar Alexander II, Emperor Franz Joseph I and Kaiser Wilhelm I came together in a vague agreement to co-operate in preserving the general European peace. The three emperors were also united in a generally conservative outlook. Bismarck further hoped that the agreement, vague though it was, would discourage a conflict between Austria-Hungary and Russia that could likewise draw Germany into a disastrous war. Bismarck liked the ambiguity in the treaty, preserving, he believed, his range of diplomatic manoeuvers.

Activity:

Cartoon analysis

From the graffiti on the walls of ancient Rome to modern daily newspapers, cartoons have long been vehicles for political discourse. When analysing a political cartoon as a historic source, answer the following questions:

- Who is being portrayed?
- What event(s) are being depicted?
- What symbolism is used?
- Who or what is being ridiculed?
- What is the cartoonist's relationship to the people and events? (i.e. Whose side of the war is the cartoonist on?)
- What can this cartoon tell a historian
- What are the limitations of the cartoon as a historical source?

Analyse the cartoons on this page in response to these general questions, and the more specific issues raised in the questions below.

The composer Richard Wagner as a Generalissimo: "One trusts his music will make the French scarper." (*Der Generalissimus der deutschen Armee. Man rechnet auf seine Musik, um die Franzosen in die Flucht zu schlagen*). A sketch by Jules Draner published in *L'Eclipse*, Paris, 1870.

Questions

1 Why does the artist portray Wagner in a military uniform?

2 What connection is there between the military and his music?

3 Why did Wagner's music prompt such strong nationalist feeling?

4 Bismarck believed that he could control the Three Emperors' League to achieve his foreign policy goals. Why was he unsuccessful in manipulating the League?

5 What lessons did Bismarck draw from this failure?

The three emperors, or, "the ventriloquist of Varzin". Caricature published in *Punch*, London, 20 September 1884.

But this ambiguity turned into a double-edged sword. By 1875 the French government was well on its way to putting its economic and military house in order after the humiliation of 1871. Moltke and the German General Staff looked on this with increasing alarm, largely unwarranted, and passed this alarm along to the chancellor. Despite his disdain for the notion of preventative war, once famously stating that it was like committing suicide for fear of death, he sought to cower the French by means of threat and overblown rhetoric, depending on the support of the Three Emperors League. His language inspired a number of newspaper articles on the potential for war with France. Far from supporting Germany against republican France, the Tsar reacted with horror at the possibility of such a reckless course of action and travelled to Germany to dissuade Kaiser Wilhelm from further sabre-rattling. The result was that Bismarck had to back down from his attempt to bully France into a conciliatory mood. The episode clearly showed that the ambiguity in the terms of the Three Emperors League could just as conceivably be used to thwart Bismarck as aid him.

The erosion of the Ottoman Empire soon provided another crisis to test the post 1871 stability of the European peace and Germany's place within it. Looking to capitalize on a recent revolt of the Slavs against their Turkish masters, Russia declared war on the Ottoman Empire in 1877. The British had no interest in increased Russian influence in the region. The newly built Suez Canal, of which the British were now majority share holders, sat squarely within the Ottoman Empire and it was important to British foreign policy that the Russians never be in a position to threaten this waterway, so vital to British Imperial trade. The rapid collapse of the Turkish armies before the advancing Russians brought the United Kingdom and Russia to the brink of war. The Treaty of San Stefano ended the fighting between the Turks and Russians in March 1878. It hacked away at the Ottoman's European holdings, creating independent Bulgaria, Serbia, and Romania, which looked for all intents and purposes to be Russia client states. This vastly expanded Russian influence in the Balkans, something the British could not let stand. War loomed.

The British were not the only power alarmed by the sudden expansion of Russian interests in the Balkans. Austria-Hungary saw expansion southeast into the Balkans as her only avenue of growth having been permanently blocked from expanding influence to the north and west by the Austro-Prussian war of 1866 and the creation of the German Empire. Should Franz Joseph decide to join the British in resisting this Russian encroachment, a general European war seemed likely and this is what alarmed Bismarck.

Germany had no interests in the Balkans. Should the two allies go to war against each other, however, it would destroy the vague balance Bismarck had achieved with the Three Emperor's League. And, should this war expand into a general European conflict, the results would be dangerously unpredictable. Bismarck wagered he would have more control at the negotiation table than on the battlefield and invited the powers to a Congress at Berlin in June 1878 where this Balkan crisis could be solved through diplomacy.

The settlement that emerged out of the Congress of Berlin was successful in that it prevented a war between the great powers of Europe. It did not, however, come to any lasting settlement of the **Eastern Question** and as such prolonged the life of the Ottoman Empire ensuring a series of Balkan crises that would eventually tumble the world into catastrophe. The Russians made some gains at Berlin. A blow had been struck for Pan-Slavism in the independence of Serbia and Montenegro. She received territorial concessions from the Turks on the Black Sea and the right to build a fleet there. Nevertheless the Tsar saw his Balkan ambitions largely thwarted and in many ways he blamed Bismarck and his support for the Austrians for this setback. Bismarck alienated the Russians at the Congress and in many ways rendered the Three Emperors League moribund.

As Bismarck watched Russia drift away from German friendship, he turned his gaze south to buttress his diplomatic system. National kinship made a closer alliance with Austria-Hungary more popular with the German public the Russia union had been. The Dual Alliance between Austria-Hungary and Germany concluded in 1879 was designed to ensure that Germany would not be isolated in the event of war. The alliance also served to frighten Russia into closer relations with Germany and the Tsar renewed the Three Emperors League in 1881. The Dual Alliance was expanded into the Triple Alliance when Italy joined in 1882, providing further security against France. The renewed interest in the League could not withstand further Russian meddling in Balkan affairs and collapsed after 1886. By way of replacing the overlapping security of the League and Dual Alliance, Bismarck concluded a secret Reinsurance Treaty with Russia in 1887. Both countries pledged neutrality in case of war with a third party and Germany supported Russian interests in the Balkans. While this treaty may have enhanced German security and preserved her ability to manoeuver in case of a war between Russia and Austria-Hungary, its secrecy did much to destabilize European relations. Maintaining the Reinsurance Treaty in light of growing suspicion between Austria-Hungary and Russia was difficult and would prove impossible after the departure of Bismarck.

Bismarck had always claimed he had no interest in overseas colonies, a position he seemed to maintain until 1884. Within a year, however, his government made to secure its position a position in Southwest Africa. Germany would also lay claim to African territories on the east coast as well as a collection of Pacific islands. The Scramble for Africa had gripped other European nations and German industrial interests demanded that Germany be a part of it. Colonies could provide a source of raw materials and potential markets for expanded production. Bismarck also seemed to have his eye on gaining a position in Africa from which Germany could potentially challenge the substantial British and French influence on the Continent. As with all Bismarckian diplomacy, however, this colonial scheme was to serve German power in Europe. When it seemed that African disputes could bring European powers into conflict, Bismarck moved to encourage a degree of predictability in the process of African colonization. For the second time in less than a decade Bismarck hosted a congress of European diplomats, this time to set out rules for the acquisition of African territories.

> **Eastern Question** This was the diplomatic dilemma that arose out of the dissolution of the Ottoman Empire. Essentially it revolved around the question of what power, if any, would control the Ottoman's European holdings.

The volatile relationship between Bismarck and his monarch that had weathered the storms of German unification and founded the German Empire, came to an end in March 1888 when Kaiser Wilhelm died. He was briefly succeeded by his son who also died within the year. This left the throne to 29-year-old Wilhelm II. King Wilhelm II and Bismarck soon came to blows over social legislation favoured by the Kaiser but opposed by Bismarck. The split escalated and became public. When Reichstag elections turned against Bismarck's supporters, he made plans to dissolve the Reichstag by force. He further tried to limit the King's access to government officials. Wilhelm could no longer brook such assaults on what he saw as his authority and asked for Bismarck's resignation in March 1890. The Iron Chancellor stepped down.

Activity:

Bismarck: a case study in historiography		
Emphasis	Bismarck as Great Man	Bismarck as precursor to authoritarian Germany	Bismarck as skeptical political tactician
Historian	Gerhard Ritter Wilhelm Schüssler Hans Rothfels	Hans Kohn Friedrich Meinecke Hans-Ulrich Wehler	A.J.P Taylor Andrea Hopp Otto Pflanze
Approach	To a number of historians Bismarck is seen as a continuation of the great statesmen of the 18th century rather than a precursor to the nationalists of the 20th century. Some believe the nationalism that helped propel the unification project was a populist phenomenon rather than officially supported by the chancellor. The end product was "national" in the west but more "multi-national" in the east of Germany and thus not a precursor to the ultra-nationalism of the 20th century. Some historians in this mould see Bismarck as a Prussian or German patriot, whose goal from the start was the unification of Germans into a single state. For most historians in this school, Bismarck distrusted and avoided war except as a last resort.	This approach, always more popular outside of Germany than inside it, sees the authoritarian and anti-democratic structures set up by Bismarck as laying the foundation for the rise of extreme nationalism in 20th-century Germany. Some in this school hold that because democracy as a principle and its necessary institutions were never allowed to develop in Bismarck's Germany, the rise of ultra-nationalism in the wake of the First World War and in the 1930s was more readily acceptable. Others maintain that even if Bismarck can bear no responsibility for the rise of the Nazis, he established Germany as an anti-liberal state with mechanisms for repression. For Wehler, Hitler is a continuation of what he sees as Bismarck's charismatic rule.	Bismarck emerges as less sure of himself and his goals in this approach. The unification project is more about the exercise of political power in the service of a stronger Prussia than any notions of German nationalism. Bismarck saw numerous obstacles to this exercise prior to unification (Austria and France) and threats to the state (Catholicism and Socialism) after 1871. Bismarck would meet such perceived threats aggressively regardless of the practical cost of repression. In this approach Bismarck is a skilled politician, driven by personal motives as well as ideals of service and patriotism. War was a political tool, as were principles such as liberalism and nationalism. In Otto Planze's words "Bismarck was the political surgeon who amputated nationalism from liberalism and conservatism from legitimism."

Evaluation exercise

1 Evaluate each of the above approaches. What are the relative strengths and weaknesses of each?

2 The above schools of historical thought concentrate on Bismarck the man and his actions. Social historians would look to broader social and economic issues that affected Bismarck and his times as a way of explaining issues of cause and effect. Create a third column that examines Bismarck and his work from the perspective of social history.

Austria in the 19th century

The spectre that floats though all these great nation building projects of the mid-19th century is Austria. For the first half of the century, the system engineered by her Foreign Minister at Vienna in 1815 guided the affairs of Central Europe. The erosion of Austrian influence and the chiselling away of its territories marked the second half of the century. In 1815 the Hapsburgs counted Germans, Czechs, Croats, Serbs, Poles, Italians, and Magyars as their subjects. By 1890, substantial numbers of the Germans and Italians had been wrenched away into the new states of Germany and Italy and many of the nationalities that remained clamoured for more autonomy and in some cases outright independence.

The revolts of 1848 had rocked the Hapsburg monarchy. By 1849, however, it had wrested control of its territories back from the revolutionaries. The lesson that the Austrian authorities took from 1848 was not that it needed to embrace some form of constitutionalism and take steps to appease the nationalists within its borders—quite the opposite. When the administration of Count Schwarzenberg took the helm of the Austrian Empire in November 1848 he set out to re-establish central authority in Vienna. He dissolved the constituent assembly and threw out the constitution that had created it. In its place a new Imperial Constitution repudiated many of elements of autonomy that the revolutionaries had granted to the Empire's many nationalities and even took back some that Hungary had enjoyed prior to the upheavals of 1848. The new parliament would be built on universal male suffrage but would have very little power. This centralizing project had some liberal features. The legal system was unified. Internal tariffs were abolished. Infrastructure was improved and railways built. But these reforms were in the interest of efficiency rather than political principle. The most important liberal political ideas of freedom, equality, and constitutionalism were firmly rejected.

Hungary had been one of the most nationally active territories within the Austrian Empire. It had won certain dispensations from the imperial government in the 1840s, including the use of the Magyar language in education and within their provincial Diet. When revolution swept through the Hapsburg domains in 1848, Hungary claimed even more autonomy. As Imperial authority began to reassert itself by the end of 1848 this autonomy came under increased attack. In response, Hungarian nationalists declared themselves an independent Hungarian republic in April 1849. The republic could not, however, withstand the combined assaults of the government in Vienna and the Russian army the Austrian Emperor had invited to intervene. After August 1848 Hungary was drawn back into the unified Austrian Empire with fewer freedoms than it had before 1848.

The Crimean War had weakened Austria. Its armies, mobilized to occupy Moldavia and Wallachia when the Russians retreated, were disarmed by the Congress of Paris that concluded the war. The war precipitated Italian unification under Piedmontese leadership that would eventually wring from the Hapsburgs Lombardy, Venetia and Austria's influence in the Italian peninsula.

Austria's decline that had begun to manifest itself in the Crimean War was dramatically accelerated in the ensuing wars with Piedmont and the emergence of a powerful Prussia culminating in the disastrous Austro-Prussian war of 1866. Now shut out of German affairs, Austria looked to its own house and sought to rebuild. The Magyars that dominated matters in Hungary saw in the Austrian defeat a chance to press for more rights within the Austrian Empire. The result was a compromise that would create the Dual Monarchy of Austria-Hungary composed of the Austrian Empire and the Kingdom of Hungary. It was a unique arrangement. The Hapsburg ruler, in this case Franz Joseph, would be simultaneously Austrian Emperor and King of Hungary. While the new Dual Monarchy would have a common foreign policy and military, internal affairs were to be kept separate, with a constitution and parliament for each state. Neither state was to dominate. The two parliaments would come together to discuss issues of concern to the entire country.

The Dual Monarchy was an imaginative solution to the most pressing nationalist issue facing the Hapsburgs in the wake of the Austro-Prussian War. In fact, in the long run it can be seen as destabilizing the state. It did not take long for many of the other national minorities that made up the polyglot Austria-Hungary—Czechs, Slovaks, Serbs and others—to begin demanding a status similar to Hungary's. As the 19th century came to c a close, these nationalist sentiments grew, especially in the Balkans were ethnic and linguistic affinities began to trump loyalty to Vienna. Pan-Slavism moved many of these Balkan nationalists to look to Russia as a sponsor, and this would escalate tensions in this region up until the First World War. The creation of the German Empire barred Austria from expanding its influence to the north. Italian unification blocked western development and any move to the northeast would run into Russia. This left the Balkans, a region in flux throughout the second half of the 19th century. It was the potential created by this flux and a desire to recapture her prominence or at least stem her decline that led Austria–Hungary to take a more active role in Balkan affairs throughout the turn of the century, a development that would have momentous consequences.

Exam practice and further resources

Sample questions

1 Why did the revolution of 1848 have such a limited impact on the German states.
2 Assess the contribution of Cavour to the unification of Italy.
3 "Economic strength was the key factor in the rise of Prussia as a powerful state by 1862." Examine the validity of this statement.
4 Analyse the contribution made by nationalism to the decline of Austria by 1866.
5 Compare and contrast the means by which Italy and Germany were unified by 1870.
6 How successful were Bismarck's domestic policies 1870–90?

Recommended further reading

Italian unification:

Beales , Derek and Eugenio F. Biagini. 2002. *The Risorgimento and the Unification of Italy*. New York, USA. Longman.

Mack Smith, D. 1971. Victor Emanuel, *Cavour and the Risorgimento*. Oxford, UK. Oxford University Press.

Riall, Lucy. 1994. *The Italian Risorgimento: State, Society and National Unification*. New York, USA. Routledge.

German unification:

Clark, Christopher. 2006. *Iron Kingdom: The Rise and Downfall of Prussia, 1600–1947* Allen Lane.

Nipperdey, Thomas. (trans. Daniel Nolan, Daniel). 1983. *Germany from Napoleon to Bismarck, 1800–1866*. Princeton, USA. Princeton University Press.

Showalter, Dennis. 2004. *The Wars of German Unification*. Hodder Education.

Taylor, A.J.P. 2003. *Bismarck: The Man and Statesman*. Phoenix Mill, UK. Sutton Publishing.

Imperial Germany:

Berghahn, Volker R. 2005. *Imperial Germany 1871–1918: Economy, Society, Culture and Politics*. Providence, USA. Berghahn Books.

Nationalism:

Ignatieff, Michael. 1993. *Blood and Belonging: Journeys in the New Nationalism*. London, UK. BBC Books.

Austria:

Taylor, A. J. P. 1976. *The Habsburg Monarchy, 1809–1918: A History of the Austrian Empire and Austria-Hungary*. Chicago, USA. University of Chicago Press.

3 Western and Northern Europe, 1848–1914

For 40 years after the Congress of Vienna rebuilt Europe in the aftermath of the French Revolution and the Napoleonic Wars, the major European powers were able to keep the forces unleashed by the revolution at bay—forces like liberalism, democracy and nationalism. This all changed in 1848. Revolutions rocked France, Austria, and Prussia. In France these revolutions would lead not to expanded democracy and liberty, but rather to a form of authoritarian government in the person of Napoleon III. This unique regime could not withstand the onslaught of both Prussian armies and ideas such as liberalism. After a short, sharp and bloody transition France transformed into a bureaucratic, republican democracy that would weather scandal and the First World War. Across the channel in the United Kingdom, no such upheaval rocked society in 1848. An expanding economy and Empire was eventually matched by an expanding electorate. Legislative reform attempted to ameliorate the harshest effects of industrialization with mixed results.

By the end of this chapter, students should be able to:

- analyse the causes and effects of the 1848 Revolution in France
- evaluate the domestic and foreign policies of the Second Empire
- discuss the fall of the Second Empire and the Commune
- review the successes and failures of the Third Republic to 1914
- evaluate social and political reforms in the United Kingdom from 1867 to 1914
- analyse the domestic and foreign policies of Disraeli and Gladstone.

France, 1848

The European conflagrations of 1848 were sparked in France and had much to do with the inability of the government of Louis Philippe to adjust to the changing economic, social and political needs of his country. On the surface his government seemed an unlikely target for revolution. Bound by a constitution and with an elected assembly to guide him, Louis Philippe's monarchy seemed to have the mechanisms in place to adjust to the changes that were buffeting French society in the 1840s. But this would only have been the case if he and his ministers were interested in allowing them to work. The constitution that Louis Philippe brought forward after a popular insurrection carried him to the throne in the July Revolution of 1830 had doubled the franchise and reformed the upper chamber, eliminating hereditary representation. Though the number of voters had been dramatically increased, this was relative to what it had been before 1830, and the right to vote still rested on the ownership of property. Propertied interests and the upper bourgeoisie thus controlled the important political bodies of the **July Monarchy**—throne, government, upper chamber and lower chamber.

The stability that the propertied classes and limited **franchise** were thought to bring to the political system cut both ways. As the social and economic system changed, those guiding the political system steered a conservative course that by the 1840s had lapsed into corruption and stagnation. Although there was the framework of political parties within the chambers, they still represented a very narrow social base. Government ministers came and went with some regularity, but continuity was maintained in several key ministries and in the person of Louis Philippe himself who took an active role in governing. The working class and liberals, with little to no representation, looked on with growing irritation. Such political irritants may have been able to continue for some time had not a European economic crisis stressed the system to breaking point.

The French economy of the 1830s changed only sluggishly. Property, rather than industry, remained the mark of prestige. Large industrial enterprises, though starting to appear, were not the rule. **Protectionism** predominated, stunting economic growth. Although it had a central bank that was expanding its influence, the availability of credit in France was insufficient to support large-scale industrial expansion. This lack of capital doomed railway development in the 1830s to small, private, and unco-ordinated endeavors. This began to change at the beginning of the 1840s under government direction and investment, but railway development in France was still in its infancy, especially when compared to her industrial competitors across the English Channel and the Rhine River.

The "hungry forties" provided an economic stress that exposed the cracks in the conservative and reactionary edifice of the major continental states. In reality it was not one, but several crisis that gripped the European economy in the 1840s. Bad harvests descended on Europe from Ireland to Poland driving agricultural prices drastically higher and spreading hunger in both rural and urban areas. During these same years industrial production was cut back, throwing people out of work across the continent at the same time their food prices were skyrocketing. High bread prices had restricted the money that people had available for manufactured goods resulting in surplus inventories and overproduction. Credit, already limited in France, began to dry up. The harvests of 1846 were terrible, setting off rural unrest at the consequent sharp increase in bread prices. Unemployment and poverty spread to Paris and other urban centres.

The relative prosperity of the propertied classes and upper bourgeoisie was the basis of much of Louis Philippe's support. The hungry 1840s bit deep into that prosperity and support. Political frustration had been growing throughout 1846 and 1847. Political meetings, under the guise of banquets, overt political meetings having been banned by Louis Philippe's regime, were held throughout the country. French liberals, like their counterparts in

July Monarchy This is the name given to the regime of Louis Philippe. The July Monarchy lasted from 1830 until it was overthrown during the February Revolution in 1848. The July Monarchy was succeeded by the Second Republic.

Franchise The right to vote.

Protectionism Protectionism is a trade policy by which a government seeks to protect domestic industries from competing foreign products by imposing tariffs on imported goods, making them more expensive than those produced domestically.

other European countries, advocated more democratic rights and a strengthening of the constitution. More radical reformers demanded a republic. The unemployed demanded jobs and food.

The February Revolution

After the government forbade a massive protest banquet in Paris on 22 February 1848 barricades were thrown up across the capital. When the National Guard refused to come to the aid of the government, the king looked as though he would bow to pressure and initiate political reform. Sensing their time had come, the most radical of the reformers pushed the mobs to remain in the streets. Protestors outside of the prime minister's residence were fired upon further radicalizing the street mobs spreading more violence throughout Paris. Faced with this challenge to his authority, it appeared to Louis Philippe that he had lost both popular legitimacy and, with the mutiny of the National Guard, his monopoly of force. On 24 February 1848 he abdicated and fled to England. France found herself a republic once again.

One of the lasting legacies of Napoleon III was the widening of the boulevards in Paris. To some degree this would make it more difficult to put up barricades in times of civil insurrection.

 What other evidence is there that Napoleon III learned from the revolutionary history of France?

The events of February came very quickly, surprising most people on both sides of the political conflict. Louis Philippe gave way to cascading events rather than a coherent opposition platform. With no one opposition party dominant, the hastily assembled provisional government cobbled together moderate liberals with radical and moderate socialists. Its policies were likewise a series of compromises. Financially, the new regime honoured its obligations at the expense of its gold reserves. A large tax hike brought some money into the government coffers and a great deal of resentment from the population.

Barricades in Paris, February Revolution.

Politically, the provisional government brought in a liberal agenda that included universal adult male suffrage, freedom of the press, and the abolition of the death penalty. Like most political compromises, the reforms of the provisional government went too far for some and not far enough for others. Right-leaning liberals questioned the extension of the franchise to the peasant and working class. Radical socialists wanted more direct government intervention in the economy. Foremost among those in the government advocating government economic regulation was Louis Blanc who envisioned a scheme of state-run industries that supported a right to work. The compromised nature of the provisional government meant that this vision would never be met.

The government appointed a commission of working class representatives who were to advise it on the social conditions facing the poor of Paris and the country, but who had no real power. The social experiment that grew out of Blanc's ideas was a system of

National Workshops. Designed to alleviate the economic and social problems associated with the massive unemployment that had gripped France since the economic crisis of the 1840s, the National Workshops would inject money into the economy through the pockets of the workers and alleviate the social ills that accompanied unemployment. While Blanc had imagined such workshops would be spread through all manufacturing sectors of the economy and be controlled by the workers themselves, the realization was limited to public works overseen by government officials. Blanc's scheme had run into stiff opposition from classical liberals in the government who, though they were political republicans, looked on the collectivist views of the social republicans like Blanc with a mixture of distrust and scorn. This distrust soon spread to the middle class throughout the country.

> The **National Workshops** were work schemes devised by French Socialists of the Second Republic. They provided work to applicants through as series of public works in Paris.

Activity:
Louis Blanc: The Organization of Labour

The government ought to be considered as the supreme regulator of production and endowed for this duty with great power. This task would consist of fighting competition and of finally overcoming it.

The government ought to float a loan with the proceeds of which it should erect social workshops in the most important branches of national industry.

As these establishments would demand considerable investments, the number of these workshops at the start ought to be carefully limited, still they would possess, by virtue of their organization—as we shall see later—an unlimited expansion.

The government, considered as the only founder of the workshops, must determine the statutes regulating them. This code, deliberated and voted for by the representatives of the people ought to have the power and force of a law.

All workmen who can give guarantee of morality shall be called to work in these social workshops up to the limit of the original capital gathered together for the purchase of tools. ...

For the first years after the workshops are established, the government ought to regulate the scale of employment. After the first year it is no longer necessary, the laborers would then have time enough to truly estimate their respective work, and, all being equally interested as we will soon see, the success of the association would eventually depend on the elective principle. ...

Every member of the social workshops would have the right to use, according to his discretion, the profits of his labor; but it would not be long before the evident economy and the

incontestable excellence of this communal life would call forth other voluntary associations among the workmen according to their needs and pleasure.

Capitalists can also be taken into the association and would draw interest on their invested money, which would be guaranteed by the budget; but in the profits they would participate only if they were laborers at the same time.

Source: Louis Blanc, L. 1840. "The Organisation of Labour". *Modern History Sourcebook*. http://www.fordham.edu/harlsall/mod/1840blanc.html.

Questions

1 What is the role of government to be in the establishment of the social workshops?

2 By what mechanism will the workshops be maintained after they are set up?

3 What elements of democracy are inherent in these social workshops?

4 What was the economic and social context in which Blanc was writing? How might living in France in 1839 have affected his views?

5 How did the National Workshops set up in 1848 in Paris differ from the Social Workshops that Blanc wrote about in 1840? How were they similar?

6 What elements of French Society in the 1840s would oppose these workshops? Chose one such element and write a response to Blanc written from that perspective.

Despite middle-class opposition, the demand for participation in the National Workshops by the unemployed themselves soon outstripped both the supply of work available to the workshops and government funds allocated to the experiment. To offset the growing cost of the workshops, the government levied taxes on property, ensuring that property owners, whether they owned small peasant holdings or large estates, saw in the National Workshops an urban scheme for which the countryside would have to foot the bill.

This opposition registered itself in the elections of April 1848. A strong conservative majority was returned to the Constituent Assembly who in turn selected a conservative executive in which the views of socialists like Louis Blanc found no voice. The election, therefore, resulted in a volatile political polarization within the capital. The massive number of applicants for National Workshop jobs indicates that there was a large population of unemployed poor in the capital recently mobilized by the workshop project itself. The election results indicate that outside of Paris there was a strong opposition to the kind of social policies that appealed to the workers. The recently liberalized press in the country amplified this rift between urban and rural France. Political publications multiplied and along with them meetings, clubs and speeches. As the spring of 1848 progressed, the political mood on Paris grew explosive. Parisian workers stormed the Assembly in mid May but were suppressed by the National Guard sparking an anti-socialist campaign that would disband the workshops.

The June Days

On 23 June the capital erupted in violence. Once again barricades sprang up in the working class quarters and other parts of the capital while the National Guard, augmented by provincial volunteers, fought a three-day running battle with the revolutionaries. By 26 June the army had reduced the majority of the barricades and order was restored at a cost of over a thousand lives. Eleven thousand of the insurgents were arrested. The government responded to the June Days by imposing martial law, shutting down political clubs, censoring the press and arresting and deporting the radicals. As with many revolutions, the revolutionaries could generally agree on what they sought to overthrow, in the case of the February Revolution it was the stagnant and corrupt regime of Louis Philippe. When he fled, pushed by such scant pressure, the cracks in the revolutionary position began to emerge. Those who saw in the revolution a chance to advance a broader social program ran into the opposition of the groups who saw the revolution as a more modest change in government rather than a more complete overhaul of the system. Both of these groups had their respective constituencies—the social republicans in the working class districts of Paris and the political republicans throughout the rest of the country. The expanded franchise put the relative strengths of these two groups to the test and the social republicans were found to be wanting. They took to the streets of Paris to protect what they thought they had won in February and were defeated. The only question that remained to be answered was what form the new conservatism in France would take. The answer came in a familiar name.

The rise of Louis Napoleon Bonaparte

The blood-soaked June Days left a mark on the psyche of France. The volatile events of the first six months of 1848 seemed to point to the need for a strong government to secure the modest political

> **Discussion point:**
>
> **The radical divide**
>
> Throughout the 1789, 1830, 1848, and 1870 revolutions, Paris was the centre of radical activity. This reflects a deep urban–rural divide, and a division in particular between Paris and the rest of France.
>
> **?** **Why were urban areas, and those of Paris in particular, more radical than non-urban areas?**
>
> How has this influenced the course of French history in the 19th century? To what degree did this trend continue into the 20th century?

changes that had been achieved on the heels of Louis Philippe's hasty departure. A new constitution was drafted in the wake of the June Days that would see more power vested in the hands of the executive, but that preserved universal adult male suffrage. The presidential elections of December 1848 brought Louis Napoleon Bonaparte, Napoleon I's nephew, to power by a wide margin. After a flamboyant career that had seen him since 1832 a revolutionary, a prisoner, an author, and an English constable Louis Napoleon was something of an enigma in the French political landscape of 1848. This, in fact, served him well as he was associated with neither political extreme in France. He presented himself at once as the friend of the working man and paragon of tradition and constancy and as such, like his uncle before him, he appealed to a country looking for stability. He had the advantage, in a newly enfranchised population, of possessing instant name recognition at a time when nostalgia for Napoleon I was riding high. The Emperor's remains had recently been returned to France and interred at **Les Invalides**. Those voting for the first time may not have recognized the names of his opponents, men like the poet Lamartine or the general Cavaignac, but they certainly knew the name Napoleon Bonaparte regardless of which given name came in front of it. The election results bore this out when Louis Napoleon captured over 72 per cent of the popular vote. For the second time in the century, a Bonaparte took the helm of France.

> **Les Invalides** The military hospital and home for ageing soldiers built by Louis XIV in the late–17th century.

> **TOK Link**
> **Ways of knowing—What's in a name?**
> Louis Napoleon deliberately emphasized his family connections. He chose to stage his coup on the anniversary of the great Battle of Austerlitz. Imagery and symbolism of the First Empire were reintroduced.
>
> **?** What knowledge issues are inherent in Louis Napoleon's claim to greatness by virtue of his relationship to Napoleon Bonaparte?

The Second Republic

France had been a republic for 11 months by the time Louis Napoleon came to power, but was on its second constitution. When elections for the new Legislative Assembly were held in May 1849 its composition reflected the divided nature of the French body politic. Conservative royalists dominated, although they were themselves factionalized. The minority republicans were likewise split between socialists and liberal republicans. With a keen eye to the country's right-wing tilt, Louis Napoleon set himself at the head of a **coalition** of the conservative elements in the Assembly, taking aim at the minority socialists. When June again beckoned the socialists to revolt, Louis Napoleon struck, expelling socialists from the Legislative Assembly, limiting freedom of assembly and drastically expanding press censorship. A series of laws enacted in 1850 re-established the Catholic Church's control of education and stripped the franchise from about three million Frenchmen. The support of the Catholic Church was further solidified when he sent

> **Coalition** A government comprised of representatives of more than one political party or interest group.

> **Napoleon III (1808–1873)**
>
> Louis Napoleon was the nephew of Napoleon I. He was raised in exile and grew into a romantic adventurer. He returned to France to lead two failed revolts in 1836 and 1840 after which he was imprisoned. While in prison he wrote and developed views influenced by socialism and the legend of his uncle. He escaped prison and sought refuge in the United Kingdom. He returned shortly after the February Revolution of 1848. After being appointed to the presidency of the Second Republic in 1848 he led a coup in December 1851 and was elected president for a term of ten years. Within a year he proclaimed himself Emperor Napoleon III and would rule until ousted during the debacle of the Franco-Prussian War. He died in Britain in 1873.

troops to protect the Pope in the face of Mazzini's republican assault. Louis Napoleon could now count the Church among his formidable conservative coalition.

But Louis Napoleon was no ordinary conservative politician with authoritarian tendencies. He could be a clever and manipulative tactician. With the conservative elements in France firmly ensconced in the Bonaparte camp, he turned his attention to winning over the average Frenchman, insofar as such a person existed. This shameless **populism** was made that much easier since he had all but eliminated the socialists and their claim to this constituency. In 1850 Louis Napoleon began to advocate a return to the universal suffrage he had so recently taken away, portraying the Legislative Assembly as a cabal of elitist interests and himself as the champion of the people. Napoleon was showing himself to be an adept manipulator of public opinion.

> **Populism** A political doctrine that seeks support from the mass population by addressing their immediate needs.

Activity:

The many faces of Louis Napoleon

Louis Napoleon used the press to portray an image of himself that appealed to various interests in France. Draw an editorial cartoon that portrays Louis Napoleon favourably to each of the following interest groups:

- the French working class
- monarchists
- the bourgeoisie
- the Church.

Regardless of which Napoleon was at the fore, the conservative protector of tradition and order or the socially conscious friend of the people, Louis Napoleon faced a major obstacle in the very constitution that brought him to power. The constitution stipulated that the president could only be elected to a single term of four years. This seemed equally disagreeable to Louis Napoleon himself and the interests that he protected. To some, the looming presidential election of 1852 was likely to spark a return to the political violence that had savaged French political life in 1848 and 1849.

The crux of the problem was that Louis Napoleon was an authoritarian serving a constitution designed to prevent authoritarianism. One solution would be to simply change the constitution, but this required a parliamentary majority beyond his reach. The only other solution seemed to be to take by force what parliamentary democracy was unwilling to give him—to stage a *coup d'état*. Throughout the summer and autumn of 1851, he and his supporters made preparations. The press, at his encouragement, railed at the elitist assembly. Louis toured the country and appointed supporters to key ministries, controlling the army and the police. He attacked the disenfranchise law in November as if to reinforce his populist credentials. By the end of November 1851, the ground had been prepared.

Napoleon III in Coronation robes.

On 2 December, the anniversary of his uncle's victory at Austerlitz, Louis Napoleon seized control. He declared the Assembly dissolved. Opposition politicians were arrested. When what resistance remained took to the streets, the army easily quelled it and peace soon returned to the capital. Why then no return to the brutality of 1848? Part of the answer lay in the careful preparations made by the conspirators. His tours of the country convinced Louis that he had broad-based support and there existed a deep fear of revolutionary upheaval. This was a revolt from above and was thus much easier to control especially with the active support of the army command. In 1848, the insurrection had risen from the street with the complicity of the National Guard, and although it lacked a coherent leadership, this fact provided it with considerable armed force. The resistance in 1851 possessed no comparable force of arms.

In reality, Louis Napoleon's actions had considerable popular support throughout France. When Louis Napoleon's seizure of power was overwhelmingly confirmed by plebiscite later in December, he seemed to have combined the two key components of the stable exercise of political power—legitimacy and a monopoly of force. While it would be naive to suspect that the plebiscite came close to what modern democracies would consider a fair and open vote, the sheer size of his victory—over 90 per cent of the vote—indicates that he had considerable support and a justifiable claim to a good degree of popular legitimacy. This popularity was not evenly distributed, however, and Louis's seizure of power garnered slightly more than 60 per cent of the Parisian vote. When combined with his supporters, Saint-Arnaud and de Maupas, in command of the army and police respectively, Louis Napoleon held the keys to a stable exercise of power.

Napoleon III and the Second Empire

Domestic policy

Louis Napoleon wanted to enshrine the legitimacy conferred by the plebiscite of 20 December 1851 and chose the constitution as the vehicle. Although stopping short of establishing the presidency as absolute, it nonetheless vested a great deal of power in this office. The President was to sit for a period of ten years. He was the head of the executive, which was, in turn, responsible to him alone. The **bicameral parliament** consisted of a Senate of appointed "notables" and an elected *corps législatif* that could debate and then either accept or reject legislation. The elected members were not allowed to initiate legislation. The President had the power to call and dismiss the Senate and the *corps législatif*. He appointed the members of and chaired the Council of State, which prepared all legislation. If this structure seemed familiar to the citizens of France it was not by accident. Louis Napoleon had studied and then emulated his uncle's state institutions and constitution.

> **Bicameral parliament** A parliament consisting of two houses, an upper house and a lower house.

Like dictators before and after him, Louis Napoleon set up a sham democracy and then used it to claim continued legitimacy. While the plebiscite did grant a certain degree of legitimacy, a true democracy must allow the electorate to express their opinions by various means, frequently and regularly. Modern democratic constitutions generally make the government responsible in some way, shape or form to the electorate. Louis's constitution took the authority granted by the electorate and then funneled it into the President's hands from which that same electorate to could not remove it or even question the way in which it was being exercised for another 10 years. Louis Napoleon justified much of this anti-democratic impulse by arguing that the will of the people was embodied in his person and thus his exercise of dictatorial power was really them speaking through him. In this way he claimed to transcend the class rivalries that had torn France apart in 1848.

> **Discussion point:**
>
> Authoritarian regimes often attempted to give the illusion of legitimacy. How was this accomplished in the following authoritarian regimes?
>
> ● Italy, 1922–43
> ● Germany, 1933–45
> ● Spain, 1939–75
> ● USSR, 1928–53

It was not much of a stretch, then, from Louis's notion of representing the collective French will to claiming the title of Emperor. Louis's well-oiled propaganda machine leaped into action and he again gauged public opinion. Were the French ready to abandon their so newly achieved republic and in its place sanction an Empire that claimed to have their best interests at heart, but in which they would have no meaningful say? In the autumn of 1852 Louis embarked on another tour to gauge the public mood outside the capital, moving through Lyon, Marseilles, and Bordeaux. Louis judged the latter to be the case and less than a year after the *coup d'état*, Louis Napoleon declared France an Empire and himself its Emperor as Napoleon III. This was dutifully confirmed by yet another plebiscite.

It is important to understand that Napoleon III was not an absolute ruler in the way that the Bourbons or even Napoleon I had been. If the preceding 65 years of French history has shown anything it had shown that at least some of the various constituencies of the French body politic had to be satisfied before any regime could enjoy long-term stability. Napoleon III therefore maintained the conservative coalition on which he had depended in 1848 and these interests exercised at times considerable influence over the Emperor. Although limited in power, the representative institutions of the Empire contained opposition politicians throughout his reign. Regardless of the reality of such ties, Napoleon presented himself as transcending class and political divisions and as such was exactly what the fractious France needed after the upheavals of 1848. He ruled the *départments* of the country through a system of prefects who often manipulated local elections and constantly promoted the **Bonapartist** agenda.

Napoleon III, as we have noted, was a skilful manipulator of public opinion. His propaganda machine was well established by the time he took the title of Emperor. Well-placed supporters wrote articles at his behest, and friendly editors suppressed those that were unflattering. When those subtle means proved insufficient, or editors themselves proved hostile, the Napoleonic regime resorted to censorship of articles and the outright closing of some presses. Newspaper headlines and placards were peppered with Napoleonic slogans. Always more popular outside of the capital than within it, as the plebiscite returns had indicated, Napoleon made good use of countrywide tours. Such tours served a dual purpose. Always wary of his public image, they provided Louis Napoleon with a picture of his popularity outside the sometimes insular world of Parisian politics. Such tours had helped him gauge popular support for the *coup d'état* and the declaration of the Empire. Moving through the countryside also gave Louis Napoleon the opportunity to put the pomp and ceremony of his regime on display throughout France, helping establish in the minds of his subjects the legitimacy of his Imperial airs.

Indeed such spectacle was central to the Napoleonic system and a key component of his propaganda. Napoleon wanted to present the public with images and pageantry that linked him to the glories of his uncle's epoch. His was not to be a new Empire, but rather, that of Napoleon I continued. His choice of name, Napoleon III, was intended to suggest that the Napoleonic line had continued after the first Emperor's death through his son, even though Napoleon I had never occupied the throne. The date chosen for both the coup that brought him to the presidency and the proclamation of the Empire, 2 December, brought to mind Napoleon I's military masterpiece at Austerlitz in 1805. The Imperial eagle began to reappear at official functions. Processions and military parades were designed to convey strength and order, the core of his public appeal and that of Bonapartism in general. An Emperor needed an Imperial court and Napoleon constructed one around him modelled on his uncle's. While he did not rely on the court as a tool of administration, as both his uncle and the Bourbon rulers before him had done, the court became an important source of spectacle and a key element in Napoleon III's propaganda. As such, court events such as receptions balls, and audiences were governed by established rules of protocol and widely reported in the press.

> **Bonapartism** A French political doctrine that advocates a strong centralized government supported by a broad and often vague mandate from the population.

> **Discussion point:**
>
> ### Propaganda
>
> Propaganda involves the use of media to emotionally affect and influence audiences. There were a number of different propaganda tools available to authoritarian rulers in the 19th century:
>
> - newspapers
> - posters
> - rituals
> - pamphlets
> - music.
>
> What makes good propaganda? Are some methods more effective than others? Why? How did the advent off mass communication affect the use of propaganda?

Paris itself grew in grandeur during the reign of Napoleon III. Always a keen student of modernization and "progress", Napoleon wanted a capital to reflect his modern Empire. These public works also created employment, a very important consideration given the forces that had led to the bloody June Days and were constantly in the back of Napoleon's mind.

The economy

Napoleon III hoped that employment in public works would spread economic prosperity to the working classes. As disastrous as his foreign adventures would prove to be, the French economy would enjoy a significant period of growth under his supervision. To be sure, the world economic situation was propitious for such an expansion. Economies around the world were recovering from the hungry forties and France was no exception. The world money supply was expanded on the strength of drastically expanded gold reserves fed by substantial finds in California and Australia. The subsequent rise in prices stimulated commercial activity and expansion, as did the availability and improved mobility of credit. Infrastructure, communication and maritime transportation also made great strides during this period, facilitating trade and commerce.

Napoleon's economic policies certainly benefited from this period of economic boom. There were, however, particularly French innovations during this period the credit for which can at least partially be claimed by the Emperor and his regime. Moderate taxes, with the exception of special measures designed to pay for Napoleon's various wars, left much of the new-found wealth free to move in the **capital market**. But how to organize and concentrate this capital? Prior to the Second Empire, relatively small, family owned operations with fairly limited scope had dominated France's banking system. In 1852 two new institutions were established, backed by the Bank of France, that tapped into the growing public wealth by offering shares for sale and then invested the resultant pool of capital in business, industrial and farming interests eager to expand. This concentration of capital made possible large-scale projects that had previously been impossible without over-burdening the taxpayer. The stock market also boomed during the Second Empire encouraged by laws protecting shareholders. Although the economic cycle again took a down-turn in the mid 1860s, much of these innovations survived as did the works they financed.

Much of this capital financed industrial expansion. Just as in the rest of Europe railway construction was an important trigger. Rail length increased from 2,915 km in 1850 to 16,465 km in 1869. Modernization was accompanied by rationalization: as the total length of rail line increased, the total number of independently operated lines was reduced from 55 to six, enormously increasing

Activity:

Haussmann's Renovations

Georges-Eugène Haussmann was a French civil servant who undertook the modernization of Paris from the 1850s to the 1870s. Use the Internet to explore historic images of Paris and the changes that Haussmann made to it.

 How and why did Haussmann change the following?

● Streets, avenues, and boulevards

● Transportation in the city

● Monuments

● Parks

● Sanitation

Discussion point:

To what extent can the progress of the French economy in the 1850s be attributed to Napoleon's policies and to what extent can they be attributed to other factors?

Capital market The market in which money and credit is exchanged. This money is used for economic expansion.

Industrial output, 1850–69 (in metric tons, per thousand)		
Sector	**1850**	**1869**
Coal	4,434	13,464
Iron ore	1,821	3,131
Pig iron	406	1,381

efficiency. Napoleon's government contributed money to these enterprises and in return held shares in the railway companies. This vastly expanded rail system transported over ten times more freight in 1870 than it had in 1850. The shipping industry was also modernizing. In 1850 the embryonic steam ship fleet was only two per cent of France's merchant sail fleet, but amounted to 15 per cent in 1869. Telegraph use also increased by a factor of ten during the Second Empire carried on a telegraph system whose overall length had risen from 2,000 km to 70,000 km.

Napoleon III was to some degree influenced by the **Saint Simonians** in terms of his vision of the relationship of the working class to the state. Unfortunately for Napoleon, much of this came to naught. Labour battalions that were to transform unproductive agricultural land fell far short of their goals. The renovation of Paris supplied some jobs, but these were far exceeded by the demand for stable employment. Less restrictive labour legislation allowed organized labour to take root, but in the end this simply provided another forum for opposition to the regime. Some limited social legislation such as employee–employer equality before the law, pensions, and a form of legal-aid was attempted, but again it was insufficient to fill the gaps left by the labour market. The result was that poverty was a constant feature of the Second Empire and must be written against the economic gains made under Napoleon III.

> **Saint Simonianism** A belief that as society modernized science and industry would combine to share social and economic benefits more equally among the population based on the ideas of the *comte de* Saint-Simon.

Napoleon's trade policy flew in the face of a number of interests within the French economy. The Emperor was a committed free trade advocate and his policy therefore ran into traditional proponents of protectionism—organized and not so organized labour, industrialists, and farmers. This was especially true at the outset of the policy initiative for it would initially put French products and commodities in direct competition with the hyper-efficient British manufacturing and agricultural system. The potential benefits and profits of free trade were on the distant horizon. The gap between the short-term pain and long-term gain roused considerable opposition to this programme in France. Nevertheless, the Emperor pressed on and over the course of 1860–6 he concluded free-trade agreements with among others, the United Kingdom, Belgium, the **Zollverein**, Italy, Switzerland, Spain and Austria.

> **The Zollverein** A Trade Union of German states created in the 1830s.

Agriculture, of course, remained a major source of income for slightly over half of the French population and enjoyed a period of growth during the Second Empire. The area of major cereal crops under cultivation and the output that came from this land increased between 1850 and 1870 at the same time that the percentage of the population involved in agriculture was decreasing. Wine production shot up by 64 per cent. These gains came in spite of bad harvests between 1853–6. The centralized apparatus of government worked reasonably well to blunt the food shortages that threatened to re-radicalize the countryside and destabilize the regime.

> **Discussion point:**
>
> What role had hunger played in radical French politics in the past?

Church relations

Though he himself was not devout, Napoleon III saw himself become the protector of the Papacy and in many ways its champion in the years 1852–70, although his relationship with working-class

French Catholics was always more ambiguous than with the established church hierarchy. He assumed this role for practical opportunistic reasons far more than out of any notion of principle or faith. For its part, the French Church saw in Napoleon an order and stability that could stem the tide of liberal democracy and the attendant **secularization** of society, not to mention the rising red tide of socialism. It was a combination of these interests and the overwhelming popular support for the regime that made it difficult for the church to overturn elements of the constitution that reasserted civil marriage and maintained the **Organic Articles**. Throughout his reign, Napoleon used the influence of the clergy, especially in rural France, as a means of gaining the support of voters. To this end, Napoleon remained on good terms with the Catholic Church in France by maintaining its position in French Society and asserting its rights and temporal sovereignty abroad during the 1850s. The 1860s saw him use the Church to support him when he needed it and turn on it when he did not. In 1860 he reasserted government control in a number of areas in which he had previously permitted the church a good degree of latitude. When the liberal opposition made gains in the elections of 1863, he again courted Catholic voters through the church itself. Although this may seem an inconsistent and contradictory approach to governing, it simply reveals Napoleon III to be a somewhat skillful practitioner of *Realpolitik* in the same way that his contemporaries Cavour and Bismarck were.

> **Secularization** The movement away from religion or religious control.

> **Organic Articles** Legal stipulations initially established by Napoleon I that preserved the right of the French government to intervene in the affairs of the Catholic Church in France.

The liberal Empire

This *Realpolitik* was again at the fore when, after 1860, Napoleon moved to liberalize the Second Empire. By 1860 Napoleon's regime was under attack from the left, as it had been for years, but also increasingly from the right. Napoleon had, by means of censorship, exile, and repression, stabilized French society and he was therefore less necessary to conservatives. To counter this new threat, Napoleon moved to realign himself and the coalition of interests that kept him in power. In 1860 he moved to liberalize the function if not the form of government. The *corps législatif* received more budgetary power and its deliberations became public. The relaxation of censorship can be interpreted as at the same time a sop to middle-class liberals and a means by which he could make more direct appeals to the working class and peasantry in the form of progressive legislation such as free trade. The budgetary concessions to liberalism were more directly aimed at the bourgeois political elements in the *corps législatif* and the capital. These concessions were, however, circumscribed by the ultimate power of the government to adjust the budget if necessary. Both measures can be seen as the opening salvoes in the coming election campaign of 1863.

Although on the surface the elections were yet another vote of confidence for the Emperor, on closer examination they gave Napoleon pause. The Paris vote had gone heavily against the government. While that might have been predictable, its support in the countryside also showed signs of erosion. The various opposition parties of left and right garnered 32 seats and increased their votes from 665,000 in the 1857 elections to two million in 1863. There were two possible courses of action that the regime may have taken. The alarming election results might have, as they have done in other authoritarian regimes, moved the government to a more repressive stance in which it would tighten its control of parliament, the press and the right to dissent. The other course was to interpret the results as an indication that the tentative steps that Napoleon had taken toward a liberal Empire in 1860 were not enough and that he should continue along this road. It is the latter course that Napoleon seems to have chosen, although as in 1860, somewhat tentatively.

Between the elections of 1863 and 1869, Napoleon endorsed a limited programme of reform that would to some degree, as half measures are wont to do, alienate the right and frustrate the left. Proposals for educational reform in support of publicly funded universal education ran into the predictable clerical and conservative opposition and were abandoned. The right to form unions and to strike was limited by the qualification that the exercise of such rights could not operate against the general interests of the economy as a whole, and was thus little more than window dressing. Censorship was once again eased and government ministers could be questioned by the legislature. The election results of 1869 suggested that the electorate saw through such backhanded reform and demanded a more substantial and real transformation of the authoritarian regime.

The new government was led by an eloquent and moderate reformer named Émile Olivier. Napoleon adopted what to modern eyes was a more truly democratic constitutional structure. The Legislature could initiate laws and meaningfully debate and approve or reject the budget. Ministers could be drawn from the *corps législatif* and Senate debates would be public. The popularity of this liberal democratization was overwhelmingly confirmed in a plebiscite. The result of this was that the Second Empire, on the eve of catastrophe, had achieved a sort of internal compromise between liberalism and illiberalism, democracy and personal rule that may have endured had not Napoleon's confused foreign policy tumbled it into disaster in 1870.

Foreign policy

Napoleon III's foreign policy was vague and at times contradictory. He believed in nationalism, but not to the extent that it would harm French interests. He expressed a desire for European peace, but harboured expansionist ambitions. He saw France as the future arbiter of Europe, but depended on British friendship. He sought France's natural frontiers and yet stationed troops in the Papal States and embarked on a futile Mexican adventure. It is questionable that he had the diplomatic skill that was required to pursue such a disjointed policy and his handling of foreign policy often paled in comparison to his two great contemporaries, Cavour and Bismarck. Napoleon seemed to adhere to the old adage that "war is diplomacy carried on by other means", but war brings economic and social costs that traditional diplomacy generally does not and this too is the history of the Second Empire. Napoleon's domestic policy is often overshadowed by the blunders in foreign policy that led to the collapse of the Second Empire, but it is important to understand that the two were not independent of each other.

Activity:

Artistic opposition

The following is a list of writers, musicians, intellectuals and artists who were critical of the rule of Napoleon III. Choose one to research. How did they express their views? To what extent do you agree with your chosen artist? Explain your answer.

- Karl Marx
- Victor Hugo
- George Sand
- Alphonse Lamartine
- Charles Baudelaire

The Crimean War

A foreign policy goal that emerged early in Napoleon III's reign was reversal of the 1815 Vienna settlement. It was not that France suffered much if at all under the terms of the Congress, in fact sound arguments can be made that given the context, France did quite well at the Congress. In some ways it was the mechanism of the Metternich system that sat poorly with Napoleon. Its anti-liberal agenda and the fact that it was essentially administered by Vienna and under the watchful eye of the Tsar rankled with Napoleon. There is also Napoleon's family history with both the Austrian Hapsburgs and the Tsar that cannot be ignored. Napoleon III frequently invoked his uncle's image, history and aims—as he saw them—when explaining both foreign and domestic policy and the fact that it was in the snows of Russia that the First Empire died remained with Napoleon III. In one sense, however, he was determined to make a break with the diplomatic legacy of his uncle. While the Russian winter may have done its share in the demise of the First Empire, the intransigent position of the United Kingdom throughout the Napoleonic Wars, as Napoleon II saw it, was equally to blame. He was, therefore, determined to align French and British diplomacy more closely. Events in the deteriorating Ottoman Empire would present an opportunity to begin this process.

The issues underpinning the outbreak of the Crimean War were generations old. Russia desired access to the Mediterranean. Austria sought greater access to the Black Sea. The Ottomans sought to halt the long erosion of their position in the region. The British wished to maintain its virtual monopoly of sea power. The French had long had commercial and religious interests in the **Levant**. But why would these age-old issues bring the Great Powers to War in 1854? The surface issue that brought them to blows in 1854 was religious. The French had recently secured rights for Catholic Christians in the Holy Land, but under Russian pressure these had been withdrawn. Russia further claimed the right to protect all Christians in the Ottoman Empire and occupied the Danubian Principalities of Moldavia and Wallachia in 1853 to carry out this mission. While on the surface this was a religious move, it was in reality a clear expansion of Russia influence in the region and as such demanded a response from the other powers.

The first response was diplomatic and seemed to bear fruit. The Tsar agreed to the evacuation of the principalities in exchange for concessions from the Sultan. Emboldened by the international support he believed he had, the Sultan refused, much to the dismay of France, Britain and Austria. Russia subsequently declared war and inflicted a significant naval defeat on the Sultan at Sinope. The United Kingdom and France now faced the very real prospect of a Russia fleet operating in the Mediterranean. While Napoleon continued to seek a diplomatic solution, understanding that war was deeply unpopular in France and not wishing to jeopardize his young regime, war clouds loomed. When his efforts came to naught, the United Kingdom and France declared war in March 1854.

Levant An area encompassing the Eastern Mediterranean.

Discussion point:

Russian access to the Mediterranean had long been a Russian foreign policy goal. How had Russia tried to realize this goal in the past? Why had it been unsuccessful?

If Napoleon's motivation for entering the war was to improve France's military prestige, the Crimean was at least a partial success. The French forces, led by professional officers and capitalizing on North African experience, campaigned well. The industrializing French economy was able to provide adequate supplies initially. But as Napoleon had feared, the war soon put strains on the French economy. In fact, the industrialization that served French arms so well showed itself to be a double-edged sword. The French government had to compete for credit with new industrial concerns. Prices rose and with them public discontent. By 1855 Napoleon was satisfied enough to look for peace. Russia had been humbled, her influence in the Balkans contained and Christian rights reaffirmed. France had drawn closer to the British diplomatically, visiting the United Kingdom and privately corresponding with both Lord Palmerston and Queen Victoria who would visit Paris in 1855, despite an anti-French British public. As Napoleon had hoped, this was accomplished partially by French arms and the terms settled in Paris. The Crimean War had begun the major readjustment of the Vienna settlement of 1815 for which Napoleon had been looking.

Italy

While France's diplomatic star had begun to rise again on the strength of her participation in the Crimean War and the subsequent Congress of Paris, Europe's two main reactionary powers, and the two most wedded to the maintenance of the Vienna settlement of 1815, were in diplomatic decline. During the war, Austria had abandoned Russia and not sufficiently supported the allies, finding herself isolated in the aftermath. Russia had suffered a humiliation of arms that would drive her to withdraw from the continent for half a century. Napoleon now looked for opportunities to translate this new-found power into action. The disjointed Italian peninsula seemed to supply both the ideological and geo-political opportunity. Napoleon had been a conspiratorial nationalist early in his life and now found himself at the head of the most powerful continental power and in a position to affect real nationalist change.

By 1858, Napoleon's eye turned more directly to Italian intervention. In January an unbalanced Italian nationalist turned his outrage at Napoleon's sluggish support for the cause into an assassination attempt. The would-be assassin, Felice Orsini, made an impassioned plea for the Emperor to help liberate his people, one that Napoleon seemed to heed. By July of that year Cavour and Napoleon were at Plombières and in a short meeting agreed on the form of that support. France would commit 200,000 men to a war against Austria. The war was to be limited in scope, driving the Austrian forces from the northern Italian states of Lombardy and Venetia, but leaving the Papal States unscathed. For its trouble France would receive Savoy and Nice. The course for war seemed to be set. Powerful forces, however, were gathering against it. French public opinion, of which Napoleon was always mindful, was decidedly anti-war. The British position also opposed the war. To avert what it considered to be a reckless endangering of the stability that had been re-established after Crimea, the United Kingdom encouraged reform in the Italian states and began to work for a congress to settle the supposed causes of the war. The intervention of Prussia and to a lesser extent, Russia, was

Discussion point:

How was the industrial revolution transforming the military of other European powers such as the United Kingdom?

also a dangerous possibility. Much to Cavour's chagrin, the opportunity for war was slipping through his fingers. And so, it must have been with some relief that he received an ultimatum from Austria demanding unilateral Sardinian disarmament. Cavour knew that his refusal would bring war with Austria and activate the alliance with France that he had worked hard to secure.

French intervention in the Italian War of 1859 was greeted by the traditional war enthusiasm that was the hallmark of the hyper-nationalist mid-19th century, but this soon gave way to indifference and, in the capital, outright hostility. Napoleon took command of the French forces and managed to muster enough luck to win victories over the incompetently led Austria forces. But the reality of war in the industrial age gave Napoleon pause—2,300 French soldiers killed in two battles—as did the intelligence that the Prussians were concentrating troops on the Rhine frontier. After a rational examination of the matter, Napoleon sought a separate peace with the Austrian Emperor at Villafranca, later formalized in the Treaty of Zürich. While on the surface, this war may seem a moderate French success, beyond the battle victories the results were far more ambiguous. Napoleon had not secured Nice and Savoy—although this would come a short time later. He had not seen the entirety of Northern Italy wrested from the Austrians. Events in the Central Duchies had outstripped his initial plans and were now out of his control. The expanded Piedmont—both in influence and area—threatened the position of the Pope, which in turn made French Catholics anxious and the continued presence of French troops in the Papal States necessary. Abandoning Piedmont, as he had, meant that Cavour's search for friends could turn to other sponsors, Prussia perhaps. His reputation suffered and incurred the suspicion of the British.

Africa and elsewhere

The Second Empire looked to the massive African continent for glory and riches, as did other European powers. Napoleon oversaw the expansion and modernization of France's Algerian holdings and the systematic development and commercial exploitation of West African territories. Napoleon was an important backer of Ferdinand de Lesseps' Suez Canal project, seeing in it glimpses of his dream of a kind of modern enlightened imperialism. While a brilliant engineering and commercial success, the canal further destabilized the region politically as it presented both threat and opportunity to the European powers that had interests in the region—the United Kingdom, the Ottoman Empire and Russia. In the Far East, Napoleon was tempted into the first of France's Indo-Chinese wars and eventually secured a colony in this region, which expanded to become Cambodia. He also gained territory in China and the Pacific.

Perhaps the most curious of Napoleon III's colonial adventures was his Mexican enterprise. In the 1860s Mexico entered into a period of instability and civil war. When Benito Juárez emerged as the victor he suspended payment on Mexico's debt. When this was added to the new Mexican government's generally anti-clerical position, Napoleon lit on a bold—and, ultimately, foolish—course of action. French intervention in Mexico was initially part of a joint French, Spanish

---

Activity:

The Orsini plot

Write a newspaper article on the Orsini plot and its aftermath from the perspective of one of the following:

- an Italian Nationalist
- a French Nationalist
- the French government
- the Austrian government

Discussion point:
The Just War Theory

The 13th-century Christian Theologian Augustine developed what has become known as the "Just War Theory." In short, this theory posits certain conditions that must be met before a war is just. According to a more recent definition, for a war to be "just" it must:

- have a just cause
- be a last resort
- be declared by a recognized authority
- have just intentions
- have a reasonable chance of success
- have an end that is proportionate to its means.

To what extent do the wars of Louis Napoleon comply with these conditions? What criteria would you use to judge whether or not a war is justified?

and British show of force. But when the Anglo-Spanish force withdrew, the French remained. What the French military proved unable to achieve, having been defeated by Juárez's forces at Puebla, Napoleon attempted to secure by dynastic manipulation. He placed Maximilian, brother of the Austrian Emperor, on the throne of Mexico. The folly of the Mexican adventure was laid bare when more immediate issues in Europe demanded that Napoleon abandon his would-be client and withdraw his forces. Five years in Mexico had cost the French much and benefited the Empire not at all.

France and Germany

With one portion of his army tied up half way around the globe in Mexico and another protecting the Pope in Rome, it must have been with some alarm that Napoleon witnessed the rebirth of the Prussian military. His Italian, Mexican and African meddling ensured that the major European powers greeted French diplomacy with suspicion at precisely the time when she would need friends. After meeting Bismarck at Biarritz in 1865, Napoleon convinced himself of the reality of what was in fact a dangerous illusion. The illusion lay in the idea that France could remain neutral in any future Austro-Prussian conflict while maintaining her position in Europe, or perhaps even improve it by picking up the Rhineland in the wake of a Prussian defeat. At worst he saw a long and bloody war in which both his continental rivals would punch themselves to exhaustion, leaving him the arbiter of Europe. At best, the Austrians would win the war and he could take the Rhineland as it pleased him and, by the terms of an agreement with the Austrian Emperor, Venetia would be turned over to Italy as he had always hoped and promised it would be. While it is true that the Austrian military collapse was by no means obvious leading up to the war and took much of Europe by surprise, by sitting it out, Napoleon left the diplomatic field to Bismarck giving himself no real claims in the event of a Prussian victory. This was indeed what occurred.

What Napoleon faced after the smoke of Sadowa had cleared was an Italy that was suspicious of France and indifferent to her pledges of support and an enlarged, strengthened Prussia no longer balanced against a second German power. The nightmare that French diplomats and generals had struggled against for two hundred years had come to pass—a unified German power on France's eastern frontier. The fact that the Southern German states were not formally part of that union was cold comfort as they had tight military alliances with Prussia. Napoleon tried in vain to secure the Rhine frontier as compensation for his benevolent neutrality, but Bismarck was predictably in no mood to negotiate. Napoleon then approached the King of the Netherlands with an offer to purchase Luxembourg. The condition set by the Dutch was Prussian consent that Bismarck, after gauging public opinion, declined to give. France would get nothing in the wake of the Austro-Prussian War and this increased domestic pressure on Napoleon's government and endangered his prestige. War is often attractive to those who wish to regain lost stature and as the 1860s drew to a close, the French preached peace while thinking of war.

> **Discussion point:**
>
> As Prussia and Austria moved closer to war, what options were open to Napoleon III? To what extent could he have prevented this war? How might he have benefited from it?

While wounded pride was certainly one motivation driving French foreign policy in the late 1860s, fear also played an important role. In the wake of the Luxembourg rebuff, Napoleon's diplomats began to seek alliances against the new threat on her eastern frontier, but there was little interest from the other European powers. Italy would only join with France if Napoleon withdrew his forces from Rome, something that the *corps législatif* would not countenance. Austria was in no hurry to place itself in the line of Prussian rifles in the near future. The growing talk of war in France worried the British, making them deeply suspicious of Napoleon's protestations of peaceful intent. France was very much alone.

It is perhaps the fear of this isolation that precipitated the French demands surrounding the **Hohenzollern candidature**. The Spanish throne sat vacant in 1868, turned down by a number of candidates. When Spanish diplomats offered the crown to King Wilhelm IV's cousin, Leopold, the French diplomatic nightmare got immeasurably worse, for it created the fear of being surrounded. This prospect persuaded both King Wilhelm and Leopold against the candidature. What seemed to bother the French was that the King's renunciation of the candidature was made as the head of the House of Hohenzollern, not as the King of Prussia. For French diplomatic pride to be salvaged, or so thought the French Foreign Office, Prussia, not just the Hohenzollerns, must disassociate itself from the matter. The subsequent French demand that the King pledge that no permission would ever be granted showed a remarkable lack of diplomatic savvy. The German public was outraged and Bismarck's clever editing of the King's telegram, when released to the press, ensured that the French would share the sentiment. France declared war on 19 July 1870.

The French public may have been ready for war but her army was not. Although on paper it was a large experienced force with modern weapons relying on a sound rail infrastructure. The reality was that the mobilization was haphazard and inefficient. A little over half the expected troops arrived at the front leaving the French 275,000 soldiers to face over 450,000 German troops. The German General Staff under von Moltke, though far from perfect, was managing the mobilization with skill that the French command lacked. Napoleon took command of the French forces and with his generals predictably blundered into a series of engagements during the first half of August. By 3 September the Prussians had mauled a French army under the command of

> **Hohenzollern candidature**
> The proposal by the Spanish government that would give the Spanish throne to Prince Leopold, a member of the Catholic branch of the Hohenzollern royal family.

Activity:
Napoleon III and nationalism
A written debate

Individually, research the Napoleon III's career and foreign policies and complete the following chart. Once you have completed your research, find a partner to debate the following statement:

"Napoleon III was a nationalist."

One of you will take the positive side and the other will argue the negative. Each of you will write a defence of your position using the research for specific support. Once you have both finished, exchange papers and write a rebuttal to the specific points made by your partner. Once you have completed the rebuttal, take some time to discuss the role of the revolutions in the history of 19th-century nationalism.

	Evidence of nationalism	Evidence of imperialism
Italy		
Crimean War		
Mexico		
Germany		
Other		

Napoleon was captured after the French forces at Sedan surrendered to the Prussians.

 Why was Napoleon III leading the French army when he had only limited military experience?

General McMahon and the Emperor himself at Sedan forcing it to surrender. The war would continue for months, but the battle of Sedan marked the functional end of the French Second Empire.

Collapse and Commune

The *corps législatif* did not even wait until the end of the war to put an end to the Empire, establishing the Third Republic under a provisional government on 4 September 1870 bowing to the pressure of yet another Paris insurrection. In a bid for popular support the provisional government chose to continue the war and rally the country behind it. The net result of these efforts was a catastrophic siege of Paris and the further humiliation of the French army. After four months of shelling and starvation the capital surrendered and German troops began their two and a half year occupation of France.

Napoleon III and Bismarck after the Battle of Sedan. A woodcut after a painting from 1876 by Wilhelm Camphausen.

Although the French would manage to pay the huge **war indemnity** demanded by the Germans in a remarkably short period of time, it is hard to overstate the extent of the disaster that the Franco-Prussian War was for France. The immediate results were, apart from the indemnity of five billion francs, the loss of the frontier territories of Alsace and Lorraine with their mines, the loss of 140,000 soldiers and the humiliation of the army, political instability to which would be added the looming spectre of civil war.

> **War indemnity** A sum of money paid by the losing side in a war to compensate for damages caused.

It was Bismarck who demanded that elections be held once the siege of Paris was lifted so that it would be with a duly elected and thus more legitimate government with which he would conclude the terms of peace. The elections of February 1871 revealed a France, especially outside of the capital, that was looking to a stable, traditionally conservative government in the harsh light of a brief but horrific war. The results returned conservatives and monarchists to the National Assembly. Republicanism was thus far from a self-evident response to the ruin that Napoleon III's Empire had brought to France.

On this issue, as with many, France was divided. Radical politics had always been more popular in the capital and this was the case in 1871. By March the conservative government of Adolphe Thiers had refused to pay the National Guard while lifting a moratorium on rents and debts passed during the war, incensing the poorer citizens of the capital. In response to their treatment the National Guard rose against the government, which in turn fled to Versailles. The situation was quite confusing. The elected national government sat outside the capital, while an insurrectionary Commune governed

> **Activity:**
>
> ## Bismarck and Napoleon
>
> After Napoleon was captured at the Battle of Sedan, he met with Bismarck to negotiate the terms of the surrender of the French forces. Write a dialogue of the conversation that might have taken place between these two leaders. Include their visions for the future of Europe.

Paris with little in the way of direction or organization. The Paris Commune was essentially a committee set up to administer the city in the wake of the National Assembly's flight. Although its members represented both bourgeois and working-class elements, the Commune passed a number of moderate socialist laws including wage and price controls. Such legislation however was subordinated to the overarching concern with political survival. By April the regular army, loyal to the Versailles government, was fighting with elements of the National Guard determined to protect the Commune.

Given its limited constituency, the Commune was doomed from the start. The Versailles army stormed Paris on 21 May 1871, leading to terrible street fighting in which desperate **Communards** torched buildings and took hostages. Atrocities were committed by both sides, some 20,000 Parisians dying during the "Bloody Week". When the fires had subsided the victorious National Assembly ferreted out all suspected Communard sympathizers, arresting 40,000 and deporting 7,500 to penal colonies.

> **Communards** Supporters of the Paris Commune of 1871.

Activity:

Views on Louis Napoleon

Source A
Karl Marx

Driven by the contradictory demands of his situation, and being at the same time, like a juggler, under the necessity of keeping the public gaze on himself, as Napoleon's successor, by springing constant surprises—that is to say, under the necessity of arranging a coup d'état in miniature every day— Bonaparte throws the whole bourgeois economy into confusion, violates everything that seemed inviolable to the Revolution of 1848, makes some tolerant of revolution and makes others lust for it, and produces anarchy in the name of order, while at the same time stripping the entire state machinery of its halo, profaning it and making it at once loathsome and ridiculous.

Source: Marx, K. 1852. "The Eighteenth Brumaire of Louis Bonaparte." *The Marx/Engels Internet Archive.* http://www.marxists. org/archive/marx/works/1852/18th-brumaire/ch07.htm

Source B
Victor Hugo

Judging him apart from what he calls his "necessary acts", or his "great deeds", he is a vulgar, commonplace personage, puerile, theatrical, and vain. Those persons who are invited to St. Cloud, in the summer, receive with the invitation an order to bring a morning toilette and an evening toilette. He loves finery, display, feathers, embroidery, tinsel and spangles, big words, and grand titles—everything that makes a noise and glitter, all the glassware of power. In his capacity of cousin to the battle of Austerlitz, he dresses as a general. He cares little about being despised; he contents himself with the appearance of respect.

Source: Hugo, V. 1909. *The Little Napoleon.* Boston, USA. Little Brown and Company. p. 26

Source C

Campaigning for President, France, December 1848, from an unsigned woodcut published in the Leipzig-based *Illustrierte Zeitung* on 30 December 1848.

Questions

1 Find evidence to support the opinions of Louis Napoleon expressed by Hugo and Marx. What evidence can you find that refutes their point of view?

2 Evaluate the views of Napoleon III expressed in sources A and B.

3 Compare and contrast sources A, B and C.

4 Write your own evaluation of the character and career of Napoleon III.

The Third Republic

. . . .

It may seem strange that France would establish a republic shortly
after it had just decisively defeated the radical republicans of the
Paris Commune. The reality was that the monarchists were deeply
divided and had been since the 1830s. Some French monarchists
advocated a return of the Bourbons to the throne of France while
others favoured a monarchy under the Orléans branch of the royal
family. The divisions between the houses and their supporters made
compromise unlikely. In the absence of such a compromise, the
French government moved carefully forward under the guidance of
Adolphe Thiers, looking for all the world like a republic, but a
conservative and cautious one. In this way we can see that Thiers
cleverly co-opted the main attraction of the monarchists—stability—
and dressed it in republican robes. He had a moderate tax position
and moved to restore the effectiveness of the army, both very popular
throughout France. Thiers also understood that the first step to the
restoration of national dignity after the defeat in the Franco-Prussian
War and the bloody repression of the Commune was to pay the five
billion franc indemnity as soon as possible so that the occupying
German army could retire.

For his efforts Thiers was driven from office in 1873 by conservatives
who thought the Republic looked too republican. With the Commune
still fresh in their memory, regardless of their role in suppressing it,
the government passed to Marshall McMahon of Sedan infamy.
What was the new non-republican republic to look like? The two
monarchist factions were no closer to compromise in 1873 than
they had been in 1871 and the National Assembly itself was deeply
divided. Agreement on a single, coherent and comprehensive
constitution seemed hopeless. Such being the case, the Assembly
passed a number of laws that, when taken together, formed a
constitution of sorts.

- The Republic would be led by an elected president.
- The president's term of office was seven years and he could stand
  for re-election.
- The president could dissolve the Assembly.
- A council of ministers was to be led by a premier.
- The legislative assembly was bi-cameral—a Senate and a Chamber
  of Deputies.
- One third of the Senate was elected for life, the remainder to nine
  year terms.
- Senate elections were to be from single-member constituencies
  rather than from a system of proportional representation.
- The Chamber of Deputies was elected by universal adult male
  suffrage.

When elections were held to for the "new" Chamber and Senate in
1875, overtly republican candidates won the day in both houses.
Although the "constitution" had been cobbled together in an effort to
enhance stability and to a large extent benefit the conservatives, the

electorate seemed just as suspicious of monarchists as they were of republicans, if not more so. Perhaps a stable, moderately conservative republic was the answer.

The form of the new republic would be further clarified in 1877. McMahon dissolved the Assembly, as was his right under the constitution, and attempted to replace the premier and council of ministers, that had the support of the Assembly, with his own hand-picked ministers who had no such support. The ensuing campaign and elections established the principle of **responsible government** in the Third Republic. The electorate overwhelmingly returned republicans to both the Senate and the Chamber. The premier and the ministers would from that point in practice be responsible to the Assembly and not the President whose position would gradually become more ceremonial. The real power lay in the hands of the Council of Ministers and the Premier who needed to have the support of a majority of the Assembly to remain in office. In the coming years the wide variety and number of parties represented in the Assembly made the achievement of such a majority difficult and dependent on ever-changing coalitions. In such a case, effective governance devolved onto the complex bureaucracy and had the effect of centralizing control in France.

> **Responsible government** A principle on government in which the executive is accountable to the electorate through the legislative branch of government.

The premiers who controlled the council of ministers during the years 1877–85 complimented this bureaucratization. While France was a republic, it was certainly not a radical republic. Memories of the Commune ensured that men like Léon Gambetta, Charles-Louis Freycinet and Jules Ferry steered a moderate conservative course, while at the same time memories of Napoleon III's authoritarianism kept the monarchist parties at bay. French political life remained divided between monarchists, Bonapartists, republicans and the radical left, but the moderate republic seemed initially to be able to mediate between these forces and establish itself as the most effective, or perhaps least objectionable, to the voting public. The voting public itself was mollified by the nature of politics in the Third Republic. Deputies to the Assembly depended on the votes of their constituents for their livelihood and thus worked to support local interests, which seemed to trump larger ideological issues. This strengthening of local democracy was a double-edged sword in that it meant that, because of the principle of responsible government, the ruling administration generally enjoyed a good deal of popular legitimacy, but could also founder on the rocks of the myriad local interests that could present themselves in any one session of the assembly.

Social legislation

As republicanism became more inclusive in the first decade of the Third Republic, it made modest gains in social legislation. In 1881 the government established freedom of the press and general expression. Bureaucratic appointments became subject to an examination and not patronage. Democracy was extended to local elections and life-memberships for Senate seats were abolished.

Closely related to the expansion of democracy was the issue of public education. The 19th-century liberal reasoning was that if democracy was to be effective and meaningful, the choices made by the electorate must be reasoned, and free from undue influence. For this to be the case the voters had to be educated and this education must be managed by the state and not other interests such as the church. This line of argument fell in line with the growing bureaucratization of the state. For many liberals, education was the great social equalizer. While their conservative opponents believed in a system that placed great stock on the authority of birth and tradition, by definition closed to the majority of the population, liberals believed in the equality of opportunity afforded by education. While liberal opinion may have been divided on the extent to which the state should pay for that education, the principle of public education and its concomitant attack on the power of the Catholic Church brought liberals and the more radical left together in France in the early years of the Third Republic.

The Republic established compulsory state- funded primary education in 1882. Teaching was regularized through state-run teaching colleges, which were opened to women. Church influence was purged from universities. This new state education preached the principles of the Third Republic including liberal rights, science and technology. This anti-clericalism of the republicans and the animosity it engendered among conservative Catholics was never far below the surface of French society during the first decades of the Third Republic. It was occasionally obscured by short outbursts of national unity and pride as in the years leading up to and following the International Exhibition. Pope Leo XIII who officially recognized the French Republic in 1891 and instructed French Catholics to do the same furthered this period of relative peace between secular and clerical forces. Nevertheless, in times of crisis and stress the deep divisions that split French society would again appear.

Open ideological warfare would break out between the Church and the Republic in the wake of the Dreyfus Affair. The deep divisions reopened by the affair led a leftist-dominated Assembly to the passage of a number of laws in 1905 that would forever sever the connection between Church and state in France.

- Clergy were taken off the states' payroll.
- Church land was confiscated.
- The management of Catholic Parishes was turned over to laymen.

While some of these measures would eventually be blunted, by 1905 the official relationship with the Catholic Church had been largely swept away.

Crisis and scandal

It is something of a truism in history that extremist political parties emerge when states face economic or social crisis. Such was the case in the mid 1880s in France. The French economy was in recession and crops were failing. When the French electorate went to the polls in 1885 it registered its deep sense of insecurity by dramatically increasing right-wing nationalist representation in the Assembly. As a bulwark against this potential threat, the premier minister appointed a Council of Ministers with strong republican reputations. Over the course of the next three years French politics seemed to be

Discussion point:

Who controls and pays for education in your country?

What choices do people have when choosing schools in your country?

falling into a familiar pattern. The Minister of War, General George Boulanger, courted the army with reforms designed to please all levels of the military while he fanned nationalist flames by taking an increasingly hard line against Germany, which proved wildly popular with French voters. The republican government rightly saw in his growing popularity a serious threat and removed him, after which he ran as a candidate transforming his popularity into

Georges Boulanger (1837–1891)

Boulanger was a French general who had served throughout the French Empire and against the Prussians in 1870. He played a role in the suppression of the Paris Commune in 1871. After serving as commander in Tunisia he returned to France and became a politician serving as minister of war in the administration of Freycinet. He openly courted fame and became a popular figure amongst Bonapartists and royalists. Between January and April 1889 his followers clamoured for him to seize power. Instead he fled to Belgium and then Britain, committing suicide in 1891.

something of a movement. Soon the term "Boulangism" was bandied about in a way that Bonapartism once had been. "Boulangist" candidates began to make inroads in the Assembly. As they had in 1799, 1830, and 1852, the French seemed poised to turn the reigns of power over to a strongman with vague notions of domestic peace and foreign glory. The key difference is that Napoleon I, Louis-Phillipe and Napoleon III had been more than willing to seize these reigns when proffered, while Boulanger shrunk from the possibility of a coup in January 1889 when his followers filled the streets of Paris. He later fled to Belgium after the Assembly made to prosecute him for treason in April of that year. The Republic had survived and in response retrenched its essentially conservative approach to governing.

One of the greatest engineering feats of the 19th century was the Suez Canal, built, in large measure, by Egyptian labour and French money, organized by Ferdinand de Lesseps. Hoping that he could repeat this success in Panama, a joint stock company was set up with Lesseps as the president. The company began to cut across the Isthmus of Panama in 1881 and immediately encountered serious setbacks, setbacks that would accumulate over the next seven years and require ever-larger injections of money. By 1888 the financial problems proved too difficult to overcome and the company wound up its operations over the next three years, dissolving in 1891. The financial repercussions of the bankruptcy were staggering. Not only had the substantial public money granted by the government to the company vanished into the jungles of Central America, but close to a million French investors had also lost money in the collapse. The scandal arose when it was discovered that a substantial amount of that money had in fact disappeared into the pockets of politicians and officials in the form of bribes.

The scandal forever tarred the reputation of the leading politicians from the political generation that had established the Republic and in many ways paved the way for a new group of men, men like Raymond Poincaré and Delcassé, to take the helm of the republic, a group that would guide France through the next turbulent decades. While the Panama Scandal had altered the characters, the script of the Third Republic remained largely unchanged. It would continue, under the guidance of this new political generation, as a bourgeois conservative republic managed by a professional civil service. The Panama Scandal did not, in the end, shake French society to its core the way that the Dreyfus Affair would.

The Dreyfus Affair

In September 1894 a document came to rest on the desk of Hubert-Joseph Henry, a French intelligence officer. The document had come from the trash of a German military attaché stationed in Paris. It revealed that sensitive military information was being passed from a member of the French **General Staff** to the Germans. Still smarting from the humiliation of 1871, the French army took the matter extremely seriously and began to ferret out the traitor. A cursory investigation seemed to point to a recent addition to the General Staff, a Captain Alfred Dreyfus, as the culprit. A case of dubious and, at times, fabricated evidence was gathered and the Captain was arrested in October 1894. His court martial in November of that year duly confirmed the guilt that the General Staff had created and Dreyfus was sent to the French penal colony on Devil's Island off the coast of French Guiana.

Two years later, evidence came to light that seemed to exonerate Dreyfus, but this evidence was either suppressed or rejected by the French military, which refused to reopen the case. There are a number of explanations for the French army's rush to convict and reticence to re-examine the case against Dreyfus. With its reputation still tarnished from the Franco-Prussian War, the General Staff was unwilling to allow a long trial and subsequent acquittal to further besmirch the competence of the army. The more the senior officers of the army proclaimed Dreyfus's guilt, the harder it became to back down. As the army dug in, it produced ever-more outlandish evidence "proving" Dreyfus's guilt. The government was tied to the army's case; if Dreyfus was found to be innocent, the government would fall and this produced yet another layer of resistance to reopening the case. The conviction of Dreyfus, who was Jewish, also exposed a deep current of **anti-Semitism** in the army and the country as a whole. Such currents came to the surface in times of social crisis in France and elsewhere and during the Dreyfus Affair the Parisian anti-Semitic press ranted at the Jewish conspiracy that they claimed threatened France from within.

> **General Staff** The organized group of officers charged with the over-all co-ordination of military affairs and operations.

> **Activity:**
> ### The Dreyfus Affair
> Much of the vitriolic war of words that surrounded the Dreyfus affair was carried out in the press. Write a newspaper article from the perspective of either a Dreyfusard or an anti-Dreyfusard.

> **Anti-Semitism** A prejudice against Jews.

> ### Alfred Dreyfus (1859–1935)
> Dreyfus came from a wealthy Jewish family in Alsace. He entered the military and rose to the rank of Captain. In 1894, after becoming a staff officer, he was accused of transmitting secret documents to the Germans. Dreyfus was then tried for treason on fabricated evidence and sentenced to life imprisonment on Devil's Island. A core of supporters mounted a public campaign for his retrial, which was met by a vitriolic and often anti-Semitic support of the guilty plea. He was eventually exonerated and served with distinction in the First World War.

Between 1896 and 1898 the two sides in the affair solidified and raged at each other with a ferocity that was unprecedented in French society. While the "Dreyfusards" were those who generally believed in the essential innocence of Dreyfus, more significantly, they represented the forces of secular republicanism. As the affair split communities and even families, the Dreyfusards portrayed themselves as the progressive modern vision of France. They opposed what they saw as the backward and corrupt old France embodied in the army and the Church.

The rehabilitation of Alfred Dreyfus. Dreyfus, photographed in 1906, is standing second from the right.

They railed against the often overt anti-Semitism of the case and France in general. The Dreyfusards most eloquent champion was the writer Émile Zola who published his famous tract *J'Accuse* as an indictment of the anti-Dreyfusards and all that they stood for. Zola succeeded in getting himself prosecuted for his words and used his own trial to further expose the injustice of the Dreyfus case. Against Zola's and the Dreyfusards' vision of France the anti-Dreyfusards saw in the case an attempt to subvert the traditional order of France. Conservatives, monarchists and self-styled patriots flocked to the anti-Dreyfus banner as a bulwark against what they saw as modern and dangerous ideas like republicanism, secularism and socialism. Some even believed that Dreyfus and the efforts to free him part of a wider Jewish conspiracy, the so-called "Syndicate". Even those who were not convinced of Dreyfus's guilt believed the efforts to reopen the case would weaken France in the face of its German enemy. In many ways the actual guilt or innocence of Alfred Dreyfus became a secondary matter to the broader issues in the bitter debate.

The 25 daily newspapers in Paris carried on the battle, ensuring that it was in the public eye constantly for two years. The army elected to retry Dreyfus in 1899, but again found him guilty, to the outrage of the Dreyfusards. The Affair again threatened to tear the country apart. The government decided that the best chance of salvaging social stability was to pardon Dreyfus and did so in 1899. In 1906 the injustice was reversed when he was exonerated and returned to the army. The Affair had diverted the republic from other matters of state for the better part of a decade, but the republic and republicanism had survived yet another threat to its legitimacy and was thus in a stronger position *vis a vis* its enemies than before the Affair.

"If you shut up truth, and bury it underground, it will but grow."

Émile Zola

In 1906 Dreyfus was formally acquitted and readmitted into the French army. It had been a civilian court that cleared Dreyfus, a verdict by which the army abided.

The French army, however, did not officially declare Dreyfus innocent until 1995.

 Why would it take so many years for the French army to overturn the guilty verdict?

Activity:

J'Accuse …!

The following is an excerpt from the 13 January 1898 edition of the Paris newspaper *L'Aurore*. It is an open letter to the President of the French Third Republic written by the influential writer Émile Zola.

> *You appear radiant in the apotheosis of this patriotic festival that the Russian alliance was for France, and you prepare to preside over the solemn triumph of our World Fair, which will crown our great century of work, truth and freedom. But what a spot of mud on your name—I was going to say on your reign—is this abominable Dreyfus affair! A council of war, under order, has just dared to acquit Esterhazy, a great blow to all truth, all justice. And it is finished, France has this stain on her cheek, History will write that it was under your presidency that such a social crime could be committed. …*
>
> *As for the people I accuse, I do not know them, I never saw them, I have against them neither resentment nor hatred.*

> *They are for me only entities, spirits of social evil. And the act I accomplished here is only a revolutionary mean for hastening the explosion of truth and justice.*

Questions

1 Explain the reference "the Russian Alliance" and "our World Fair". What, according to Zola, is their relationship to the Dreyfus Affair?

2 What does Zola mean when he calls the Affair a "social" crime? What does he mean by "social evil"?

3 What are the strengths and weaknesses of this open letter as a historical source for historians studying the Dreyfus Affair?

Socio-economic developments

In the years 1871–99 The Third Republic seemed to lurch from crisis to crisis. German occupation, Boulanger, Panama, Dreyfus all sapped the attention and energy of the Republic and as such diverted the country from the economic progress that its neighbors were enjoying. The economic picture in France in the last decades of the 19th century was complicated. Domestically, there grew a certain degree of stability and even prosperity. Railways were again built and there was a general improvement in infrastructure. An advanced banking system moved capital around the country with ease and exported it to countries throughout Europe allowing industries, new and old, to expand. This capital also served to bolster France's foreign policy during this period. Protectionist policies sheltered French agriculture from competition with British, German and American products. These years witnessed an expansion of French iron and coal production as well as manufacturing. Such domestic economic prosperity translated into moderately high living standards for much of the French population, a situation helped by the slowing population growth.

Problems begin to arise when these gains are compared to France's European neighbours/competitors during this same period. This realization was not lost on French policy makers whose move to protectionism in the late 1880s and 1890s signaled economic insecurity *vis a vis* Germany, the UK and USA. Agricultural tariffs protected smallhold farms that were inefficient in comparative terms. Even though French capital permeated markets throughout Europe, French exports were low in comparison to other powers. French manufacturing was also inefficient compared to Germany and the United Kingdom. Even the vaunted French wine industry continued to suffer from the effects of the *phylloxera* blight that destroyed 40 per cent of the French grape crop in the 1860s and 1870s. Even in demographics (population), France lagged behind Germany.

Discussion point:

The world economy was experiencing significant change in the last 30 years of the 19th century. What were these changes?

 Why was France unable to keep pace with other economic powers during this period?

The comparative deficiencies in French industry and the country's population came at a very inopportune time in French history. Relations with Germany were exceedingly tense. Public mood cried for *"revanche"* (revenge) for the indignity of the 1871 defeat. Right-wing politicians made careers on the demand for the repatriation of Alsace and Lorraine. At the same time the military was convulsed by the destructive Dreyfus Affair and a general crisis of confidence generated by the upheaval. Relations with the United Kingdom were also sensitive. France on the one hand wanted British aid against Germany, but at the same time public opinion wanted to satisfy France's claims to **Fashoda**. The Third Republic attempted to address these issues with a conscription programme that drafted 80 per cent of eligible males into the military, creating an army disproportionate in size to the country's industrial and demographic position in Europe. While this might stand France in good stead against powers like Austria, it was still behind Germany, which had more men of military age to call upon in times of war. Germany spent far more on its military and yet this sum amounted to a smaller percentage of the national income than in France.

> **Fashoda** A village in central Africa over which the British and French both had claims. The situation nearly came to war in 1898.

The rise of the left

As the smoke of the Dreyfus Affair settled, and Dreyfus himself was reintegrated first into French society and by 1906 into the army, those who had staked their careers and reputations on his guilt were removed from positions in the army and the government. The defeat of the right brought moderate left-wing coalitions such as the administration of Waldeck-Rousseau to power in 1899. The final separation of church and state came under his watch, as did various pieces of labour legislation that improved workplace safety. Movement on more substantial social legislation such as social security and collective bargaining were slow in proceeding, alienating elements of the left. This alienation grew out of the fact that the Waldeck-Rousseau administration was made up of primarily of the Radical Republican Party and the Opportunist Republican Party, with some socialist representation. It was Republicanism that united this cabinet, not any consensus on social legislation. The core support for republicanism came from shopkeepers, the urban middle class and independent farmers. National stability and patriotism was the basis of their platform, not progressive social legislation. As disappointment mounted, the working class of France looked to other socialist alternatives. In 1899 these various alternatives came together in an attempt to find common cause. Predictably this came to naught, but two major left-wing parties rose out of the meeting. The dividing line between the two parties, the French Socialist Party and the Socialist Party of France, was the degree to which they would co-operate with the Waldeck-Rousseau government. The more radical Socialist Party of France advocated non-cooperation and protest, while the more pacifist French Socialist Party under the brilliant orator Jean Jaurès preached the achievement of political power through the democratic structures of the Republic. The two parties reconciled in 1905 as the Section *Française de l'Internationale Ouvrière* (SFIO) with a non-cooperation platform and would remain outside official government participation until the eve of the First World War.

> **Activity:**
> **Labour legislation**
>
> Labour legislation was an important part of social legislation throughout Europe at the turn of the century. Conduct some research into labour laws in France from 1890–1914. To what extent did these laws satisfy labour organizers during this period? Use the following headings to guide your research.
>
> ● Hours
> ● Wages
> ● Safety
> ● Child labour
> ● Collective bargaining
> ● Labour Unions
> ● Strikes

The trade union movement in France at the turn of the century was pulled between these various socialist parties, but also found a home in the radical **syndicalist** movement led by Georges Sorel. Sorel preached the primacy of the labour union as the key revolutionary body that would use the general strike to press for concessions from the government. As such, they too adopted non-cooperation with liberal-democratic institutions as a central tenet. Various French labour unions joined together in the Conféderation Général du Travail (CGT) in 1895 and by 1905 had support throughout the country. From this point, labour unrest grew. A miner's strike in 1906 led to the government using force to protect strike-breakers. After postal workers went on strike in 1909, the government passed legislation forbidding the civil service from striking. The government broke a railway strike with the help of the army in 1911. In the end, the non-cooperation strategy of the Socialists and syndicalists left the government and the Chamber of Deputies with little to balance the moderate and more radical political right that continued to participate in the democratic process to the end that even after the Dreyfus Affair, French society continued to be deeply split.

Syndicalist An approach to socialism based on the organization of trades unions into larger federations or syndicates.

Discussion point:

The Syndicalist movement lasted well into the 20th Century. Where was it popular? Why was it popular in these places? To what extent was the Syndicalist movement successful in these places?

The Third Republic: an assessment

On the eve of the First World War, France was only moderately less divided than it had been in the wake of the Franco-Prussian War. Leftists were split between the Socialists, Marxists, and the syndicalists, arguing the relative merits of participating on the government. While they fought, the right began to recover from its defeat in the Dreyfus Affair. Monarchists and Catholic parties continued their co-operation with the government and were thus able to contribute to post Dreyfus policies. The Republicans that emerged in the post 1871 political climate were far from the radical republicans that had been defeated during the Commune. Instead they were the opportunists, moderate centre-right Republican patriots who sought stability in the cloak of republicanism. They were solidly bourgeois and committed to a measured recovery from the defeat of 1871. As such they looked with disdain on the radicals of both left and right. This stability, however, was constantly undercut by the various scandals that rocked French society in the last decade of the 19th century. The Third Republic's particular form of constitutional liberal democracy made for frequent changes of government formed out of necessity by coalitions and an inherently unstable legislature. The one issue on which most, though not all, could agree was the need for *revanche* against Germany. Unfortunately, the weakness of French industry and military compared to Germany made this unlikely. The insecurity of this cumulative reality further sapped the energies of the Third Republic as she was plunged into the general catastrophe of the First World War.

Activity:

A timeline of the Third Republic

Create a timeline of the governments of the Third Republic. What patterns do you notice? What does this tell us about the nature of politics in the Third Republic?

The United Kingdom, 1867–1900

Just as France experienced scandal, war, revolution, empire and republicanism in the second half of the 19th century, the United Kingdom of Great Britain and Ireland seemed the exemplar of stable, moderate parliamentary democracy. It had a two-party system and a limited franchise that kept politics toward the centre of the political spectrum. Its command of the seas limited the UK's potential enemies and protected its rich trade with an expanding Empire and other trading partners. Starting in the 1830s, Britain's constitutional monarchy eased cautiously toward moderate reform with only limited civil unrest, while revolution and war racked the Continent.

Significant political reform in 19th-century Britain, though long attempted, can only be traced from the Reform Act of 1832. Prior to 1832, the British parliamentary system had only been representative in a nominal sense. While the British social structure and economic base had changed dramatically since the **Glorious Revolution** of 1688, parliament had not. The population of Britain more than doubled and yet representation in the House of Commons had remained static, representation being based on place rather than population. New cities had emerged with no representation. Old communities whose populace was decimated by economic migration still enjoyed parliamentary representation disproportionate to their population. With a wary eye to the events on the continent and in the streets of London and other British cities, British politicians passed the Reform Act of 1832, which enlarged the electorate by some 60 per cent. Representation was redistributed to more accurately reflect the changes wrought by the industrial revolution.

> **Glorious Revolution** The revolution that deposed King James II and brought William of Orange to the throne of England.

Activity:

The Halévy Thesis

In 1962 the historian Élie Halévy developed a theory that attempted to explain why the revolutionary upheavals that rocked Continental Europe at the end of the 18th century and early 19th century did not spread to the United Kingdom.

The theory posits that it was the growth of Evangelical Methodism that gave the British a vent for revolutionary emotion. Methodism preached the virtues of individualism and self-help that, according to Halevy, replaced revolutionary ideologies such as radical republicanism and socialism.

Develop your own thesis as to why the Revolutions of 1848 did not spread to the UK. Be sure to support your thesis with historical evidence.

Party formation: Liberals and Conservatives

In the wake of the Great Reform Act of 1832, long-established political alignments began to shift. In many ways this shifting was only a reflection of the changing nature of economic power in Britain. The political battles of 1688 had left Britain with a legacy of a two-party political system, the Whigs and the Tories. It must be said, however, that these "parties" were not political parties in the modern sense. A more accurate term might be political "tendencies".

Because there was no membership, as such, of these parties, the boundaries between these two political interests were blurry and permeable. The years leading up to the Reform Act of 1832 saw years of Tory rule. But this Tory rule was an amorphous thing. In the 1820s young liberal Tories began to exert influence on the Tory party. Men like Sir Robert Peel began supporting urban reform, foreign independence movements, lower taxation and increased free trade—all denounced as dangerously "liberal" by more traditional Tories. By the time the Reform Act of 1832 was law, the Tory party was showing more signs of fracture. The pressures of Chartism and the great fight over the repeal of the **Corn Laws**, between 1839 and 1846, pushed **Peelite** Tories further from their traditional base and in fact closer to Reformers, Whigs, Radicals and Liberals, who had already been co-operating in the House of Commons as a *de facto* parliamentary Liberal party. At the same time the Tories, led by men like Lord Derby and Benjamin Disraeli, were realigning with more traditional Whigs in opposition to this new political force. The UK was on the brink of a more organized two-party system.

In June 1859 Liberal, Radical, Whig and Peelite Tories agreed in public to co-operate in the formation of the Liberal Party under the leadership of Lord Palmerston, who was equally loathed by the co-operating members and thus a suitable compromise as leader. A national party apparatus also began to develop during this period which made mobilization of support during general elections more efficient and aided the dissemination of liberal ideals. Local Liberal party organizations, clubs and associations spread throughout both urban and rural areas of England and this helped solidify a firmly recognizable liberal platform if not ideology.

While the Liberal/Conservative split in Britain was not strictly along class divisions, Liberalism emerged as the ideology of "new" Britain and took as its values those of its new constituencies:

- non-conformists
- laissez faire capitalists
- small urban shopkeepers
- artisans
- professionals
- anti-slavery reformers
- free-trader supporters.

The Conservative Party that formed in opposition to the Liberals tended to support:

- the Established Church of England
- landed Aristocracy
- independence of the House of Lords
- the monarchy
- squirearchy
- a generally paternalistic view of society.

Whigs	Tories
Comprised of:	**Comprised of:**
● upper aristocracy and merchant/commercial interests.	● lesser aristocracy and gentry.
Supporters of:	**Supporters of:**
● the aristocracy and industrialists ● business and trade ● urban interests.	● Church of England ● monarchists ● rural interests.
Believed in:	**Believed in:**
● religious toleration ● economic reform ● parliamentary supremacy.	● the supremacy of the executive and the Crown ● isolationism and protectionism.

Corn Laws A set of protectionist tariffs on imported grain.

Peelites Supporters of Sir Roberts Peel. They were generally advocates of moderate reform and free trade. They left the Conservative Party in the wake of the Corn Law debate.

Discussion point:

Political parties or loyalties have been a part of democracies for thousands of years. They make democracies function more effectively, but they can also inhibit the free expression of ideas.

? What are the advantages and disadvantages of political parties in a democratic system?

Sir Robert Peel (1788–1850)

Peel was born into a wealthy manufacturing family and entered Parliament in 1809. He served in a number of government and cabinet posts under the ministries of the Earl of Liverpool and the Duke of Wellington. He emerged as the leader of the new Conservative Party. In the 1840s he came to the conclusion that Britain must pursue a free-trade policy that would entail the repeal of the Corn Law. The ensuing bitter debate split the Conservative Party, with Peel and his followers—the "Peelites"—including William Gladstone, leaving the party.

Political reform

The Reform Act of 1867

In 1865 about one million Englishmen could vote. Within two years this would double. But this sudden surge of suffrage had been brewing since the passage of the Reform Act of 1832. The Chartist movement flourished between 1838 and 1848 only to founder on the fear of the ruling classes. The Anti-Corn law movement had also witnessed mass mobilization of the non-voting public, signifying an interest in the kind of mass politics that the new modern political parties were developing. Skilled workers were forming trade unions and tasting the political and economic power of collective effort. Other working-class organizations such as **Friendly Societies** were moving beyond their local roots to the extent that by the 1870s a number had become national organizations, the so-called Affiliated Orders, with a cumulative membership of over 1.3 million. These experiments in mass organization in the years between the Reform Acts of 1832 and 1867 helped keep the issue of parliamentary reform close to the surface of English political life. A number of different cabinets, Liberal and Conservative, sought to tap into this political force by discussing and at times introducing bills to reform parliament by expanding the franchise.

What were the arguments against advancing the vote to more Englishmen? One, popular with laissez faire capitalists, was the so-called "stake in society" theory. It held that only those with a stake in society, and by stake they meant property, should have a say in how it was governed. Only those with something to lose should have a say in its governance. It is easy to see why this was a popular argument for land-owners as far back as the **Putney Debates** of the 1640s and likewise with industrialist owners of factories. Others argued, as they would against women's suffrage fifty years later, that the "lower" classes did not have the intelligence or requisite experience to understand the complex matters of state. To many, the monster meetings of the Chartist movement and various outbursts of street violence showed that the working class was too unruly to be given the vote.

The street agitation and massive political meetings that gave rise to much of this fear surfaced again in 1866 and the demand was, once again, an expanded franchise. The experience of mass organization and mobilization gained in the years between the Reform Acts manifested itself in the creation of the Reform League and Reform Unions. Trade unions also added their voice to the demand for reform. As 1866 moved into 1867 the Conservative government under Lord Derby ever more desperately sought a way to placate the demands of the reformers while maintaining their conservative base and keeping control of Parliament away from the more reform-minded Liberals.

It was Benjamin Disraeli, Lord Derby's **Chancellor of the Exchequer**, who solved the conundrum. He brought forth a series of proposals and laid them before parliament. All were decidedly conservative, but one had the potential to win enough

Friendly Societies Generally working-class mutual benefit organizations that took small collections from their members to be redistributed for sickness and death benefits.

Activity:
An editorial
Write a newspaper editorial arguing in favour of enlarging the franchise in Britain. Be sure to address the arguments put forward by opponents of reform.

Putney Debates Debates within Cromwell's New Model Army during the English Civil War as to what form society should take.

Chancellor of the Exchequer Member of the British cabinet responsible for financial matters.

conservatives and reformers to gain a majority and pass. This potential was realized by a bewildering set of amendments that gradually democratized the bill. The effect was that the bill that materialized into law expanded the franchise from less than one million voters to over two million voters. The vote now reached down to male householders in cities and renters who paid £10. The Act also redistributed seats in the House of Commons. Smaller towns lost some representation, which was then parceled out among those cities that had grown since 1832. The overall effect of the Reform Bill transformed mass politics in Britain. The enfranchisement of much of the wealthier urban working class meant that the political parties now had to more overtly include legislation that meaningfully addressed the concerns of this new constituency. Party organization had to take into this into consideration when creating election campaigns. The Conservatives began to organize on a more national level with the National Union of Conservative Associations and Liberals brought local party associations together in 1877 in the National Liberal Federation. That there still emerged no distinct working man's party increased the influence of interest groups that were dominated by the working-class. Groups like the Social Science Association and the Trades Union Congress influenced legislation throughout this period. Much of this legislation attempted to address the social ills that remained despite the economic prosperity and social consensus that has come to define the mid-Victorian period.

The Reform Act of 1884

The third great parliamentary reform act of the 19th-century was a logical extension of the 1867 act. It essentially extended the voting qualifications of 1867 from the boroughs to the countryside reaching to the rural working class. Gladstone's Liberal government passed the bill through the House of Commons in 1883, but it foundered in the House of Lords where rural Conservative Lords feared the loss of their authority to new working-class political interests. When Gladstone reintroduced the bill in1884, the Lords agreed to pass it in return for a bill that would further the concept of single-member constituencies while giving rural constituencies more representation. The right to vote, however, was in no way associated with citizenship, but rather hinged on expanded concepts of property and gender. The poorest of the working class and women could still not vote.

Social reform

From the 1840s to the 1870s, British industry produced a dazzling prosperity that saw her supplying much of the world's cotton, iron and coal. The British largely controlled the world's transportation system both on land and sea. London had become a centre of finance and a major supplier of capital to the rest of the world. It was interest earned on this capital as well as other service exports such as insurance and transportation that made up for the fact that Britain had for a long time imported more commodities than it

TOK Link
Statistics

Britain has conducted a decennial census since 1801. Early censuses merely collected head counts, but by the mid century a middle-class fascination with statistics and the power of these numbers to give valuable information to those studying problems such as poverty and disease provoked the governments to ask new questions.

This information gathering included details of a person's occupation, age, place of birth and marital status as well as health information about such conditions as deafness and blindness.

 What knowledge issues are involved when historians use statistics to study the past? What are the strengths and limitations of the use of historical statistics as evidence?

Discussion point:

The history of democracy is, in many ways, the story of the expanding franchise.

What qualifications would you put on the right to vote? Are there any members of society from whom you would withhold the right to vote? Why?

 Iron production, like textiles, is a trigger industry, because its development sparks the development and expansion of other industries. What other industries are trigger industries?

exported. Because the industrialization of other countries in part depended on British shipping and capital, the British were in an economically powerful position in the last quarter of the 19th century despite the fact that other economies, such as Germany and the United States, were producing as much and in some cases more than the United Kingdom.

The social ills that accompanied the first century of industrialization—poor working conditions, child labour, low wages, urban overcrowding, poor sanitation—had been dealt with haphazardly and ineffectually by an unreformed parliament prior to 1832 and only marginally better after this date.

Labour

After the Reform Act of 1867, the pace of social reform quickened for a time. Factory conditions continued to be a target of reformers. In 1872 coalmines were required to provide safety measures such as ventilators and safety lamps. The Ten Hours Act was extended to all workers in 1874 and by 1878 holidays and shorter working weeks were more common.

British iron industry.

The expanded franchise also helped ensure that the legal status of organized labour continued to improve. One of the legal bludgeons previously available to employers was amended in 1867. The Master and Servant Act had allowed employers to bring workers before the law who violated terms of employment where obedience could then be compelled by fine or imprisonment. The new act, blunted this, though was still regarded as being biased toward employers. Within 10 years of this amendment workers and employers were given equal status before the law in regards to employment contracts. This trend was continued when by 1881 workers could sue employers for injuries sustained on the job. By 1871 Trade Unions were recognized as legal bodies that could hold funds and own property and have representation at law. This legislation also protected the right to strike. Six years later trade unions were given the same rights as individuals before the law.

The Age of Reform 1829–67	
Year	**Legislation**
1828	Non-Anglican Protestants (Dissenters) are allowed to sit in parliament
1829	Catholic Emancipation Act allowed Catholics to sit in parliament
1829	Metropolitan Police Act set up a professional civilian police force in London
1833	Factory Act forbade children younger than nine from working in factories
1834	New Poor Law compelled the poor into workhouses and poorhouses before qualifying for relief
1835	Municipal Corporation Act reformed local politics
1842	Mines Act prohibited women and boys under 10 years old from working underground
1842	Railway Act improved safety of railways
1844	Railway Act ensured daily service to many areas of Britain and set some fares
1844	Factory Act restricted labour of children and women in factories
1847	Ten Hours Act restricted the hours that women and children could work in Factories to 10 hours per day
1848	Public Health Act provided for but did not compel local governments to set up Public Health Boards
1856	Police services spread to the rest of the UK
1859	Peaceful and "reasonable" picketing allowed during strikes
1860	Food and Drugs Act tried to ensure the safety of food and drugs
1866	Sanitary Act compelled local authorities to construct sewers and provide safe water supplies

Public health

The initial small steps in public health taken by the Public Health Act of 1848 were broadened after the Reform Act of 1867. The initial small steps in public health taken by the Public Health Act of 1848 also continued after 1867. Public health had been a key interest of reforming Victorians long before 1848. This interest was fuelled by a number of forces. The fear that attended the cholera, influenza, and typhus outbreaks in the 1830s and 1840s captivated members of all classes: diseases theoretically knew no social distinctions, although in practice the working class were far more likely to be affected. In this context, the concern for public health also meant self-preservation for those of the upper classes. The growing 19th-century liberal interest in empiricism also fed interest in public health when more accurate statistical details of health pointed to the endemic nature of many diseases. Throughout the mid-19th century, reports and investigations into public health, such as Edwin Chadwick's report of 1842, began to turn public opinion in favour of government intervention in the areas of health such that by 1871 the Local Government Act greatly centralized and made government control of Public Health issues more efficient. Local government intervention was further mandated in the Act of 1875, which tasked local governments with the duty to provide clean water and police the food supply, as well as reporting cases of infectious disease. This last stipulation was made more explicit in 1889 by the passage of the Infectious Disease Notification Act, which helped improve compliance.

Education

Much of the basic education that school-age children received prior to the 1850s came in the form of Sunday schools. These schools were appealing to working-class families, as it did not interfere with the working week during which children were contributing to the household income. They appealed to evangelical reformers, centred as they were on Bible reading and the acceptance of the hierarchical social order. Ragged Schools were another attempt by philanthropists at establishing basic education for the working class organized on a national level in the Ragged School Union. Grammar schools, traditionally tasked with the teaching of Latin and Greek, began to broaden their curriculum into areas of mathematics and modern languages as early as the late 18th century and filled a niche between the Sunday Schools and the Public Schools as did a number of private or proprietary schools operated as corporations. Educational reform of the late 19th century touched on all these institutions.

From the 1850s the central government had taken an increasing interest in the regulation of education and in fact funded a portion of elementary education. As on the continent, however, attempts at school reform by an essentially secular government invariably ran into the concerns of religious groups, especially the Church of England. This was compounded by the fact that for hundreds of years one of the primary duties of the British education "system" right through to the universities was to train Church of England ministers. This became apparent when the Gladstone administration

Activity:

The Chadwick Report

Research the Chadwick Report. What were its recommendations? To what degree were these acted upon? How do the recommendations compare to public health in your country today?

offered a comprehensive Education Act in 1870. The Act encouraged the establishment of elementary schools supported by local taxes in areas where there was not adequate elementary schooling. These schools were to be administered by elected School Boards. It did nothing about the existing Anglican and Catholic schools. There were therefore two systems, each receiving government funding. In the long term the arrangement allowed the Board Schools to grow as they had access to both state funds and taxes, while the so-called "voluntary schools" had only government grants to sustain them. As the areas that the School Boards governed grew in population so did their tax base. In the short term, however, it made for an uneven patchwork of national education in the 1890s provided by some 14,000 voluntary schools and 2,000 School Boards. This elementary education became compulsory for children between the ages of five and ten in 1881, with parents having to pay a sum that many working poor could not afford. The Free Grant Act of 1891 made this compulsory education free.

Discussion point:

What do you think is the relationship between free public education and the functioning of a democracy?

Activity:
A British education

Source A

The following is an excerpt from the autobiography of Dorothea Beale who describes her educational experience in the 1840s.

> It was a school considered much above average for sound instruction; our mistresses had taken pains to arrange various schemes of knowledge; yet what miserable teaching we had in many subjects; history was learned by committing to memory little manuals; rules of arithmetic were taught, but the principles were never explained. Instead of reading and learning the masterpieces of literature, we repeated week by week the "Lamentations of King Hezekiah", the pretty but somewhat weak "Mother's Picture".

Source: http://www.spartacus.schoolnet.co.uk/Wbeale.htm

Source B

The following excerpt is from the autobiography of Philip Snowden who describes his education under the Education Act of 1870.

> The Act was adopted, and the school I attended was taken over by the newly formed School Board. Steps were taken at once to build new school premises. A trained master was appointed, and a new era in child education in the village was opened up. I was between ten and eleven years old when this change took place. It brought me into a new world of learning. We were taught in a new schoolroom, which by comparison with the dingy old place we left seemed like a palace to us. The walls were covered with maps and pictures. Our curriculum was extended to include grammar, geography, history, elementary mathematics, and the simple sciences. We were not troubled with the religious question.

Source: http://www.spartacus.schoolnet.co.uk/Leducation70.htm.

Source C

The following is an excerpt from historian Gillian Sutherland on the effects of paying teachers according to the results achieved by students in certain subject areas after the 1870s.

> The "forcible feeding" metaphor is horribly apt. The framework of payment by results restricted the range of grant-earning subjects. All too often it bred a mechanical drilling in the classroom, a rehearsal every day for the examination that came once a year. Although the basis for grant was changed in the first half of the 1890s, the habits engendered took much longer to die.

"Education" by Gillian Sutherland, quoted in Thompson, F.M.L. ed. 1990. *The Cambridge Social History of Britain, 1750–1950*, vol. 3. Cambridge, UK. Cambridge University Press, p. 145.

Questions

1 Compare and contrast the view of sound teaching expressed in the three sources.

2 Examining the sources, how much had educational practice changed in the years 1840–90?

3 How do the educational experiences described in the sources compare to your educational experience?

4 Conduct some research into the development of women's education in the 19th Century. How did it compare to the educational experience of men during this period? Use the following topics to guide your research.

● Facilities
● Educational levels available
● Teachers
● Subjects
● Funding

Disraeli and Gladstone

During the last four decades of the 19th-century, British political life was dominated by the towering figures of Benjamin Disraeli, a Conservative, and William Gladstone, a Liberal. The two men came from very different backgrounds. Gladstone was the product of a strict Scottish Presbyterian turned propertied Anglican Tory family whose wealth came from the expansion of shipping. This wealth sent the future prime minister to public school and then Oxford. All indications were that he would fall into a privileged Tory mould and he seemed to do just that,

Gladstone and Disraeli: 1846–94		
Years	Disraeli	Gladstone
1846	Opposes Repeal of the Corn Laws	Supports Repeal of Corn Laws
1852	Chancellor of Exchequer	
1852–55		Chancellor of Exchequer
1858–59	Chancellor of Exchequer	
1859–66		Chancellor of Exchequer
1866–68	Chancellor of Exchequer	
1868	Prime Minister	
1868–74		Prime Minister
1874–80	Prime Minister	
1880–85		Prime Minister
1886		Prime Minister
1892–94		Prime Minister

entering the House of Commons in 1832 as a Tory, a proponent of High Anglicanism and an opponent of parliamentary reform. He served in Sir Robert Peel's cabinet in the treasury and would later become Chancellor of the Exchequer. He remained a Peelite and carried their banner into the new Liberal Party in 1859. From that point he would emerge as the consistent, though increasingly weathered, face of Victorian Liberalism until his death in 1898.

Benjamin Disraeli had a less orthodox upbringing. Although of Jewish descent, he was baptized into the Anglican Church when he was 13 years old. He attended an independent school until the age of 15. His life then led him to the continent for a tour and then into a literary career. He took side trips into stock speculation, journalism, and eventually into politics as a Whig and a Radical but later as a Conservative opposing the repeal of the Corn Laws. After Peel's split with protectionist Conservatives over repeal, Disraeli emerged as an important Conservative politician under the leadership of Lord Derby. Disreali and Gladstone would alternate ministries in the1870s and 1880s, adding to rather than repealing each other's legislation and constantly looking to winning new voters. This was partially because, when it came to fundamental views of society and the relation of government to that society, the two parties did not differ radically. Both were essentially committed to the fundamentals of the economic engine that had brought the United Kingdom the economic prosperity it enjoyed at the end of the 19th century.

Disraeli's domestic policy

Disraeli, in many ways, was the architect of the 1867 Reform Act, though he was not the prime minister at the time. In getting this measure passed in both the House of Commons and the House of Lords he showed himself to be a shrewd parliamentary tactician, opportunist and judge of public opinion. While he was not particularly committed to reform, he believed it to be inevitable. The Conservatives were enjoying their first government in years and Disraeli saw no use, practical or ideological, in being turned out for raging against the inescapable and great gain to be had in posing as the agent of change.

Disraeli's second ministry was his longest and most productive. During this time he painted the Conservative Party as the protectors of the public. Labour legislation protecting picketing was passed and compulsory education was established under Disraeli's watch. His government passed public health measures such as the Sale of Food and Drugs Act and the Public Health Act. The Factory Act of 1878 further regulated the labour of children and women. While this legislative agenda may seem pro-labour and uncharacteristic of a Conservative ministry, in some ways it harkens back to Tory paternalism especially as it emerged out of the first Reform Act of 1832. It also owes a good deal to the electoral strategy of Disraeli who understood that if his ministry were to win another parliamentary majority, he would need to appeal to the urban working class that he had helped enfranchise. The reform agenda can also be seen as much as a response to the needs of a growing industrial society as a product of any detailed ideology.

Disraeli's foreign policy

Disraeli's first brief ministry came during a decade of massive upheaval in the established global situation. Across the Atlantic the United States was reconstructing its society after a brutal civil war in which the British had supported the losing side. In 1867, four of Britain's North American colonies had confederated into the Dominion of Canada, dramatically changing, though far from severing, Britain's relations with these territories. In Europe, Italian nationalism had brought much of the peninsula under a national government. Prussian bayonets were prodding the German states into a powerful central European nation state while at the same time checking Austria's traditional influence. Many of the Continental changes were taken with a wary eye to British reaction and in some cases a certain degree of deference, but certainly with no direct participation. The trick, then, for both Disraeli and Gladstone after him would be to remain influential while not being dragged into a destructive Continental conflict while maintaining and perhaps expanding the British Empire.

"Colonies do not cease to be colonies because they are independent."
Benjamin Disraeli

When Bismarck attempted to intimidate France during her recovery from the Franco-Prussian War, The Third Republic appealed to the United Kingdom and Russia for aid. While Disraeli sought an expanded role for Britain on the Continent it was, however, the Russians who diffused the situation, while Disraeli and his Foreign Office watched.

Then, as ever, an important issue for the British was control of the straits that connected the Black Sea to the Mediterranean, which in turn hinged on the troubled relationship between Russia and Turkey. In 1875, Bosnia and Herzegovina rose against their Turkish masters in a rebellion that had spread to Bulgaria by 1876. The Turkish army brutally suppressed the rebellion reportedly killing some 12,000 Bulgarians. Gladstone rose to oratory heights denouncing the massacres in speech and print. This put Disraeli in a difficult situation. He believed, as many had before him, that Turkey must be supported as a bulwark against Russian control of the straits. This seemed even more imperative since the opening of the Suez Canal in 1869 and the Disraeli government's purchase of 44 per cent of the shares in the canal's operating company in 1875, making it the principal shareholder. But the Bulgarian atrocities and the ensuing Russo-Turkish War of 1877 made this difficult, especially in the face of Gladstone's thundering morality. The war quickly proved the reality of Turkish decay and the resulting Treaty of San Stefano heavily favoured the Russians to the outrage of the British public. Disraeli maintained that some form of the status quo must persist in the near east and with this in mind he attended the Congress of Berlin in 1878. The Treaty of San Stefano was abandoned at Berlin. Serbia, Montenegro and Romania gained independence and Bulgaria remained, nominally under the control of the Turks. Disraeli had helped secure a peace that maintained the British position in the near east and blocked Russian expansion into the Balkans. But this had far from answered the festering Eastern Question, a question that would be a constant source of tension up until 1914.

Disraeli's Imperial policy

There is some debate as to what extent Disraeli was a genuine imperialist. In public he gradually showed more enthusiasm for the Empire throughout the 1860s and 1870s. The motive is less clear. Regardless, he did make the Empire central to the conservative platform during his second ministry. In the Empire he sought to unite all voting classes behind Conservative leadership—to make clear in the public mind the connection between the Empire, patriotism and the Conservative party. Having Victoria proclaimed Empress of India in 1877 was an important part of this connection, which also reflected his interest in India and the near east to the neglect of other colonial holdings. Besides the unifying effect of Empire, Disraeli was keen that the Empire should not be an economic burden, which also helps explain his prejudice towards India, paying as it did for its own defence and providing as it did an important strategic position *vis a vis* Russia in central Asia.

During his administration the Empire advanced in fits and starts. Although Fiji was annexed under his second ministry in 1874, he largely inherited the events leading to the annexation. In 1874 the British established a protectorate on the Gold Coast. On occasion Disraeli's officials "on the spot" dangerously advanced Imperial policy beyond that which Disraeli was comfortable, but for which he was at least partially responsible. Afghanistan sat as a buffer between India and Russia. One school of thought was that the United Kingdom should stay out of the remote territory, passively maintaining it as a buffer. The other school of thought, the so-called "forward policy" was that Britain should become actively involved in the administration of Afghanistan. Disraeli tended to favour the forward-policy concerned as he was with Russian threats to India. Lord Lytton, the British viceroy in India, took steps to put this forward-policy into action. He sent troops into Afghanistan in 1878 to force the Ameer to accept a British military delegation and to reject a Russian delegation. While initially successful, a bloody civil war erupted in 1879 in which British officials were killed, embarrassing the Disraeli administration.

In an effort to consolidate British possessions in South Africa, Disraeli's administration annexed the Transvaal in 1877 amid the protest of the inhabitants. The British governor of the Transvaal, Sir Bartle Frere, exceeded his instructions and demanded that King Cetewayo disband his army in the neighboring Zulu territory. When this was not forthcoming, Frere sent British troops invaded Cetewayo's lands. The ensuing Zulu War did not go well for the British initially. They suffered a substantial defeat at Isandlwana and near disaster at Rorke's Drift.

The war was financially and politically costly for Disraeli's government. Again, one of his officials too aggressively pursued the forward-policy that Disraeli had adopted. To be sure, 1874 to 1880, the period of Disraeli's second ministry, was eventful in terms of foreign affairs for the British. Nevertheless, Disraeli was more than willing to reap the rhetorical and popular benefit of Empire without pursuing a consistent and controlled Imperial policy.

Activity:
Disraeli: an evaluation

Construct a report card for Disraeli's administrations. Provide a grade from A to D in the following areas. Supply specific evidence to support the grades that you award.

	Grade	Evidence
Social policy		
Economic policy		
Foreign policy		
Imperial policy		
Irish policy		

Gladstone's domestic policy

Gladstone did not seek a radical overhaul of British society, nor an all-encompassing government that regulated daily life. Rather his was a 19th-century liberal agenda in that it espoused an equality of opportunity that would allow more individuals to participate in society based on ability rather than birth. He wanted to make government more efficient and systematized in its responses to the challenges that a modern industrial society faced. However, much to his and other doctrinaire liberals chagrin, this often meant a more intrusive government.

In establishing a more systematic approach to civil administration, Gladstone took aim at the army and the civil service. The arcane traditions and organization of the British army were both a source of national pride and nostalgia. On the other hand they made the army difficult to manage in war and peace. Its organization of militia and regular army coupled with the purchase of commissions made parts of the army resemble a gentleman's club more than a modern fighting force. The rapid military developments on the continent in the 1860s and the resultant emergence of Germany as a major military power made army reform even more imperative. Under Gladstone and his Secretary of War, Edward Cardwell, the sale of **military commissions** was abolished, opening the officer ranks to talent. To make military service more appealing, terms of service

Military commissions These were appointments to officer ranks in the army and navy. Prior to Gladstone's reforms they could be purchased regardless of ability.

were drastically reduced. The army was also reorganized into a more rational structure based on districts and brought under common command in times of war.

This same rationalization and attack on privilege was carried on outside the army. In 1871 the University Test Act opened the doors of Oxford and Cambridge to non-Anglicans. Gladstone also disestablished the Church of Ireland in 1871, an act that removed a number of privileges from the Anglican Church in Ireland where the vast majority of the population was Roman Catholic. Civil service reforms established examinations for those pursuing positions in government administration. By 1873, Gladstone's government had centralized much of the administration of justice in England with the Judicature Act.

Gladstone's foreign policy

Disraeli's foreign policy can be seen as broadly governed by the practice of *Realpolitik* in the service of a strong independent United Kingdom through independent forceful action. Gladstone's approach was based on morality, caution, and international co-operation. He was not a non-interventionist, but he did believe that if the UK were to play a more interventionist role it had to be based not on self-interest, but rather in the cause of global, as opposed to purely British, interests. While the Eastern Question dominated foreign policy during Disraeli's second ministry, Gladstone's first ministry faced the fundamental reordering of the balance of power on the Continent culminating in the Franco-Prussian War and the establishment of the German Empire.

Caution and co-operation were certainly the watchwords for the British response to the growing threat of war between France and Prussia; or timidity and passivity to its critics. Gladstone and his cabinet at first tried to defuse the issue of the Hohenzollern candidature. When this failed they were keen to remain out of the war and keep it from spreading. The decades-old issue of Belgian neutrality and the freedom of the channel ports was the only major strategic issue that the war seemed to present to the British cabinet. Gladstone's moral indignation was aroused, however, by the shelling of Paris and what he viewed as the harsh terms of the peace— specifically the annexation of Alsace and Lorraine. But the price of non-intervention was that Bismarck had little inclination to listen to the Gladstone's moralizing. The fundamental balance of power on the Continent had been altered with no real input from the UK. Nevertheless, the new German Empire could provide a good counterweight to the power of Russia, which was to prove to be more of a concern to British interests.

Gladstone came up hard against the idea that a faith in **multilateralism** is only as good as the commitment of the other powers involved, when Russian unilaterally repudiated the 1856 Treaty of Paris that had ended the Crimean War. This repudiation directly affected the clauses that concerned the Black Sea. The façade of co-operation was re-established in 1871 when the hastily assembled Conference of London ratified what the

Discussion point:

The United Kingdom had taken a keen interest in Belgium since the 1830s.

Why was interest in Belgian neutrality so important to the UK?

How had the British attempted to protect this neutrality?

"Nothing that is morally wrong can be politically right."
William Gladstone

Multilateralism The principle in foreign affairs that countries should cooperate in decisions and actions rather than act individually.

participants had had no part in negotiating. By the elections of 1874 British public opinion welcomed a more forceful approach to foreign policy and this was ostensibly to be supplied by Disraeli and his Conservatives.

Foreign policy played an important role in Gladstone's return to power in 1880. While in the political wilderness, he had thundered against the immorality of the Bulgarian atrocities and Disraeli's support of the Turkish oppressors. The debacles of Isandlwana and Afghanistan were also fresh in the voters' minds and Gladstone was returned to office in 1880. During Gladstone's second ministry the Colonial Office was to be far busier than the Foreign Office.

Gladstone's Imperial policy

Gladstone's first ministry had seen some fundamental changes in the administration of the Empire along the lines of consolidation and rationalization. The newly established Dominion of Canada was expanding with the addition of Manitoba, British Columbia, and Prince Edward Island. This domestically self-governing entity within the British Empire now stretched from the Atlantic to the Pacific and would be connected by a transcontinental railway by 1885. After considerable debate amongst the colonists, the Cape Colony was granted responsible government in 1872.

It was during Gladstone's second ministry that Imperial issues rose to the fore. In the wake of the disastrous Zulu War, the Boers rose in rebellion and defeated the British forces at Majuba Hill in 1881 resulting in the renewed independence of the Transvaal. Although he believed in what would later be called self-determination, the British dependence on the Suez Canal forced Gladstone to send troops to Egypt when the Khedive was threatened with a nationalist rebellion in 1882. Alexandria was bombarded and Egypt was made a British protectorate. Such an interventionist policy served to drag the United Kingdom further into the interior of Africa. A revolt in the Sudan led Gladstone to send General Gordon to evacuate the troops there, but he instead attempted an unsuccessful defence of Khartoum in which Gordon himself was killed and for which Gladstone's government was blamed for hesitating in its support. Like Disraeli before him, Gladstone fell victim to adventurous officials on the spot. Gladstone, much to his chagrin, was looking for all intents and purposes like an aggressive imperialist.

He was able to exercise his belief in international co-operation at the Berlin Conference in 1885. The Conference was called to establish certain ground rules for the acquisition of territories in Africa—to regulate the so-called Scramble for Africa. This type of European concert —with representation from the United States—appealed to Gladstone's approach to foreign and Imperial affairs. Because he was as some have called him a "reluctant" imperialist, his policy and its implementation seems haphazard. Disraeli's Imperial policy, on the other hand, was eventually knit into his notion of Conservatism and was only inconsistent in its application.

Activity:

Disraeli vs. Gladstone

Use this chart and your own research to compare and contrast the policies of Disraeli and Gladstone under the following categories and then answer the questions that follow.

	Disraeli	Gladstone
Industry		
Finance		
Trade		
Education		
Empire		
Military		
Diplomacy		

Questions

1 On which policies are these two prime ministers the most alike? On which are they the most different? Account for their differences and similarities.

2 What is the relationship between finance, trade and industrial policies? How is this relationship manifested in the policies of these two prime ministers?

3 If "collectivism" is expressed by increased government intervention in the economy and society and "individualism" is expressed by less government in the economy and society, place Disraeli and Gladstone on the following spectrum. Justify your placement of each.

Collectivism |——————————|——————————| Individualism

Ireland

The position of Ireland in the British Empire was in all ways unique. The penal laws of the 18th century had oppressed the Catholic majority. The Act of Union of 1800 deprived the Irish of home rule, but granted them representation in both houses of the British parliament. After 1829 Catholics were allowed to vote and hold most offices, although they paid rents to absentee landlords and tithes to an established Protestant church. In the years after the Irish Famine, opposition to British rule grew. It was both peaceful and violent.

Partially to discourage violent Irish republicanism by encouraging moderate constitutional reform, Gladstone took steps to disestablish the Protestant Irish Church, freeing Catholics from paying **tithes** to it and reducing the property it controlled. This was followed in 1870 by the Irish Land Act, which attempted to protect tenants from eviction, by requiring them to be paid compensation in certain cases and providing limited loans to those who wished to purchase their land.

Tithes Compulsory dues paid to a church.

By 1880 economic distress had once again turned the situation in Ireland volatile. The core of the Irish lobby centred on the Irish Home Rule League and the Irish Land League. These two forces were united under the leadership of the Protestant Irish politician Charles Parnell at the end of the 1870s. After the 1880 general election his nationalist party held 62 seats and they would not be dissuaded by Gladstone's piecemeal concessions such as the 1881 Land Act, which further eased conditions for Irish tenants. Parnell's position was strong enough to negotiate legisled debt relief for many Irish tenants. By 1885 he was able to use the seats he controlled in parliament to bring down Gladstone's second ministry.

Gladstone tackled the Home Rule issue head on during his third ministry. His proposed Home Rule Bill that would establish an Irish Parliament in Dublin under similar strictures that had governed the Dominion of Canada in 1867. It was defeated and split his Liberal Party, driving the Liberal Unionists away. With the support of these Unionists the Conservatives were able to control parliament.

During his fourth and final ministry, Gladstone tried one last time to push Irish Home Rule through on the slim strength of a minority government. It failed in the House of Lords and would not be raised again for a number of years.

Activity:

Disraeli, Gladstone and Empire

Source A

John Tenniel, *Disraeli and Queen Victoria Exchanging Gifts*, published in *Punch*, 1876.

Source B

A Break Down: Cause and Effect. Disraeli's "statesmanship" versus Gladstone's moral foreign policy "hobby".

Source C

… there is another and second great object of the Tory Party. … to uphold the empire of India as a burden on this country, viewing everything in a financial aspect and totally passing by those moral and political considerations . …. in my opinion, no minister in this country will do his duty who neglects any opportunity of reconstructing as much as possible our colonial empire .

Source: Benjamin Disraeli, 24 June 1872, quoted from MacArthur, Brian. ed. 1996. *The Penguin Book of Historic Speeches*, London, UK. Penguin Books. p. 321.

Source D

Modern times have established a sisterhood of nations, equal, independent; each of them built up under that legitimate defence which public law affords to every nation, living within its own borders and seeking to perform its own affairs, but if one thing more than another has been detestable to Europe, it has been the appearance on the stage from time to time of men who, even in the times of Christian civilization have been thought to aim at universal domination.

Source: William Gladstone, 27 November 1879, quoted in MacArthur, Brian. ed. 1996. *The Penguin Book of Historic Speeches*. London, UK. Penguin Books. p. 327.

Questions

1 What gifts are Disraeli and Queen Victoria exchanging in Source A? What do these "gifts" symbolize?

2 What political message is being expressed in Source B?

3 According to Disraeli in Source C, what are the chief benefits of a colonial empire? What other benefits might there have been for Great Britain enlarging her Empire?

4 In what sense is Gladstone a nationalist?

5 Using these documents and further research compare and contrast the Imperial policy of Gladstone with that of Disraeli.

The United Kingdom, 1900–14

The rise of Labour

For all its power and reach, the British economy was inherently unstable in the years after 1870. Periods of growth were matched by periods of recession with alarming regularity. This was compounded by a worldwide depression that lasted from 1873 to 1893. Overall, British economic growth, even in good years, was not what it had been in the early part of the century. The new industrial revolution rewarded the new economies of Germany and the United States, which were offering stiff competition to British goods by the turn of the century. In response British industry, did not become more productive, but rather looked inward to the Empire for resources and markets.

This economic situation exacerbated the perpetual problem of poverty, which in turn spurred a number of well-meaning middle-class reformers to publish studies on the conditions of Britain's poor. These reports made for sobering reading. They numbered the working poor at around 30 per cent in London and other centres. These people worked in crowded and unsanitary conditions for low wages. Regardless of the wage, employment for a number of these working poor was seasonal or casual as with agricultural labourers or dock-workers. At the very bottom of the socio-economic scale were the poorest tenth: vagrants, criminals, unemployed and homeless. As their cause became more public, old Victorian arguments about individual responsibility for poverty could no longer stand.

From the mid-19th century organized labour had increased drastically in both numbers and respectability. These were, however, primarily trade unions of skilled workers. Much of the work of these unions was mainly an extension of 19th-century doctrines of self-help and mutual-aid in which workers bound together in groups such as friendly societies, burial societies and trades unions to build up funds that would provide collective self-help measures such as death and sickness benefits and eventually pensions. Collective action in the interest of wages, conditions, and hours was more rare as the century progressed for these unions. The unskilled labourers, however, were also organizing in the period after 1870 and they were far more willing to take direct collective action in the interest of their day-to-day conditions. In 1888 London match girls won an end to an unfair system of fines. Gas- and dock-workers organized and struck for shorter workdays. The improved transportation and communication across the United Kingdom, the same system that had helped make nationally organized political parties possible, now made nationally organized labour unions possible for both skilled and unskilled workers. By the turn of the century British unions had some two million members. This "new unionism" was viewed as a serious threat by factory owners across the country and the turn of the century was to be a period of intense industrial conflict, in which the new unions took a beating on the picket line and in the courts.

The Reform Act of 1867 enfranchised the wealthiest of the urban working class who then fit into the existing political culture of Liberal and Conservative parties. The same happened for a period after the passing of the Reform Act of 1884. But within the decade this began to change. Until this point working-class Members of Parliament tended to sit as Labour-Liberals, or Lib-lab as they were called. Keir Hardie, a coal miner, union organizer and first independent labour Member of Parliament cobbled together the Independent Labour Party (ILP) from union supporters and socialists and some Lib-Lab Members of Parliament. By 1900 the ILP merged with moderate Marxists, Fabians, and trade unionists to form the Labour Representative Committee, which in 1906 became the Labour Party. This new Labour Party was careful to steer clear of radical revolutionary rhetoric so as not to alienate the moderate working-class voters who had previously supported the Liberals or even the Conservatives. In the 1906 general election the Labour Party won 29 seats.

Reform, 1886–1914

With the exception of a three-year hiatus, the Conservative Party ruled Britain from 1886 to 1906. During that time the ministries of Lord Salisbury and Arthur Balfour held to the Conservative model of paternalism and tradition. Salisbury's reform agenda was busy more than it was effective. The Conservatives passed the local Government Act, which regularized county councils giving local populations the ability to elect local governments. This was consistent with Salisbury's essentially decentralized approach to government with its concomitant belief in self-help and low taxes. The Factory Act of 1891 further regulated child labour. Salisbury's expertise and interests lay in foreign affairs and domestic reform suffered as a consequence. His successor and nephew, Arthur Balfour, made attempts at reform that were only marginally more aggressive. His education reform established secondary education, but at the price of alienating the non-conformists. In terms of Labour Legislation a Workman's Compensation Act was more than offset by Balfour's unwillingness to address court decisions that had severely hampered the ability of labour unions to operate in the country.

The Boer War had exposed the organization and training of the British army to be dangerously flawed and Balfour's government set about to remedy that. His reforms began at the top. Matters of Imperial defence applicable to both armed services were brought under the control of the Committee of Imperial Defence. The army was to be controlled by an Army Council and a General Staff was created. Balfour's army reform stalled in 1906 when the Conservatives suffered a crushing electoral defeat.

> *"English policy is to float lazily downstream, occasionally putting out a diplomatic boathook to avoid collisions."*
>
> Lord Salisbury

Robert Cecil, 3rd Marquis of Salisbury (1830–1903)

Salisbury was a Conservative politician that served as Foreign Secretary and Prime Minster in the 1880s and 1890s. After his education at Eton and Oxford, he entered politics in 1853. Initially critical of Disraeli's leadership, this view softened over time and he became Foreign Secretary in Disraeli's second ministry. As Prime Minister he took an individualist and non-interventionist view of the role of government and this marked his domestic policy. His strength was in foreign affairs. He guided the United Kingdom through the partition of Africa, but also stumbled into the Anglo-Boer War.

There were a number of elements that led to the Conservative defeat in 1906. The schools issue had alienated non-conformists. Workers had been disaffected by the aggressive, largely Conservative, court rulings against organized labour. The Conservatives had also toyed with the idea of re-establishing protective tariffs for goods coming from outside the Empire, something it was rightly feared would raise prices at a time when real wages were already deceasing. In the end, the Liberals were handed their greatest electoral majority in history. But what would they do with it?

Much of the dissatisfaction with Balfour's Conservative government had grown out of its inability to address the needs of the working class. For the time being the Liberal Party had largely been the beneficiary of that dissatisfaction. But the Labour Party had won 29 seats in their first general election under that name. Lest they go the way of the Conservatives before them and to help staunch the flow of votes from Liberal to Labour, the government of Herbert Asquith and his Chancellor of the Exchequer, the mercurial David Lloyd George set about co-opting what could well become labour initiatives. The liberals introduced a programme of reform designed to create a degree of social harmony in a United Kingdom split by class, gender, nation, and ideology. Such a programme of reform would require state intervention in both the economy and society to a degree previously unheard of in Britain. The hated common law that opened labour unions to libel actions was remedied. Minimum wage, pensions, and unemployment insurance all became law in some way, shape or form under Asquith's government. National contributory health insurance was established in 1911. The government put money into rural transportation and agricultural research. The Labour Department sought to act as a buffer between the interests of workers and employers and by 1912 took the extraordinary step of legislating miners' wages.

These social welfare schemes were costly and to pay for them Lloyd George drastically increased taxes. In so doing, he introduced the idea of a progressive income tax whereby those who earned more, paid more. He also established increased property taxes as well as a form of **capital gains** tax on the sale of property. Opposition to these measures in the House of Lords necessitated an amendment to the constitutional power of the Lords. The right of the House of Lords to veto financial legislation was abolished by the Parliament Act of 1911. The same legislation provided for a salary for members of parliament so that those without independent wealth could sit in the Commons. The maximum time period between general elections was reduced from seven to five years by this same act. The Bill was the main issue in two general elections in 1910, with the Liberals winning a minority government and being able to pass the legislation with the help of the 42 Labour MPs.

Regardless of its extent, Asquith's reform package did not completely heal the socio-economic division that existed in the first decade of the 20th century. The railway strike of 1911 was eventually met with force and mediated by Lloyd George. Massive coal strikes also rocked the United Kingdom in 1911. But there were groups that were stubbornly excluded from the social peace

Discussion point:

Generally income tax can be progressive, regressive, or flat.

What are the strengths and weaknesses of the different forms of taxation?

Capital Gains Profits acquired through the sale of property.

Workers flee police during the 1911 Transport Strike.

that the Liberal government sought. The militancy of the women's suffrage movement would sorely test the Liberal harmony of this period.

Women's Rights

In the great Acts of 1832, 1867, and 1884 women are conspicuous by their absence. Working-class women occupied the lowest paid occupations in the workforce under some of the harshest conditions. Insofar as legislation looked to the role of women in the workforce it was to take a paternalistic approach evidenced by the many factory acts of 19th century that often combined the interests of women and children. Women workers rode the wave of new unionism into organized labour action and this occasionally yielded positive results, as with the London match girls' strike of 1888. In terms of legal and political rights women, however, remained far from the equal of men.

Feminism had been a growing movement in Britain throughout the 19th century. Early in the 19th-century feminist advocates concentrated on broader social and legal rights in the spirit of the French Revolution, but as the Reform Movement and Chartism gathered momentum attention also turned to political rights for women. Writers such as John Stuart Mill and Harriet Taylor argued for the essential equality of men and women and thus merged the issues of political and social rights. Just as it had done for the formation of political parties and the labour movement, improved communication and transportation helped transform the suffragist cause into a national and even international movement.

While economic and social conditions were important to feminists there was a growing belief that the best way to affect these changes was to get the vote. Local organizations advocating for this right sprang up across the country and were brought together in the National Union of Women's Suffrage Societies (NUWSS) in 1887. Pamphlets, newspaper articles, marches and petitions emanated from the NUWSS on all manner of subjects from women's right to vote, to the economic conditions of women workers, to white slavery. The NUWSS was committed to peaceful actions, but as time went on with the vote not forthcoming, this was not enough for some members. Emmeline Pankurst led a breakaway group and formed the Women's Social and Political Union (WSPU). In the years leading to 1914 the WSPU adopted radical tactics including violence targeted at property. Upon arrest, many of these suffragists went on hunger strikes. It would not be until after the First World War that women over the age of 30 were granted the right to vote in the United Kingdom in 1918.

? How did the "new unionism" and improved transportation and communication make later general labour strikes possible? How could the civil authorities use these same improvements to combat labour unrest?

"Don't be afraid to take a big step if one is indicated; you can't cross a chasm in two small jumps."

David Lloyd George

"The argument of the broken window pane is the most valuable argument in modern politics."

Emmeline Pankhurst

Emmeline Pankhurst (1858–1928)

Pankhurst was born Emmeline Goulden in Manchester. After being educated in France, her parents exposed her to political activism and one of these causes was the emancipation of women. Pankhurst grew frustrated with the slow progress that existing suffrage organizations were making and began advocating militant tactics such as violence to property and civil disobedience for which she was repeatedly imprisoned. She subordinated these tactics to the British war effort in the years 1914–18 during which her views grew more conservative and patriotic. Near the end of her life she joined the Conservative Party.

Activity:
"The Cat and Mouse Act"

The police used a number of tactics in their clashes with the Suffragists. One tactic to deal with hunger-striking prisoners was called the "Cat and Mouse Act." What was this act and how was it used? Would it be legal in your country today?

Activity:
Case studies

The IB History Guide requires that students also study a case study of a Northern or Western European country during the period 1848–1914. When conducting this case study it is important to examine elements such as:

- Domestic policy
- Foreign policy
- Economic developments
- Social developments
- Gender issues.

Poster of *The Suffragette Newspaper*, 1914.

 The Cat and Mouse Act was designed to combat the suffragettes' prison strategy of hunger strikes. At what other times have hunger strikes been used by prisoners? How did the authorities respond in these situations?

Exam practice and further resources

Sample questions

1 Examine the factors which led to the establishment of the Second Empire in France by 1851.
2 "Foreign policy rather than domestic discontent caused the collapse of the second empire". To what extent do you agree with this statement?
3 Compare and contrast the reasons for the passage of the 1867 and 1884 Reform Acts in the United Kingdom.
4 Analyse the impact of Gladstone's Irish policy on the Liberal party.
5 Examine political developments from 1850 to 1900 in ONE country you have studied?

Recommended further reading

On the 1848 Revolution in France:

Harsin, Jill. 2002. *Barricades: The War of the Streets in Revolutionary Paris, 1830–1848*. New York, USA. Palgrave.

On Napoleon III:

Price, Roger. 2001. *The French Second Empire: An Anatomy of Political Power*. New York, USA. Cambridge University Press.

Truesdell, M. 1997. *Spectacular Politics: Louis-Napoleon Bonaparte and the Fête impériale, 1849–1870*. New York, USA. Oxford University Press.

On the Paris Commune:

Christiansen, Rupert. 1995. *Paris Babylon: The Story of the Paris Commune*. New York, USA. Viking.

On the Third Republic:

Brown, Frederick. 2010. *For the Soul of France: Culture Wars in the Age of Dreyfus*. New York, USA. Alfred A. Knopf.

On social and political change in the United Kingdom:

Thompson, F.M.L. (ed.). 1990. *The Cambridge Social History of Britain, 1750–1950*. Cambridge, UK. Cambridge University Press.

On Gladstone and Disraeli:

Wills, Michael. 1989. *Gladstone and Disraeli: Principles and Policies*. Cambridge, UK. Cambridge University Press.

Mathew, H.C.G. 1995. *Gladstone 1875–1898*. Oxford, UK. Clarendon Press.

Shannon, Richard. 1992. *The Age of Disraeli, 1868–1881: The Rise of Tory Democracy*. New York, USA. Longman.

On gender issues:

Purvis, June and Holton, Sandra. (eds). 2000. *Votes for Women*. New York, USA. Routledge.

4 War and change in the Middle East, 1914–49

This chapter deals with the impact of the First World War on the Middle East and analyses the effects of Allied diplomacy as well as the peace treaties on the shape of the region in the post-war era. The inter-war years saw the establishment of new state boundaries, the introduction of a new system of governance called the mandate system, and the emergence of a powerful movement of nationalism. The chapter will aim to explain the causes and the consequences of each of these: how and why the new states were born; how and why the mandate system replaced the colonial administration; how and why Turkey, Iran and Saudi Arabia succeeded in establishing themselves as autonomous countries in the region. Finally, the chapter will focus on the Palestinian Mandate and the circumstances leading to the birth of the State of Israel. This will serve as background to the Arab–Israeli dispute.

By the end of this chapter, students should be able to:

- recognize the countries that make up the Middle East
- understand the historical relationship between the Middle East and the Western world
- assess the impact of the First World War, the war-time promises and the peace treaties on the region
- explain the Arab Revolt and assess its consequences
- recognize the discrimination faced by the various ethnic minority groups, such as the Armenians and the Kurds
- understand the mandate system and explain the complexity of the Palestinian Mandate
- understand the post-Second World War tensions, leading to the creation of the State of Israel and the 1948 Arab–Israeli War
- explain the nature of the regimes in Turkey, Iran and Saudi Arabia.

Introducing the Middle East

The term Middle East was first used in 1902 by an American naval historian, Alfred Thayer Mahan, to describe the land that lies between Arabia and India. Before that, words like the Levant, the Orient, or the Near East were used to describe the region. The historical relationship between the Middle East and the Western world is clear in the name itself: it describes a region relative to the West's geographic location. In reality the Middle East is only "Middle" and "East" from a Western perspective. Geographically, the Middle East covers three continents: Europe, Asia and Africa. It includes the 17 countries listed on the map following.

Activity:

Map study: The Middle East

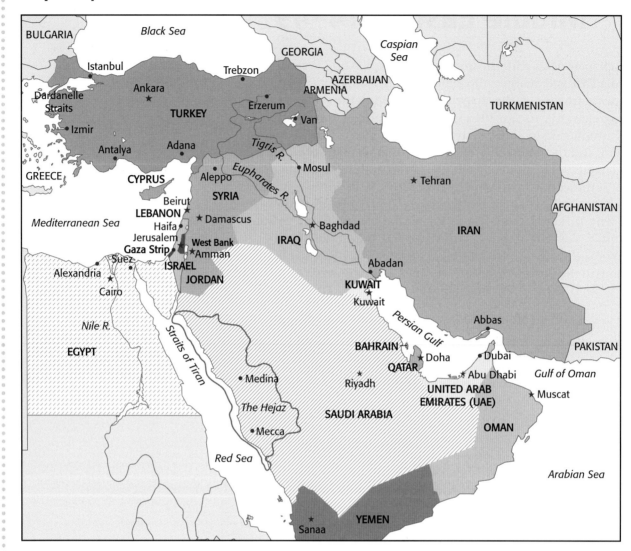

1	Bahrain	
2	Cyprus	
3	Egypt	
4	Iran	
5	Iraq	
6	Israel	
7	Jordan	
8	Kuwait	
9	Lebanon	
10	Oman	
11	Palestinian Authority Territories (West Bank and Gaza Strip)	

12	Qatar
13	Saudi Arabia
14	Syria
15	Turkey
16	United Arab Emirates (UAE)
17	Yemen

The strategic importance of the Middle East

What makes a place more "important" than another? Choose a region of strategic importance to make a brief presentation. You could consider:

● sea routes

● cities that offer access to trade routes

● regions with mineral resources

● elevated territory that can offer security

● any other factors?

To what extent is this "importance" specific to a particular period in history? How has this changed with time? Why?

The Middle East is composed of three major groups of people, Arabs, Turks and Persians, each with their respective history, language and dialects, literature, civilizations and rivalries. The main languages are: Arabic, Turkish, Farsi, Kurdish and Hebrew but there are in addition 25 other language groups in less accessible regions. The main languages divide up into three distinct language groups: Semitic (Arabic and Hebrew), Turkic (Turkish) and Indo-European (Kurdish and Farsi (Persian). The Middle East is the home of the three monotheistic religions: Judaism, Christianity and Islam. The Jewish population is the smallest. It makes up two percent of the population of the region. The Christians live mainly in Lebanon, Egypt and Syria and make up five per cent of the population. The Muslims are the largest group and make up 92 per cent of the total population.

The countries in the Middle East vary in size. The largest is Saudi Arabia which measures nearly 2,000,000 square kilometers, and the smallest is Bahrain with 665 square kilometers. The most populated country is Egypt with over 71,000,000, whereas the least populated one is Qatar with 600,000. The region as a whole contains 65 per cent of the world's oil supplies but the distribution of this resource varies between countries. While Saudi Arabia, Iran, UAE and Kuwait produce around 24 per cent of the world's oil, Egypt, Turkey, Syria or Jordan produce very little or no oil at all. Politically, the countries in the Middle East also represent a wide variety of political systems. They vary from monarchies and sultanates where a family effectively owns the state, to republics of different shades, colours and types.

The Middle East and the world

It is fair to say that the lives of the great majority of the people of the world, regardless of where they live, have been affected by the Middle East. The river valleys of Mesopotamia and Egypt are where humans first settled, started to cultivate plants and domesticate animals. To succeed, these communities needed to co-operate and so established strong centralized leadership, which gave birth to cities. Writing, as a means to keep records, was also invented in this region. With settlement and trade came prosperity and further progress as well as the time to pose more philosophical questions on the origin of mankind. This second feature led to the birth of spirituality and worship. With the birth of religions, the Middle East became the centre for pilgrimage, a cross-road where people met and ideas were exchanged. This allowed the region to flourish both intellectually and commercially.

The changing fortunes for the Middle East came with the Industrial Revolution. As the West progressed, the Middle East entered a "dormant phase" and consequently came to be dominated politically and economically. This ended with the outbreak of the First World War. The War led to the break-up of the Ottoman Empire into a number of successor states and brought the Europeans into the region. A new type of European governance called the mandate system was born. The discovery of oil in 1907 and the conversion from coal to oil raised the economic and strategic importance of the region for the Industrial countries of the West. The decision in 1917 to offer Palestine

TOK Link
**Ways of knowing—
What's in a name?**

Why do we say the Far East, the Near East or the Middle East?

Why "far", "near", "middle"?

Where is the starting point of the person who has coined these terms?

How objective is this view of the world?

as a future Jewish homeland caused tension between the Jewish settlers and the Palestinians and this further involved the Europeans in the affairs of the Middle East. The inter-war years increased this involvement as nationalist sentiments spread and caused clashes between various ethnic groups and the European administrators. The end of the Second World War prompted the region to redefine itself in the context of the Cold War and, as Avi Shlaim, a prominent historian of the Middle East, put it "the European phase in the history of the Middle East gave way to the superpower phase." The superpowers expressed great interest in the region and broke it up into competing spheres of influence. In the period following the Second World War, the conflict between the newly formed state of Israel and the emergent Arab nationalist states forced the attention of the world on the region involving the major world powers in the peace process. In 1979 the Islamic revolution in Iran once again brought the region to the forefront of world affairs. Since the end of the Cold War tension in the Middle East has further intensified. The 1991 Gulf War was the first crisis of the post-Cold War era. Today it is fair to say that the events in the Middle East affect the world on a daily basis.

The First World War in the Middle East

The First World War—the Great War as it was known—is often regarded as a European War, with the focus on the battles of the Western Front. But we forget that it was also fought in the Middle East where a large number of British, Russian, Ottoman and (to a lesser extent) French, German and Austrian soldiers lost their lives. Indeed, some of the bloodiest battles of the First World War were fought on the Turkish-Russian frontiers. Strategically, the Middle East was important for both the Entente and the Central Powers. It was the route through which Russia's supply lines could be kept open. Its important Mediterranean coast watched over vitally strategic sea routes. The Suez Canal speeded up access between the East and the West and was a vital link between the United Kingdom and her Empire in India. This was particularly important when the war started because it allowed a speedy transportation of Indian troops to Europe. Oil had been discovered in south-western Iran in 1907. In 1912 the British Navy switched from coal to oil. Consequently, controlling these strategic spots in the Middle East became a major war aim for both sides because it was believed that it could actually help to determine the outcome.

The impact of the First World War on the Middle East should not be underestimated. Its demographic impact is marked by the significant number of civilian and military casualties over the extended period of the conflict. Ottoman military losses, according to the Ottoman archives, were more than 750,000 men (this included death in action, missing in action and death due to disease). About the same number were wounded. Non-combatant losses came up to 2,150,000 men, women and children. This included deaths caused through famine, disease and population transfer such as the relocation of approximately 1.5 million Armenians. In Mount Lebanon, for example, more than 50 per cent of the population died of famine. Given that war continued in the region until 1922, Ottoman population loss in the period 1914–1922 rose to five million.

Politically, the First World War resulted in the disintegration of the multi-ethnic Ottoman Empire and the dissolution of the caliphate. The Arab-speaking population separated from the Empire and broke up into a number of smaller states. The Turkish-speaking population established themselves separately as Turkey. Palestine was designated as the homeland for the Jewish people and Jews from different corners of the globe were encouraged to migrate and settle in the region.

The Ottoman Empire joins the First World War

On 2 August 1914, a day after Russia had entered the war, a secret agreement was signed between a small circle of the Young Turk leaders and the Germans, in which the Ottomans agreed to join the conflict. On 2 November the Ottomans entered the war and on 14 November the Sultan officially declared Holy War, with the aim of obtaining the support of the Muslim population in the French and British colonies as well as Russia's Central Asian regions. The war

Activity:
Communities

The Ottoman Empire was made up of various religious communities known as *millets*. The word *millet* means nation in Turkish, but it was used by the Ottomans to describe religious rather than ethnic or linguistic communities.

Undertake research to find out how many different *millets* existed under the Ottomans. What were their rights and how autonomous were they?

See map of the Ottoman Empire p. 176.

The Ottoman Empire (1299–1922)

The Ottoman Empire was a multi-ethnic empire that survived for 623 years. At its height, in 1683, it stretched over three continents: from the Persian Gulf in the east to Western Algeria in the west and the outskirts of Vienna in the north. In addition to its military strength, the Ottoman Empire became the seat of the caliphate (Islamic government), which meant that the Ottoman Sultan was viewed as the leader and representative of the Sunni Islamic world.

Though diminished in size, the Ottoman Empire in the early 19th century was still extremely vast. It included Cyprus in the Mediterranean, the Balkans—today's Serbia, Bosnia, Kosovo, Macedonia, Albania, Greece, Bulgaria and large parts of Romania—as well as Anatolia (modern-day Turkey). The Empire embraced the entire Arab-speaking world with the exception of Morocco.

The Ottoman ruler's control over such a vast Empire was weak and in some parts of North Africa practically non-existent. Over time, it became unsustainable. Consequently, from the middle of the 19th century, the Empire referred to as "the sick man of Europe" started to face major challenges from both inside and out. Western Imperial powers started to take advantage of the weakened government and came to dominate many parts of the Empire. The French took over Algeria and Tunisia, the British controlled Egypt and the Italians Libya. Of the enemies within, a notable group was the nationalist movement called the Committee for Union and Progress (CUP), better known as the "Young Turks" who wanted to modernize the country through a series of reforms. Following the Young Turks' revolt of 1908 many CUP activists came to play an important role in government.

Nationalist movements among non-Turkish-speaking people led to a wave of national liberation struggles resulting in the break away from Empire and the establishment of independent states. This movement had already started in the 19th century in the Balkan region when Greece, Serbia, Montenegro, Romania and Bulgaria seceded from the Empire. The First World War led to an escalation of these movements and by the end of the war the break-up of the Ottoman Empire had resulted in a large number of new states.

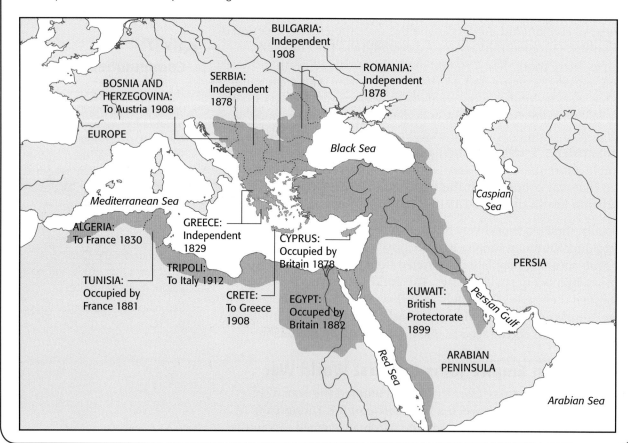

would continue until the armistice of Mudros on 30 October 1918. In retrospect, the decision to enter the war proved to be a miscalculation on the part of the Ottomans because it was based on the belief that the conflict was limited to Russia, Germany and Austria–Hungary. Backed by the Germans and the Austro-Hungarians a war against Russia (without the participation of Britain and France) would be a short and an easy victory. Defeating Russia would rid the Ottomans of a hostile neighbour and yield them territorial gains in the Caucasus and the Balkans. Instead, the war was long, the adversaries more numerous and it was to become the catalyst for the final disintegration of the Ottoman Empire. According to Avi Shlaim, the decision for the Ottomans to enter the First World War on the side of Germany "was the most significant in the history of the modern Middle East and the first move in its remaking."

Allied diplomacy: plenty of promises

The Ottoman Empire's entry into the First World War caused a number of concerns for the Allies. Firstly, it put the Russian war effort at risk because it physically blocked the sea route, the Dardanelle Straits (see map p. 172), through which reinforcement and equipment could have reached the Russian Front. Secondly, it brought the Central Powers, namely Germany, too close to Britain's major sphere of interest—Persia and the Indian subcontinent. Finally, it extended the battle front and, as the Allies knew the risk involved in spreading their troops over such a large area, it brought them to the negotiating table. These negotiations involved making a number of promises to the Russians, the Italians, the French, the Jews and the Arabs in return for allied support for the war effort. These promises became the basis for the new states that came into existence following the break-up of the Ottoman Empire after the war. Consequently, while the war was being fought, most of the Ottoman territory had been promised in one way or another. Historian and specialist on the Middle East, Elisabeth Monroe, called this "expansionist bookings in advance".

Promises to the Russians

One of Britain's main concerns was keeping Russia involved in the war. Given its major military setbacks in 1915 there was fear that the Russians might withdraw. To entice them to stay, the Treaty of Constantinople was signed in March 1915. This treaty would have offered Russia control of the Dardanelle Straits and therefore access to the warm-water port, which had been one of its most important foreign policy objectives throughout the 19th century. In return, the Russians recognized the rest of the Ottoman territory as French and British zones of influence and agreed to a British control of Central Persia.

Promises to the French

In order to reassure their major ally, from the spring of 1915 the British had started discussing the future partition of the Ottoman Empire with the French. These talks, led by George Picot, a French diplomat and Sir Mark Sykes, a member of the British Parliament, were made public in May 1916 and came to be known as the Sykes–Picot Agreement. According to this agreement the British and the

French divided the region into two categories of control: direct and indirect. Where they were assigned direct control they would establish an administration "as they saw fit". In the regions that fell under indirect control they would supply the Arab State or the Confederation of Arab States with advisors and functionaries at the request of the Arab leaders. In making the distinction between "direct" and "indirect" the French and the British showed that they recognized the future existence of Arab states in the region. In this partition the British would take direct control of Iraq from Baghdad to the Persian Gulf and indirect control over the region that ran from the Egyptian border through to the Persian Gulf. This would allow them to build the Haifa–Basra railway line and link the future oil fields to the Mediterranean ports. The French would directly control Lebanon and the coastal region of Syria as far south as Acre and indirectly control the rest of Syria up to the Iranian border. Palestine and the Holy cities would be administered internationally.

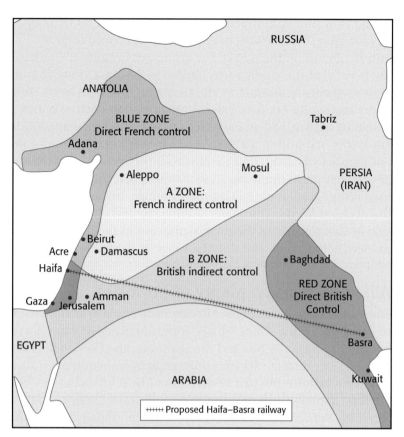

Sykes–Picot Agreement, 1916.

Source: Palestinian Academic Society for the Study of International Affairs (PASSIA).

Promises to the Italians

In order to bring Italy into the war, the British signed the Treaty of London in April 1915, promising Italy parts of the Ottoman territory in return for their support to the Entente powers. The Allies recognized Italy's claims on Libya and the Dodecanese islands, off the coast of Turkey as well as a portion of Anatolia. When the Sykes–Picot Agreement became known in Italy, the Italians pressed for further assurances of Italy's share of the Ottoman territory. Accordingly, the Saint-Jean Maurienne Agreement was concluded between the United Kingdom, France and Italy in August 1917. This agreement further promised Smyrna and south-west Anatolia to Italy.

Promises to the Jews

The Zionist movement had since the Basel Program in 1897 been rallying support for the idea of establishing a Jewish homeland in Palestine. As early as November 1914 this idea was discussed by British policy makers, but it was not taken very seriously and the Sykes–Picot Agreement of 1916 had placed Palestine in international hands. From the end of 1916, however, the British started to show more sympathy to the Zionist cause for a number of reasons. On the one hand, it would help the war effort because it would appeal to the Russian Jews, who were influential among Russian revolutionaries. In the event of a revolutionary takeover, the new government would be compelled to keep Russia in the war. They also believed that the cause of a Jewish homeland would attract support from the United States and put pressure via the American Jews on President Woodrow Wilson to enter the war. On the other hand, supporting the Zionist cause would serve the United Kingdom's long-term interests. By protecting the right of self-determination of the Jewish people, the UK's access to this strategic region of Palestine would go unopposed by either France or the United States. This region not only offered the United Kingdom ports on the Mediterranean Sea, it also formed a buffer against any external threat to the Suez Canal. Many of the leading politicians in the British government recognized the right of the Jewish people to the land of Palestine. This led to the Balfour Declaration in November 1917, which stated that the British government "viewed with favour the establishment in Palestine of a national home for the Jewish people." To fulfil this promise the British had moved away from their position as concluded in the Sykes–Picot Agreement and now supported the idea of placing Palestine under direct British control after the war.

Promises to the Arabs

Soon after the war started the British officials in Cairo contacted Sharif Hussein, the **Sharif of Mecca**, informing him that in return for assistance against the Ottomans, the British would support their claims for Arab independence. Aware of the separatist sentiments among the Arabs, the British were aiming to incite an Arab revolt, which would then divert the Ottoman troops and weaken their war effort. In a letter sent to Abdullah, Sharif Hussein's son, it was stated that the British had no design on their territories after the war and that if the Arabs rebelled, the British would recognize and help establish Arab independence "without any intervention in your internal affairs." Following these discussions a series of letters were exchanged between Henry McMahon, the High Commissioner in Cairo and Sharif Hussein. The Hussein–McMahon correspondence formed the basis for the promises made to the Arabs.

As these promises were not honoured, mainly because they contradicted the other promises that the British had made to the Jews and the French, there is a fair amount of controversy surrounding these letters. There is even some doubt today as to the degree to which McMahon's promises were actually backed by the government in London. Historian William Cleveland argues that the "thorniest issue in their correspondence concerned frontiers". For Hussein, Arab territory included all the Arab-speaking provinces east of Egypt. That means the coastal parts of the Arabian peninsula (the Hejaz), Greater Syria (including Lebanon and Palestine) and Iraq. McMahon claimed that the inhabitants lying west of

> **Sharif of Mecca** With the birth of Islam, Mecca (the birth place of the Prophet) and Medina (the town the Prophet migrated to) in the Arabian Peninsula became Holy cities of Islam. Mecca is the home for the annual pilgrimage (the Haj). Traditionally, the Hashemite family, descendants of the Prophet, was assigned the custodianship of Mecca. The custodian was responsible for ensuring that the pilgrimage was properly conducted. The title Sharif of Mecca means the nobleman of Mecca. When the First World War broke out, Hussein ibn Ali (Hussein, the son of Ali) was the Sharif of Mecca.

Foreign Office,
November 2nd, 1917.

Dear Lord Rothschild,

I have much pleasure in conveying to you, on behalf of His Majesty's Government, the following declaration of sympathy with Jewish Zionist aspirations which has been submitted to, and approved by, the Cabinet.

"His Majesty's Government view with favour the establishment in Palestine of a national home for the Jewish people, and will use their best endeavours to facilitate the achievement of this object, it being clearly understood that nothing shall be done which may prejudice the civil and religious rights of existing non-Jewish communities in Palestine, or the rights and political status enjoyed by Jews in any other country".

I should be grateful if you would bring this declaration to the knowledge of the Zionist Federation.

Letter to Lord Rothschild from the British Foreign Secretary, Arthur James Balfour, 2 November 1917.

Damascus (the coastal part of Syria) were not purely Arab and therefore the coastal region should not be regarded as Arab territory. As the two men did not come to any agreement, they postponed the matter until after the war. McMahon also wanted to secure British control over the provinces of Baghdad and Basra. These areas were of strategic importance because they controlled the oil supplies of the Persian Gulf. Hussein consented to a temporary British occupation until a stable administration could be established.

All together, between July 1915 and March 1916 ten letters were exchanged between the two men. In a letter dated 14 July 1915 Hussein demanded that Britain should recognize the independence of the Arab countries naming the following states: Greater Syria (including Palestine, Lebanon, Iraq and the Arabian Peninsula). In his response, dated 30 August 1915, McMahon affirmed with pleasure that British and Arab interests were the same and declared Britain's desire "for the independence of the Arab countries and their inhabitants and [British] readiness to approve an Arab Caliphate", omitting however the naming of states. It is claimed that McMahon was far more encouraging than London intended. London supported the "freedom of the Arabs" and *not* their "independence".

In the following letter, dated 24 October 1915, McMahon stated that in areas "where Great Britain is free to act without detriment to the interests of her ally France" Britain would "recognize and uphold the independence of the Arabs." This included Central Syria, Northern Iraq and the Arabian Peninsula and it did not, according to the British interpretation of the letter, include western Palestine (west of the River Jordan). Though in the letters that followed Hussein insisted on his opposition to French control of any Arab land, McMahon emphasized Britain's close relations with France and it was agreed to leave the fate of Lebanon and Northern Syria until the end of the war.

In May 1917 Sykes and Picot met with Sharif Hussein to convince him to accept the Sykes–Picot Agreement. Hussein was reluctant and was only persuaded when he was told that France's control over Lebanon would be indirect and the French would only supply the advisers and functionaries at the request of the Arab state. This, however, turned out to be untrue. Once the Balfour Declaration had been issued Hussein was assured that the British government's support of the Jewish people stood so far as it was "compatible with the freedom of the existing population". This assurance was however not stated in the declaration itself.

The British needed Hussein and the support of the Arabs to win the war. Hussein needed the British in order to establish a future Arab state. In a statement issued in June 1918 to a delegation of Syrians known as the "Declaration to the Seven" the United Kingdom recognized "the complete and sovereign independence of Arabs" and agreed that once the war was over and the Ottomans defeated, the new government would be based on the consent of the governed. Clearly one of the biggest problems was that many of the important decisions, namely those concerning the future of the region, were left in total ambiguity until the end of the war.

Activity:

Source analysis

The Hussein–McMahon correspondence has caused a great deal of controversy. Read the two letters below and research the places discussed by both authors and discuss the reasons behind this controversy. What do the sources reveal about both sides?

Sharif Hussein to Sir Henry McMahon, 14 July 1915

Whereas the entire Arab nation without exception is determined to assert its right to live, gain its freedom and administer its own affairs in name and in fact;

And whereas the Arabs believe it to be in Great Britain's interest to lend them assistance and support in the fufillment of their steadfast and legitimate aims to the exclusion of all other aims;

And whereas it is similarly to the advantage of the Arabs, in view of their geographical position and their economic interests, and in view of the well-known attitude of the Government of Great Britain, to prefer British assistance to any other;

For these reasons, the Arab nation has decided to approach the Government of Great Britain with a request for the approval, through one of their representatives if they think fit, of the following basic provisions which, as time presses, have not been made to include matters of relatively smaller importance, since such matters can wait until the time comes for their consideration:

1. *Great Britain recognises the independence of the Arab countries which are bounded: on the north, by the line Mersin-Adana to parallel 37°N. and thence along the line Birejik-Urfa-Mardin-Midiat-Jazirat (ibn 'Umar)-Amadia to the Persian frontier; on the east, by the Persian frontier down to the Persian Gulf; on the south, by the Indian Ocean (with the exclusion of Aden whose status will remain at present); on the west by the Red Sea and the Mediterranean Sea back to Mersin.*

2. *Great Britain will agree to the proclamation of an Arab Caliphate for Islam.*

3. *… The Sharifian Arab Government undertakes, other things being equal, to grant Great Britain preference in all economic enterprises in the Arab countries …*

5. *Great Britain agrees to the abolition of Capitulations in the Arab countries, and undertakes to assist the Sharifian government in summoning an international congress to decree their abolition …*

Source: Smith, Charles D. 2007. *Palestine and the Arab-Israeli Conflict*. Boston, USA. pp. 96–7.

Sir Henry McMahon to Sharif Hussein, 24 October 1915

I regret to find that you inferred from my last note that my attitude towards the question of frontiers and boundaries was one of hesitancy and luke-warmth. … All I meant was

that I considered that the time had not yet come in which that question could be discussed in a conclusive manner.

But, having realised from your last note that you considered the question important, vital and urgent, I hastened to communicate to the Government of Great Britain the purport of your note. It gives me the greatest pleasure to convey to you, on their behalf, the following declarations which, I have no doubt, you will receive with satisfaction and acceptance. The districts of Mersin and Alexandretta, and portions of Syria lying to the west of the districts of Damascus, Homs, Hama and Aleppo cannot be said to be purely Arab, and must on that account be excepted from the proposed delimitation.

Subject to that modification, and without prejudice to the treaties concluded between us and certain Arab Chiefs, we accept that delimitation.

As for the regions lying within the proposed frontiers, in which Great Britain is free to act without detriment to the interests of her ally France, I am authorised to give you the following pledges on behalf of the Government of Great Britain, and to reply as follows to your note:

1. *That, subject to the modifications stated above, Great Britain is prepared to recognise. and uphold the independence of the Arabs in all the regions lying within the frontiers proposed by the Sharif of Mecca.*

2. *That Great Britain will guarantee the Holy Places against all external aggression, and will recognise the obligation of preserving them from aggression;*

3. *That, when circumstances permit, Great Britain will help the Arabs with her advice and assist them in the establishment of governments to suit those diverse regions;*

4. *That it is understood that the Arabs have already decided to seek the counsels and advice of Great Britain exclusively; and that such European advisers and officials as may be needed to establish a sound system of administration shall be British;*

5. *That, as regards the two vilayets of Baghdad and of Basra, the Arabs recognise that the fact of Great Britain's established position and interests there will call for the setting up of special administrative arrangements to protect those regions from foreign aggression, to promote the welfare of their inhabitants, and to safeguard our mutual economic interests.*

I am confident that this declaration will convince you, beyond all doubt, of Great Britain's sympathy with the aspirations of her friends the Arabs; and that it will result in a lasting and solid alliance with them, of which one of the immediate consequences will be the expulsion of the Turks from the Arab countries and the liberation of the Arab peoples from the Turkish yoke which has weighed on them all these long years …

Source: Smith, Charles D. 2007. *Palestine and the Arab-Israeli Conflict*. Boston, USA. pp. 98–9.

The Armenians and the First World War

By January 1915, the defeat of the Ottoman army in the Caucasus exposed the eastern parts of the country to more Russian attacks. In this region the local population included a large Christian community, the Armenians. There is a varied account of the size of the Armenian population. An American demographer, Justin McCarthy has estimated the number in 1915 to have been around 1,600,000 or just over ten per cent of the population in the Ottoman Empire.

Before the war, representatives from the Armenian community and the government in Constantinople had discussed the community's demand for some autonomy. These, according to Erik Zürcher, would have been put into effect if the First World War had not occurred. The war altered the situation with the prospect of an eventual Ottoman defeat and, encouraged by the Russians, the Armenian nationalists saw it as an opportunity to break away from the Ottoman Empire and establish an independent Armenia. In pursuit of this aim, some Armenians even joined the Russian army. The reaction of the Ottomans was immediate. On 24 April 1915 a large number of Armenian leaders were arrested. The cabinet then took the decision to relocate the entire Armenian population from the war zone to Syria and Mesopotamia (Iraq of today). Deportations (officially referred to as relocation) started immediately and by the summer the area was cleared of Armenians. In some areas families were given 24 hours notice to pack everything they owned and were ordered to march towards their final destination.

There is controversy over the number that died. Turkish historians speak of 200,000 deaths, while Armenians consider the number to be ten times larger. Zürcher considers the number of deaths to be between 600,000 and 800,000. There is also controversy over whether the relocation and the deaths that followed can be called genocide. The Turkish government argues that the deaths were caused by inter-ethnic fights between the Kurds and the Armenians, but the Armenians believe that it was the intended policy of the government to exterminate a large number of Armenians. Zürcher concludes that: "even if the Ottoman government as such was not involved in genocide, an inner circle within the [government] wanted to 'solve' the Eastern Question by the extermination of the Armenians and it used the relocation as a cloak for this policy."

1915, orphaned Armenian children, Syria.

War and diplomacy in the Middle East

This model of diplomacy, however rational and expedient it appeared during the war, left behind a long trail of unfulfilled promises and entangled the United Kingdom in a number of difficult situations after the war. If they were to keep their pledge to the French and defend France's position in Greater Syria, as stated in the Sykes–Picot Agreement, the Arabs would be betrayed. If, on the other hand, they wanted to respect their engagement to the Arabs and back the birth of Arab independent states, they would be angering both the Jews and the French. The promises also show the degree to which the break-up of the Ottoman Empire and the fate of the Middle East was decided as a war aim in the early years of the war. It is, as James Gelvin put it, as though France and the UK saw the Middle East as compensation for fighting the war.

The Empire's sheer size and its extensive borders made the Ottoman army extremely vulnerable. No sooner had the war been declared than they were attacked both by the British in the Persian Gulf region and the Russians in the Caucasus. The Ottoman army, nonetheless, performed much more effectively than anticipated and managed to engage the British and the Russian forces in the region throughout the duration of the war. Fighting also occurred in Persia (the Iran of today), which though neutral became nonetheless the battle ground for rivalry between Germans, Russians, Turks and the British.

The first battle occurred on the north-eastern border of the Ottoman Empire, in the Caucasus. The Russian attack was at first successfully stopped, but in the counter-offensive the Turks were heavily defeated at Sarikamis in February 1915. Only 12,000 out of 90,000 troops survived.

In January 1915 an Ottoman force crossed the Sinai desert and tried to take the Suez Canal, an extremely sensitive strategic spot that controlled the sea route for France and the United Kingdom. Their attempt failed, but it also turned the UK's attention to the East. The British had already entered the scene when their troops stationed in India, the Indian Expeditionary Force, were sent to the Persian Gulf to protect the oil pipelines in case of war. Once war broke out these troops were ordered to advance inland and take Basra in November 1915. This initial victory misled the British by undermining their assessment of the potential of the Ottoman forces. In the attempt to take Baghdad, the British were forced to retreat and found themselves trapped in Kut-el-Amara. The siege lasted 146 days and ended with a British surrender in April 1916. 13,000 prisoners of war were interned. Another British humiliation occurred in February 1915 at the Gallipoli campaign. The aim was to land on the Turkish mainland, advance on to Constantinople and once the capital was taken bring about the collapse of the Ottomans. The Allies managed to land on the Gallipoli peninsula but Turkish resistance was such that they were forced to retreat by January 1916 leaving behind an enormous number of casualties. The humiliating failures of Kut-el-Amara and Gallipoli were a major setback for the Allies. Consequently they turned to a new tactic.

> *"What makes the agreement* [the Constantinople Agreement] *important is that it established the principle that the Entente powers had a right to compensation for fighting their enemies and that at least part of this compensation should come in the form of territory carved out of the Middle East."*
>
> James Gelvin

A change of tactic: encouraging dissent among the Ottoman troops

The wave of nationalism that had affected the Balkan region from the last quarter of the 19th century had also left its marks on the other ethnic minorities in the Ottoman Empire. With the outbreak of war, the Entente powers realized that through encouraging such nationalist sentiments, they could cause an internal fracture inside the Ottoman army. Already the Russians had attempted this with the Armenians, an attempt that ended in the policy of "relocation" and the tragic massacre of this community. The British now turned their attention to the Arabs, who made up about one third of the Empire's population and, just like the Armenians, had tried to negotiate with the Ottoman rulers to obtain a degree of independence legally. When these attempts failed the Arabs turned to the British for help.

In 1913 a delegation of Arabs from Damascus and Beirut contacted the British consulate in Beirut. In the same year another group visited Kitchener, the British Consul in Cairo. Finally, in June 1913, 200 delegates from the Arab community met in Paris and adopted a resolution demanding reforms in the Ottoman Empire that would permit more freedom for Arabs. Before the outbreak of the First World War the British reaction had been very negative. They supported the Ottoman Empire and defended its territorial integrity. With the outbreak of war and the realization that the defeat of the Ottomans was not as easy as they had expected, an alliance with the Arab people in the Ottoman Empire became much more attractive.

The Arab Revolt, 1916

Sharif Hussein was designated as chief spokesman of the Arabs and through a number of meetings and correspondences, an alliance was established between the two sides. The Arabs agreed to revolt against the Ottomans and denounce the Ottomans as an enemy of Islam. In return, the British agreed to back their demand for independence. The Ottoman authorities tried to dissuade the Arab nationalists. This dissuasion took two forms. First, they tried fear tactics: from the summer of 1915 Jamal Pasha, the military governor of Greater Syria began to deport, arrest, interrogate, torture and even execute many Arab nationalist leaders. As an example of these persecutions on 6 May 1916, in Beirut and Damascus, 21 Arab nationalists were hanged on the grounds of disloyalty and treason. The other move was to publish the text of the Sykes–Picot Agreement in order to show the Arabs the duplicity of the Imperial powers. Neither of these moves dissuaded the Arabs, who started their revolt on 10 June 1916.

The Arab tribal armies were commanded by Sharif Hussein's sons, Faisal and Abdullah. It was funded and organized by the British. Their first attack was on the Ottoman garrison in Mecca. This attack was repulsed by the

> **Discussion point:**
>
> Guerilla warfare is strategically defensive and tactically aggressive. What are its advantages and disadvantages?

> ### T.E. Lawrence (1888–1935)
>
> Lieutenant Colonel Thomas Edward Lawrence first visited the Middle East when he arrived in Beirut as a field archeologist in 1910. His knowledge of Arabic and of the region meant that after the outbreak of war, he was a tremendously important recruit for the British Intelligence Service. His first posting was to Cairo. During the First World War, he fought alongside the Arabs under the command of Faisal. The two men were instrumental in transforming the Arab army into a successful guerrilla force assisting the British army in the battles against the Ottomans. Lawrence famously wrote about his experiences in the Middle East in his autobiography, *The Seven Pillars of Wisdom* (first published in 1922), upon which the 1962 film *Lawrence of Arabia* was based.

Turkish army in Mecca and the British had to send reinforcements from Egypt to assist Hussein's men. By September, the principal towns of the Hejaz, with the exception of Medina, were in Arab hands. However, the expected mass support from the Arab-speaking Ottoman soldiers was not forthcoming. It nonetheless served to divert and tie down the Turkish troops.

Under the command of Faisal, the Arabs changed their tactics: instead of involving themselves in major frontal attacks, where clearly they lacked the necessary skills and equipment to face a professionally trained army, they chose guerilla warfare. T.E. Lawrence a junior member of the Arab Bureau (a branch of the Foreign Office) had apparently analysed this situation when he wrote in November 1916 that the value of the tribes was defensive only and they would only succeed in guerilla warfare. In a series of hit-and-run tactics they succeeded in disrupting the Hejaz railway thus cutting the supply lines of the Turkish forces and immobilizing 30,000 Turkish troops along the Hejaz railway from Amman to Medina. They also prevented the Turco-German forces in Syria from linking up with the Turkish garrison in Yemen. By attacking the telegraph lines, the Turks were forced to send messages by wireless, which the British could now intercept. In July 1917 the Arab–British forces attacked and captured the Red Sea port of Aqaba and following the campaign for Sinai took over Palestine. In October 1918 Faisal entered and liberated Syria. This final act justified many of the demands for an independent Arab state.

> **Discussion point:**
>
> How historically accurate was the film *Lawrence of Arabia* and Lawrence's own account of the Arab Revolt in *The Seven Pillars of Wisdom* upon which the film was based?
>
> Was the significance of T.E. Lawrence's role in uniting the Arab forces exaggerated?

Activity:

The Arab Revolt

Did the Arabs fulfil their side of the bargain?

The effectiveness of the Arab Revolt is open to varied interpretations. The British War Office claimed that the Arabs had not fulfilled their promise of inciting a mutiny inside the Ottoman army. The Arabs argued that they had kept their side of the bargain: the revolt had taken place and the Ottoman army was finally defeated.

Read the following extracts and answer the questions that follow.

Source A

Three weeks after Hussein announced his rebellion, the British War Office told the Cabinet in London that the Arab world was not following the lead. In a secret memorandum prepared for the War Committee of the Cabinet on 1 July 1916, the General Staff of the War Office reported that Hussein "has always represented himself, in his correspondence with the High Commissioner, as being the spokesman of the Arab nation, but so far as is known, he is not supported by any organization of Arabs nearly general enough to secure … automatic acceptance of the terms agreed to by him." As a result, according to the memorandum, the British government ought not to assume that agreements reached with him would be honoured by other Arab leaders.

Source: Fromkin, David. 1989. *A Peace to end all Peace: Creating the Modern Middle East 1914–22.* London, UK. Penguin. p. 223.

Source B

Nearly a year after Hussein proclaimed the Arab revolt, Hogarth [Lieutenant-Commander David G. Hogarth was the head of the Arab Bureau in Cairo] was prepared to write it off as a failure. In reviewing what he called 'A Year of Revolt' in the Hejaz for the Arab Bulletin, no. 52 (31 May 1917), he concluded that it had not fulfilled the hopes placed in it nor did it justify further expectations: "That the Hejaz Bedouins were simply guerrillas, and not of good quality at that, had been amply demonstrated, even in the earlier sieges; and it was never in doubt that they would not withstand Turkish regulars.

Source: Fromkin, David. 1989. *A Peace to end all Peace: Creating the Modern Middle East 1914–22.* London, UK. Penguin. p. 223.

Source C

Although the tribal contingents had served to divert and tie down Turkish troops and to disrupt the Hejaz Railway, their real military contributions awaited the campaigns into Palestine (1917) and into Syria (1918), when the army led by Faysal played an important role in cutting supply lines and in threatening the Ottoman/German eastern flanks.

Source: Smith, Charles D. 2007. *Palestine and the Arab Israeli Conflict.* Boston, USA. Bedford/St Martin's. p. 79.

Source D

Meanwhile, although the Arab Revolt launched by the sharif aroused little response in Mesopotamia and Syria, which were still firmly under Turkish control, it made an important contribution to the war in the Middle East. It immobilized some 30,000 Turkish troops along the Hejaz railway from Amman to Medina and prevented the Turco-German forces in Syria from linking up with the Turkish garrison in Yemen. There could have been the most serious consequences for the Allies if the enemy forces had made contact with the Germans in East Africa and succeeded in closing the Red Sea to Allied shipping.

Mansfield, Peter. 1991. *A History of The Middle East.* Middlesex, UK. Penguin Books.

Questions

1 In your opinion did Arabs fulfil their side of the bargain?

2 The promises made to the Arabs were not fully met in the post-war period, and the Arabs felt betrayed. Can it be argued that this sentiment of betrayal was justified?

3 Find out what you can about the Arab soldiers who participated in Faisal's campaign.

4 What is the legacy for Arab relations with neighbouring countries? Break up into groups and analyse the perspective on the Arab Revolt from the point of view of the Syrians, Turks, Egyptians, British and the Germans.

Towards an Ottoman defeat

The good fortunes of the Ottomans started to turn in 1916. This was mainly because they were overstretched on too many fronts and had also, at Germany's request, sent soldiers into Romania, Macedonia and Galicia. The army was also depleted as a result of hunger, lack of transport and a shortage of equipment as well as recurrent epidemics of diseases such as malaria, typhoid and cholera. According to Zürcher, an army that in 1916 contained 800,000 men had halved in size by 1917 and by October 1918 counted only 100,000.

On the Mesopotamian and Palestinian front, the British Expeditionary Force, assisted by the Arabs, took Baghdad in March 1917 and Palestine in December 1917. On the Eastern front, the Ottomans were incapable of stopping Russia's advances: Trabzon, Erzerum and Van fell into enemy hands. The Caucasus, however, engaged the Ottoman and Russian armies until 1917, when the Russians withdrew as a result of the Russian Revolution.

The second Russian Revolution in November 1917 caused a certain amount of turmoil. First the Russians withdrew, which naturally allowed the Ottomans to retake their lost territory. The power vacuum, however, immediately gave rise to a nationalist rising among Georgians, Armenians and Azerbaijanis, who wanted to unite and form the Republic of Transcaucasia. The Ottoman forces once again entered battle and defeated the new republic in May 1918. This success, however, coincided with the collapse of the Central Powers elsewhere and the Ottoman government realized it had to seek armistice. On 30 October 1918 following the armistice of Mudros, the Ottomans capitulated to the Allies.

The peace settlements

Post World War 1 peace settlement is not just a chapter in history but the essential background to contemporary politics. It lies at the root of the countless political clashes, territorial disputes, struggles for national liberation, and interstate wars that have become familiar features of the politics of the Middle East. It lies at the heart of the current conflicts between the Arabs and Israel, between Arabs and other Arabs, between some Arabs and the west. As Field Marshall Wavell, who served in the Palestine campaign presciently observed, it was "a peace to end all peace."

> **Source:** Shlaim, Avi. 1995. *War and Peace in the Middle East: A Concise History*. New York, USA. Penguin. p. 18.

The Treaty of Sèvres

The peace treaty signed with the Ottoman Empire took a little longer than the others. An agreement was finally reached at the San Remo Conference in April 1920. This conference had brought the European Powers that had a territorial interest in the redistribution of the Ottoman territory to the negotiating table. The conference resolved the French and British differences and recognized the validity of the Balfour Declaration. The decisions taken at San Remo were then incorporated into the Treaty of Sèvres.

The Treaty of Sèvres carried with it the seeds of future troubles in the region. This was because it was written in total disregard of the sentiments of the Turkish people. The victor nations were so keen to pursue their own national interests that they behaved as though the Turks no longer existed and that their goods could be auctioned to the highest bidder. Though it maintained the Ottoman Sultan in office, by reducing his army and taking away his control on major ports as well as the country's finances, the treaty made him weak, dependent on the West and vulnerable to internal challenge.

The treaty also offered certain national minorities within the Turkish territory, such as the Kurds and the Armenians, the prospect of independence without in any way providing them with the necessary tools. Consequently those communities collapsed in the face of rising Turkish nationalism. The state lines established by the treaty were drawn up in a totally arbitrary way and paid very little attention to the will of the local population. These state boundaries left most of its inhabitants dissatisfied and were to cause inter-state wars until the present day.

Finally through the creation of the mandate system it reintroduced the Europeans to the region in total disregard of the national sentiments of the local population. The Treaty of Sèvres reaffirmed the promise made to the Jewish community through the Balfour Declaration and sowed the seeds of a long inter-communal conflict between the Palestinian Arabs and the Jews.

With the Treaty of Sèvres the European Powers had resolved *their* internal conflicts and succeeded in redrawing the map of the region to suit their interests, but they had done very little for the long term stability of the region. By showing such disregard towards the Turks, the treaty managed to arouse the anger of the Turks and build on their sentiment of nationalism. This led to the outbreak of the Turkish War of Independence (see section, starting p. 175). Strengthened by their victories in this war, the Turkish nationalistsquestioned the very validity of the Treaty of Sèvres, forced its annulment and obtained a new treaty. This second treaty, signed in Lausanne in June 1923, was a remarkable turnaround as it granted the Republic of Turkey recognition as an independent nation-state, free of any interference from foreign powers.

The Treaty of Sèvres

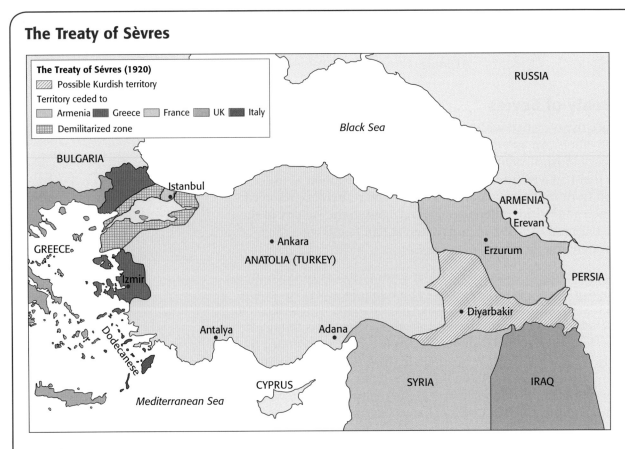

Signed: 10 August 1920

Signatories: UK, France, Italy, Japan, Armenia, Belgium, Czechoslovakia, Greece, Hejaz, Poland, Portugal, Romania, Yugoslavia and the Ottoman Empire.

a The Kingdom of Hejaz was given international recognition

b A Democratic Republic of Armenia was created.

c The extra privileges granted to foreign nationals, called Capitulation, which had been abolished before the war were restored.

d The Allies were to control the Empire's finances. This included the supervision of the Empire's national budget, and total control of the Ottoman Bank.

e The Ottoman army was to be reduced to 50,000.

f Greece was given Izmir in the western Anatolia and eastern Thrace

g France was given Mandatory Power over Greater Syria

h Britain was given Mandatory Power over the provinces of Baghdad, Basra and Palestine

i The Dardanelle Straits were placed under international supervision

j An independent Kurdish zone was proposed.

The Treaty of Lausanne

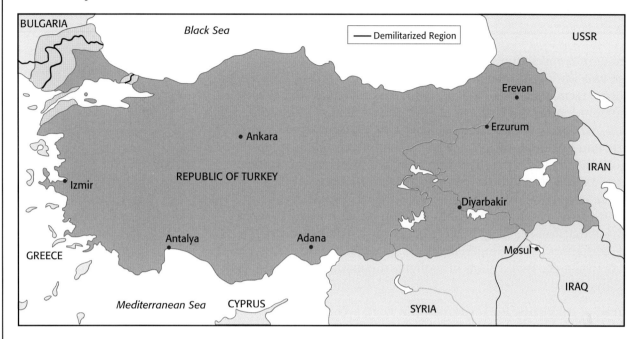

Signed: 24 July 1923

Signatories: UK, France, Italy, Japan, Greece, Romania, Yugoslavia and Turkey.

a The terms of the Treaty of Sèvres were revoked.

b New borders of the Republic of Turkey were assigned. The loss of the Arab-speaking provinces and Cyprus were confirmed

c The Dardanelle Straits remained under international control until 1936.

d Turkey restored control over its financial and judicial matters. The extra privileges of the foreign nationals were revoked.

e The frontier between Turkey and Iraq was to be decided at a later date. The controversy was over the fate of Mosul, claimed by Turkey, but the British wanted to incorporate it within the new state of Iraq.

Activity:

The treaties of Sèvres and Lausanne

Analyse the treaties and fill out the table below.

Questions	Treaty of Sèvres	Treaty of Lausanne
How was the fate of the Ottoman Empire affected by the treaties?		
How was the fate of the Armenians affected by the treaties?		
How was the fate of the Kurds affected by the treaties?		
How was the fate of the Arabs affected by the treaties?		
What was decided about the Dardanelle Straits?		
How did the treaties affect the influence of the European Powers?		

The mandate system

Among the representatives at the Paris Peace Conference there were two schools of thought. The French and the British pursued a colonial agenda and were looking for territorial expansion as a compensation for the First World War. The President of the United States, Woodrow Wilson, had a different vision for the post-war world and was opposed to any annexation of territory as spoils of war. He advocated self-determination as a principle according to which nations should be formed. Self-determination assumed that the local population would be consulted as to the form of their future government. Wilson's position raised the expectations of those that were seeking independence but caused concern and discomfort for the imperial powers. In order to bridge the gap between the two schools of thought, the mandate system was invented.

Instead of colonizing the territories that were according to the peacemakers "not yet able to stand by themselves", the advanced countries would administer their affairs until the time that they were ready to manage on their own. While in each case one country would be assigned the role of Mandatory Power, the **League of Nations** would supervise their work through the **Permanent Mandates Commission (PMC)**. The mandated territories were divided into three groups, known as A, B and C Mandates. This division was in accordance with their level of political development. The countries that were given Mandatory Power (the United Kingdom, France, Japan, Belgium, South Africa, Australia and New Zealand) agreed to guide their mandates towards independence. The understanding was that they would encourage the development of political, economic and social institutions in these regions to the point at which self-government could be achieved, following which the Mandatory Power would withdraw.

- **Category A Mandates** included the ex-Ottoman Arab territories in the Middle East that were on the brink of independent statehood.
- **Category B Mandates**, consisted mainly of former German colonies in Africa (with the exception of South West Africa), the Mandatory Power guided the mandates away from abusive customs such as slavery, exploitation of native labour and opened the region up for trade with other countries.
- **Category C Mandates** included South-West Africa and German islands in the Pacific. These Mandates were regarded as too under-developed and therefore not ready for independence. Consequently they came under total control of the Mandatory Power.

The **League of Nations** was an inter-governmental organization established after the First World War. Its aim was to prevent the outbreak of a future war by firstly encouraging countries to disarm and secondly to use negotiation and diplomacy as a means to resolve conflicts.

The **Permanent Mandates Commission (PMC)** was established as a supervisory body over the application of Article 22. The Mandatory Powers were required to give an annual report to this commission and show that they were fulfilling their task in a satisfactory manner. The members of the PMC were selected by the League Council on the basis of their expertise and impartiality. If a dispute arose between the local population and the Mandatory Power, both sides called upon the PMC to arbitrate between the two parties. Mandates could also send petitions to the Commission to ask them to look into a problem.

The Headquarters of the League of Nations, Geneva.

The mandate system applied the principle of self-determination, which was so dear to President Wilson, but at the same time legitimized French and British control over the desired territories in the Middle East. According to F.S. Northedge, a specialist on the League of Nations, "it was a device … to solve a dilemma, namely, how could Allied Powers … be allowed to keep their gains, without affronting people, especially in the United States, who wanted to break free from old-fashioned imperialism." In the words of Mehran Kamrava, a historian on the Middle East, however, it was "a polite disguise for what a couple of decades earlier had been unabashedly called colonialism." This model of control was formalized in **article 22** of the **Covenant of the League of Nations.**

On paper the mandate system was a fairly interesting compromise between colonialism and independence, but its application to the case of the ex-Ottoman Arab territories was not easily resolved. This was mainly due to the fact that the principle of tutelage or guardianship was in conflict with Arab nationalism which had taken possession of the Arab world during and after the war. In other words a nation (the Arab nation) that had fought alongside the Allies in order to obtain an independent Arab State was now being cast aside as one that was "not yet able to stand by [itself]" and asked to entrust itself into the hands of the more "advanced nations". Many Arabs found this offensive and the numerous revolts that erupted against the two Mandatory Powers, France and the United Kingdom, reflected this.

Covenant of the League of Nations (article 22)

To those colonies and territories which as a consequence of the late war have ceased to be under the sovereignty of the States which formerly governed them and which are inhabited by peoples not yet able to stand by themselves under the strenuous conditions of the modern world, there should be applied the principle that the well-being and development of such peoples form a sacred trust of civilisation and that securities for the performance of this trust should be embodied in this Covenant.

The best method of giving practical effect to this principle is that the tutelage of such peoples should be entrusted to advanced nations who by reason of their resources, their experience or their geographical position can best undertake this responsibility, and who are willing to accept it, and that this tutelage should be exercised by them as Mandatories on behalf of the League. …

Certain communities formerly belonging to the Turkish Empire have reached a stage of development where their existence as independent nations can be provisionally recognized subject to the rendering of administrative advice and assistance by a Mandatory until such time as they are able to stand alone. The wishes of these communities must be a principal consideration in the selection of the Mandatory. …

In every case of mandate, the Mandatory shall render to the Council an annual report in reference to the territory committed to its charge. …

A permanent Commission shall be constituted to receive and examine the annual reports of the Mandatories and to advise the Council on all matters relating to the observance of the mandates.

Activity:

The mandate system and the principle of self-determination

Article 22 of the Covenant of the League of Nations stated that "the wishes of these communities must be the principal consideration in the selection of the Mandatory." In other words, the local population was to be consulted as to whom they wanted to be administered by.

To consider the wishes of the Arabs and apply article 22 of the Covenant of the League of Nations, the United States proposed forming an international commission of inquiry, which would consult the local population in the region. As France and Britain refused to send representatives, only Charles Crane and Henry King, representatives from the United States carried out the inquiry. This is known as the King–Crane Commission.

The two men travelled from Palestine to Anatolia during the summer of 1919 and interviewed Arabs and Jews. They received 1836 petitions, held audience with 34 mayors, 15 administrative councils, 65 councils of village chiefs, 30 Arab sheikhs and 17 trade and professional associations. The commission found that an overwhelming majority of those questioned wanted the unity of Syria with Lebanon—a territory that they called Greater Syria. When asked which country they preferred as their Mandatory Power, their order of preference was as follows:

1 No Mandatory Power (independence)
2 The United States
3 The United Kingdom.

The findings of the inquiry were submitted to the Paris Peace Conference, but not made public.

Putting the Allies to the test

1 Why were the findings of the King–Crane Commission not published?

2 Why did decision-makers at the Paris Peace Conference not respect the "wishes of the communities"?

3 What do you think were the long term implications of this disrespect?

The case of Syria and Lebanon

Syria and Lebanon both became French mandates and were administered by the French until they obtained independence in 1944. This decision came as a surprise to some Arabs, who during the course of the war had been led to think otherwise. This misunderstanding caused tension between France and its mandates.

In December 1917 when the Allied forces were preparing the assault on Syria General Allenby, who commanded the Egyptian Expeditionary Force, announced that the United Kingdom sought "the complete and final liberation of all peoples formerly oppressed by the Turks and the establishment of national governments … deriving authority from the initiative and free will of those people themselves." This was a confirmation of the pledges that had already been offered to Sharif Hussein by McMahon. The pledge was again repeated in June 1918 to a delegation of Syrians in Cairo. This is known as the "Declaration of Seven". And, as a way of honouring that pledge, on 3 October 1918 the British troops let Faisal enter Damascus, claim victory and liberate the city from Ottoman control. Faisal then established his government in Damascus. Faisal was however not to remain ruler for long and the fate of Syria and Lebanon was discussed and resolved in London and Paris without any consultation with Sharif Hussein or his sons.

On 1 December 1918 the British Prime Minister, Lloyd George, and the French Prime Minister, Clemenceau, had met in London. The purpose of the meeting was to review and amend the Sykes–Picot agreement. The two men agreed to redraw the boundaries according to their interests and each negotiated their share of the territory in total disregard to their prior engagements or the wishes of the local communities. Though at this stage the agreement was informal some changes to the Sykes–Picot agreement were discussed and later introduced at the conference in San Remo in 1920. Most notably, the United Kingdom's territorial share was to be increased through the addition of Mosul to Iraq; Palestine was no longer to be placed under international administration but was to fall under British guardianship; while Syria and Lebanon would be handed over to the French.

Accordingly, when the Allied Supreme Council met in San Remo with representatives from the UK, Italy, France and Japan, it was decided that Greater Syria would be divided into two mandates (Syria and Lebanon), both under French administration. Thus Faisal's rule over an independent Arab Greater Syria was a short-lived dream. To ease the French take-over, by September 1919 the British had already withdrawn their troops from Syria. Faisal was therefore left to face the French troops alone. After the Battle of Maysalun in July 1920 the French defeated Faisal's forces. Faisal fled to Haifa. Syria and Lebanon became French mandates.

Article 22 of the Covenant stated that mandatory's role was to offer "administrative advice and assistance" to prepare the mandates for independence (see the text on p. 191). Instead of encouraging the formation of local administative institutions and promoting national unity, the French adopted a policy of divide and rule which rendered the Syrians and the Lebanese more dependent on their presence. Thus Lebanon was dominated politically by **Maronite Christians**, who constituted 30 per cent of the population. This created a situation where the majority Muslim population were unhappy about being ruled by the Christians. Syria was broken up into two major states of Aleppo and Damascus each with separate governors and two smaller districts for the **Alawis** and the **Druze.** Political life in Syria was to be dominated by Sunni Muslims thus isolating the Druze and the Alawites. The French High Commissioner responsible for all decision-making was situated in Beirut.

Christian Maronites living in Mount Lebanon had close ties with the French.

The **Alawis** are a minority Muslim sect living in Western Syria and Northern Lebanon who describe themselves as a sect of Sh'ia Islam.

The **Druze** are a minority Muslim group living in Southern Syria, Central Lebanon and Northern Israel who describe themselves as unitarian Muslims.

The presence of the French and the manner in which they administered the region led to the rise of nationalist movements. In Syria in July 1925 a revolt broke out in the Druze region. Led by Sultan Atrash, a Druze chieftain, they succeeded at first in forcing the French out of the region. By autumn the movement had become nationwide. In spite of massive air and artillery attacks on Damascus the revolt continued and it was not until the spring of 1927 that the French managed to suppress the rebels. Over 6,000 Syrians were killed. The revolt gave rise to a Syrian political organisation, the National Bloc. In spite of the moderate stance of the National Bloc, the French authorities continued to undermine the Syrian people's right to independence and maintained their rigid control until 1944.

The case of Iraq

In the negotiations at San Remo, state boundaries were drawn and what was previously known as the Mesopotamian region became Iraq. Iraq's borders were drawn to suit British interests. In the north the British showed interest in the oil wells of Kirkuk and Mosul, so they negotiated with the French and obtained their agreement to exclude Mosul from Greater Syria. Hence Iraq's northern border was extended up to Anatolia (Turkey of today) and Persia (Iran of today). The mountainous province of Mosul inhabited by Sunni Kurds became part of Iraq, the borders extending south to include the province of Basra, inhabited by Shi'a Arabs because it was situated at the opening of the Persian Gulf. From this position they kept an eye on the navigation in the gulf, in particular the transportation of oil. The central province of Baghdad became the capital of the new country. This province included a mixture of Shi'a and Sunni Arabs.

The Kurds

The Kurds are ethnically distinct from the Arabs. They have a different language and culture. Their ancestral home has been in the region that is today a cross-section of Iraq, Iran, Turkey and Syria. They have not assimilated into any of the countries that they were assigned to live in and continue to this day to claim their political autonomy.

In the Treaty of Sèvres promises were made for a future Kurdistan; it was to be a two-stage process, with the Anatolian Kurds obtaining independence straight away and the Iraqi Kurds being given the choice to join at a later date. The Sèvres proposals never materialized because the United Kingdom decided to include a Kurdish province, Mosul, into the newly formed Iraq and, subsequently, the Turkish war of Independence forced the revision of the Treaty of Sèvres.

In the Treaty of Lausanne, there was no mention of a distinct Kurdish region. On the contrary, given the Turkish nationalist sentiments during this period, Kurds were not even regarded as ethnically distinct from the Turks. The Kurdish rebellion of 1925 resulted in the death of 25,000 Kurds. The Kurdish question continues to cause major disputes to this day.

Consequently the Iraq that was born in 1920 included three separate provinces: Mosul, Basra and Baghdad. This merger created an uneasy and a very complex situation: The Kurdish minority of Mosul were brought under the hegemony of the Arabs and were denied minority rights by the Arab majority. They therefore opposed the authority of Baghdad. The Arabs, divided between Shi'as and Sunnis, were to be ruled by the minority Sunnis because the British administration backed the Sunnis. This left a major legacy of dissatisfaction among the Shi'as. The population continues to this day to suffer from this diversity.

Iraq's border, as drawn by the British in 1920, also had the disadvantage of not giving Iraq direct access to the Persian Gulf. Its small coastline (only 58 kilometres) was unsuited to deep-water port facilities, which has left an unfortunate legacy of major border disputes between the Iraq of today and its neighbours. These disputes culminated in the Iran–Iraq War of 1980–8 and the Gulf War of 1991.

The British were soon faced with internal revolt; in May 1920 the first rebellion against the British rose among the tribes of the Euphrates. The revolt lasted several months and over 10,000 Iraqis and 450 British soldiers were killed. Though this rebellion was crushed, the British policymakers decided to find an alternative long-term solution. They decided to hand over responsibility to an Arab ruler, with whom they would sign a treaty, which would safeguard British economic and strategic interests in the country. In 1921 Faisal, who had recently lost Greater Syria to the French, was brought into Iraq and after a carefully managed national referendum was crowned as the King of Iraq.

The case of Iraq was therefore different to that of Syria and Lebanon in that the apparent reigns of power were handed over to an Arab ruler. Faisal's rule, as a constitutional monarchy, was however closely supervised and aided by the British. In the words of William Cleveland, Iraq was an example of "Empire by treaty". Eventually, in 1932, Iraq obtained its formal independence, joined the League of Nations and Britain ceased to be Iraq's Mandatory Power. Though independent, the United Kingdom maintained important economic and military privileges in the region, including two air bases. All Iraqi military personnel had to be trained in the UK or by British instructors in Iraq. A 75-year concession was signed between the British government and the Iraq Petroleum Company, which meant that the UK owned Iraq's oil fields for 75 years and simply paid Iraq a modest royalty for every ton of oil extracted.

The case of Transjordan

Under Ottoman rule Transjordan (territory east of the River Jordan) had belonged to the province of Damascus (Syria) and was inhabited by Bedouin tribes. However, as a result of the San Remo conference, this territory was attached to Palestine and became a British Mandate. Once in control, however, the British decided to divide up the mandate along the river Jordan and thus form Palestine to the west of the River Jordan, where the British would comply with the Balfour Declaration and supervise the establishment of a Jewish national home, and Transjordan, to the east of the River Jordan, where Abdullah, Sharif Hussein's other son, would establish an independent Arab state. In this way, even though they did not consult any of the local inhabitants as stipulated in article 22 of the Covenant of the League of Nations, they fulfilled both their promises to the Jews and the Arabs.

In April 1921 the division was completed and two administrative entities were formed. This division was ratified by the League of Nations on 24 July 1922. Abdullah was then designated as the prince (Emir) of the Emirate of Transjordan, which remained a British Mandate until its independence in 1946. The United Kingdom fulfilled its responsibilities as a Mandatory Power by supervising the political, economic and military affairs of the newly-formed Emirate. Transjordan did not constitute a major economic asset, as for example Iraq did, but it was nonetheless important to the UK as a base to control the security of the region. The British supervised Transjordan's armed forces through the exclusive supply of instructors and arms and maintained a well-disciplined military loyal to the British Crown.

Though it is true that Transjordan was an artificial state and was "created by the stroke of a pen", the state—renamed Jordan after its independence in 1946—has continued to exist and given its geo-political status in relation to Palestine and later Israel has come to play an important strategic role as an arbiter in the region.

Discussion point:
Drawing state boundaries

After six months, Britain issued a statement excluding Transjordan from the provisions for a Jewish national Home in the Palestine mandate. Churchill, well satisfied with his handiwork, frequently boasted that he had created the Amirate of Transjordan by the stroke of his pen one bright Sunday afternoon and still had time to paint the magnificent views of Jerusalem before sundown.

Source: Shlaim, Avi. 1995. *War and Peace in the Middle East: A Concise History.* Penguin. p. 14.

What role did the Allies play in the drawing of the state boundaries in the Middle East after the First World War? How are state boundaries drawn in other parts of the world?

The case of Palestine

Of all the mandates, Palestine proved to be the most complicated because of its location as the spiritual home of Judaism, Christianity and Islam. Jerusalem (*Al Quds* in Arabic) was the site of the Jewish temple, of Jesus' crucifixion and of the prophet Mohammad's ascension to heaven. The future of Palestine was the concern of the world at large and therefore it was difficult to hand over its exclusive control to one nation only. There were, consequently, a number of different expectations. As Palestine was not specifically mentioned in the Hussein–McMahon correspondences, the British claimed that it was considered as part of the Syrian coastal territory "lying west of the districts of Damascus" and was not "purely Arab". It was therefore excluded from the Arab claim. The Palestinians disputed this and considered themselves an Arab state just like Iraq, Syria or Lebanon and claimed a right to independence. Both Arabs and Jews claimed that they had been promised Palestine. According to the Balfour declaration of November 1917, the British were bound to help the Jews set up a Jewish National Home. According to article 22 of the Covenant of the League of Nations, the British as the Mandatory Power were handed "the sacred trust of civilization" which meant helping the Palestinians obtain their independence. Much of the liability for ongoing tensions is due to the conflicting promises made by the Mandatory Powers.

Under the terms of the Sykes–Picot Agreement, France and the United Kingdom had agreed to place Palestine under an international administration. However, as the war was coming to a close, the UK realized that its economic and strategic interests were better served if Palestine came under its direct rule because the Mediterranean coast offered Britain vital ports and allowed them to control access to the Suez Canal. Lord Curzon, British Foreign Secretary and a specialist of the Middle East, considered Palestine "the military gate to Egypt and the Suez Canal". Presence in the region also permitted the British to supervise "the establishment in Palestine of a national home for the Jewish people", as promised in the Balfour Declaration.

The conference at San Remo recognized the Balfour Declaration. This meant that the pledge was no longer only between the United Kingdom and the Jews. The UK's allies also agreed to honour it. Accordingly, the British military administration in Palestine was replaced by civilian rule in July 1920 and Herbert Samuel became Palestine's first High Commissioner. Article 95 of the Treaty of Sèvres confirmed this decision placing Palestine in British hands:

> The Mandatory will be responsible for putting into effect the declaration originally made on November 2, 1917, by the British Government [the Balfour Declaration], and adopted by the other Allied Powers, in favour of the establishment in Palestine of a national home for the Jewish people, it being clearly understood that nothing shall be done which may prejudice the civil and religious rights of existing non-Jewish communities in Palestine, or the rights and political status enjoyed by Jews in any other country.

The British were given the task of balancing the interests of the two communities: the Palestinians and the Jews. The decision to divide up the land along the river Jordan and create two separate states, Palestine and Transjordan, was a step in that direction. Unfortunately, it satisfied neither. The Palestinians still claimed their right to an independent state, as specified under article 22 of the Covenant of the League of Nations:

> Certain communities formerly belonging to the Turkish Empire have reached a stage of development where their existence as independent nations can be provisionally recognized subject to the rendering of administrative advice and assistance by a Mandatory until such time as they are able to stand alone.

The Jews on the other hand, reassured by the validation of the Balfour Declaration, complained of the fact that their "designed territory" had been reduced to the land west of the river Jordan only.

The UK was in theory committed to both communities. They reassured the Jewish community that they would honour their promise, but assured the Arabs that they "would never impose … a policy that was contrary to their religious, political and economic interests." In practice, these two positions proved to be irreconcilable. As Northedge puts it, the fact that the mandate could have such diametrically opposite meanings for the two communities symbolized its contradictions.

The administration of Palestine turned into a major dilemma for the British government. Their failure to reconcile the Arab and Jewish communities led to violence both targeted at one another and towards the United Kingdom. While the UK ended its Mandatory Power in 1948 and left Palestine, those remaining (the Jews and the Palestinian Arabs) have continued their hostility to this day. In order to fully understand how the Jews and the Palestinians came to this mutual hostility, it is necessary to take a step back and study the region in greater detail.

The mandate system and the rise of independence movements

Allied diplomacy during the First World War and the peace treaties had lured all participants towards notions of independence and self-determination. The Covenant of the League of Nations had given further reassurances towards those aims. The mandate system as proposed in article 22 of the Covenant had raised expectations among those nations that were "on the brink of independent statehood" by promising them assistance towards that goal. Yet, in practice, it was made clear that the Mandatory Powers intended to pursue their colonial and imperialist goals in total disregard to the wishes of the local communities. This led to frustration and encouraged independence movements in the region. Indeed, it can be argued that the whole idea of guardianship or tutelage, as envisaged in the mandate system, was in conflict with the nationalism that had been encouraged during the course of the war.

Palestine

Though Palestine had no precise boundaries, it was traditionally made up of four regions around the Holy city of Jerusalem. To the east it included the ancient sites of Samaria and Judea—today known as the West Bank. To the south stood the sparsely populated desert region of Negev inhabited by nomadic Bedouins. To the west there was the coastal region spreading from Gaza in the south to Lebanon in the north. These maritime ports dated back to the ancient Phoenician civilizations. To the north were the fertile valleys that in Biblical times were known as Galilee.

Palestinians are descendents of the Canaanites and the Edomites who have lived in the region under different rulers for more than 2,000 years. In 1517 Palestine became part of the Ottoman Empire. The main economic activity in the region was agricultural and the local inhabitants were either Bedouins (nomadic people) or farmers. However, given that Palestine was the home of so many religions, it attracted many pilgrims too. Consequently, its population was multi-ethnic and multi-confessional. The accounts left to us by travellers to this region describe a society made up of different religious and ethnic communities who co-existed peacefully. Far from being a divisive threat this diversity was an attractive feature of the region.

The wave of Pan-Arab nationalism which started to take shape in the late 19th century started to alter the situation. It raised hopes among many Arabs for obtaining an independent Arab state after the First World War. Although the majority of Arabs were disappointed with the outcome of the peace treaties, in the case of Palestine the sentiment was a little stronger. Palestinians felt betrayed by the fact that the land they lived on was promised away to the Jewish community. This threat of eviction forged a sense of national identity and so a Palestinian national movement was born. In December 1920 a number of Palestinians met in Haifa and elected a group of representatives. This body called the Arab Executive was committed to fight against Zionism and obtain the independence of Palestine as an Arab state.

How and why did the Jews come to settle in Palestine?

The first organized group that proposed a Jewish migration to the Holy Lands was called *Hovevei Zion* (Lovers of Zion). It was based in Russia, where following the assassination of Alexander II in 1881 the Jewish community was severely persecuted. The first Jewish settlers reached Palestine soon after 1881. This first wave of Jewish immigration was called The First *Aliyah*. *Aliyah* is the Hebrew word that means immigration to the land of Israel. Although

The first Jewish city built in the suburbs of Jaffa: Tel Aviv, 11 April 1909.

no precise numbers exist, it is estimated that by the end of the 19th century there were 21 Jewish settlements totalling about 4,500 inhabitants. This small Jewish presence went practically unnoticed and the relationship between the settlers and the local population was peaceful.

The idea of migration was picked up by Theodor Herzl, who in 1896 published a book entitled *The Jewish State*. With the publication of this book Zionism as a political movement was born. Zionism proposed the establishment of a Jewish national home where the Jews would no longer be

> ### Theodor Herzl (1860–1904)
>
> Theodor Herzl, a Jewish Austro-Hungarian journalist is regarded as the father of Zionism. Alarmed at the growth of anti-Semitism across Europe, he argued that the minority status of Jews in each country made them easy targets for discrimination. The Dreyfus Affair in France, where a Jewish captain had been falsely accused of espionage had convinced him that Jews could never assimilate into European societies and were therefore always in danger. The solution he proposed was for Jews to create their own state, where they would no longer be a minority. In order to bring his project to fruition, Herzl set about contacting prominent statesmen and influential individuals. Herzl died in 1903 and did not see his project materialize. Chaim Weizman, a British Jew took his place and, using his contact with influential British statesmen, succeeded in obtaining the Balfour Declaration in 1917.

persecuted as a minority. This was the beginning of a Jewish national movement. With the birth of political Zionism the number of immigrants to Palestine started to grow and the relationship between the local population and the Jews started to alter. By 1917 they had obtained the backing of the United Kingdom through the Balfour Declaration and were therefore able to claim more legitimacy for their cause. The migration project had a clear long-term objective of establishing a national home for the Jewish community in Palestine. The project was also now better financed, with the setting up of the Jewish National Fund. This helped the settlers purchase land in Palestine.

As political Zionism offered Jews a national home and not a minority status in an Arab state, the project's major long-term goal was for the Jewish settlers to outnumber the local Palestinians. In order to fulfil this objective it was decreed that land purchased could never be resold to non-Jews. The settlers were discouraged from employing local Arab labour. In this way the indigenous population, unable to find work, would eventually leave and look for employment elsewhere.

The movement also needed ideological justification. In order to claim Palestine the Zionist movement needed to give the Jewish community, who for the past two millenniums had been dispersed throughout the world, a common claim to national identity. To do this, ancient Jewish Biblical history was revived which showed that the Jews had in the past lived in the region of Palestine. Similarly, scholars set about modernizing the Jewish language, Hebrew, which in its classic form had been used for prayer for more than 2,000 years. A common history, a common language and a common religion became the cornerstones of the future Jewish nation.

In order to morally justify the return to Palestine, it was necessary to claim that the land they proposed to settle in belonged to no-one. A Palestinian nation or Palestinian right to nationhood was therefore rejected. This last point was clearly summarized in the slogan "A land without people for a people without land." Finally, on the more practical level, by 1906 the settlers had started to organize

> **Discussion point:**
>
> Some colonies are settlers' colonies. This means that the aim of the colonizer is to populate the colony. What type of problems could this type of colonization bring about?

themselves: the first Jewish political parties were formed; Hebrew newspapers were published and collective farms, called the Kibbutz system, were set up. In 1909 the first Jewish self-defence militia, the *Hashomer*, was created. One prominent Zionist among the settlers was David Ben-Gurion. He was to become Israel's first prime minister.

As a result of these changes the presence of the Jewish community in Palestine could no longer go unnoticed. In July 1922 the League of Nations ratified the Palestinian Mandate and article 4 of this document stated that "an appropriate Jewish Agency would advise and co-operate with the administration for the purpose of establishing the Jewish National Home." Palestinians and Jews were now put in a situation where both communities laid claim to the same piece of land.

Activity:

Points of view: Is there such a thing as a Palestinian nation?

Source A

Golda Meir, Prime Minister of Israel, 1969–74

> There is no such thing as Palestinians. When was there an independent Palestinian people with a Palestinian state? … It was not as though there was a Palestinian people in Palestine considering itself as a Palestinian people and we came and threw them out and took their country from them. They did not exist.

Source: Meier, Golda. *Sunday Times.* 15 June 1969. Quoted in Kimmerling, Baruch & Migdal, Joel S. 2003. *The Palestinian People.* Harvard University Press. xxvi–ii.

Source B

Jimmy Carter, President of the United States, 1977–81

> The Syrian leader [Hafiz Assad] also said that Israelis asserted that the Jews of the world constitute one people, regardless of obvious differences in their identities, languages, customs, and citizenship, but deny that the Palestinians comprise a coherent people even though they have one national identity, one language, one culture and one history.

Source: Carter, Jimmy. 2006. *Palestine Peace not apartheid.* Thorndike Chivers. p. 106.

Source C

Israel Ministry of Foreign Affairs

> The history of the Jewish people and of its roots in the land of Israel spans some 35 centuries. In this land, its cultural, national, and religious identity was formed; here, its physical presence has been maintained unbroken throughout the centuries, even after the majority was forced into exile. With the establishment of the state of Israel in 1948, Jewish independence, lost 2000 years earlier, was renewed. "Israel in Brief".

Source: 15 December 2008. *Israel Ministry of Foreign Affairs.* http://www.mfa.gov.il/MFA/Facts+About+Israel/Israel+in+Brief/.

Source D

American Council on the Middle East

> The Palestinians' claim is predicated on the right of ownership evidenced by uninterrupted possession and occupation since the dawn of recorded history. They lived in the country when the Hebrews came … they continued to live there during the Hebrew occupation. They remained there after the last Hebrew or Jew left the country nearly two thousand years ago … . The people today called Palestinians or Palestinian Arabs … are largely the descendents of the Canaanites, the Edomites and the Philistine when it was invaded by the Hebrews in ancient times. But the Hebrews finally left or were driven out two thousand years ago.

Source: Sakran, Frank C. 1976. *Palestine Still a Dilemma.* Washington DC, USA. American Council on the Middle East.

Source E

Yousef Heikal was the town's last elected mayor before the establishment of the State of Israel. This is an excerpt from the first volume of Heikal's memoirs, written in Arabic, as he remembers the life of his family and his town under Ottoman rule and then under the British Mandate.

> Our house stood in the northeastern part of Jaffa, east of the railroad, and west of the orchard of the Haidar family and parts of the orchard of the Abu Qaoura family. Further east was the Jaffa-Tel Aviv highway. To the south was the house of Mr. Hochau and his large tile factory whose products were exported to all parts of Palestine. Mr. Hochau was a German businessman who lived in our neighborhood with his wife and children. Between Hochau's land and the railroad was the street that led to our house. The street started from a large gate that led to the land on which our house was located. Walking down the street for about 100 meters, one would come to a large iron gate in the railroad wall. Right opposite to it, on the other side of the railroad, was an identical gate.

We used these gates to cross over to the Arshid neighborhood. The railroad company built the two gates especially for us, in fullfilment of one of the conditions my father insisted upon when he sold that piece of land to the French company that built the railroad in 1892.

Source: Heikal, Y. Summer. 1984. "Jaffa as it was …". *Journal of Palestine Studies*. vol. 13, no. 4. pp. 3–21.

Source F

PLO Proclamation of Independence

Palestine, the land of the three monotheistic faiths, is where the Palestinian Arab people was born, on which it grew, developed and excelled. The Palestinian people was never separated from or diminished in its integral bonds with Palestine. Thus the Palestinian Arab people ensured for itself an everlasting union between itself, its land and its history.

Source: Palestine Media Center. http://www.palestine-pmc.com

Source G

Weizmann was a Chemistry professor at the University of Manchester and an active supporter of the Zionist movement. He was close to Prime Minister Balfour and was influential in obtaining the Balfour Declaration. Weizmann was the first president of the State of Israel.

In its initial stage Zionism was conceived by its pioneers as a movement wholly depending on mechanical factors: there is a country which happens to be called Palestine, a country without a people, and, on the other hand, there exists the Jewish people, and it has no country. What else is necessary, then, than to fit the gem into the ring, to unite this people with this country? The owners of the country [the Ottoman Turks?] must, therefore, be persuaded and convinced that this marriage is advantageous, not only for the [Jewish] people and for the country, but also for themselves.

Source: Weizmann, Chaim. 28 March 1914. Quoted in Litvinoff, B. (ed.). 1983. *The Letters and Papers of Chaim Weizmann.* vol.1, series B. Jerusalem, Israel. Israel University Press. pp. 115–6.

Source-based questions

1 With reference to their origin and purpose, assess the value and the limitations of the above extracts.

2 Using the information provided in these excerpts to summarize the arguments presented on both the Palestinian and the Jewish sides that justifies their right to the land of Palestine.

3 Why do the accounts differ so much?

Political representation within the British Mandate

Political power resided in the hands of the High Commissioner and the government in London. Though the mandate offered neither community political rights, it encouraged the two communities to organize their own affairs. From the start, the Jews were better organized. They were represented internationally by the World Zionist Organization, which later became the Jewish Agency. This body played a vital role as a liaison on behalf of the Jewish settlers in Palestine with the British government. It also organized the immigration and the settlement of the Jews into Palestine and managed the Jewish National Fund. Within Palestine they formed the Assembly of Representatives, the Jewish National Council, which levied taxes from its community, and was recognized by the British government.

The Arab community lacked a unitary international voice because the Arabs were broken up by the implementation of the mandate system into various states. Each community had its own enemy to fight and rallied around different causes. Consequently, the channel of communication between the Palestinians and the British government was not as effective as the Jewish one. On the local level, in 1922 the Supreme Muslim Council was formed to serve as a consultative body between the Arab community and the British. In reality, the mandate system offered Palestinians little scope for change. Unlike in other mandates, where the presence of the Mandatory Power was temporary, in the case of Palestine the presence of the Jewish community was to be permanent. In the absence of a representative government, the Arab population had no say over the Jewish question and therefore had no means of changing the status quo democratically.

In 1922 a constitution for Palestine was drawn up in which a legislative council composed of Palestinians, Jews, Christians and the British themselves was proposed. The Arabs were offered ten out of the 23 seats even though they made up 89 per cent of the population. Most of the leaders of the Arab community did not believe that their community should participate in a political body that in practice gave them no right to alter their situation. Consequently, the Arabs boycotted the elections because they argued that through their participation they would simply be legitimizing the terms of the mandate and the eventual transfer of power to the Jewish settlers. The British therefore decided to govern with a panel of British officials. In 1935 when the Arabs expressed an interest in participating in a legislative council the British, lobbied by the Zionists, rejected the idea.

Rising hostilities between the Palestinian Arabs and the Jewish settlers

The Palestinians were angered at the growing number of immigrants entering their state and the fact that the newcomers were purchasing their land and refusing to employ Arab labour. This anger was expressed through violence. Violence in turn bred more violence. The Jewish settlers' militia organizations became more proactive and retaliated with a similar degree of violence. The British administration was forced to intervene. This intervention took two forms. Firstly, through its forces of law and order, they tried to arrest the perpetrators and collectively punish all sympathizers. This counter-violence made the British extremely unpopular in the eyes of the Arabs. Secondly, London set up a number of commissions of enquiry to understand why the violence had occurred. Often the findings expressed sympathy with the plight of the Palestinians. This raised hopes and expectations among the Palestinians, but left them all the more disappointed when no change was forthcoming. Consequently the inter-war years saw the degradation of relations between the Jewish settlers and the Palestinian Arabs as well as the intense hostility of both communities towards the British Mandatory Power.

 Can violence be a means to solve a problem?

In May 1921 a group of Jews were attacked in Jaffa. The violence then spread to other towns and caused the death of about 200 Jews and 120 Arabs. This outburst of violence gave birth to the Jewish paramilitary organization, the Haganah, which claimed that the British appeared to be incapable of protecting Jewish farmers, so they would carry out the task themselves. The Haycraft Commission of Enquiry that was sent to look into the Jaffa attack blamed the Arabs for the violence but also pointed out that the Arabs were reacting out of fear for the loss of their livelihood. The British government then published a White Paper in 1922. This was known as the Churchill White Paper. It declared that Britain did "not contemplate that Palestine as a whole should be converted into a Jewish National Home, but that such a home should be founded in Palestine." It however reminded the Arabs at the same time that the Balfour Declaration was "not susceptible to change".

On 23 August 1929 a group of armed Arabs attacked Jewish worshippers at the Wailing Wall in Jerusalem. The rioting that followed the attack caused the death of 113 Jews and 116 Arabs. In Hebron another attack killed 60 more Jews. The Shaw Commission that looked into the incidents concluded that the fundamental cause was "the Arab feeling of animosity and hostility towards the Jews consequent upon the disappointment of their political and national aspirations and fear for their economic future."

Upon the recommendation of the Shaw Commission, the British government sent Sir John Hope-Simpson to the region. His report expressed concern over the economic difficulties facing the Arab farmers. It argued that there was insufficient land in Palestine to absorb the flow of immigration. It also criticized the policy of hiring only Jews, which, it claimed, was responsible for the deplorable conditions in which the Arabs found themselves. It recommended a control on immigration and on the Jewish land purchase. The recommendations were incorporated in the Passfield White Paper in October 1930, which proposed setting land aside for the landless Palestinians and a restriction on Jewish immigration. As a consequence of the 1929 riots the Haganah grew in size, acquired more weapons and transformed from an untrained militia to an underground army.

Social and economic developments in Palestine in the 1930s

The 1930s saw a widening gap between the Jewish and the Arab communities. In the years 1930–5 the Jewish population had doubled in size. By the end of the 1930s they constituted one third of the population of Palestine. Many of the new immigrants were highly skilled refugees fleeing anti-Semitic persecutions in Europe. They brought with them knowledge and funds to boost the Palestinian economy. While the world was plunging into the Great Depression, in Palestine the economy was thriving. Haifa, the terminus of the oil pipe lines linking Mosul to the Mediterranean, had become a major industrial centre. Tel Aviv had expanded from a population of 46,000 in 1931 to 135,000 by 1935.

What's in a name? A debate over the postage stamp

The disagreements over the name on the postage stamp reveals the degree to which reconciliation between the Palestinians and the Jewish settlers was difficult.

The British proposed printing the name Palestine in the country's three official languages: Arabic, Hebrew and English. The Arab leaders argued against the inclusion of Hebrew, while the Zionists rejected the name Palestine on its own and wanted to replace it with the inscription "Palestine: Land of Israel" in three languages. The final compromise was using the name Palestine in three languages. In Hebrew, however, the word Palestine would be followed by a two-letter abbreviation that stood for *Eretz Yisrael* (the land of Israel). By 1938, however, the Palestinians had issued their own stamp which they added to all letters. The inscription read: "Palestine for the Arabs."

Palestinian postage stamp issued in 1922, showing overprint in Arabic, English, and Hebrew.

Palestinian postage stamp issued in 1927 depicting Rachel's Tomb. (Jewish symbol)

Palestinian postage stamp issued in 1927 depicting the Dome of the Rock. (Islamic symbol)

Palestinian postage stamp issued in 1938.

Economic growth was, however, not evenly distributed between the two communities. Palestinians, whose farm product was mainly staple crops, suffered from the absence of tariffs imposed on imported goods. When Palestine became the dumping ground for such food products the Palestinian landowners, unable to compete with the cheaper world prices, were forced into bankruptcy. Many farm workers had to abandon their jobs and seek employment in the local towns or neighbouring countries, and many farm owners had to sell their land. The figures provided by Rachid Khalidi, a Palestinian-American historian of the Middle East, underline the gap between the two communities. Between 1922 and 1947, the annual growth rate of the Jewish sector of the economy was 13.2 per cent, while that of the Arab was 6.5 per cent. Per capita, these figures were 4.8 per cent and 3.6 per cent respectively. Capital invested in Arab industrial establishments was two million pounds as opposed to 12.1 million pounds in Jewish industrial establishments. By 1936, Jewish individuals earned 2.6 times as much as Arabs. An official census in 1937 indicated that an average Jewish worker received 145 per cent more in wages than his Palestinian Arab counterpart. For women in the textile industry the difference was 433 per cent. By July 1937 the real wages of the average Palestinian Arab worker decreased by ten per cent while those of a Jewish worker rose by the same amount. This situation only increased the resentment of the Palestinians towards the Jewish settlers.

The Jewish community was also more proactive on the social and cultural level. In 1919 they established a centralized Hebrew school system. By 1925 there were two Hebrew universities: the Technion University founded in 1924 and the Hebrew University founded in 1925. Consequently, figures taken in 1932 showed a wide gap in the literacy rates of the two communities: whereas the Jewish literacy rates stood at 86 per cent, it was only 22 per cent for the Palestinian Arabs.

The Great Arab Revolt 1936–9

The revolt was triggered off by the murder of two Jews on 15 April 1936, which immediately incited retaliation with the murder of two Arabs. Within a few days thousands were mobilized; there were mass demonstrations and mob attacks against each community as well as guerrilla attacks directed against British installations. The 1936–9 revolt was different to prior revolts in the following ways. The Palestinians were far more united than on prior occasions.

Activity:
Grievances
Debate in class

Tension and conflict is always caused by grievances. These grievances could be the result of economic inequalities, ethnic, religious and social differences or absence of political rights. Grievances could be self-inflicted or caused by an external factor and be beyond one's control. While Palestine was a British Mandate, both the Palestinian population and the Jewish population had a number of grievances.

	Economic grievances	Social/ religious/ ethnic grievances	Political grievances
Arab Palestinians			
Jewish population in Palestine			

Undertake research in order to fill in the box above. Form groups of Palestinian Arabs and Jewish immigrants and start a formal class debate: How justified were each side's grievances?

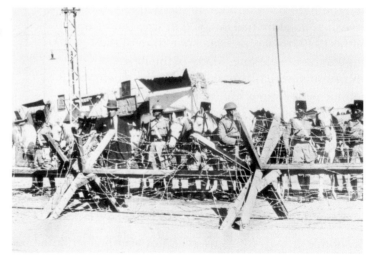

The 1936 Arab revolt. A key position at the junction of several important roads, with a detachment of steel-helmeted British troops and Palestinian guards.

The Arab Higher Committee, formed soon after the beginning of the revolt, rallied important Palestinian families under the chairmanship of the Mufti of Jerusalem, Amin al Husseini. The committee provided the revolt with the leadership and organization that had been lacking on previous occasions. This meant that the revolt could be sustained for a longer period of time and involved more Arabs than before. At its peak in 1938 over 10,000 people were involved in the revolt. The Arabs had a clear set of demands. These were:

● An end to Jewish immigration.
● An end to transfers of land to Jewish owners.
● A representative government based on democratic rules.

This last demand was new. In 1922 the Arabs had refused participation in a legislative body. The change of position was because they now felt empowered through their struggle to bring about change democratically.

There was a significant change of tactic in the revolt. Whereas previously the attacks were more spontaneous and reflected sheer anger, this time they were better organized and aimed at more long-term objectives. Crops were destroyed, pipelines sabotaged, roads mined, transportation disrupted. The Arab Higher Committee called for the non-payment of taxes as well as a general strike. The long-term objective was to bring everyday life to a standstill through civil disobedience and sustained violence. The general strike lasted from April to October 1936.

The revolt was met with an escalation of violence on the part of the Jewish settlers. A group of more militant settlers split from the Haganah to form the Irgun. Irgun stood for "the national military organization in the land of Israel". Its ideology, as expressed in the following statement, was further proof of the irreconcilability of the two communities: "Every Jew had the right to enter Palestine; only active retaliation would deter the Arabs and the British; only Jewish armed force would ensure the Jewish state."

The British officials became direct targets of the violence. In one incident, in September 1937, the district commissioner for Galilee, Lewis Andrews, was assassinated. This in turn led to an unprecedented degree of counter-mobilization on the part of the British forces. The British called in an extra 20,000 men to suppress the revolt. The Arab Committee was banned and its chairman, Amin al Husseini was forced to flee Palestine. The casualty rate was much higher than previous revolts: 101 Britons, 463 Jews and around 5,000 Palestinians, with many more wounded. In response to the violence, the British government sent Lord Robert Peel to head a Royal Commission to report on the grievances that had led to the revolt.

The outcome of the Peel Royal Commission

The report by the Peel Royal Commission in 1937 admitted for the first time that the contradictory obligations contained in the Balfour Declaration were impossible to fulfil. It therefore proposed the division of Palestine into two separate states. But, as Elisabeth Monroe put it, "Maybe it was right to recommend a surgical operation, but where was the surgeon?". Indeed, it seemed wise to divide up the two communities, but having left it so late, it was impossible to bring either side to accept such a decision. Faced with

The logo of the Irgun. Notice the map of Palestine corresponds to the original mandate of Palestine and includes territory east of the river Jordan.

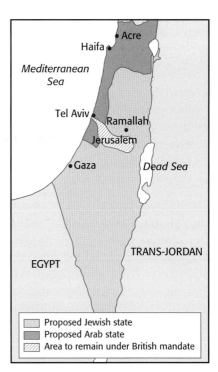

Map showing the suggested partition by the Peel commission.

opposition from both sides, who each believed they had the right to claim *all* the territory, the recommendations were rejected and the situation in Palestine continued to deteriorate.

With the rejection of the Peel recommendations violence became even more widespread. Arab rebel bands attacked railroads, bridges and police stations. By the summer of 1938 they controlled much of the countryside and several of the cities and disrupted the economy through the non-payment of rent. They insisted that men wear the *kafiya* the checkered head-cloth that has become the symbol of Palestinian national identity. The British increased their troops and resorted to more violent methods, but did not succeed in quelling the violence until March 1939.

The British White Paper of 1939

The Arab Revolt had in reality two very contradictory effects. On the one hand, the severe retaliation on the part of the British had led to a large number of arrests, imprisonments and executions of Arab militants and had caused the virtual collapse of the Arab national movement. On the other hand the unity shown by the Palestinians over such a long period of time had given birth to an Arab-Palestinian national identity. More importantly it had finally convinced the British of the existence of a Palestinian national sentiment whose demands needed to be taken seriously.

The White Paper that followed finally reflected these demands and questioned the idea that Palestine could become a "Jewish state". It stated that "the framers of the mandate … could not have intended that Palestine should be converted into a Jewish State against the will of the Arab population of the country." In conclusion, "His Majesty's Government therefore now declare unequivocally that it is not part of their policy that Palestine should become a Jewish state."

The approaching war in Europe was also a factor that pushed the British to show more understanding towards the Arabs. Palestine and the Arab world in general were of strategic and political importance in the war to come. The White Paper made the following propositions:

The kafiya: a chequered head cloth worn as a symbol of Palestinian identity.

- Jewish immigration was to be limited to 15,000 a year for the next five years.
- In view of the plight of the Jews in Europe, Palestine should accept 25,000 refugees.
- Land transfer to the Jews would be restricted to specified zones.
- Palestine would be granted independence within ten years.

The Zionists rejected the proposals of the White Paper because, they stated, it was contrary to the promises made in the Balfour Declaration. Disappointed by the British response, the Zionist organization realized the need to look for support for their cause elsewhere. The United States, which was the home of a large number of Jews, was the obvious candidate. The Arabs, in particular the more defiant Arab Higher Committee, rejected it because it did not offer them immediate independence. As Charles D. Smith puts it "the 1939 White Paper had outraged the Zionists without satisfying the Arabs."

The publication of the White Paper coincided with Hitler's preparations for the invasion of Poland. The Second World War brought with it the persecution of Jews on an unimaginable scale and confirmed what Theodor Herzl had claimed: that Jews, living as a minority, were constantly in danger of becoming the target of racial persecution in spite of the number of years that they had resided in Europe. This only made the Zionists more resolute in completing the task that Herzl had begun, which was to acquire a Jewish state where the Jews would no longer be a minority.

Activity:

The importance of demography: Do numbers matter?

The size of the population of each community has always been and will continue to be a crucial factor in the Zionist–Palestinian debate, raising fears and providing justifications for the actions of both sides.

The Zionist project was to offer Jews a national home and not a minority status in an Arab state. In order to fulfill this objective, it was necessary to outnumber the Palestinians.

Palestinian demography of the late-19th and early-20th centuries has never been just a matter of numbers. It has always been a front-line weapon used in a life-and-death struggle for nationhood.

Data analysis

1 What do the statistics reveal?

2 Analyse the data and argue the case for each side's position in terms of population and policy.

Jewish immigration to Palestine	
Year	Immigrants
1931	4,075
1932	12,533
1933	37,337
1934	45,267
1935	66,472
1936	29,595
1937	10,629
1938	14,675
1939	31,195
1940	10,643
1941	4,592

Source: http://www.zionism-israel.com/dic/Arab_Revolt.htm.

Israel / Palestine: Arab / Jewish Population (1914–2005)				
Year	Jews	Arabs	Total	% of Jews to Total
1914	60,000	731,000	791,000	7.585%
1922	83,790	668,258	752,048	11.141%
1931	174,606	858,708	1,033,314	16.897%
1941	474,102	1,111,398	1,585,500	29.902%
1950	1,203,000	1,172,100	2,375,100	50.650%
1960	1,911,300	1,340,100	3,251,400	58.783%
1970*	2,582,000	1,045,000	3,627,000	71.188%
1980	3,282,700	2,100,000	5,382,700	60.986%
1995	4,495,100	3,506,900	8,002,000	56.173%
2005	5,275,700	5,139,100	10,414,800	50.656%

*Starting in 1967, population figures include residents of East Jerusalem and the Jewish settlements in the West Bank and Gaza Strip.

Source: http://israelipalestinian.procon.org.

Timeline: Palestine, July 1914 – May 1939.	
1914	November 2: Ottoman Empire enters the First World War
1915	February–December: Gallipoli Campaign
	March 18: Treaty of Constantinople
	April 24: Armenian leaders arrested. Decision to relocate the Armenians (Armenian Genocide)
	July 14: First letter sent by Sharif Hussein to MacMahon
1916	January 9: Allied surrender at Gallipoli
	July–March: Letters exchanged between McMahon and Sharif Hussein
	April 26: Treaty of London
	April: British surrender in Kut el Amara
	May 16: Sykes–Picot agreement made public
	June 10: Beginning of the Arab Revolt
	November: British troops take Basra
1917	April 26: Saint-Jean Maurienne Agreement
	November 2: Balfour Declaration
	December: British troops capture Jerusalem
1918	June: Declaration of the Seven
	October 3: Faisal's troops enter Damascus
	October 30: Ottomans surrender. Armistice of Mudros signed
1919	June–July: King–Crane Commission
1920	April 19–26: Conference at San Remo
	May–October: Iraqi Revolt against the British
	July 23: Battle of Maysalun. Syrian forces defeated by the French
	August 10: Treaty of Sèvres
1921	April: Division of the British mandate into Transjordan and Palestine
	May 1: Jews attacked in Jaffa. The birth of Haganah
	August 23: Faisal becomes King of Iraq
1922	June 3: White Paper on Palestine (The Churchill White Paper)
	July 24: The division of Transjordan and Palestine ratified by the League of Nations. Abdullah becomes the Emir of Transjordan
1923	July 24: Treaty of Lausanne
1925	July 20: Druze revolt against French rule
1929	August 23: Wailing Wall riots
1930	June: Hope-Simpson Inquiry
	October 21: Hope–Simpson Report and the Passfield White Paper
1936	April 21: Hope–Simpson Report and the Start of the Arab Revolt (this will last until 1939)
1937	May–June: Peel Commission
1939	May: The White Paper

The Second World War and the creation of the State of Israel

The impact of the Second World War on the situation in Palestine was tremendous. The extermination of six million Jews, which constituted two-thirds of the Jewish community in Europe shook the world and forced it to rethink the Jewish Question. For the Zionist movement the urgency for establishing a Jewish State in Palestine was all the more evident. The war had also brought with it the end of US isolation and was to give birth to a new international organization, the United Nations. Soon the question of Palestine became an international affair. Throughout the war Palestine was of major strategic importance to the Allies, in particular the British. Both the Suez Canal and the Persian Gulf served as vital supply channels to the British fleet and enabled operations in the Mediterranean and North Africa to continue. British control of the Palestine's Mediterranean ports was of utmost importance.

Arab loyalty towards the Allies was brought under question on a number of occasions. In Iraq, in 1941, a group of Iraqi generals overthrew the pro-British government and appealed to Germany for help. The coup was however extremely short lived and the British forces reoccupied Iraq within a few weeks. The Palestinian leader, Amin al Husseini, the **Grand Mufti** of Jerusalem and the head of the Arab Higher Committee, who had fled the country as a result of the Arab Revolt, took refuge in Nazi Germany where he met with Hitler. Though he was keen on approaching the Palestinian cause to Nazism, his efforts did not have a major repercussion among Palestinians during the war. The war was clearly seen as an opportunity for some Arab leaders to collaborate with the United Kingdom's enemy, Germany.

The United Kingdom was equally unpopular among the Jewish community. They had been outraged by the White Paper in 1939 and resented the UK's lack of support for their settlement in Palestine. They, however, had no choice but to support the British war efforts against Nazism. As Ben Gurion, the first Prime Minister of Israel, was to put it, they would help the British as though there was no White Paper, but they would equally fight the White Paper as though there was no war. They therefore did not oppose the British control of Palestine during the war and sent units to fight under British command, but it was clear that this alliance would last as long as the war. Once the Germans were defeated the Zionists were determined to resume their struggle to oust both the British and the Arab Palestinians in order to establish their Jewish State.

After the publication of the White Paper and the proposed restrictions on Jewish immigration, the Zionists decided to continue the flow of emigration illegally. In 1939 more than 11,000 Jews entered Palestine illegally. With the outbreak of war the number of Jewish refugees in Europe increased and therefore this effort was stepped up. The British authorities kept to the decisions of the White Paper and either interned the newcomers or transferred them to the island of Mauritius

Activity:

United Nations

Research the background to the formation of the United Nations. Which were the founding countries?

- Make a list of the date of entry of the Middle Eastern countries studied in this chapter.
- Are all the countries listed on p. 172 member states?

Mufti A Muslim cleric or expert in Islamic (*Shari'a*) law empowered to give rulings on religious matters. A **Grand Mufti** is the chief legal authority for a large city.

in the Indian Ocean. In order to prevent the Jewish immigrants from reaching Palestine they also called on the countries where the ships were due to transit to refuse them entrance. This was the source of a great deal of tension between the Zionists and the British.

In December 1941, the SS Struma, a vessel badly in need of repair carrying 769 Romanian Jews stopped in Istanbul on its way to Palestine. The British persuaded the Turks to refuse the vessel the right to leave the port for the Mediterranean. The negotiations took two months, at the end of which it was sent back to the Black sea where the vessel sank on 25 February 1942. There was one survivor.

With the rising tension between the British and the Jews, the Zionists turned to the United States and the American Jewish organizations for support. In May 1942 a conference was held at the Biltmore Hotel in New York, where associates of Chaim Weizmann met with American Jewish organizations. The conference passed the following resolutions:

- Palestine would be opened to Jewish immigration.
- The Jewish Agency would control immigration and have authority to develop Palestine.
- After the war Palestine would be established as a "Jewish Commonwealth" to be integrated into the new democratic world.

The conference was a great success as a large of number of Americans began to support the Zionist ideal. The Zionist cause was greatly publicized and pressure was put on the United States government to oppose the White Paper. Both the Democratic and the Republican parties endorsed the Biltmore Program in their political platforms.

In October 1944 various Arab heads of state met in a conference in Alexandria, Egypt, and called for the creation of the League of Arab States. In a resolution passed at this conference they expressed their sympathy with the "woes that had been inflicted upon the Jews by European dictatorial states" but showed their full support for the independence of Palestine because "there can be no greater injustice and aggression than solving the problem of the Jews of Europe by another injustice, that is, by inflicting injustice on the Palestine Arabs". The League, which was formed in March 1945, agreed to represent the Palestinian case and pledged to fight their cause before the Western world.

The end of the war and the last years of the British Mandate 1945–1948

The Jewish leadership in Palestine wanted unlimited immigration and the setting up of an exclusively Jewish state. The Arab leadership called for the dissolution of the Jewish national home and the creation of an independent Arab state. It was clear that no amount of British pleading or British pressure could bridge the gap between the two sides. At first the British government sought reconciliation with the Arabs. They were keen on maintaining a foothold in the region. Access to the Suez Canal and the Haifa pipelines was a major economic concern for the post-war British government that had been weakened economically by the war.

For the Zionists, this was totally unacceptable and they realized that, in order to achieve their aim, their focus needed to turn to the expulsion of the British from Palestine.

The last years of the British Mandate can be divided into four stages. The first stage, from May 1945 (the end of the Second World War) to February 1947, was characterized by escalating Zionist violence against the British troops. It was also a time when the Zionist movement succeeded in mounting an effective publicity campaign especially targeted at the United States for its cause. This in turn put enormous pressure on Britain to change its position. Clashes between the Zionists and the British forces started in October 1945. By the end of the year 80,000 British soldiers had been sent to Palestine to counter the Zionist insurgency. The Zionists, who had fought under British command during the war had obtained a great deal of experience and had managed to stock up a large quantity of arms. Now with the moral and financial support from the United States, they were able to increase their arsenal and were fully prepared to fight the British. The aim of the Zionists was to use terror and violence as a means to make the cost of maintaining Palestine too high. In February 1946 a British Officers' club was blown up killing a dozen officers. In retaliation, in June 2,700 Jewish activists were arrested. In July a bomb exploded at the King David Hotel in Jerusalem. This Hotel housed the British administration: 91 British, Jewish and Arab personnel were killed. Material damage caused through sabotaging such installations as railroads, pipelines and airfields amounted to four million pounds.

The war of terror eventually bore fruit. Public opinion in Britain started to turn against retaining the British Mandate of Palestine and the British government started to look for other solutions.
The second stage of the mandate, from February 1947 to September 1947, was a period of months in which the British came to terms with the futility of their presence in Palestine. This stage also highlighted to the rest of the world the intensity of the animosity in the British–Zionist relations. In February the British cabinet decided to hand over the problem of Palestine to the United Nations. Though Britain had surrendered the political initiative to the UN it was not ready to hand over its mandatory responsibilities yet. It therefore retained its rights to police and administer Palestine.

The UN Security Council was asked to investigate the question of Palestine and come up with a plan that would resolve the problem. They decided to send a commission of inquiry and create a political committee. Both were to prepare a report for the General Assembly of September 1947. Hence the United Nations Special Committee on Palestine (UNSCOP) was formed. It had 11 members and was chaired by Sweden. Its members were from Australia, Canada, Holland, Czechoslovakia, Yugoslavia, India, Iran, Guatemala, Peru and Uruguay. The Committee members stayed in Palestine for five weeks. While the investigations were taking place two very widely publicized incidents underlined the intensity of Jewish–British animosity and played an important role in shaping the decision of the committee members.

Discussion point:

Was violence against the British justified in these circumstances?

Activity:

UN Security Council

What is the role of the UN Security Council? What are they responsible for, and who sits on it?

● Research the recommendations of UNSCOP and the formation of the UN Partition Plan (1947).

● What role has the UN Security Council played in Middle East peace talks?

In July two British sergeants were kidnapped by the Irgun. The kidnappers demanded the release of three Irgun activists awaiting a death sentence. When the death sentences were carried out, the two sergeants were hanged. The bodies of the two sergeants were booby-trapped and displayed publicly. A note pinned to their body justified the hangings: it claimed that the two men were members of an "illegal Army of Occupation in the Hebrew homeland, which denied the Hebrews the right to live". The incident received widespread media coverage in Britain. It also led to violent reprisals by the soldiers in Palestine against the local Jewish community. For many Britons it meant that it was the time to leave Palestine.

The bodies of the two kidnapped British sergeants, Clifford Martin and Marvyn Paice, hanging from eucalyptus near Netanya, in Palestine, on 30 July 1947.

In the same month a refugee ship named *Exodus 1947*, carrying mainly Holocaust survivors from the port of Sète in the south of France, was refused entry into Palestine by the British authorities. Its 4,515 passengers were sent back to France. The passengers refused to disembark in France and they were then redirected to Hamburg in Germany, which was a British-controlled zone. Though they were placed under British supervision in the refugee camps in Lübeck (near Hamburg), symbolically sending Jewish Holocaust survivors to a camp in Germany was enough to outrage public opinion. The ship's history later became the source of Leon Uris's novel *Exodus,* and Otto Preminger's film of the same name. The incident played an important role in the founding of the State of Israel.

The UNSCOP report was unanimous in calling for an end to the British Mandate. However the committee split 8:3 over the type of state that should emerge once the mandate ended. The majority wanted a two-state solution: Arab and Jewish. The minority (India, Iran and Yugoslavia) wanted a federal state solution based on the US model of government. The General Assembly was scheduled to discuss the plans in November. On 26 September Britain announced that it was quitting Palestine. In this third stage of the mandatory period, from September to November 1947, the fate of the Palestinian Arabs and the Jewish community was in the hands of the United Nations. These few decisive months were characterized by intense lobbying. On 29 November resolution 181 calling for the partition of Palestine into two states was passed: 33 representatives voted for it; 13 voted against and ten abstained. Britain was among the abstainers. The date for the ending of the British Mandate and the total withdrawal of the British troops was set for 15 May 1948.

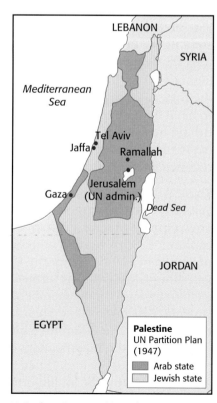

United Nations Partition Plan, 1947.

Though a major step had been taken and the date 29 November 1947 is retained by Israelis as the date for their country's independence, the troubles in Palestine were far from over. A vote taken in New York was not necessarily applicable in Palestine. There is one more stage before the establishment of the State of Israel. Leading up to 14 May 1948, this last stage was marked by uncertainty and anticipation. The Jewish militants remained pragmatic: their aim was to chase as many Arabs as possible out of their sectors in order to have full control of the regions allocated to them. It is important to remember that in the proposed UN partition at least 860,000 Arabs would have continued living in the Jewish sectors of Palestine. The policy of militant groups such as the Hagana and the Irgun was therefore to terrorize the Arab population through acts of violence to force them to leave. The Arabs, on the other hand, continued to desire what by now appeared to be the impossible and the unattainable: an independent unitary state of Palestine. They therefore settled scores with the Jewish settlers and attacked and destroyed Jewish property.

Over the next six months there was an intense level of violence. In April the village of Dayr Yassin was attacked by Jewish militants, killing 115 people. News of Dayr Yassin had the impact the Jewish militants were looking for: the threat of other Dayr Yassins produced a state of panic and resulted in the flight of over 300,000 Arabs. The land and the property of those Arabs was taken up by new Jewish settlers. The Arabs retaliated for Dayr Yassin by attacking a medical convoy and killing 75 Jews.

On 14 May Ben Gurion proclaimed the State of Israel. This was done one day before the British ended their Mandatory Power in Palestine. The United States, followed immediately by the Soviet Union, recognized the new state. On the same day the armies of the Arab states invaded the State of Israel.

The May 1948 War

The May 1948 War, the first in a long series of Arab–Israeli wars, was according to historian Avi Shlaim a "Jewish triumph and a Palestinian tragedy". It had been planned by the League of Arab States and included units from Iraq, Syria, Lebanon, Egypt, Jordan and a smaller section from Saudi Arabia. The motivation and objective for the war was to restore Palestine as a unitary state. The official declaration stated:

> The only solution of the Palestine problem is the establishment of a unitary Palestinian State, in accordance with democratic principles, whereby its inhabitants will enjoy complete equality before the law, [and whereby] minorities will be assured of all the guarantees recognised in democratic constitutional countries.

The War can be divided into the following phases:

1   From mid-May to 11 June: The Israelis successfully pushed back the Arab invasion. A truce was called and secured by the UN peacekeeping forces. The truce was designed as a time when both

TOK Link
Ways of Knowing—
Collective memory
Collective memory is different to individual memory in that it is *constructed* by society as a whole.

   What effect do best sellers such as *Exodus* by Leon Uris have on collective memory?

sides would reflect over peace. A UN mediator, Count Folke Bernadotte, was sent to help each side reach an agreement and enforce the UN resolution 181, but as he explained it himself, the war had made the situation harder: while the Arabs continued to reject the UN partition, the Israelis, empowered by their military successes, had also come to question the UN decision.

2 From 8 to 18 July: The truce was broken by the Egyptian and Syrian forces. In this phase of the war, the Israelis, who had received more supplies, carried out three major offensives, resulting in the crushing defeat of the Arabs on all fronts. Another truce was called on 18 July during which time Count Bernadotte attempted to mediate between the two sides. His mission, however, came to an abrupt end when he was assassinated in September 1948 by an underground Israeli group.

3 From 15 October to 20 July 1949: The Israeli Defense Force launched a few minor offensives with an aim to extend and secure Israel's new borders.

Two different images of the war: Displaced Palestinians seeking refuge in neighbouring states; Israelis celebrating the end of the war.

The new borders of Israel were about 50 per cent larger than the UN partition proposal had allotted it. These cease-fire lines were known afterwards as the Green Line. The Gaza Strip and the West Bank were occupied by Egypt and Jordan respectively. The UN was assigned the task of monitoring the cease-fire and assisting the Palestinian refugees.

The 1948 War: A Jewish triumph and a Palestinian tragedy

There are a number of factors that help us understand why the Arabs lost the war in 1948. The Arab armies were not united under one leadership and they did not all trust each others' motives. Many were suspicious of the Jordanian participation; King Abdullah of Jordan was suspected of seeking to incorporate the Palestinian Arab territory into his kingdom. At the start of the war the Egyptians attacked a British air base near Haifa. Consequently their air force came under attack by the British air force.

There are also a number of factors that help us understand the Israeli victory in 1948. The Israelis were quick in bringing their units under one command. The Israeli Defense Force (IDF) incorporating the militia organizations was formed on 26 May. The Israelis received supplies from Czechoslovakia. The collective farms under the Kibbutz system offered the Israelis a well-organized and well-disciplined organ of defence. These units had the experience of defending themselves from Arab attacks in the past and were, as a consequence, well-equipped and well-trained.

Morale was also a contributing factor. The cause of liberation, independence and defending the first Jewish State gave the Israelis a will to fight that was lacking amongst the Arabs, who were not fighting for *their land*. For the Palestinians, who were fighting to keep their homeland, the struggle had been going on for nearly 30 years and, after so many setbacks, independence was now seemed to many to be an unattainable goal.

The Legacy of the 1948 Arab–Israeli War

As historian Avi Shlaim puts it, the war confirmed the legacy of violence. "A state created by the sword would have to live by the sword." The war physically increased the space allotted to the Jews and introduced the world to the idea of the Palestinian refugee. The war also gave rise to two totally different narratives of history. Arab historians have recorded this war under the name *Nakba*, "the catastrophe". It was a major blow to Arab unity and Arab pride. The day after the proclamation of the State of Israel and the start of the 1948 war, 15 May, is commemorated as the *Youm al Nakbah* (the day of the catastrophe). For the Israelis on the other hand, it is remembered as the *Milhemet* (War) *HaAtzmaut* (of Independence) or (*Milhemet HaShihrur* (of Liberation), summoning up the strength of purpose to build their young nation. This widened the existing gap between the two communities even further.

Activity:
Map study

Compare the map of Israel's borders in 1949 with the maps on pages 205 and 212. How has life changed for the residents of Jerusalem? What were the implications of the changes for Jordan, Lebanon and Syria?

Map of Israel's borders in 1949.

"No room can be made in Palestine for a second nation except by dislodging or exterminating the first."

Albert Hourani, speaking on behalf of the Arab agency.

"Injustice is unavoidable and we have to decide whether it is better to be unjust to the Arabs of Palestine or to the Jews."

Chaim Weizmann, leader of the Zionist movement and later the first president of Israel, represented the Jewish Agency.

Activity:

Essay-writing skills

"What were both the long-term and the short-term causes of the 1948 War?"

E.H. Carr writes in *What is History* "The study of history is a study of causes." Below are a selection of extracts that give the factual account of the birth of the State of Israel: the date, the circumstances and the events are recorded by all three authors. Yet, as in most historical events, there is always more than one side to the story. Discuss these differences and use this information to answer the essay question.

Source A

> On 14 May [1948] the Jewish community declared its independence as the state of Israel, and this was immediately recognized by the United States and Russia; and Egyptian, Jordanian, Iraqi, Syrian and Lebanese forces moved into the mainly Arab parts of the country. In a situation where there were no fixed frontiers or clear divisions of population, fighting took place between the new Israeli army and those of the Arab states, and in four campaigns interrupted by cease-fires Israel was able to occupy the greater part of the country. From prudence to begin with, later because of panic and the deliberate policy of the Israeli army, almost two thirds of Arab population left their homes and became refugees. At the beginning of 1949 a series of armistices was made between Israel and its Arab neighbours under the supervision of the United Nations, and stable frontiers were created. About 75% Palestine was included within the frontiers of Israel.

Source: Hourani, Albert. 1991. *A History of the Arab Peoples*. London, UK. Faber and Faber. pp. 359–60.

Source B

> At five o'clock on the afternoon of 14 May 1948, in the main hall of the Tel Aviv Museum, a ceremony took place that inaugurated the State of Israel. The ceremony began with the singing of the Jewish anthem "Hatikvah". A few moments later David Ben-Gurion, as Prime Minister and Minister of Defence of the newly created provisional government, put his signature to Israel's Declaration of Independence. As the other signatories completed their work, "Hatikvah" was played again, by the Palestine Symphony Orchestra. Palestine was no more.

Source: Gilbert, Martin. 1998. *Israel: A History*. London, UK. Doubleday. p. 186.

Source C

> With 1948, in the words of Fawaz Turki [a Palestinian author], "the Nation of Palestine ceased to be. Its original inhabitants, the Palestinian people, were dubbed Arab refugees, sent food rations by the UN, and forgotten by the world." After Palestine's dust began to settle, a migration began from the hilly regions, out of the old villages and towns and out of the refugee camps, not to the coast, as in previous times, but to distant places in Palestine.

Source: Kimmerling, Baruch & Migdal, Joel S. 2003. *The Palestinian People: A History*. Cambridge, USA. Harvard University Press. p. 215.

Source D

> The declaration [Israel's declaration of Independence] opened by describing the Land of Israel as the birthplace of the Jewish people, and looking back at the land's distant past. "Here their spiritual, religious and political identity was shaped. Here they first attained to statehood, created cultural values of national and universal significance, and gave to the world the eternal Book of Books." "They had 'kept faith' with the land during all these years of dispersal, 'and never ceased to pray and hope for their return to it, for the restoration in it of their political freedom.'"
> The declaration continued: "Impelled by this historic and traditional attachment, Jews strove in every successive generation to re-establish themselves in their ancient homeland. In recent decades they returned in their masses. Pioneers, ma'pilim—immigrants coming in defiance of restrictive legislation —and defenders, they made deserts bloom, revived the Hebrew language, built villages and towns, and created a thriving community, controlling its own economy and culture, loving peace but knowing how to defend itself, bringing the blessings of progress to all the country's inhabitants, and aspiring towards independent nationhood."

Source: Gilbert, Martin. 1998. *Israel: A History*. London, UK. Doubleday. p. 186.

Atatürk and the Turkish Republic

When the First World War ended and the armistice was signed, much of Anatolia (Turkey today) was under occupation. Istanbul, the capital was taken over by Allied forces and placed under their administration; the Dardanelle Straits were occupied by the British and major cities on the southern Mediterranean coast such as Cilicia and Adana and Antalya were in French and Italian hands. The fate of Turkey was in the hands of the Allies. They wished to maintain the Ottoman Sultan, Mohammad VI on the throne, but his role was purely nominal. His sultanate had become an empty shell and as ruler he was rendered powerless and dependent on the West. However, of all the defeated powers of the First World War, Turkey was to be the only one that succeeded in forcing the Allies to revise their original peace treaty. This was mainly through the strength and perseverance of Turkish nationalism, which was personified in the leadership of Mustafa Kemal, otherwise known as Atatürk, the Father of the Turks.

Turkey emerged from this war with pride and was ready to build a new and modern state. However, the country and its people had suffered enormously after so many years of war. The population of Anatolia had declined by at least 20 per cent. The war had disrupted much of the country's infrastructure and famine was widespread. This caused massive waves of migration and about another 10 per cent of the population had left the country. The task ahead for the nationalists was therefore not an easy one. In 1919 Atatürk's main objectives were to rid Turkey of the presence of foreign troops, reverse the terms of the Treaty of Sèvres and restore Turkish sovereignty in Anatolia. Ultimately, he wanted to strengthen Turkey and put an end to its reputation as "the sick man of Europe".

For the first step of ridding the country of foreign troops, Atatürk was greatly helped by the presence of the Greek army, which had landed in Izmir, south-western Anatolia, in 1919. The Greek presence was a major blow to Turkish national pride. For centuries Greece had been an Ottoman colony. They had only joined the First World War in the last year, in May 1917, and had never defeated the Ottomans in battle during this war. Furthermore, somewhat miscalculating the Turkish reaction, the Greeks took this opportunity to further advance into Anatolia. This triggered off an upsurge of nationalism and

Mustafa Kemal (1881–1938)

Mustafa Kemal attended military school and graduated from the Imperial War College in Istanbul. In 1908, he played a role in the Young Turk Revolution. The Young Turks were reformists who aimed to limit the power of the sultan by restoring Parliament and the constitution. In 1910 he attended the French Army manoeuvres in Picardy as one of the Turkish Army representatives. In 1911, he worked at the Ministry of War and was later posted to the Ottoman province of Trablusgarp (present-day Libya) to fight in the Italo-Turkish War. He returned to the capital in October 1912 following the outbreak of the Balkan Wars. During World War One he served in the Gallipoli campaign and gained a reputation for bravery. He was later posted to Sofia and Berlin as military attaché, where he became an admirer of European institutions. Following the Turkish War of Independence (1919–1923) Mustafa Kemal emerged as the ideal candidate to lead Turkey towards modernity.

started the Turkish War of Independence. Mustafa Kemal reminded his compatriots that the homeland was in danger and that "only the will of the nation" could save it. In the occupied territories local groups calling themselves the Society for the Defence of Rights started to put up armed resistance. The Graeco–Turkish war lasted for two years and ended in September 1922 when the Turks liberated Izmir and drove the Greeks out of Turkey.

In the East, the threat came from the Armenians, who had been promised an autonomous republic by the Allies (see page 182). In Autumn 1920, with the support of Soviet troops, the Turkish Army of Resistance attacked and successfully defeated the newly formed Republic of Armenia. This was the first step in revising the Treaty of Sèvres. Following these victories on 11 October 1922, the Armistice of Mudanya was signed between Turkey, Greece and Britain. A peace conference was convened in Lausanne, Switzerland, to renegotiate the terms of the Treaty of Sèvres.

Establishment of modern Turkey

In the pursuit of the ultimate objective of strengthening Turkey's rule, Mustafa Kemal set about dismantling the sultanate, the Ottoman system of government, because he considered it outdated and a continuous source of weakness for Turkey. His aim was to replace the Sultanate with a Republic. He was however aware of the need to remain cautious because the majority of the Turks continued to be loyal to their sultan and the system of the sultanate.

Kemal's tactics were extremely subtle. He established his authority in Ankara, a city in the heart of Anatolia, as opposed to the Ottoman capital, Istanbul. For two years between 1920 and 1922 a dual power existed: the legal seat of power remained in Istanbul, where the sultan and the Ottoman parliament resided; but an alternative seat of power backed by the Grand National Assembly composed of delegates chosen by local resistance groups was in Ankara. Kemal wanted to show that the sultanate was weak and dependent on the West and therefore, though legal lacked legitimacy. He stressed the sultan's association with the signing of the humiliating Treaty of Sèvres, which undermined Turkish sovereignty and dismembered Turkey. He pointed to the fact that any decision taken by the government of Istanbul had to be approved by the occupying forces. An incident in the early months of 1920 helped illustrate this point: in January 1920 the Ottoman parliament met and adopted the National Pact, the *Misak-ı Millî*. This pact defined the Ottoman frontiers as "all Ottoman land inhabited by Turks when the Treaty of Mudros was signed in October 1918". It stated that Turkey's national boundaries were the areas inhabited by an Ottoman Muslim majority. It was a nationalist message addressed to the foreign powers (Greek, Italian, French and British) present on Turkish soil; it did not question the loss of the Arab-speaking Ottoman territory, but rejected any further loss of Turkish territory. As soon as the Parliament's decision was published British, French and Italian troops occupied the city of Istanbul. The incident showed the disregard that the Western powers had towards the Ottoman Parliament's decision, which further confirmed its lack of autonomy.

> **Discussion point: Terminology**
>
> Both the words legal and legitimate have their origin in law. Legal means "established, permitted by law". Legitimate means "having an official status defined by the law"
>
> Can a legal institution lack legitimacy?

While the government of Istanbul was at the mercy of the foreign troops, the Grand National Assembly in Ankara represented the people of Turkey and its strength depended on the Turks themselves. By making the National Pact the credo of the Nationalists and the Grand National Assembly, Atatürk had made this alternative seat of power legitimate in the eye of the Turkish people. The following steps assured Atatürk's ultimate success:

- On 23 April 1920 the Grand National Assembly repudiated the sultanate and offered Mustafa Kemal the title of President of the Grand National Assembly. Furthermore, the Mufti of Ankara declared the government of Istanbul to be a traitor.
- On 1 November 1922 the Grand National Assembly passed a law abolishing the sultanate.
- On 29 October 1923, following the signing of the Treaty of Lausanne, Turkey was proclaimed a Republic with Mustafa Kemal as its first president.

Reforms under the Republic

In the course of the next two decades Turkey underwent enormous changes. It was modernized and became a secular parliamentary republic capable of dealing with the European powers on equal terms. Many of these changes were due to Mustafa Kemal. So much so that the word "Kemalism" has since entered the political vocabulary to describe modern Turkey. Kemalism was based on six principles. These principles, known as the "Six Arrows", were incorporated in the Constitution in 1937:

The Six Arrows

1 Reformism/revolutionism
2 Republicanism
3 Secularism
4 Nationalism
5 Populism
6 Etatism/Statism.

Reformism/revolutionalism

Reformism summed up the need to revolutionize Turkey and the Turkish way of life according to the model conceived by Mustafa Kemal. This principle symbolized Kemalism because its aim was to bring about state-controlled, orderly change and it demanded the willing and active participation of the people. Kemalism was a paternalistic ideology. Atatürk, as the father of the Turks, prescribed remedies, which he thought would better the life of the Turks. Just like a father, he was at times disappointed when his flock showed little appreciation.

The reforms had two aspects, a cultural and a political one. Culturally, Kemalism aimed to bring Turkey close to the Western European nations. For Mustafa Kemal the model of the Western nations was the model for progress. Therefore, the closer the Turkish people came to resemble their European neighbours, the better their lives would be. Politically, the reforms aimed to strengthen the state through establishing a state ideology that united the citizens of Turkey under a uniform and centralized model.

Among the changes were strict laws restricting people's clothing. Men were no longer allowed to wear the traditional headgear, the Fez or the turban and women were strongly discouraged from wearing the veil. Instead the people were encouraged to dress in the Western European style, like the leader himself. Culturally, this had the effect of reducing the outward differences between a Turk and a Western European. Kemal wanted the word "Turk" to represent a new modern man as opposed to an outdated and exotic person. Politically, it served the purpose of eliminating regional and ethnical differences. The Kurds, for example, were strongly discouraged to dress in their traditional clothes. This helped introduce a mono-ethnic, modern Turkish identity for all the people.

In 1926 The European calendar replaced the Islamic lunar calendar. Sundays replaced the Friday as the day of rest. With this reform, the Turkish national identity was shifting Westward and the break with the past was further underlined.

In 1928 a new Turkish alphabet using Latin letters replaced the Ottoman alphabet which was written from right to left and used Arabic letters. At the same time schools became free and compulsory. Between 1923 and 1940 the number of schools doubled; the number of teachers increased by 133 per cent and the number of students by 300 per cent.

Culturally the ability to write in a similar style as the Western European helped bridge the gap between the Turk and the Western European. Politically, the inability to read the Ottoman script ended the new generation's relationship with the past. It would therefore be a clean start for Modern Turkey. Furthermore the language of the Qur'an is also in Arabic letters, and even though the holy book was translated into Turkish, for the many devout Muslims, it needs to be read in the original language. The new generation, brought up on the new alphabet, would have difficulty reading the Qur'an in Arabic. The new alphabet therefore had the effect of secularizing the Kemalist youth.

In 1924 the Turkish Women's Union was formed to promote women's rights. In 1930 women were given the right to vote in municipal elections. In 1934 they obtained the right to vote in national elections and present themselves as candidates. The union was disbanded in 1935 because it was stated that with the right to vote, parity had been achieved.

Women were also encouraged to pursue their education and enter public life. Mustafa Kemal set a personal example: his adopted daughter, Sabiha Gökçen, (1913–2001), became Turkey's first female combat pilot. These measures had the clear cultural objective of modernizing the Turkish woman and politically they distinguished Kemalist Turkey from the Ottoman era.

> *"Our rich and harmonious language will be able to display itself with new Turkish letters. We must free ourselves from these incomprehensible signs that for centuries have held our minds in an iron vice. You must learn the new Turkish letters quickly."*
>
> Kemal Atatürk, 9 August 1928

Sabiha Gökçen and Mustafa Kemal

Republicanism

On 29 October 1923, following the signing of the Treaty of Lausanne, Turkey was proclaimed a Republic with Mustafa Kemal as its first president. Symbolically, in order to break with the past, Mustafa Kemal changed the seat of the government. The capital of the country moved from Istanbul to Ankara. In 1924 a new constitution was passed which confirmed the move from a hereditary constitutional monarchy to a republic. According to the 1924 constitution, sovereignty lay with the people, who elected a parliament, the Grand National Assembly, which then elected the president, who chose the prime minister. Though a Republic, civil liberties were severely restricted under Kemalism.

From 1925 a one-party system—the Republican People's Party (RPP)—was established and all opposition came under severe attack. A law called The Law of the Maintenance of Order, was introduced in March 1925 with an aim to crush the Kurdish rebellion (see below), but was then used extensively to rid the Kemalists of all form of dissent. This law remained in force until 1929. Kemal was conscious of the danger of opposition. That is why even within the Republican People's Party he introduced strict discipline. Discussions were only allowed in closed meetings and once the decision was taken, all members were bound by that decision. Consequently the state and the party were often indistinguishable. Discussions in the National Assembly were rare and the votes were often dictated by the party decision. Elections were held every four years, but the candidates were presented by the party. In 1930 for a few months, a new party, the Free Republican Party, was given the go-ahead to be formed. This was with Mustafa Kemal's total approval. In the October 1930 local elections, the new party obtained 30 of the 502 local councils. Their success was enough to bring about its closure. In November 1930, the Free Republican Party was forced to close down.

Liberty of the press was severely restricted. In 1931 a new Press Law was adopted which gave the government the right to close down any newspaper that published anything contradicting the "general policies of the country". Kemalism intended to use the press as a means to spread its message and not to allow any adverse information to be spread.

Secularism

For Mustafa Kemal Islam represented the past and was a reminder of the Ottoman Empire. One of his first moves was to separate the caliphate (religious authority) from the sultanate (political authority). After the departure from office of Mohammad VI, Abdul Majid, the sultan's cousin, was designated as caliph. Though this post was now void of any political responsibility, it nonetheless had a great deal of potential influence over the Muslim population.

On 3 March 1924, the Grand National Assembly passed a law abolishing the caliphate. This put an end to a position of religious authority, which the Ottomans had held for over 400 years. It was an extremely risky move, but it fulfilled the new credo. Politically it completed the break with the Ottomans and culturally it was a major step towards a modern Turkey. To succeed the measures taken under this principle aimed to reduce the influence of Islam in the daily lives of the Turkish people. These measures included the closure of religious schools, the abolishment of the Turkish Ministry of Religious Endowments (with all its property handed over to the state) and the replacement in 1926 of Islamic courts by civil courts based on the civic codes of such European countries as Switzerland, Italy and Germany. As a consequence, the Islamic jurists lost their authority and gradually fewer people

"There is no logical explanation for the political disenfranchisement of women. Any hesitation and negative mentality on this subject is nothing more than a fading social phenomenon of the past. … Women must have the right to vote and to be elected; because democracy dictates that, because there are interests that women must defend, and because there are social duties that women must perform."

Mustafa Kemal

The electorate

All men over the age of 18.
Universal suffrage after 1934 (men and women)
↓
Grand National Assembly
↓
President
↓
Prime minister.

Discussion point:

How important is it for a modern state to be secular? Can you think of non secular modern states?

chose to become Islamic jurists. Worship at tombs and shrines was prohibited. Following the translation of the Qur'an into Turkish, the call to prayer was read in Turkish. The family code was changed, banning religious marriages and polygamy. In 1928 the words "official religion of the country is Islam" were barred from the constitution.

This of course did not mean that Turkey stopped being a Muslim country or that the Turkish people stopped practising their religion. It succeeded however in reducing the power of the clergy in such a devoutly religious country. Following the model in many Western countries, Kemalism had established a clear separation of religion from the State and religion now belonged to the private sphere.

Nationalism

Under the title of nationalism came the promotion of Turkish history and culture. In 1925 the Turkish Historical Society was founded. Its main job was to emphasize Turkey's pre-Islamic history and show the importance of the Turkish people *before* their association with Islam. Kemalist ideology also aimed to develop the cult of Mustafa Kemal. This was done through reinterpreting history and emphasizing his role in the nationalist movement.

In 1926 Mustafa Kemal's memoirs were published. In his memoirs he depicted himself as the one who led the nationalist movement from the start and presented all former colleagues as incompetent. In a speech in October 1927 he outlined the history of the Turkish national movement and criticized once again many of his former collaborators. This speech was translated into German, French and English and became the official version of the history of Modern Turkey both in Turkey and outside.

 How useful are memoirs to a historian?

While offering the public a one-sided interpretation of history, Kemalism also aimed to make the Turkish people proud of Turkey. Its aim was to make people have faith in and be loyal to a new national identity. After 1934 "History of the Turkish revolution" became a compulsory subject at school. Also in 1934 the title Atatürk was bestowed upon Mustafa Kemal. In that way he was in some ways inventing the notion of Turkishness through rewriting the past and placing himself as its founder. In the 1982 constitution the principle of nationalism still stands and it is defined as the "material and spiritual well-being of the Republic". Mustafa Atatürk is also described as "the immortal leader and incomparable national hero".

Populism

This principle emphasized the common interests of the nation over the interests of a group or a class. Kemalist reforms were beneficial to all and did not limit themselves to a privileged group. Kemalism reached out to the people and spread its ideology beyond the élite. For that purpose the Ministry of Education organised lectures and exhibitions throughout the country to spread nationalist and secularist ideas. This was called the Turkish Hearth Movement. In 1932 these were replaced with People's Homes and People's Rooms, to carry out the same activity. By the end of the Second World War there were 500 People's Homes throughout Turkey. These "homes" served also as recreational centres or sports clubs. They fulfilled both a cultural and a political purpose, spreading Kemalist thinking to reach out to people in their leisure time.

Etatism/Statism

Central to the concept of "Reformism/Revolutionism", one of the aims of the Kemalist ideology was to strengthen the state. Under the principle of "Statism/Etatism", centralized economic planning was introduced and the state came to supervise much of the economic sector. Statism gave the state the predominant role in the economic field. It should be underlined that centralized economic planning was not so unusual in the inter-war years. On the one hand, given the state of Turkey immediately after the war, and the massive shortages, the state was the only force that had the ability to redress the situation. On the other hand, with the economic depression of the 1930s many countries, such as the United States and Germany, had also opted for centralized planning. The model taken up by Kemal was in fact a mixture of Roosevelt's New Deal and Hitler's planned economy.

Turkey's relations with the outside world

Atatürk's nationalist discourse did not translate into a will to expand. Turkey's prime objective was to restore its sovereignty over its own territory. In fact Mustafa Kemal showed a great deal of pragmatism in his relations with the outside world and this was at times at the cost of losing popularity at home. This was the case with his support for dropping Turkey's territorial claims to Mosul. Mosul province stood on the border of Turkey and Iraq and divided up the Kurdish community. This artificial border was devised by Lloyd George and Clemenceau and was based on the existing oil reserves. It served the purpose of giving the British access to the oil fields of the Mosul Province. As the Turks put it, "Turkey began where the oil fields ended." According to the National Pact, which defined Turkey's territory as "all Ottoman land inhabited by Turks when the Treaty of Mudros was signed in October 1918", the province of Mosul *should* have been "part of Turkey". Notably, three days after the signing of the Treaty of Mudros, Mosul was captured by the British forces.

Atatürk was under pressure by the Grand National Assembly to push for Turkey's rights. He decided, however, to call for the arbitration of the League of Nations. A commission of enquiry was sent by the League of Nations in 1925. When they arbitrated against Turkey, Mustafa Kemal signed a treaty in July 1926 with Iraq and the United Kingdom and accepted the decision of the League: Mosul, the Turks agreed, belonged to Iraq. In return the Turks received 10 per cent of the region's oil revenue. There was negative reaction in Turkey to this decision, many felt humiliated by such a biased arbitration. To control the dissent among Kemal's own nationalists, civil liberties were greatly restricted. The Law of the Maintenance of Order, introduced in 1925, was extensively used to curb open discussions. His decision to hand over Mosul was based on the assumption that a fight with the UK over Mosul would simply weaken Turkey. Kemal was also aware of the separatist tendencies of the Kurdish population and realized that adding Mosul to Turkey might increase the strength of the Kurdish ethnic minority and prove dangerous for the new Turkish Republic.

In the interest of promoting "Peace at home and peace in the world", Atatürk's foreign policy remained cautious and realistic. Atatürk maintained very amicable relations with the Western world. By 1925 he had signed a number of bilateral treaties with various countries in Western Europe. He also maintained cordial relations with the Soviet Union. The two countries signed a non-aggression pact in 1923, which lasted until 1945. In this way Turkey maintained its independence from the West. In 1928 and in 1930 Turkey signed Treaties of friendship with Italy and Greece, in which both countries renounced their claims over Turkish territory. In 1932 Turkey was admitted into the League of Nations, and in 1934 Atatürk concluded the Balkan Pact with Greece, Yugoslavia and Romania; this assumed non-aggression and co-operation between them.

In 1936 Turkey asked for and obtained the right to supervise the Dardanelle Straits. The Treaty of Saadabad, signed between Iran, Turkey, Iraq and Afghanistan in 1937, brought about closer co-operation between them, reaffirming existing frontiers and agreeing to consult one another on matters of common interest. In 1939 Turkey took back the district of Alexandrette—Hatay to the Turks. This district, which has a large Turkish minority (about one third of the population), had become part of Syria after the First World War and was administered by the French. In 1938 the Turkish Republic successfully pleaded its case in front of the League of Nations and the district was detached from Syria and became the independent Republic of Hatay. The newly formed Republic then announced its union with Turkey the following year.

Kemalism: an assessment

The most important objective behind Mustafa Kemal's reforms was to show the world and the Turkish people that times had changed. This new era was defined by nationalism, republicanism and secularism. Loyalty to a Turkish national identity replaced loyalty to the Ottoman ruler. Kemalism succeeded in this task because Turkey continues to be a secular Republic and has bridged the gap with Europe so successfully that it might soon find itself a member of the European Union. Furthermore, Turkey's relationship with the outside world remained peaceful and it succeeded in affirming its sovereignty over its territory. However, in our final assessment we need to evaluate his success in the long run. Though Atatürk had the backing of the Turkish elite, the transformation that Kemalism aimed to bring about was not as smooth as the state ideology claims, and there are to this day signs of resistance to Kemalist reforms. Change was imposed and consequently at different periods in the history of modern Turkey, dissatisfaction has erupted to the surface that reflects certain shortcoming in the system. To give a few examples:

The policy of Turkification

The policy of forcefully replacing multi-ethnicity with mono-ethnicity aimed to bring about a standard Turkish identity. The ethnic minorities, such as the Kurds were discouraged from speaking Kurdish or dressing in their traditional Kurdish clothes. They were in fact not recognized as ethnically or culturally distinct from the Turks and were referred to as the "Mountain Turks". They could not form a political party based on their ethnicity. In 1925 the Kurds revolted against the government. Their rebellion was severely crushed and the rebel leader and a large number of his followers were executed. In spite of so many years of repression, the Kurds still claim their cultural autonomy and some demand separation from Turkey. Mustafa Kemal's ideal of "inventing" the mono-ethnic Turk has not been totally successful.

The 1982 constitution reiterated the mono-ethnic nature of Turkey. It stated: "The Turkish State, with its territory and nation, is an indivisible entity. Its language is Turkish." Indivisibility means that the Turkish nation cannot be divided into ethnic groups and the teaching of any other languages, as a first language, is prohibited in state schools. Article 66 defines a Turkish civic identity: "everyone bound to the Turkish state through the bond of citizenship is a Turk".

The Kurdish rebellion, 1925

In its quest to repress ethnic differences, the Republican government banned the use of Kurdish in public. The language was no longer allowed to be taught in schools. As a way of dispersing the population, large Kurdish landowners were relocated to the west of the country.

The rebellion broke out in February 1925 and it was motivated by both Islamic (restoration of the caliphate) and nationalistic (the formation of an independent Kurdistan) sentiments. The government took immediate measures to crush the rebellion. Martial law was declared in the region. Through the Law on the Maintenance of Order, organizations and publications that caused disturbance of law and order were banned. In April, the leader of the rebels, Sheikh Sait, was arrested and this marked the end of the rebellion. In the aftermath of this revolt, many of the Kurdish leaders were executed and more than 20,000 were deported to the west of the country.

The policy of secularization

The Turkish constitution aimed to keep religion out of the political sphere and while Mustafa Kemal was in office (until 1938), this measure was strictly maintained. However, as early as the 1950s, political parties started to emerge that openly expressed their religious beliefs and often their popularity in the elections proved that the Kemalist secular ideals had not transformed the Turkish people's beliefs. However, the 1982 constitution once again reiterated the secular identity of Turkey and since the late 1990s a law banning the wearing of the headscarf has been rigidly enforced for girls in higher education.

In recent years there have been major debates within the Turkish community over the degree to which Islam could be tolerated politically. Since 2002 the Justice and Development Party, a party with open Islamic principles has won the majority in Turkish elections. In February 2008 the Turkish Parliament, with a Justice and Development Party majority voted in favour of lifting the ban on the wearing of headscarf in colleges and universities. According to a Gallup Poll taken in 2007, 45 per cent of Turkish women wear the headscarf. In June 2008, however, the Constitutional Court overturned the parliamentary vote as unconstitutional. Clearly, the ideals of Atatürk have not eradicated strong religious beliefs.

> **Discussion point:**
>
> Respect for various ethnicities can be divisive. A strong republic is a "unitary" republic. How important is it for a modern state to be unitary?

Equal rights for men and women

Kemalism attempted to impose parity between men and women in society. This of course required a major change in thinking. By 1933 there were 13 female judges in Turkey. In the 1935 elections 17 women were elected. Sadly though, these numbers were not sustained. In 1990 there were only six women deputies. After the 2007 elections, the number rose to 24, but this still only constitutes 4.4 per cent of the total number of deputies in Turkey's parliament today. On a more positive level, statistics for 2003–4 comparing male and female school attendance at the secondary level show that the gap between them is less than ten per cent. Comparative literacy rates between men and women in 2003 showed that 79 per cent of women could read and write, compared to 94 per cent of men.

In conclusion, to evaluate Kemalism it is important to return to 1918 when the defeated Ottoman Empire was barely capable of maintaining its political independence let alone defend its territorial integrity. Seen from that angle, the nationalists of Turkey were successful in putting Turkey on its feet and forcing the rebirth of a nation in an extremely hostile environment. The changes that this new nation underwent on the other hand appear at times both abrupt and the manner in which they were carried out somewhat authoritarian. Consequently in our assessment, while recognizing certain of the achievements, one has to objectively point to the fact that in the process large segments of the population were alienated and the authoritarian legacy has been a difficult one to eliminate.

Activity:
Atatürk: an assessment

Review the following images and extracts that together provide insights into the legacy of Mustafa Kemal Atatürk, and answer the questions below.

Source A

Atatürk promotes Latin script on a visit to the provinces.

Source B

He proved by a personal demonstration that a Turk can be his own master in Anatolia without having to wait for a better world, and under his inspiration the National Movement sprang to life.

Source: Originally published in 1922. Quoted in Toynbee, Arnold J. 2009. *The Western Question in Greece and Turkey: A study in the contact of Civilisations.* [place], [country]. Martino Fine Books.

Source C

The Armenians know Ataturk for his role in the Armenian Genocide and as a Young Turk. The Young Turks were the forerunners of Hitler's infamous SS troops. The Greeks knew Ataturk as the butcher of Smyrna and for his role in the Pontian Greek Genocide. The Kurds know Ataturk for his initiating in 1924 the attacks on the Kurds which amounted to ethnic cleansing and crimes against humanity. Two million Christians were killed by Turks in the 20th century, mostly when Ataturk was dictator of Turkey. Ataturk ranks with Hitler and Stalin as a brutal dictator.

A statement by American Hellenic Institute President Gene Rossides from 2006. The AHI was founded on 1 August 1974, following Turkey's invasion of Cyprus.

Source: Rossides, G. 15 August 2006. "Turkey-Ataturk and U.S. Policy: Fundamental Reexamination Is Needed". http://www. ahiworld.com/press_releases/081506.

Source D

Mr. Atatürk, I don't know how to put this delicately for you, but the country you helped put together is a deformity in a class of its own. When you started your war of liberation, you donned turbans, pleaded with the Kurds for help, and invoked Allah to grant you success for a place under the sun where Muslim Turks and Kurds could live unmolested. When it was over, you banned turbans, took Islam out of government, and the part I don't understand, declared all Kurds nonexistent! Your children are now telling me, it was all for my own good. Many Kurds who have been deprived of rays of freedom and the light of science go along with this nonsense.

An Open Letter to Mustafa Kemal Atatürk, signed Kani Xulam.

Source: http://www.kurdistan.org/Current-Updates/ataturk022405.html

Source E

Not everyone has shared a positive view of Ataturk. Writing in the 1930's the American journalist John Gunther described Ataturk as "the dictator-type carried to its ultimate extreme, the embodiment of totalitarian rule by character."

Source: Mallinson, W. 2005. *Cyprus: A Modern History.* London, UK. IB Tauris. p. 107.

Source F

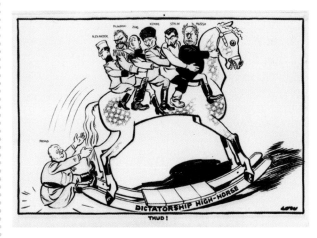

A political satire depicting Mustafa Kemal by David Low, first published in the Evening Standard on *30 June 1930*.

Source: UK Cartoon Archive. http://www.cartoons.ac.uk.

Source G

He stands today as the Emancipator of Turkey. He has lifted the people out of the slough of servile submission to alien authority, brought them to a realization of their inherent qualities and to an independence of thought and action. Without a doubt Mustapha Kemal Pasha is one of the great figures in contemporary history."

Source: "Mustapha Kemal Pasha: Where is a Turk his own master?". *Time*, 24 March 1923.

Source H

*The name of Atatürk reminds mankind of the historical success of one of the greatest men of this century.
His inspirational leadership of the Turkish Nation, his open view in understanding the modern world and his might and courage as a military leader.*

Source: John F. Kennedy, President of the United States, 1961–63.

Source-based questions

1 With reference to their origin and purpose, assess the value and the limitations of the sources above.

2 Why are assessments of Atatürk so polarized?

3 Using these sources and your own knowledge assess Mustafa Kemal's contribution to Turkish history?

Timeline: Atatürk and the Turkish Republic, 1914–39	
1914–18	The First World War
1919	May 16: Occupation of Izmir by the Greeks
	May 19: The beginning of Turkey's War of Independence
1920	January 28: Ottoman Parliament adopts the National Pact
	February 16: British, French and Italian troops occupy Istanbul.
	April 23: Grand National Assembly repudiates the Sultanate and offers Mustaf Kemal the presidency
	September–November: Defeat of the Armenians
1922	September: Liberation of Izmir by the Turkish nationalists
	October 11: Armistice of Mudanya between Greece, the UK and Turkey
	November 1: Caliphate and Sultanate abolished
1923	July 24: Treaty of Lausanne
	October: Non-agression pact signed with USSR
	October 23: Turkey proclaimed a Republic
1924	March 3: Grand National Assembly abolishes the Caliphate
	April 24: New constitution
	The Turkish Women's Union formed
1925	February–April: The Kurdish Revolt
	March: Law of the Maintenance of Order
	September 2: The closing of Sufi
	November 25: Change of headgear for men
	December 16: The League of Nations hands Mosul over to Iraq
1926	January 1: The European Calendar replaces the Islamic lunar calendar
	October 4: Islamic courts replaced by civil courts
	July: Decision of the League of Nations to hand Mosul over to Iraq
1928	Statement taken out of the constitution: "the official religion of the country is Islam"
	November 1: Introduction of the new Turkish alphabet
	Treaty of friendship signed with Italy
1930	Women given the right to vote in municipal elections
	Treaty of friendship signed with Greece.
1931	Press law passed restricting articles that contradict government policies
1932	Turkey admitted into the League of Nations
1934	December 5: Women given the right to vote in national elections
	The title 'Atatürk' (father of the Turks) given to Mustafa Kemal
	Balkan Pact signed with Greece, Yugoslavia and Romania
1935	The Turkish Women's Union disbanded
1936	July 30: Turkey obtains the rights to supervise the Dardanelles Straits
1937	July 8: Treaty of Saadabad signed with Iran, Iraq and Afghanistan
1938	September 2: Republic of Hatay made independent from Syria
	November 10: Mustafa Kemal Atatürk dies

Iran and Reza Khan, 1924–41

Timeline: Atatürk and the Turkish Republic, 1914–39	
1939	June 23: Republic of Hatay joins Turkey

Persia (present-day Iran) declared its neutrality when the First World War broke out, but nonetheless served as a battle field for the belligerents. The north-western region of Azerbaijan saw fighting between the Russians and the Ottomans and was consequently occupied by the Russians throughout most of the war. The Central Powers, in particular the Germans, were also very actively engaged in Persia. Their plan was to recruit sympathizers both from amongst the clergy and the tribal chiefs and persuade Persia to join their side of the war, a feat that had it succeeded would have strategically tipped the balance in favour of the Germans. As a result of the German plans, a British force of about 8,000 men landed in the south and remained active on Persian territory throughout the war.

Apart from physical damage, a more important consequence of the war was the effect it had on the central authority of the ruler. Iran was ruled by Ahmad **Shah**, of the Qajar dynasty. His authority had been totally undermined by the presence of the foreign troops and once the war was over, taking advantage of this power vacuum, the country broke up into a number of local separatist revolts.

Shah means King in Persian.

Iran after the First World War

Once the war ended a Persian delegation went to Paris in order to present its country's grievances to the peacemakers. They claimed that as war had damaged their economy and left many regions devastated, the conference should compensate them. Though some of the representatives were sympathetic to the Persian plea, the British delegation refused even to let the Persians present their demands and the delegation returned home empty handed. The reason behind the British refusal was that they had already prepared the bi-lateral agreement, the Anglo-Persian Agreement, which aimed to put Persia under the protection of the United Kingdom. According to this plan, the weak Persian government would sign the treaty and Persia would hand over to the UK total control of its finances, its army, its economy and its administration. Once Persia became a British protectorate, its affairs would be a matter handled solely by the British government and not by the peace conference.

The years following the First World War were chaotic years for Persia. However, in spite of an extremely weak central government, the country managed to rally sufficient nationalist support to obstruct the plans of the United Kingdom and prevent the ratification of the humiliating Anglo-Persian Agreement. It also succeeded in defeating the rebel forces and restored the authority of Tehran, the capital. Persia remained an autonomous sovereign state. The credit for this has been given to a Cossack Brigade commander, Reza Khan.

Reza Savad Koohi (later known as Reza Khan) joined the Persian Cossack Brigade, an elite military unit run by Russian officers, at the age of 16. A military career gave the young man access to a minimum of education, which he may otherwise have not obtained. It also sowed the seeds of patriotism and a particular dislike for the foreign powers that dominated his country. Later in life he is recorded as having said: "After I had chosen the soldier's profession I became ever more sunk in grief as I saw the destinies of Iran's forces determined by Russian officers, who intervened directly in the affairs of the army and compelled the Iranian officers to accept their dictatorial ways." The "soldier's profession" also gave him the opportunity to rise to the rank of Brigadier. This coincided with the Russian Revolution and the dismissal of the Russian officers, which for the first time opened the possibility for an Iranian to fill the post of Commander. Reza Khan, having already shown his capacities while combating the rebel forces, was the man to fill that post.

> ### Reza Khan (1878–1944)
>
> Born in a remote village to a modest family in the northern provinces of Mazandaran, Reza Savad Koohi had by the age of 47, in 1925, obtained the highest rank in the country—that of monarch. Adopting the name of Pahlavi, Reza Shah Pahlavi became the founder of the Pahlavi dynasty that ruled Iran from 1925–79. Reza Shah enjoyed a great deal of support at the start of his reign, when he attempted to place Iran on the path of modernity. Many, however, were disappointed when he turned out to be a traditional ruler. His reign ended abruptly in 1941 when as a consequence of the Allied occupation he was forced to abdicate in favour of his son and spend the rest of his life in exile—a tragic fate for a nationalist. He died in 1944 in Johannesburg.

In 1921 in the midst of civil disorder and a virtually disintegrated central authority, Reza Khan led his troops into the capital in a bloodless coup d'état and forced Ahmad Shah to appoint him as Commander in Chief and minister of defence. From there, Reza Khan's ascent to power was rapid. By 1923 he had become prime minister and in 1925 following a parliamentary vote took over from Ahmad Shah, who was forced to abdicate, bringing an end to the Qajar dynasty. Reza Khan was made King and became Reza Shah. Reza Khan chose the name Pahlavi as the name for his dynasty, after the name for the language spoken in Persia before the Muslim conquest of Iran in the 600s.

> **Discussion point:**
>
> **Dynasties**
>
> A dynasty is a family that rules a country. This hereditary system is called a monarchy. What other systems of government exist?
>
> **What are the drawbacks and disadvantages of the monarchical system?**

Reza Shah: the consolidation of power

To consolidate his position Reza Shah Pahlavi needed to obtain legitimacy and popularity. His first task was to restore order and ensure the military defeat of the rebels. He needed to establish himself as the sole, legitimate ruler of the country. He did this by merging all the different armed units into one central national army. The army was then sent out to the tribal areas to crush and disarm the rebels. He personally led the fight against the last of the tribal chiefs, Sheikh Khaz'al, who led a separatist movement in the southern regions of Khuzistan. Once the last of the chiefs was eliminated and ethnic rebellions were suppressed, Reza Khan rode back to the capital as hero and saviour. He had restored discipline and prevented the disintegration of the country. This made him both popular and legitimate.

He then needed to obtain a power base. Persian rulers traditionally had a tribal affiliation which offered them the necessary platform from which to rule. They had always ascended the hierarchy within their tribe and were usually tribal chiefs before they vied for the position of leadership in the country. The Qajars, for example, originated from the north-western Azerbaijan region of the country and therefore brought with them the support of the Turco-Persian ethnic group. Reza Khan was of humble origin and had not obtained a high status in his home town. Without the necessary tribal affiliation that guaranteed a support system, Reza Khan needed to create his power base. As a nationalist and a modernizer, he chose the army and the middle class intelligentsia as his tribe.

To the soldier he offered nationalistic pride. As Commander in Chief and through increasing the size of the army and offering privileges to the armed forces, he managed to obtain and maintain their total loyalty. This remained his main power base until the end of his rule.

To the middle class intelligentsia he promised both a national rebirth and national unity. He also pledged a break with the past. He therefore received the backing of the middle classes who had suffered the humiliation of a country dominated by foreign powers under the weak Qajar dynasty. For this group, Reza Khan was the man who could realize their wish for an independent and stable Persia free from the clutches of foreign powers and ready to meet the challenges of the 20th century. Though this group aided him in his rise to power and supported his projects at the start, once Reza Khan established his rule, they did not remain his loyal supporters through to the end.

To make the break with the past Reza Shah needed to unify the country and offer his supporters an ideology that would replace tribal affiliation, one based on loyalty to the nation and its founder. Nationalism, based on a unified Persian identity, was the means through which Reza Shah could justify many of his actions. He needed to eliminate the risk of future separatist movements and suppress ethnic differences. Iran is an ethnically diverse country; each ethnic minority has its specific language, culture and sometimes literature. Reza Shah outlawed ethnic languages and clothing. Loyalty to the central state became the credo of his rule. As a symbol of national rebirth, Reza Shah also revived the pre-Islamic myth of Persia and took steps to revive the pre-Islamic Iran. By 1935 he even changed the name Persia to Iran—the land of the Aryans—thus emphasizing the pre-Islamic roots of the country. Iran was inclusive of all ethnic groups, whereas Persia was exclusive.

From the start, Reza Khan pursued a military discipline, where disobedience was equated to mutiny. Criticism of his rule was curbed from the start and all rivals suppressed through restrictions of civil liberties. At first many accepted the restrictions; it was a price to pay for obtaining independence and national unity and even rendered him popular amongst those who feared the disintegration of the country. In the long run, the use of force led to his declining popularity.

Reza Shah: the nature of the regime

Reza Shah's rule was based on two principles: tradition and continuity on the one hand and nationalism and change on the other. Through nationalism he would introduce modernity and bring about change,

Discussion point:

What role has the intelligentsia played in different historical events?

Activity:

Research pre-Islamic Persia

The Persian Empire dates back to 550 BCE. Islam came to Iran in around 630 CE.

while his respect for tradition maintained continuity and prevented the birth of a truly modern state. The forces of tradition were represented by those that supported the system of monarchy and the Islamic authority vested in the clergy, *the ulema*. He never managed, as Atatürk in Turkey had done, to break away totally from these traditional forces because he feared alienating their authority and consequently could not face the social upheaval and tension that such a break would entail. In the words of Ali Ansari, a historian of modern Iran, "Reza Khan's reformist zeal was tempered by respect for tradition". He therefore maintained the monarchy and withheld some of the reforms in order to appease the *ulema*. So the nature of Reza Shah's regime was a mixture that reflected continuity and change.

Continuity under Reza Shah

Many of Reza Khan's supporters were led to believe that he would end monarchical rule in Persia and instate a republican regime. There was much debate in the media on this issue. A republic had already been established in neighbouring Turkey and appealed to many of Reza Khan's middle class supporters, who saw it as a way to break with the past and set the country on the path of modernization. A republic, however, also upset some of the more traditional interest groups such as the clergy, who equated it with the secularist ideas of Mustafa Kemal Atatürk. On 4 March 1924, the *Ulema*, the Islamic authorities, declared that a republic was contrary to Islam. Reza Khan consequently changed his views and justified his change of mind by claiming that without a dynasty the nation would not survive. When faced with the potential opposition from the Islamic clergy, Reza Khan clearly chose to continue along the traditional path by not only maintaining monarchical rule, but also by giving it a nationalistic justification.

The Qajar dynasty had the full backing of the clergy and in return was totally dependent on their approval. Reza Khan's will to modernize his country required a break from the rigid control of the clergy. Though in the later part of his reign, he took steps in that direction, he did not eliminate the clergy from the political scene. In 1925, as we already saw, he acquiesced to the will of the clergy and maintained the monarchy. When he introduced the "Compulsory Military Service Law", the clergy opposed it on ideological grounds; they feared the indoctrination in secular principles. Reza Khan reacted by amending the law in such a way that theological students would be exempt from military service. With time, as Reza Shah felt more secure, this exemption was withdrawn. The clergy continued throughout this period to hold designated seats in the parliament.

 What are the advantages of having a compulsory military service?

Persia was predominantly a rural economy and under the Qajars, social, economic and political power resided in the hands of the land-owning classes. Reza Khan's struggle against local chieftains challenged this authority. He attacked the traditional elite and therefore confiscated much of their property. However, as the country did not undergo enormous economic changes, the major source of prestige and wealth remained the land. In some cases, new landowners had replaced the old ones, but the nature of the power structure and social relations in the rural areas remained the same.

Under the Qajars, civil liberties in the country were extremely restricted. At first, when Reza Khan took over, the middle class intelligentsia spoke of "a wind of change" and believed that the new leader would be the vehicle through which their agenda would be implemented. They soon realized their mistake. Under the reign of Reza Khan, freedom of the press was severely restricted. Opposition to his rule was totally suppressed. As M. Reza Ghods, put it "the first Pahlavi monarch reduced parliament and the cabinet to rubber stamps". The Institute for the Orientation of Public Opinions was formed to control and repress all forms of dissent. In addition, even articles written about Iran in the foreign press were systematically reported and censored. There was therefore little change in the domain of civil liberties.

Changes under Reza Shah

Under Reza Shah, loyalty to the nation replaced previous feudal relations. Traditional leaders in society were undermined and instead patriotism and the love of the unitary nation were introduced. This was a new model and one that was more in line with modernity. However, given the importance of the ruler, his was a form of "dynastic nationalism", as Ali Ansari described the new ideology; nationalism under Reza Shah was defined around the person of the ruler and not the nation. Reza Shah was more calculating and shrewd than his predecessors. This is because he needed to secure his position and did not have their divine legitimacy. He chose his allies carefully and according to circumstances. He used the Western educated intellectuals but dispensed with them as soon as they started to threaten him.

Reza Shah's creation of a distinctly Persian identity was a further break with the past. This had become the credo and the legitimacy of his regime. In 1928 textbooks were written for secondary schools that emphasized the country's pre-Islamic past. History was therefore rewritten to give Persians a different beginning. A Persian language academy was formed to purify the Persian language, and in particular to take out the Arabic words.

Reza Shah sought greater autonomy from the West. The Qajar dynasty, especially in later years, was identified as a weak government that depended financially and politically on foreign powers. Of the two Great Powers that traditionally controlled Persia, Russia had been eliminated as a result of the Russian Revolution; this left the United Kingdom, which also underwent a setback when the Anglo-Persian Agreement was rejected. Reza Shah's aim was to pursue a "third-power policy". This meant obtaining the backing of a country other than Russia or the UK. Reza Shah addressed countries such as France, the United States, Italy and later Germany to obtain technical expertise and equipment. He sent students to these countries, instead of the UK, for training. Reza Shah's relations with the UK, however, continue to be a debatable issue and many of his critics claim that in reality he did little to eliminate British control. In 1932 Iran and the United Kingdom came to the negotiating table to discuss the existing oil concessions. In the new agreement that was signed in 1933, Iran's royalties rose from 16 per cent to 20 per cent, but the

> **Discussion point:**
>
> Many authoritarian regimes change school text books. Why do you think that is?

233

contract was extended for an extra 60 years. Not many saw the terms of the new treaty as necessarily favourable to Iran.

Reza Shah also established good relations with neighbouring countries and tried to strengthen regional links. In 1937, the Saadabad Pact was signed with Turkey, Iraq and Afghanistan and ended any potential disputes between the four countries.

One clear break with the Qajar monarchs was the role of the state apparatus. Whereas the Qajars continued to rule as though the state was the monarch, Reza Shah's more lasting reforms concerned the administration of the state. In February 1924 before even ascending to the throne, Reza Khan introduced an important set of reforms. The aim of this reform package was to modernize Persia and the purpose behind this was to strengthen the state, reduce the influence of foreign powers and to find a new power base.

One of the most important steps towards the modernization of Persia came about through the reorganization of the army. The army, Reza Shah claimed was the "soul of the nation" and its strength was a reflection on the nation as a whole. It is also true that, as the head of the armed forces, a strong army was also a reflection of his strength as a leader. Ansari refers to the army as Reza Shah's "missing tribe". The first step he took, which was introduced in the 1924 reform package, was a law introducing compulsory military service for a period of two years. This increased the size of the armed forces and consequently Reza Shah's power base. In 1925 there were 40,000 men serving in Iran's National Army. By 1941 their number had risen to 400,000. One third of the country's budget was allocated to the army. The armed services also permitted more social mobility in society and allowed young men of humble origin to receive a basic education and the possibility to move up the social ladder. Unit commanders were ordered to teach soldiers elementary reading, writing and arithmetic. Young officers were sent abroad, mainly to France, for training and French instructors came to Iran. In this way, the army was also a channel through which modern ideas entered the country. Another benefit of a national army was that it limited regional opposition. Prior to conscription the tribes secured the country's safety by providing the necessary resources in men and weapons. Now that the country was rendered safe as a result of a strong centralized national army, there was less need for local private armies.

Reza Shah was also aware of the power of the clergy and was very cautious about the way he dealt with religion. In the later part of his reign, once he felt more secure, he started to implement measures that were directly targeted at offending the clergy. These included a new dress code, which prohibited the wearing of the turban. Many of these measures followed the pattern that Atatürk had set in neighbouring Turkey. In fact, going one step further, in 1936 Reza Shah banned women from the wearing of the veil.

Central government was practically non-existent when Reza Khan assumed responsibility in Persia. Most of those who ran it either lacked the know-how or were too conservative to bring about any major changes. Reza Shah planned to reorganize many of the existing institutions with an aim to strengthen the state through the creation of a modern bureaucracy. In this way, he reduced his country's

Discussion point:

How important is it for a country to have a national army? Why do you think a country such as Iran did not have a national army until the 1920s?

dependence on foreign powers that had traditionally provided many of the administrative services for the Persian monarchs in the past.

The reorganization of the country's finances was a major priority for Reza Khan. The country was on the verge of bankruptcy. To introduce change, such as for example the creation of a national army, he needed money. Sound finances would reduce the country's dependence on outside loans. A new tax on sugar and tea was introduced to finance the country's budgetary needs. The National Bank of Iran *Bank Melli Iran* was formed. For the first time, Iran was in a position to print its own money, taking over from the British Imperial Bank.

In 1927 a new Ministry of Justice was formed whose job was to draw up a set of civic codes. Prior to that, the only courts were religious and all legal issues were in the hands of the clergy. Although the clergy did not lose all its control over judicial matters, Reza Shah's judiciary reforms were a major step on the road to modernization and secularization. In 1928 the capitulation laws, the laws that did not permit a foreign national to be tried in an Iranian court, were annulled.

Aware of the high rates of illiteracy in Iran, Reza Shah introduced important reforms in the field of education. Education, of course, also served the purpose of disseminating loyalty towards the new monarch. In 1927 he established new secondary schools, including one for women. In 1928 he started sending students abroad on government scholarships. By 1934, 200 foreign-educated students had become secondary and university teachers. Tehran University was inaugurated in 1934. Though illiteracy remained high, the number of school leavers went up:

In elementary education:		In secondary education:		In higher education:	
1925	55,960	1925	14,488	1925	600
1941	287,245	1941	28,194	1941	3,300

Before Reza Shah, Iranians had no birth certificates; their births were registered unofficially by the family. They had no surnames and were usually known as the son of or daughter of their father. Reza Shah introduced a law whereby all Iranians were obliged to choose a name and were forced to register officially under that name. This reform, quaint as it may sound today, was a major step towards standardizing Iran with the rest of the world and replacing the old kinship system with a modern national identity.

Iran under the Qajars lacked any form of infrastructure. Reza Shah was particularly keen on giving Iran such modern amenities as a railway system and roads. In his inaugurating speech for the Trans-Iranian Railway project linking the Caspian Sea to the Persian Gulf, he had referred to the railways as "one of the most powerful factors in the progress and prosperity of the country". The Trans-Iranian Railway, funded by the new taxation system, was completed in 1929. It was, in the words of Cyrus Ghani, the author of a recently published biography of Reza Shah, "more than a transportation and communication project … it was an assertion of independence and a means of restoring the lost confidence of the nation." Between 1925 and 1941 12,000 kilometers of roads were constructed. The transport of goods and passengers from one end of the country to the other now became a matter of days and not months.

Having paid a visit to Atatürk's Turkey in 1934, Reza Shah was particular impressed by the new dress codes. He therefore implemented them in Iran on his return. All government employees were forced to wear Western clothes. All men, except for those registered as clergymen, were obliged to wear "international" headgear, in other words a hat. Women were prohibited to leave the house wearing a veil. These measures aimed to "modernize" Iran, but in the words of Amin Banani, a specialist on the effects of modernity in Iran, these measures were merely an "indiscriminate imitation of the surface gloss of Western societies."

Reza Shah stressed the need to offer women equal rights to men. He opened up the right to education to women and even permitted women to attend the newly formed Tehran University after 1934. Of the 12 women that took up the offer almost all achieved high positions in the professional world subsequently. The 1936 law that banned the wearing of the veil was a step towards modernity, but was considered by many to have been too abrupt and too rigid. Women were arrested if they were seen wearing their Islamic covering in public. While aiming to liberate women from the constraints of religious practice, the law also restricted women's freedom and right to choose.

The fall of Reza Shah

His fall from power was particularly tragic. In 1941 the Allied forces asked for the right of passage through Iran and when this was refused, they occupied the country. Strategically, Iran was the vital link for sending supplies to the Soviet Union to prevent Hitler's advance into the Caucasus. The Iranian army showed little resistance

Activity:

Essay skills: compare and contrast

Very often Atatürk and Reza Shah have been compared with one another. A typical essay question could be: *"Compare and contrast Ataturk and Reza Shah's attempts at modernization."* The ability to compare and contrast in history helps historians have a clearer understanding of the historical context of the topic studied. It is important to view a ruler in history as a product of his or her time. The historical context offers the investigator this vital link.

By completing the box below gather the factual information necessary for writing the essay. The information gathered should form the basis of your argument in the essay. Make sure that you don't make any claims that are not backed by the evidence gathered in these columns.

	Turkey	Iran
Effects of the First World War		
Nature of government and changes in the administration		
Relationship with the clergy		
The position of women		
Party system		
Relationship with the armed forces		
Other social, political and economic reforms		

Activity:

Verdicts on Reza Shah Pahlavi

Accounts written on Reza Shah vary enormously and make the task of the historian particularly difficult. Whilst the Pahlavi dynasty was still in power (up to 1979), many of the books written on the subject lacked true objectivity. Since the Iranian Revolution and the overthrow of the Pahlavis, many of the studies aim to justify the Iranian revolution of 1979 and therefore underline the negative aspects of the Pahlavis; and others, that are less supportive of the new Islamic regime in Iran, present a particularly nostalgic picture of the past.

This underlines the fact that our task as historians is to always evaluate the origin and the purpose of our sources. Read the following source extracts and answer the questions below.

Questions

1   Based on these documents and your outside research what would you say were Reza Shah's greatest achievements?

2   Are the criticisms of Reza Shah justified?

Source A

Gentlemen! I am leaving the country soon, and must say something that you should know. No one has ever had any appreciation from me for his services and no one was ever thanked or rewarded by me, although some excellent services were rendered. Do you know why? The reason is because this country has no opposition. My decisions were all made and carried out without you … With regard to my plans and ideas, the secret of my success was that I never consulted anyone. I studied the problems quietly, and without showing why I was interested. But last year for the first time in my life, I tried to change this way, and consulted the Higher War Council … If I had not done so, I would not now find myself in this situation.

Source: Reza Shah's last statement to his cabinet quoted in Ansari, Ali M. 2005. *Modern Iran Since 1921: The Pahlavis and After*. Harlow, UK. Pearson Education. p. 73.

Source B

The younger generation and some foreigners take what was accomplished by Reza Shah for granted, failing to realise the spiritual, political and material conditions which prevailed in Iran in 1920, when this predestined genius of a man undertook the gigantic work of changing a medieval, feudalistic, anachronistic country into a modern State, having, it is true, many shortcomings, but still modern, and capable of improvement.

Source: Arfa, General Hassan. 1964. *Under Five Shahs*. London, UK. John Murray. p. 293.

Source C

Perhaps no monarch before him had ever left so distinctive an imprint. He found a semi medieval, feudalistic, anachronistic conglomerate of tribes, huge landed estates, and backward peasants, freed it from foreign political and economic domination, and converted it forcibly and irresistibly into the beginnings of a modern state. … Reza Shah was the right man thrown up at the right time in a country that needed such a man.

Source: Elwell-Sutton, L.P. "Reza Shah the great: Founder of the Pahlavi Dynasty", in Lenczowski, George. ed. 1978. *Iran under the Pahlavis*. Stanford, USA. Hoover Institute Press. pp. 47–8.

Source D

The first Pahlavi ruler wanted to modernize Iran without altering the patrimonial structure of society, which was his main source of power. The Shah's plans for development, which were clearly in the direction of autocratic centralism, would have required symbolic mass participation to succeed. However the first Pahlavi monarch viewed mass participation as a threat to his rule, not as a potential support. His attempt to create national consciousness was, therefore doomed for failure.

Source: Ghods, Reza. 1989. *Iran in the Twentieth Century: A Political History. Boulder, USA.* Lynee Rienner Publishers. p. 120.

Source E

Reza Shah was far from a philosopher-king, and undeniable a flawed individual. But he was unquestionably the father of modern Iran and the architect of the country's twentieth-century history.

Source: Ghani, Cyrus. 1998. *Iran and the Rise of Reza Shah: from Qajar Collapse to Pahlavi Power*. London, UK. I.B. Tauris, 1998, p. 407.

Source F

Opinions will continue to remain divided over the character, personality and achievements of Reza Shah. His supporters attribute to him all the achievements of his age and further. His detractors attribute to him all the ills of his age and further. An appreciation of Reza Shah is important … Indeed it is not inaccurate to argue that an understanding of modern Iran is not possible without an appreciation of Reza Shah, his methods and the flawed legacy which he left his countrymen. … For many who were willing to tolerate Reza Shah, he was indeed viewed as a transitional figure, necessary but most definitely transient. Others were less forgiving, viewing him as a modern version of the despots of old, harnessing all the tools and the institutions of the modern age to his dynastic ambitions.

Source: Ansari, Ali, M. *Modern Iran Since 1921: The Pahlavis and After*. Harlow, UK. Pearson Education. p. 74

and once the Allied forces were in control of Iran, Reza Shah was asked to abdicate in favour of his son, Mohammad Reza Pahlavi, and was subsequently sent into exile to South Africa. The rapidity of his fall and the absence of any signs of resistance have questioned the extent of Reza Shah's popularity, and the success of his reforms.

Timeline: Iran and Reza Khan, 1924–41	
1921	February 21: Reza Khan's coup d'état
	February 26: Treaty of Friendship with the Soviet Union
	April: Reza Khan becomes Minister of War
	July 17: Soviet troops withdraw from northern Iran
	October: Reza Khan launches his attack against the Northern rebels
1923	October: Reza Khan becomes Prime Minister
1924	February 11: Series of reforms introduced including a two-year compulsory military service
	March 4: the *ulema* (the clergy) declared that a republic is contrary to Islam
	April 1: Reza Khan declares his opposition to the institution of a republic
1925	October 31: Government is entrusted to Reza Khan
	December 12: Qajar Dynasty abolished
1926	April 25: Coronation of Reza Khan
1927	April 26: Opening of the new Courts of Justice
1928	March: Clash with the clergy in Qom
	May 10: End of the capitulation laws
	December: Law enforcing Western clothes for men
	Persian language academy established
	Standardized textbooks for schools
1929	Trans-Iranian railway (nothern section) inaugurated
1933	April 24: Gass Golshayan Oil agreement
1934	May 29: Law for the foundation of Tehran University
1935	March 21: Name of the country changes from Persia to Iran
	July: Clash with the clergy in Mashad
1936	January 8: Law banning the veil
1937	July 8: The Treaty of Saadabad
1938	August 21: Completion of the Trans-Iranian railway.
1941	August 25: Iran occupied by the Allies.
	September 16: Reza Shah abdicates in favour of his son
1944	July 26: Reza Shah dies in Johannesburg

Saudi Arabia

The Kingdom of Saudi Arabia was proclaimed in 1932 by its founder and first ruler, Abdul Aziz ibn Saud. The Saud family continues to rule the Kingdom to this day. The historical trajectory of Saudi Arabia differed from the other Arab states for a number of reasons. The peninsula is arid and before the discovery of oil in 1938 its hostile geography repelled invaders. During the Ottoman Empire only the Western coastal region of the Hejaz was under Ottoman control. The rest was governed by tribal rulers. As the birthplace of Islam and the home of Islam's two holiest sites, Medina and Mecca (situated in the Hejaz), the European powers were cautious and preferred not to offend Muslim sentiments by taking over the region directly. This explains why the Hejaz was not brought under the administration of a Mandatory Power in the peace treaty negotiations. The lack of direct presence did not mean that the Europeans, in particular Britain, were totally disinterested. It was in the words of William Cleveland like being part of the British "Empire by treaty".

During the First World War Britain had tried to forge an alliance with Sharif Hussein, the official guardian of the holy places of Mecca and Medina, who emerged as the King of Hejaz at the end of the First World War, but would only keep this post until 1924. Already the manner in which he had obtained this post was questioned by the local tribesmen. The proud warrior tribesmen did not appreciate being ruled by a man who had been assisted by an outsider. Sharif Hussein incurred the suspicion and disrespect of his rivals further when, in 1924, following the deposition of the Ottoman Caliph Abdul Majid, he claimed the title for himself. The Hejazi kingdom was invaded by the **Ikhwan** army led by Abdul Aziz ibn Saud and Sharif Hussein was forced into exile to the island of Cyprus.

> The **Ikhwan** were a non-tribal military corps. What brought them together was religion; as militant religious soldiers they were committed to the spread of Wahabism and were loyal to the head of the Wahabi order, the House of Saud. They fought alongside Abdul Aziz ibn Saud to spread the doctrine of the puritan and revivalist Abd el Wahab and to unite the Arabian Peninsula under the rule of the House of Saud.
>
> In 1930 the militia was disbanded and reorganized as the Saudi Arabian National Guard, also known as the White Army.

The origins of the Saud dynasty

The emergence of the Saud dynasty dates back to 1744 when Mohammad ibn Saud, the local prince (*emir*) of the Nejd, the central highlands of the Arabian Peninsula, joined forces with Abd el Wahab, a religious revivalist, who, disillusioned by the laxity of religious practice in Arabia, called for a return to the Islam of the time of the Prophet. With the decline of Mecca as a commercial centre, tribal unity had come to an end and with disunity had come the semi-abandonment of Islamic practice. Abd el Wahab

> ### Abdul Aziz ibn Saud (1876–1953)
>
> Born in Riyad, in the region of Nejd in central Arabia, Abdul Aziz Ibn Saud was forced with his family into exile in Kuwait, where he remained until 1901. In 1902 he led a raid into Riyadh and captured the city from the hands of the rival tribe, the Rashidis. This success was followed by many more and within two years, he had recaptured nearly half of the Nejd. By 1912 his rule stretched over the entire Nejd and the eastern coast of Arabia. In the same year he created the *Ikhwan*, Arabic for the Brothers. Those who admired him called him "the greatest Arab since the Prophet Mohammad". His critics underlined his ruthlessness. In 1932 he united the Arabian Peninsula and proclaimed the Kingdom of Saudi Arabia. Abdul Aziz ruled over the Kingdom until his death in 1953 and ensured that the succession would remain within the Saud family.

blamed the Ottoman religious domination through the Caliphate and called on ibn Saud to challenge the Ottoman rule. The alliance of the "warrior" and the "preacher" proved to be a potent force. While the warrior conquered territory and gave the preacher the opportunity to spread his word further, the preacher gave the warrior moral and religious legitimacy and a commitment that went far beyond tribal loyalty. With the death of Adb el Wahab, the head of the Saud House assumed the dual role as both head of the Wahabi order and the Saud family. Though the first two Saudi–Wahabi states were short-lived, their alliance remained in force and was revived in the 20th century.

In 1902 Abdul Aziz launched a military campaign to reinstall the House of Saud for the third time. He formed the Ikhwan army and successfully defeated the rival tribes and united the peninsula under his command. In 1927 Abdul Aziz was recognized as the King of Hejaz and Nejd and in 1932 he founded the Kingdom under his name, Saudi Arabia. In a country which had throughout its existence been ruled by local tribesmen, this unity was somewhat extraordinary.

Abdul Aziz: the consolidation of power

Abdul Aziz's success can be explained by a number of factors. His first and foremost reason for success was the fact that he had militarily subdued his rivals. In the tribal tradition conquerors obtain the respect of others. Abdul Aziz also had the prestige among Arab rulers that he had won his Kingdom through his own effort, and not through the influence of foreign powers. His role as the head of the Wahabi order also offered the conquered tribesmen salvation through the practice of a puritanical religious doctrine. Abdul Aziz's success became synonymous with a return to the righteous practices of Islam. The dismantlement of the tribal system also facilitated the institution of an agrarian policy by forcing the nomads to settle in small agricultural communities. In this way he broke down the tribal organizations that could have later challenged his authority. Abdul Aziz maintained a policy of providing the communities with material assistance in the form of agricultural supplies and arms.

Once he took over the Hejaz, Abdul Aziz impressed the Muslim pilgrims of his ability to restore law and order in Mecca and Medina, by protecting and securing the holy places in Mecca and Medina. The spreading of the Wahabi doctrine by building mosques and sending trained clerics to disseminate Wahabism also worked to homogenize the otherwise diverse community. In this way he was able to obtain a sense of communal loyalty that surpassed the tribal one. Abdul Aziz introduced to the inhabitants of the Arabian Peninsula, for the first time, a sense of national identity backed by an ideology in the form of Wahabism.

Once Abdul Aziz had succeeded in defeating his internal enemies, he set about consolidating his power. This he did by signing treaties with neighbouring states. In order to define his future Kingdom's boundaries, a measure deemed unnecessary before the era of nation-states, he entered into negotiation with Iraq, Yemen and Jordan, eventually signing treaties with each. He followed this up with a treaty with the United Kingdom. Abdul Aziz was quick to realize the need to have the backing of the European powers. Alhough the UK had backed his rival, Sharif Hussein, he nonetheless signed the Treaty of Jiddah with the British government in 1927. With this treaty he obtained official recognition as the "King of the Hejaz and the Sultan of Nejd and its Dependencies". In return, he acknowledged British interests in the coastal region of the Persian Gulf and pledged not to expand his rule in those domains.

Once his position was secure enough, Abdul Aziz set about suppressing the excessive elements within his *Ikhwan* army. Although he owed a great deal of his success to the devout commitment of the *Ikhwan* warriors, he nonetheless needed to control their religious zeal and present himself as the sole ruler and decision-maker. As Wahabism aimed to revive Islam throughout the Muslim world its most ardent supporters wanted to spread their ideology beyond the Arabian Peninsula. Therefore, once the war within Arabia was over and Wahabism had been established as doctrine inside the Arabian Peninsula, they started to prepare for war beyond the Arabian borders and invaded Iraq. Abdul Aziz, realizing the dangers of such a move, challenged the rebels and in the Battle of Sibilla in 1929, succeeded in defeating and subduing them. Victory confirmed his position as the political ruler as well as the religious leader or *imam*. In 1930 the *Ikhwan* militia was disbanded and reorganized as the Saudi Arabian National Guard, also known as the White Army.

In 1932 Abdul Aziz was ready to confirm his victory by uniting the Nejd and the Hejaz. He named the kingdom after his family: the Kingdom of Saudi Arabia. The Soviet Union, followed by the United Kingdom, France and the other European countries all recognized the new Saudi kingdom.

The Kingdom of Saudi Arabia

Saudi Arabia is a Kingdom and it can only be ruled by either the sons or the grandsons of its founder, King Abdul Aziz. The leading members of the Royal family choose the King with the approval of the religious authorities, the *Ulema*. The constitution is based on the Holy Qur'an and the legal system is Islamic law, the *Shari'a*. The Shari'a courts have authority over the entire population, and the *Ulema* have a say in politics. The religious police monitor public behaviour and enforce strict Islamic norms. Kinship or family connection is a crucial factor in the government of Saudi Arabia. The main sectors of society are run by family members. There are no recognized political parties and therefore no national elections. The King has absolute power. In 1953 a Council of Ministers was formed which gave the ruler the chance to consult with a group of ministers. The members of this council were directly chosen by the King and he maintained the right of veto over all their decisions.

Religion played a primordial role in the establishment of the Kingdom of Saudi Arabia. It was the combination of tribal and religious legitimacy that gave the House of Saud success. This connection was further strengthened through intermarriages between the Wahabi and the ibn Saud families. There is no separation between religion and the state; on the contrary the King as the political ruler and the Imam as the religious ruler are one and the same. Other high-ranking religious

Activity:

Shari'a law

Research how much of daily life for Muslims is affected by Shari'a law?

How does it differ in different countries with a predominantly Muslim population?

clerics also play an important role politically. They are financed by the state and influence many of the political decisions. The merging of the two ensures stability and prevents any change.

Until the discovery of oil in 1938, the Kingdom's main source of revenue came from the pilgrims to Mecca and Medina. This did not leave the new King with a large sum to spend. In 1933 Abdul Aziz signed a concession agreement with the Standard Oil of California soon to become the Arabian American oil Company (ARAMCO). The agreement gave him an initial loan of 50,000 pounds in gold, an annual rent of 5,000 pounds in gold and a further loan of 15,000 pounds in gold once oil was discovered. Oil was discovered in 1935 and commercialized by 1938. By 1939 the Kingdom was receiving an annual royalty of 200,000 pounds in gold. Though this was an enormous income, Abdul Aziz was said to have mismanaged the economy and by 1953 the country was on the verge of bankruptcy. Though a substantial influx of American employees entered the country, the two communities were segregated. The aim was not to offend the local religious sentiments through the exposure of another culture. Segregation also served the purpose of maintaining a rigid control on society.

The legacy of Abdul Aziz ibn Saud

Economically, the Kingdom of Saudi Arabia has greatly changed since its foundation. Forced settlement of the tribal population gave rise to urbanization. The revival of the Holy cities of Mecca and Medina increased contact with the outside world and subsequently speeded up technological change. The discovery of oil has brought wealth and introduced foreign nationals into the country. Abdul Aziz accepted these aspects of modernization and skilfully persuaded the conservative Wahabis to do so as well.

Politically, the Kingdom has barely changed since its foundation. Personal rule based on the two pillars, Wahabism and the Saud family, continues to be the foundation of the regime. There are still no outside contenders to this leadership. However, the ultra-conservative Wahabists have had to face the challenges of modernity.

Activity:

Essay skills: Analysing the evidence

"Assess the importance of the Imam-chief alliance in the unification of the Arabian Peninsula under the rule of the Abdul Aziz ibn Saud."

The Saudi state structure has been described as the "Alliance System of Chiefs and Imams" by the political scientist Iliya Harik. He defined such a state as one where "authority is invested in tribal chief supported and awarded a legitimate authority beyond the confines of his tribe by virtue of his identification and / or alliance with a prominent religious leader and his teachings."

We are often, as historians, forced to question certain assumptions. Use the table below to list the evidence and any relevant claims and counter-claims to support this thesis.

Steps towards unification	Evidence	Claim/Counter-claim
Mohammad ibn Saud/Adb el Wahab alliance		
1902 Abd el Aziz military campaign to take Nejd.		
The defeat of Sharif Hussein in the Hejaz		
1932 the proclamation of the Kingdom		
Other factors?		

Exam practice and further resources

Sample questions

1 Compare and contrast the treaties of Sèvres (1920) and Lausanne (1923).
2 Analyse the consequences of allied diplomacy on the territories of the Ottoman Empire (excluding Palestine).
3 "Tensions in Palestine were largely a consequence of religious and economic differences." To what extent do you agree?
4 How successfully had Atatürk modernized Turkey by 1939?
5 Analyse the nature and impact of Reza Khan's regime on Iran.

Recommended further reading

General history of the Middle East:

Cleveland, William L. and Bunton, Martin. 2009. *A History of the Middle East*. 4th edition. Philadelphia, USA. Westview Press.

Gelvin, James. 2005. *The Modern Middle East: A History*. Oxford, UK. Oxford University Press.

Smith, Charles D. 2007. *Palestine and the Arab Israeli Conflict*. 6th edition. Boston, USA. Bedford/ St Martin's.

Smith, Dan. 2008. *The State of the Middle East: An Atlas of Conflict and Resolutions*. London, UK. Earthscan.

History of the First World War in the Middle East:

Fromkin, David. 1989. *A Peace to End All Peace: Creating the Modern Middle East 1914–1922*. Harmondsworth, UK. Penguin Books.

History of Palestine and the birth of Israel:

Gelvin, James. 2005. *Israel–Palestine Conflict*. Cambridge, UK. Cambridge University Press.

Baruch Kimmerling, Baruch and Migdal. Joel S. 2003. *The Palestinian People*. Cambridge, USA. Harvard University Press.

Gilbert, Martin. 1988. *Israel: A History*. London, UK. Doubleday.

History of the Turkish Republic:

Zürcher, Erik J. *Turkey: A Modern History*. London, UK; New York, USA. IB Tauris. 2004.

History of Iran:

Ansari, Ali M. 2005. *Modern Iran Since 1921: The Pahlavis and After*. London, UK. Pearson Education.

History of Saudi Arabia:

Al-Rasheed, Madawi . 2002. *A History of Saudi Arabia*. Cambridge, UK. Cambridge University Press.

5 The Second World War and Western Europe

This section deals with the Second World War, post-war recovery, European integration, and the effects of the Cold War on Western Europe with particular focus on Germany and Spain. By 2000, these states had a great deal in common; politically, as members of the European Union, militarily, as allies within NATO, and philosophically as modern, market-economy, liberal democracies. Such an outcome would have seemed implausible in 1939, and it is from that point that this section traces each state's history through the second half of the 20th century. The emphasis on Western Europe recognizes the fact that for most of this period Europe was divided between the Eastern Soviet Bloc and the non-Communist West under US protection and that each side of this artificial and temporary divide developed in distinct ways.

By the end of the chapter, students should be able to:

- describe the role of these two countries in the Second World War
- assess the impact of the Second World War on Western Europe
- explain how Western Europe recovered from the War
- understand how each state was affected by the Cold War
- explain how Western European states moved from conflict towards political and economic integration
- identify the social, political and economic issues facing these states and the methods used to cope with the challenges.

The Second World War in Europe

The Second World War can only be described in superlatives; it was the most destructive war in history causing more deaths, and involving more countries, than any previous conflict. Six years of war had left Europe in a state of utter devastation. Europe experienced "total war" on a terrifying scale, destroying lives not just where formal military conflict occurred but throughout civilian populations suffering bombing, occupation, persecution, exploitation and extermination. Hopeful ideas of human progress and the superiority of European civilization had already been battered by the horrors of the First World War, the economic disasters of the 1930s, and the political extremism that followed. The liberation of the Nazi concentration camps exposed a further, barely comprehendible depth of industrialized cruelty. The process of rebuilding a broken continent would take place in the shadow of these events.

This era of European civil war 1914–91, can be said to have concluded with the revolutions in Eastern Europe (1989), the reunification of Germany (1990) and the collapse of the Soviet Union (1991). However, the social, political and economic structures that emerged and have endured from the post-war situation have done so in response to that defining conflict. In particular, the European Union has its origins in a shared desire to avoid any return to mass unemployment, political extremism, German militarism, war and revolution.

For the Western Allies, despite the alliance with Stalin, it was also a "just war", an unusually clear cut case of conflict between Good and Evil and as such has served as an enduring historical example, used by later politicians to rally their nations, or to invoke when faced by new threats. The enormity of the crimes committed in Germany's name inevitably cast a shadow over the remainder of the century. Spain's limited involvement in the war allowed Franco's dictatorship to survive in isolation from mainstream European developments.

Globally, the war marked a shift in power from the shattered nations of Western Europe to the United States and the Soviet Union. The discredited, ruinous rivalry of European states was replaced by a bipolar struggle between the two new superpowers with an added ideological dimension. Western European states would have to accept their diminished roles, abandon their global empires and seek security under America's protection.

Few countries in Western Europe were able to avoid the traumas of war in the years before 1945 and the two countries covered in this section, Germany and Spain, represent the experiences of defeat and neutrality. For others, (France, Belgium, the Netherlands, Luxembourg, Denmark, Norway) invasion by Nazi Germany was followed by occupation, exploitation, and eventually, liberation. The United Kingdom, though undefeated, endured the threat of invasion and the bombing of its cities. For Italy, war brought defeat, invasion and civil war as Axis and Allied forces fought across Italian territory. Spain, Switzerland, Sweden, Portugal and Ireland maintained varying degrees of precarious neutrality as war raged around them. It is not to belittle the scale of these events to acknowledge that the war in Western Europe was less destructive than in the East. Nazi racial ideology could accommodate a degree of respect for the peoples of Western Europe that was absent in the East where the conflict was a "war of annihilation", carried out with the aim of destroying entire categories of people.

Discussion point:

All historical work on the events of this period will have to be pursued or considered in relation to the events of Auschwitz. … Here, all historicization reaches its limits.

Saul Friedländer, quoted in Judt, Tony. 2007. *Postwar: A History of Europe Since 1945*. Pimlico Press, London. p. 803.

The term "historicization" describes the act of representing something as historic—in other words "doing history".

 How far do you agree with Friedländer's statement?

Activity:

Statistical analysis

Death statistics for the Second World War				
	Total deaths	**% of pre-war population**	**Military deaths**	**Civilian deaths**
Belgium	88,000	1.1%	76,000	12,000
France	810,000	1.9%	340,000	470,000
Germany	6,850,000	9.5%	3,250,000	3,600,000
Italy	410,000	0.9%	330,000	80,000
Poland	6,123,000	17.2%	123,000	6,000,000
Soviet Union	20,600,000	10.4%	13,600,000	7,000,000
United Kingdom	388,000	0.8%	326,000	62,000
Yugoslavia	1,706,000	10.9%	N/A	N/A

Source: http://www.historyplace.com/worldwar2/timeline/statistics.htm.
Statistics for Second World War casualties are difficult to verify and vary from source to source.

Questions

1 Why is difficult for historians to agree on accurate statistics of the number of people who died in the Second World War?

2 What do the statistics tell you about the Second World War as experienced in Eastern and Western Europe?

What were the aims of Germany and Spain in 1939?

The United Kingdom and France declared war on Germany on 3 September 1939 following the German invasion of Poland. The Western Allies' attempts at appeasement; using diplomacy, compromise, and conceding to Hitler's demands in order to maintain peace in Europe had ended in failure and revealed how seriously they had misunderstood Hitler, a leader whose reasoning was of a radically different nature. Hitler's aims, as he had made clear, were to undo the Treaty of Versailles, to establish Germany's domination of Europe, to destroy communism, to carry out a race-war against non-Aryans and to create **Lebensraum** for the German people guaranteed by the power of the "Thousand Year Reich".

Spain stood apart from Europe in 1939. After three years of devastating civil war, Spain had been economically ruined and socially ripped apart. The success of the nationalists left General Francisco Franco as dictator of Spain, a position he was to consolidate with characteristic brutality throughout the duration of the Second World War. As the Second World War broke out Franco had a natural inclination to side with the fascist dictatorships whose aid had been so important to his success in the Spanish Civil War but he proceeded with caution. Franco may have had imperialist ambitions for British Gibraltar and French North Africa for (as described by historian Paul Preston) "he cherished hopes of empire on the cheap, on the coat-tails of Hitler", but his overarching concern was always to strengthen his own domestic position.

Lebensraum means "living space". It sums up Hitler's policy of territorial expansion into Eastern Europe, to take over and occupy the land of Slavic nations.

What were the consequences of Germany's early successes?

German forces defeated Poland within weeks. The **Blitzkrieg** tactics overwhelmed the Polish Army. The Soviet Union subsequently invaded the eastern half of Poland as agreed in a secret deal with Germany. Poland's geographical isolation from the United Kingdom and France meant that there was no practical assistance to be offered. Having secured his eastern flank, Hitler's attention turned to Western Europe. In May 1940, German troops attacked the Netherlands, Belgium and France. The British Army was forced to abandon the Continent. As the German advance briefly paused, over 300,000 British and French troops were rescued from the beaches at Dunkirk and taken to Britain to fight another day. As German troops closed in on Paris, the British and French governments discussed the idea of uniting their nations in a Franco-British Union to sustain France even through military defeat. This embryonic proposal of European union came to nothing and the French Government collapsed soon after. General de Gaulle escaped to London and assumed leadership of the *Françaises Libres* (*free French)*; those who had escaped and those who were determined to continue the struggle from France's overseas territories. Marshal Petain stayed in France as head of a Nazi-controlled puppet state which was to be economically exploited for the German war effort and from which the Jewish population would be transported to concentration camps.

Suspicions remained between Germany's enemies. De Gaulle felt that the British Royal Air Force (RAF) could have provided more planes for the defence of France, but Winston Churchill would not risk losing these aircraft that would be vital to the defence of the UK. By acting cautiously in case France should be defeated did Churchill actually guarantee that it did? Further ill feeling arose from Royal Navy attacks on the French Mediterranean Fleet, the loyalties of which were uncertain. To the British this was a military necessity to prevent the ships falling into enemy hands but the incident exposed the strain put on the Allies by their failures against Germany. Fruitless Anglo-French attempts at unity, French ingratitude, suspected British lack of commitment to Continental allies, mutual incomprehension; these themes were to resurface in the post-war era as a new Western Europe took shape.

In July 1940, Hitler paused. Tentative offers of peace were discussed. Records of British Cabinet meetings show that there was some support for the idea that Hitler could be appeased once more. It fell to Churchill to clarify the situation.

Hitler made preparations for Operation Sealion; the German plan to invade Britain. To succeed, Germany would first have to achieve air superiority by destroying the fighter planes of the RAF. The Battle of Britain was a decisive defeat for Hitler, the first of the War. Throughout August and September, 1940, the two air forces fought each other over southern England until German losses became unsustainable and the invasion of Britain was postponed. This victory was, in Churchill's phrase, Britain's

Blitzkrieg literally means "lightning war", and describes the rapid advances involving infantry supported by tanks and aircraft.

Discussion point:

I have thought carefully in these last days whether it was part of my duties to consider entering into negotiations with That Man. But it was idle to think that, if we tried to make peace now, we should get better terms than if we fought it out. … The Germans would demand our fleet … and much else. We would become a slave state, though a British Government which would be Hitler's puppet would be set up … And I am convinced that every man of you would rise up and tear me down from my place if I were for one moment to contemplate … surrender. If this long island story of ours is to end at last, let it end when each one of us lies choking in his own blood upon the ground.

Prime Minister, Winston Churchill, speaking to the British Cabinet, 28 May 1940.

What kind of demands do you think Hitler could have made in return for peace?

"finest hour", achieved by pilots from the United Kingdom, the British Empire, Poland, Czechoslovakia, France and other Allied nations. The strategic implications of victory were crucial as the UK's survival provided the Allies with an impregnable base beyond the reach of Germany's superior land forces. From this base the Allies could develop their air power to eventually achieve air supremacy in Western Europe. The victory also provided hope for the people of occupied Europe and bought time to develop the Alliance that would defeat Hitler.

The two air forces continued to bomb each other's cities; German attacks on civilian targets were held up as examples of Nazi barbarism, although the British were also bombing civilian targets in Germany. By the final year of the War, Germany was suffering raids on a devastating scale. Hundreds of thousands of people were killed in the destruction of Cologne, Hamburg, Dresden and other cities. Of the approximately 60,000 British civilian victims of German bombing raids, 9,000 were killed in the final year of the War by missiles launched from Germany. These unmanned weapons were totally indiscriminate—they were simply aimed at London.

Whether or not the bombing of cities could destroy an enemy's morale and its will to continue the war is uncertain; British propagandists made much of London's ability to "take it", disregarding the possibility that German cities might be able to "take it" too. The destruction of factories could temporarily disrupt production but required greater accuracy than was achievable.

TOK Link
Ways of Knowing—Reason
The role of Bomber Command

Dresden, devastated after the Allied bombing campaign of 13–15 February, 1945.

The ongoing controversy over the devastation wrought by the Allied bombing campaign in Germany illustrates the difficulty of maintaining a consistent ethical stance in warfare. For many of those involved, agonizing over ethics was a luxury that could not be indulged.

In the period since the Second World War, individuals, armies and states have gone to great length to justify their actions and to present them favourably in order to demonstrate that even amid the hard realism of war there remains a desire to occupy the moral high ground.

Source A

They are wonderful men …They flew seven nights a week over Germany and were knocked out of the sky like ninepins at the start. They shortened the war by six months and saved hundreds of thousands from the gas chambers by bringing it to a halt.

Source: "Scotty", 70, campaigner for a memorial to be built for the British RAF Bomber Command *The Guardian*. 20 August, 2006.

Source B

The tremendous courage and sacrifice of Bomber Command is something to admire. On the other hand, area bombing was a very serious mistake and a moral crime. Somehow you've got to hold those facts together. Any memorial is worthwhile, but to think of applauding Bomber Command in mass murdering civilians night after night would be wrong.

Source: Grayling, A.C. 2006. *Among The Dead Cities: The History and Moral Legacy of the WWII Bombing of Civilians in Germany and Japan*. London, UK. Bloomsbury.

Source C

The Nazis were to good as a black hole is to light. The effects of British and American bombing on Germany and the lands the Germans conquered were dreadful and it is right that they should be recorded and remembered. But the Allies' real crime would have been to hold back from using any of the means at their disposal to destroy Hitler and those who sustained his war. The argument over exactly what Bomber Command achieved will never be settled. One undeniable success, an awkward one to acknowledge nowadays, is that it altered Germany's personality. Saturation bombing may not, as intended, have broken the Germans' spirit. But it helped powerfully to bring about their post-war conversion to peaceful democracy.

Source: Patrick Bishop, author of *Bomber Boys*, quoted at http://www.rafbombercommand.com/memorialfund/

Source D

The bombing of Dresden was an example … of the brutalisation of man in war … History written by individual nations in which each one selects what he has done well cannot be allowed to continue. If we really want to unify this Europe, then history must be unified as well.

Source: President of Germany, Roman Herzog, 1995, quoted in Davies, N. 2006. *Europe at War*. London, 2006. Pan Macmillan.

TOK Questions

1 Identify the arguments for and against the actions of Bomber Command.

2 Explain President Herzog's comment that "history must be unified". Is it possible to unify history?

3 In your opinion was the bombing of German cities justified? How did the Allied bombing campaign support the Just War Theory? Do further research on the background to this theory.

Fill out the table below with examples of the circumstances and appropriate conduct that support theories of a "Just War".

Circumstances in which it is right to fight a war	Justifiable conduct during a war

Why did Spain remain neutral?

A series of myths had to be generated in post-1945 Spain. By this time, Franco's close association with the Axis powers in 1936–40 had become a serious diplomatic obstacle. The reality of the negotiations between Franco, Mussolini and Hitler had to be rewritten. In this version of events, Spain's neutrality during the Second World War was a hard–won diplomatic victory for Franco, the man who had faced down Hitler and his "threat of 200 divisions". Or, in the words of one Franco era biographer, Silva & Silva & Saenz de Heredia "the skill of one man held back what all the armies of Europe had been unable to do." If Spain had dallied with Nazi Germany, the argument continued, it was a result of the efforts of Franco's brother in law and Nazi sympathizer Serrano Súñer. This interpretation of events, in the words of Paul Preston, is quite simply "nonsense".

The first important point to make is that, short of a full scale declaration of war Franco's Spain was anything but neutral, especially in the early stages of the Second World War. Described at the time as "non-belligerence" the position is better understood in the words of historian Stanley Payne as "pre-belligerence". A United Nations Security Council investigation conducted after the war found evidence that Spain had allowed German planes to operate from Spanish airfields to attack Allied shipping. Spanish ports were secretly used to refuel and repair German warships. And in addition to this practical support, the state controlled Spanish media consistently broadcast a pro-Axis message. On 22 September 1939, the newspaper *Arriba* encouraged its readers to attack anyone overheard criticizing Nazi Germany. A good indication of Franco's attitude to Nazi Germany is contained in the private letters he wrote to Hitler after the defeat of France in the summer of 1940:

> Dear Führer,
> At the moment when the German armies, under your leadership, are bringing the greatest battle in history to a victorious close, I would like to express to you my admiration and enthusiasm and that of my people, who are watching with deep emotion the glorious course of a struggle which they regard as their own … I do not need to assure you how great is my desire not to remain aloof from your cares and how great is my satisfaction in rendering to you at all times services which you regard as most valuable.

It is therefore safe to say that Spain's neutrality in the Second World War had little to do with any ideological differences with Nazi Germany. So why, despite Franco's promises of support, did Spain remain neutral? One of the key reasons was timing. During the early years of the War, it was assumed by both Franco and the Axis powers that Spain's intervention on the side of fascism was inevitable. The sticking point was the terms of this Spanish entry. Had Hitler accepted some of Franco's overly ambitious imperial demands for North Africa at the time of their infamous Hendaye meeting, Franco would have been more than ready to join the Axis cause. But by the time Hitler was ready to welcome Franco's support and make the necessary imperial offers, Franco was too concerned to maintain the neutrality that was essential to the continual flow of much needed American aid.

This leads us to the most important reason for Spanish neutrality. It was not so much Franco's diplomatic strength that explains Spanish neutrality but rather Spain's economic and military weakness. Franco may have been tempted to join Hitler, but unlike Mussolini, he was an experienced soldier with a realistic notion of his country's weaknesses. These views were shared by Hitler's closest advisors before the Hendaye meeting; German state secretary Ernst von Weizsäcker concluded that Spain has "neither bread nor petrol" and was of "no practical worth" to the Axis. Even if the Spanish successfully captured Gibraltar, the British would be expected to retaliate by seizing the Canary Islands and other colonial possessions.

Franco's only official meeting with Hitler, Hendaye, France, 23 October 1940. Franco claimed in 1958 that his train's late arrival was a deliberate ploy to throw Hitler "off balance".

And for Franco, the failure of Hitler to defeat Britain in the summer of 1940 had raised too many questions. Italian setbacks against the British in the autumn of 1940 both increased Franco's concerns but also turned Hitler's attention to an attack on Gibraltar and a hope of closing off the Mediterranean.

At the same time Spain's economic situation was getting steadily worse with famine becoming a very real possibility. Franco was now overwhelmingly concerned with the stability of his regime. He consistently failed to set a date for the attack on Gibraltar blaming ongoing domestic shortages, while British and American diplomatic efforts continued to promise grain in return for neutrality. In the end Hitler gave up waiting, claiming in a letter to Mussolini that Franco has made "the greatest mistake of his life." The Führer instead turned his attentions to the war in the East.

Why was 1941 a turning point?

In June 1941, Hitler launched Operation Barbarossa, the invasion of the Soviet Union. Over three million German soldiers participated in what was the largest military assault in history. They were assisted by smaller contingents from Romania, Hungary and Italy. Despite Spain's declared neutrality, Franco agreed to the deployment of 20,000 Spanish troops, the Falange-shirted "Blue Division" on the condition that they were used only against the Soviet Union and not in Western Europe. Within months this invasion force had advanced hundreds of kilometres, vastly extending the territory of German-controlled Europe. Approximately 5.5 million Soviet soldiers were taken prisoner by the Germans during the Second World War and of these 3.3 million died in captivity.

However, Germany was unable to achieve victory; the Soviets were able to concede territory in order to buy time. Factories were moved east beyond the range of German planes and production steadily increased. In an ever more destructive war of attrition the Soviets could replace troop losses at a rate the Germans could not match. During the first winter of the campaign the Soviets halted the German advance and over the following year fought bitterly to turn back the invaders. Following the devastating German defeat at Stalingrad in January 1943, the Red Army began to drive the Germans back in a series of emphatic victories. All restraints were abandoned in what had become a war of annihilation, with 75 per cent of Germany's total War casualties occurring on the Eastern Front.

Meanwhile, the United States had entered the War, following the Japanese attack on Pearl Harbour in December, 1941. Germany had declared war on the USA soon after. The defeat of German and Italian forces in North Africa was followed by the Allied invasion of Italy beginning in July, 1943. A vast invasion force of Allied troops from the United States, United Kingdom, Canada and other allied nations gathered in southern England. On 6 June 1944, (D-Day) these troops landed in France opening another front against Germany. Hitler's Empire was now being squeezed on three sides.

The home front in Germany

Civilian populations in Western Europe endured shortages, rationing, restrictions on liberty, extended working hours, bombing, as well as the emotional strain of loved ones risking death in battle. Technological advances, in particular the bomber, brought war to ordinary people far from front lines to an extent that had been impossible a generation before. By 1939, Germans had already experienced six years of totalitarian Nazi rule; the militarization of society, rearmament, greater government control of labour and the economy, the violent suppression of opposition, propaganda, and restrictions on personal liberty. Therefore, the outbreak of War did not require the radical changes in government powers that were experienced in liberal democracies such as the United Kingdom. However, food rationing was introduced immediately at the outbreak of war; meat was in particularly short supply though chronic food shortages were not experienced until 1944. The conquests of 1939–41 allowed Nazi Germany to live off the wealth of its victims, but severe shortages were experienced as the expanse of occupied territory contracted. Soap, clothing and cigarettes all became subject to restrictions. Germany's lack of natural resources, especially oil, led to fuel shortages for civilians and the military, a situation that worsened when Romania, an oil producing ally of Germany, dropped out of the War in 1944.

For all the powers of coercion, persecution and terror at their disposal, Nazi leaders could not completely ignore the importance of civilian morale. The collapse of the home front had been a factor in Germany's defeat in the First World War. Indeed, a great deal of energy was expended on maintaining domestic support for the War and though it is difficult to quantify, it is unsurprising that levels of morale should correlate directly with military success and failure. Support for the War was strongest in the early years but by 1943 following the defeat at Stalingrad, the Nazis found it harder to

Discussion point:
Turning points?

So, we have won after all.

Churchill's diary entry, December 1941 after the Japanese attack on Pearl Harbour drew the USA into the Second World War.

Churchill's comment identifies the entry of America into the War as a crucial event. Was it the most significant turning point?

What other events of the War could be described as key turning points?

counteract war-weariness, political jokes, criticism and despair, to the extent that the regime was obliged to make "defeatism" a criminal offence, punishable by death. By 1944, the regime was imposing the death penalty on children as young as 14.

> The Gestapo also took an ever more active role in enforcing discipline at work. In 1942, 7,311 workers were arrested by the Gestapo for breaches of labour discipline but by 1944 the figure had risen to 42,505.
>
> **Source:** Roseman, M. 2001. *Total War and Historical Change: Europe, 1914–1955*. Philadelphia, USA. Open University Press. p. 243.

The Nazi state encouraged women to conform to the roles of mothers and home-makers, offering loans and rewards to those starting families. From 1939, young, unmarried women were compelled to undertake a year's labour service, often agricultural work. Throughout the War, the demand for more labour eroded the Nazi-adopted slogan of the three Ks *"Kinder, Kirche, Küche"* (Children, Church, Kitchen), as the traditionally assigned female roles when women increasingly took on jobs in industry, administration, auxiliary military services, such as signals and anti-aircraft units. Such burdens were in addition to the struggle to acquire daily rations and maintain homes for the family.

The labour shortage undermined Hitler's core belief that Germany was a people without land, deserving of ever more *Lebensraum*. As more and more Germans were called up to the military, it soon became evident that Germany was in fact a land in need of more people. Franco's Spain provided 100,000 Falange co-ordinated volunteer workers in 1941 but this did not even begin to address the problem. After the "total war" orders of 1943 which increased the working week to 60 hours and raised the age-limit for calling up women to work to 50, there was little more that could be done to extract labour from the German population. The introduction of foreign labour was initially resisted as a threat to the "racial hygiene" of the German nation, as well as an unwelcome security threat. The demands of the war economy overcame these reservations to the extent that by the end of the War there were over seven million foreign workers in Germany. These labourers were subject to a complex system of racial hierarchy. The pay, conditions, food, accommodation, freedom, and punishment an individual worker could expect were related to his or her standing in Nazi ideology, from skilled northern Europeans down to the murderous slavery imposed on Jews, Poles and Russian prisoners of war.

German wartime propaganda aimed to reinforce morale on the home front, to justify Nazi policies, and to encourage defeatism among the enemy. Propaganda Minister, Josef Goebbels, extended state control over all forms of media, art and entertainment relentlessly expounding the Nazi world-view. Many artists and writers had fled Germany; those that remained were restricted to churning out crude Nazi-approved propaganda. The glorification of Nazism was most successfully achieved at the mass Party rallies at Nuremburg. The innovative films of Leni Riefenstahl, demonstrated in *The Triumph of the Will* (1935) and *Olympia* (1937) are among the few examples of Nazi era art of lasting merit. The hysterical dishonesty of Nazi newspapers, news films and radio became less plausible as Germany's military campaigns faltered and led many to risk listening to foreign broadcasts from more trustworthy sources such as the BBC, an offence punishable by death.

Internal opponents of the regime faced enormous risks and required extraordinary courage to organize against the Nazi State. The most serious attempt at deposing Hitler was "Operation Valkyrie", a plot to place a bomb in Hitler's headquarters in July 1944. The conspiracy was developed by military officers disillusioned at the course of the War, including Claus von Stauffenberg, the man who was to deliver the bomb. Although the bomb exploded, Hitler was shielded from the blast by the solid oak table under which the bomb had been placed, and suffered only minor injuries. Von Stauffenberg was captured and shot that night; his fellow suspects were arrested and tortured, disclosing further names. Death sentences were carried out by firing squad, beheading and strangulation. It is said that Hitler watched home movies of the victims' executions throughout the night of their deaths.

The "White Rose" movement of students at Munich University opposed the regime by distributing leaflets protesting against Nazi atrocities. By 1943, the group had become increasingly bold in their activities and in February of that year the leading members including siblings Hans and Sophie Scholl were arrested. In court, as they were sentenced to death, Sophie accused the court of agreeing with the White Rose but lacking the courage to admit it. Hans and Sophie, along with their friend Christoph Probst were beheaded in the courtyard of Stadelheim Prison on 22 February 1943. The bravery of those prepared to confront the Nazi regime is extraordinary, but neither the students' nor the Army officers' movements had deep roots among the people.

The Church produced some opponents to Hitler; brave individuals, Catholic and Protestant, who denounced the evils of Nazism. At an institutional level, however, potential opposition from the Catholic Church was undermined by the **Reichskonkordat** with the Nazi State which guaranteed some protection for the Church in return for non-interference in political matters. Pope Pius XII' s apparent indifference to the suffering of the Jews has since been the subject of particular controversy. The creation of a new Reich Church enticed sufficient Protestant clergy to weaken efforts to establish a united Christian opposition movement. Political opponents were also fragmented and ineffective. Prominent communists and socialists were among the first to be arrested on the Nazi seizure of power. Many of those who avoided prison were forced into exile, often choosing to oppose fascism by fighting for the Republicans in the Spanish Civil War. Potential Communist opposition was particularly stifled in the years 1939–41 by the compromises of the Nazi–Soviet Pact. Trade unions had been consolidated into the German Labour Front in 1934. The constraints of this system were offset by the Nazis' achievements in providing full employment and routes to upward social mobility based on race, Party membership, civil service or military careers.

> The **Reichskonkordat** is the concordat between the Holy See and Germany. It was signed on 20 July 1933 by Eugenio Cardinal Pacelli and Franz von Papen on behalf of Pope Pius XI and President Paul von Hindenburg respectively. It is still valid today in Germany.

Activity:

How did Germany change as a result of the Second World War?

In Total War and Historical Change: Europe, 1914–1955 (2001) historians A. Marwick and C. Emsley define ten broad areas in which war can act as a catalyst for social change. These provide some useful criteria by which we can identify the social

consequences of war and allow us to create a well-planned essay in response to the question above. As you work through this chapter complete as much of the table as possible. Some sections will require further research.

Social consequences of the Second World War: Germany	
Catalyst	**Outcomes**
Social Geography (basic population statistics, urban/rural distribution)	
Economic and technological change	
Social structure (including questions of class)	
National cohesion (including ethnic composition)	
Social reform and welfare policies	
Material conditions	
Customs and behaviour	
The role and status of women	
High and popular culture	
Institutions and values	

Spain under General Franco

Although Spain was technically not at war, the unstable European situation and the legacy of the bitter civil war resulted in Spain being on a near-permanent war footing with all the attendant socio-economic and political consequences. The period of 1939–45 in Spain was a time of acute shortages and the threat of famine was never far away. Politically, Franco did not relax the authoritarian regime that had been created at the height of the civil war. For the defeated supporters of the Republic who had not fled the country (estimated at 200,000), this meant the civil war continued through other means. There was to be no peace and reconciliation, but rather class war and vengeance. Urban workers, the rural poor, liberal intellectuals, regional nationalists and feminists were grouped together as *rojos*—reds and enemies of the state. With the Law Against Military Rebellion, tens of thousands were executed in military trials, many more spent time as political prisoners. The retrospective functioning of the Law of Political Responsibilities (passed in February 1939) allowed the state to try some half a million people for their pro-republican sentiments backdated to October 1934. Properties were seized and many were sentenced to forced labour as a means of doing penance for their republican "sins". This was most famously illustrated in the building of the *Valle de los Caídos*, Franco's memorial to his crusade against the Republic.

Valle de los Caídos—the last memorial to Franco

Built by 20,000 slave labourers between 1940 and 1958, and 150-metre high granite cross and an underground basilica bigger than St Peter's in Rome,

the memorial of the Valley of the Fallen continues to provoke controversy. The basic design concept was Franco's, imitating Nazi Germany's classicism and the architecture of Albert Speer, its intention was in his words "to defy time and forgetfulness". The memorial marks the remains of 40,000 soldiers and the grave of Franco himself and was until recently the site for annual political rallies on the anniversary of Franco's death on 20 November.

> *On those crystal-clear days that the thin air of Madrid, Europe's highest capital, is famous for producing, it [the holy cross] can be seen, 50 kilometers from the city itself. It is an uncomfortable, and largely unwanted, reminder that Franco may be dead, but his spirit is still out there somewhere.*

Source: Tremlett, Giles. 2006. *Ghosts of Spain: Travels Through a Country's Hidden Past*, London, UK. Faber and Faber. p.38

In December 2007, the socialist government of José Luis Rodríguez Zapatero passed a Law on the Historical Memory of Spain which bans political meetings at *Valle de los Caídos* and outlaws the public display of Francoist symbols in Spain.

Why was Germany defeated?

Hitler's campaigns against the United Kingdom and the Soviet Union and his declaration of war with the United States exposed Germany to an overwhelming coalition of enemies against whom the traditional *Blitzkrieg* tactics could not be applied. Island Britain, having defeated the *Luftwaffe* was safe from German tanks. The Soviets could concede territory, gather strength and expose the over-extended German supply lines. The USA could direct its industrial power to war production, supply its allies with equipment and eventually open a second front in Western Europe. This economic mismatch was compounded by Germany's comparatively slow economic mobilization, failing to match the UK's production of war material in the first years of the War. This inefficiency was masked by the outstanding performance of the German military in the *Blitzkrieg* attacks on Poland and France and by *Reichsmarschall* (Marshal of the Empire) Hermann Goering's inflated reports of economic progress. Evidence suggests that Hitler was surprised by the British and French willingness to go to war over Poland and had not anticipated total war—the logical outcome of Nazism—until the mid 1940s, by which time Germany would have consolidated the core of a new empire at the expense of its Eastern neighbours and opened up a greater military lead. Hitler's gambler's logic and impatience with economic realities led Germany prematurely into global conflict. Albert Speer, Reich Minister for Armaments and Production (1942–5) brought greater organization and productivity after 1942 but by then Germany was facing an alliance of the UK,

Should the *Valle de los Caídos* be dismantled?

Why is the memorial an uncomfortable reminder?

the USA and the Soviet Union. Speer's improvements could not compensate for this strategic disadvantage as Germany was subject to bombing by superior air forces from east and west while Russian and American factories were out its reach.

Tanks and aircraft production, 1940–5						
	Germany		**Soviet Union**		**USA**	
	Tanks	Aircraft	Tanks	Aircraft	Tanks	Aircraft
1940	1,643	10,826	2,794	10,565	331	12,084
1941	3,790	11,776	6,590	15,735	4,052	26,277
1942	6,180	15,556	24,446	25,436	24,997	47,836
1943	12,063	25,527	24,089	34,845	29,497	85,898
1944	19,002	39,807	28,963	40,246	17,565	96,318
1945	3,932	7,544	15,419	20,052	11,968	49,761

Source: Davies, N. 2006. *Europe at War: 1939–1945*, London. Pan Macmillan, pp. 33–5.

Hitler held ultimate responsibility for military and political decisions during the War. The successes of 1939–41 convinced him of his own infallibility and he became less willing to listen to the advice of his generals. As the limitations of *Blitzkrieg* were exposed in Russia, Hitler stubbornly insisted on a policy of no retreats, carelessly sacrificing troops' lives. As the long term outlook worsened Hitler chose to ignore strategy and instead interfered with decisions at a tactical level, denying local commanders any initiative in battle. Those close to Hitler, describe a man whose physical and mental health deteriorated rapidly and yet who remained convinced of his historic destiny, as stated in the words of historian Ian Kershaw.

> Hitler's detachment from reality broke new bounds in the last war years. His self-imposed isolation in his remote headquarters… intensely magnified his tendency to exclude unpalatable reality in favour of an illusory world in which "will" always triumphed.

The Nazi project to establish a new order in Europe foundered on its own contradictions. Civilian life in those areas under German occupation was often brutal and the Nazis spurned opportunities to co-operate with anti-Soviet nationalists in the Ukraine and the Baltic States. Ultimately, all the Nazis could offer was war without end and war as an end in itself. As these contradictions unravelled in the defeats of 1944–5, support for the War collapsed.

As the Soviet Army entered German territory from the East, its soldiers sought revenge for the atrocities carried out in Russia by the German Army in the preceding years. Rape and pillage were widespread and tacitly condoned. Stalin himself asked if it was not possible to "understand the soldier who has gone through blood and fire and death, if he has fun with a woman or takes a trifle?" The Nazis used the reports of mass rape and murder to urge citizens to fight to the end, though many thousands preferred to flee to the West where the British and American forces were seen as more benevolent invaders. Hitler himself chose suicide over the humiliation of capture. By May 1945, the Western Allies had advanced deep into Germany, Berlin was captured by the Red Army and victory was achieved.

Was the Second World War a "Total War"?

The Second World War is commonly regarded as an example of total war in terms of extent, intensity, lack of restraints and far-reaching social change. Governments assumed powers of control over citizens and economies in the pursuit of military victory and advances in military technology gave combatants the power to attack the enemy's citizens and economy. The killing of enemy civilians became not simply a by-product of war but an aim in itself. As historian, Ian Beckett has noted:

> The inescapable logic of the attempt to create a war economy was the recognition that a society that sustained a war became as much a legitimate target for military action as an army that waged war on its behalf.

Source: Quoted in Marwick, A. et al. 2001. *Total War and Historical Change: 1914–1995.* Buckingham, UK. Open University Press. p. 28

Are you the German people determined, if the Fuhrer orders it, to work ten, twelve and, if necessary fourteen and sixteen hours a day and to give your utmost for victory? … I ask you: Do you want total war? Do you want it, if necessary more total and more radical than we can imagine it even today? [Loud cries of "Yes!" and applause] … *Let the nation arise! Let the storm break!*

Heinrich Goebbels' "Total War" speech, February 1943.

Activity:

Total War

Complete the following table, adapted from Peter Browning's *The Changing Nature of Warfare: 1792–1945* (2006).

Characteristics	The Second World War
Intensity (very intense battles, frequency of battles, high casualty figures, massive deployment of men and resources)	
Extent (number of participants, geographical extent, duration)	
Restraints (moral, legal, military)	
Aims (ideological, racial, unconditional surrender)	
Targets (all, soldiers and civilians)	
Economic mobilization	
Social mobilization	

The Second World War: Deaths in individual battles and campaigns	
Operation Barbarossa: battles of Byelorussia, Smolensk & Moscow, 1941	1,582,000
Stalingrad, 1942–3	973,000
Siege of Leningrad 1941–4	900,000
Kiev, 1941	657,000
Operation Bagration (Soviet offensive), 1944	450,000
Kursk, 1943	325,000
Berlin, 1945	250,000
French Campaign, 1940	185,000
Operation Overlord (France), 1944	132,000
Budapest, 1944–5	130,000
Polish Campaign, 1939	80,000
Battle of the Bulge (Belgium), 1944	38,000
Warsaw Rising, 1944 (excluding civilians)	30,000
Operation Market Garden (the Netherlands), 1944	16,000
Battle of El Alamein (North Africa) 1942	4,650

Source: Davies, N. 2007. *Europe at War 1939–1945.* London, UK. Pan Books. p. 25.

Analysing statistics

1 In what ways was the Second World War in Western Europe less "total" than in the East?

2 What do the statistics reveal about the war in Eastern Europe compared with Western Europe?

Post-war Europe

The "Big Three" allied leaders Churchill, Roosevelt and Stalin met at Yalta in February 1945 to plan for the organization of post-war Europe.

- Germany would be divided into four zones: British, American, Soviet and French.
- Berlin, within the Soviet Zone, would itself be divided between the four powers.
- They agreed to co-operate in the new United Nations Organisation.
- Nazi war criminals were to be tried and punished.
- The countries of Central and Eastern Europe, liberated by the Red Army, were to remain within the Soviet sphere of influence.

Instead of destroying Communism, Hitler's actions had brought it to the heart of Europe and only with American support could the traditional powers of Western Europe counter this threat. Although Poland's independence had been the cause that brought Britain and France into the War, Poland with the rest of Eastern Europe was now abandoned to the Soviet sphere of influence. The two halves of the continent would follow separate paths. The accelerated war-time arms race had led to the development of the nuclear bomb enormously multiplying humanity's powers of destruction.

As the Soviet Union consolidated its new empire in Eastern Europe, the Western European powers were losing a grip on theirs. Britain, France, Belgium, and the Netherlands no longer possessed the resources to maintain control of their global colonies. Nationalist leaders in Asia and Africa rejected the right of Europeans to dominate their countries and demanded independence. In the following decades, Europeans would in some cases accept the consequences of this "wind of change" and at other times resist it.

After the First World War borders were moved, and new countries established while populations were largely left in place. Following the Second World War most borders stayed in place and people were moved. The exception to this was Poland which was moved westwards, losing land in the East to the Soviet Union and gaining land in the West from Germany. Germany's formal partition into two states, East Germany (the German Democratic Republic) and West Germany (the Federal Republic of Germany, combining the American, British and French zones), was completed by 1949. The result was a tidier Europe of ethnically homogenous nation states.

Map of post-war Europe.

Post-war Germany

The total defeat of May 1945 has often been described as the *Stunde Null* (zero hour) of German history, a phrase which hints at both the psychological difficulty of confronting the moral bankruptcy of Hitler's war, and at the need to look forward. Approximately seven million Germans had been killed; millions more were injured and traumatized. An estimated 11 million German soldiers were in captivity in May 1945, adding to the shortage of men due to military casualties, which led to a marked imbalance of the sexes. The traditional female roles espoused by Nazi propaganda were a fading memory as women worked to support fatherless families. Whole cities had been reduced to

Discussion point:

The partition of Germany, the establishment of Russian satellite states in Eastern Europe, and the bomb, combined to prevent the outbreak of a third world conflict. This is not to say that the World War Two settlements were morally defensible. The bomb was a weapon of terror. The absorption into an extended Soviet Empire of the East European states violated the principal of self-determination.

Source: Arnold-Forster, M. 1973. *The World at War*, Fontana. p. 278.

 Explain how the "partition of Germany, the establishment of Russian satellite states in Eastern Europe, and the bomb, combined to prevent the outbreak of a third world conflict".

Do you agree that the settlements were not "morally defensible"?

To what extent is morality relevant in international relations?

rubble, leaving their populations homeless. The social dislocation
was enormous. Amid the collapsed infrastructure millions tried to
make their way home; refugees, foreign workers, and released
prisoners all had to be provided for. Normal economic relations had
broken down; factories lacked fuel and raw materials, transport
systems were wrecked, cigarettes replaced money as currency. Labour
had first to be directed to clearing the rubble and providing temporary
housing. Agricultural production also fell leading to widespread hunger
and malnutrition. The resources of the United Nations Relief and
Rehabilitation Administration (UNRRA) and the Allied military were
directed at ensuring bare survival. Into this confusion poured
Germans expelled from the East.

Activity:
The expulsion of German minorities

Ethnic Germans expelled from Czechoslovakia, 1945.

Source A

*The Three Governments [US, UK, USSR], having considered
the question in all its aspects, recognize that the transfer to
Germany of German populations, or elements thereof,
remaining in Poland, Czechoslovakia and Hungary, will have
to be undertaken. They agree that any transfers that take
place should be effected in an orderly and humane manner.*

Source: Article 13, Potsdam Agreement

Source B

*We have decided that we have to liquidate the German
problem in our Republic once and for all.*

Source: Czechoslovak President Benes, speech, 12 May 1945.

Source C

*Stragglers were beaten with truncheons and whips and
those who failed to get up were shot and their bodies
stripped and plundered.*

Source: Description of the forced expulsion of ethnic Germans
from Brno, Czechoslovakia, 1945, in MacDonough, Giles. 2007.
After the Reich: The Brutal History of the Allied Occupation.
London, UK. Murray. p. 139.

Source D

*Of the roughly 12 million Germans who in 1944 were living
in territory that was soon to become part of Poland, an
estimated six million fled or were evacuated before the
advancing Red Army reached them. Of the remainder, up to
1.1 million died, 3.6 million were expelled by the Poles, a
further million were designated as Poles, and 300,000
remained regardless. Thousands starved and froze to death
while being expelled in slow and ill-equipped trains.*

Source: Green, S. et al. 2008. *The Politics of the New Germany.*
Abingdon, UK. Routledge. p. 13.

Which, if any, of the following statements justify these acts of "ethnic cleansing"?

- History showed it was necessary to create ethnically homogenous nation states.

- The German minorities were potentially troublesome traitors.

- Transferring German property to the people of Eastern Europe was compensation for their suffering.

- The German minorities deserved to be punished for Nazi atrocities.

- Spontaneous expulsions were happening already. Governments could only attempt to regulate this process.

- Expulsions would prevent future ethnic conflict.

*"As far as the Western Allies were
concerned, the joke ran around
that the Americans had been given
the scenery, the French the vines,
and the British the ruins."*

MacDonough. G. 2007. *After the Reich*.
London, UK. John Murray. p.199

How did Germany become divided?

When the Allies met again at Potsdam in July–August 1945 they
set out their immediate objectives regarding Germany, including
denazification, demilitarization and democratization. They also
agreed that although political power in Germany would be
decentralized, it would be treated as a single economic unit.
However, in 1949, West Germany (the Federal Republic of
Germany) and East Germany (the German Democratic Republic)
were established as separate states.

The process of denazification aimed to identify and punish Nazis,
to re-educate German people and by removing the ideology of
Nazism establish a basis for democracy. The most prominent aspect
of this process were the Nuremberg Trials of those leading Nazis
who had been captured at the end of the War. The trials resulted in
several death sentences; others received life imprisonment.
The trials produced a thorough documentation of Nazi crimes, they
established a principle of individual responsibility even when the
accused claimed to be following orders, and they set before
the German people the nature of the crimes committed in their
name. Even so, the Nuremberg Trials were criticized as an example
of "victors' justice" carried out for the purpose of revenge.
The presence among the prosecutors of officials from the Soviet
Union, a country responsible for comparable crimes, further
undermined the process.

The Allies each attempted to identify and punish Nazis in their zones.
However, this process ran into practical difficulties largely due to the
scale of the task. There were approximately eight million Nazi Party
members by the end of the Second World War so it would not be
possible to punish Germans simply for being Nazis. However,
attempts to distinguish degrees of guilt among such a large group
would be a difficult, time-consuming task. As attention turned to the

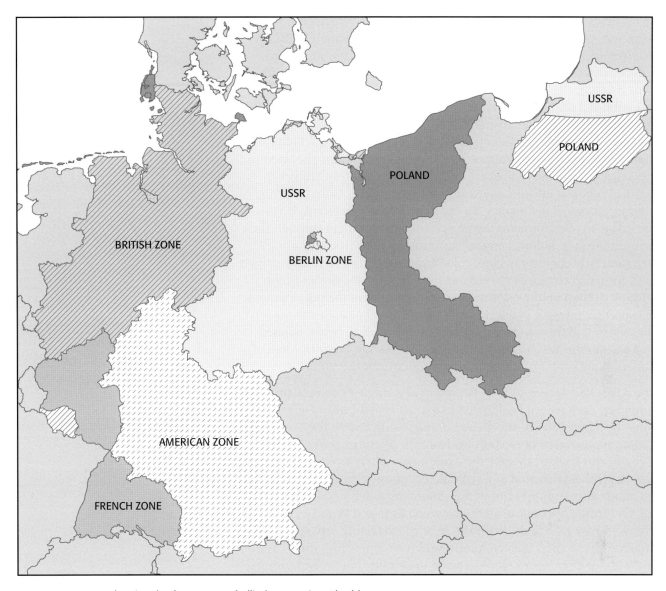

Post-war Germany showing the four zones of Allied occupation. The blue areas
show former German territories allocated to Poland and the Soviet Union.
The Saar region in the South West was administered as a French Protectorate until
1957. Berlin, entirely within the Soviet zone, was itself divided into four sectors.

problems of reconstruction it became necessary to engage competent
administrators among the population. After 12 years of Nazism it was
inevitable that people with the required experience were often
ex-Nazis and so zealous denazification was replaced by turning a
pragmatic blind eye.

In the Soviet analysis, Nazism was a result of "capitalist self-interest
in a moment of crisis" as Judt put it. Accordingly, the Soviet authorities
paid little attention to the distinctively racist side of Nazism, and its
genocidal outcome, and instead focused their arrests on businessmen,
tainted officials, teachers and others responsible for advancing the
interests of the social class standing behind Hitler. This dismantling
of capitalism set the Soviet zone on a different path from the Western
zones where the UK, America and France would nurture the
reconstruction of a market economy.

The Allies originally planned to maintain a united Germany but mutual suspicion, in particular Soviet anxiety at facing a permanent 3:1 majority of Western Powers, led to the decision to give supreme authority in each zone to its military commander rather than to any joint governmental organization. France also opposed moves to re-establish a unified German state and so vetoed the creation of centralized German administrative departments. All the Allies were united in their determination to prevent a return to Nazism. Political organization was decentralized in a Federal system that allocated greater power to the individual German *Länder* (states). However, political renewal in Germany was hampered by the Allies differing interpretations of democracy. To the British and Americans, it was preferable to offer Germans the prospect of improvement through their own democratic political engagement rather than risk alienating Germans by prolonging military rule. Non-Nazi parties were encouraged to re-form and participate in elections. In the East, the Soviet Union's authority rested on the exercise of power and less on the development of consent. Emerging political parties were soon abolished and power consolidated in the hands of the Communists. Stalin's heavy handed approach in the East had the beneficial effect for the Western Allies of undermining support for Communist politicians in the West.

The Allies had agreed to treat Germany as a single economic unit. However, each would be allowed to extract reparations from their zone. In recognition of the greater damage suffered by the Soviet Union, ten per cent of reparations from the Western zones would be given to the Soviets. Despite the agreements, therefore, each zone was in fact being treated as a separate economic entity. The Soviets set about dismantling factories and removing machinery, initiating the enduring economic disparity between East and West Germany. For the Americans and British the issue of extracting reparations was of less concern than the economic burden of supporting their zones. In 1946, food shortages were so acute in Britain that bread rationing was introduced, a measure that had not been necessary during the War itself. Meanwhile, the UK tax payer was subsidizing food imports to the British Zone in Germany. In these circumstances, British and American attention turned to plans for making their zones economically self-sufficient.

In January 1947, the British and Americans united their areas of occupation into "Bizonia". Over the following two years Bizonia accrued further symbols of statehood, such as a central bank, a supreme court, its own currency, and amalgamation with the French zone. The replacement of the inflated old currency with the new Deutsche Mark and the lifting of price controls introduced incentives into the economy, encouraging greater production and halting the inefficiencies of what had been reduced to a barter system. The economic divergence of the two Germanys was accelerated by the provision of massive financial aid from the US for Western Europe

Discussion point:

One thousand two hundred enterprises were hastily dismantled in a fortnight, possibly out of fear that the Allies would call a halt in favour of a systematic policy. Electricity cables and toilets were ripped out of private homes on "orders" from Moscow. For the United States, it was clear that the Russians had no intention of feeding the cow they wished to milk. This was not only morally indefensible, it was bad economics too.

Source: Kettenacker, L. 1997. *Germany Since 1945*. Oxford, UK. Oxford University Press. p. 13.

What does Kettenacker mean by "feeding the cow they wished to milk"?
What similarities and differences were there in Allied policy towards Germany?

under the **Marshall Plan**. The Soviet Union, suspicious of American motives, rejected this aid and Stalin ordered his satellite states in Eastern Europe to do the same. As capitalism was eradicated in the East, economic recovery was boosted in a West Germany restored to the international economy.

The status of Berlin was a further cause of tension. In June 1948, Stalin blocked access by road and rail from the Western zones to Berlin in the hope that the Western Allies would be forced to either surrender their sections of the capital or abandon their plans for a separate West German state. Instead, the Western Allies sustained West Berlin through this blockade with a massive airlift of food and supplies reinforcing its position as a Western enclave and Germany's division deepened. The US had again demonstrated its commitment to the security of West Germany and Western Europe and its determination to adhere to the **Truman Doctrine** of the containment of Communism. Stalin's actions were hardly likely to win him the allegiance of ordinary Germans and his confrontational methods contributed to the division of Germany, an outcome he claimed to oppose. This hardening of Cold War front lines made the development of a neutral, unified Germany impossible.

German politicians shared a reluctance to participate in the division of their country. That an alternative settlement was possible is demonstrated by the example of Austria which developed as a unified and neutral state. However, Germany was much larger than Austria and much more important to the two superpowers making the first moves in their struggle for superiority. In these circumstances, German politicians had insufficient power to influence events to their satisfaction. Konrad Adenauer and his East German counterpart, Walter Ulbricht, publicly insisted on their desire for unity but only ever on their own terms, with their political system being imposed on the other. Furthermore, as a politician closely associated with his home region in the West of Germany, Adenauer's chances of personal electoral success would not be enhanced by the addition of several million East German votes. Disappointing results for Communist candidates in elections in Berlin and elsewhere demonstrated to Ulbricht the limited prospects of genuine democratic success for his Party in Germany as a whole.

As the stand-off in Berlin continued, plans for a West German state were drawn up. Representatives of each of the West German *Länder* produced the Basic Law of the new state on 23 May 1949. The Basic Law aimed to prevent any return to Nazism; checks and balances ensured that power was shared between branches of government and between the federal Länder. It committed West Germany to the protection of human rights and the right to ban anti-democratic political parties. It was

> The **Marshall Plan** was a scheme to provide impoverished European countries with American economic aid in the form of food, fuel, raw materials, and equipment. The plan aimed to rebuild the European economy, to restore international trade, to re-establish markets for America goods and to strengthen Europe against communism.

? To what extent was the Marshall Plan an example of "enlightened self-interest"?

> The **Truman Doctrine** was a set of American foreign policy principles announced by President Harry Truman in March 1947. The United States would "support free peoples who are resisting attempted subjugation by armed minorities or by outside pressures." In other words the USA would contain communism as demonstrated by American support for anti-communists in Greece and Turkey in 1947 and by the determined response to the Berlin Blockade in 1948–9.

Konrad Adenauer (1876–1967)

Konrad Adenauer (1876–1967) began his political career representing the Catholic Centre Party and was elected Mayor of Cologne 1917–33. He was dismissed from office and twice imprisoned by the Nazis. After the War he established a new movement, the Christian Democratic Union (CDU), as a party that would appeal to Protestants as well as Catholics. Adenauer steered the CDU to the centre-right of German politics in competition with the more radically left-wing Socialist Party (SPD). He formed an alliance with the Christian Social Union (CSU), a centre-right Bavarian party.He achieved further prominence as Chairman of the parliamentary council which drew up the Basic Law of the new state on 23 May 1949 and thereby established the Federal Republic of Germany. In September 1949, at the age of 73, Konrad Adenauer was elected as the first Chancellor of West Germany.

envisaged as a provisional document in anticipation of the future reunification of Germany at which point a permanent constitution could be created. The provisional nature of the legal framework reflects the politicians' reluctance to be seen as collaborators in their country's permanent partition and was further symbolized by the unlikely choice of the relatively small city of Bonn as the capital.

The Soviet response was to proclaim the establishment of the German Democratic Republic in their zone on the 7 October 1949. Germany was now divided into two states each claiming to represent the entire German people. Hitler had often claimed that his Germany was defending Western civilization and fighting a "crusade against communism". The West German state indeed became the West's front line against Communism, facing an East German neighbour integrated into the Soviet Empire. Hitler's defeat had removed the common cause which bound the Allies together and the Cold War saw a return to older suspicions between two hostile ideologies. The disagreements over Germany underlined the incompatibility of these two systems and the impossibility of maintaining a unified state. Neither side could accept the other's domination of Germany, so partition became the most acceptable option.

Discussion point: The division of Germany

Source A

The immediate cause of the division of Germany lies in Stalin's own errors in these years. In central Europe, where he would have preferred a united Germany, weak and neutral, he squandered his advantage in 1945 and in subsequent years by uncompromising rigidity and confrontational tactics.

Source: Judt, T. 2007. *Postwar: A History of Europe Since 1945.* Pimlico Press, London. p. 127.

Source B

No serious politician or author can dispute that, as a consequence of the war, the German national state became divided. By the way, not by the Communists and anti-Fascists but rather by Konrad Adenauer, according to the motto, "Better half of Germany, than a complete communist Germany.

Source: GDR Government Minister Kurt Hager, quoted in *Stern,* April, 1987. (Trans. Kirkpatrick, E.V. 1990. *World Affairs.* vol. 152.)

Source C

Ultimately, both [Adenauer and Ulbricht] chose to settle for half a cake baked to their own preferred recipe. The respective recipes had been supplied by the occupying powers.

Source: O' Dochartaigh, P. 2004. *Germany Since 1945.* Basingstoke, UK. Palgrave Macmillan. p. 35.

Source D

In the final analysis it should not be forgotten that ultimately the division of Germany was the legacy of an occupation that was the culmination of a war ignited by German racism, German expansionism and German tanks and guns. The primary responsibility for the division of Germany lies not in the events of 1945–9, but in the behaviour of the German people after 1933.

Source: O' Dochartaigh, P. 2004. *Germany Since 1945.* Basingstoke, UK. Palgrave Macmillan. p. 36.

Source E

German leaders had been tempted to hold out for a united Germany; but the Berlin blockade removed their hesitations.

Source: Davies, N. 1996. *Europe: A History.* Oxford, UK. Oxford University Press. p. 1071.

Source F

The Federal Republic of Germany emerged as much as a result of the political calculations of the Western Allied powers–the USA, the UK and France–as because of the efforts of the founding fathers of the "Bonn Republic" in Germany.

Source: Green, S. et al. 2008. *The Politics of the New Germany.* Abingdon, UK. Routledge. p. 22.

 Who was responsible for the division of Germany? Was the division of Germany inevitable?

Post-war Spain, 1945–53

Map of Spain's provinces and regions.

How did political system work in Franco's Spain?

Although there were always fascistic elements to the government of Franco's Spain, it would be an oversimplification to merely attach the label "fascist" in the hope that this somehow explains things. Franco was to rule Spain for nearly 40 years until his death in 1975. During this time Spain underwent significant changes and the regime evolved accordingly. But some fundamentals did remain the same. Firstly, Franco was a dictator; the **Caudillo**, with powers comparable to Hitler and greater than those of Mussolini. Secondly, Spain was a single-party state. In Franco's Spain, the single party was a loose coalition, of which the fascist party, the **Falange,** was only a part. The *Falange Española Tradicionalista y de las Juntas de Ofensiva Nacional Sindicalista* (FET de las JONS) was the only legal political entity in Franco's Spain. Alongside the Falange, it was

Caudillo is a Spanish word (*caudilho* in Portuguese) usually describing a political-military leader at the head of an authoritarian power.

The **Falange Española Tradicionalista y de las Juntas de Ofensiva Nacional Sindicalista** (FET de las JONS)] was a Spanish political party, founded in 1933 as a fascist movement by José-Antonio. Primo de Rivera and merged in 1937 with traditional right-wing elements to form the ruling party under General Franco.

267

comprised of influential conservative figures from the army, the Catholic Church and monarchists. Throughout Franco's rule, the relative influence of the various constituent groups or "families" within this coalition or *Movimiento Nacional* fluctuated, but all groups were normally represented in the Spanish cabinet. One of the key reasons for the longevity of Franco's regime was his ability to maintain a rivalry between these coalition groups with the permanent goal of securing his own position.

Spain under Franco had no democratic institutions. The *Cortes Generales* (Spanish for *General Courts* or *Cortes Españolas, Spanish Courts*) established in March 1943, was an assembly created to represent the important interests in Spain, what Franco described as "organic democracy" where the people could participate directly in the nation's politics without any parties. The *Cortes* did not have the right to initiate legislation or to vote against the government; it could only approve laws presented by the executive. Two thirds of the representatives were directly appointed by Franco or by one of his ministers and the other third were elected by Falangist groups from approved lists of candidates. The representative nature of the *Cortes* did become broader over time, but met rarely and always approved the legislation submitted to it. Franco's Spain was a highly centralized state with power vested in Madrid. The regime abolished regional government and passed laws against the use of the Basque and the Catalan languages. In addition, the Catholic Church became once again the official religion of Spain and central to the national education system.

The other key political characteristics of Franco's Spain were the strict control over the media which did much to enhance Franco's personality cult and the absence of basic human rights which made open dissent a hazardous occupation. Over 200,000 passed though the prison system during Franco's rule (two per cent of the total male population). Along with this anti-liberalism, Franco's other main political characteristic was his trenchant anti-socialism. But unlike his other political views or his anti-Semitism and obsession with Freemason conspiracies, his opposition to socialism would make him powerful international friends during the Cold War.

How did Franco survive the defeat of the Axis powers?

Franco remained hopeful of an Axis victory right up until **VE-day**. Even after then, his support for the ideals of European fascism was undiminished. The Spanish state provided one hundred active German Nazis with new identities and political asylum. In December 1943 Franco had told the German ambassador that he did not expect his regime to survive defeat of the Axis powers. Indeed, in 1945, with Spain denied entry into the United Nations and subject to an international economic boycott, the prospects for Franco seemed bleak. Politically Franco faced threats from all sides. In March 1945, Don Juan de Borbón, the son of Alfonso XIII, produced his "Lausanne Address" calling on Franco to abandon power in favour of a constitutional monarchy. In response, a senior group of monarchists went as far as to nominate the members of

Victory in Europe Day (V-E Day or VE Day) was on 8 May 1945, the date when the Allies formally accepted the unconditional surrender of the armed forces of Nazi Germany and the end of Adolf Hitler's Third Reich.

Activity:

Was Franco a fascist?

Adolf Hitler and General. Franco demonstrating Fascist style.

Source A

The teoria de caudillaje *was a defining contour of the Franco regime, and with it came a flourishing personality cult … this bureaucratic state learned much from the economic policy of Fascist Italy. These lessons also included autarky, the Labour Charter establishing rights and duties of workers (1938), the "Battle for Wheat" and the INI [Instituto Nacional de Industria], a source of state investment for industry (1941). The Falangist Sección Femenina … "re-educated" women in their traditional roles, analagous to the Nazi Kinder, Kirche, Küche … Franco regime banned not only divorce but, along with all Catholic countries, contraception. As in Mussolini's Italy and the Third Reich, awards were given as incentive to produce large families … Through the voluntary Youth Front founded in 1940 (Pelayos aged 7–10, Flechas 11–14, Cadetes 15–18) Falangists instilled political doctrine … [and] occupied top positions in the Franco propaganda machine, press, radio, film, theatre, and … orchestrated parades and rallies affirming mass support for the Caudillo with their fascist salute and conspicuous blue shirts.*

Source: Forrest, A. 2000. *The Spanish Civil War*. London, UK. Routledge. p. 116, p. 118.

Source B

Falangists never played a major role in the new state. Most of the key leaders of the Falange did not survive the Civil War, and Franco moved quickly to subordinate the fascist party, merging it as well as more conservative and traditional political forces into the broader and vaguer National Movement under his direct control …Thus, while there was a definite fascist element during the first decade of Franco's rule, most analysts have concluded that early Francoism can more accurately be described as semifascist.

Source: Solsten, E & Meditz, S.W. (eds). *Spain: A Country Study*. U.S. Library of Congress, 1988. http://countrystudies.us/spain.

Source C

First, it must be conceded that Franco was a very different sort of man from Hitler or Mussolini. They were first and foremost politicians, but he was pre-eminently a soldier … He was never a member of any political party, and thus there was no equivalent of the Nazis or the Fascists in Spain. The Falange, as we have seen, was the nearest Spain came to possessing a fascist party, but Franco took actions to limit its importance–and members of the Falange responded in 1940 with an assassination attempt.

Source: Pearce, R. 1997. *Fascism and Nazism*. Hodder. p. 86.

Source D

Franco ruled Spain as the regent of a Conservative Monarchy, like Admiral Horthy in Hungary. Both Franco and Salazar–in differing degrees–were allies of the Catholic Church. During the civil war, in order to humour his fascist backers, Franco uttered fascist slogans and played up the Falange. But at best he was half-hearted, as the German ambassador repeatedly complained.

Source: Woolf, J.S. 1981. *Fascism in Europe*. Taylor & Francis, p. 35.

Source E

Franco was not a fascist. There is an element of revolutionary politics in fascism, of wanting to provoke a dramatic change in society. That was not Franco's intention: on the contrary, he wanted to preserve Spain from change … the debate as to whether Franco was a fascist is in many ways irrelevant, since the denial of Franco's fascism has often been an essential part of attempts to legitimise his actions. The fact remains that his brutality matched or even exceeded that of Mussolini.

Source: Ribeiro De Meneses, Filipe. 2001. *Franco and the Spanish Civil War*. Routledge. p. 87.

Source F

An eagerness to exonerate the Franco regime from the taint of fascism can go with a readiness to forget that, after coming to power through a civil war which claimed hundreds of thousands of lives and forced hundreds of thousands more into exile, the dictatorship executed at least quarter of a million people, maintained concentration camps and labour battalions, and sent troops to fight for Hitler on the Russian front. ... the confident exclusion of the Franco regime from a discussion of fascism could only be justified if fascism is taken to be synonymous with Nazism at its most extreme, complete with racialistic bestiality. Such a view, since it leads logically to the suggestion that Mussolini's Italy was not really fascist, is so rigid as to be useless.

Source: Preston, P. 1995. *The Politics of Revenge: Fascism and the Military in 20th-century Spain*. Routledge. pp. 10–11.

Source G

In spite of the Fascist trimmings of the early years–the goose-step and the Fascist salute–Francoism was not a totalitarian regime. It was a conservative, Catholic, authoritarian system, its original corporatist features modified over time. It came to have none of the characteristics of a totalitarian state: no single party parallel to the state administration; after the early years, no successful attempt at mass mobilization.

Source: Carr, R. 1980. *Modern Spain 1875–1980*, Oxford, UK. Oxford University Press. p. 165.

Source H

The word "Fascism" is almost entirely meaningless. In conversation, of course, it is used even more wildly than in print. I have heard it applied to farmers, shopkeepers, Social Credit, corporal punishment, fox-hunting, bull-fighting, the 1922 Committee, the 1941 Committee, Kipling, Gandhi, Chiang Kai-Shek, homosexuality, Priestley's broadcasts, Youth Hostels, astrology, women, dogs and I do not know what else ... almost any English person would accept "bully" as a synonym for Fascist". That is about as near to a definition as this much-abused word has come.

Source: Orwell, G. 1944, "What is Fascism?". *Tribune.* http://orwell.ru/library/articles/As_I_Please/english/efasc.

Questions

1 Compare and contrast the views of Paul Preston and Filipe Ribeiro De Meneses on Franco. To what extent do they disagree with each other?

2 Franco ruled Spain for nearly 40 years. Why does this make it more difficult to conclude whether he was a fascist or not?

3 In 1944 the English writer George Orwell wrote that the word fascism was "entirely meaningless". Does the word have any meaning or use in today's world?

4 List the characteristics of a fascist state. How does Franco's rule conform to these definitions?

---

a provisional government and to draft the text of the decree to restore the monarchy. And from the other extreme, Franco faced full-scale guerrilla war led by the Republican exile **Maquis** in the north and east.

Socio-economically, the late 1940s are known in Spain as *los años del hambre* (the years of hunger). This was a time when there were no cats and dogs on streets, as they either died of starvation or were eaten. In the cities there were daily power cuts, cigarettes were sold one at a time and the rural poor ate boiled grass and weeds. Real wages in 1951 were a mere 60 per cent of their 1936 level. The problems were exacerbated by Franco's fascistic inspired economic policy of autarky which provided an ideological basis for Spain's isolation but prevented any steps towards the much needed modernization of the economy. The result was that industrial production in 1948 was no better than 1929 levels. In the end, were it not for imports from Peron's Argentina, full-scale famine would have been likely. The reasons why Franco survived these most difficult of years goes some way to explaining why Franco was able to stay in power until his death in 1975. We can identify four distinct explanations for his survival in this period.

> The **Spanish Maquis** were Spanish guerrillas exiled in France after the Spanish Civil War who continued to fight against the Franco regime until the early 1960s, carrying out sabotage, robberies (to help fund guerrilla activity), occupations of the Spanish Embassy in France and assassinations of Francoists, as well as contributing to the fight against Nazi Germany and the Vichy regime in France during the Second World War.

Firstly, the international community, although generally hostile, was unwilling to take action to remove Franco. For the British Foreign Office, Franco may have been an "unfortunate anomaly", but he was also unlikely to give up power without plunging Spain once again into civil war. Spain was not under threat from Stalin's encroachment from the east, but if Franco was removed the Spanish Left would be the most obvious beneficiary. As Churchill argued, "if the Communists become master of Spain, we must expect the infection to spread very fast though Italy and France." As the Cold War began to take hold, the regime's fascistic origins and Franco's enthusiastic support for Hitler and Mussolini was quietly forgotten. What mattered now was Spain's strategic position and Franco's well-documented, fervent anti-communism. Allied non-intervention after the War helped Franco, just as it had during the civil war.

The second reason for Franco's survival was his control over the Spanish state which provided both a compliant media and the extensive machinery of coercion. The Catholic Church was a loyal supporter and though its monopoly control of education did much to reinforce the regime. The Falange, although less significant after the War, still played an important role in organizing spontaneous mass demonstrations of support. With the defeat of the Axis powers, Franco's propaganda machine went into overdrive rewriting the history of the War and Spain's role within it. Franco was now proclaimed as the "Caudillo of Peace" and the end of the War was "Franco's Victory". According to the Spanish newspaper *ABC*, Franco must have been "chosen by God" for "when everything was obscure, he saw clearly and sustained and defended Spain's neutrality". When Don Juan de Borbón made his dangerous Lausanne Address, censorship ensured that nothing was reported in the Spanish press. Although the civil war was officially over, Franco's Spain remained on a war footing in order to counter the subversive threats from within. In the state budget of 1946, 45 per cent was dedicated to the police the Civil Guard and the army, described by Preston as "the apparatus of repression".

During the civil war, the *ABC* famously published two different versions, the Madrid edition supporting the Republic and the Seville edition supporting the Nationalist side. When the War was over, *ABC* in Madrid was given back to its legitimate owners and once again became the largest national daily newspaper in Spain. The third reason is very much to be explained in terms of Franco's personality, which gave Franco a curious mixture of acute political adroitness and messianic blind faith in his own survival. Even the most critical commentators will grant that Franco had a remarkable ability to strengthen his own position by the judicious and carefully balanced use of his powers of patronage. For example, when the great powers met at Potsdam with threatening plans to democratize the Axis countries and their allies, Franco responded by reducing the influence in his cabinet of the pro-Axis members of Falange. One of the key

Activity:
Essay writing skills: PEE paragraph.
Good paragraph construction is essential to any effective essay. Each paragraph should contribute a distinct point that contributes to your answer to the set question.

Make a big **point** in the first sentence, then **explain** it and illustrate your point with **examples. (PEE)**.

A good test of how well you have planned your essay, is to ask yourself whether you can reduce the whole essay to just the first sentences (as summary points).

appointments saw Foreign Minister Jose Lequerica, with his reputation of being more German than the Germans", replaced by the monarchist Martín-Artajo who was charged with producing a liberal sounding bill of rights, the *Fuero de los Españoles* (1945). It did nothing to weaken Franco's own position but was one of a number of measures designed to create favourable foreign perceptions. Franco's personality also exhibited a fatalistic belief in his own destiny to govern Spain. Not only was he not going to give up, more importantly he would show no signs of giving up; Franco "has skin like a rhinoceros" bemoaned one British Foreign Office official. Or, as Preston, in his biography of Franco, put it: "The monumental egotism that lay at the heart of his being enabled him to shrug off the demise of his erstwhile benefactors Hitler and Mussolini as matters of little significance relative to his own providential mission."

The worse the news, Franco once advised, the bigger one must smile. "I will not make the same mistake as General Primo de Rivera", Franco said. "I don't resign. For me, it's straight from here to the cemetery." He kept a photograph of the mutilated body of Mussolini as a reminder of his own fate if he failed to hold on to power. It helped that he lived in a megalomaniac's fantasy world, in which Spain's energy problems would be solved by synthetic gasoline and the British Labour Party's landslide election victory had been brought about by the votes of 12 million Freemasons. So when Franco consistently denied after 1945 that he had expected Spain to join the Axis powers during the War, it is impossible to say whether he was lying or had come to believe his own propaganda. This can make it difficult for historians to make objective judgments on Franco.

The final reason for Franco's survival was perhaps the least tangible, but most long-lasting. In Spain, the legacy of the civil war resulted in the prevailing concern to maintain peace at almost any cost. The civil war had left deep social and cultural scars. Attempts to remove Franco risked reopening these scars and plunging Spain into a renewed civil war. The traumatic legacy does much to explain the attitude that, until recently, has dominated Spanish life, summed up in the phrase, *"el pacto del olvido"* (the pact of forgetting): to live in the present one must be prepared to forget.

By a variety of means, then, Franco survived. And more than this, by the beginning of the 1950s, Franco's position was becoming secure. Domestically, the threat from Republican exiles had receded and an accommodation had been reached with the monarchists. Don Juan de Borbón's son, Juan Carlos, was to succeed Franco but Franco was to retain responsibility for the future king's education. Internationally, the first moves towards reintegration came through a Concordat with the Vatican and, as the Cold War intensified, so also did Spain's potential usefulness to the United States. With the 1953 visit of President Eisenhower and the resultant Pact of Madrid, an agreement was reached with the United States to give Franco considerable financial aid in return for the establishment of four US military bases in Spain.

TOK Link
Ways of Knowing

Why did you decide to study history for your IB Diploma? Are you certain about your reasons?

If asked why you chose to study history, would you give the same answer at a university entrance interview as you would to your friends?

If you were asked in ten years time, would your answer still be the same?

We often read historical accounts which lay claim to know why decisions were made or what an individual in the past intended to achieve. In the light of the observations about Franco above, make a list of the difficulties of knowing for certain why people in the past acted the way that they did.

Rebuilding Europe

The Cold War shaped a continent artificially divided between East and West. The countries of Western Europe remained vulnerable in the face of Soviet power and dependent on the military protection of the United States. They faced the urgent challenge of rebuilding their economies to achieve prosperity and security. Despite these tensions, the 1950s and 1960s were something of an economic "golden age" for Western Europe, with years of growth and full employment. Governments shared a **Keynesian** commitment to direct state intervention in order to manage economies and to the maintenance of the "welfare state"— providing health care, housing and pensions. This affluence coupled with technological innovation brought about enormous material changes to societies in which consumer goods such as cars, televisions, fridges and washing machines became widely affordable. The 1960s, in particular, were years of artistic experimentation and an internationally driven flood of popular culture, led by a global world media. Many Western European countries experienced a degree of social liberalization; the availability of the contraceptive pill facilitated changes in sexual behaviour, the influence of religion went through a period of decline, legislation decriminalizing homosexuality, adultery and blasphemy were passed, and censorship laws were relaxed.

> **Keynesian Theory** An economic theory developed by the British economist John Maynard Keynes which claims to explain economic cycles and the methods by which governments can intervene to deal with them, in particular to maintain full employment, social harmony and, in the context of post-War Europe, blunt the appeal of more radical forms of socialism.

European integration

In the immediate post-war years, in the ruined capitals of Western Europe, leaders could look back at the traumatic decades of conflict, depression and political extremism, they could look East to the hostile Soviet Bloc, they could look within their own states to the enticement of indigenous communist parties that enjoyed some support, and they could reflect on their own diminished status. There could be no return to the discredited ways of the past, but each country's way forward would vary according to its unique circumstances. The key partnership in this new Europe was that of the old enemies France and Germany.

For Germany, greater economic and political integration with neighbouring states, in particular France, was a strategy for overcoming the destructive legacy of nationalism and hostility and a route towards political rehabilitation and economic recovery. The relationship with France was a key aspect of West Germany's recovery. A proposal by the French Foreign Minister Robert Schuman, known as the Schuman Plan, led to a joint agreement between the two countries, to co-ordinate production in the coal and steel industries. This was marked by the signing of the European Coal and Steel Community (ECSC) Treaty in April 1951. Politically, the agreement aimed to break the pattern of hostility between France and Germany by identifying and developing areas of mutual interest. The ESCS Treaty obliged members (France, Germany, Italy, Belgium, the Netherlands, and Luxembourg) to agree to the principle of **supranationality**—handing over control of the industries to an international body. For West Germany, being welcomed

> Following the signing of the ECSC Treaty on 18 April 1951, this first European **supranational community** set up its administrative offices in Luxembourg on August 10, 1952.

into an international organization alongside neighbouring states, the treaty represented a confirmation of the new state's legitimacy and rehabilitation. As Adenauer remarked, *"Das ist unser Durchbruch"* (this is our breakthrough).

How much do you think the Schuman Plan is motivated by self-interest, and how much is it to do with a genuine spirit of co-operation?

If the signing of the ECSC Treaty promises to forge better relations between France and other countries on Germany's Western border, what is the likely impact on East–West relations?

On 18 April 1951, in Paris, the German Chancellor, Konrad Adenauer, signs the treaty establishing the European Coal and Steel Community (ECSC).

Adenauer found common ground with his fellow European leaders; the foreign ministers who signed the treaty all represented Christian Democratic parties. The continental experience of invasion, occupation and liberation fostered a shared determination to work towards unity. The treaty included the declaration that the ECSC was "a first step in the federation of Europe". In 1957 "the Six" member states took the further step, with the Treaty of Rome, of creating the European Economic Community through which West Germany integrated its economy with its Western European neighbours. The Franco-German partnership was to be the engine of this European project, a relationship in which German economic power was harnessed to French political leadership. Trade between member states grew rapidly to their mutual benefit.

Not all Western European states were ready to commit to the process of integration. In particular, the United Kingdom's experience of the Second World War, undefeated and triumphant, vindicated a confident nationalism and an insular sense of security based on standing apart, some might say aloof, from the troubles of the Continent. The proven strength of British ties with the British Commonwealth and with the United States, united by a common language and heritage, further diminished the appeal of

The Schuman Plan

Europe will not be made all at once, or according to a single plan. It will be built through concrete achievements which first create a de facto solidarity. The coming together of the nations of Europe requires the elimination of the age-old opposition of France and Germany. Any action taken must in the first place concern these two countries. With this aim in view, the French Government proposes that action be taken immediately on one limited but decisive point.

It proposes that Franco-German production of coal and steel as a whole be placed under a common High Authority, within the framework of an organization open to the participation of the other countries of Europe. The pooling of coal and steel production should immediately provide for the setting up of common foundations for economic development as a first step in the federation of Europe, and will change the destinies of those regions which have long been devoted to the manufacture of munitions of war, of which they have been the most constant victims.

Source: Robert Schuman, extract from 9 May declaration. 1950. http://www.ena.lu.

European integration. At an instinctive, emotional, historical level there was a sense that the "Island Nation" did not quite belong to Europe and so the UK passed up the opportunity. The British attitude was not unrealistic; economically, the UK relied less on European markets than on its extensive commercial links overseas. In 1947, British exports were greater than the combined exports of the six who predominantly traded with each other—the UK didn't need Europe to the extent that it was prepared to surrender any degree of sovereignty. Furthermore, the British Labour Government under Clement Attlee (1945–51) had no wish to join an organization that might limit its scope to pursue the development of a socialist "New Jerusalem" in the UK.

The British military triumph had come at a heavy price, a quarter of the national wealth had been lost (a greater proportion than any other country), gold reserves were nearly exhausted, and only American loans were preventing economic collapse. Added to this were the costs of maintaining an overseas empire, policing the defeated countries of Europe, and striving to justify its Great Power status alongside the United States and the Soviet Union. Though the British economy recovered, industrial production rose more slowly than in its European neighbours. 1958 was the cross-over year between the winners and losers of the Second World War when the West German economy became bigger than that of the UK.

For Franco's Spain, relations with Europe were always coloured by mutual suspicion, Franco regarded the EEC to be a "fief of Freemasons, liberals and Christian Democrats". The technocrats who oversaw Spain's economic transformation in the 1960s (see below) successfully persuaded a reluctant Franco to begin negotiations for Spanish membership in 1962. The EEC agreed to begin discussions about economic issues but Franco' s refusal to contemplate major changes to the Spanish constitution meant that any movement to full membership was not on the agenda until after the dictator's death in 1975.

The need to secure long-term peace in Europe, both between historic enemies within Western Europe such as France and Germany, and against the Soviet threat was the motivation for the establishment of common security structures. Western Europe's alliance with the United States was formalized within NATO (the North Atlantic Treaty Organisation) in 1949, confirming America's military commitment to defend Europe. In the words of the first NATO General Secretary, Lord Ismay, the original purpose of the alliance was "to keep the Americans in, the Russians out, and the Germans down." However, in 1955, West Germany was accepted into NATO and began to share the burden of defending Western Europe against Soviet Communism. The enduring strength of NATO contrasts with failed European attempts at establishing common defence structures and reflects Europe' s reliance on American military power. The most notable attempt at creating a Western European military entity—the EDC (European Defence Community)—failed due to concerns about German rearmament, opposition to the idea of ceding military control to an external organization, and fears that the EDC might diminish America' s commitment to European security. The French Government formally rejected the EDC

Annual Average Growth Rates 1950–60	
UK	2.7%
France	4.6%
Italy	5.8%
Germany	7.8%

Source: Young, H. 1999. *This Blessed Plot: Britain and Europe, from Churchill to Blair*. Woodstock, NY, USA. Overlook Press. p. 106.

project in 1954. As NATO developed, with the USA's continued security guarantee, the need for an EDC came to be seen as unnecessary duplication.

Western Europe's military weakness was exposed by the humiliation of Suez in 1956. Egypt's General Nasser had asserted Egyptian national control of the strategically vital Suez Canal against British and French wishes. In response, the United Kingdom, France and Israel had seized control of the canal but were forced to withdraw under intense diplomatic and financial pressure from the USA. Suez demonstrated that neither nation could project its power globally without the support of the Superpowers. For France the EEC offered an alternative sphere of influence. For the UK Suez triggered a painful reassessment of its global role. Economic projections were also pessimistic and eventually resulted in an acceptance that the UK could no longer afford to be excluded from Europe. Belatedly, and from a position far weaker than previously, the British Government applied to join the EEC in 1963. France's president Charles de Gaulle rejected the application. The reasons for this infamous *"Non"* were de Gaulle's concerns that the United Kingdom remained too pro-American and lacked commitment to European integration. At a more basic level, the UK's entry might threaten France's leading role in Europe. Both the UK's combination of wounded pride and disdain as well as De Gaulle's vain grandeur were summarized in the British press with the popular metaphor, "there cannot be two cocks on the dung-hill". A second British application was rejected by de Gaulle in 1967 citing the weakness of the British economy.

Key dates in European integration	
1949	NATO established. The original members were the USA, Canada, the UK, France, Belgium, the Netherlands, Luxembourg, Norway, Iceland, Italy, Denmark and Portugal.
1951	European Coal and Steel Community (ECSC) established. "The Six" (France, Germany, Italy, Belgium, the Netherlands and Luxemburg) agree to co-ordinate their coal and steel industries.
1954	France rejects plans for a European Defence Community.
1955	West Germany joins NATO.
1957	The Treaty of Rome established the European Economic Community (EEC), agreeing to work towards a common market in which members would remove trade barriers and allow the free movement of labour, capital and goods.
1960	The European Free Trade Association (EFTA) established offering an alternative European vision. A grouping of peripheral states —the UK, Austria, Sweden, Denmark, Norway, Portugal and Switzerland—formed a free trade area without the EECs ideals of political integration.
1963	UK application to join the EEC rejected following De Gaulle's veto.
1967	Second UK application to join the EEC vetoed by De Gaulle.

Discussion point:

1 What were the aims of the founders of the European movement? Was European integration more concerned with avoiding the mistakes of the past or fulfilling the vision of a united Europe?

2 The idea of the EU as a peace project ensuring Franco-German reconciliation has been criticized on the grounds that war between individual members of either Cold War bloc was impossible. To what extent do you agree?

Germany, 1950–69

Konrad Adenauer secured the chancellorship by the narrowest of margins; he faced determined opposition from the Social Democratic Party, and his Christian Democratic Union Party could only rule with the support of smaller parties. The Chancellor of the new state faced a series of challenges, internal and external.

The economy

In 1950 the prospects of economic recovery in West Germany was far from certain. There were two million people unemployed, over 10 per cent of the workforce. To this number were added the continuing flow of German internal immigrants from the East (about 447,000 between 1951–3) with all the attendant problems associated with integration. There was still an acute shortage of housing, basic consumer goods and the danger that frustration at economic failure could find expression in political extremism.

The GDR

The GDR would remain a challenge and a source of efforts to undermine the West German state throughout the Cold War. Should the FRG fail, the existence of an alternative national model could prove an attraction for dissatisfied citizens. West German politicians had to live with the dilemma of pursuing unity with East Germany or integrating the FRG more securely into the American-led Western bloc. The Socialist Party opposed Adenauer's pro-Western policies.

The Cold War

West Germany faced front-line exposure to Soviet pressure. In 1949, the year in which the Soviet Union successfully tested an atomic bomb, the Soviet bloc armies vastly out-numbered those of the West. When, in 1950, Communist North Korea attacked Western-backed South Korea, the parallels with the world s other ideologically divided state, Germany, were obvious.

Semi-sovereignty

West Germany did not immediately gain full independence; the military occupation of Germany continued and German politicians' scope of action was curtailed by the Allies' power of veto. The Ruhr industrial region was placed under international control and France retained control of the Saar coal-mining region. West Germany was not permitted to rearm or to manufacture weapons.

International relations

Germany was still mistrusted by neighbouring countries. Germany's history placed constraints on German politicians as they articulated national interests. This lingering pariah status is underlined by the Brussels Pact of March 1948, in which the UK, France and the Benelux countries formed an alliance against future German aggression.

How successfully did West Germany deal with these problems?

Adenauer was the dominant political figure of West Germany in the new state's first decade, the years of the *Wirtschaftswunder* (economic miracle). Economic progress was rewarded with an increased share of the votes for Adenauer's Christian Democratic Union (CDU) in elections in the 1950s. From this secure foundation Adenauer was able to take steps towards addressing the nation's challenges. Adenauer and his economics minister, Ludwig Erhard, oversaw a period during which the economy grew by an average of eight per cent per year, the fastest in Europe. By the end of the decade unemployment had fallen below one per cent and there was a labour shortage. Inflation remained low throughout and West Germany's share of world exports trebled. Erhard's "Social Market Economy" comprised free market economics regulated by the state as far as necessary to ensure adequate distribution of wealth, and welfare provision for weaker members of society. It represented a third way between American-style capitalism and the strictly controlled command economies of the Eastern bloc. A co-operative approach to industrial relations helped avoid economic disruption. Workers had the right to significant representation on company boards through which they could influence and share responsibility for decisions. Productivity more than trebled in the two decades after 1950, far outstripping British figures, and highlighting the efficiency of the "German model". An extensive building programme offered millions of Germans the chance of gaining a home of their own. The Equalisation of Burdens Act, 1952, redistributed wealth from those fortunate enough to have survived the War with their property intact, to those who had suffered losses.

Adenauer and Erhard were assisted by external factors; the Korean War provided a surge in demand for German steel and manufactured goods establishing the pattern of an export-led economy. As the Western Allies bore the burden of Cold War military spending, disarmed Germany could allocate resources elsewhere. Under Adenauer, the CDU broadened its support from its Catholic origins to include other denominations and non-religious conservatives to position itself as a powerful centre-right party. The dominance of this strong centre, and the economic stability that underpinned it, contrasted with the polarised politics of the Weimar years and exerted a magnetic appeal. During the 1950s, over two million, often skilled and well-educated, East Germans moved west to take advantage of the greater personal freedom and increased job opportunities. In 1956, the inhabitants of the Saar region rejected French plans to develop as an independent state in favour of the "small reunification" with West Germany.

Adenauer's policy of deeper integration into Western alliances alarmed the Soviet Union and drew criticism from domestic opponents who argued that German unification should be the priority. Stalin's proposal, in 1952, of uniting the two states as a neutral Germany in which free national elections could be held, attempted to exploit these divisions. The plan was rejected by the Allies who insisted that free elections would have to come first and that Germany should be allowed to join military alliances of its choice. Adenauer agreed that Stalin's real intention was to split West Germany from the West and create a demilitarized Germany in the Soviet shadow. However, to his opponents this demonstrated Adenauer's subservience to the Allies and his disregard for the 17 million Germans on the other side of the Iron Curtain. From then on suspicions lingered that at heart Adenauer was not really interested in reunification. He was more anxious to safeguard West Germany's freedom and security as a member of the Western Alliance than to achieve national unity. The working assumption was that it was a choice of one or the other.

In May 1955 West Germany's rehabilitation was marked by the abandonment of the Occupation Statute and, following the signing of the Germany Treaty, the Western Allies' recognition of West Germany as a fully independent state. In the same month, ten years after the defeat of National Socialism, West Germany joined NATO and as a member was expected to contribute to the defence of Western Europe. Adenauer faced opposition to such a contentious policy, and could only proceed with rearmament by placing strict constitutional limits on the use of the German military. Domestic opponents argued that history proved the folly of pursuing military power, and that Adenauer's policies reduced the chances of achieving German unification. The Soviet Union responded to West German membership of NATO by announcing the establishment of the Warsaw Pact, an opposing military alliance of Eastern bloc states including the GDR.

The two German regimes settled into a pattern of mutual hostility each denying the other's legitimacy and each claiming to be the true representative of Germany. West Germany also denied recognition of other countries which recognized the GDR. The only exception to this **Hallstein Doctrine** was the Soviet Union; Adenauer visited Moscow in 1955 and secured the release of some 10,000 German prisoners of war still held in Russian camps. Berlin remained an anomaly, a Western enclave surrounded by East Germany and the scene of an increasing flow of East Germans into the West. The GDR was the only European country to experience a decline in population during the 1950s. In August 1961, the East German authorities began to halt this process by constructing the Berlin Wall, giving physical shape to the city's political division. Willy Brandt, Social Democrat candidate for the chancellorship broke off from his election campaign to travel to Berlin. Adenauer's response was slower; he didn't go to Berlin until nine days later, giving the impression that, for him, Berlin was not a priority. Nevertheless, the CDU, as architects of West Germany's solid economic performance, won the election.

Adenauer's cautious conservatism had set West Germany on a path from being Europe's problem to a position of respect as a stable component in Western Europe's response to the constraints of the Cold War. However, critics perceived a failure to deal

> **Discussion point:**
>
> The two German states were not the only countries in the world in the post-war period to foster exclusive mandate policies.
>
> Can you think of any other divided countries that demanded, and still maintain the right to, sole sovereignty?

honestly with the legacy of National Socialism. Although Adenauer acknowledged Germany's guilt and agreed to pay reparations to Israel, the emphasis of the Adenauer years was on reconstruction rather than recrimination and many ex-Nazis retained their positions in the civil service and in government. The benefits of confronting the past were balanced by an awareness of the destabilizing effect such a comprehensive purge may have.

Adenauer's final term as Chancellor was marred by the Spiegel Affair in which a journalist and the editor in chief of *Der Spiegel* magazine were arrested following a controversial article in the magazine criticizing the sorry state of the German *Bundeswehr* (Army). The arrests were widely seen as an attack on the freedom of the press. The affair would cost Franz Josef Strauss, the Minister of Defence, his office and serve to further question the complacency and arrogance of a government in its 13th year in power. The old, authoritarian attitudes were amplified by the fact that one of the journalists was arrested while in Spain by officials of General Franco's regime. The affair provoked protest from the public, the press and other political parties. Adenauer could only secure the continued support of his coalition partners by promising to stand down in 1963. At the age of 86, Adenauer's rule was coming to an end.

On 17 August 1962, Peter Fechter, an 18-year-old East Berliner, bled to death at the base of the Wall after being shot by East German border guards during an escape attempt. For the West German public this brought home with unprecedented directness the barbarity of the shoot to kill order in effect along the border between the two Germanys.

By 1966 West Germany's economic growth had begun to slow down. Unemployment and the success of neo-Nazi candidates at local elections revived fears of a return to the problems of the Weimar years. The CDU had formed a "Grand Coalition" with the Socialist Party—between them they controlled over 80 per cent of parliamentary seats—diminishing the power of opposition within parliament and encouraging those who chose to oppose the government elsewhere, often violently, in street protests that were a feature of many European cities at the time. At the same time the Grand Coalition enacted a programme of social liberalization in which adultery, homosexuality and blasphemy all ceased to be criminal offences. The CDU's dominance of West German politics finally came to an end in 1969 when Willy Brandt became Chancellor at the head of a Socialist/Liberal (FDP) coalition.

Activity:

Verdicts on Adenauer

Verdict A

In 2003 German television channel ZDF invited viewers to vote for the greatest German of all time. These are the results:

1 Konrad Adenauer

2 Martin Luther

3 Karl Marx

4 Hans and Sophie Scholl

5 Willy Brandt

6 Johann Sebastian Bach

7 Johann Wolfgang von Goethe

8 Johannes Gutenberg

9 Otto von Bismarck

10 Albert Einstein

Adolf Hitler and other Nazis were excluded from the poll. Winner Konrad Adenauer served from 1949 to 1963 and helped re-establish German democracy after the Nazi era. He also oversaw the first years of the German economic miracle—a cause for some nostalgia today as the country's economy lags in the doldrums.

Source: http://news.bbc.co.uk/2/hi/europe/3248516.stm.

Verdict B

Adenauer and the CDU made West Germany in the 1950s their own. They brought economic prosperity, material wealth, political stability and relative security to a population that wished to move on and put the recent past behind it … Adenauer also secured for the Federal Republic a respected place in the international community …

Source: O'Dochartaigh, P. 2004. *Germany Since 1945.* Basingstoke, UK. Palgrave Macmillan, p. 71.

Verdict C

There can be no doubt that he provided the kind of safe leadership the Germans badly needed if they were to climb out of the abyss into which Hitler had led them. Above all, he felt it his mission to protect Germans from themselves, from their penchant for political follies, by tying them as closely as possible into the Western European community of nations.

Source: Kettenacker, L. 1997. *Germany Since 1945.* Oxford, UK. Oxford University Press. p. 54.

Verdict D

Bitterness towards Adenauer remained in Berlin long after his death: such behaviour seemed to confirm the widely held belief that for him anything east of the River Elbe was Siberia.

Source: O'Dochartaigh, P. 2004. *Germany Since 1945.* Basingstoke, UK. Palgrave Macmillan. p. 71.

Verdict E

"The Resurrection", GDR cartoon.

Source: http://www.calvin.edu/academic/cas/gpa/wind.htm.

Verdict F

CDU A 1957 campaign poster for Konrad Adenauer and the Christian Democratic Union (CDU. The inscription reads *Keine Experimente!* (No experiments!).

Source: Mary Evans Picture Library.

The Verdict on Konrad Adenauer

1 What were Adenauer's greatest achievements?

2 Are criticisms of Adenauer justified?

Spain, 1953–75

In retrospect, 1953 may be seen as the high point of Franco's political career, a moment of triumph with the forces of the Nationalist coalition united around him. Before the end of the decade, whilst his survival could hardly be threatened, he would find himself no longer entirely in control, forced to abandon the Falange and leave the detailed management of economics and, by extension, politics to expert technocrats.

Preston, Paul. 1995. Franco: A Biography. London, UK. Fontana. p. 635.

Why was Spain in crisis by 1957?

By 1953 Franco's position was apparently more secure than at any point in the previous decade. The onset of the Cold War, and in particular its intensification during the Korean War, ended the period of Spain's total international ostracism. In November 1950, Spain received a $62 million loan from the United States as part of the European Co-operation Administration despite not belonging to the Marshall Plan. The 1952 decision to allow Spain membership of UNESCO was followed up in December 1955 with full membership of the United Nations.

Successes in international relations stood in stark contrast to continued economic weaknesses. Per capita meat consumption in 1950 was only half what it had been in 1926 and bread consumption only half what it had been in 1936. Shortages and corruption was so bad that families were forced to pay black market prices double those in the shops. For the very poorest in the south of Spain, conditions were so bad that families, and even whole villages, packed up their belongings and headed to the industrial cities of the north. With nowhere else to live, they built *barracas* (shacks) out of whatever materials they could find. The shanty towns that grew up on the edge of the big cities had no running water or sewerage and it would take years before electricity was provided.

By 1957 the regime was virtually bankrupt, inflation was heading for double figures and there was evidence of serious discontent among students, workers and the younger, more radical, members of the Falange. In addition, in the previous year, Franco, the man who had once dreamed of a great African empire, had been forced to grant independence to Spanish Morocco.

How did Franco stay in power?

Repression and exile continued to be an important means of controlling those on the Left and Franco's Machiavellian balancing of the various conservative interest groups in the government *Movimiento* continued to keep the Right in check. This was increasingly difficult after the international agreements of 1953 when the common foreign enemy which had united the various groups within the Movimiento disappeared. Franco was getting old and showing signs of this. Most of his time was taken up by hunting and fishing trips and spending time with his grandchildren. The political divisions that opened up between the monarchists and the Falange reflected the different competing agendas for Spain after Franco. Franco resolved the problem by bringing a third group, the Opus Dei technocrats, into the political equation that seemed to provide a series of policy solutions to Spain's economic crisis. It also helped that he kept the question of his succession open for as long as possible until he finally named Juan Carlos his heir in 1969.

Franco, ese Hombre, 1964

A hagiographic propaganda film directed by José Luis Sáenz de Heredia and written by José María Sánchez Silva. Described by Paul Preston as a "skilful piece of work", the film portrays Franco as a national saviour, the "man who forged twenty-five years of peace". It was a considerable box office success and still attracts significant viewing figures and pro-Franco comments on YouTube.

Strict control of the media and Falangist propaganda continued to reinforce the regime, but even taken together with coercion, Franco would have had little chance of survival had the 1960s not been characterized by an unprecedented period of economic growth.

Why was there an economic boom in the 1960s?

In February 1957 Franco reshuffled the cabinet and brought in Alberto Ullastres Calvo to lead Spain's Ministry of Commerce, and Mariano Navarro Rubio to take on the finance portfolio: a new breed of technocrats, their key characteristics were their proven ability in academic or professional life and membership of or sympathy with the secretive Catholic sect **Opus Dei**. The Stabilization Plan of 1957 was designed in the short term to tackle inflation and the balance of payments deficit and in the longer term to break with the Falangist policy of autarky, which had so restricted the possibility of economic growth. Public spending was cut, wages frozen, credit restricted and the *peseta* (the Spanish currency) was devalued. The short term economic goals were achieved with the inevitable social costs that result from a dramatic cut in people's real earnings. Unemployment reached nearly 35 per cent in 1959–60. By the early 1960s, the Spanish economy had entered a period of sustained economic growth that at seven per cent per annum was growing faster than any non-Communist economy with the exception of Japan.

For apologists of the regime, the economic growth was the direct beneficial consequence of "Franco's peace" and the Stabilization Plan. But if the Spanish economy made significant progress in the 1960s it was largely because it had a long way to go. Critics draw attention to the fact that the *Desarrollo* (Spanish Miracle) benefited from a wider European boom that largely fuelled the backward

Founded in Spain in 1928 by the priest St. Josemaría Escrivá, **Opus Dei** is an organization within the Catholic Church. In 1960s Spain, Opus Dei tried to address the fact that industrialization and urbanization tends to lead to the growth of liberal ideals and anti-Catholic sentiments. It was argued that if devout Catholics could supervise economic growth, they could control it in order to safeguard Catholic values. In popular imagination Opus Dei is largely associated with the practice of mortification of the flesh and the persona of the evil monk that features in the novel and film The *Da Vinci Code*.

Spanish economy. Foreign investment was attracted by the low cost of labour and the lack of civil rights that the authoritarian regime guaranteed. Northern Europe's expanding middle class provided significant foreign exchange earnings with their spending on package tour holidays on the rapidly developing Spanish Costas. And Spaniards working in the service sector abroad, most of whom were either political or economic exiles, sent home remittances of one third of their earnings to the families left behind. By 1973 there were 750,000 Spaniards working in Germany and France.

By 1964 Spain had ceased to be the on the list of UN-designated "developing nations", and when the *Desarrollo* ended with the world oil crisis of 1973 Spain was the world's ninth biggest industrial power.

Why were the consequences of the economic boom paradoxical?

If the ambition of the Opus Dei technocrats was to secure Franco's authoritarian regime, they were successful in the short-term. The most prominent of the technocrats López Rodó argued that if Spain could achieve a per capita income of $2,000 then social tensions would disappear. During a decade of unprecedented economic growth the number of Spanish homes with washing machines increased from 19 to 52 per cent, those with fridges from four to 66 per cent, and those with cars from one to ten per cent. Average incomes almost tripled during the 1960s, so that López Rodó could boast "never had so much been achieved in short a time."

As with the authoritarian Communist regimes of the Eastern bloc during the same period, economic growth helped to generate both loyalty from a new elite class of administrators who had successfully passed the state examination system (the *oposiciones*) and political indifference among the great majority. The end of shortages and the availability of consumer durables, combined with a culture of evasion to produce the main political objective of the Franco regime— apathy. As literacy levels began to improve, "kiosk literature" and romantic "photo novels" found a

Total Spanish emigration, 1959–76			
Year	Departures	Returns	Balance
1959	55,130	41,309	13,821
1960	73,431	35,308	38,123
1961	115,372	7,815	107,557
1962	142,505	45,844	96,661
1963	134,541	52,230	82,311
1964	192,999	112,871	80,128
1965	181,278	120,678	60,600
1966	141,997	143,082	−1,085
1967	60,000	85,000	−25,000
1968	85,662	67,622	18,000
1969	112,205	43,336	68,869
1970	105,538	40,000	65,674
1971	120,984	60,000	70,348
1972	110,369	70,000	40,369
1973	100,992	110,000	−9,073
1974	55,347	140,000	−84,473
1975	24,477	70,000	−45,485
1976	15,642	70,000	−54,358

Source: Instituto Español del Emigratión.

Television in Franco's Spain

Televisión Española (TVE) was established as a state monopoly in 1956. As with all media it was subject to censorship, attracting a particularly strict form of intervention. Plans for making television programmes had to be approved by an advisory commission made up of officials from the church, the army etc. And before programmes could be aired they were previewed by a censor who would require cuts to be made.

Cuts were likely to be made for political or moral reasons. The Billy Wilder film, *The Lost Weekend*, for example, was censored by a Dominican monk who ordered the following to be cut:

1 The kiss at point of farewell

2 When he steals the woman's handbag, eliminate the shots in which she and her companion behave with excessive affection.

3 Kiss and conversation while holding one another.
   Temper the kiss.

The same censor also recommended changes to a French comedy film because it ridiculed the Gestapo and Hitler.

ready mass market. Spain in the 1950s had more cinema seats per capita than any other European country, and this was followed by the massive influential state controlled television which reached 90 per cent of the population by 1970, compared to just one per cent a decade before.

Football offered a similar means of escape and was fully exploited by the regime. Its popularity was enhanced by the success of the national team in the 1964 UEFA European Nations Cup and Real Madrid who were European Cup finalists on eight occasions in the period 1956–66, and six times winners. As football-loving Franco asserted, with Match of the Day and TV most of my subjects "have nothing to complain of".

One of the most significant economic consequences of the *Desarrollo* was the increased gap between the richest provinces of the north and the poorer south. Provinces such as Badajoz and Granada had per capita incomes well under half of the Basque province of Vizcaya. By 1970, 70 per cent of homes in Madrid had television sets, compared to only 11 per cent in Soria. A second significant consequence was the rapid urbanization of Spain. In 1940, half of the active population had worked on the land, by the time of Franco's death the Spanish were largely city dwellers with a similar percentage of agricultural workers as their French neighbours.

The Real Madrid team line up before the Champions League Final football match against Eintracht Frankfurt at Hampden Park, Glasgow, Scotland in 1960.

Did Franco fix the 1968 Eurovision Song Contest?

After negotiations to join the European Community collapsed in 1962, Franco's Spain depended on cultural outlets like sport to bolster its international status. Unexpected victory in the 1968 Eurovision song contest served a similar function. A documentary from 2008 by the Spanish film-maker Montse Fernandez Vila claimed that Franco had the voting rigged. She argues:

> the regime was well aware of the need to improve its image overseas … When you look at all the parties they organised and how Massiel was transformed into a national heroine, you realise it was rather over the top for a singing competition. It was all intended to boost the regime.

Source: http://www.guardi an.co.uk/music/2008/may/06/news.spain.

It could be argued that the economic growth designed to protect Franco's regime, undermined the very social structure and cultural mindset that helped create the regime. Falangist's had glorified the peasant farmer and traditional class structure of southern Spain, but the urbanization of the *Desarrollo* did much to destroy this. Falangist propaganda may have denigrated the moral turpitude of the liberal democracies but Spain's economic revival depended on the remittances of Spaniards living in these democracies. These Spaniards generally came back home eventually, bring with them dangerous liberal ideas and attitudes. Education reform had a similar effect. The modernization of the Spanish economy required the young to be better educated than ever before, but by the late 1960s a radical Marxist subculture had emerged in the universities. Perhaps the best illustration of the paradoxical consequences of the Franco economic reforms was the policy to encourage tourism after 1959, the year when visas were abolished. The tourist boom was essential to the Spanish economic miracle, but it was not only made possible by the unrestricted development of the Costas, but also by a willingness to accept the liberal mores of the northern European holiday makers whose presence and example was an anathema to the values of traditional Catholic Spain.

It has been argued that the economic transformation of Spain in the 1960s made the peaceful transition to democracy possible. This suggests that Opus Dei failed in its ambition to protect traditional Catholic interests in Spain. But what was the alternative? Would Franco's regime have survived as long as it did without the economic transformation? This is the paradox. The dictatorship only survived by overseeing the social, economic and (importantly) cultural transformation of Spain that meant that the dictatorship was unlikely to survive Franco's death.

> **TOK Link**
> **Ways of Knowing—Language**
> **Different ways of writing history:**
> **Did the Bikini save Spain?**
>
> In 1959 the Mayor of Benidorm on the Costa del Sol, Pedro Zaragoza, was threatened with excommunication by the Catholic Church for signing a municipal order that allowed the wearing of the fashionable two-piece swimsuit, the bikini. In 1950s Spain excommunication meant the end of a person's career. After a nine-hour Vespa ride to Madrid and an audience with Franco, Zaragoza secured the support of the Caudillo and the patronage of Franco's wife Carmen Polo, who later became a regular visitor to Benidorm. The excommunication process was dropped. The bikini stayed.
>
> > *Some see this, at least symbolically, as a defining moment in recent Spanish history … The tourists had the power to outface the Church. They brought not just their money, but the seeds of change. They also brought the fresh air of democracy. There was no turning back … General Franco was there at the key moment. Without the bikini there, quite possibly, would have been no modern Benidorm and, in fact, precious little tourism at all.*
>
> **Source:** Giles Tremlett, G. 2007. "How the Bikini saved Spain". *Ghosts of Spain: Travels Through a Country's Hidden Past*. London, UK. Faber and Faber. p. 103.
>
>
>
> **Discussion**
>
> 1 Giles Tremlett is a journalist for *The Guardian*. Why is the story of Pedro Zaragoza's nine-hour Vespa ride to Madrid so central to Tremlett's account? How else might you expect his account to be different to that of a professional historian?
>
> 2 Which is the more significant turning point in Spanish history: Franco's decision to allow bikinis on the beaches of Spain or his decision to reshuffle his cabinet in 1957? How did you reach your decision?

What is Franco's legacy?

> [Franco is] a complete cynic, interested only in keeping power as long as he lives, and indifferent to what may happen after he dies. He is said to keep folders on his desk, one marked "problems which time will solve" and the other "problems which time has solved", his favourite task being, it is said, to transfer papers from one folder to the other".
>
> Sir Ivo Mallet, British Ambassador to Spain, 1956.

When Franco died in 1975 Spain stood alone in Western Europe as the only remaining authoritarian regime that owed it origins to pre-war fascism. As we have seen, in many respects Spain had been radically transformed. But for all the social and economic changes, the state and laws were fundamentally unchanged from the system established at the end of the civil war. Franco remained head of state until his death and was also Prime Minister until 1972. Politically, the Organic Law of 1967 extended participation in the political system, but was still overwhelmingly focused on the *Cortes* representing not political parties but interest groups drawn from the monarchists, the army, the church and the Falange. In 1967, Franco warned reformist elements who were to succeed in introducing limited liberalization of the press that "If by contrast of opinions somebody is seeking to establish political parties, let him know *that* will never return."

In addition to this anti-democratic legacy, the Spanish state in the early 1970s clearly reflected the deeply conservative influence of Franco. Women in Franco's Spain, for example, were legally second class citizens. Among European states only Turkey had a comparable degree of institutionalized discrimination against married women and on several counts the status of wives in Turkey was actually higher. The basis of the relationship between men and women was the concept of *permiso marital*. Without her husband's permission, a wife could not, for example, take a job, open a bank account or even travel any significant distance. Married women did not have rights to property, passing everything on to their husbands. And although adultery was a crime punishable for both men and women with up to six years in prison, it was generally only a crime for men if the affair became public knowledge. In addition, there was no divorce in Franco's Spain and contraception was illegal.

Perhaps the legacy that was to have the most lasting influence on Spain at the end of the 20th century was Franco's resistance to political devolution to the national regions of Spain, most notably the Catalans and the Basques (see map of Spain on p. 267). For Franco, the devolution of power to the regions by the Second Republic of the 1930s was one of the very reasons why the army had felt the need to launch a coup d' état in 1936. Along with socialists and communists, the regional nationalists would have no place in Franco's Spain. Strict restrictions on the national languages of Catalan, Basque, Gallego etc. were only gradually lifted after 1945 and remained in place on radio, television and in the press until Franco's death. However, by the late 1960s, protest against the suppression of regionalism was on the rise. In Catalonia this protest was largely expressed peacefully through cultural means. In the Basque country protest became associated with the terrorist group **ETA** which soon became caught up in a spiral of retaliatory violence which continues to the present day.

Franco's last years were marked by rapidly declining health and a jostling for position among the Franco factions: the *búnker* (far-right) who resisted all reform and the *aperturistas* who promoted a transition to democracy to ensure their own survival. Admiral Luis Carrero Blanco, Franco's loyal deputy became increasingly responsible for the day to day management of the country and resorted to increasingly authoritarian measures to combat the effects of the world oil crisis and the unprecedented unrest from students, workers and Basque nationalists. Increasing criticism from the

ETA short for *Euskadi Ta Askatasuna* (Basque Homeland and Freedom) is dedicated to achieving independence for the Basque country. ETA began its terrorist campaign in the late 1960s and despite the transition to democracy and the granting of significant regional autonomy, ETA continued its campaign against the Spanish state. In the late 1970s and early 1980s as many as a hundred people were killed every year in ETA attacks. The influence of the group has gradually declined since the 1990s and in March 2006 it declared a permanent ceasefire. But the peace talks failed, and ETA ended its ceasefire in June 2007. On the 50th anniversary of the founding of ETA in July 2009, an attack that killed two Guardia Civil officers in Majorca brought the total number of ETA killings to 828. At the same time there were more than 500 ETA prisoners in Spanish jails.

Catholic Church was matched with international condemnation of the "Burgos Trials" of ETA members and show trials of underground trade unionists. After the assassination of Carrero-Blanco in December 1973, Carlos Arias Navarro became Prime Minister but little substantive could be achieved given the divisions within the cabinet and Franco's regular hospitalization. Franco's last significant action was to confirm five death sentences for ETA members in the face of worldwide diplomatic protests led by Pope Paul VI. He died on

Luis Carrero-Blanco (1903–1973)

A graduate of the Escuela Naval Militar, the Spanish Naval Academy in Galicia, Luis Carrero-Blanco became chief of naval operations from the start of Franco's rule, and remained one of the General's closet collaborators. He was said to be in opposition to Spain entering the Second World War on the side of the Axis powers, a notably different political position compared to some other Falangists. A monarchist, and devotee of the Catholic Church, he was also close to Opus Dei. In politics, he was a hardliner, famously boasting "To offer change to a Spaniard is like offering a drink to a confirmed alcoholic." Franco's alter ego, he was appointed Prime Minister in June 1973. His assassination by ETA in December of the same year led Franco to lament, "they have cut my last link with the world". It also seriously undermined Franco's attempts to ensure the continuation of regime after his death.

20 November 1975, exactly 39 years to the day after the death of José Antonio Primo de Rivera the founder of the Falange. Franco is buried opposite Primo de Rivera at the *Valle de los Caídos*.

Activity:

Essay skills: Making judgements

The IB examiners like to set essay questions where students are expected to evaluate and analyse the rule of the leader of a single-party state over a significant period of time. Typically you might be invited to:

"Assess the aims and achievements of Franco between 1939 and 1975."

The practical problem is how to answer such a big question in the 50 minutes allowed for HL essays. Planning and selection of relevant supporting information are the keys to success. The question needs to be broken up both temporally and thematically.

Temporally, the essay must recognize that the aims of Franco the general at the end of the Second World War were not identical to those of the aging *Caudillo* in 1969. Thematically, the essay must make judgements based on criteria that incorporate political, economic, social and cultural aspects of Spain during this period.

A successful essay must therefore break-up Franco's regime into manageable periods while making judgements on its successes and failures. It requires carefully selected examples to illustrate and support the points being made.

The ethical problems of making a judgment

The great English social historian E.P. Thompson was famous for urging historians to judge people in the past on their own terms, therefore avoiding "the enormous condescension of posterity". If we are to judge Franco on the terms of his aims alone we cannot help but conclude that in terms of his ability to stay in power, Franco's achievement was remarkable. But Franco's aims were also to resist democracy, punish dissent and subjugate women.

 Is the fact that he achieved these aims to be judged a success?

As historian Paul Preston, concludes, there are other ground for judgement in evaluating the " human cost in terms of the executions, the imprisonments, the torture, the lives destroyed by political exile and economic migration points to the exorbitant price paid by Spain for Franco's 'Triumphs'."

Unifying Europe

Western Europe's "golden age" of economic growth came to an end during the 1970s for a number of reasons. Increased global competition from the Far East cut into Western Europe's share of world exports. The "oil shocks"—substantial increases in the price of oil in 1973 and 1981 distorted the balance of payments for non-oil producers, forcing states to reduce imports and hindering global trade. Economic stagnation and higher unemployment were coupled with the inflationary rise in oil prices to produce the new phenomenon of "stagflation". Meanwhile, the slower birth rates of these years led to pessimistic projections of social welfare costs.

Under these strains the Western European political consensus began to break. The application of **monetarist** economic theory, in which unemployment could be tolerated as a weapon to contain inflation, was pursued with particular enthusiasm in Britain. To politicians on the Right, such as the British Prime Minister Margaret Thatcher, it was the interventionist state itself which disrupted the natural efficiency of free markets and impeded economic growth. Economic polarization—a widening gap between the richest and the poorest—was experienced in many countries including the United Kingdom, but not Germany. Heavy industry declined in relative size and importance to other (technological, service) sectors of the economy and accelerated the fragmentation of the traditional unionized working class. At the same time, greater social and geographical mobility broke traditional "tribal" political allegiances and challenged political parties to seek new methods of attracting support.

European states had welcomed mass immigration during the boom years to make up the labour shortage, but as jobs became scarce there was an increase in racial tension and indeed violence, encouraged by overtly racist political parties. The role of women continued to develop as the greater numbers of women in employment asserted demands for equality. The legalization of abortion was achieved in Germany in 1975 and Spain in 1985. Growing evidence of environmental degradation led to the emergence of Green politics, with the Green Party in Germany achieving electoral successes in the 1980s.

Western European states faced the onslaught of violent terrorist organizations during these decades. ETA in Spain carried out a campaign of murder and bombing in the name of Basque nationalism. In West Germany, the extreme Left **Red Army Faction/Baader-Meinhof Gang** attacked the state for ideological reasons.

Western Europe remained dependent on the United States for its defence, and it was through NATO that military security was maintained. The 1970s saw a relaxation of Cold War tensions. The German version of détente was to pursue the *Ostpolitik* strategy of Willy Brandt and establish relations with the GDR. The superpowers

---

Monetarism – an economic theory that emphasizes the importance of controlling the supply of money to achieve the low inflation necessary for growth and stability.

The **Red Army Faction/Baader-Meinhof Gang**—a terrorist group, active during the 1960s and 70s—aimed to undermine the West German state and the capitalist economy through campaigns of arson, kidnapping and murder. The group's ill-defined motivations stemmed in part from a generational divide between post-war youths frustrated at their elders' perceived failure to confront Nazism or to deal honestly with the legacy of National Socialism. Andreas Baader and Ulrike Meinhof were arrested in 1972, but a dwindling band of supporters continued their sociopathic war on the state with sporadic acts of violence in the following years. The group's activities resulted in at least 28 deaths of soldiers, businessmen, policemen and civilians and provoked the Brandt government into enacting the *Berufsverbot* in 1972, a law which barred from state employment any individual engaged in anti-constitutional political activity. The group received financial and logistical assistance from the East German secret services but the "masses" whom the terrorists may have hoped to inspire to revolution were emphatically not inclined to support Baader-Meinhof's delusional fantasies

reached agreements on arms reduction, and through the Helsinki Agreements of 1975 accepted each other's spheres of influence, recognized borders, and established international standards of human rights—on paper at least.

European Integration

The project of European integration has advanced unevenly, with periods of great activism in broadening (accepting new members) and penetrating (increasing the co-ordination of policies, laws, and economies) interspersed with periods when progress has stalled. Supporters of a closer union have likened the project to a bicycle; it must keep moving forward or it will fall. It can, however, only progress by maintaining the support of the member governments, each of which in turn must maintain the support of their voters. The European Community has sought to develop a clearer democratic mandate for its institutions through the introduction of direct voting to the European Parliament from 1979. This assembly has only gradually assumed powers from the unelected European Commission, and elections are notable for their low voter participation and being contested on narrow nationalist agendas. The blocks of like-minded parties that constitute the European Parliament are a long way from forming any genuinely pan-European political parties. The size of the project, which at an economic level allows great economies of scale, at a political level has often led to unsatisfactory complexity. However, whatever weaknesses this system has, it should be remembered that it has helped Europe achieve an extended period of peace in which conflict between members is resolved by negotiation rather than violence.

The Common Agricultural Policy (CAP) has been representative of some defining aspects of European integration. The CAP established a system of subsidies and protection for food producers. It guaranteed minimum prices for farmers, funded investment, and encouraged increases in production. However, the policy has been expensive, sometimes corrupt, with funds being transferred from European taxpayers to farmers in member states with large agricultural sectors, mainly France. Consumers also endure higher food prices while producers in developing countries face trade barriers and the dumping of surplus production on their domestic markets.

The policy represented a compromise between German industry which was allowed access to French markets in return for German financial support for French farmers. The higher ideal of Franco-German partnership could be served and at the same time France could use its leading role to shape policy in the French national interest. Given Europe's troubled history, no reasonable observer could oppose the reconciliation of France and Germany but the process has at times exposed divisions between European states. For British politicians, having missed the chance to participate from the start, there was a sense of frustration as European integration developed without British influence. The finalization of the CAP and the equally controversial Common Fisheries Policy (CFP) immediately prior to UK entry significantly raised the price of membership.

The short-term financial benefit which France could squeeze from the outcast British *demandeurs* must be balanced against the negative effect the resulting longer term discord had on the loftier notions of the European project.

UK entry to the EEC was achieved at the third attempt in 1973, by which time De Gaulle had died and the UK was led by a committed pro-European Prime Minister, Edward Heath. Heath's election defeat in 1974 brought the more sceptical Harold Wilson to power at the head of a Labour Party that remained divided on the issue of Europe. The following year, in a referendum to decide whether the United Kingdom should remain part of the European Community, British voters responded 2:1 in favour. However, this did not bring an end to the European argument within British politics. The particular problem with the European issue is that the argument cut across party lines with advocates and opponents on both sides. Margaret Thatcher (Prime Minister, 1979–90) took reluctant steps towards Europe, signing the Single European Act in 1985, but indulged in increasingly anti-Europe rhetoric culminating in her Bruges speech of 1988 in which she declared that her Government had "not successfully rolled back the frontiers of the state in Britain only to see them reimposed at a European level." This association of Europe with socialist themes such as state intervention contrasts with the mistrust of earlier Labour Governments. The UK continues to be dogged by an inconsistent attitude to European integration. Margaret Thatcher's hostility towards the pro-European wing of the Conservative Party was a factor in her downfall in 1990.

John Major (Prime Minister, 1990–97) pursued a moderately pro-European policy but faced opposition from Eurosceptics within the Conservative Party. The Major Government ratified the Treaty of Maastricht in 1992 which introduced the rebranded European Union to establish European citizenship, increase the powers of the European Parliament, and create a European Central Bank. The Social Chapter guaranteed workers' rights including minimum holiday entitlements, right to free association in trade unions, health and safety standards, but saw John Major negotiate to opt out of this clause. German participation was more wholehearted, with the German Chancellor Helmut Kohl, giving the endorsement: "At Maastricht we laid the foundation stone for the completion of the European Union. … which within a few years will lead to the creation of what the founding fathers of modern Europe dreamed of after the last war: the United States of Europe."

A prominent pillar of integration throughout this period has been European Monetary Union (EMU). The stability of the Bretton Woods system of exchange rates fixed against the dollar which had lasted until 1971, had contributed to the successful growth of European economies. The collapse of that system and the ensuing disruptive fluctuations of Europe's currencies encouraged EC member states to establish co-coordinated monetary policies. The Exchange Rate Mechanism (ERM) fixed exchange rates between European currencies but devaluations continued caused by governments seeking to redress trade imbalances and boost employment, and by speculators wary of artificially over-priced currencies. The final expression of EMU, the introduction of the single currency (the Euro) in 1999 has provided stability and clarity to member states' economies, but not all members' economies were judged ready to join the "Eurozone". Others, such as the UK, preferred to retain national control over their currencies. The different speeds at which member states have adopted such new projects has led to a situation tolerated as the "variable geometry" of Europe.

Despite these difficulties, the European Community expanded to include Greece in 1981, and Spain and Portugal in 1986. Moves to deepen political integration were more problematic, but the European Community endured as a force of stability while the opposing Eastern bloc crumbled. It was this collapse of the Soviet Empire from 1989 that ended Europe's division; bringing East and West back together and facilitating German reunification in 1990. The historical fears aroused by this were given expression by Margaret Thatcher who reportedly told a former German ambassador it would be "at least another 40 years before the British could trust the Germans again." This characteristically British invocation of the Second World War effectively ignored the Community's achievement in preventing the development of "a German Europe" by nurturing "a European Germany". For the newly free countries of Eastern Europe, the European Union became something to aspire to, a guarantor of stability in a turbulent era. Moreover, the expansion to include these countries created new alignments and diluted the ability of any one member to dominate. In the final decade of the century, the EU faced a series of challenges. The end of the Cold War removed one of the external reasons for the EU's existence, reducing the grand vision to a narrower pursuit of commercial advantage. Likewise, the war in Yugoslavia exposed the EU's inability to pursue an effective, co-ordinated foreign policy.

Difficulties remain for the EU in its efforts to retain the consent of its citizens. Well-intentioned critics of the EU are often marginalized by a political correctness which categorizes them with the less reasonable nationalist groups throughout Europe opposed to any form of international co-operation. A persistent criticism remains that the EU has removed power from nation states to a remote, centralized and undemocratic centre, diminishing national sovereignty. However, this argument ignores the multiple ways in which national sovereignty is compromised in a globalized world of overlapping alliances, multinational companies and mass communications, in which markets hold sway over government policy. Others argue that Europe's nations are being forced to conform to a bland Europe-wide culture, imposed from above. However, at a cultural level, France remains as distinctly French as it ever was—the EU has not eroded the essential characteristics of Bordeaux and Blackpool. Where culture has been internationalized it has been as much a result of an enthusiastic consumption of America's cultural output as anything emitting from Brussels.

Key dates in European integration	
1973	The UK, Denmark and Ireland join the European Community (EC)
1979	The European Monetary System (EMS) is established. A step towards a common currency in which member states (not including the UK) agreed to maintain the value of national currencies against a notional European Currency Unit (ECU)
1979	The first direct elections to the European Parliament
1981	Greece becomes the tenth EC member
1985	The Single European Act moves towards the completion of a common market. The Schengen Agreement abolishes passport controls and opens borders between France, Germany, Belgium, the Netherlands and Luxembourg. Other European countries have since joined the Schengen group, but not the UK
1986	Spain and Portugal join the EC
1991	The Treaty of Maastricht. The EC becomes the European Union (EU). The Treaty sets out a timetable towards monetary union. European citizens gain freedoms to live and work throughout the EU
1995	Austria, Finland and Sweden join the EU
1999	Introduction of the Euro

Germany, 1970–2000

What factors led to the reunification of Germany in 1990?

German reunification formally took place on 3 October 1990, following a year of revolutionary change in Europe. The tectonic plates of the Cold War blocs which had ground against each other for four decades had suddenly slipped, altering the political landscape at a speed which challenged the efforts of policy makers to steer the course of events. Reunification was only possible following Mikhail Gorbachev's reforms in the Soviet Union. However, the nature of the reunification process, the speed with which it occurred, its acceptability to the international community, and its desirability to German voters were also based on the relationship between the two Germanys and the development of each state in the late Cold War era.

Ostpolitik

Willy Brandt as Chancellor (1969–74) sought a fresh approach to West German foreign policy. Adenauer's hard line non-recognition of East Germany was abandoned in favour of a more open relationship. Brandt was able to pursue this *Ostpolitik* (Eastern Policy) in the period of Cold

Extended discussion point:

Sometimes I like to compare the EU as a creation to the organisation of empires. We have the dimension of Empire but there is a great difference. Empires were usually made with force with a centre imposing diktat, a will on the others. Now what we have is the first non-imperial empire.

J.M. Barroso, EU Commission President, 11 July 2007.

The European Community was a heroic endeavour, undertaken against great odds, which built a record of assisting peace and prosperity among European nations that has not been surpassed.

Source: Young, H. 1999. *This Blessed Plot: Britain and Europe, from Churchill to Blair.* Woodstock, NY, USA. Overlook Press. p. 106.

1 Have the aims of the European Union changed since its establishment?

2 What are the advantages and disadvantages of EU membership?

3 Helmut Kohl described the creation of a United States of Europe as an entirely positive ambition. Do you agree?

4 To what extent is the EU a "non-Imperial Empire"?

War **détente** as both superpowers sought to reduce tension and stabilize the situation in Europe. *Ostpolitik* can therefore be seen as a German version of détente. In practical terms *Ostpolitik* led to the signing of a series of treaties with Russia (the Moscow Treaty, 1970), and with Poland (the Warsaw Treaty, 1970), in which participants agreed to the renunciation of force and recognition of existing borders, in particular Poland's western border with Germany (the Oder-Neisse Line). In Warsaw Brandt visited the site of the 1943 Jewish Warsaw Ghetto Uprising and spontaneously knelt in front of the monument there—an iconic gesture of repentance.

Willy Brandt (1913–1992)

Willy Brandt became a Socialist as a teenager. He opposed Nazism and escaped to Norway and then Sweden to avoid arrest when the Nazis came to power in 1933. Returning to Germany after the Second World War, he rose through the ranks of the SPD (Social Democratic Party), becoming Mayor of West Berlin in 1957. He was influential in the modernization of the SPD, broadening the Party's appeal while remaining true to his principles.

In 1969, he became Chancellor of the FRG—the first SPD Chancellor since 1930—and in 1972 he was re-elected with an increased share of the vote. In 1974 it was revealed that Günther Guillame, a close advisor of Brandt's, was an agent of the East German secret police, the Stasi. Brandt shouldered the blame for the scandal and resigned. He was replaced by fellow Social Democrat Helmut Schmidt. In his five years as Chancellor, Brandt had continued Adenauer's work in consolidating a strong, democratic state and set West Germany's foreign policy on a new course. Brandt was awarded the Nobel Peace Prize in 1971 for his success in establishing more positive relations with Eastern Europe.

The 1972 Basic Treaty with East Germany recognized the existence of two states without rejecting the desirability of unification at some unspecified future date. In Brandt's words, they were "two states, one nation". In the meantime the two Germanys agreed to co-exist within their unique circumstances, to exchange "representatives" (significantly not "ambassadors"), to ease travel restrictions for West Berliners, and to accept the post-war status quo of European borders. The Basic Treaty was accompanied by the following letter:

Détente is the relaxation of tension between countries.

> The Federal Minister Without Portfolio in the Office of the Federal Chancellor Bonn, December 21, 1972
>
> To the
> State Secretary of the Council of Ministers
> of the German Democratic Republic
> Dr. Michael Kohl
> Berlin
>
> Dear Herr Kohl,
> In connection with today's signing of the Treaty concerning the Basis of Relations between the Federal Republic of Germany and the German Democratic Republic, the Government of the Federal Republic of Germany has the honour to state that this Treaty does not conflict with the political aim of the Federal Republic of Germany to work for a state of peace in Europe in which the German nation will regain its unity through free self-determination.
>
> Very respectfully yours,
> Bahr [West German Foreign Minister]

 How would you expect Brandt's supporters and opponents to interpret

The Bulletin, vol. 20, n. 38. Published by the Press and Information Office of the Federal Government (Bundespresseamt), Bonn. © Press and Information Office of the Federal Government (Bundespresseamt).

Opponents within Germany saw *Ostpolitik* as a means of formalizing Germany's division and therefore postponing unification. To these critics it was paradoxical to suggest that the way to achieve one state was first to recognize two. The dubious legitimacy of the East German regime was offered recognition from the West, undermining potential opposition within East Germany. The concessions on travel and cultural links were criticized as merely making division palatable. Economic links developed over the following years, in which the West repeatedly loaned money to the East thereby propping up the GDR regime. A trade developed in which the West German government would pay the GDR to secure the release of dissident prisoners, creating incentives for further arrests.

7 December 1970: West German Chancellor Willy Brandt kneels in front of the Jewish Heroes monument paying tribute to Jews killed by the Nazis during the 1943 uprising in the Warsaw Ghetto in Poland.

The fact of reunification has since vindicated *Ostpolitik*, but there was nothing inevitable about this development and claims for direct causality are undermined by assessments made pre1990 which saw reunification as improbable. Brandt himself, in 1988, described calls for German unity as the "life lie" of West German politics. East German leader, Erich Honecker, felt confident enough to remark as late as January 1989 that "The Berlin Wall will be standing in 50 or even 100 years." These remarks came after two decades of peaceful co-existence during which priorities had adjusted and opinion polls showed that reunification had slipped from being the most important issue for 45 per cent of West Germans in the 1950s and 60s to less than one per cent in the 1970s.

How far do you agree that the Basic Treaty did not "conflict with the political aim of the Federal Republic of Germany to work for a state of peace in Europe in which the German nation would regain its unity through free self-determination"?

Brandt's justification of his policy was based on realism, warning opponents that "patriotism must be based on what is attainable". Division was a result of Germany's war and could not be wished away but in small practical steps the effects of division could be modified. The borders could not be changed but perhaps the quality of the borders could; cultural, economic, institutional, personal links could be nurtured and a form of German unity sustained beyond the narrow political definition. In the long term, *Ostpolitik* made German unity seem a less threatening prospect to the Soviet Union. Without peace, acceptance of the reality of the situation, and the sincere renunciation of violence, reunification could not have occurred. *Ostpolitik* was a new phase of German foreign policy but once established, the practical, step by step, "no surprises" style carried out within Cold War constraints, was pursued with consistency by Brandt's successors. This approach brought stability to a potentially volatile area and above all avoided another European war.

In 1973 both Germanys were accepted as member states of the United Nations. At the 1974 World Cup, for the only time, East and West Germany played each other in a professional football match. East Germany won 1–0, although it was West Germany who eventually won the tournament providing ammunition for politicians on both sides who like to use sport as evidence of societal superiority. In 1975 both signed the Helsinki Treaty on the post-war settlement and on human rights. The East German regime and their Soviet masters appeared to have got what they wanted, however, the Helsinki Treaty opened up a new avenue of legalistic opposition within the Soviet bloc from dissident groups seeking to expose their governments' failures to uphold the environmental and human rights commitments. The treaties and agreements could not change the essential vulnerability of the East German regime, the existence of which ultimately depended on a permanent Soviet military presence.

On 30 May 1970, the Federation of Expellees (a group which represented West Germany's approximately eight million refugees) organized a demonstration to protest against Brandt's *Ostpolitik* in Bonn; the event drew 50,000 protesters. The banner in the background reads, "Whoever recognizes violence loses peace"; the one in front of the podium reads "The recognition of the Oder–Neiße Line is a crime against Germany." Three small posters underneath it read: "Divided 3 times? Never!"

 How could Brandt defend his Ostpolitik to these critics?

Cold War renewed

Brandt's successor as Chancellor, Helmut Schmidt (1974–82) stuck to *Ostpolitik*. However, the twin strategies of keeping West Germany firmly anchored in the Western Alliance and maintaining good relations with Moscow and the GDR came under pressure as Cold War détente gave away to renewed superpower hostility. In 1976, the Soviet Union began deploying SS-20 intermediate range nuclear missiles in Europe. Schmidt supported the NATO "dual track" response involving the counter-deployment of similar weapons in West Germany and at the same time proposing arms reduction talks. Germans on both sides of the Cold War front line had more reason than most to fear nuclear escalation and this predicament united all Germans in a shared sense of heightened vulnerability. In the West, to Honecker's satisfaction, anti-nuclear peace groups grew rapidly, often to the bemusement of those East Europeans such as Václav Havel who observed that "'peace' is not an option in countries where the state is permanently at war with society". The suggestion that such activists were naive was given weight by the later revelations that the **Stasi** had thoroughly penetrated Western anti-nuclear groups. However, the protests encouraged East German peace groups to similar acts of opposition and their ensuing oppression exposed the GDR regime's hypocrisy. This renewed Cold War hostility destabilized

Activity:

Class debate
"Ostpolitik hindered Reunification" vs. "Ostpolitik helped Reunification".

The **Stasi** (from "**Sta**atssicherseit") were the East German secret police. The Stasi motto, "the Sword and Shield of the Party" rather than "of the people", made its intentions clear.

West Germany to the extent that it split Schmidt's SPD; the left wing of the Party was sufficiently attached to the idea of non-nuclear purity that many joined the emerging Green Party. However, West German democracy was resilient enough to overcome such divisions. On the other side of the iron curtain, the Soviet system was being stretched to the limit to keep up with the US in an accelerated arms race.

Cold War relations deteriorated further with the Soviet invasion of Afghanistan in 1979. West Germany struggled to hold onto the advantages of détente, declining to impose sanctions on the Soviet Union. The ultimate failure of the Afghanistan Campaign revealed Moscow's weakness, inflamed Islamic opposition, and brought the collapse of Soviet Communism a step closer. The West German response to Solidarity's achievements in challenging the Polish regime in 1980–81 exposed further strains. Willy Brandt voiced his suspicion of what was seen as an unpredictable nationalist movement and Helmut Schmidt declined to criticize the Polish Government's imposition of martial law in December 1981. Schmidt's government seemed more concerned with maintaining stability than encouraging the self-determination of Eastern Europeans. Was this further evidence of wise caution in West Germany's foreign policy, or an example of *Ostpolitik* degenerating into appeasement? At the very least, Germany's unique historical journey had led to some awkward contradictions in foreign policy.

Economic Disparity

The GDR was the only Eastern bloc state with a Western *Doppelgänger*, sharing its language and history. As a result, comparisons were unavoidable and the economic disparity between the two Germanys was a source of embarrassment to the GDR regime which routinely manipulated economic statistics to disguise their weakness. To the frustration of the impoverished people, high quality imported goods were available only to those few with access to western currency. This coupled with the denial of the basic right to express criticism of the regime and restrictions on travel generated widespread dissatisfaction. East Germans could make their own comparisons while watching West German television or while driving the East German Trabant—a sub-standard car that came to symbolize material disadvantage. When political changes elsewhere eventually allowed for free movement, the people of the East voted with their feet, heading west in their thousands to a West German state that was constitutionally bound to offer them full citizenship.

West Germany's economic progress, however, was not without its problems. The disruption to the global economy following the sharp increase in oil prices in 1973 brought the "golden age" of post-war economic growth to an end. The SPD/FDP coalition government steered the economy into temporary recovery but the results of a further slowdown following a second oil shock in the early 1980s divided Chancellor Schmidt's government. In 1982 the FDP deserted the coalition, offering its support to a new government with the CDU/CSU under Helmut Kohl's leadership. The economy again recovered, recording steady growth rates through the 1980s, but unemployment remained high and social welfare provision was cut back.

Discussion point:

Why did the Solidarity movement and the crisis in Poland seem threatening to some West German politicians?

 To what extent was West German foreign policy contradictory?

Despite these difficulties, West Germany's economy performed better than that of competitors such as the UK. Meanwhile, the GDR struggled from crisis to crisis. Honecker's regime spent heavily on housing, welfare and the provision of consumer goods but could not match the material wealth of West Germany. These increasing expenditure demands had to be sustained while earnings from the exports of East Germany's inefficient industries fell. By the 1980s, the GDR had become financially dependent on loans from West Germany. As the East German currency weakened against the Deutschmark, it became more difficult to pay the interest on these loans. The GDR was heading towards bankruptcy.

The Soviet Union

In 1985, Mikhail Gorbachev came to power in the Soviet Union. He acknowledged the mistakes of his predecessors and the comparative economic failure of the Soviet Union. Gorbachev called for economic *perestroika* (restructuring), a relaxation of central planning and the introduction of market forces, along with political *glasnost* (openness), a willingness to discuss mistakes and allow the expression of alternative ideas. These reformist ideas were rejected by the GDR regime which remained committed to orthodox Communist ideas. As the East German government minister Kurt Hager stated in 1987, "If your neighbor re-wallpapered his apartment, would you feel obliged to do the same?" Even more threatening to the GDR regime was Gorbachev's rejection of the Brezhnev Doctrine by which the Soviet Union had reserved the right to intervene in its satellite states to uphold Communist rule as it had done in East Berlin in 1953, Hungary in 1956 and Czechoslovakia in 1968. This was replaced by the "Sinatra Doctrine" by which each satellite state was free to "do it their way". Honecker could no longer rely on the Soviet military to guarantee his regime. As the year progressed, Poland elected a non-Communist leader and the reformist regime in Hungary opened its border with Austria. Thousands of East Germans took the opportunity to flee to the West. A domino effect rippled across Eastern Europe as the failures of each Communist regime weakened its neighbours. The accessibility of instant television images undermined Party efforts to control information and played a role in encouraging individuals to seize the moment.

Internal protests

Even more threatening to the GDR regime than the numbers fleeing west were the growing protests by those who remained. Every Monday, throughout the autumn, demonstrators gathered in East German cities demanding reform and greater freedoms.
The individuals involved took part despite the threat of violent police intervention of the kind seen in Beijing's Tiananmen Square in June 1989. Groups such as "New Forum" formed to co-ordinate the protestors' demands presented a challenge to the Communist right to monopoly rule. Initially the protestors demanded reforms within the GDR; only later, following the fall of the Wall, would calls for reunification predominate.

The weakness of the GDR leadership

The GDR regime had followed Moscow's line for 40 years but Gorbachev's reforms threw Honecker's government into confusion and divisions emerged. The Party belatedly attempted reform; Egon Krenz replaced Honecker on 18 October. In what Pol O' Dochartaigh describes as *"a sad testament to Honecker's Marxist discipline … he also voted for his own removal, so that the decision would be, as usual, unanimous."* The regime was clearly struggling to hold on, but the breaching of the Berlin Wall on 9 November still came as a surprise. An announcement that travel restrictions would be lifted immediately resulted in thousands of citizens flocking to the Wall, demanding the right to cross. The guards stood aside and the people were free to come and go. Within hours people were singing and dancing on the Wall, passing through, or physically attacking the Wall with hammers and pick axes. The authority of the GDR regime had emphatically collapsed.

Erich Honecker and Mikhail Gorbachev at the GDR's 40th Anniversary Celebration (October 7, 1989). During this visit Gorbachev warned Honecker that reform was necessary to survive.

Reunification

It is important to acknowledge the unexpectedness of the events of 1989–90. As has been noted above, even influential figures such as Willy Brandt and Erich Honecker did not predict such rapid change. Kohl's 10-point plan of 28 November 1989 envisaged a period of confederation followed by possible unification in five years' time. On the same day, France's President Mitterrand offered his opinion that, "I don't have to do anything to stop it (reunification). The Soviets will do it for me. They will never allow this greater Germany just opposite them." Caught between global political changes and street level revolution, German politicians struggled to steer the course of events. The instinctive caution that had characterized West German politics for four decades had to be replaced by a radical and flexible approach.

The elections of March 1990 confirmed the popular desire for unification expressed in public demonstrations. The "2+4 Treaty on the Final Settlement with Respect to Germany" formalized international agreement that the newly united country would join NATO and that Soviet troops would be withdrawn. Gorbachev had at least extracted financial compensation from Germany and had negotiated radical change without hostility but the expiry of Moscow's German ally, however peaceful, could only weaken Gorbachev domestically. Eastern Europe was entering a period of dangerous instability.

Discussion point:

Why did the East German Government resist reform?
What options did Honecker have in 1989?

The new united Germany officially came into existence on 3 October 1990, although it is significant that this was not the unification of equals but rather the accession of the East German *Länder* to the FRG.

Timeline for German reunification	
1989	November 9: Berlin Wall opened
	November 28: Helmut Kohl's "10 points" set out a plan for eventual reunification
	December 1: Communist Party surrenders power to coalition of democratic parties
1990	February 25: US President Bush assures Kohl of American support for reunification
	March 18: First free elections in GDR result in victory for pro-unification parties
	July 1: Currency union between East and West Germany
	September 12: Final "2+4 Treaty" (the two Germanys plus the United States, the Soviet Union, the United Kingdom, and France) formalizes international acceptance of reunification
	October 3: Unification

What challenges confronted the new Germany?

The West German currency, the Deutschmark was extended to East Germany in July 1990 replacing the old GDR currency at the generous rate of 1:1 (the market rate was 5:1). This succeeded in slowing the westward flow of East Germans but was enormously expensive. The low productivity of East German workers did not justify the falsely inflated wages they could earn following currency union and factories became unviable. At the same time, the GDR's export markets in Eastern Europe were faltering. The result was long term economic collapse and mass unemployment in the East and an enormous financial burden for Western tax payers. Moves to rebuild a national identity would have to take place against the tensions caused by economic problems.

Once again Germany had to come to terms with the legacy of a dictatorial regime. The GDR was a state in which the Stasi spied on the citizens and in which people were encouraged to inform on each other. These activities were recorded in meticulous files. Post-unification Germany had to find a balance between ensuring that justice was seen to be done, that the past be remembered and examined and, on the other hand, avoiding the divisive effect of a "witch hunt" against East Germans constantly having to justify their past behaviour or the danger of individuals seeking revenge. The Federal Authority for the Archives of the GDR State Security Service was established to provide victims of Stasi activities with access to their files and to manage media access.

Forty years of separate experiences had resulted in the development of attitudinal differences. Misunderstandings between "Wessi's" (Westerners) and "Ossi's" (Easterners) were inevitable as each side indulged in disparaging stereotypes of the other, leading many to ask whether the physical Wall had been replaced by a wall in people's minds. The *Ostalgie* phenomenon—a nostalgic yearning for the GDR—reflects the fact that not all the expectations of 1989 have been fulfilled. The 1990s also saw an upsurge in crime, a symptom of economic hardship, but also as regards racially motivated violence, evidence of the activities of overtly "neo-Nazi" groups. Politicians had to balance moral obligations to asylum seekers, economic migrants and the German-born children of "Gastarbeiter" (guest-workers) with indigenous resentment at foreign competition for scarce jobs and resources. Again the shadow of Germany's history made the debate particularly sensitive.

Internationally, Germany continued to pursue greater European integration. The Maastricht Treaty 1992 turned the European Community into the European Union and established greater economic and political co-ordination between member states. The European Bank for Reconstruction and Development (EBRD) offered financial assistance to East European countries in the transition to democracy and German industry was able to re-establish trade links with its traditional markets to the East. Approaching the new century, a generation of politicians with no direct memory of Second World War proved more willing to assert Germany's national interest though without ever challenging the broad consensus on Germany's commitment to being part of a greater Europe. This commitment was demonstrated by the abandonment of the cherished Deutschmark in favour of the new Euro currency in 1999.

Activity:

The "German Question"

All German leaders have had to wrestle with the historical German Question.

Where is Germany?

Germany does not have natural boundaries and therefore its territorial borders have been a matter of dispute. Germans are the largest ethnic group in Central Europe and members of this *Kulturnation* (national culture) of German speakers have historically settled throughout Central and Eastern Europe. Therefore, establishing exactly where a German state should be that incorporates as many Germans as possible has been problematic. Germany's *Sonderweg*—its unique historical path—has shaped its present reality.

Research and compare these attempts to answer the German Question. There are several appropriate websites including http://germanhistorydocs.ghi-dc.org

- 1871 Bismarck's first German nation state.
- 1917 The Treaty of Brest–Litovsk

- 1919 The Treaty of Versailles
- 1942 Hitler's New Order
- 1945 Occupation and Division
- 1990 Reunified Germany

Questions

In each case, identify Germany's borders, and explain why they are there. To what extent has Germany's history been shaped by its geography?

Since 1945, the German Question has evolved and these issues have influenced the politics of the post-war era:

1 How have Germans tried to overcome the division of Germany?

2 How have German relations with territories in Central and Eastern Europe formerly part of a greater German nation developed?

3 What role should a unified Germany play in the post-Cold War world order?

Spain, 1975–2000

How did Franco's Spain become a democracy?

In the 50 hours that Franco's body lay in state, during up to 500,000 people filed past for their last look at the dictator. A joke common at the time suggested that many had come just to make sure he was dead. Indeed there was some quiet celebration. In Barcelona the writer Vázquez Montalbán wrote "champagne corks soared into the autumn twilight. But nobody head a sound." There was also a lot of genuine, private grief. But the overwhelming emotion was the foreboding that accompanies uncertainty.

With hindsight the Spanish transition to democracy can appear to have been an orderly, almost inevitable process. But in the immediate aftermath of Franco's death, little if anything appeared to be inevitable. The view in 1975 was captured by the academic José Amodia: "It is naïve to expect Franco's death to work a miracle. In the political future of Spain I see a great deal of darkness and hardly any light; my forecast must be pessimistic."

Reform had been in the air for several years and the now the central obstacle to it had been removed. Between a divided government and divided opposition there was only consensus that Spain had reached an historic moment. From the perspective of the reformist Right, the challenge was to initiate change that did not threaten the foundational principals of the Francoist system. From the centre-left perspective, the challenge was to bring about an end to Francoism without provoking the intervention of the army. For many at the time it seemed as though Spain was attempting to "reconcile the irreconcilable". And always in the background was the possibility of yet another Spanish **pronunciamento** in a country still haunted by the memory of civil war.

> A **pronunciamento** is a declaration by which a military coup d' état, i.e. a military dictatorship, is made official.

For most of the first year of post-Franco Spain, there were little grounds for optimism for those who hoped for change. The first key decision of King Juan Carlos was to re-appoint Franco's Prime Minister Arias Navarro, known during the civil war as the "Butcher of Malaga". In this first cabinet, loyal Francoists still filled the key institutions, including the Council of the Realm which nominated the *terna*, the list of three candidates for prime minister presented to the king. In January 1976, Arias introduced proposals for limited democratic reform, a programme that was well short of opposition demands. Clashes between police and demonstrators were dealt with in traditional Francoist fashion and five workers were killed. By the

Juan Carlos I of Spain (1938–)

Juan Carlos was born in Rome, grandson of the previous King of Spain, Alfonso XIII, who was deposed in 1931. In 1948 Juan Carols moved to Spain, as part of a deal struck between Franco and his father Don Juan. This gave Franco control over Juan Carlos' education, allowing Juan Carlos to be groomed as Franco's successor. In 1969, Juan Carlos was officially designated heir to Franco and was given the new title of Prince of Spain. As a condition of being named heir-apparent, he pledged an oath of loyalty to Franco's *Movimiento Nacional*. Privately though from the 1960s Juan Carlos had been meeting members of the opposition. On the 22 November 1975 Juan Carlos became head of state and King of Spain. He is widely credited with overseeing the successful transition to democracy and for in particular for the failure of the attempted coup of 1981 "23-F".

summer, Arias was struggling to get the Francoist establishment in the Cortes to pass the centrepiece of his legislative reform, the legalization of political parties. On July 1 with the Cortes at an impasse, he tendered his resignation to the King. What happened next was as unexpected as it was crucial to Spain's democratization.

Six key points in *La Transición*

4 July 1976: Adolfo Suárez appointed Prime Minister.

The liberal newspaper *El País*, famously responded to the appointment of Adolfo Suárez with the headline "What a mistake! What an immense mistake!" Reformers had been hoping for the appointment of one of the regime's heavy weight *aperturistas*, but in Suárez they had the young General Secretary of Franco's *Moviemento Nacional*. The reactionaries in the *búnker* were delighted However, for King Juan Carlos, Suárez's impeccably conservative credentials were all part of the plan hatched with the support of the King's former tutor Fernández-Miranda whom the King had manoeuvred into the chairmanship of the Council of the Realm. Suárez's name been allowed to slip on the *terna* shortlist of three as a safe conservative that no one expected to be chosen. But, in the words of one commentator, the appointment of Suárez "was the culmination of months of assiduous conspiracy".

Suárez had been one of a number of politicians invited by Juan Carlos in the last months of Franco's life to outline a programme for the future of Spain. Suárez's plans had impressed the king with their detail and realism. Suárez himself had the youth, persona and detailed understanding of how politics in Spain worked. He knew how to use the system against itself. It meant that within a few months of his appointment, Suárez was able to present to the *Cortes* a thorough reform bill that would completely transform the political landscape and take the Francoist *búnker* off guard.

18 November 1976: Law for Political Reform passed

In addition to the leadership of the *Moviemento,* Suárez had also been director general of Spanish state television, TVE. He used his media experience to the full in ensuring that the whole reform process was covered on television from his announcement of the details of the reform bill through to the televised debate on 18 November. In the *Cortes* itself, debate was managed by the Speaker Fernández-Miranda, who prevented key elements of the bill from being diluted by hostile amendments. In the end Francoism capitulated 424 votes to 59 on live television, as one by one Franco's deputies were called by name to vote for or against reform. On 15 December the "yes" campaign won 94 per cent of the referendum vote.

Adolfo Suárez (1932–)

Adolfo Suárez y González is a lawyer who served in a number of Franco governments and became the secretary general of the *Movimiento Nacional*. He was an unexpected choice as prime minister in 1976. According to historian Raymond Carr, "The achievement of Suárez was to accomplish the programme of 'democratization from above', using the legal institutions of Francoism." On 8 June 2007, during the celebration of the 30th anniversary of the first democratic elections, King Juan Carlos I appointed Suárez Knight of the Order of the Golden Fleece for his important role during the Spanish transition to democracy.

9 April 1977: Spanish Communist Party legalized

In the same month as the referendum, the socialist party (PSOE) under Felipe González held its first congress in forty years. Informal contacts between González and Suárez resulted in an acceptance by the nominally republican socialists of a democratic monarchy. In February the PSOE was legalized. The Spanish Communist Party (PCE) presented the government with a much more difficult problem. To legalisze the PCE was to risk right-wing revolt and army intervention. Changing public opinion in the light of the **Atocha massacre** in January and the willingness of communist leader Santiago Carrillo to negotiate with the government, persuaded Suárez to risk legalization of the PCE in April. Subsequently, in late spring the trade unions were legalized, the right to strike recognized and Franco's *Movimiento* was abolished.

Atocha massacre The murder of five trade unionists on 24 January 1977 by an extreme right-wing terrorist organization. More than 100,000 people attended the funeral which became the first mass left-wing demonstration after the death of Franco.

15 June 1977: Election

Adolfo Suárez's popularity was such that any party led by him was likely to win the first democratic elections. The problem for Suárez was that he did not belong to any party. During the previous winter, various conservative groupings had been emerging and in March Suárez negotiated a position as leader of the most prominent of them: Unión de Centro Democrático (UCD). As expected, the UCD won the election, less anticipated was failure of the extremist parties, the Communists (PCE) on the Left and the *Alianza Popular* (AP) on the Right, to make much impression.

1977 Spanish General Election Result		
Party	Votes	Percentage
UCD	6,337,288	36.61
PSOE	5,358,781	29.27
PCE	1,718,026	9.38
AP	1,525,028	8.33

The results showed that the electorate rejected both the extreme Right and the extreme Left. The results were a triumph for moderation while registering the desire for change.

In the absence of an absolute majority, Suárez chose not to form a coalition government but instead worked on producing an inclusive set of agreements, (known as the Moncloa Pacts signed 25 October) involving all the major political parties and trade unions. As a consequence the Spanish Constitution which was ultimately approved by referendum on 6 December 1977 was a consensual document that represented the broad spectrum of political groups in Spain. Among the most liberal constitutions in Europe, it defines Spain as a parliamentary monarchy rather than as just a constitutional monarchy. It abolished the death penalty and the links between the Catholic Church and the state. Most radically, the 1978 Constitution transformed Franco's highly centralized state into a state where significant power was devolved to the regions and the "historical nationalities" (*Nacionalidades históricas*).

23 February 1981: The Tejero coup "23-F"

For those who participated in the attempted military take-over in Februray 1981 "23-F", Spain was on the verge of political and economic collapse. Demands for home rule from the regions were getting out of hand and the continued ETE terrorist campaign in the Basque country showed no signs of slowing up. In addition, throughout 1980 divisions had been opening up with the ruling UCD Party over the extent to which Spain required social reform. Contraception had been legalized, homosexuality decriminalized and discriminatory laws on adultery also abolished. Proposals to reform the divorce laws split the UCD and it appeared unable

The attempted military take-over in February 1981 by "23-F".

to govern effectively. In January 1981 Suárez resigned and in the month before his successor Calvo Soltero could take over, a faction within the army attempted to seize power by force. Colonel Antonio Tejero led an occupation of the Congress of Deputies holding most of Spain's political class hostage for 24 hours. He claimed to act in the name of the king, but Juan Carlos quickly acted to reassure the public that this was not the case while ordering the army to follow his orders. It is still not known exactly who was behind the attempted coup and the generals who were arrested were clearly expecting others to follow suit. But what is certain is that the failed coup indirectly helped the socialists into power the following year.

28 October 1982: Election of PSOE

Throughout much of its time in opposition under Felipe González, the PSOE had been painfully distancing itself from its Marxist origins. The failed Tejoro coup and the splits in the UCD did much to help the cause of the PSOE. The moderate programme of reform proposed by the PSOE and the effective media friendly leadership of González did the rest. In the election, the socialists were swept into power with 201 seats and a comfortable majority in the *Cortes*. The election of González marks for many historians the end of *La Transición* because it demonstrated that power in Spain could be passed from one party to another without unrest or the intervention of the armed forces. And this was the ultimate test of democracy.

1982 Spanish General Election Result		
Party	Votes	Percentage
PSOE	10,127,392	49.4
AP	5,409,229	25.9
UCD	1,425,248	6.8
PCE	846,440	4.0

The Spanish are very proud of *La Transición*. Indeed, it continues to serve as the model and inspiration for many recent transitions whether in Africa, Latin America or in Eastern Europe. But we should be careful not to get too carried away. Often ignored by commentators is the violence that accompanied Spain's *Transición*. In the five years following Franco's death more than 100 demonstrators were killed by the police or extreme Francoist groups. Also ignored has been the lack of justice for the victims of Francoism, as the former Prime Minister Filipe González himself explained. "There was not sufficient strength to demand either justice or, even, any explanation for the past." In other countries that have been through a transition like post-apartheid South Africa there have been "truth and reconciliation" commissions designed to heal the wounds of dictatorship. In contrast, in Spain *La Transición* was accompanied by what the Spanish call the *pacto del olvido,* the unwritten agreement by all sides to forget what happened under Franco. Only very recently has this been called into question.

Discussion point:

Who was the most important individual during *La Transición*?

To the extent that it is possible to simplify this account by establishing an order of precedence among the individuals who took leading roles in the transition, one might say that Don Juan Carlos headed the list … Adolfo Suárez would be in second place, and Santiago Carrillo would come third.

Tusell, J. 2007. *Spain: From dictatorship to democracy 1939 to the present.* Wiley-Blackwell. p. 274.

 What criteria might Tusell have used to rank his top three individuals? If you were to add one more name to the list who would it be?

Activity:

Essay writing

How can we explain *La Transición?*
—or the Good King Juan theory of history?

The English historian E.H. Carr famously once wrote an attack on what he called the "Bad King John theory of history"—the naive view, as he saw it, that "what matters in history is the character and behaviour of individuals". In his book, *What is History?* Carr attacked the "childlike" simplicity of such an approach. What Carr was also attacking was the tendency for history to concentrate on the "great men" of history (rather than the social history of all people), and the belief that in some way individuals were separate from wider social and cultural influences.

Writing an essay about *La Transición* offers the student an ideal opportunity to consider the relative significance of prominent individuals. Historians agree that key individuals were unusually important to the success of *La Transición* and that amongst them King Juan Carlos is pre-eminent.

Historian Charles T. Powell, for example, characterized the King as *"El Piloto Del Cambio"* (the pilot of change). Other individuals, most notably Adolfo Suárez, also played an important role. Juan J. Linz, has argued that Suárez exhibited "a great capacity for personal dialogue, engaging with those whom he had to negotiate, listening to them, and creating a certain sense of trust without necessarily making promises he was uncertain about being able to satisfy."

Individuals can also be important through their absence. Had Carrerro-Blanco not been killed in 1973

the right wing *búnker* would not have been denied the leadership it lacked in 1976. This not only raises counterfactual or "what if?" questions about *La Transición* but also ethical questions about whether terrorism can ever be justified.

However, if we are to follow E. H. Carr's advice fully, we must recognize that important individuals are at once "a product and an agent of the historical process". Beyond the role of individuals, a successful essay must also evaluate the relative importance of the individuals acting as groups (as political parties or social classes for example) and the essay should also consider how individuals are influenced and affected by social and cultural forces beyond their control.

For example, the media in the immediate years after Franco' s death was considerably more liberal than under the dictatorship and enjoyed "a freedom unimaginable in the heyday of Francoism." This helped create a climate of opinion in which, by 1977, a vast majority of the Spanish population favoured democracy over authoritarianism. The freedom of the press not only helped shape a more liberal public opinion, it also *reflected* the extent to which liberal ideas had become entrenched in Spain as a consequence of the economic growth of the 1960s *Desarrollo*. This is the basis of the controversial view of Franco apologists that the *La Transición* was a direct consequence of the dictatorship's policies.

Discussion point:

Was Juan Carlos II a Lenin or a Napoleon?

The great man is always representative either of existing forces or of forces which he helps to create by way of challenge to existing authority. But the higher degree of creativity may perhaps be assigned to those great men who, like Cromwell or Lenin, helped to mould the forces which carried them to greatness, rather than to those who, like Napoleon or Bismarck, rode to greatness on the back of already existing forces.

Carr. E.H. *What is History?*

Spain since 1982

How was Spain's *Transición* consolidated?

The transition from an authoritarian to a democratic system of government requires more than the introduction of competing political parties and periodic elections. Democracy also requires a complex system of laws and supporting institutions to guarantee the fundamental human rights that are at the heart of the democratic system. The **rule of law** must be paramount and the political, business and military elites must be bound by it. The army and police must be under civilian control. If freedom is to mean anything then equality of opportunity provided through universal access to education, healthcare and welfare support are essential. Social freedoms and entitlements help to encourage the spiritual and intellectual freedoms that ultimately produce a culture of creativity (artistic or entrepreneurial) that legitimates the regime. And underpinning it all, as Franco himself realized in the late 1950s, must be a successful, expanding economy. In the late 20th century, a successful Spanish economy meant an increasingly free and internationally integrated economy within the context of the European Union. After nearly 40 years of authoritarian rule, therefore, the laws and institutions of Spain still bore the imprint of Franco's personal rule: his priorities and his prejudices. When the PSOE came to power in 1982, there was still much to be done.

> The **rule of Law** means that the law is above everyone and it applies to everyone whether they are rulers or the ruled.

Army in transition

In Franco's Spain the army enjoyed the privileged position of one of the families behind the *Movimiento*. The 1981 Tejero coup was just one of the coups that actually left the barrack room. The key initial work in bringing the Army under civilian control was undertaken by Lieutenant General Gutiérrez Mellado in the Suarez government who removed the automatic right of military chiefs to sit in cabinet. From December 1982 until March 1991 the Defence Minister Narcís Serra,

Javier Solana (1942–)

In many ways Javier Solana is the embodiment of Spain's **Transición**. As a member of the illegal socialist opposition in the 1960s he was secretly smuggled in to meetings with King Juan Carlos on the back of a motorbike. He was a senior PSOE cabinet member for 13 years before becoming NATO secretary general in 1995. From 1999 to 2009, he was secretary general of the Council of the European Union.

former Mayor of Barcelona, designed what has been described as an "imaginative and sweeping restructuring of the military" The most significant of these reforms was to reduce the size of bloated officer class and to make promotion much more dependent on ability rather than age. A second change has been to make the army professional. 1984 legislation allowed the 20,000 conscripts called up every year to avoid military service by applying to be conscientious objectors. Such large numbers succeeded in doing this that the Aznar government did away with national service altogether. By 2001 there were no conscripts left in the Spanish army. A final feature of the reform was to give the army a new international role. By 1992 Spain provided more UN peace keeping officers than any other country in the world. And by the time Spanish socialist **Javier Solana** became Secretary General of NATO, early Spanish antipathy to NATO seemed a distant memory. Increased Spanish involvement in NATO under the government of Aznar also led to closer ties to the United States with significant implications.

Economy and society in transition

Unlike the democratic transition undertaken in countries of the former Eastern bloc, Spain was not subject to the kind of free-market shock treatment associated with the Washington Consensus. As political scientist Omar G. Encarnación points out "Rather than relying on shock and exclusion, it was anchored in direct negotiation and pacts with societal actors, including the national unions." When after 1984 there were a series of significant privatizations of state industries it helped that it was undertaken by a socialist government that cushioned the blow with increased spending on welfare, unemployment benefits and education which increased in real terms by 57 per cent between 1982 and 1989. The biggest problem throughout the *Transición* has been unemployment, which was consistently above the EU average. Unemployment by the mid 1990s reached a European record of 24 per cent of the active population. But in 1986–91, the Spanish economy grew quicker than any other country in the European Community. By 1992 Spain had become 40 per cent richer in real GDP terms than it had been in 1980. One of the significant consequences of increased wealth was the ability of the Spanish to maintain their status as Europe's number one owner-occupiers. By 1999, 86 per cent of Spaniards lived in houses that they owned compared to only 69 per cent in the UK. Owning property gives people a significant stake in society and makes them less likely to support calls for radical or revolutionary change. As John Hooper observes, "If the growing prevalence of home-ownership was one reason why Franco was able to die peacefully in his bed, then it was also a key to the relatively peaceful transition that ensued."

If the prevalence of home ownership marked a significant continuity with the past, the changing status of women in post-Franco Spain stands out at the most significant social transformation. The post-Franco governments were able to reverse most of the legal impediments to sexual equality: Discriminatory laws on adultery were revoked in 1978 and those on domestic finance in 1981. Contraception was legalized in 1978 and a limited law that legalized abortion was passed in 1985. In 1982 the PSOE government set up the institute for women *(Instituto de la Mujer)* to promote women's rights. In 1988 the last bastions of male exclusiveness fell when the first women began training to be Guardia Civil and the High Court in Madrid ruled that exclusion of women from the armed forces violated the constitution. The rate that women entered the workplace in the 1980s was unprecedented. In 1981 less than one quarter of the workforce were women, by 1991 it was a third. At the start of the 21st century, Spain had a higher percentage of female parliamentary representatives than Germany, the United Kingdom or France. And yet, although laws have changed, domestic attitudes have largely remained rooted in the past. Women have entered the workforce but have also continued to bear the burden of child care and domestic chores. A survey conducted in 2004 found that Spanish men do less than ten per cent of daily domestic tasks, which makes Spanish women the hardest working in Europe. The consequence of this has resulted in the most profound change in Spanish society since the death of Franco: women now have fewer children in Spain than anywhere else in the world.

The arts and media in transition

The arts had suffered under Franco because of the simple fact that most artists and intellectuals had been in the side of the Republic during the civil war. Some like Federico García Lorca were killed, many others fled into exile. Intellectuals were distrusted during Franco's time and arts that were encouraged reflected Franco's conservative tastes. With democracy comes creative and intellectual freedom. In the 1980s the new freedom were best exemplified by *La Movida Madrileña*, an "anything goes" cultural movement which rejected traditional Francoist mores in favour of a mass infusion of diverse forms of contemporary culture, and a party scene to match. The fact that Spaniards are today Europe's biggest consumers of cocaine is partly to be explained by the reaction to the restrictive society of the Franco era. A more productive legacy of the spirit of *La Movida Madrileña*, is to be found in the brilliantly idiosyncratic and visionary work of Spain's premiere filmmaker, Pedro Almodóvar, who has been described by film theorist Steven Marsh as 'the cultural symbol par excellence of the restoration of democracy in Spain." Indeed, cinema has probably been the most successful international cultural symbol of the "new Spain", with Spanish films winning more Oscars than any other non-English speaking country in the 20 years since 1982. Probably only architecture can compete with film as a cultural symbol. Spain has been described by Richard Rogers as "Europe's architectural hothouse". Most of the world's top architects have important buildings in Spain, the most iconic of them being the Guggenheim museum in Bilbao.

Opened in 1997, the Guggenheim Museum Bilbao is a museum of modern and contemporary art designed by the Canadian-American architect Frank Gehry.

The most significant aspect of the cultural transition has been the liberalization of the media from the constraints imposed by an authoritarian regime. Newspapers had already enjoyed a degree of freedom at the end of the Franco regime and although newspaper sales were relatively low in Spain (in 2000 only 36 per cent of the population read a daily newspaper compared to 62 per cent in Europe as a whole) the influence of newspapers was disproportionate. Newspapers have been particularly significant in helping to uncover corruption and government abuses. The most notable example of this was Pedro J. Ramírez' s *El Mundo* which led the investigation into the "dirty war" conducted by the PSOE government of the 1980s against ETA. As journalist John Hooper concludes, the uncovering and reporting of the GAL scandal "undoubtedly contributed to the PSOE's removal from power.". In contrast, television in Spain has not enjoyed the same reputation. This is important because the Spanish watch more television than any other nation in Europe. The state broadcaster TVE was consistently accused of favouring the government of the day. One survey found that during the 1989 election campaign, 103 minutes was spend on coverage of the governing PSOE compared to just four minutes for the opposition *Partido Popular.* The advent of independent television since 1989 has improved the situation, but the Zapatero government' s manifesto commitment in 2004 to de-governmentalize TVE suggested there is still much to be done.

Further political transition

The consolidation of Spain as a liberal democracy has required the state to willingly relinquish a significant degree of sovereignty: internally to the regions and externally to Europe. Franco's state had been one of the most centralized in Europe. By 1982, the system of self-government for the regions, *Estado de las Autonomías*, was giving rise to fears that the Spanish state might break up under these centrifugal forces. In a 2001 report by the Organisation for Economic Co-operation and Development (OECD), Spain' s regional governments were responsible for a higher percentage of public expenditure than the German *Länder* and even Switzerland's cantons. The process of decentralization continues in Spain and may yet lead to the break-up of Spain, but as is often pointed out, were it not for the *Estado de las, Autonomías* a violent declaration of independence would probably have resulted. As Hooper argues, "the moment at which Spain was really in danger of going the way of the former Yugoslavia was before, and not after, it embarked on its experiment with decentralization." It is hard to believe that the declining support for ETA in the 1990s would have been achieved were it not for the granting of significant regional powers to the Basque country. During the three key years of Spain's Transición there were 240 deaths attributable to ETA compared to 19 in the last three years of the 20th century. In contrast to devolution, the integration of Spain into Europe has been a relatively unproblematic. The prize of European integration, which could not even be considered while Franco was alive became after 1975 a Holy Grail which helped keep Spain's *Transición* on track. "The fact that the EEC was solidly democratic and set up a stable pattern of rewards and disincentives for would-be members was helpful to Spain's transition and consolidation". After lengthy negotiations, Spain was finally accepted into the EEC in 1986. The economic boom which followed was significantly supported by the various "cohesion funds" which redistributed wealth from the richer to the poorer nations. In 1996 the determination of the Aznar government to meet the Maastricht criteria for entry in to the Euro enabled the government to push through reforms that brought the Spanish labour market in line with the rest of Europe.

Spain into the 21st Century

The success of Spain's *Transición* can be measured by the extent to which Spain resembled any other major Western European country at the end of the 20th century. The challenges facing Spain in the year 2000 were largely the same: globalization, an aging population, childhood obesity, environmental damage. The challenges that were particularly Spanish were to be understood in terms of its unique post-war history. The continuing threat of the break-up of the Spanish state and ETA violence is one of them. Race relations are another. The isolation of Spain during the Franco years kept Spain a relatively homogenous white-Catholic state. Yet Spanish birth rates which are the lowest in Europe (another post-Franco legacy) mean that the Spanish economy is now heavily dependent on high rates of non-European immigration. Between 1999 and 2002 the number of non-EU citizens living legally in Spain tripled. Nearly a quarter of all Europe's immigration is to Spain. How will the Spanish state cope with such rapid change? A final example of challenge is not simply to be explained in terms of the past, it is in fact history itself. As we have seen, Spain's *Transición* depended on *el pacto de olvido*, an agreement to forget about the Franco years and the civil war in particular. The fact that the Spanish school history curriculum only covered events up to 1936 was an example of that. But since the late 1990s, things have begin to change. Books and documentaries about the Franco years had become very popular, archives were opened up and most significantly "historical memory" groups were been formed demanding the right to exhume the bodies of those executed and disposed of without proper burial. In October 2007 the controversial historical memory law (*Ley de Memoria Histórica*) was passed by the Spanish Parliament which amongst other things provides state funds for identifying and digging up the mass graves of the Franco era. It has been argued that until the process of exhumation is complete; neither will the process of *Transición*.

Spain, 1982–2000	
1982	30 May: Spain Joins NATO
	28 October: PSOE wins General Election with 202 seats
1986	1 January: Spain becomes a member of the EEC
	22 June: PSOE wins General Election with 184 seats
1988	18 October: Trial of two police officers accused of assassinating ETA personnel Scandal of the Grupos Antiterroristas de Liberación (GAL) begins
1989	19 June: Spain joins the European Exchange Rate Mechanism
	29 October: PSOE wins General Election with 175 seats
1992	29 March: 24 ETA members arrested in France
	20 April: World "Expo 92" opens in Seville
	25 July: Olympic Games opens in Barcelona
1993	6 June: PSOE wins General Election with 159 seats
1995	19 April: ETA fails in assassination attempt on PP leader José María Aznar
	1 July: Spain assumes presidency of the EU
1996	3 March: PP wins General Election with 156 seats. Coalition negotiations delay Aznar's appointment as Prime Minister until May 4
1997	22 June: Felipe González is replaced as leader of the PSOE by Joaquín Almunia
	12 June: PP councillor Miguel Angel Blanco is murdered by ETA
1998	29 July: Former Governor of Vizcaya and two senior police officers are sentenced to ten years in prison for their part in the GAL dirty war against ETA. They are pardoned just 105 days later
	16 September: ETA announces "unilateral, total and indefinite" ceasefire
1999	28 November: ETA ends its ceasefire
2000	12 March: PP wins General Election with 156 seats, its first absolute majority
	22 July: PSOE elects José Luis Rodríguez Zapatero to the Party leadership

Activity:

Six key dates of *La Transición*

Date	Event	Significance
4 July 1976	Adolfo Suárez appointed prime minister	
18 November 1976		
9 April 1977		
15 June 1977		
23 February 1981		
28 October 1982		

Copy and complete the table above and then rank the six events into the order of significance. Explain the reasons behind your ranking.

Questions

1 The dates of 1 January 1986 (Spain's entry into the EEC) or 3 March 1996 (victory of the conservative Partido Popular) have also been identified as important dates in the process of Spanish democratization. Why?

2 Some historians and political commentators have suggested that Spain's transition from the Franco years is still not yet complete. What arguments can you identify for and against this assertion?

Exam practice and further resources

Sample questions

1 Why was Nazi Germany defeated by April 1945

2 Examine the impact of the Cold War on Germany up to 1955.

3 "By the mid 1950s Europe had regained political stability." Assess the validity of this statement with reference to one country you have studied (excluding Germany and Spain).

4 Analyse the reasons for and extent of economic integration in Europe by 1961.

5 Assess the major factors which allowed Spain's transition from a dictatorship to a constitutional monarchy.

Recommended further reading

History of the European Union:

Judt, Tony. 2007. *Postwar: A History of Europe Since 1945*. London, UK. Pimlico.

Davies, Norman. 1996. *Europe: A History*. Oxford, UK. Oxford University Press.

Davies, Norman. 2006. *Europe at War*. London, UK. Pan Macmillan.

Germany:

Green, Simon. et al 2008. *The Politics of the New Germany*. Abingdon, UK. Routledge.

O' Dochartaigh, Pól. 2004. *Germany Since 1945*. Basingstoke, UK. Palgrave Macmillan.

Kettenacker, Lothar. 1997. *Germany Since 1945*. Oxford, UK. Oxford University Press.

MacDonough, Giles. 2007. *After the Reich: The Brutal History of the Allied Occupation*. London, UK. John Murray.

Spain:

Raymond Carr, Raymond. 2001. *Modern Spain: 1875–1980*. Oxford University Press.

Tusell, Javier. 2007. *Spain: From Dictatorship to Democracy: 1939 to the Present*, London, UK. Wiley-Blackwell.

Preston, Paul. 1995. *Franco: A Biography*. London, UK. Fontana Press.

Preston, Paul. 2005. *Juan Carlos: Steering Spain from Dictatorship to Democracy*. London, UK. HarperPerennial, 2005.

Hooper, John. 2006. *The New Spaniards*. Harmondsworth, UK. Penguin.

Giles Tremlett, Giles. 2007. *Ghosts of Spain: Travels Through a Country's Hidden Past*. London, UK. Faber and Faber.

6 Post-war developments in the Middle East, 1945–2000

This section deals with the impact of nationalism, communalism, modernization and westernization on some of the countries of the Middle East. Though the Middle East was not directly involved in the battles of the Second World War, it nonetheless witnessed major changes in its aftermath. Europe's decline boosted nationalist movements, introducing major political, economic and social changes. In turn, Europe was replaced by the United States as a dominant influence on international relations in the region. Domestically it led to reforms that brought the countries closer to the Western model, both socially and economically. In some cases these had long term repercussions. The chapter will concentrate on these changes and evaluate their long-term effects with a focus on Egypt and Iran. It will also cover the Arab–Israeli conflict and consider the attempts at peacemaking.

By the end of this chapter, students should be able to:

- discuss Nasser's rise to power in Egypt
- analyse the success and failure of the reforms of Nasser and Sadat in Egypt, and compare their foreign policies
- assess the degree of change and continuity under the presidency of Mubarak
- define the impact of Pan Arabism, the Arab League and Pan Islamism in the region
- consider the causes of the ongoing conflict between Israel and the Arab world
- evaluate the success of the peace talks between Israel and the Arab world
- recognize the forces that divided Lebanon and caused its civil war
- assess Iran's path to modernization and its long-term consequences
- understand the causes of the revolution in Iran in 1979.

Egypt

Modern Egypt emerged in 1952 when a military coup, better known today as the Egyptian Revolution, brought down the monarch, King Farouk, and put in office a military regime. The new rulers rallying around a strong sentiment of nationalism, succeeded in introducing a series of reforms to modernize Egypt. Furthermore, they challenged the West and affirmed Egypt's independence on the international scene. The man whose name is closely associated with these changes is Gamal Abdel Nasser, the son of a postman, who, at the apex of his career, was elevated to the status of hero and hailed as the unifier of the Arab world. He was, according to historian William Cleveland, "the embodiment of what the Arab world wanted to be: assertive, independent and engaged in the construction of a new society freed from the imperial past and oriented towards a bright Arab future." This section will give an account of the circumstances that allowed Nasser to come to power.

Egypt, the most populated of all the Arab countries in the Middle East stands on the crossroads of Asia and Africa. Through the Suez Canal, a man-made waterway built in 1869, it links the Mediterranean to the Red Sea. This continues to be the major naval route between Europe and Asia. Egypt had been part of the Ottoman Empire but was controlled by Britain. In 1914 it became a British **protectorate**. In the post-war period a nationalist uprising, inspired by the **Wafd** Party, sought independence from the United Kingdom. The British arrested Zaghlul its leader and exiled him to Malta. The arrest incited further anger and in 1919 anti-British riots became widespread throughout the country. The nationalist revolt led to the cancellation of the protectorate in 1922 and Egypt became an independent state, with King Fuad on its throne. In 1923 a constitution was drawn up and following the first parliamentary elections in January 1924, Zaghlul became Egypt's first elected prime minister. The British, however, continued to interfere in Egyptian politics. In 1936 following the death of King Fuad and his succession by King Farouk certain changes were introduced. The Anglo-Egyptian Treaty was signed which offered Egypt more independence, but the UK maintained a military presence in the Suez Canal zone and had the right to "defend Egypt" in case of attack. The occasion for interference was to come in the course of the Second World War in 1942. The humiliation that the Egyptians experienced on that occasion, known as the "4th of February incident" was one of the factors that brought Nasser to power.

When war was declared in 1939 Egypt declared its neutrality and had every intention of staying out of the conflict. On 13 September 1940, when Italian troops crossed the Libyan border into Egypt, this proved to be impossible and Alexandria came under heavy attack. Economically, the country also suffered as its trade was disrupted by war-time conditions. There were severe food shortages, which caused bread riots in Cairo. The Egyptian political elite's position towards the Allied forces was a little ambivalent. Given their history of domination by the British, some saw the war as an opportunity to close ranks with the UK's enemies. Fearing such an eventuality, the British took the upper hand and forced the King to appoint a member of the more reliable Wafd Party as prime minister. This happened on the 4th of February 1942. The ultimatum, which left the King with the choice of either following British orders or abdicating, was humiliating for Egypt. The consequences of the incident were far-reaching. It undermined Egypt's sovereignty and discredited the monarchy and the Parliament. For the Wafd party, the 4th of February incident was political suicide. The party lost all credibility with the Egyptians as they were seen to be too co-operative with a foreign power and therefore stopped being a nationalist alternative in Egyptian post-war politics.

> A **protectorate** is an independent state that is provided with administrative, diplomatic and military support by a stronger state or entity. The protectorate usually accepts specified obligations, but retains its sovereignty.

> **The Wafd** (meaning delegation) was the name of a nationalist party led by Saad Zaghlul after the First World War. The party stopped functioning in 1952, but was revived as the New Wafd Party in 1983.

Activity:
Saad Zaghlu

Research the career of Saad Zaghlu, who formed the first Wafdist government in 1924.

What were his goals and aims? How did he attempt to achieve these aims? To what extent was he successful?

Discussion point:

Credibility (the ability to elicit belief) is a vital quality for a politician. What are the factors that enhance credibility in a political leader or a politician?

When the war ended, relations between Egypt and the United Kingdom remained tense. The Egyptians wanted the UK to renegotiate the 1936 treaty and evacuate its troops from the Suez Canal zone, but the British refused. The political situation was unstable as both the King and the ruling Wafd Party were regarded as compromised and weak in relation to the UK, so neither inspired much loyalty. The Suez Canal was one of the major bones of contention between Egypt and the UK. It is not surprising that it came to blows in 1956 with a war between the two countries.

The Suez Canal Company was originally owned by the French, who had been responsible for its construction. It was then taken over by the Egyptians in 1863, during the reign of Ismail Pasha, for a sum of £3,800,000. But in 1875, faced with a major financial crisis due to a drop in the demand for Egyptian cotton in the world market, Egypt was forced to sell its shares to the British government. Furthermore, the British government secured its investment by maintaining a British force in the canal zone. The presence of British troops on Egyptian soil angered many Egyptians and the Egyptian government asked the British to leave on many occasions. In 1936 the Anglo-Egyptian Treaty, which affirmed Egypt's sovereignty, nonetheless stipulated Britain's hold on the canal zone. Stationed in the area to protect it were 10,000 British troops. In 1951, when the government finally chose to abrogate the treaty and force the British out, there were violent clashes. The British troops remained in the area until 1956.

Another factor contributing to rising discontent was the economic situation of Egypt, and the growing gap between the rich and the poor. As a country in which the economy was mainly based on food production, this gap was particularly apparent amongst landowners. There was a massive inequality in land distribution and in the size of the holdings: 0.4 per cent of the landowners were in possession of 35 per cent of the country's cultivable land, while 94 per cent of the population owned 35 per cent of the land. The size of the holdings varied from 200 *feddans* or more (an Egyptian unit of area equivalent to 1.038 acres or 0.42 hectares) to 0.8 *feddan*. Given that many of the landowners were in fact the ruling politicians, no real attempts were made to change the situation and consequently the politicians became the target of the anger of the poor.

Finally, the humiliating defeat of the 1948–9 Arab–Israeli War (see chapter 4, p. 213–6) increased the unpopularity of King Farouk. The war convinced the younger officers of the incompetence of the men ruling Egypt. Two opposition groups emerged. The first were the Muslim Brothers, a **Pan-Islamic** group which had been formed in 1928 by Hassan al Banna. This was a movement which proposed a return to Islamic values as a means of uniting Muslims in the Arab world against the intrusion of foreign powers. The other were the Free Officers, a group of junior military officers formed immediately after the 1948–9 war, who proposed a national revival to recoup Egypt's lost pride through the overthrow of the monarchy. They were motivated by the desire to rid Egypt of British imperialism and bring about social justice reforms that would combat social inequality.

Discussion point:

Land is an important source of wealth in many countries. What other sources of wealth can you think of? Does the source of wealth define the type of country?

Pan-Islamism is a political movement advocating the unity of Muslims under one Islamic state.

In 1951 the Wafd government, faced with growing opposition, announced the unilateral abrogation of the 1936 treaty as a way to gain some popularity. The British once again refused to negotiate. The matter had become a question of national pride and the refusal led to clashes between the Egyptian people and the British forces stationed in the canal zone, killing and wounding hundreds of protestors. On 26 January 1952, a day known as "Black Saturday", Cairo exploded in anger: demonstrators took to the city centre burning banks, cinemas, bars. This was the last straw that broke the camel's back.

On the night of 22–23 July 1952 the army headquarters, the airport and communication centres were seized by the Free Officers and in a relatively bloodless coup (two soldiers were killed and seven wounded), King Farouk's government was replaced with the Revolutionary Command Council (RCC). The King was sent into exile, where he remained until his death in 1965. In June 1953 the monarchy was abolished, the 1923 constitution was withdrawn, political parties were banned and though Egypt was proclaimed a Republic, the RCC obtained the right to rule for a transition period of three years. The RCC also prohibited all those who had held political posts in 1946–52 from entering politics again. Under the new regime, Mohammad Naghib became President, with Nasser in the post of Vice-President. In February 1954, disagreement between Nasser and Naghib led to the resignation of the latter. With his main rival out of the way, Gamal Abdel Nasser started to construct his Nasserist state.

Gamal Abdel Nasser (1918–1970)

Gamal Abdel Nasser was born in Alexandria, where his father had a job as a postal worker. As a young student he participated in many of the anti-British demonstrations of the 1930s. In 1937, a year after the Anglo-Egyptian treaty, he enrolled in the Military Academy in Cairo. Fighting in the 1948 War against Israel, he had a first-hand experience of the humiliation of defeat. He blamed King Farouk and the political elite for Egypt's humiliation.

Nasser was popular among ordinary people because of his social background. He spoke vernacular Arabic, which was easily understood. He was also admired for his courage and charisma. During the period of his presidency he succeeded in highlighting Egypt's role as a pioneer in the Arab world. To the outside world Nasser's Egypt could no longer be ignored. He also introduced important socio- economic reforms within the country which left an indelible imprint on Egypt. His premature death at the age of 52 was mourned by the majority of Egyptians.

Activity:
Essay skills: Causation

"Discuss the long-term and the short-term causes for the rise of Nasser to power."

For a historian, events are agents that bring about other events, often in reaction to what has gone on before. This is what we call causation. Some of these events have consequences that take a long time to mature; others trigger a reaction straight away. The first category we call long-term causes and the second become short-term causes.

To respond to the essay question, you need to select events that fit both categories, and to decide on whether they had a short-term (S) or long-term (L) impact. Fill out the table below with 4–6 events. Once the table is completed, you have all the evidence you need to construct a clear analytical essay. Make sure that your justifications are logical.

Event	When did it happen?	What did it lead to?	L/S?

Discussion point:

Many governments in the Middle East emerged out of a military coup d' état. What do you think gives the armed forces the legitimacy to govern?

The Nasserist state

In contrast to the weak government and lack of leadership shown by its former monarch, the new regime led by the military and the Free Officers demonstrated its well-honed organizational skills, military discipline and authority. The military rulers represented the nation as a whole. The members of the new government represented the ordinary people and not just the privileged landowners. Nasser himself, originating from the rural poor, symbolized the new Egypt: one that would take into consideration the under-privileged. He spoke their language and understood their plight. In a speech made in April 1954 he said: "The Egyptian masses were too weak to start a revolutionary action to improve their lot, so we your brothers started it for you, but you are the revolution." The new regime claimed to be the guardian of the people's interests.

The new regime was a populist regime, which means that they claimed to represent "the people". It was also a one-party system. As representatives of the people, other parties were no longer needed. Political parties are divisive and this regime wanted to introduce a new model that reflected co-operation rather than conflict in society: Egypt would be "a co-operative state". Nasser justified this position in a statement quoted in the *New York Times*, in 1955: "We see no advantage for Egypt in the establishment of a parliament in which men serving the interests of big landlords, or of Iraq, London, Washington or Moscow, would sit masquerading as Egyptians." In January 1953 the RCC formed the National Liberation Rally as the only political organ that represented the people. Nasser was its Secretary-General. This organization was to form a bridge between the people and the revolution.

In 1956 the end of the three-year transition was announced and a new constitution was drawn up, without however permitting any other political parties. In 1957 the Liberation Rally was replaced by the National Union. The National Union's role was to supervise and guide the people. In 1962, this body was replaced with the Arab Socialist Union (ASU), another name for the single party that continued to be the sole body representing the people of Egypt. Even though Egypt only had one political party, elections did take place. Candidates were chosen and closely screened by the ruling party.

The new regime justified its seizure of power by the fact that they would redistribute the wealth of the country, modernize Egypt and bring social justice to the country. One of the regime's most ambitious objectives was an extensive agrarian reform, introduced in 1952. For Nasser this transformed the military coup into a revolution. A decade later, in 1962, with the launching of the Arab Socialist Union, Nasser's revolutionary policies, which he named the **National Charter**, spread to the rest of society. When presenting the Charter, Nasser explained his policies in the following way: "Revolution is the way in which the Arab nation can free itself of its shackles, and rid itself of the dark heritage which has burdened it … [it] is the only way to overcome underdevelopment which has been forced on it by suppression and exploitation." The Free Officers had taken the law in their hands because the legal government had been the source of humiliation for Egypt. Their discourse was a nationalistic one and stood in opposition to foreign domination. For Nasser, nationalism

---

Activity:

Class debate

"Political parties are divisive" vs. "Political parties are necessary".

Consider the following statement:

The Premier and his colleagues on the Revolution Command Council are convinced that restoration of the freedom of political parties to contest elections would produce a parliament in which special interests could buy representation, and would neglect the well-being of the Egyptian masses.

Source: Nasser quoted in the *New York Times*. 19 May 1955.

The **National Charter** became the platform for action of the Arab Socialist Union (ASU). Its agenda included:

1 a programme of nationalization in which banks, insurance companies, shipping companies and major heavy industries all passed from private hands to the state
2 agrarian reform, which reduced the maximum holdings from 200 to 100 *feddans*
3 90 per cent income tax imposed on income over 10,000 Egyptian pounds
4 workers being represented on management boards
5 workers and peasants being guaranteed at least 50 per cent of the seats in parliament.

was synonymous with revolution because it was only through independence that Egypt could bring social justice to Egypt: "We must fight imperialism, monarchy and feudalism because we are opposed to injustice, oppression and slavery."

One of the trade-marks of Nasserist Egypt was the notion of Arab Socialism. This identified with a state-run centralized planned economy, a series of welfare measures and the will to export these ideas to other Arab states. The mission set forth by the new regime went beyond the borders of Egypt. Nasser insisted on uniting the Arab world and he cultivated a sense of communalism as well as nationalism. His objective was to restore the pride and confidence of the Arabs and through this unite them against the external forces. The 1956 constitution, for example, stated that Egypt was an Arab country and part of the Arab nation. This emphasis was a reminder that Egypt planned to lead the other Arab states in this quest. Nasser referred to the outcome of the Suez Crisis in 1956 as "the Great Arab victory" (see p. 337), its momentum going beyond Egypt's borders. In 1958 Egypt entered into a union with Syria and Nasser announced the birth of the United Arab Republic.

Opposition such as the Muslim Brotherhood and the Communist Party were severely repressed. In 1954 after an assassination attempt on Nasser by a member of the Muslim Brothers, six of its leaders were executed and thousands of its members imprisoned. The Communist Party received a similar treatment. After a major strike in the textile factory near Alexandria, said to have been instigated by the Communist Party of Egypt, the army was called in to crush the strike. Two of the workers were executed and many more received prison sentences. Later, in 1957 an intelligence service, the *Mukhaberat*, was set up and its job was to keep a strict watch on the people. Having come to power in a conspiratorial manner, the new regime was fully aware of the dangers of conspiracy. According to the historian Mary Ann Fay, Nasser had once admitted that he tended to see a conspiracy in everything. Consequently, his regime was extremely vigilant and condemned any form of opposition. The press, now under state control, was subject to strict censorship.

Activity:
The National Charter

Read the agenda of the National Charter on page 318, and answer the following questions:

1 Who was the National Charter designed to appeal to?
2 Which groups in society would feel threatened by it?
3 What were the implications of these divided opinions for the future of the Nasserist regime?

Activity:
Essay skills: Compare and contrast

Very often in the exams you will be asked to compare and contrast two single-party rulers. It is advisable to tackle such a question thematically. Use the list of headings below to write up a comparative analysis of Nasser and one other single-party ruler from the 20th century.

Single-party rule	Nasser	Another ruler
Conditions that brought the leader to power		
Cult of personality		
Nature of the government		
Domestic policies		
Foreign policies		
Status of women		
Treatment of the opposition		
Treatment of minorities		
Role of education		
Propaganda		

An important feature of Nasser's regime was his cult as a leader. Even though Nasser had risen from the ranks of the army, he distinguished himself from them so that if the military had any setbacks it would leave his reputation intact. As a leader, he was always present, personifying the nation and the regime, and insisting on absolute loyalty. What Nasser said in October 1954 immediately after a member of the Muslim Brotherhood shot eight bullets in his direction, but missed, is one example of this relationship. "If Abdel Nasser dies ... each of you is Gamal Abdel Nasser ... Gamal Abdel Nasser is of you and from you and he is willing to sacrifice his life for the nation."

Colonel Gamal Abdel Nasser standing at the window of his train as it enters the station in Cairo on 29 October 1954 is greeted by the crowd. He is returning from Alexandria where he had been the victim of an assassination attempt by Mahmood Abdel Latif, a member of the Muslim Brothers.

Nasserist Egypt's foreign relations

Within a few years of Nasser's accession to power, Egypt became the scene of a war with the United Kingdom, France and the State of Israel. The Suez War, as it came to be known, had a major impact on Egypt's relations with the world. It:

- created a distance between Egypt and the Western Allies
- improved Egypt's relations with the communist world
- elevated Egypt to a leadership role in the Arab world
- became one of the causes for the outbreak of the 1967 Arab–Israeli War.

Though Nasser had made it clear that his aim was to reduce foreign interference in Egypt, he did not at first choose to turn his back on the West. On the contrary, to finance the Aswan Dam project and to improve Egypt's outmoded military equipment he first turned to the West. But the loan that was offered by the World Bank stipulated that its officials supervise Egypt's budget. Another request, this time for military equipment, was simply refused. On learning this, Nasser was forced to seek out other alternatives. Starting out, in April 1955, he became one of the founding members of the non-aligned movement, following the **Bandung Conference**. In September of the same year, he announced an arms deal with Czechoslovakia. He would receive Soviet military equipment via Czechoslovakia in exchange for Egyptian cotton. In May 1956 Egypt recognized Communist China. In this move, he went against the Western Alliance's containment policy requiring "friendly nations" to refrain from recognizing Mao's China. And, in a final bold step, in June 1956, Nasser accepted the Soviet Union's offer of a loan for the construction of the Aswan Dam. In July, the US State Department announced that financial help to Egypt was no longer "feasible". To pursue the Aswan Dam project, Nasser nationalized the Suez Canal.

"My countrymen, my blood spills for you and for Egypt. I will live for your sake, die for the sake of your freedom and honor. Let them kill me; it does not concern me so long as I have instilled pride, honor and freedom in you. If Gamal Abdel Nasser should die, each of you shall be Gamal Abdel Nasser."

Gamal Abdel Nasser, after an attempt on his life in 1954.

The **Bandung Conference** was a meeting of Asian and African states, most of which were newly independent, which took place 18–24 April 1955 in Indonesia. The aim of the conference was to promote Afro-Asian economic and cultural co-operation. It took a strong position against all forms of foreign intervention in the internal affairs of independent countries . As the Western Imperial nations including the United States were implicated, the meeting was not viewed very favourably by the Western Allies.

The Suez crisis and the 1956 War

We need to understand the ensuing Suez crisis in the context of the Cold War. From the 1950s the cold war had entered a new phase: in order to avoid physical confrontation each side chose the system of alliances. Alliance with the Western camp included generous US military and economic aid. The division of the world into the East–West contending spheres of influence manifested itself in the signing of pacts. The Central Treaty Organization otherwise known as the Baghdad Pact, signed in 1955 between Britain, Turkey, Iran, Pakistan, and Iraq, aimed to bring these countries that were situated on the Soviet Union's southern borders into the Western sphere of influence and thus contain the spread of communism. The British government attempted to force Egypt to join the alliance.

The new Egyptian government had promised to restore Egypt's sovereignty over the Suez Canal, which according to the 1936 treaty was still under the control of the British government. The British refused to discuss the evacuation of the Suez Canal base until Egypt agreed to join the Baghdad Pact. But the Egyptians would only start discussing the matter when the British agreed to leave. In October 1954 the UK agreed to sign an agreement promising to withdraw their troops from the base within 20 months. They added the provision, however, that the British base could be reactivated in the event of an attack on Egypt or Turkey by an outside power or an Arab League state. In February 1955 the British Foreign Minister, Anthony Eden, visited Cairo seeking again to persuade Nasser to join the Baghdad Pact. Nasser once again refused. Furthermore, since Nasser was more attracted by the non-aligned pact he also encouraged other Arab states to refuse the Baghdad Pact. He was successful in convincing both Syria and Jordan to decline membership in the Baghdad Pact.

By April 1956 the UK had withdrawn their troops from the canal zone. The canal was nonetheless still owned by the British Suez Canal Company. On 26 July 1956, immediately after the announcement by the United States that a loan would not be forthcoming, Nasser announced the nationalization of the Suez Canal. Though he was prepared to pay compensation to the owners, he justified this act by stating that he would thereafter use the income from the canal to finance projects such as the Aswan Dam project. Nasser was asserting Egypt's rights over what he considered to be Egyptian property. The UK viewed the matter differently and started devising a plan to overturn Nasser's decision.

A secret agreement was reached between Israel, France and the UK. This is the reason the war is remembered in the Arab world as the "Tripartite Aggression". The Israelis refer to it as the "Sinai War". This plan consisted of an Israeli attack on Sinai with the objective of reaching the east bank of the canal. This took place on 29 October 1956, and would be followed by a British and a French ultimatum asking *both* Egypt and Israel to retreat from the canal zone in order to avoid conflict and ensure safe passage for navigation. As Israel would agree and Egypt could only refuse (according to the plan) the British air force would carry out an air raid. This event took place on 31 October.

Discussion point:

Who was the rightful owner of the Suez Canal?

The facts:

- The United Kingdom and France had built the canal.

- The UK had bought out Frances's shares in ownership.

- The canal is situated in Egypt.

The last act of aggression in this well thought-out plan was the landing of French and British paratroopers on Port Said on 5 November.

Although everything had gone according to plan, the attack was halted at midnight on 6 November, and was immediately condemned by both the United States and the Soviet Union. President Eisenhower was so furious that he was ready to sell the US government's Sterling Bond holdings, which would have forced the devaluation of the British currency. He also led the UN General Assembly to demand an immediate end to the offensive. France and Britain agreed to a UN sponsored cease-fire. The UK and France withdrew their troops in December and Israeli forces evacuated the region by March 1957. The UN sent its troops to the Sinai as a peacekeeping force. In April 1957 the Suez Canal re-opened for international commerce.

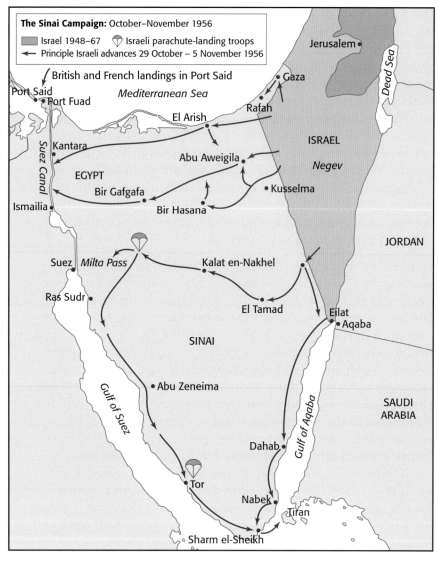

The Sinai Campaign: October–November 1956
- Israel 1948–67
- Israeli parachute-landing troops
- Principle Israeli advances 29 October – 5 November 1956

British and French landings in Port Said

Though Egypt had undergone a military defeat, Nasser was not overthrown as the three belligerent countries had hoped. Instead the crisis turned into a political triumph for Nasser. Egypt retained its newly acquired rights over the Suez Canal and Nasser was hailed as a hero in the Arab world. According to William Cleveland, "No other Arab leader approached his status and no other Arab leader aroused such high expectations."

The British and the French had been humiliated on the international scene. Suez was indeed a watershed in terms of the decline of the UK's role in the Middle East. As the former CIA official Chester L. Cooper put it, Suez turned out to be "the lion's last roar." According to Avi Shlaim, Suez was the turning point: the European phase in the history of the Middle East gave way to the superpower phase. The repercussions for the British and the French inside Egypt were even worse; their nationals were expelled and their property seized. The Egyptian Jews were also either expelled or chose to leave.

The Suez Crisis brought Egypt and the Soviet Union closer together. In 1958 the Soviet Union finalized its offer of a loan for the construction of the Aswan Dam. They also increased their military aid. Ideologically, Egypt remained neutral. According to Nasser, Egypt's foreign policy was an example of "positive neutralism": it did not enter into conflict with either of the superpowers. It can, however, be argued that the 1967 War against Israel found its long-term roots in the Suez Crisis.

Nasser's popularity and status as a champion of the Arab world led to some unwise and hasty moves. This included the short-lived United Arab Republic and the intervention in Yemen's civil war. Both these themes will be covered in the section on Arab Unity.

The 1967 War or the "Six Day War"

The mid 1960s had witnessed growing tension on Israel's borders with Jordan and Syria. The Israelis complained of guerrilla raids and retaliated. In 1967 the tone became more hostile and the Israeli Prime Minister, Levi Eshkol, warned that Damascus could be occupied if the raids were not controlled. Nasser saw this as an opportunity to revive the heroic days of 1956 and improve his tarnished reputation. He therefore called on the UN peacekeeping forces (present since the 1956 War) to leave the Sinai. Once they left, on 16 May, he announced that he would be closing the Tiran Straits, which connects the Gulf of Aqaba to the Red Sea and is vital to Israeli shipping. For Israel this constituted a declaration of war, a **casus belli**. On 5 June, Israel launched a full-scale pre-emptive attack on Egypt, Syria and Jordan. Within a few hours the Israeli air force had destroyed 90 per cent of the Egyptian air force, about 70 per cent of the Syrian air force and almost all of the Jordanian air force. By 8 June the Israeli ground force had crossed the Sinai and reached the Suez Canal. Within six days the Arab defeat was total. Israel now held the City of Jerusalem, the West Bank, the Gaza strip, the Sinai Peninsula and parts of the Golan Heights. The 250,000 Palestinians living on the West Bank were forced to flee to the East Bank.

The military defeat of 1967 was a tragic reminder of the defeat in 1948 and a major setback for Nasser. In the eyes of the Egyptians, those who had promised to restore Egypt's national pride had brought her further shame in the humiliating defeat of 1967. Egypt had lost approximately 10,000 soldiers and 1,500 officers; another 5,000 soldiers and 500 officers were captured and 80 per cent of its military equipment destroyed.

Economic and social policies under Nasser

The Nasserist regime set about introducing social and economic changes in Egyptian society through new legislation. The aims of these policies were to break away from the old social, economic and political order and end the privileges of the large landowners. Nasser strove to build popular support amongst the poorer sectors of society, in particular the rural workers. His aim was to encourage the industrialization and modernization of Egypt.

Within weeks of coming to power, in September 1952, the RCC enacted the first Agrarian Reform Act. This law aimed to offer the poorer *fellahin* (farmers) the possibility of a better life. It aimed to do this through a fairer land distribution by setting a limit on the size of property. The law stated that the maximum holding for a family

> **Casus belli** is a Latin expression meaning the justification for acts of war. *Casus* means "case" or "incident", and also "rupture", while *belli* means "of war".

> "Democracy is not defined by the constitution and the parliament, but is created by eliminating feudalism and monopoly and the domination of capital. There is no freedom and no democracy without equality and no equality with feudalism and exploitation and domination of capital."
> Gamal Abdel

> "One of the principal aims of the land reform scheme is to direct new investment into the improvement of land and into mining, industrial and commercial enterprise."
> Gamal Abdel Nasser

would be 200 *feddans*. The surplus land was then sold at a favourable price to those farmers who owned less than 5 *feddans*. The poor farmers were given 30 years to pay back the state. The dispossessed owners were to be compensated with government bonds. As this was deemed an insufficient amount of time to pay back the debt, in 1962, with the launching of the National Charter the period for payment was raised to 40 years. The National Charter also extended land distribution by lowering the ceiling of ownership to 100 feddans in 1962. As a result of the Land Reform Act, rents were lowered and co-operatives were established for the very poor farmers (those who owned less than 5 *feddans*). These co-operatives provided farmers with fertilizers, seeds, pesticides and transportation for the products to the market. Other conditions included the introduction of a minimum wage for agricultural workers, and access to the national power grid for electricity extended to many villages.

In April 1954 Nasser announced the confiscation of land belonging to the royal family. This was redistributed in the same manner to the poor farmers. Through this redistribution, 869 landless peasant families in the Beheira province near Alexandria were given land. On this occasion Nasser pledged to work to establish decent living standards for all workers and peasants, but urged them not to expect miraculous results.

The new labour laws addressed the industrial workers with a similar aim to gain popularity and raise living standards. These reforms included a raise in the minimum wage, a reduction in working hours, job creation (especially in the public sector), the introduction of rent control, and a programme to construct housing for workers.

In 1957 the National Planning Committee was established giving the state a leading role in organizing the economy. The economic system under Nasser has been called "State Capitalism" because, while maintaining the capitalist system, it placed much of the ownership in the hands of the state and created a large public sector. In the 1960s economic policies shifted further towards a greater state monopoly. In 1960 Egypt launched its first Five Year Plan. The plan placed emphasis on industrial development supported by a programme of nationalization announced in the 1962 National Charter. By 1970 the public sector accounted for 74 per cent of all industrial production, 46 per cent of all production (as rural production remained largely in private hands), 90 per cent of all investment and 32 per cent of the GNP. The public sector workers were provided with a decent pension, a minimum wage and health care.

The economic and social reforms included a major project to build a dam at Aswan. This would improve the irrigation system and be a major source of hydroelectric power. The project began in 1960 and was completed in 1970. As a result of this project the agricultural areas increased from 5.2 to 5.8 million *feddans*.

Another area of public life through which the Nasserist regime could distinguish itself from the past was the provision of education. The government increased its spending on education with the goal of obtaining national and cultural unity. The slogan "Two new schools every three days" was posted everywhere.

> ### Discussion point
> ### The Aswan Dam
>
> The Aswan High Dam controls the flooding of the Nile, stores water for times of drought and provides hydro-electric power. These benefits do not come without a price. Dams, like any other technical advancement, need to be reviewed in the light of the environmental, and social impact it has on the country.
>
> **What type of environmental and social impact did the Aswan Dam have?**

Ceremonies on completion of the Aswan High Dam. Nikita Khrushchev, leader of the Soviet Union with Nasser, 01 January 1964.

Though this remained a publicity slogan, the number of students increased substantially. Enrolment in primary schools went up from 1.3 million in 1953 to 3.6 million in 1970. Government figures also showed a fall in the illiteracy rate from 80 to 50 per cent. Nasser also encouraged university education by making it free and promising every university graduate a government job.

Women in Egypt had already expressed their political demands before the Nasserist revolution. Doria Shafig and her organization "Daughter of the Nile Union" were at the forefront of the movement to obtain the right to vote. The RCC's discourse was clearly progressive, however no practical reform in the voting system seemed forthcoming. In March 1954 Shafig and 18 other women went on a hunger strike in protest. They were promised that the matter would be considered. Two years later, in 1956, women won the right to vote. By 1957 modest changes occurred, two women were elected to the National Assembly, and state education was opened to both sexes. The 1962 National Charter stated that women were equal to men; it allowed for an increase in the number of women in universities and the workforce. Women were even given access to the Al-Azhar University, a religious institution previously closed to women. In 1963 laws were passed that promoted equal pay between men and women. Nasser's regime did not, however, alter the discriminatory measures of the existing family laws.

Nasser died in 1970 of a heart attack at the age of 52. The Egyptians were overwhelmed by a sense of loss, not because they supported his policies, but because they feared the future without him. In the words of historian Mary Ann Fay "he had left behind an imperfect and unfinished revolution."

Activity:
Daughter of the Nile Union

Research Doria Shafiq and the Daughter of the Nile Union. How did her movement compare to women's movements elsewhere?

Activity:
Verdicts on Gamal Abdel Nasser

Nasser's name has gone down in history as the dynamic and charismatic President who put Egypt back on the map. He broke with Egypt's past and transformed its society according to a new set of rules. These rules were not always well thought-out in advance and some have left Egypt with a legacy of economic inefficiency, an oversized bureaucracy and a political system centered around one person: the president.

Using the information in this section and the following passages, discuss Nasser's contribution to the history of the Egyptian state.

Source A

Nasser changed the course of the country's history … He understood what democracy is. He loved the common man.

Source: Statement by Amin Howeidi, former Minister of Defence and chief of Egyptian General Intelligence, quoted in the bi-lingual Egyptian–French daily newspaper *Al Ahram*. 5 November 2009.

Source B

He pushed Egypt ahead, but soon let his fantasy take over, leading to the disaster of 5 June 1967 … From a zaim [Arabic work meaning the courageous one] he turned into a prophet whom no one could criticize. He was all in one. In him were embodied all the national gains of Egypt ever since the country had a recorded history. Suez was the turning point. It led him to believe that revolutionary Egypt vanquished Imperialism and that had it not been for Nasser this would not have happened. Victory was his victory, protected by Providence. Everyone forgot Egypt was not victorious in 1956!

Source: Hussein Dhu'l Fiqar Sabri, quoted in the independent Egyptian weekly *Rose-el Youssef*. 18 July 1975.

Source C

For 18 Years Nasser Had Almost Hypnotic Power in His Leadership of Egyptians

Source: Obituary headline, *New York Times*, 29 September 1970.

Source D

Abdel Nasser was not a tyrant as some believe. He was considerate, frank and decisive. He sought to understand what was being presented to him before he made a decision.

Source: Statement from 1968 by Abdel Wahab al Burullusi, Minister of Public Health, published in *Rose-el Youssef.* 29 September 1975.

Source E

… signaled to the nation and it awoke; he signaled to the army and it moved; he signaled to the king and he departed; he berated imperialism and it exited from the country, feudalism and it was smashed, political parties and they were dissolved.

Source: From *Shakhsiyyat Abdel Nasir* (*The Personality of Abdel Nasser*) by M Rabi, published in 1966. Quoted in Vatikiotis, P.J. 1978. *Nasser and his Generation*, New York, USA. St. Martin's Press. p. 313.

Nasser's charisma may well have anaesthetized the Egyptians. The fact remains that his autocracy founded little that is politically lasting, even though it may have provided the outlines of social and economic change in the future.

Source: Vatikiotis, P.J. 1978. *Nasser and his Generation*. New York, USA. St. Martin's Press. p. 268.

Source F

He overwhelmed us with his magic … and the hopes, dreams and promises which underlay the victories of the revolution which he repeatedly announced to us … with their pipes and drums, anthems, songs and films, which made us see ourselves as a great industrial state, leaders of the developing world … and the strongest military power in the Middle East.

Source: Tawfig al Hakim, an Egyptian writer whose play, *El Sultan El Haer* (*The Perplexed Sultan*) , from 1960, could be regarded as a mild critique of Nasser. Quoted in Vatikiotis, P.J. 1978. *Nasser and his Generation*. New York, USA. St. Martin's Press. p. 320.

Source G

Nasser's funeral, 1 October 1970.

Anwar Sadat, 1970–1981

Anwar Sadat, Nasser's successor was faced with a country that mourned its hero but was also in desperate need of an overhaul. The economy was stagnant. There were signs of social unrest; 1968 had already seen widespread demonstrations by students and workers in major cities. Many were frustrated at government inefficiency and corruption. Politically the tension that reigned between Israel and Egypt left many Egyptians feeling uncertain about the future. In the 11 years that Sadat took control, he succeeded in reorienting the country on a new path economically, politically and socially. Under the slogan "the revolution of rectifications", he set about correcting his predecessor's mistakes. In most cases this meant a total reversal of the Nasserist regime.

Sadat had been a member of the Free Officers Group. In 1954 he was the Minister of State and in 1956 he chaired the National Union. Between 1960 and 1968 he became vice-president, a post to which he was reappointed in December 1969 and was therefore acting president at the time of Nasser's untimely death. His candidacy for the position in the long term was formalized on 3 October 1970 when the Arab Socialist Union (ASU) nominated him as President and confirmed on 15 October when 90 per cent of the electorate approved this nomination in a nationwide referendum. Very few, at the time, were aware of the changes that Sadat was about to bring in.

Sadat's most pressing concern was the economy. In order to rectify Nasser's legacy and revive the economy he needed to encourage foreign investment. To succeed in this task he needed to reduce government expenditure, open up the economy to the private sector and obtain the support of the business classes. In foreign policy terms, his aim was to reduce the Soviet influence and open the way for closer relations with the West. In particular he wanted to ease tensions with Israel. Before putting into effect his plans, he first needed to consolidate his unstable position.

Sadat's first move was to purge the government and the ASU of his rivals. In May 1971 he dismissed the Vice-President/head of the ASU and a number of high-ranking ministers including the ministers of the Interior and War, and charged them all of plotting a coup to overthrow the regime. Once they were out of the way, he replaced them with a group of men loyal to himself.

The state system under Sadat

In September a new constitution was put to a referendum. The new constitution brought about some important changes in the political structure of the state, but maintained the central authority of the president. The president remained supreme commander. He continued to have the power to declare war, conclude treaties, and appoint the prime minister and the cabinet. He could also propose and veto legislation, and rule through decree under emergency powers. The executive continued to be more powerful than the parliament.

Sadat had risen from the ranks of the army. The military, therefore, remained powerful, but after the 1967 defeat its role had already been redefined by Nasser; from a dominant political role in the state it became more professional, in the process becoming de-radicalized. The humiliating defeat of 1967 was partly blamed on the political involvement of the officers, which distracted them from pursuing their most important task: defending the fatherland. Sadat's purge of the ASU rid him of important political figures in the army. He then maintained his authority by repeatedly changing the minister of defence and the chief of staff and rotating the

Anwar Sadat (1918–1981)

Born into modest family circumstances, Anwar Sadat was one of 13 brothers and sisters. His father was Egyptian and his mother was Sudanese. He graduated from the Military Academy in Cairo in 1938, and soon after entered the army as second lieutenant. It is in the army that he met Nasser and joined the Free Officers Movement. He participated in the 1952 military coup and held important positions in the new Egyptian government. In 1969 he was appointed, for the second time, to the post of Vice-President and succeeded Nasser as President in 1970.

In 1977 Sadat became the first Arab leader to visit Israel. In 1979 he signed a peace treaty with Israel, a treaty that brought him fame and appreciation in the world at large, but notoriety and dishonour in the Arab world. Egypt was expelled from the Arab League and accused of breaking Arab unity.

Sadat was assassinated on 6 October 1981 by a member of an Islamic organization called Al-Jihad.

Discussion point:

Certain constitutions give power to the legislature (Parliament). Others give more power to the executive (President). What are the advantages and disadvantages of each one?

commanders. Following the signing of the peace treaty with Israel in 1979, the country was less dependent on the army. However, in spite of these changes, the military remained an important feature of the Egyptian state.

The single-party system was a Nasserist legacy that Sadat planned to dismantle because the Arab Socialist Union (ASU) was a powerful institution that could endanger Sadat's position. To break down the ASU's monopoly, he decided to gradually introduce other parties into the system. In 1975 he started to allow the formation of groups that would be permitted to express "opinions" within the ASU. Three such groups were formed:

- on the right, the Socialist Liberal Organization (later known as the Liberal or the *Ahrar* Party)
- in the centre, the Egyptian Arab Socialist Organization (later the term "organization" was replaced by Party)
- on the left, the National Progressive Unionist Organization (later to become the NPU party).

A major step towards a plural political system was taken in the 1976 parliamentary elections because these groups were allowed to present their candidates and platforms. Though the ASU obtained a clear majority in the 1976 elections, other views had been expressed for the first time and 48 seats had gone to non-ASU candidates. It was on the occasion of the opening of the new assembly that Sadat announced that the groups could function as a political party. Egypt's single party system had come to an end.

In 1977 Sadat announced that he would establish his own party, the National Democratic Party (NDP). Following this announcement the ASU merged into the new party. Sadat had therefore succeeded in transforming the single-party system into what Raymond Hinnebusch calls the "dominant party system", a system of maintaining total political control demonstrated by the fact that the NDP continued to dominate the Egyptian political life. Through what Hinnebusch calls "Parties of pressure" (in other words, small opposition parties), Egyptians were offered limited space to express their opinions.

In spite of the move towards plurality, internal security continued to be a serious matter. The Central Security Police was granted extensive powers and guarded the regime from the danger of opposition. The military was also called in to crush the opposition. Under Sadat, Egypt had entered a "post-revolutionary" phase. It no longer needed to justify its seizure of power; it now had a more solid legal base. The 1971 Constitution underlined Egypt's more traditional values, such as kinship and the respect for religion. This caused a total reorientation in the regime's power base.

In its foreign policy this also coincided with a switch from support of the Soviet Union to a rapprochement with the United States. In July 1972, 15,000 Soviet advisors were expelled from Egypt. This was the first step in a major realignment of Egypt's relations with the superpowers. Following the war in 1973 (see below) the United States took a greater interest in Egypt. By 1976 they contributed to the reconstruction of the Suez Canal and offered Egypt economic assistance. By 1976 Sadat had also ended the Soviet–Egyptian Treaty of Friendship and Cooperation.

Since the 1967 War, Israeli forces had occupied Egyptian territory from Gaza to the Suez and held the upper hand. Sadat, desperate to rebuild Egypt's economy, needed to ease the military tension in order to reduce its military spending. At first he tried to negotiate, but found that neither Israel nor the United States were willing to come to the negotiating table. He then switched to another tactic: he planned a surprise military attack with limited objectives (seizing a strip of land across the Suez Canal in the Sinai) as a prelude for negotiations with Israel. This was an enormous military gamble, but it paid off.

The 1973 Yom Kippur War

On 6 October 1973 Egyptian forces launched a surprise attack across the Suez Canal into the Sinai. The attack was planned on a Jewish religious day, Yom Kippur. The Israelis were unprepared for war. The "crossing" as it became known was an astounding success as it took only four hours to complete. Even though the Egyptian offensive was followed by a successful Israeli counterattack and the territory gained fell back into Israeli hands, it nonetheless served Sadat's purposes, by restoring Egypt's credibility as a military power. Sadat was hailed as the "Hero of the Crossing". He was able to use his popularity to introduce important economic changes and break with Nasserism.

The Yom Kippur War caused the involvement of the superpowers as well as the United Nations. On 22 October the US and Soviet foreign ministers met and came up with a cease-fire agreement. Resolution 338 was passed by the UN Security Council. This called for an immediate cease-fire and reaffirmed the demands set out in Resolution 242—the return of the occupied territories to the respective Arab states. A UN emergency force arrived to police the cease-fire. This brought Israel to the negotiating table: on 4 September 1975 an agreement known as the Sinai II between Egypt and Israel was signed in Geneva. The agreement stated that conflict between the two countries "shall not be resolved by military force". It was the prelude to the 1979 peace treaty.

This initial success of the Yom Kippur War had a tremendous effect on the morale of the Arab people. On 17 October the Arab oil-producing countries announced a five per cent cutback in oil production every month until the time Israel withdrew from the occupied territories. This was an unprecedented act of solidarity not seen since the 1948–9 war. President Nixon responded by asking Congress to release 2.2 billion US dollars to finance the sending of weapons to Israel. Saudi Arabia reacted in turn by announcing a ten per cent cutback and the total suspension of all oil shipments to the United States. This caused a massive rise in oil prices. It made the Western powers realize their dependence on the oil-producing countries and forced them to reassess their relationship with those countries.

The Egyptian–Israeli Peace Treaty, 1979

Sadat's aim of easing Egypt's tensions with Israel had, nevertheless, remained the same. That is why, on 19 November 1977, he agreed to travel to Jerusalem and address the Israeli Parliament, speaking about

> **Yom Kippur**, also known as the **Day of Atonement**, is the holiest day of the year for religious Jews.

> **Discussion point:**
>
> Research resolutions 242 and 338. Find out the countries that voted for them —those who voted against and those that abstained.

 What do you think were the effects of the rise in oil prices?

the need to reach a peace agreement. The visit came as a surprise to many and a large number of Arabs were shocked. They felt betrayed by what they believed was the abandonment of the Arab cause. Sadat's visit was a prelude to peace negotiations that took place with the mediation of the United States. The talks took place at Camp David, the US president's residence in Maryland, in the presence of President Jimmy Carter. The talks were concluded on 17 September and the Egyptian–Israeli Peace Treaty was signed on 26 March 1979. The treaty redefined Israeli–Egyptian relations in the following way:

- Israeli troops would leave the Sinai within three years
- a multinational force would remain in the region
- the two countries would establish diplomatic relations
- Israeli ships would be permitted to pass through the Suez Canal.

On the question of Palestine, the "Framework for Peace in the Middle East" put forth a plan towards creating a "Self-governing Authority" for the Palestinians. The deadlines set for these discussion were, however, never kept.

The reaction in the Arab World was unanimous: they all condemned Egypt's decision to sign a separate peace treaty because they believed it was a breach of solidarity and a betrayal of the Arab cause. The Arab countries suspended diplomatic relations with Egypt and stopped any financial aid. Egypt was also expelled from the Arab League, the organization it had helped to form.

In 1978 Anwar Sadat and Menachim Begin, the Israeli Prime Minister, were awarded the Nobel Peace Prize. This award was an acknowledgement for the achievement of a peace treaty. While the treaty resulted in Sadat's isolation in the Arab World, it was regarded by the world as an extremely brave move and a major step towards peace in the Middle East.

Sadat's economic and social policies

Sadat's main concern, however, remained the economy, which had become unproductive and stagnant. Contrary to his predecessor he believed in the need to expand the private sector, reduce the level of state intervention, encourage foreign capital and liberalize the economy. His aims were both political and economic. Politically, he wanted to shift the regime's base of support from reliance on Nasser's populist coalition to a reliance on the landed and business classes. Economically, he aimed to replace the inefficient public sector into a more competitive private sector and thus introduce incentives for investment. These changes were presented in the "October" working paper of 1974 better known as the *al Infitah* or "the opening". The main aim of his proposals was to dismantle Nasser's economic system. The proposals included an invitation to foreigners to invest in Egypt. They were offered incentives such as tax exemption and the freedom to repatriate their profits. This stood in contrast to Nasser's decision in 1956, following the Suez War, to expel all British and French nationals and seize their property. In the agrarian sector, rents went up and transaction of land became easier. This favoured the richer landlords. Private contractors, such as building contractors, were encouraged to work with the public sector. This coincided with a major construction boom and the development of the tourist industry.

Discussion point:

What other significant negotiations have taken place at Camp David that affect the Middle East?

Discussion point:

Discuss the Arab World's condemnation of Egypt's peace treaty. How justified was it?

Activity:

Nobel Peace Prize

Research other winners of the Nobel Peace Prize from the Middle East.

Discussion point:

What is the public sector? Why do some countries have a bigger public sector than others?

Foreign investment did not rise as high as it had been expected. In this period Egypt had an inflation rate of nearly 20 per cent, which made investment in the country less appealing. The liberalization of the economy increased unemployment. As government subsidies for basic goods such as sugar, tea, rice and bread were lifted, prices soared and lower-income groups suffered. The *Infitah* helped the enrichment of a few. The military also benefited from these economic changes because it became an investor in many private ventures sometimes on its own and sometimes in partnership with the private sector. As a consequence, the army owned agricultural land (20 per cent of the bread sold in Egypt belonged to the army) and invested in a large number of sectors such as pharmaceutical companies, hotels, apartment buildings and many other areas.

The new economic policies brought Egypt efficiency at the cost of increasing social unrest. The widening gap between the rich and the poor caused bread riots and left large sectors of the population dissatisfied. Furthermore there were allegations of misconduct and corruption among those who represented the public sector such as the army. In January 1977 there were riots in many of the major cities and the government had to send in the army to crush the demonstrators. In the clashes 800 people were killed and several thousand wounded. Dissatisfaction also gave rise to the growth of opposition movements such as the Muslim Brotherhood.

Sadat's broader social strategy also involved reversing Nasserist modernization reforms and social policies, in particular, in relation to the legal status of women. Sadat returned to the more traditional values of society and reiterated the role that the family should play in the lives of women. The 1971 Constitution for example stated that:

> The family is at the base of the society and is shaped by religion, ethics, and nationalism. The state pledges to preserve this genuine character of the Egyptian family, the customs and values it represents, and to generalize them to the rest of the society.
>
> (Article 9)

> The State guarantees the reconciliation of women's duties toward her family with her work in society, and her equality with man in the political, social, cultural, and economic fields of life without prejudice to the principles of Islamic *Sharia*.　　(Article 11)

In spite of this reversal to traditional and religious values, Jehan Sadat, Anwar Sadat's wife was active socially and politically; she founded the Talla Society, a co-operative which made it possible for village women to learn skills that enabled them to earn their own money; she headed the Egyptian delegation to the United Nations International Women's Conference in Mexico City and the Egyptian delegations to the UN Women's Conference in Copenhagen. She was present on all public occasions with her husband: an image that was not representative of the "traditional" Middle Eastern woman.

 Was *Infitah* a success or a failure?

The riots of January 1977

On January 18 and 19, there was rioting in towns from Aswan to Alexandria. They were said to have been the biggest upheaval since the 1919 riots against the British. They started when the government announced that it was ending subsidies on flour, rice, and cooking oil and was cancelling bonuses and pay increases. It lasted 36 hours. The rioters attacked many buildings and burned many cars. In the clashes 800 were killed, and several thousand were wounded. The rioting ended when the government cancelled the price increases. Benefits and 10 percent wage increases for public sector employees were also restored.

So although the emphasis on tradition was to break with Nasser's legacy and obtain the support of the traditionalists, in practice there were few major changes in the day-to-day lives of women. The majority of women from the poorer and the rural districts had remained within the confines of religion, the family and the clan, and those who had succeeded in breaking away from the traditions through education maintained their more liberated and modern status. The reversal nonetheless emphasized the religious family codes (these codes were never questioned under Nasser) and therefore slowed down modernization efforts.

Jehan Sadat was present by the side of her husband on most official occasions. Here the Sadats are offering Pope Paul VI a 2,000-year-old alabaster bowl.

Sadat: an assessment

Sadat's presidency witnessed a large number of changes for Egypt. On the one hand, in 1973, Egyptians were hailed as heroes of the Arab cause and Egypt became the focus for an unprecedented expression of Arab solidarity. On the other hand, in 1979, Egypt was scorned and rejected by the Arabs and accused of abandoning the Arab cause through the signing of a separate peace treaty with Israel. Both these images are correct. The Arab world was probably mistaken in thinking that Sadat's policy in relation to Israel reflected the Arab cause. In both cases Sadat was fulfilling what he believed Egypt needed to do.

Domestically, Sadat's record was less ambiguous: he made it clear from the start that his aim was to support the well-to-do as opposed to the poorer sectors of society. Had he, however, totally satisfied the rich and the privileged classes, he may have maintained a greater popularity. In practice, his economic policies, "the opening", disappointed many and satisfied only those who were able to make use of them to enrich themselves. The changes he had brought about in the political structure of the country remained superficial. The party that dominated remained the presidential party, the National Democratic Party, and those who had hoped for a "political opening" and a greater freedom of expression were left frustrated and dissatisfied. Socially, if we take the example of women, Sadat's policies represented a return to more traditional values. At the same time, the mere image of Jehan Sadat and the President, who notably cultivated a Western image, distanced them from the people and angered many traditionalists.

Sadat's reforms were pragmatic, but also self-serving; their objective was to reinforce his rule. His more liberal economic system, instituted because Egypt was bankrupt, was also the way for Sadat to obtain the support of the wealthier classes. And if pluralism replaced the single-party system, it was because of the political frustration and discontent that the single-party regime had brought about, and a way to reduce the power of the ASU. As a result, Sadat found himself extremely isolated in the last years of his presidency, having lost the support of

Discussion point:

The National Council for Women (http://www.ncwegypt.com) was established in 2000 as a government institution. It has been instrumental in passing laws to improve the status of women. In 2004 the Family Law Act was amended which gives women the right to divorce. It amended the Nationality Law to guarantee women gender equality and abolished the law which stipulated that the wife had to obtain her husband's approval to be issued a passport.

To what extent do you think the status of women in a society reflects the degree of modernization?

the poor and the traditional sectors of society. He never gained popularity among the wealthier classes and those who sought a more modern society.

Following the massive riots of 1977, the regime became increasingly entrenched. In order to suppress growing criticism, it resorted to arresting more and more of its opponents and restricting the people's rights of expression. In September 1981 the government ordered a massive roundup and over 1,500 people were arrested. On 6 October 1981, while observing a military parade commemorating the 8th anniversary of the Yom Kippur War, Sadat was assassinated by a member of the Al Jihad movement.

? Who assassinated Anwar Sadat and why?

Husni Mubarak

Husni Mubarak, the Vice-President, succeeded Anwar Sadat in 1981 and has so far achieved the longest tenure of an Egyptian leader in the period following the Second World War. He has maintained a strong executive, but has opted for a middle course between Nasser's populism and Sadat's *Infitah*. In the immediate aftermath of Sadat's assassination, Egypt was in a state of insurrection: the Islamic militants took control of a number of cities, a state of emergency was declared and within 48 hours the army succeeded in restoring order. These events once again placed the army in a prominent position in Egyptian political life because it is regarded as the only institution that can guarantee domestic security.

Under Mubarak, the army has grown in size and its officers continue to enjoy greater privileges. The military has come to play a significant role in civilian life. It is responsible for internal security and many civilians have been tried by military courts. The military continues to own major sectors of the industry. This includes military and non-military productions. By the year 2000 the army ran 16 factories and had 75,000 workers under its control. These factories were exempt from taxation and there have been rumours of widespread corruption. Ironically these changes have reduced the military's political role, but have given it an enormous economic importance in Egyptian society.

Mubarak continued Sadat's "multi-party" system. In the 1984 elections a number of political parties, previously banned under Sadat, were allowed to participate. However, a new electoral law, passed in 1984, stipulated that only those parties that received more than 8 per cent of the vote could receive seats in Parliament. Consequently, in 1984, only one other party, the New Wafd Party, managed to obtain sufficient votes. In this election, the National Democratic Party won more than 70 per cent of the votes and took 390 of the 448 seats. In spite of the apparent move towards a multi-party system, the table here shows that the dominant-party system continued to function.

Husni Mubarak (1928–)

Born in 1928, he graduated from the Military Academy in 1949. He joined the Egyptian Air Force and was trained in the USSR. Though not a member of the Free Officers Movement, he joined the government in 1972 and served as deputy minister of defence. He was appointed Vice-President in 1975 and therefore became President in 1981 when Sadat was assassinated. In 2005 he started his fifth term of office as President.

Mubarak succeeded in reversing Egypt's status amongst the Arab states and in 1987 the League of Arab States resumed diplomatic relations with Egypt. In 1989 Egypt was readmitted into the Arab League and two years later its headquarters returned to Cairo. Mubarak, however, has continued to respect the peace treaty with Israel and has not taken a position against Israel in the more recent Arab–Israeli conflicts. This has diminished Egypt's importance in the Arab world.

Number of seats held by the NDP in the Egyptian parliament , the *Majlis Al-Chaab* (People's Assembly)		
Year	Number of seats of the dominant ruling party	% of seats held by the dominant ruling party
1976	295/360	81.9%
1979	347/392	88.5%
1984	391/458	85.4%
1987	359/458	78.4%
1990	386/454	85%
1995	417/454	94%
2000	388/454	87.7%

Source: *Egypt: Majlis Al-Chaab (People's Assembly)*. Inter-Parliamentary Union. http://www.ipu.org/parline-e/reports/2097_arc.htm. For the year 2000: *Egypt Country Page*, International Republican Institute (IRI). http://www.iri.org/mena.

Mubarak's economic and social policies

Mubarak's economic policies stand between Nasser's state capitalism and Sadat's open door policy or *Infitah*. His government supports state intervention such as price control and food subsidies and the continuation of a large public sector because, since the major food riots of 1977 and the insurrection of 1981, it remains politically dangerous to neglect employees of the public sector and the poor. Mubarak also encourages the growth of the private sector because, much like his predecessor Sadat, his aim is to improve Egypt's economic performance and he does not want to lose the support of those who benefit from it. This "softly-softly" approach has been called gradualism or incrementalism, and is aimed at reforming the *Infitah* but not reversing the policy. Subsidies have been slowly decreased, but Mubarak has resisted pressure to further privatize.

 What do these figures reveal about the ruling party?

The presence of opposition parties

The opposition in Egypt has rallied around two poles: the absence of freedom and economic policies that benefit only a few. The parties that have been most successful in rallying popular support in times of economic hardship have been the Islamic ones. In the 1970s Islamic opposition groups had started to take shape first amongst the students and then, as poverty started to spread, among the urban poor. Sadat's decision to sign a peace treaty with Israel in 1979 gave the Islamic opposition a further rallying factor; Sadat had betrayed not just the Egyptian but the Muslim world. Since the assassination of Sadat, Mubarak has taken important measures to curb their activities, but given the economic situation and the position that Mubarak has held in relation to Israel, their popularity has not diminished. They have presented candidates in a number of elections and increased their presence in the Egyptian political scene.

Though Egypt has since the death of Nasser undergone major political, economic and social changes, according to Raymond Hinnebusch, it still remains a president-dominated, military-led, authoritarian-bureaucratic regime and the Egyptian Parliament is subordinate to the executive. In spite of the multi-party system, Parliament remains weak and political activity is severely restricted. Mubarak has succeeded in staying in power, but the social malaise continues to explain the presence of radical Islamic militancy.

Timeline: Egypt, 1945–2000	
1952	January 26: Black Saturday demonstrations against the British control of the Suez Canal
	July 22–23: The Free Officers' coup d'état. Revolutionary Command Council (RCC) formed
	September: Naghib takes over as Prime Minister
	September: Agrarian Reforms announced
1953	January: RCC is replaced by the National Rally and political parties formally dissolved
1954	April 17: Nasser replaced Naghib
	October 26: Assassination attempt on Nasser
1955	Baghdad Pact
	April: Nasser attended the non-aligned conference in Bandung
	September 27: Czechoslovakia agrees to sell Egypt arms
1956	January: a new constitution proclaimed
	May 16: Egypt offically recognizes the People's Republic of China
	July 19: Dulles announces that USA could not fund the Aswan High Dam
	July 26: Nationalization of the Suez Canal
	October–November: Suez War
1957	Liberation Rally replaced by National Union
	April: Suez Canal reopened for international commerce
1958	February 1: Proclamation of the United Arab Republic
1961	September 28: United Arab Republic ended
1962	National Union replaced by the Arab Socialist Union (ASU)
	National Charter launched
1967	1967 War
1968	Demonstrations by students and workers
1970	September 28: Nasser dies
	October 3: Sadat nominated President by the ASU
	October 15: Referendum approves presidency of Sadat
1971	September: New constitution
1972	July: Soviet advisers expelled from Egypt
1973	October 3: Yom Kippur War starts
	October 17: Arab oil-producing countries reduce production of oil by 5%
1974	New economic policies: *Infitah*
1976	Sadat ends Treaty of Friendship with USSR
	Parliamentary elections permit more than one party to stand
1977	January: Bread riots
	Establishment of National Democratic Party
	November 20: Sadat addresses Israeli Knesset
1978	September: Camp David talks
	Sadat and Begin receive Nobel Peace Prize
1979	March 26: Egyptian–Israeli Peace Treaty signed on
1981	October 6: Assassination of Sadat. Insurrection break out.
	Mubarak becomes President
1984	New electoral law

Arab unity

Faced with a common enemy, Arabs have sought to express themselves as a united force and to do so have based their commonality on different factors:

- a common language, ethnicity, culture: Pan-Arabism
- belonging to a common organization: the Arab League
- a common religion: Pan-Islamism

Pan-Arabism

A movement born in the 19th century, it was mainly a response to the domination by an outsider, namely the Europeans (colonialism) and the Turks (the Ottoman Empire). During the Ottoman rule, restrictions imposed on the self-determination of Arabs such as a ban on the teaching of Arabic rallied Arabs from different provinces of the empire and pushed them towards the idea of forming one Arab state. This unity would be ethnic and linguistic and therefore include Arab speakers of different religions, geographically situated in different parts of the Ottoman Empire, as well as Arabs from totally different economic and social backgrounds. Given this diversity, the movement based its premise for unity on a cultural heritage, but aimed to use this identity to rejuvenate and redress those forces that had in recent history been the cause of their weakness and subordination. It was founded by Michel Aflaq, who was born in Damascus of Greek Orthodox religion and educated in the French system as Damascus had come under a French Mandatory administration. In 1947, Aflaq and a Sunni Muslim, Salaheddin Bitar, formed the Ba'ath Party. The word Ba'ath means "resurrection" or "renaissance" and it called upon all Arabs to suppress state boundaries and unite as one state. Its motto was "Unity, Freedom and Socialism". Its aim was to strengthen the Arab nation against foreign interference through developing branches in every Arab State. According to Aflag "The solution of the Arabs today is in unity and their road for achieving unity is through democracy." It was a secular party and aimed to prevent a religious split amongst the Arabs. It was also nationalistic, but the nation was not the artificial state boundaries that were imposed by the Europeans after the First World War; rather, it was the entire Arab nation. The solution was also based on socialism: for the young Arab nation to rise, it was necessary to base the new state on social justice.

Following the Second World War and the birth of the State of Israel another "common enemy" had come to threaten the Arab nation. The defeat in the 1948–9 War was a confirmation of the dangers of disunity. Although all the five neighboring Arab states were concerned about the creation of the State of Israel and all the Arab states—Egypt, Iraq, Jordan, Lebanon and Syria—declared war on the new state, they fought as separate states and each pursued their separate interests. According to Avi Shlaim, "The Arab coalition was one of the most divided, disorganized, and ramshackle coalitions in the entire history of warfare." It goes without saying that had they

> **Discussion point:**
>
> What is the meaning of the word "pan"? Can you think of other examples where the word Pan is used?

> *"The newly independent Arab states had enough in common, in shared culture and historical experience as well as shared interests, to make it possible for them to come into close union with each other, and such a union would not only give them greater, collective power but would bring about that moral unity between people and government which would make government legitimate and stable."*
>
> Albert Hourani, *A History of the Arab Peoples.*

been united, they would have stood a much better chance of defeating their enemy. Their humiliating defeat was therefore a good incentive for forming a united force.

Nasser, the President of Egypt was the first politician to give some reality to this view. In 1956 when the French, the British and the Israeli armies were forced back, Arabs throughout the region shared Egypt's victory. The Suez War, Nasser claimed, was the great *Arab* victory. The 1956 constitution stated that Egypt was an Arab country and a part of the Arab nation. Pan-Arabism had found a hero, a leader and a just cause.

In 1958 these ideas were put into practice and the United Arab Republic (UAR), a union between Syria and Egypt, was born. Though Nasser had initiated the idea, it was Syria that instigated the actual formation of the UAR. A delegation of Syrian politicians belonging to the Ba'ath Party appealed to Nasser suggesting a total union of their two states. Their objective was primarily domestic: they wanted to prevent a pro-communist coup and preserve the Ba' athist dominance in Syria. Nasser accepted the proposal and became the Republic's President. Cairo became its capital and the Nasserist model was applied to Syria. Although Nasser was at first hailed in Damascus, the capital of Syria, as a leader, it soon became obvious that the Syrians felt overwhelmed by Egypt and feared losing their sovereignty. In 1961 the United Arab Republic was ended.

Why did Pan-Arabism fail?
Pan Arabism was born in the colonial context when the Arabs had a common enemy—the colonial powers, under the Ottomans, the French or the British. In the 1950s, when Nasser launched Pan-Arabism, the colonial powers were no longer in direct control and could no longer dictate the terms. Pan Arabism also undermined the legitimacy of individual rulers in the Arab states, who were naturally hostile to the idea. It was a threat to their very existence. Pan-Arabism implied that a collective Arab identity was stronger than the national individual state identity. Ultimately, the notion of statehood, born after the First World War, proved to be resilient and Arabs had started to identify more and more with their individual states. Pan-Arabism was also never practically thought out: it was in the words of historian William Cleveland "an awkward entity". Its source of energy was purely emotional. As Dan Smith puts it "the language of pan-Arab nationalism was deeply appealing to large numbers of Arabs, yet it was rarely matched in practice."

Arabs in other parts of the region did not appear united. There was tension between Egypt and the Kingdom of Saudi Arabia over Yemen, where a military coup had overthrown the royalist government in 1962. While Nasser intervened to support the new republican government, the Saudis backed the royalists. This tension weakened the whole notion of Pan-Arabism. Did Arabs have enough in common to unite them? Or were they divided into separate states with separate ideologies, each pursuing their separate national interests? The defeat in the 1967 War was a major blow to Pan-Arabism. If unity did not bring the Arab states military victory, what use was it?

Many of the Arab rulers identified Pan-Arabism with Nasser's Egypt and questioned Egypt's intentions: was it to unite or to dominate? Egyptian radio propagated Nasserist propaganda throughout the Arab world. Egyptian movies were seen and Egyptian popular music was heard in the majority of Arab-speaking countries. Nasser's popularity in the Arab world and Egypt's presence in world affairs was indeed an eyesore for many other Arab leaders. The dissolution of the UAR came in September 1961 when units within the Syrian military rebelled against their Egyptian commanders. The experiment was followed by other attempts, which proved even less successful.

In response to the formation of the UAR, the Federation of Iraq and Jordan, under King Faisal of Iraq and King Hussein of Jordan, was formed. This union only lasted six months, as King Faisal was overthrown in a military coup in July 1958. In 1971 the leader of Libya, Gaddafi, revived the struggle for Arab unity by calling upon Syria and Egypt to come together to form the Federation of Arab Republics. This was ratified in 1972 and on paper continued its existence until 1977. However, in the eyes of the world, it never obtained the legitimacy of its predecessor, the UAR.

In the years that followed, other events underlined the disunity of the Arabs as a linguistic and ethnic group. In 1978, when Anwar Sadat started peace talks with Israel, and in 1979 when an Egyptian–Israeli Peace Treaty was signed, disunity among the Arab States in the face of their common enemy, Israel, was confirmed. The separate road to peace was proof of division and a confirmation that each Arab state identified with its state rather than its nation. Egypt had pursued its national interest and not its ethnic linguistic one. It was not an *Arab* peace treaty but an *Egyptian* one. In 1981 when war broke out between Iran and Iraq, Syria sided with the non-Arab country Iran. This again underlined the differences between Arab states. In 1990 when Iraq invaded Kuwait, two Arab states were found to be fighting against each other. Furthermore Egypt, Saudi Arabia and the Gulf states joined the US coalition against Iraq.

The Arab League

The League of Arab States was formed in 1945 with six members: Egypt, Saudi Arabia, Transjordan, Iraq, Syria and Lebanon. The League today has 22 members including Palestine—the Palestinian Liberation Organization joined in 1976. Its aim was to bring together the Arab states, as independent sovereign nations and offer them a forum where they could discuss and co-ordinate policy and resolve disputes. Each member state has one vote in the Arab League council and decisions are not binding on those countries that do not vote. In 1979 Egypt's membership was suspended as a result of the peace treaty it signed with Israel and the League's headquarters moved to Tunis. Egypt has, however , since been readmitted and the League's headquarters have returned to Cairo.

The League has achieved co-ordination on an economic and cultural level between its member states. The Joint Arab Economic Action Charter set out the principles for economic activities of the

League. The Arab League has played an important role in shaping school curricula, preserving manuscripts and Arab cultural heritage and has launched literacy campaigns. The Arab League has also played a significant role in the Palestinian question. Co-ordinating policies over the Palestinian question was not an easy task for the Arab League because each state had foreign policy constraints of their own. In theory they all accepted the Palestinian people's rights to nationhood.

Discussion point:

The Arab League brings 22 countries together into one organization. The European Union brings 27 countries together into one organization. What are some of the differences between the two organizations.

Pact of the Arab States, 1945

Annex on Palestine

At the end of the last Great War, Palestine, together with the other Arab States, was separated from the Ottoman Empire. She became independent, not belonging to any other State.

The Treaty of Lausanne proclaimed that her fate should be decided by the parties concerned in Palestine.

Even though Palestine was not able to control her own destiny, it was on the basis of the recognition of her independence that the Covenant of the League of Nations determined a system of government for her.

Her existence and her independence among the nations can, therefore, no more be questioned de jure *than the independence of any of the other Arab States.*

Even though the outward signs of this independence have remained veiled as a result of force majeure, it is not fitting that this should be an obstacle to the participation of Palestine in the work of the League.

Therefore, the States signatory to the Pact of the Arab League consider that in view of Palestine's special circumstances, the Council of the League should designate an Arab delegate from Palestine to participate in its work until this country enjoys actual independence.

Source: Annex on Palestine, Pact of the Arab League of States. http://www.mideastweb.org/arableague.htm.

In more recent years the Arab League has also taken steps towards a peace initiative. In 1989, at the meeting in Taif, the League put forward proposals to end the Lebanese conflict. At the Cairo summit in 2002 the Saudis presented a peace proposal, which offered full normalization of relations with Israel in return for an Israeli withdrawal from all occupied territories including the Golan Heights, recognition of a Palestinian State in Gaza and the West Bank with East Jerusalem as its capital, and a "just solution" for the Palestinian refugees. So far these have been mere proposals. It is, however, possible that, at a later date, the Arab League may prove to be the organization capable of offering Arabs a united voice and thus come to play a more dominant role as an effective actor in the Arab–Israeli conflict.

What differentiates the Arab League from the UAR is that the Arab League does not aim to merge any of the countries and is therefore not based on the principle of Pan-Arabism. On the contrary, its founding principles were based on mutual respect for each others' rights of statehood and sovereignty. Article 8 of the Arab League charter states that:

Every member State of the League shall respect the form of government obtaining in the other States of the League, and shall recognize the form of government obtaining as one of the rights of those States, and shall pledge itself not to take any action tending to change that form.

Source: Pact of the Arab League of States. 22 March 1945. http://www.mideastweb.org/arableague.htm.

Pan-Islamism

Another form of unity that has been proposed is one centered on the common religion— Islam. This unity of course surpasses the Arab nation and can potentially embrace a far greater community in the world. There are more than one billion Muslims in the world. The notion of Pan-Islamism was born in the 19th-century for similar reasons as Pan-Arabism. Faced with the impact of colonialism and Western domination, the Muslim world sought ways of restoring its pride and identity. It realized that united, it would be a stronger force. This unity was found in Islam. Islam proved to be a strong and viable force because:

- it provided an identity and an allegiance
- it offered leadership through the clergy
- it allowed the message to be transmitted through mosques
- it was accessible to all.

Already in the late-18th century, revivalist ideas such as **Wahabism** in the Arabian Peninsula had successfully given Ibn Saud a potent political force to rally and unite his country. (see pp. 239–40). In the 19th century Islamic thinkers sought a more modern approach. Their aim was to show that Islam could be adapted to the modern world and could therefore pose itself as an alternative political entity. In the colonial period this reawakening of Muslims became synonymous with nationalism and anti-colonialism. Pan-Islamists called for unity in order to expel the colonial ruler. Later, once national governments were established, a focus on social injustice prevailed, offering a solution to the poverty and deprivation of the lower classes of society. Pan-Islamism presented itself as an alternative political force, and competed for power using parliamentary and non-parliamentary methods. As a political force, it elaborated its own model for the government and the economy. As a force that spoke out against social injustice, it also came to address injustice in the world. This brought Pan-Islamism in conflict with those forces that were considered "guilty" of inflicting pain and suffering on the Muslim world. This could include the countries that have waged wars in the Muslim world, the Zionist movement that has expelled Palestinians from their homes, and rulers whose policies support such countries. Three events played an important role in increasing support for Pan-Islamism:

> **Wahabism** is an Islamic movement which developed during the 18th century in central Arabia, providing a rigorous interpretation of Sunni teaching. In 1774 an alliance between Prince Mohammad ibn Saud and Sheikh Mohammad ibn Abd el Wahab was forged. In the 19th century two attempts to establish a Saudi-Wahabbi state failed. Consequently the Wahabis were persecuted by the Ottoman Turks, which made them receptive to the uprising of Abdul Aziz ibn Saud.

- The defeat of the Arab States in the 1967 War. This defeat underlined the weakness of the Pan-Arab movement and opened up the way towards another form of unity.
- The Iranian Revolution in 1979, which was the first time that Pan-Islamism succeeded in putting into effect its alternative political model of an Islamic republic.
- The defeat of the Soviet forces in Afghanistan in 1989, which boosted the pride and the confidence of Pan-Islamism because it had successfully defeated a superpower.

A closer look at three Pan-Islamic groups in the Middle East will give us a better understanding of their activities and will explain their popularity even though the world at large condemns them as terrorist organizations.

The Muslim Brothers

The Society of Muslim Brothers was founded in 1928 by Hassan al Banna in Egypt. Its fundamental belief was to revive Islamic values that rendered society just and free of corruption. It opposed colonialism as a force that exploited Muslim countries economically, subordinated them politically and culturally imposed its value system on the Muslim people. In the post-independence era, the Muslim Brotherhood message has continued to be pertinent because in many Muslim countries the rulers serve the interests of Western nations. As a consequence, in many Muslim countries, the Muslim Brotherhood is considered to be a threat to the ruling regime and is banned.

The Muslim Brotherhood is not a political party as such, but it exerts an ideological influence on many parties. Its popularity comes from its commitment to offering welfare and assistance to the poorest members of society. It has founded hospitals, schools and has organized relief groups. This has been an effective way for the Brotherhood to pass their message on to the people and highlight the ineffectiveness of the ruling governments. In Egypt the organization was banned by Nasser and many of its leaders were arrested. Under Sadat its activities were revived, but they are still not permitted to stand for elections under the banner of their organization. They have nonetheless introduced candidates for Parliament as independents and have had significant success. In the 2005 parliamentary elections they won 19.4% of the votes and obtained 88 seats.

Hamas

The Muslim Brothers established themselves among the Palestinians in the 1930s and its members fought alongside Arab armies in the 1948–9 War. After the 1967 War when many Palestinians were disillusioned with the Arab leadership and with Pan-Arabism, the Muslim Brotherhood became a viable alternative. The Islamic Resistance Movement, otherwise known as Hamas, founded in 1987 during the first *Intifada,* is a branch of the Muslim Brotherhood that has managed to obtain popular support among Palestinians. They not only showed active leadership in the period of the *Intifada* uprisings, but also offered welfare assistance through funding schools, healthcare centres, youth clubs and mosques. Since the establishment of the Palestinian Authority after the Oslo Accords in 1993, Hamas's growing popularity has been reflected in election results. In the 2006 elections they won 76 of the 132 seats in the Palestinian Parliament. Many countries have however condemned the activities of Hamas and regard it as a terrorist organization.

Activity:

Research Pan-Islamism

In this section you have a brief introduction on the three organizations that propose a Pan-Islamic road to the unity of the Arab world.

The class can divide into three groups and do further research for a presentation on one of the following groups:

- The Muslim Brothers
- Hamas
- The Hezbollah

In your research you should look for:

1 Reasons for the group's discontent
2 Methods used to express their discontent
3 Activities carried out by the group
4 The group's influence on the Muslim community

Hezbollah

The Hezbollah (which literally means the Party of God) was founded in Lebanon in 1982 after the start of the Israeli War. Unlike the Muslim Brothers and Hamas, it is a **Shi'a Muslim** organization and has been inspired by the Ayatollah Khomeini, the leader of the Iranian Revolution. The Hezbollah started as a militia group fighting the Israeli forces in 1982, but has developed into a political organization with strong political support in the Lebanese elections. Much like the Muslim Brothers, it has passed on its message through its welfare activities such as funding schools, hospitals and relief centres. In the 1992 elections Hezbollah did extremely well: they won all the 12 seats that were on their electoral list. In the elections in 2009, they formed an alliance with Amal, another Shi'a organization and won 35 out of the 128 seats.

> **Muslims** are the largest group in the Middle East and make up 92% of the population of the region. They are divided between **Shi'as** (29 per cent), which evolved as a separate sect from the year 657 CE, and **Sunnis** (65 per cent).

Models of Arab unity: an assessment

In a comparative assessment of all three movements the weakest of all proved to be Pan-Arabism. In spite of the ideals of the 1940s, the state boundaries drawn by the colonial powers after the First World War proved to be strong and resilient. The Arab countries' policies proved to be motivated by their state interests, conforming to the principle of **raison d'état** by proving that national interests always override other interests.

> **Raison d' état** is the French term for a country that prioritizes its own national interest.

The Arab League is a powerful force because it represents economically powerful states. It is, however, limited in that it represents the heads of states of these countries and does not appeal to the popular masses. Pan-Islamism on the other hand has the potential to surpass all other forms of organization and unity to date. It addresses the people directly and claims to offer Muslims a supranational unity (a unity that goes beyond state boundaries) that is appealing. Where Pan-Islamic governments have actually come to power, as in Iran, Afghanistan, Gaza, Southern Lebanon, their popularity has at times been challenged, but where Pan-Islamic parties pose as opposition they have been successful in gaining many votes and remain a very popular alternative.

Ways of Knowing—Emotion

? To what extent does emotion play a role in an historian's analysis?

Discuss the statements below, and find other primary and secondary sources that analyse the role of emotion in popular movements.

Where national memories are concerned, griefs are of more value than triumphs, for they impose duties, and require a common effort.

… nationalism converts sentiments into politics.

Gelvin, James. 2005. *The Israeli-Palestine Conflict.* Cambridge University Press. p. 6.

The Arab world and Israel

The establishment of the State of Israel left two very important unresolved questions. These have formed the basis for the uneasy relations and have posed as a major obstacle to conflict resolution.

On 14 May 1948, when the State of Israel was proclaimed, none of the Arab states recognized it and instead responded with the 1948 War, as a means to end its existence. Even though the Israeli victory in the war made Israel's existence a reality, to this day there are still 22 UN states that do not recognize it. In the Middle East these include Iran, Iraq, Yemen, UAE, Saudi Arabia, Syria, Kuwait, Lebanon, Bahrain, Qatar and Oman. Non- recognition has closed the door to a diplomatic solution to the situation. Only Egypt, Jordan and the Palestinian Liberation Organization (PLO) have so far recognized Israel and have agreed to negotiate with it. As a consequence, up to this point, while the question of recognition has not been confirmed by all states, the only means of "resolving" the situation has been war. A similar situation exists for the Palestinians. Although the State of Palestine is recognized by 100 states, Israel is not one of them. Non-recognition of a Palestinian State stands as yet another obstacle for a peaceful solution to the problem.

The other major issue is the plight of the **Palestinian refugees**. Although the UN resolution that gave birth to the State of Israel stipulated that Israel was required to accept a number of Palestinians within its new state, following the 1948–9 War thousands of Palestinians chose to leave or were forced to leave their homes and became refugees. The question for Israel was whether it should allow them to return.

There were at least two reasons why Israel did not wish to allow the **repatriation** of the Palestinians. For demographic reasons, in order to maintain a "Jewish State", it was important to reduce the number of Palestinians and the **Law of Return**, passed in 1950, which encouraged Jewish immigration into Israel, needed the space that the Palestinians had vacated for more Jewish settlements. For security reasons Israel regarded the Palestinians as potential enemies who intended to cause trouble. So its policy was to block their return and discourage any potential **infiltration** through tight border security. The decision against repatriation however meant that thousands of Palestinians remained homeless and lived in refugee camps. These camps, situated in neighbouring Arab states, became a major source of conflict: in addition to hostility between the Palestinians and the Israelis, tension also rose between Israel and the states hosting the refugees. As the number of refugees increased the situation also became tense between the refugees and their Arab hosts.

The past 50 years have seen many conflicts but also some attempts at resolving the conflict. The Middle East has become the centre of world attention. The conflicts have brought many external powers such as the United States to the negotiating table. This section will discuss how the relationship between the Arabs and the Israelis has evolved over these past 50 years.

A **Palestinian refugee** is defined by the UN as those: "whose normal place of residence was Palestine between June 1946 and May 1948, who lost both their homes and means of livelihood as a result of the 1948 Arab–Israeli conflict."

Repatriation After the 1948–9 War the international community put pressure on Israel to allow the Palestinians to return to their homes and take back their abandoned property, which in most cases had been expropriated by the local Jewish residents. The number of Palestinians that returned was extremely low.

The **Law of Return** was passed by the Israeli Parliament, the Knesset, in July 1950. It stipulated that all Jews and those of Jewish ancestry as well as their spouses had the right to settle in Israel and obtain Israeli citizenship.

Infiltration Palestinian refugees who returned to their homes, not to restitute their goods and settle in Israel, but with an aim to sabotage and destroy the new State of Israel. To prevent such attacks, Israel felt totally justified by attacking those neighbouring states that allowed these infiltrations to take place.

The wars that shaped the region

The outbreak of the 1948–9 war was a direct consequence of the refusal of the Arab States to recognize the new State of Israel. Their objective was to undermine its existence and re-establish Palestine. The outcome of the war was catastrophe, *Nakba,* for the Arabs and an affirmation of independence for the Israelis and the existence of the State of Israel.

The 1950s saw the establishment of new regimes in many of the Arab states. Many of the new leaders rose from the ranks of the military and championed the cause of the Palestinians. Many of them believed that the Palestinian cause could be pursued if the Arab states co-ordinated their efforts to defeat Israel. In 1967 this opportunity came. The 1967 war was an example of this unity. Egypt, Syria and Jordan attempted to co-ordinate their force to block Israel, but were disastrously defeated. Ironically the outcome of this war has since served as the basis for peace negotiations, but the implementations of the peace terms have not always been a great success.

The 1967 (Six Day) War had two major consequences. It increased the size of Israel by adding the Sinai and the Gaza Strip, the West Bank, East Jerusalem and the Golan Heights to Israel (see map, p. xxx). These are referred to as the "occupied territories". This meant that Egypt, Jordan and Syria were now all directly affected by the expansion of Israel and their hostility towards Israel was no longer the question of defending the Palestinian cause; it was now *their own* cause too. The three countries were therefore brought in as actors to the negotiating process. In November 1967 the UN passed resolution 242. This resolution based itself on two very important principles:

1 The withdrawal of Israeli armed forces from territories occupied in the conflict because "acquisition of territory by war was inadmissible".
2 Termination of all claims and the state of belligerency to be replaced by respect and acknowledgement of the sovereignty, territorial integrity and political independence of every state in the area and their right to live in peace within secure borders and recognized boundaries free from threats or acts of war.

These two principles have been used by both the Arabs and the Israelis to justify their rights. This is because the two principles can contradict one another. The first clause is a demand for Israel to withdraw from territories occupied in the conflict because it is "inadmissible" to acquire land through war. The second gives every state in the area the "right to live in peace within secure borders and recognized boundaries free from threats or acts of war." The Arab states therefore demanded the immediate return of the occupied territories as a precondition for negotiation. The Israelis claimed that returning some of the occupied territories would endanger their security. While Israel's expansion since the 1967 War has been used as a bargaining factor for Israel to open negotiations, it has not resolved all the problems. The negotiating process has been called "Land for Peace".

In 1973 the region was hit by another war, the Yom Kippur war or the "Crossing". The war started with an initial Arab victory, but ended with a successful Israeli counter-attack. The Israeli victory was however brought to a rapid end through the intervention of the superpowers. This war brought no major territorial changes and Israel continued to hold the territories it had gained from the previous wars. It nonetheless introduced a number of new elements which were to pave the way for future peace negotiations. Psychologically, the Arab states saw this war as a turning point. The humiliation of the 1967 (Six Day) War was wiped out of their collective memory and replaced with the memory of the victorious "Crossing" in the early stage of the conflict. This opened the way for the Egyptians to negotiate peace with the Israelis on equal terms. Given that the war had once again ended in a successful Israeli counter-attack, the Arab states came to the realization that Israel could not be defeated militarily. Clearly the existence of Israel could no longer be brought under question. This justified peace talks as a means to resolve the conflict. The 1973 war also introduced the United States to the negotiating table. From this conflict onwards the USA would play an important role in mediating peace talks between the belligerents.

The occupied territories

The Sinai Peninsula

The Sinai Peninsula was part of Egypt and formed the Israeli–Egyptian border after the 1949 war. In the 1956 War (known as the Sinai War by Israelis), the Sinai was occupied by Israeli forces. The Israelis however withdrew under US and Soviet pressure and handed it over to the United Nations Emergency Forces (UNEF). In 1967 Nasser ordered the UNEF to leave, but the 1967 (Six Day) War resulted in the occupation by Israel of the entire peninsula. The peninsula remained in Israeli hands until the 1979 peace treaty signed between Sadat and Begin, in which the principle of "Land for Peace" was implemented for the first time. The Israeli forces withdrew in stages and it was not until 1982 that Sinai returned into Egyptian hands entirely.

The Gaza Strip

The Gaza strip is a narrow strip of land 41 kilometers long and 6–12 kilometers wide. Following the 1948–9 War it was occupied by Egypt but was mainly populated by Palestinian refugees from the 1948–9 War. In the 1956 War it was briefly

taken by Israel but returned to Egypt. As a consequence of the 1967 War, the Gaza Strip was occupied by Israel and remained in Israeli hands until the Oslo Accords of 1993. Following the Oslo Accords, Israel agreed to hand over Gaza to the Palestinian Authorities. Gaza, however, continues to be a major source of insecurity for the State of Israel. Israel continues to control its airspace, its water supplies and its borders.

The West Bank

The West Bank is the territory west of the River Jordan, situated between Jordan and Israel. It is populated by Palestinian refugees of the various wars. After the 1948–9 war it was annexed by Jordan (called Transjordan until 1949). The Jordanian rule continued until 1967, when the West Bank fell into Israeli hands. In 1988, while still under Israeli hands, Jordan renounced its claims on the territory and handed it to the Palestinian Liberation Organisation (PLO). Following the Oslo Accords of 1993, the Israeli government agreed to hand over parts of the West Bank to the Palestinian National Authority. The West Bank continues, however, to be the home of thousands of Jewish people, who settled in the region during the long years of occupation.

The Golan Heights

The Golan Heights is a plateau and mountainous region lying between Syria and Israel. Although part of Syria after the 1948–9 War, it fell into Israeli hands after the 1967 War. At first the region was controlled by Israel as occupied territory but after 1981 they passed the Golan Heights Laws which brought the region directly under Israeli civilian administration. The Golan Heights is now regarded as a northern district of Israel. This move was condemned by the United Nations, but Israel claims that the Heights are essential to is security. Syria continues to demand the return of the Golan Heights.

East Jerusalem

East Jerusalem refers to the part of Jerusalem that was originally part of Transjordan (as it was populated mainly by Arabs) and which was taken over by Israel after the 1967 War. The Israeli

Activity:
Map study

Research the occupied territories and discuss each region's strategic and economic advantages and disadvantages. Fill in the table below, and decide whether "Land for Peace" should be put into effect or not.

"Land for Peace": a formula for negotiation and conflict resolution				
Region	Strategic advantage	Economic advantage	Any other factors?	Conclusion: should Israel agree to "give" the region away in return for peace?
The Sinai Peninsula				
The Gaza Strip				
The West Bank				
The Golan Heights				
East Jerusalem				

Parliament had stated as early as January 1950 that Jerusalem was the capital of Israel (even though at that time Jerusalem was divided and the State of Israel was only in control of the Western district). Following the 1967 war and the acquisition of the eastern part through war, the Israeli Parliament announced that Jerusalem had been unified for all time. Much like the Golan Heights, the Jerusalem Laws were passed in 1980 and the city has come entirely within the State of Israel.

Conflict resolution: "Land for Peace"

The Sinai Peninsula: Egyptian–Israeli relations, the Camp David Accords and the Egyptian–Israeli Peace Treaty

At first Nasser attempted to dislodge Israel from Sinai by waging a war of attrition through a series of artillery duels across the Suez Canal. The attempts were not successful. In 1973 the Yom Kippur war or the Crossing succeeded in bringing the United States into the negotiations and in 1977 Sadat initiated talks on the basis of "Land for Peace". The Camp David agreements of 1978 and the Peace Treaty signed in 1979 were a major breakthrough because in return for the Sinai Peninsula, Egypt became the first country to recognize Israel in the region. The two countries agreed to end their hostility towards one another and the "Land for Peace" formula had been successful.

The West Bank: Israeli–Jordanian relations and the Israeli–Jordanian Peace Treaty

In 1987 Jordan also followed the Egyptian example and initiated talks with Israel in view of ending hostilities between the two countries. In 1988 Jordan renounced its claims on the West Bank and handed those rights to the Palestinian Liberation Organization (PLO). A major obstacle had been removed and this permitted an Israeli–Jordanian peace treaty. In October 1994, King Hussein of Jordan and Prime Minister Yizhak Rabin of Israel finally signed the Israeli–Jordanian Peace Treaty. According to this treaty, both countries agreed to respect each others' sovereignty (This meant that Jordan was recognizing the existence of the State of Israel) and put an end to the hostility of the two countries.

The Golan Heights: Israeli–Syrian relations

Of the three countries that had lost territory in the 1967 War, a "Land for Peace" negotiation between Syria and Israel over the Golan Heights has still not happened. There are a number of reasons for this. Syria opposed both peace treaties and so far has shown reluctance to come to the negotiating table. The Golan Heights has more strategic importance to Israel than the Sinai or the West Bank. The Golan Heights overlooks the region called Galilee and in the hands of Syria it would render that part of Israel very vulnerable to attack. Since 1981 Israel has included the Golan Heights within the civil administration of the State of Israel. Handing over the Heights would be like giving up part of its own territory.

The Gaza Strip and the West Bank: Israeli–Palestinian relations; the Oslo Accords or the Declaration of Principles

In 1991 a conference was held in Madrid, in which the USA and the USSR brought together Israelis and Palestinians in the presence of Syria, Lebanon and Jordan. Though Israel objected to the presence of the PLO, the Palestinian delegation was in constant contact with the PLO leadership. The conference lasted three days and its objective was to hold an open forum between groups that had so far never agreed to meet, to discuss peace. This was symbolic, but it was an important first step. In 1993 negotiations opened between the Israelis and the PLO in Oslo, Norway. This led to the Oslo Accords, represented in the form of two letters exchanged between the chairman of the PLO, Yasser Arafat and the Prime Minister of Israel, Yitzhak Rabin (see letters following). The PLO recognized the State of Israel, while the Government of Israel recognized the PLO (but not the State of Palestine). This was an important breakthrough because Palestinians and Israelis had never agreed to meet face to face and the Palestinians had never, up to that moment, recognized the State of Israel. The Oslo Accords were then followed by the Declaration of Principles, which based itself on the "Land for Peace" formula. The Israelis agreed to withdraw from the Gaza Strip and parts of the West Bank and authorized the creation of a Palestinian National Authority (PNA) in those regions. Elections were held in 1996 and Yasser Arafat was elected as President of the Palestinian National Authority. As Israeli troops withdrew from the zones mentioned in the Accords, the PNA took over. This was the first time since the 1948–9 War that Palestinians had been allowed the right of self-determination in a limited portion of their homeland. The "Land for Peace" settlement, however, cost Yizhak Rabin his life because a month

Activity:
Between the lines

Correspondence between Yasser Arafat and Yitzhak Rabin.

1 What was each side conceding to?

2 How important do you think these concessions were?

Correspondence between Yasser Arafat and Yitzhak Rabin

September 9, 1993
Mr. Prime Minister [Yitzhak Rabin],

The signing of the Declaration of Principles marks a new era… I would like to confirm the following PLO commitments: The PLO recognizes the right of the State of Israel to exist in peace and security… The PLO commits itself…to a peaceful resolution of the conflict between the two sides and declares that all outstanding issues relating to permanent status will be resolved through negotiations…the PLO renounces the use of terrorism and other acts of violence and will assume responsibility over all PLO elements and personnel in order to assure their compliance, prevent violations and discipline violators…

Yasser Arafat.

September 9, 1993
Mr. Chairman [Yasser Arafat],

In response to your letter of September 9, 1993, I wish to confirm to you that, in light of the PLO commitments included in your letter, the Government of Israel has decided to recognize the PLO as the representative of the Palestinian people and commence negotiations with the PLO within the Middle East peace process.

Yitzhak Rabin

after signing the agreement known as Oslo 2, in November 1995, he was shot by a Jewish religious extremist, who justified for his actions at the subsequent trial with the claim, that Rabin "wanted to give Israel to the Arabs".

In conclusion, the "Land for Peace" principle opened the way for negotiation and successfully ended the deadlock caused by "non-recognition" between Egypt, Jordan, the PLO and Israel. It has however only been a partial success because of the presence of Jewish settlers in the occupied territories, and the continuing problem of the Palestinian refugees.

The Jewish settlements

One of the major difficulties in implementing the "Land for Peace" principle has been the presence of nearly half a million Jewish settlers in the occupied territories. The settlers, some of whom have lived in the occupied territories since the early 1970s, have been reluctant to give up their homes and be relocated.

Yasser Aarafat (1929–2004)

Yasser Arafat was born in 1929 in a Palestinian merchant family that had settled in Cairo. He was one of seven children. He studied engineering in Fuad University in Egypt and graduated in 1951. Already at university he started organizing Palestinian groups and advocated the idea that Palestine can only be liberated through armed struggle. This conviction and the cult of violence, which he came to renounce near the end of his life by signing the Oslo Accords, symbolized the Palestinian national movement. In the late 1950s Arafat formed the Fatah, a guerrilla group whose objective was the restoration of an independent, democratic state of Palestine. Fatah became part of a larger front representing the Palestinians known as the Palestinian Liberation Organisation. Arafat became its chairman in 1969 and kept that post until his death in 2004. As chairman he was respected by the Arab world and obtained international recognition for the Palestinian cause. In 1974 he addressed the United Nations plenary session, stating: "Today I have come bearing an olive branch and a freedom fighter's gun. Do not let the olive branch fall from my hand."

Later in his career Arafat changed his stance on Israel and agreed to enter the process of negotiation with Israeli officials. This culminated in the Oslo Accords of 1993 and the Camp David Summit of 2000. These talks brought him international fame but criticism from other Palestinian groups. Some saw his move as a step towards the resolution of the conflict while others regarded it as an unacceptable compromise. In 1994 Arafat along with Yitzhak Rabin and Shimon Peres received the Nobel Peace Prize.

As the first President of the Palestinian National Authority, Arafat settled in Ramallah in the West Bank. In 2004 he travelled to France for medical treatment, and died in a hospital near Paris.

Attempts to destroy the settlements have led at times to violent clashes between Israeli soldiers and the settlers. In 1982, for example, the settlement in Sinai called Yamit, which housed 2,500 people, had to be evacuated and returned to Egypt as part of the Israeli–Egyptian Peace Treaty agreement. The residents barricaded themselves in the houses and had to be dragged out by Israeli soldiers. The question of the settlements has therefore been a major obstacle to peace because no Israeli government wants to be accused of uprooting and forcefully evacuating Jewish homes.

A further issue is the number of settlers and settlements. According to the Central Bureau of Statistics in Israel, the number of settlers has evolved in the following increments:

Year	West Bank	Gaza Strip	East Jerusalem	Golan Heights	Total
1972	1,182	700	8,649	77	10,608
1985	44,100	1,900	103,900	8,700	158,700
1995	133,200	5,300	157,300	13,400	309,200
2004	234,487	7,826	181,587	17,265	441,828

Source: *Comprehensive Settlement Population 1972–2008*, 15 November 2009. http://www.fmep.org.

The statistics shown above do not take into consideration the illegal settlements. The number of settlements varies in size; some are self-contained small towns with a population ranging from 15,000 to 25,000 settlers, others are temporary homes in trailers on a hill top, which are often illegal. Each of the territories has the following number of "legal" settlements: 150 settlements in the West Bank, 20 settlements in Gaza, and 30 settlements in the Golan Heights. Jewish communities decide to settle in the occupied territories for a number of reasons that can be summed up as:

- ideological/nationalistic
- economic
- defence.

Reasons for the settlements

Ideological/nationalistic

The Zionist Movement considered many parts of Palestine to be the "Land of Israel" *Eretz Yisrael*, land that according to the Bible had been promised to the Jews. This did not limit itself to the portion allocated to the State of Israel in 1948 by the United Nations. Therefore territories acquired through war only constitute land that should rightly belong to Israel. A group that advocates this view-point is the *Gush Emunim* (Bloc of the Faithful), an organization founded in 1974 that considers it is the religious duty of every Jewish citizen to extend the Land of Israel. The organization's strategy has been to encourage settlements and resist any attempt to be removed from the occupied territories. The *Gush Emunim* is a powerful organization with a great deal of influence in the Knesset, the Israeli Parliament.

> **Activity:**
> **Gush *Emunim***
>
> Research *Gush Emunim*. What kinds of activities have brought the organization into the news?

Economic

Not all the settlers have an ideological incentive. Many have settled in the occupied territories because it is cheap and spacious. The government has also offered tax breaks and low-interest loans to those that settled in the occupied territories.

Defence

These territories also constitute a major defence incentive. They have even been referred to as the Israeli **Maginot Line**. The settlers' presence in these regions helps form a buffer zone for the security of Israel. In the case of the Golan Heights, it is also a spot that overlooks the Galilee region of Israel and is therefore of strategic and tactical importance. However, some have questioned the validity of these arguments. Firstly, they state, the fact that Israel's enemies are today capable of attacking Israel with missiles from their own countries makes the defence argument a little redundant. Secondly, keeping the occupied territories causes such intense hostility with the local Palestinian inhabitants that it can only increase the threat of an attack. Claiming that the occupied territories are *needed* for Israel's defence has, however, been a principle justification for their stay in the occupied territories. According to the UN resolution 242, Israel has the "right to live in peace within secure borders". If Israel needs the occupied territories to be assured of secure borders, then the settlements would be totally justified.

> The **Maginot Line**, named after the French Minister of Defence André Maginot, was a line of fortifications built in the 1930s along the Franco-German border to defend France in case of a German attack.

The role of the Israeli governments

The policy of encouraging settlements is usually associated with the Likud Party, which came to power in 1977. However, as the statistics above show, settlements had actually started before that date under the Labour party. After the 1977 elections, settlements started to expand because the Likud-dominated government advocated the building of the Greater Israel.

The international community has announced that they consider the settlements illegal and the United Nations had condemned Israeli government. According to the 4th Geneva Convention signed in 1949 "The occupying power shall not deport or transfer parts of its own civilian population into the territory it occupies." The Israeli governments have ignored these remarks. Given the numbers of settlers and the adamancy of those political organizations who advocate settlement, it is hard to imagine an Israeli government that would agree to put an end to the Jewish settlements. Meanwhile their presence is a constant reminder for the Palestinian refugees of Israel's power and dominance in the region.

The Palestinians: from refugees to the PLO and the PNA

The 1948–9 War turned 700,000 Palestinians into refugees. They abandoned their homes to live in the West Bank (which belonged to Transjordan) or Gaza (which belonged to Egypt). The 1967 War caused another 300,000 Palestinians to become homeless. According to the United Nations, in 2002 the number of refugees had risen to 2,000,000. They now live in Gaza, the West Bank, Syria, Lebanon and Jordan.

The presence of Palestinians in the neighbouring Arab states became a source of many problems. As a displaced nation, the Palestinians regarded the country they were residing in as a base from which to attack Israel. The host country, on the hand, viewed the Palestinians as refugees, who while waiting to return to their homeland, should abide by the laws of their new place of residence. This led to the tragedy of September 1970, known as Black September in Jordan. It also led to the Lebanese war of 1982. It has also continued to incite hostility and conflict between Israelis and the Palestinians. Whereas for the world at large, the plight of the Palestinian refugees is a constant reminder of the injustice the Palestinian people have had to face in recent history, for the Israeli government it is a confirmation of the threat to their security and therefore a justification for their constant state of war.

Former US President Jimmy Carter, founder of The Carter Center, has a special interest in the Middle East, and has observed many of the events in the region. In 2006, he published a book entitled *Palestine: Peace not Apartheid* in which he provided glimpses of life in the occupied territories. He wrote of Gaza:

> Living among 1.3 million Palestinians, the 8,000 Israeli settlers controlled 40% of the arable land and more than one half of the water resources. 12,000 troops are required to defend their presence.

Source: Carter, J. 2006. *Palestine: Peace not Apartheid.* New York, USA. Simon and Schuster. p. 217.

> *"The right of the Jewish people to the land of Israel is eternal and indisputable and is linked with the right of security and peace."*
>
> Likud Party platform, 1977.

Ten years earlier, in 1996, the Carter Center had been to the West Bank to monitor the elections:

> … it was obvious that the Israelis had almost complete control over every aspect of the political, military and economic existence of the Palestinians within the West Bank and Gaza. Israeli settlements permeated the occupied territories, and highways connecting the settlements with one another and with Jerusalem were being rapidly built, with Palestinians prohibited from using or crossing some of the key roads. In addition more than one hundred permanent Israeli checkpoints obstructed the routes still open to Palestinian traffic either pedestrian or vehicular.

> **Source:** Carter, J. 2006. *Palestine: Peace not Apartheid*. New York, USA. Simon and Schuster. p. 183.

In 2002 the restrictions became more visible when the Israeli government decided to build a wall in the West Bank to separate the settlers from the Palestinians. From the Israeli point of view the wall defends the settlers and Israel from the Palestinian suicide bombers. According to the BBC there have been more than 70 bomb attacks on Israeli targets since 2000. The Palestinians are angered because it severely restricts their ability to access their place of work in Israel. In 2004 the International Court of Justice declared that the barrier was illegal and construction should be immediately halted, but Israel said it would not abide by this ruling.

A view of the Barrier Wall and the Israeli settlement of Gillo from the West Bank city of Bethlehem.

The birth of a Palestinian national movement

In 1964, in a meeting held in Cairo initiated by the Egyptian President, Nasser, 13 Arab leaders agreed on the formation of an organization representing the Palestinian people. This organization adopted the name the Palestinian Liberation Organization (the PLO). The organization's national Charter stated that Palestine, as it existed under the British mandate, is the homeland of the Palestinian Arab people and Palestinian Arabs possess a legal right to its homeland. The PLO is made up of a number of different organizations. The Fatah, the group founded by Yasser Arafat is the largest group within the PLO. Yasser Arafat became the chairman of the PLO in 1969 and remained in that office until his death in 2004. Up to the 1967 War, the Palestinian cause had been championed by the Arab states and the Palestinians were regarded as too insignificant and weak to defend their case themselves. The defeat in the 1967 War was a turning point. It underlined the incapacity of the Arab states and demonstrated to Palestinians that they needed to take the matters into their own hands.

In 1968 the Israeli forces attacked the village of Karameh in the West Bank (Jordan). The aim of the attack was to uproot Palestinian armed forces. Assisted by the Jordanian army, the Palestinians forced the Israelis to withdraw. This battle was of major symbolic value to the Palestinian national pride. Karameh (in Arabic the word means dignity/honour) allowed Palestinians to distinguish themselves as a nation capable of standing up for its own rights.

Yasser Arafat addressing the UN General Assembly 13.11.1974

The presence of Palestinians in Jordan was, however, a potential threat to Jordan, which was losing its authority amongst the Palestinians. As the Palestinians were supported and financed by other Arab states, they became more autonomous and the Jordanian regime lost its authority among the Palestinians. The Jordanians resented the Palestinian disregard for Jordanian law. Regardless, Palestinian commandos believed it to be their right to establish an independent base from which to fight for their independence. This cross-border war had devastating effects on Jordan as it became the target of Israeli military retaliations. In November 1968 King Hussein (the ruler of Jordan) addressed this "problem" and proposed a seven-point agreement with the Palestinian leaders. These included such measures as forbidding Palestinians to carry arms and asking Palestinians to carry Jordanian identity cards. The Palestinians, who had recently been empowered by the successes of the battle of Karameh, refused to abide by the new rules.

As the relationship between the Jordanian government and the Palestinian groups worsened, King Hussein decided to go on the offensive. On 15 September 1970 he declared martial law and the Palestinian headquarters came under heavy attack by the Jordanian army. The battle referred to as Black September lasted ten days. Making no distinction between civilians and guerrilla fighters, the Jordanian army bombarded the refugee camps. Over 3,000 were killed and over 11,000 wounded. The Palestinians were expelled from Jordan and were given a "home" in Lebanon.

The PLO had suffered a major setback and internal disagreements over tactics arose between the groups that made up the PLO. Yasser Arafat's *Fatah* emerged as the more moderate group that accepted "national authority over any piece of Palestinian territory". This meant that they were no longer pursuing the policy that denied Israel its right of existence and could eventually come to a diplomatic solution and negotiate on the basis of "Land for Peace". This has commonly been referred to as the "Two State Solution". Other groups within the PLO rejected this idea and therefore broke away from the organization. In 1974, the PLO obtained recognition first amongst the Arab states at the Arab League summit meeting in Rabat, and then in the international arena when Yasser Arafat addressed the UN General Assembly on 13 November 1974 and the PLO obtained observer status at the UN.

Discussion point:

Can rebellions be justified? What about the *Intifada*?

Activity:
Class debate

To what extent is the "Two State Solution" a way to resolve the Israeli–Palestinian problem?

The class will break up into groups representing different countries and different opinions.

1 Why are they for it?

2 What are the obstacles?

3 What will it resolve?

4 Would it be a temporary solution or a permanent one?

The Palestinian uprising (*Intifada*)

The Palestinian uprising or the *Intifada* began in Gaza in December 1987 following a road accident involving an Israeli military vehicle that killed four Palestinians. In the protest rally that gathered after the incident, the Israeli forces opened fire and shot more people. Within a few days Gaza, East Jerusalem and the West Bank became the scene of violent clashes between the local population and the Israeli armed forces. This rebellion, known as the *Intifada*— the shaking off—lasted for five years. Though the incident that triggered off the *Intifada* was a road accident, it was clear that the situation was ripe for such an uprising and the incident was merely the spark that fell on dry wood ready for ignition.

Intifada. Rebellion in Gaza from 1987. Palestinians throwing rocks at Israeli tanks. Israeli tanks attacking teenagers that carried slingshots and stones.

In order to understand the long-term causes of the rebellion, it is necessary to take a step back and consider the situation in the occupied territories. In the 1980s the Israeli government fell into the hands of hardliners who pursued an active policy of settlement. Furthermore, in the occupied territories, faced with growing threats of insecurity, the Israeli military administration continuously harassed the Palestinians through constant security checks. Palestinians had to abide by Israeli rules which were becoming more and more restrictive and as the majority of the Palestinians were totally dependent economically on the Israeli job market, they had to accept the restrictive measures that the Israelis imposed upon them on a daily basis. Furthermore, Gaza is both extremely poor and overpopulated. It has one of the highest rates of population growth in the world (4.7 per cent). When the accident happened in 1987 there was already mounting discontent amongst the population at large.

During the first few weeks the uprising was spontaneous and unorganized: young people gathered and threw stones, gasoline bombs and other home-made weapons at the Israeli soldiers. As the movement persisted, a body calling itself the Unified National Leadership (UNL) took over the role of co-ordination. The UNL issued instructions and called upon the people to support the movement in every way possible.

The tactic proposed by the UNL was refusal to abide by Israeli laws—in other words civil disobedience. These tactics included calling for a general strike, the refusal to pay taxes, a boycott of Israeli goods, the withdrawal of money from Israeli banks and mass demonstrations. While the public at large carried out these passive forms of mobilization, the youth were actively confronting the Israeli soldiers with stones and slingshots. The leadership specifically forbade the use of guns and knives. The movement's demands centred on their grievances with the Israeli military presence. They asked for an end to settlements and to the confiscation of Palestinian lands, the cancellation of the special tax and Israeli recognition for the Palestinian State. The *Intifada* lasted for nearly five years. An estimated 1,100 Palestinians and 160 Israelis were killed in the confrontations. A further 1,000 Palestinians, accused of collaboration with the Israelis, were killed or executed by Palestinians.

The image of Israeli tanks attacking teenagers that carried slingshots and stones tarnished Israel's reputation in the international arena. It also pushed the Israelis to realize that the forceful method is not necessarily the successful one, and moved them closer to the negotiating table. More than any of the previous wars, the images of the *Intifada* as shown through the international media raised the attention of the world to the plight of the Palestinian refugees. International organizations such as the UN and the European Union raised their concern over Israeli policy in the occupied territories. The European Union later became a major financial contributor to the **Palestinian National Authority**.

> Formed in 1994, the **Palestinian National Authority** is the body that administers the territories of the West Bank and Gaza that the Oslo agreement accorded to the Palestinians. The West Bank was divided up into three areas: A, B and C. Area A was brought under the complete control of the PNA. Area B was under PNA's control in civilian matters, but for security matters Israel took responsibility. Area C, known as "security zones" remained under Israeli control.

Activity:

Essay writing: analysis

"To what extent did the Intifada pave the way towards the Oslo Accords?"

The Oslo Accords were a major breakthrough in the Israeli-Palestinian relations. Such a major event can never be caused by one single event. In a "to what extent" essay, you need to consider a wide spectrum of events and evaluate the merits of each. As always "opinions and conclusions should be presented clearly and supported with appropriate evidence and sound argument".

Source: IBO "Glossary of command terms" in the *History Guide*.

Prepare a chart

Use the one on p. 317 as a guide. Write about some of the following events that may be considered as having "paved way towards the Oslo Accords".

The coming of the end of the Cold War

The *Intifada*

The Gulf War

The election of a Labour government in Israel

The role played by the Norwegians

Activity:

Palestinian National Authority

Research the PNA Does it have a flag? What kind of governing body is it? Where has it been formally represented?

Lebanon

In 1975 a civil war started in Lebanon. This was to last for 16 years. The Lebanese Civil war shared similar traits with all classic civil wars: it revealed the existence of a weak central government incapable of maintaining authority over its citizens; it reflected the presence of domestic tensions brought about by ideological, religious and/or ethnic differences; it involved a large number of civilians whose place of residence or religious affiliation turned them into war targets. Finally, like many civil wars, Lebanon also became a theatre of war for outsiders who intervened in the war by assisting one side or the other to pursue their own interests. The civil war was triggered off by an incident in the town of Sidon in 1975, but the long-term causes of the war arose from the growing social tensions and divisions that came to a head in the 1970s.

Lebanon has a diverse population divided both along ethnic and religious lines, being comprised of Sunni, Shi'a and Druze Muslims and Catholic, Orthodox and Protestant Christians. Though the region underwent conversion to Islam in the seventh century (632–61 CE), a small community of Christians remained. The largest of these communities known as the Maronites settled on the coastal region of what is today Lebanon. With the Mediterranean Sea on one side and a range of mountains, Jabal Lubnan or Mount Lebanon on the other, this community was physically separated from their Muslim counterparts. Their settlement on the coast meant that many became merchant seamen and thus had close contacts through trade with the outside world. This allowed them to retain their ties with the Christian world. As a minority they maintained a close-knit communal life, vigorously preserving their religious rites and beliefs and acquiring the skills of self-defence and armed resistance. The survival of the community under Muslim rulers resulted in an equilibrium being established between the two religious communities. Colonization was to change this equilibrium.

With the arrival of the Europeans, the Christian community was revived because the Europeans regarded them as a natural ally. The Lebanese Maronites were given important posts by the French colonizers. Many had received a French education, which tied them even more closely to France. They enjoyed privileges and gradually came to dominate the Muslims politically. In order to justify the privileged status of a minority community a census was carried out in 1932. According to this census the ratio of Christians to Muslims was 6:5. This ratio served as a framework for Lebanon's political structure; it was transposed into political representation and so the constitution fixed a condition which ensured that for every six Christian deputies in the Assembly there would be five Muslim deputies.

Lebanon obtained its independence in 1943. In the same year the National Pact, the *Mithaq al watani*, was agreed upon. This document reaffirmed the 1932 census and maintained the same balance of power

Discussion point:

Discuss civil wars. Why do they occur? Can you think of other countries where civil wars have occurred?

Activity:
Map activity

Draw a map of Lebanon and show where different religious groups live.

in parliament. In addition, it allocated the following posts to each of the religious groups: the president had to be a Maronite; the prime minister, a Sunni Muslim; and the Speaker of the Parliament a Shi'a Muslim. As the French political model was used, the president played a major political role. The Maronites were also put in charge of the army. The National Pact ensured a "pragmatic representative system" that allowed a compromise that would preserve the state. It established Lebanon as a multi-confessional state and by freezing the ratio of the population and rejecting proportional representation (a system whereby parliament and the government would reflect the changing demographic ratio of the country) it claimed to "protect" each religious community. It nonetheless enforced and gave permanence to the division and denied Lebanon any form of national homogeneity.

Furthermore, this confessional division (division on the grounds of religion) permeated all other aspects of life. Geographically, each community occupied a particular part of Lebanon. The Christians lived on the coast around Beirut and Mount Lebanon. The Sunnis were mainly in the East in the region called Anti-Lebanon on the border of Syria. The Shi'as lived mainly in the south near the Israeli border. Politically, each religious group was represented by its own party. The parties also often had a military wing of trained militia that were ready to defend or fight for the rights of their community. The peaceful co-existence of the communities was dependent on the strict adherence to the National Pact and an unchanging demography and geography. In other words, if the population of Lebanon remained as it had been in the 1932 census, the system made sense. Post-independence Lebanon was, however, to see many changes that destabilized its demographic and geographic equilibrium and brought the National Pact under question. The factors that destabilized the demographic equilibrium were:

1 the increasing presence of Palestinians
2 the presence of the PLO as a political organization
3 the migration of the Shi'a community towards the North of Lebanon.

The Palestinians started to enter Lebanon as a consequence of the wars. Already 100,000 Palestinians had come to settle in Lebanon after the 1948–9 War; their numbers grew with the 1967 War and the outbreak of hostilities between the Jordanian government and the Palestinians in 1970 known as Black September. As a result, the Palestinian community of Jordan as well as the PLO organization came to use Lebanon as their new place of residence. This increased the number of Muslims in Lebanon and upset the delicate demographic and confessional balance of the country.

With the PLO headquarter in Beirut, Lebanon came to be used as a base to launch guerrilla warfare against Israel. This brought Israel into Lebanese politics and gave rise to serious security and political problems for the Lebanese government. The PLO was an extremely powerful force in the 1970s and the presence of Palestinian refugees on the border of Israel in Lebanon was a security problem for Israel. Israel retaliated against the PLO with raids against Lebanon. This violated Lebanon's sovereignty and without a strong army behind it the status and the legitimacy of the Lebanese government was undermined. As the Lebanese army was incapable of defending the population against Israel, the population came to form militias to defend themselves. When war broke out in 1975, the Lebanese national army was outnumbered by the militias by about 2:1.

The political geography of Lebanon changed when the Shi'a community that lived in southern Lebanon was forced to migrate north to Beirut as a result of the settlement of the Palestinians in their region. The presence of the Palestinians was resented by the Shi'as, who now struggled to make a living because of the greater competition in the job market and whose lives were now placed at risk because the region had become the target of Israeli raids. This mass migration of the Shi'as caused further disequilibrium in the delicate demographic balance of Lebanon.

Though the demographic changes were a cause for the imbalance and destabilization of the region, it should not be forgotten that the colonial legacy of "divide and rule" had established the division in Lebanon. Through favouring one group over another, it had raised expectations among the Christian Maronites who came to perceive themselves as more modern and more Western than the Muslims. Consequently they believed that they had the know-how and the capacity to rule Lebanon better than the others. This naturally caused resentment among the Muslim community, whose numbers grew with time while their political representation remained minimal. With rising tension each side started to look for 'allies' in the region. As Lebanon had also become the home of the Palestinians and in particular the PLO, neighbouring countries such as Israel, Syria and Iran started to show a greater interest in Lebanon and use it as their own battleground. According to Colbert Held, "Lebanon became the confused battleground for its own militias and for its neighbors' armed forces."

Lebanon's ethnic composition			
Ethnic composition	**% of the total population**	**Religious composition**	**% of the total population**
Arab:	84.5%	Muslims:	62.4%
Lebanese	71.2%	Shi'a	34%
Palestinian	12.1%	Sunni	21.3%
		Druze	7.1%
Armenian	6.8%	Christians:	37.6%
		Maronites (Catholics)	19%
		Greek Catholics (Melchites)	4.6%
			6%
		Greek Orthodox	5.2%
		Armenian Apostolic	0.5%
		Protestant	
Kurd	6.1%		
Other	2.6%		

Held, C. 2006. *Middle East Patterns: Places, Peoples and Politics*. Boulder, Colorado, USA. Westview Press p. 292

Lebanon: a divided nation

The Christians

The Christian Maronites were the first to organize themselves. In 1936 the Phalange (*Kataeb* in Arabic) party was formed by Pierre Gemayel, a Maronite. Though a secular party, it strongly reflected the interests of the Christian Maronite community. The party believed in the sovereignty and independence of Lebanon and ideologically stood on the right. Opposed to the Palestinian presence in Lebanon, the Phalange believed that the Palestinian presence was undermining their position and Lebanon's sovereignty because it was extending the Arab–Israeli conflict into their homeland. By the late 1960s the party had formed its own militia group. At the start of the civil war the Phalange militia, under the leadership of Pierre's son Bachir Gemayel, was said to have had 10,000 members. Later in the war the different Christian groups came together to form the Lebanese Front.

Another Christian militia was the South Lebanon Army. This was mainly under the control of Israel and fought the Muslims in the southern Israeli occupied region.

The Druze

The Druze are a minority Muslim group living in Southern Syria, Central Lebanon and Northern Israel who describe themselves as unitarian Muslims. They are a dissident branch of the Ismaeili Shi'a sect. Their population is around 910,000 and they have lived in the region for at least a millenium. The Druze leader Kamal Jumblatt formed the Progressive Socialist Party and was the founder of a militia named the Lebanese National Movement (LNM). They disagreed with the Maronites on two major points. They disagreed over the National Pact. The Christian Maronites believed in maintaining the Pact, but the Druze called for its abrogation. They also disagreed over the presence of the Palestinians. While the Christian Maronites regarded the Palestinian presence as a danger to the stability of Lebanon, the Sunnis and the Druze and later the Shi'as defended the Palestinian cause against Israel. The LNM was very active in the early years of the civil war. Consequently they came into conflict with the Phalangist Maronites. In the early years of the war, they claimed to have 25,000 militiamen and fought alongside the PLO.

The Shi'as

The Shi'a community was adversely affected by the influx of the Palestinians into Southern Lebanon. Many were forced to migrate and settled in Beirut's so-called "poverty belt". In the mid 1970s the group *Amal* (*Amal* means hope) was formed, which rallied Lebanese Shi'as and called for the expulsion of all foreign forces in Lebanon and in defence of the rights of the Shi'a community. In 1982, following the second Israeli invasion, another Shi'a militia group was formed, the Hezbollah (the Party of God). The Hezbollah's main target was Israel and their militia fought against both the South Lebanon Army and the Israeli troops until the final evacuation of the Israelis in 2000.

The Lebanese Civil War, 1975–90

A dispute about business deals in the Sidon fishing industries triggered off the fighting in April 1975. Muslim fishermen fearing a threat to their business by a Maronite fishing consortium staged a demonstration, which turned violent. The Lebanese National Army was called in, which in turn brought in Muslim militias and the PLO. The delicate balance between Muslims and Christians had snapped and antagonism between the two groups that had been building up over the years erupted into an all out conflict. The main protagonists were at first the Palestinians with their supporters and the Phalangists.

On 13 April 1975, an assassination attempt on the life of Phalangist leader Pierre Gemayel suddenly brought Beirut into a state of war. Roadblocks set up to identify religious affiliations prompted panic and caused people to leave their homes and take refuge amongst their religious communities. Violence on both sides caused massive civilian casualties. By 1976, Syrian forces had entered the country. An Arab League summit held in Riyadh charged the Syrian army to remain in Lebanon as the Arab Deterrent Army. A fragile cease-fire was called. So far 50, 000 people had been killed and the country was effectively divided between the Muslim and Christian zones.

Activity:
An historical investigation

Following the news of the massacre of Sabra and Shatila, the Israeli organization *Peace Now* called a demonstration in Tel Aviv. The demonstration was attended by 400,000 people (out of a population of 5.5 million) calling for a commission of inquiry into the event.

Find out what really happened at the Sabra-Shatila refugee camp. Look at the role played by the:

● Phalangists
● Israeli Defense Force
● Israeli people
● world public opinion
● United Nations
● Kahan Commission.

In 2008 Ari Folman's animated film *Waltz with Bashir*, the story of an Israeli soldier's recollections of the 1982 Sabra and Shatila massacre, revived the nightmares of war. The film won a number of international awards.

Instability in Lebanon gave Israel the opportunity to pursue its prime foreign policy objective, which was to destroy the PLO and establish a "friendly" government in Beirut. This would render her northern border secure. In 1978 Operation Litani was launched. Israeli troops occupied South Lebanon as far north as the river Litani. Though the occupation was immediately followed by a UN resolution calling upon Israel to withdraw its troops, the invasion had nonetheless served a very important purpose. It allowed Israel to maintain a force on a 12-mile stretch of the Israeli–Lebanese border and more importantly it gave the Israelis the opportunity to form the South Lebanon Force, a Christian militia based in the South and trained and equipped by the Israelis. So, in spite of the presence of UNIFIL (the UN Interim Forces in Lebanon), a peace-keeping force, Israel's war objective was pursued through a war by proxy between the South Lebanon Army and the PLO.

By 1982, dissatisfied with the results of their war by proxy, the Israelis once again took the decision to invade. This took place on 6 June 1982 and was codenamed Operation Peace in Galilee. Though they claimed that their objective was to widen their security zone in Southern Lebanon, it was clear from the start that the Israelis were targeting the PLO headquarters and Beirut. Their aim was to destroy the PLO or at least force them out of the region. The next few months saw the bloodiest battles in the entire civil war. Israeli presence unleashed the internal differences in Lebanon and confrontation between the Israeli-backed Phalangists and Muslim pro-Palestinian militia groups caused, according to some estimates, over 20,000 deaths. There were tragedies on both sides: in the refugee camp of Sabra-Shatila near Beirut, the Phalangist forces unleashed their hatred on unarmed Palestinian civilians. In the three days of killing that took place in this refugee camp hundreds were butchered. Muslim suicide bombers brought about the death of hundreds of American and French soldiers who were in Lebanon. Photographs of such savage killings shocked the world.

The Israelis succeeded in forcing the PLO out of Lebanon. Under the supervision of the multinational forces, the PLO fighters evacuated Beirut. They moved to a base in Tunis in 1982. As their objective was fulfilled, Israel agreed to gradually move its troops out of Lebanon. The last of the Israeli soldiers left southern Lebanon in the year 2000.

Sectarian fighting continued in Lebanon until 1991. In 1989 the Arab League stepped in to broker a Lebanese peace. The meeting which took place in the Saudi Arabian town of Taif produced the Taif Agreement or the National Reconciliation Accord. This document suggested certain amendments to Lebanon's political system, the National Pact. These changes were regarded as necessary steps to ensure peace. The Taif Agreement, while maintaining the "pragmatic representative system" of the National Pact, asked for an increase in the powers of the prime minister and the Speaker of Parliament. In this way the Christian representative was not given more power than the other two. More importantly, without ordering a new census, the Taif Agreement changed the 6:5 ratio and replaced it with a 50:50 (Christian–Muslim) division. Consequently, Christians and

Muslims are each allocated 64 of the 128 seats. Taif also called on the disbandment of all militias.

In March 1991 the Lebanese Parliament passed an amnesty law that pardoned all political crime. All the militias with the exception of the Hezbollah were disbanded. The Syrian army pulled out its army in 2005 and though there are still border disputes between the Hezbollah and Israel generally Lebanon is undergoing reconstruction after 16 years of civil war.

Timeline: Lebanon, 1932–2000	
1932	Population becomes the basis for a division of political power
1943	Independence: the National Pact
1945	Lebanon becomes a member of the Arab League
1970	PLO headquarters moves to Beirut
1975	April 13: Start of the civil war
1976	June: Syrian forces intervene
1977	Druze leader Kemal Jumbalat assassinated
1978	March 15: Israeli invasion into Southern Lebanon
	March 23: UNIFIL sent to guard the Southern border
1982	June 6: Second Israeli invasion into Southern Lebanon
	August 30: Yasser Arafat and the PLO headquarters move to Tunis
	September 14: Bashir Gemayel is assassinated
	September 16–18: Phalangists attack Palistinian refugee camps in Sabra and Chatila
1983	PLO headquarters moved to Tunis
1989	October 22: Taif Agreement
2000	May 24: Israelis pull out of Southern Lebanon after 22 years

Iran, 1941–79

At the outbreak of the First World War, Iran declared its neutrality. On 25 August 1941 British and Soviet forces invaded Iran. The purpose of the invasion was to open up supply lines to the USSR through the Persian corridor. Reza Shah who had refused to abide by the Allies' requests and had denied them the use of the railways across Iran was forced to abdicate and was sent into exile. His 22-year-old son, Mohammad Reza ascended the throne on 16 September 1941. The new Shah signed a Treaty of Alliance with the United Kingdom and the Soviet Union in January 1942 and provided non-military assistance to the Allied war effort. In return, the Allies agreed to respect Iran's independence and territorial integrity and to withdraw their troops from Iran within six months of the end of hostilities. While the British and American forces respected the agreement and left soon after the war ended, the Soviet troops continued to stay in Iran.

The War had brought about major disruptions and the abdication of Reza Shah had once again weakened the authority of central government. The scenario that had followed the First World War was about to repeat itself; the suppressed ethnic minorities rose in revolt against the central government. This time, however, the rebels were backed by the Soviet Union whose troops were still in Iran and therefore Iran's territorial integrity was at risk. In December 1945 an autonomous republic was declared both in Azerbaijan and Kurdistan. However, within a few months the Soviet forces withdrew, the independent republics were overthrown and the break-up of the country was averted. This was thanks, in part, to the intervention of the United States. President Truman is said to have sent Stalin an ultimatum over Azerbaijan and was prepared to raise the stakes if the Soviets continued to interfere in Iran's affairs. In January 1946, Iran, now a member of the UN, also lodged a complaint to the UN about the Soviet refusal to evacuate its troops as well as its interference in the internal affairs of Iran. The situation was skilfully handled by the Iranian Prime Minister, Ahmad Gavam, who also opened negotiations with the USSR. He persuaded Stalin to withdraw his troops in return for the promise to submit a bill to parliament permitting the Soviet Union to exploit the oil fields of northern Iran. The Soviet Union began withdrawing its troops in March and by 9 May the Soviet army had left Iranian soil. In December Gavam sent the Iranian army into Azerbaijan and successfully defeated the new republics. This bill was, as promised, submitted to parliament, but it was defeated by 102 votes to two. This was thanks to the National Front bloc led by Mohammad Mossadegh. The new parliament added another bill forbidding any other foreign oil concessions.

Activity:

Class discussion: Terminology

Community · Nation · Communalism · Nationalism

Communalism defines loyalty to a community. Nationalism surpasses community loyalty and inculcates a sense of belonging to a nation. At times communalism can be regarded as a divisive force within a nation. What about nationalism?

- Come up with a set of working definitions for these terms.

- What do they have in common? How are they different?

- Evaluate their positive and negative implications for society.

- Apply them to case studies of selected countries in the Middle East.

At the beginning Iran tried to maintain cordial relations with the two superpowers. Already during the war years, the Iranians had turned to the United States for help in the rebuilding of their country. American advisers were sent to Iran to reorganize the police force and the Iranian army from the end of 1943. Iran's relation with the US was, however, greatly reinforced after the Azerbaijan and Kurdistan incidents. Both sides realized that they would benefit from a rapprochement. As a neighbour to the USSR, Iran would be the testing ground for the success of the containment policy and would set an example for the rest of the world. Relations with the Soviet Union were a little more strained. Since 1941, a pro-communist political party, the Tudeh Party (*Tudeh* means the masses) had been formed. In the 1944 legislative elections they had eight members in parliament. The popularity of the party was such that Gavam, who had no ideological sympathy with communism, had three Tudeh Party ministers in his cabinet. For the Soviet Union a popular pro-communist party was an important stepping stone for infiltration into Iranian politics.

If Iran wanted to avert the threat of Soviet expansion, it clearly needed US protection. Iran contained oil supplies that were vital for the West. Its loss to the Soviet sphere of influence would therefore have enormous economic repercussions. Anglo-Iranian relations were tense. The British had been interfering in Iran's affairs since the 19th century, and this had caused a strong reaction amongst Iranian nationalists. In order to keep Iran in the Western camp, the United States had to replace the British influence. In 1947 Iran and the United States signed an agreement. This was a reaffirmation of the war-time agreements and extended the offer of US military aid, which included the purchase of military equipment as well as military training. The agreement stipulated that Iran would not seek the military assistance of any other country. With this agreement Iran had clearly entered the Western sphere of influence in the post-war world. In 1949, following an assassination attempt on the life of the Shah, the Tudeh Party was blamed and as a consequence banned. With Tudeh activists in prison and the party forced underground, the Iranian government had cleared the way for closer ties with the United States.

President Truman's **Point Four Program** was the first step towards the deepening of US–Iranian relations. With Point Four came $500,000 in assistance and American involvement through investment as well as technical assistance. This was the beginning of extensive US political, economic and social influence in Iran. Through the employment of American consultants in a variety of different fields such as public health, education and technology, the Point Four Program established a pattern for the modernization and Westernization of everyday life in Iran according to the American model.

> **Discussion point:**
>
> Iran shares a border with the USSR and the Persian Gulf. Could it have stayed out of the Cold War?

The **Point Four Cooperative Program for Aid in the Development of Economically Underdeveloped Areas** was part of a US foreign-aid package which aimed to provide technological skills, knowledge, and equipment to poor nations throughout the world. The project received its name from the fourth point of a programme set forth in President Truman's 1949 inaugural address. Within the context of the Cold War, the programme had clear political objectives of maintaining these countries in the US sphere of influence.

Activity:

Does *modern* mean Western?

Modernity has been used as a synonym for the word "civilized". The western nations are modern/civilized and view those that are not modern as primitive because they have not *yet* reached that goal.

A modern state is one that has undergone the Western experience and duplicated the Western model because this model is universal. Science replaces superstition; secularism replaces religion; freedom replaces despotism.

Those who questioned the modernist theory first came from such disciplines as anthropology and cultural studies. A number of historians reject the modernist theory as too Eurocentric. They do not reject the fact that the West left its imprint and had enormous

consequences on the region and was one factor for change. Undertake further research:

- Define the terms. What do the terms "Westernization" and "modernization" have in common? How are they different? What are their positive and negative implications?

- Apply these definitions and an analysis of the outcomes to the countries studied in this chapter. Why have these countries failed to achieve democracy?

- Summarize the main points of view. Find quotes from leading commentators, historians and political leaders.

The Iranian state

Iran remained a constitutional monarchy, which meant that the Shah had to rule in conjunction with Parliament, the *Majlis*. In consolidating his power the young Shah was keen on extending his power and with that aim in mind, he convened a Constituent Assembly. He wanted to rid himself of the control of the *Majlis*, especially given that many of the deputies were far more experienced politicians than he was. The Constituent Assembly created a second legislative assembly, the Senate. This would counterbalance the *Majlis* and remain totally loyal to the Crown because half of its members would be appointed directly by the Shah. The Shah also obtained the right to appoint the Prime Minister, a right that had previously belonged to Parliament.

In spite of these attempts the *Majlis* continued to be a strong and potent force in Iranian politics until 1953 and this was mainly due to the calibre of its deputies and the dynamic nature of political activity in post-war Iran. Following the abdication of Reza Shah, politicians whose views had been suppressed now spoke up. A free press flourished and the *Majlis* became the forum for open discussion. One such deputy was Mohammad Mossadegh, the leader of a coalition of nationalist groups called the National Front. Mossadegh was to play a prominent role in Iranian politics and his fall from power in 1953 was a major turning point for Iran.

When the Parliament (*Majlis*) rejected the oil concession to the USSR in 1947, they also forbade the drawing up of any other concessions without the approval of the *Majlis*. This would prevent the Shah or the prime minister from closing deals with foreign powers without consulting the Parliament. It also called upon the government to renew negotiations with the Anglo-Iranian Oil Company (AIOC), which owned oil concessions in the South. Iranians were angered at the fact that the AIOC paid more in taxes to the British government than it paid the Iranian government.

Discussion point:

Does a country have the right to nationalize something that belongs to another country?

Consider the implications of the nationalization of the Iranian oil industry for:

- the British AIOC

- the Iranians

- the region as a whole

Can you think of other examples of nationalization in the region?

They therefore wanted to revise the terms of the agreement. Finally, having approved the first Development Plan (1948–55) and established the Plan Organization (PO), a body that would administer Iran's modernization and development programmes, the country sought to maximize oil revenues to finance its projects.

The National Front coalition was formed in 1949 in the wake of rising nationalist sentiments. It opposed the AIOC, which it regarded as the symbol of Iran's subordination to British interests. Resentment of foreign domination united the people in their support of the National Front. Negotiations started between the Iranian government and the AIOC. The Iranians demanded a 50:50 profit-sharing, a precedence set by ARAMCO, the Arabian American Oil Company, with the Saudi Arabian government. AIOC's refusal to comply by these requests angered the nationalists, who then raised their stakes higher and on 15 March 1951 the Parliament voted to nationalize the oil industry. In April, Mossadegh, the leader of the National Front became prime minister.

The AIOC retaliated by withdrawing its technicians from Iran and taking its case to the International Court of Justice. By claiming that Iran had committed an illegal act, Britain called for sanctions on Iran. Though the Court of Justice judged in Iran's favour, a worldwide embargo was put on the purchase of Iranian oil. The Iranian economy began to suffer enormously under the pressure of the sanctions.

Mossadegh's growing popularity was a matter of great concern for the Shah. In July 1952 the two men clashed. Mossadegh demanded the right to appoint the minister of defence; the Shah refused. Mossadegh's resignation was followed by three days of rioting at the end of which the Shah was forced to reinstate him. The tug of war between the two men had started.

In the meantime a new American president had been elected, President Dwight Eisenhower. Eisenhower took a stronger stand on the Soviet threat and was suspicious of the active support the

Oil concessions

The first oil concession was given by the Qajar King, to the Englishman, William Knox D'Arcy in 1901. This agreement was valid for 60 years and offered D'Arcy exclusive rights to search for, extract, transport and sell oil. In return he paid £20,000 in cash, an additional £20,000 in company shares and 16 per cent of the company's annual profit. In 1907 D'Arcy sold his shares to the Burmah Oil Company and in 1909, as the first oil wells opened, the company changed its name to the Anglo-Persian and then the Anglo-Iranian Oil Company (AIOC). In 1914 the British government entered into partnership with the AIOC. This proved to be an extremely wise decision because by 1922 the Iranian oil refineries were the largest in the world.

The terms of the agreement were not so advantageous to Iran. The Iranians had no say in the price fixing, were not informed of the market rates for their oil, and were therefore unable to assess the price of the oil that was sold back to them. They were for these reasons unable to verify the profits of the company and so could not check to see whether the agreed 16 per cent royalty fee was being paid. These royalties fluctuated from £130,000 to £1,410,000 pounds so Iran's economy depended on an income that was unpredictable. Given the number of grievances, in 1932 Reza Shah's government informed the AIOC that the concession was annulled. A mediator was appointed and a new concession was drawn up in 1933. The new agreement increased and stabilized Iran's revenue, but its expiry date was extended to 1993. The gap between Iran's revenues and the company's profits remained a contentious issue for Iranians. In 1948, Iran received 9 million pounds, and the British government received 28 million pounds in the form of income tax from the company. The concessions violated many Iranian's sense of economic justice and fairness, and reminded them of their weakness in relation to foreign powers.

Tudeh Party was giving to Mossadegh. The United States along with the British government decided to intervene in Iran's internal affairs. The plan devised and code-named Operation Ajax would start with an anti-Mossadegh publicity campaign. The British and American agents had bribed journalists to write anti-Mossadegh articles to influence public opinion. The articles accused Mossadegh of pro-communist tendencies and blamed him for all the economic difficulties the country was going through. They also paid people to demonstrate in the streets and demand the overthrow of Mossadegh.

The Shah would propose an alternative to Mossadegh to restore the calm. At first it appeared as though Operation Ajax had backfired; on 19 August the Shah dismissed Mossadegh and appointed General Zahedi as Prime Minister. However, Mossadegh refused and had the Shah's emissary arrested. It appeared as though the plan had failed. Zahedi went into hiding and the Shah fled the country. The tide turned, however, when on 19 August the anti-Mossadegh demonstrators came into the streets. The Shah was brought back. Mossadegh was arrested, accused of trying to overthrow the monarchy and sentenced to three years imprisonment. Hundreds of National Front and Tudeh Party members were arrested. Mossadegh remained under house arrest until his death in 1967.

The US and British involvement in the coup d'état was not disclosed. On the contrary 19 August was celebrated as a national uprising in support of the Shah. Though the repressive nature of the Shah's regime after 1953 did not leave room for alternative views, the official version of the events was unacceptable to most Iranians who had lived through the period. After the Iranian Revolution of 1979 and the overthrow of the Shah the archives were opened and many of the details were revealed. In 2000 Madeleine Allbright, the US Secretary of State acknowledged the United States' involvement in the 1953 coup. This is what she had to say:

> In 1953 the United States played a significant role in orchestrating the overthrow of Iran's popular Prime Minister, Mohammed Mossadegh. The Eisenhower Administration believed its actions were justified for strategic reasons; but the coup was clearly a setback for Iran's political development. And it is easy to see now why many Iranians continue to resent this intervention by America in their internal affairs.

Iran's government after 1953

For the next 25 years Mohammad Reza Shah was to rule Iran. One of the first steps he took was in regards to the oil industry. In 1954 an oil consortium was formed: this was made up of the Anglo-Iranian Oil Company, now renamed British Petroleum, which held 40 per cent of the shares; the other 60 per cent was divided between American and European oil companies. The consortium took 50 per cent of the Iranian oil profit and the other 50 per cent went to the National Iranian Oil Company (NIOC).

The Shah's aim, first and foremost, was to modernize his country, but he needed first to consolidate his position. In 1953–7, while the country remained under martial law, the National Front and the Tudeh Party were disbanded and many of its activists were imprisoned. The Shah was no longer going to allow the *Majlis* or political parties to become so empowered that they would challenge his authority again. Consequently, the political parties that emerged were totally subservient to the Shah. Iranians cynically referred to them as "yes your majesty" and "of-course your majesty" parties.

The Shah aligned himself and his country with the West. In 1955 Iran joined the Baghdad Pact (see p. 321). (This Pact was later renamed the Central Treaty Organization, CENTO). In 1959 Iran signed a bilateral defence treaty with the United States. The Shah spent millions of dollars on US weapons and with the weapons came American advisers and business interests. The presence of so many Americans in Iran was offensive to the more educated and politically active members of society who regarded the United States as the main perpetrator of the coup d'état. To make matters worse, in order to vouch for the security of the American citizens in Iran, the *Majlis* passed a law offering the Americans an immunity that exempted them from Iranian laws. These laws, commonly known as the capitulation laws, outraged a large number of Iranians because it meant that an American could commit a crime in Iran—even kill an Iranian—and not be judged or punished for it in Iranian courts. One of the most outspoken opponents of this law was the religious leader Ayatollah Khomeini.

> *"If someone runs over a dog belonging to an American, he will be prosecuted. But if an American cook runs over the Shah, no one will have the right to interfere with him. Why? Because they wanted a loan and America demanded this in return."*
>
> Ayatollah Khomeini, September 1964

In 1963 the Shah launched the White Revolution. This was the name he gave to his reforms. The original proposal included six points. These were put to a national referendum on 26 January 1963 that was successful, highlighting significant popular support for the Shah's reforms. The day of the referendum was commemorated every year and was considered by some as the starting point of Iran's modern history.

The White Revolution, as proposed in 1963, consisted of six points. These were:

1 Land reform: the government bought the land from large land owners and sold it to the peasants at a price below its market value. The aim of this reform was to redistribute land and give landless peasants a means of subsistence.
2 Nationalization of forests and pastures: The government took over thousands of acres of land and replanted much of it to form a green belt around the cities. The aim of this reform was to protect Iran's natural resources and plant forests where it was needed.
3 Privatization of government-owned factories: the government sold shares of the government-owned companies to the public. The aim of this reform was to speed up the industrialization process through creating a new class of factory owners. The money raised from these sales would also finance the land reform.

4 Profit-sharing for the industrial workers: the government forced private owners of industry to share 20 per cent of their net profits in the form of bonuses with employees and workers. The aim of this reform was to raise productivity through higher incentives.

5 Reforms in the electoral laws: the government extended voting rights to women and thus introduced universal suffrage in Iran. This reform aimed to modernize Iran and give women equal status.

6 Formation of Literacy Corps: as part of their military service, young men (and later women) were sent to villages as teachers. The aim of this reform was to lower the devastatingly high illiteracy rates in the country. In 1963 approximately two thirds of the population was illiterate.

Assessment: How successful were the reforms?

The reforms were put to a referendum and 99 per cent were said to have voted in favour. The reforms, however, had a number of opponents, who later claimed that they did not bring about the desired socio-economic changes. As far as land reform was concerned, many landlords managed to find a way around the new rules and succeeded in keeping their large estates. Prior to the reforms, the peasant farmer was able to use some of the land and cultivate a little on the side at the landlord's expense. Now farmers needed to borrow money to grow their own crops. Many ended up selling the little land that they had and moved to the towns, where they lived in poverty. Under the auspices of the literacy and health corps a large number of educated young people were sent to the villages, but without the appropriate infrastructure they were unable to fulfil their objectives. Many returned disillusioned and critical of the regime. The religious authorities opposed both the land reform and the extension of the right to vote to women. In 1963 one religious leader, Ruhollah Khomeini, spoke out against the reforms. His arrest led to violent demonstrations and severe repression of the protestors. Khomeini was arrested and kept under arrest for nearly a year.

Opposition to the Shah

Viewed from the outside, Iran was modernizing. Its economy was expanding and, especially after the petrol boom of the 1970s, Iranians were reaping the benefit. This included better health facilities. With improved health, the population grew. In 1966 it stood at 26 million; in 1976 it had grown to 34 million. More schools were built, resulting in a substantial rise in literacy. Elementary school enrolment went from 1.6 million in 1963 to 4 million in 1977. Higher education also expanded. The country's prestige in the region and in the international scene was equally growing, and it benefited from the protection of the United States. It also had one of the strongest and best equipped armies in the region. Iran of the 1950s was incomparable with the Iran of the 1970s. Seen from that point of view Iranians had little to complain about. Yet there was a great deal of dissatisfaction. This dissatisfaction can be broken up into economic, political, social and cultural concerns.

Economic concerns

Iran's economy is totally dependent on its oil revenues. Though the possession of such a mineral resource, commonly known as black gold, is clearly an advantage, there are also major drawbacks to it. Firstly, while oil remains the country's main source of income, other sectors have no reason to develop because the country will, unless international sanctions are imposed on her, manage through importing all the goods that it needs. This keeps a country economically dependent on the outside world. Secondly, the country's budget will depend on world oil prices and any fluctuation in those prices will cause major upheavals in the country's economy.

The petrol crisis triggered off by the Yom Kippur war in 1973 brought about a massive increase in the price of petrol on the world market. The price rose from $3 a barrel to $12. This caused a major economic boom in the country. Suddenly the Shah's dream of making Iran a major industrial and military power was to come true. Unfortunately, the steps that were taken to make this dream a reality were also the long-term reasons for his fall from power. Through the modernization process, the regime pushed aside the traditional merchant classes and forced the poorer peasants into becoming migrant workers in the major towns. It was these people that were to later form the backbone of the opposition to the Shah in the 1979 revolution.

 How does the price of oil fluctuate?

In 1976 oil prices stopped rising and actually started to fall. Iran's projects were suddenly put on hold. The economy suffered, with inflation rising over 20 per cent by 1977. Government expenditure overtook its revenues and the Shah asked the people to prepare for sacrifices. The "sacrifices" however affected certain sectors more than others. Those worst hit were the civil servants whose incomes were fixed and the rising inflation was rapidly lowering their standard of living. Many who had been impressed by Iran's modernization process and who would naturally have been staunch supporters of the regime were extremely disillusioned by the Shah and started to join the ranks of the opposition.

The massive boom was extremely badly managed. Many of the projects were too grandiose and did not take into account the country's real needs. Enormous quantities of goods were imported with the aim of developing Iran's heavy industry. But the country lacked the infrastructure. Tons of material would wait in ships and could not be unloaded. Once unloaded, there were no warehouses to store them in. The absence of planning caused bottlenecks and shortages, which caused prices to rise. With such vast sums, purchased by the state, corruption became rife. The government blamed some merchants for overpricing their goods and used them as scapegoat: 250,000 were fined and 8,000 jailed. This did not resolve the situation and alienated the merchant classes.

Importing so many foreign goods undermined local industries and many of the smaller producers suffered as they could no longer compete with the consumer goods coming from abroad. It also became fashionable to use foreign products. This was encouraged because it enhanced the Shah's image of a Western and modern country. This "Westernization" was resented by the traditional merchant classes whose livelihood was being threatened by the imports of consumer goods. They blamed the Shah and his policies.

The Shah's land reforms, proposed by the White Revolution of 1963, were a further cause of discontent, exacerbated by economic boom that encouraged the growth of larger agricultural projects, rendering smaller inefficient farms redundant. The population of Tehran went from 2.9 million in 1966 to 4.4 million in 1976. By 1979, 14 per cent of the country's population lived in Tehran. The migrant workers were faced with poor living and working conditions in the towns. As the villages lost their importance, little effort went into building roads and supplying them with the necessary services such as electricity or running water. This widened the gap even further between the towns and the countryside and created a great deal of dissatisfaction among the rural sector, who on migrating to the cities were further shocked at the alien Western lifestyle of their compatriots.

The economic boom led to a massive military build up in Iran after 1973. Though this was justified by the Shah because he believed that Iran, as a vital ally of the United States, needed to play a major role in the region and needed to have the equipment to do it. Many regarded this as a misallocation of resources. It satisfied the Shah in person who increasingly relied on the army for his own security but served no real purpose for the country.

Political concerns

Mohammad Reza Shah, much like his father, showed very little flexibility and leniency towards criticism. His reinstatement to the throne, through the 1953 coup, did not herald an easy start. Though he tried to put Iran on the path of modernity and used the West as his model, his reforms never extended to the political realm. In 1975 he abruptly ended the nominal multi-party system. A single party called the *Rastakhiz* (resurgence) was formed and it had the monopoly of all political activities. Iran became a single-party state. As a means to control the people and restrict dissent, an intelligence and security organization referred to by its Persian acronym, SAVAK, was founded in 1957. SAVAK's ruthlessness was notorious. It had unlimited power of arrest and execution and succeeded in spreading fear to prevent any form of criticism from Iranians both in Iran and abroad. In the 25 years of the Shah's reign thousands of political activists or intellectuals who criticized the regime were arrested and many were tortured and executed. SAVAK employed over 5,000 people full time and had a large number of part-time informants. They were trained and worked in close association with the United States. Opposition to the Shah's rule can be divided into three general categories or classes of people, all of whom were frustrated at the restrictions imposed on them by the rigid and inflexible political system.

The middle classes who had liberal aspirations and who had benefited economically from the modernization of Iran were prevented from contributing politically to their country's development. Many potential

Discussion point:

What is a political prisoner? Should a political prisoner be treated any differently to an "ordinary" prisoner?

Activity:
Research SAVAK

How does SAVAK compare to the fomer KGB in the Soviet Union? What about the CIA in the United States?

 What features do such security organizations share? Why do citizens fear government-backed security organizations?

supporters of the Shah were disenchanted by the absence of real pluralism and the lack of genuine elections. This extended to the large number of young disillusioned university graduates who came to realize the ineffectiveness of any legal opposition. The intellectuals and the student body both inside and outside Iran suffered from the total absence of freedom of speech and in the context of the 1960s and 1970s soon turned to revolutionary ideas and Communist aspirations. A third group, the clergy, viewed the Shah's affinity with the West and the rapid modernization of the country as a direct attack on and disrespect towards Iran's religious and traditional past. They found a natural following in the conservative merchant classes and the uprooted peasantry but also had followers among the middle classes and intelligentsia.

> ## No representation without taxation!
>
> Usually the income of a state comes from the taxes that its citizens pay. This dependence creates a relationship whereby citizens can control the state. The slogan "No Taxation without Representation!" coined by the American revolutionaries in Boston in 1750 underlined this dependence and became the battle cry for the war that eventually overthrew British rule in North America. Elsewhere, civil disobedience movements have called on people not to pay taxes in order to demand change.
>
> A country that is rich in oil does not depend on taxation. This independence means that the state does not have to be accountable to its citizens. This can have major implications politically. The citizens do not have the means to control the state, through exercising their democratic rights as voters and tax payers.

Social and cultural concerns

Socially and culturally Mohammad Reza Shah attempted to both raise nationalist sentiments by emphasizing the pre-Islamic history of Ancient Persia and to align Iran closer to the West through reforms and economic changes. In both of these aims he was faced with a certain amount of opposition.

In October 1971 more than 100 million dollars was spent on the celebration of the 2,500 years of the Iranian monarchy. The Shah wanted in this way to inscribe the Pahlavi Dynasty in the historical lineage of Persia's ancient monarchs. This took place in the ancient city of Persepolis, which had been the seat of the Achaemenian Empire. A luxurious "tent city" was put up in the desert. The guests were mainly foreign dignitaries. For many Iranians this extravagance was unacceptable and even outrageous. Furthermore, the insistence on Iran's pre-Islamic past was viewed as disrespect to Iran's Islamic heritage. One such critic was Ali Shariati, whose writings and speeches rallied many young people and intellectuals against the Shah's regime. This is what he had to say:

> The experts … may know a great deal about the Sassanids, the Achaemenians, and even earlier civilisations, but our people know nothing of such things. Our people do not find their roots in these civilisations … Our people remember nothing from this distant past and do not care to learn about the pre-Islamic civilisations … Consequently for us, a return to our roots means not a rediscovery of pre-Islamic Iran, but a return to our Islamic, especially Shi'a roots.

In 1976 the Shah proceeded to change Iran's calendar and replace the Islamic calendar with one that he called the Shahanshah (the King of the kings, the title that was given to Cyrus the Great) era calendar.

"In Many aspects, Iran is much more democratic than Europe … The opposition is so negligible that it cannot get even one seat in Parliament."

Mohammad Reza Shah (from a 1973 interview with the Italian journalist, Oriana Fallaci)

Discussion point:

Discuss the idea of introducing a new calendar. What are its advantages? What are its disadvantages?

In most Muslim countries the calendar (whether solar or lunar) starts with the *hegira*, which is the year the prophet Mohammed migrated from the city of Mecca to Medina. According to this calendar the year 1976 was 1355. The Shahanshah era calendar suddenly moved the starting date from the *hegira* to 599 BC because this was said to have represented the beginning of the Persian Empire. So the year 1355 (1976) became 2535. All of a sudden Iranians were told that they lived in the year 2535. The second millennium had come and gone without anyone noticing it! The new calendar caused an uproar. Not only was it confusing, it was also extremely insulting to Muslims and 98 per cent of Iran's population are Muslim. The opposition was so intense that it only lasted for two years: 2535 and 2536. By the end of 1977 the calendar had switched back. Iranians once again lived in 1356.

In 1962 Jalal Al Ahmad published *Gharbzadegi*. This has been translated as 'Westoxication' or 'Plagued by the West'. The book criticized Iran's emulation of the Western model and this view found many supporters. The Western model was present in the presence of a large number of American advisers, regarded by many as an affirmation of subordination to the West. It was also present in the lifestyle of the urban middle and upper classes: the way they dressed, the music they listened to, and the media. For the more traditional classes this was an infringement on Iran's Islamic values and Iran's identity and was not a step towards modernization.

The status of women also changed under the Shah's reforms. Women had been admitted into the university and a law in January 1936 had forced women to unveil and dress in the Western fashion in public (this law was withdrawn under Mohammad Reza Shah). There was an increase in the participation of women in the workforce and a higher literacy rate than previous years. Under Mohammad Reza Shah the pace was accelerated. In 1963 women were given the right to vote and were able to present themselves as electoral candidates. They were appointed as judges and held ministerial posts. In 1967 the family law was reformed. This was a major step in a Muslim country. The new civil code protected women as wives, as divorcees and as guardians of the children. A new post of Minister for Women's Affairs was also opened up in 1976.

However, these changes mainly affected the upper and middle classes, leaving the majority of women untouched. As society as a whole was not democratized and civil rights were restricted, the changes were felt to be superficial. A great deal had been promised, which raised expectations, but little was implemented and when opposition to the Shah grew, women were extremely active in their desire to topple the regime.

The coming of the revolution
In 1977 faced with mounting criticism the Shah promised to initiate some changes. The leaders of moderate opposition took the opportunity and published open letters asking for the respect of basic rights. The National Front resumed activity. At this stage protest remained relatively controlled and it was limited to constitutional rights.

In January 1978 the protest took a new turn when an article published in one of the country's daily newspapers close to government circles, *Ettelaat*, insulted Ayatollah Ruhollah Khomeini. There was an immediate reaction from the seminary students in the Holy city of Qom. The forces of law and order were sent in and a number of the demonstrators were killed. In February mosques organized ceremonies commemorating those that had been killed. In Tabriz there were clashes with the riot police causing the death of more demonstrators. Commemorative marches followed every 40 days and by the summer Iran was in turmoil. The protestors came from all classes and walks of life. Men and women alike were joining the protests calling for change. Gradually the demands and the slogans stopped being reformist and started being revolutionary. They started to demand the overthrow of the Shah.

Ayatollah Ruhollah Khomeini (1902–1989)

Born in a town called Khomein, Khomeini pursued a classical academic career: first in Arak, under the tuition of a jurist named Haeri, then in Qum. Though he lived as a member of the clergy, it was not until the 1960s that Khomeini turned to politics. One of the factors that incited Khomeini into political agitation was the increasing US involvement in Iran. He first spoke out against the Shah's White Revolution of 1963, which he equated with the growing influence of the United States. When he called on the clergy to boycott the referendum clashes with the forces of law and order took place. Khomeini was arrested in June 1963 and remained under house arrest until April 1964. On his release he set the tone for his future confrontations with the regime: "Even if they hang Khomeini, he will not compromise ... Islam is politics ... I am not a religious leader who sits and plays with his rosary beads." In September 1964, the Majlis passed the Capitulation Bill. Two weeks later, Khomeini attacked the bill in a public meeting.

Six days later he was put on a plane bound for exile in Turkey. Khomeini remained in Turkey until October 1965. He then moved to the Holy city of Najaf. In October 1978 the Iraqis expelled him and he found political asylum in France. In February 1979 Khomeini returned to Iran to become Iran's first spiritual leader and the founder of the Islamic Republic. Millions of people came to greet him. Between 1979 and 1989 Khomeini remained the spiritual leader of Iran. He succeeded in transforming Iran from a monarchy to an Islamic Republic, introducing a new constitution and new laws more compatible with Islam. He saw Iran through an eight-year war with neighbouring Iraq, bringing it to an end just a few months before his death. He died in 1989 at the age of 87.

Attempts were made to calm the situation. The regime, however, hesitated between conciliation and repression. To conciliate they revoked the Shahanshah era calendar, closed gambling houses, released a number of imprisoned clerics and political prisoners. These measures were aimed at appeasing Khomeini. In September the government declared martial law which increased the clashes between the demonstrators and the police. This did not bring Khomeini to the negotiating table and only made the demonstrators more determined.

In support of the demonstrators the public sector and the oil workers went on strike. This spread the protest movement to the workplace and brought the country to a practical standstill. On 16 January 1979 the Shah and his family left Iran, supposedly on a holiday, leaving the government in the hands of a liberal democrat, Shapoor Bakhtiar. The Shah's departure caused major celebrations throughout the country.

Khomeini arrived in Tehran on 1 February 1979. Within a few days Khomeini appointed his own Prime Minister, Mehdi Bazargan, as a challenge to the existing government. On 8 February a mutiny among airforce technicians at an air base near Tehran triggered off a general uprising and on 11 February the armed forces declared their loyalty to Khomeini. The government of Bakhtiar had fallen. The Pahlavi dynasty had ended.

Exam practice and further resources

Sample questions

1   Examine the causes and consequences of the Egyptian revolution of 1953.
2   Compare and contrast the foreign policies of Sadat and Mubarak.
3   "The presence of the PLO was a major cause of the Lebanese civil war in 1975." To what extent do you agree with this statement?
4   Analyse the impact of Pan-Arabism on the Middle East.
5   Assess the key problems which make it so difficult to make lasting peace between Israel and her neighbours.
6   Examine the extent of political change between 1945 and 2000 in any ONE country in the region (excluding Egypt).

Recommended further reading

General history of the Middle East:

Kamrava, Mehran. 2005. *The Modern Middle East: a Political History Since the First World War*. Los Angeles, USA. University of California Press.

Milton-Edwards, Beverley. 2007. *Contemporary Politics in the Middle East*. Massachusetts, USA. Polity Press.

History of Egypt:

Vatiokis, P.J. 1991. *The History of Modern Egypt: From Mohammad Ali to Mobarak*. London, UK. Weidenfeld and Nicolson.

History of Arab Unity:

Hourani, Albert. 1991. *A History of the Arab Peoples*. London, UK. Faber and Faber.

History of the Arab world and Israel:

Gelvin, James. 2005. *The Israel–Palestine Conflict: One Hundred Years of War*. Oxford, UK. Cambridge University Press.

Gilbert, Martin. 1998. *Israel: A History*. London, UK. Doubleday.

Kimmerling, Baruch and Migdal, Joel S. 2003. *The Palestinian People*. Cambridge, USA. Harvard University Press.

Shlaim, Avi. 1995. *War and Peace in the Middle East: A Concise History*. New York, USA. Penguin.

History of Lebanon:

Fisk, Robert. 2002. *Pity the Nation: The Abduction of Lebanon*, New York, USA. Thunder's Mouth Press/Nation Books.

History of Iran:

Ansari, Ali M. 2005. *Modern Iran Since 1921: The Pahlavis and After*. London, UK. Pearson Education.

7 Social and economic developments in Europe and the Middle East

This chapter explores social and economic developments in Europe and the Middle East with a focus on the case studies of the United Kingdom in the period 1945–2000 and Iran in 1953–2000. The scope of this topic is intended to provide an overview for students and identify areas of further enquiry/inquiry to develop their investigative and critical skills within the context of a case study of one country from each region. To that end, there are a number of ideas for further study throughout this chapter. These ideas are presented as discussion points and can form the basis for historical investigations and extended essays in history as well as further classroom study.

Social history is an approach to historical investigation that examines continuity and change in the social relations between elements of society. These elements can be economic relations, legal structures, class, religion, gender, race, the sciences, or the arts. When approaching this section, political history will only be discussed in the context of these social relations. That being said, students should always be aware of the importance of context—life, both in the present and in the past, rarely divides neatly into such categories. Students should always be aware of what other events and trends are occurring at the same time as those that they are studying.

By the end of this chapter students should be able to analyse social and economic developments in relation to the two countries as case studies, with a focus on:

- social structure and the development of the welfare state in the United Kingdom
- the role that immigration and emigration has played in the United Kingdom
- an evaluation of continuity and change in the roles played by race, religion and the diversification of British society
- an understanding of how British society was reflected in the arts and cultural sector
- the role played by industrial and technological advancement in the new economy
- economic and industrial developments in Iran, and their impact on society
- the development of social policy in Iran, with a focus on health and education
- social transformation in Iran in terms of class, social equality and gender relations
- religious and intellectual trends in Iran
- the development of the arts and their relationship to the social and political context in Iran.

Case study: United Kingdom, 1945–2000

Social structure in British society

From the feudal period, through to the English Civil War, Glorious Revolution, Napoleonic Wars, Industrial Revolution and two world wars, "class" has been an ever-present reality in British society. There are few concepts, however, that divide historians as much as the term "class", both its definition and even its existence. For our purposes we will take a hybrid approach to class, defined by a set of categories in a hierarchical stratification of British society. Membership of a class depends on any number and combination of factors: from occupation, to property ownership, political influence and income. We must also understand that class is more than a stagnant category, but a process through which elements of society interact with each other. In this way, a class can have a culture of its own and, rather than just being a stagnant category, function as a dynamic body with ever-changing relations between its members and with other classes. If we are to look at the very simple stratification of working, middle, and upper class we can begin to build a picture of the social structure in the post-war period.

Class put its stamp on many aspects of 20th-century life and in this we can see the idea of class as a process—a way of interacting with the rest of society. Class affected life expectancy and infant mortality. Class affected the quality and variety of educational opportunities. Vastly more money was spent on the education of the middle and upper-middle class. In the 1960s around nine per cent of the population had attended university. However, within this group, only around three per cent came from the lowest income group of the working class (unskilled workers) whereas 24 per cent came from the middle-class—professionals and managers. Nearly one fifth of university entrants in 1960 came from the most elite schools. Around 70 per cent of the elite who attended university attended Oxford and Cambridge and as some sociologists have suggested this helped form a coherent class-associated culture among those in positions of power throughout the United Kingdom. By the end of the century university education had become more common and somewhat less class-bound. Economic indicators also adhere to class lines with a person's experience of unemployment and inflation differing dependant on his or her class.

During this period, slightly over half of the British population died in the same class to which they were born. Studies have shown that this was essentially the same as it had been earlier in the century. However, there seems to have been increasing **social mobility** within a class—i.e. between the middle- and upper-middle class. This mobility was affected by the changing structure of the economy and of educational opportunities.

TOK Link
Historical evidence

Social historians analyse different aspects of historical experience to those historians studying political or military history. Below are some generic sources that a social historian might use. For each source explain the knowledge issues associated with its role in providing historical evidence and which of the Ways of Knowing a historian might use.

- A painting or a photograph
- A film or a novel
- A song or a sermon
- Immigration statistics
- The report of a Royal Commission

Social mobility Social mobility refers to the movement of people between classes—either up or down—as well as the movement within classes.

The working class

If we look at class in terms of occupation, the working class is comprised of those who performed manual labour in some way shape or form. If we are to look at occupation—as the stark measure of class—in the immediate post-war period, the working class (skilled and unskilled) made up around 60 per cent of the population. Over the course of the rest of the 20th century, this percentage steadily decreased such that by the 1990s it was slightly below 40 per cent. Within the working class the number of workers employed in industrial manufacturing shrank while those employed in the service sector increased and with it the proportion of skilled to unskilled workers. Much of this had to do with the changing nature of the economy and the increased access to education.

The middle class

In some ways, the differentiation between the middle class and both the upper and working classes is a difficult one to broach. Part of the problem lies in the increase in technological and managerial occupations in the second half of the century and with it the definition of "manual" and "non-manual labour". The stratification of the middle class itself also complicates matters. The middle class can and has been split into the upper-middle class of professionals and independent business people and the lower-middle class of white collar and clerical workers. After the war this number stood above 30 per cent, but as the century progressed the middle class grew larger with the majority of this increase in the workforce occurring in the area of technology and science.

The upper class

In many ways the upper class is equally hard to classify. With no strictly occupational definition it comes down to amorphous concepts like social status (including the titled ranks of the traditional aristocracy) and those who wield a more general influence and political power, and less amorphous concepts like income and over-all wealth. Because there is no solid occupational element to this class, its size is debatable. Some historians have pegged it at around two per cent in the post-war years. While we can certainly point to a decline in the size of the traditional aristocracy, we can also point to the fact that the wealthiest in Britain have increased their proportion of the nation's wealth in comparison to the other socio-economic classes. By 1990, ten per cent of the population controlled slightly over 50 per cent of its wealth.

> ### Discussion point: This world … or the next?
>
> *It's no good fooling about with love you know. You can't fall into it like a soft job without dirtying up your hands. It takes muscle and guts. If you can't bear the thought of messing up your nice, tidy soul, you better give up the whole idea of life and become a saint, because you'll never make it as a human being. It's either this world … or, the next.*
>
> Jimmy Porter from the 1958 film version of the John Osborne play *Look Back in Anger*.
>
> While it seems that Jimmy is speaking about love, he is really commenting on the British class structure. What is he saying about it?

Discussion point: Class and occupation

What occupational divisions were there in the United Kingdom in 2000?

1 Compare and contrast the quality of life of the working class and the middle class between 1945 and 2000.

2 Compare and contrast avenues for social mobility in 1945 and 2000.

3 Who comprised the elite of British society in 2000? How did you define "elite"?

Activity:

Defining "class"

Arriving at an accepted definition of "class" has long been an issue for historians. Some see it as a category and others as a process. Some see it strictly in economic terms while others see it as combining many economic and social factors. Some see it as a fictitious creation of leftist historians.

Evaluate each of the following definitions of class by listing their strengths and weaknesses. Which definition works best for the society in which you live? Why? What other socio-economic divisions can help historians analyse society?

Class definitions	Analysis
The process by which people negotiate their socio-economic position in relation to the means of production.	Strengths:
	Weaknesses:
One's position in society, based solely on whether a person owns the means of production	Strengths:
	Weaknesses:
One's social and economic position based on income level.	Strengths:
	Weaknesses:
One's position in society based on occupation or source of income	Strengths:
	Weaknesses:
There is no meaningful division of society called "class."	Strengths:
	Weaknesses:

Gender

Another category that structures the relations of people to society is gender and this was certainly the case during the second half of the 20th century in the United Kingdom. Although women had been granted the franchise on the same basis as men in 1928, much of a woman's social, legal, and economic experience was still structured by the fact that she was a woman. Just as with class, gender differences helped form British society and while there were important changes in that relationship, a number of aspects remained unchanged by the turn of the century.

Both world wars helped make significant changes, if not in the material aspect of women in the labour force, then at least in the conception of women's work. While it is true that women had always worked, the wars saw them enter areas of the workforce that they had not traditionally occupied, and although many had to relinquish these positions in peacetime, the experience nonetheless changed the relationship of women to work in the United Kingdom. Nevertheless, in 1946, less than one fifth of British women had jobs. Wages were consistently lower than men for the same work. Despite legislation targeting this inequity, such as the Equal Pay Act of 1970, which came into effect in 1975 and was amended in 1984, wage gaps still existed at the turn of the century. Even though women made up nearly half of the workforce, the vast majority of women occupied the lowest paying jobs. It was not until 1973 that women were allowed in the London Stock Exchange and by the turn of the century fewer than ten per cent of the heads of Britain's leading companies were women. This same pattern seems to have held for most sectors of the economy. Although women had integrated into most sectors of the economy, they were still not equal to men in terms of leadership roles and pay.

If we consider the workforce the public sphere, then how did women's role in the private sphere change over the course of the second half of the 20th century? Much of the private sphere revolved around family relations. The years after the Second World War saw a fundamental change in the nature of divorce. The dislocation of the War years helped contribute to a drastic increase in the number of divorces in the immediate post-war period after which it seemed to stabilize at half that number. Access to the legal system was increased in 1949 with the Legal Aid Act, allowing poorer women to pursue divorce. The Divorce Act of 1971 allowed marriages to be dissolved on the grounds of marital breakdown, rather than on the guilt of one of the partners. The same act removed the requirement that both partners agree to the divorce. Since 1971 the divorce rate has more than doubled. Reproductive rights were also strengthened in the years after the 1960s. The Abortion Act of 1967 provided for state-funded abortions on medical grounds but left this to the discretion of doctors. Reliable oral contraceptives became more widely available and the price subsidized through the National Health Service. The Family Planning Act of 1967 further increased woman's access to contraceptives.

Activity:

Status of women

How has the status of women changed in the years between 1945 and 2000?

Divide the following topics among the members of your class. Each group will give a class presentation evaluating the role of their area in changing the status of women during this period.

- Reproductive rights
- Education
- Employment
- Politics

Discussion point: Gender equality

Despite legal equality, why are there proportionally so few women in positions of power in the British economy?

1 How has the role of women in British politics changes since 1945?

2 To what extent did the election of Margaret Thatcher as the first woman Prime Minister affect the role of women in British Society?

3 How has the evolution of religion in post-war Britain affected reproductive rights?

The welfare state

What do we mean by the "welfare state"? Very broadly it refers to a government's direct attempts to provide for the welfare of its population. Of course such a broad definition simply begets other questions. What constitutes "welfare?" What direct means does the government use? Do these measures apply to everyone in society or just those in need? In the years immediately following the Second World War the new Labour government of Clement Attlee grappled with these questions and introduced sweeping social and economic policies that established a comprehensive welfare state.

In many ways the time was right for such a sweeping programme. The war had changed much. The economy was in dire condition with a debt of over £3 billion and war-time aid from the allies drying up. Bombing had damaged infrastructure and buildings. Workforce dislocation was looming as the country prepared to reabsorb the nearly three million soldiers of the war-time army who were to be demobilized. There was widespread fear of returning to the economic problems of the 1930s and the problems that followed the First World War, a not-so-distant memory. Government intervention in the economy had become the norm in the war years with its rationing, workforce conscription and industrial management. During the War, a government report on social services and insurance authored by William Beveridge advocated an expanded role for government in the eradication of the "Five Giant Evils" of want, disease, ignorance, squalor and idleness. The Beveridge Report was well received by the population and would form a basis for the welfare state as established by the post-war Labour government.

A primary vehicle for much of the social assistance that the government provided was the National Insurance Fund. The fund was built through contributions from all

Prime minister	Years	Party
Clement Attlee	1945–1951	Labour
Anthony Eden	1955–1957	Conservative
Harold Macmillan	1957–1963	Conservative
Alec Douglas-Home	1963–1964	Conservative
Harold Wilson	1964–1970, 1974–76	Labour
Edward Heath	1970–1974	Conservative
James Callaghan	1976–1979	Labour
Margaret Thatcher	1979–1990	Conservative
John Major	1990–1997	Conservative
Tony Blair	1997–2007	Labour

stakeholders. From the fund came social welfare payments designed to stabilize personal incomes:

- unemployment benefits
- sickness benefits
- pensions
- family allowance.

These schemes were in general governed by the principle of **universality**. They were paid to anybody who qualified regardless of financial circumstance. The wealthy received family allowance, as did the poor. Other schemes such as National Assistance were designed to provide stop-gap measures for the poorest in society and were based on a **means test**.

This principle of universality also applied to the National Health Service (NHS) inaugurated in 1948. This scheme approached health as an inalienable human right and as such its provision should not be based on income, but rather citizenship. The NHS provided free medical and dental care for all citizens. It covered hospital stays and medicine. This required that the government assume responsibility for the running of hospitals, which it did, as with the **nationalized** industries, through appointed boards. This expensive programme was to be funded through general taxation.
The government established guidelines that would help to ensure a relatively even geographical distribution of physicians between wealthy and poor areas. Most family physicians became, in essence, state employees paid a salary supplemented by a per-patient fee.

The new NHS was in many ways revolutionary, but was not without its issues. The construction of new hospitals suffered from the same obstacles faced by other building programmes—a lack of building supplies and resources to procure them. As similar services in other counties would later discover there was considerable opposition from the medical profession. Part of this opposition was economic. There was a fear that physicians would suffer economically by moving to a salary-based remuneration structure. The per-patient fee was designed to alleviate this fear. More importantly, there was a perception that the autonomous and self-governing nature of the medical profession was being compromised and with it the position of doctors within the social structure. The bureaucratization of the service, and the failure to establish a single administration for health services—some services such as ambulance and public health were left in local hands—provided at times for an inefficient administration. On the whole, the NHS succeeded in establishing sound public health care, creating what became a fixture of the post-war period in the United Kingdom and a model on which socialized medical programmes in other countries would be based.

As it was in the wake of the First World War, housing "fit for heroes" became a popular concept in 1945. As part of Beveridge's attack on squalor, the Labour government established several housing

William Beveridge (1893–1963)

Trained at the University of Oxford, Beveridge became a lawyer but soon found his way into the civil service working with David Lloyd George on social insurance schemes before the First World War. After the war he became director of the London School of Economics. In 1941 he was commissioned by the war-time government to study the prospects for national recovery after the war. The Beveridge Report highlighted the need for government intervention in the economy to combat what he called the "Giant Evils" of want, disease, ignorance, squalor and idleness. This report became the basis of Clement Atlee's establishment of the welfare state.

Universality The principle that all citizens received government benefits, regardless of need. This means that the wealthy as well as the poor receive benefits.

Means test The principle that all citizens received government benefits, based on some demonstration of need.

Nationalization The process by which a government takes over ownership and responsibility for an enterprise.

programmes. The war had exacerbated the crowded housing conditions of the 1930s. Universality did not, for the most part, apply to housing legislation passed after the war. The Housing Act of 1946 was directed at housing for the poor and built on traditional council housing schemes in which local councils used government subsidies to build housing and then rented these to tenants. Somehow, just under a million homes were constructed in the six years following the Second World War.

In many ways the construction of the welfare state in Britain was about changing the relation of the government to the economy. Social welfare programmes like the NHS were funded through taxation and were thus a way of redistributing income. In the process, the government became an important service provider. During these years the government also took steps to nationalize key industries such as coal, steel, and electrical power. These were to be operated by arms-length boards of directors appointed by the government. This rationalization of control was intended to bring efficiency to the industries, some of which were in a dire state and important to the development of the post-war economy. Such efficiency was never completely realized and this fact would become a bargaining point for the government of Margaret Thatcher, whose radical reversal of these policies of nationalization, and battle to overcome the strangle-hold of the associated trade unions, would be a major focus in the 1980s.

As much as the welfare state answered particular post-war British needs, it continued to grow in the decades following the War. While the welfare state managed to meet the material needs of the society there had been a vague sense of discontent throughout the period. By the 1970s accumulated social welfare policies had become very expensive. By 1969 inflation was gathering pace and increased spending on social programmes in the last years of the decade did not help this situation. By the time the Conservatives took power in 1970, there was widespread economic discontent. Tax and spending cuts bit hard into the social welfare programmes that had been built since 1945. As wages were not keeping pace with inflation, labour disputes became common as did the Conservative Party's legislative attempts to curb them. Industrial production was decreasing and British products were having difficulty competing in world markets. Yet inflation persisted and neither the Conservatives nor the Labour Party seemed to have a solution. By the last years of the decade, however, the Labour Party under James Callaghan took power and through a moderately austere fiscal policy managed to halt and even reverse inflation. As is often the case with moderate policies, regardless of how practical, Callaghan's approach alienated the extremes on both sides of the political spectrum.

Activity:
Previous experience

Research the House and Town Planning Act (1919) passed by the British Parliament in the wake of the First World War.

Compare and contrast the post-war housing programmes following the First and Second World Wars in the UK.

Margaret Thatcher (1925–)

Thatcher was born Margaret Roberts and attended the University of Oxford, graduating in 1947. She entered parliament in 1959 as the member from Finchley, which she would represent for the next 33 years. When Edward Heath came to power in 1970, Thatcher was promoted to Minister of Education. In February 1975 she won the Conservative Leadership from Heath. After leading the opposition for four years, Thatcher led the Conservatives into government in May of 1979 and became the first woman to lead a major Western power. During her tenure as Prime Minister she wrestled influence away from trade unions, and carried out an extensive privatization scheme. Her stern and commanding leadership style earned her the nickname "The Iron Lady". By 1990 she had alienated much of her own party and she lost her position as leader. In 1992 she was admitted to the House of Lords as the Baroness Thatcher.

Radicals in the Labour Party wanted firmer control of the economy and an end to the spending cuts. The Conservatives were won over by the *laissez faire* rhetoric of Margaret Thatcher. And so, by the eve of the 1980s, the United Kingdom was on the verge of a significant alteration to the welfare state that had been maintained since 1945.

Margaret Thatcher came to power in 1979 and over the course of the next decade began to dismantle the state-funded public infrastructure and the interventionist economic model that successive British governments had built over the previous decades. Instead of direct economic management of **fiscal policy**, Thatcher would instead rely on indirect **monetarist** controls. She would cut taxes and spending and allow market forces to right the British economy. Collectives, such as unions, were to be sidelined in favour of a fiercely individualist ideology. Such a conviction led to an accelerating pace of **privatization**. It initially started with the sale of state property, but by 1984 had spread to large government enterprises like British Telecom. Within six years, over 40 government-owned enterprises had been privatized, transferring over 800,000 workers from the public to the private sector. The state withdrew from the television, rail, steel, energy, and airline industries. To compliment this policy, the Thatcher government reduced economic restrictions and regulations.

While the Thatcher government did retreat from an ownership role in the government and adopted a more means-tested approach to replace the principle of universality, it did maintain its position as a service provider in some social programmes. The NHS was maintained while programmes that attempted to increase working-class home ownership allowed the government to draw back from housing subsidies and funding. Education funding may have been cut and government assets liquidated, but government spending on social welfare as a whole increased in the years of conservative rule.

Fiscal policy The government policy that relates to its taxation and spending.

Monetarism The approach to the economy that emphasizes managing inflation and unemployment through the manipulation of monetary policy instruments such as interest rates.

Privatization The process by which governments sell assets to the private sector.

Discussion point: Industrialization

Following are a list of Industries privatized under Thatcher's Conservative government.

British Telecom	Britoil
British Areospace	British Rail
British Gas	National Coal Board (Assets)
Rolls Royce	British Steel Corporation
Jaguar	British Gas Corporation

State ownership vs. privatization

1 How well did the state-owned corporations perform economically?

2 How did privatization affect the efficiency of the corporations that were privatized?

3 What were the arguments that opponents of the NHS used to attack the scheme?

4 How did nationalization and later privatization affect different geographic regions of the United Kingdom?

Religion

Secularization, as a social phenomenon, continued in the United Kingdom unabated after the war as it had in the early 20th century. But this is a sweeping statement that hides many nuances. At mid century, between a quarter and a fifth of citizens reported no religious affiliation and fewer regularly attended church. Nevertheless, the first six decades of the 20th century saw an increase in the number of Roman Catholics in the United Kingdom. While the number of Roman Catholics increased, the number of those who reported themselves as members of the Church of England steadily declined. **Nonconformist** numbers also declined in the 1950s and 1960s. Of course, such figures differed by geographic region. Roman Catholicism, for example, predictably had a stronger presence in Northern Ireland. Some nonconformist religions had a strong geographical element as well.

Organized or institutional religion had a complex relationship with the growing welfare state of the1940s and 1950s. On the one hand the extension of social benefits by the state seemed to attack exactly what the churches had been fighting for centuries—poverty and its effects. On the other hand, in some ways, the church was assuming much of the traditional purview of the churches and this was less welcome. In this way, the welfare state can perhaps be seen as contributing to the secularization of Britain during this period. More than mere territoriality, the concept of the welfare state struck at some key tenets of institutionalized charity. The concept of universality, while it reinforces ideas of human equality, challenged the hierarchical nature of traditional Christian charity—something practised by the well-off for the poor. By basing social welfare funding on taxes, the state removed the voluntary nature from "giving" which had also been an important part of Christian charity. These objections were not overt and there was little official opposition to the welfare state from institutionalized churches in the 1940s. Such opposition as materialized was more concerned with the spread of socialistic and, in the heat of the Cold War, communistic ideas than what was perceived as their associated atheism.

The social upheavals of the 1960s reached into Britain's institutionalized Christian religions as well. Arguments for a more humanist and functionalist and a less rule-bound approach to morality within the church framework began to appear within the Church of England as well as nonconformist churches. Vatican II began to reform the Roman Catholic Church by the mid decade. Of course, these ideas of reform met resistance from conservative elements in all the institutionalized churches, which further divided their congregations. Nevertheless, while secularization characterized this period, it was also marked by the diversification of the Christian Church specifically and spirituality in general. The growth of charismatic and evangelical Christian churches expanded after 1970 as did membership in "new" religious and philosophical movements such as Hari Krishna, Baha'I, and Scientology although such membership has varied over time with these belief communities.

Secularization The process of moving away from religious or spiritual matters

Nonconformist English Protestant sects that were not part of the established Church of England.

Nonconformist Churches

Baptists

Presbyterians (in England)

Methodists

Unitarians

Quakers

Salvation Army

Christian Brethren

Non-Christian religions also underwent a period of change in the years after the Second World War. The British Jewish community experienced significant decline between 1945 and 2000. Some estimates place the overall decline in the community at 40 per cent since 1945 but this has at times been blunted by immigration. Events such as the Hungarian uprising and the fall of the Iron Curtain brought brief influxes of Jews to Britain. For the first time, in 2001, the United Kingdom's decennial census asked questions about religious affiliation. In that census some 266,000 declared themselves to be Jewish. In terms of population density, concentrated Jewish Communities, especially in working-class neighborhoods, also began to disperse in the wake of the war. But the British Jewish community as a whole became more clustered in London by the end of the century. Jewish religious observance seems to have declined in this period, accelerating somewhat after 1960, and the social mobility that characterized the working class in Britain in the last half of the century also applied to the Jewish community.

Accelerating immigration has also put its stamp on the religious composition of the United Kingdom since 1945. The Muslim population has increased dramatically since the 1970s and according to the 2001 census stood at 1.6 million, tripling in the last 30 years of the century. This population is representative of the many Islamic traditions that characterized the Muslim world with a significant proportion tracing their roots back to the Indian subcontinent.

While we can therefore speak about secularization in the traditional British Christian community, the overall picture is more nuanced. This is especially true if we look at the broader aspect of spirituality rather than the more narrow areas of organized and institutionalized religion. The picture is even further obscured by the difficulty of obtaining statistics on belief. While the Jewish faith community seems to be shrinking, the size of the national Muslim community is increasing rapidly. Spirituality as a whole seems to be becoming more diversified.

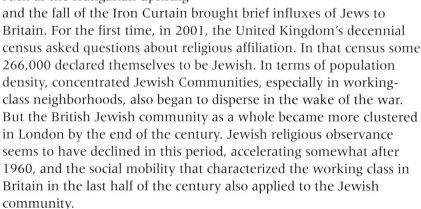

Discussion point: Religious divide

1 What is the geographical nature of nonconformist religions?

2 How did events in the Middle East in the second half of the 20th century affect the Jewish Community in the United Kingdom?

3 What are is the relationship between industrialization and secularization in Britain? How does this compare to other countries?

How has the change in the religious landscape in the United Kingdom affected political affiliation and activity?

Education

Much of post-war education in Britain was governed by an Act of Parliament drafted near the end of the Second World War. The Butler Education Act was developed by the minister of education, Richard Austen Butler. Butler, a Conservative member of Churchill's war-time cabinet, saw past the end of the War and sought to establish a foundation by which that post-war society could get beyond the ravages of the war. Butler promised a secondary education for all citizens as a vehicle for social reform and equality. To this end the Butler Act raised the school-leaving age to 15 years old. It is not hard to tell why Butler, a Conservative, successfully carried this law forward into the burgeoning welfare state of the Labour Party. Not only did it promise a more egalitarian approach to education from the point of view of the numbers who had access to the education system, but it also held out the promise of a rationalized and efficient system that would address both the needs of the United Kingdom and what was in the best interests of the student.

First it set out the principle that secondary education should be free to all citizens. The Act set up a system with three types of schools—grammar schools, secondary modern schools and secondary technical schools. Exams administered at age 11 (The 11+ Exams) would determine which stream a student should enter. Those that the exams determined to be academically inclined would enter the grammar schools while those whose aptitudes were found to lie in trades and other traditional working-class occupations were bound for the secondary modern schools. A third type of school designed to foster technical and practical engineering skills never really took off, with little more than three per cent ever attending these schools.

While the aim of the Act was to reform the education system such that it helped create a more egalitarian society the reality fell somewhat short of that. Income was not the only barrier to access. The 11+ exams tended to favour the middle-class, who then went into the grammar schools and from there into higher education. The working-class were funnelled into the secondary modern schools, which then moved graduates into working-class occupations. In this sense, the system set up by the Butler Act perpetuated the class divisions that already existed in Britain. Nevertheless, it did provide a free secondary education to all, including girls.

Such shortcomings were recognized and an experiment in comprehensive schools was developed from the end of the 1940s. In these comprehensive schools, grammar and secondary modern education was combined, in many ways eliminating the streaming of the 11+ exams. Until the 1960s, however, comprehensive schools were limited and accounted for only about five per cent of schools. This all changed in the mid 1960s. Harold Wilson's government directed local authorities to begin the move to comprehensive schools that would end the selection process of the 11+. While this direction was clear enough, the approach that the various authorities could take varied. The goal was a conventional comprehensive school for students aged 11–18. Other models involved the splitting of this age cohort into a school for students aged 11–16 and a separate sixth form school for those aged 16–18. Other two-tiered schools involved having students transfer into a junior comprehensive school and then a senior comprehensive. This system continued to strengthen through the 1970s and into the 1980s when 90 per cent of the secondary school population were attending comprehensive schools. In 1984 they developed a plan by which schools could opt out of local control and be funded directly by the central government, the administration of the school becoming the responsibility of a head teacher and governors. The 1980s also saw the movement towards a national curriculum that would culminate in the **General Certificate of Secondary Education (GCSE)**. While decentralization seems to have been a key element of Conservative Party policy, education was a curious contradiction. The movement to a national curriculum with a mandated testing regime put the schools in more direct control of the Department of Education. The "opt out" provision allowed some schools, on the decision of the parents, to separate from local school boards, establishing a more direct link with the central government. On closer examination, the contradiction fades somewhat. Parents were also given more discretion at which schools their students attended. Funding followed the students, putting schools in competition for students. The establishment of the opt-out option and funding structure was essentially individualist, allowing parents more say in the structure of education and diminished the role played by the more collectivist local school board. But while the system allowed schools and parents more control, the funding structure and the standardized curriculum and testing functionally put the government in more direct control of education.

Just as the demobilized servicemen flooded the job market in the immediate post-war years, they also flooded the universities. By 1949 there were more students in British Universities than ever before and three out of four of them were receiving government funding. Improving access to higher education and modernization of the education system were seen as a remedy to Britain's technological deficiencies. In the 1950s and 1960s university admissions dramatically increased, as did the number of universities. However, higher education remained fractured with a college and university system developing side by side. The working-class remained under-represented in universities even though new concepts such as the Open University attempted to address this issue. During the last 30 years of the century the number of universities and those attending universities had increased sharply.

Did these educational innovations work to achieve a more egalitarian society as they were intended to? Throughout this period of reform class distinctions remained. Socio-economic levels remained an important factor behind school achievement. Despite the equality promised by the compulsory state-funded secondary education that was initiated with the Butler Act in 1944, schools in poorer areas had lower achievement rates on standardized testing than those in more affluent areas. In higher education, participation rates have significantly increased, but access to and success in higher education was also partially dependent on socio-economic background. Students from more affluent independent schools had a much higher chance of attending university. The somewhat anachronistically described British **public school** remains an elite, network of independent schools that are perceived to confer on their graduates an advanced social standing and enhanced career opportunities.

> **General Certificate of Secondary Education (GCSE)** A general academic credential in the United Kingdom awarded in specific subjects.

> The **public school** is an 18th-century term, originally used to distinguish school education from private home tutoring. The "Seven Public Schools" of established reputation are Eton, Winchester, Westminster, Harrow, Rugby, Charterhouse, and Shrewsbury. Traditionally, pupils who attended these schools were prepared for university entrance and for public service. A recognized feature of the English public school is the college-style system, where elder pupils maintained order, discipline and a significant hierarchy within the social structure of the school, and in which most pupils were also boarders.

Discussion point: Education reform

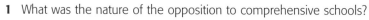

1 What was the nature of the opposition to comprehensive schools?
2 What role did the traditional public schools play in the British education system?
3 What were the arguments for and against standardized testing?
4 How did the new universities established during this period compare to the University of Oxford and the University of Cambridge?

Activity:

The nature of schools

Source A

On primary school education in the 1950s.

… in general its atmosphere and style was relaxed, informal, with an emphasis on creativity rather than on barrack-room drilling. It was the school for the vast bulk of the child population of the appropriate age group, much closer to a common school than to a class school.

Source: Sutherland, Gillian. "Education" in Thompson, F.M.L. (ed.) 1990. *The Cambridge Social History of Britain, 1750–1950*. vol. 3. Cambridge, UK. Cambridge University Press. p. 168.

Source B

On 20th-century educational reform in the UK.

Education has ebbed and flowed in the ranks of government priorities and many good intentions have faltered in the face of economic pressure. Pragmatism has often defeated radicalism, and opportunities where significant change might have been secured have sometimes been missed. Educational opportunities have increased massively since 1945, but remain disproportionately accessible by the most advantaged members of British society.

Source: Watson, Katherine. "Education and Opportunity" in Carnevali, F. and Strange, J.M (eds.) 2007. *20th Century Britain: Economic, Cultural and Social Change*. London, UK. Pearson Education, p. 371.

Source C

On academic achievement.

It also became apparent that middle-class children were far more likely to do well in the eleven-plus than working-class ones that came from a background where academic pursuits were not encouraged.

Source: Marwick, Arthur. 1990. *British Society Since 1945*. London, UK. Penguin Books. p. 56.

Questions

1. Compare and contrast the view of educational change in the period after 1945 presented by the sources.

2. Research the structure of the British school system in the period 1900–45. What elements remained unchanged after 1945?

3. Using these sources and further research evaluate the educational changes in the period 1945–2000 in terms of their effect on the social structure of Britain.

Activity:

Education on film

The differences in expectations for those attending public schools and state-run comprehensive schools is reflected in film and literature:

- *If….* (1968) directed by Lindsay Anderson.
- *To Sir With Love* (1967), directed by James Clavell, based on the autobiography of E. R. Braithwaite.
- *The History Boys*, a play by Alan Bennett (2004), set in the 1980s about a group of Oxbridge candidates. Also a film directed by Nicholas Hytner (2006).

Questions

1. How are the career and life expectations of characters in these and other similar works influenced by their educational environment?

2. What evidence is there in these works that class associations were perpetuated by the education system in post-war Britain?

3. How did post-war education reform in Britain affect this educational environment?

Divide up into groups, and make a presentation in class, that reflects on what you know about British post-war education reform and associated class interests.

The arts and popular culture

The last half of the 20th century was a dynamic time for the arts in Britain. A number of different forces determined the nature and source of this dynamism. The experience of the Second World War helped shape the themes explored by artists in the decade after the end of the war. The shrinking world also had an important impact on British arts. Initially this had much to do with the rise to prominence and influence—economic, political and cultural—of the United States, but was also affected by decolonization and influx of migrants to the United Kingdom. This was certainly a two-way street with the UK exporting its popular music and movies like never before. Like many Western countries, the UK greeted the first years of peace with a **baby boom**. This boom swelled the ranks of youth 15–30 years after the Second World War and, with its notions of rebellion and demographic purchasing power, helped determine the nature of the artistic and popular culture in the 1960s and 1970s. If we accept that art in part imitates life, it can be no surprise that the economic disaffection of the 1970s influenced the arts and popular culture scene. Technological developments, notably the advent of television, radically changed British popular culture in this period.

> **Baby boom** A period of increased birth rate in the years following the Second World War. Many countries experienced baby booms of varying durations.

Literature

The years of austerity that governed British life in the decade after the end of the war along with the international tensions and dislocations caused by the Cold War, decolonization, and the atomic age put their stamp on the literary life of the United Kingdom. Writers greeted these developments with satire, drama, comedy, parody and any number of literary forms that in previous periods had perhaps not been as accepted. Many of these literary works explored the relationship of the individual to the new centralized welfare state. The UK's changing relationship to the rest of the world and to its own past was examined as was the relationship of emerging communities—based on gender, race and age—to traditional British society. The meaning and effect of class continued to be an important theme, tempered by these other complexities.

While the drama of Noel Coward and others whose work spanned the war years were in essence nostalgic—looking for solace in the an earlier era—new, more experimental works by the likes of Samuel Beckett and Harold Pinter looked at the place of the individual in the post-war landscape. While Beckett and Pinter explored existential themes, the so-called "Angry Young Men" gave a critique of the growing sterility and affluence of the 1950s in which the promises of peace and the welfare state were seen to be empty and without principle. These young authors and playwrights attacked the hypocrisy and confinement of the persistent British class structure. The movement takes its name from the 1956 play *Look Back in Anger* by John Osborne and venerated the anti-hero, usually working class, who held the class structure in contempt but could not find a way out of its strictures. As society changed so did the targets of the playwrights. Playwrights like Caryl Churchill,

British fiction, 1945–2000		
Novel	**Author**	**Year**
1984	George Orwell	1949
The Lord of the Rings	J.R.R. Tolkien	1954
Lord of the Flies	William Golding	1954
The Quiet American	Graham Greene	1955
Saturday Night and Sunday Morning	Alan Sillitoe	1958
The Golden Notebook	Doris Lessing	1962
A Clockwork Orange	Anthony Burgess	1962
Jerusalem the Golden	Margaret Drabble	1967
In A Free State	V.S. Naipaul	1971
Possession: A Romance	A. S. Byatt	1990
Amsterdam	Ian McEwan	1998
The Blackwater Lightship	Colm Tóibín	1999
White Teeth	Zadie Smith	2000

David Hare, and Howard Brenton took aim at the growing capitalist ethos associated with Thatcherism.

In literature as with any of the arts one must be careful about ascribing the term "movement" to cultural elements that have widespread popularity and differentiate between what some historians have called elite and popular culture. Without resorting to what are sometimes over simplified and at times condescending labels, it must be kept in mind that a wide variety of genres, directed by a wide variety of tastes, are popular at any one time. For example, detective novels were very popular in the post-war period and in fact continue to be so, building on the tradition of Arthur Conan Doyle's Sherlock Holmes and the novels of Agatha Christie. This genre is an interesting combination of both continuity and change. Many of the authors who write in this tradition develop a single detective and then carry this character through different plot lines in subsequent novels allowing the reader to experience the escapist comfort of a familiar detective in a fresh story. The United Kingdom continues to produce and export a decidedly modern version of the detective novel in the form of television adaptations of books such as the Inspector Morse novels of Colin Dexter. While the detective novel is in many ways a form of pure escapism, espionage novels, another popular genre, were also escapist, but rooted in Cold War reality. Such novels of betrayal and intrigue had a particular relevance in a country that had experienced a number of high profile spy scandals such as the **Profumo Affair** and the espionage activities of the so-called **Cambridge Spies**. It is hard to deny the escapist nature of the James Bond novels of Ian Flemming, while the works of John le Carré, such as *Tinker Tailor, Soldier, Spy,* and *The Spy Who Came in From the Cold,* were somewhat more complex examples of this genre.

British drama, 1945–2000		
Play	**Playwright**	**Year**
Waiting for Godot	Samuel Beckett	1955
Romanoff and Juliet	Peter Ustinov	1956
Look Back in Anger	John Osborne	1956
The Caretaker	Harold Pinter	1960
Who's Afraid of Virginia Woolf?	Edward Albee	1964
A Day in the Death of Joe Egg	Peter Nichols	1967
The Norman Conquests	Alan Ayckbourn	1974
Plenty	David Hare	1978
The Real Thing	Tom Stoppard	1982
Benefactors	Michael Frayn	1984
Serious Money	Caryl Churchill	1987
Stanley	Pam Gems	1996

British detective fiction	
Author	**Detective**
Colin Dexter	Inspector Morse
Ruth Rendell	Inspector Wexford
P.D. James	Inspector Dalgliesh
Caroline Graham	Chief Inspector Barnaby
Ian Rankin	Inspector John Rebus
Peter Robinson	Chief Inspector Alan Banks
Reginald Hill	Andrew Dalziel and Peter Pascoe
Paul Charles	Christy Kennedy
M.C. Beaton	Hamish MacBeth
Lindsey Davis	Marcus Didius Falco

Profumo Affair A 1963 political scandal in which the British Secretary of State for War, John Profumo, was caught in an extra-marital relationship with a woman named Kristine Keeler who was also in a relationship with a Soviet intelligence agent. After lying about the affair in the House of Commons, Profumo resigned.

Cambridge Spies A group of four British men that were discovered to have been spying for the Soviet Union in the 1940s and 1950s. Kim Philby, Guy Burgess, Donald Maclean, and Anthony Blunt had all attended Cambridge University in the 1930s. Philby, Burgess and Maclean defected to the Soviet Union, while Blunt remained in the UK until his death in 1983.

Music

The themes of continuity and change played out in popular music as well. The 1950s to the 1980s were a period of great innovation in British popular music, but at the same time owed a debt to the music that came before it. British popular music at this time also reflected the social pressures and tensions facing all aspects of British Society. The advent of Rock and Roll, the influence of American blues, the British Invasion, the evolution of punk and New Wave all formed an important part of a global movement in popular culture.

American blues had been seeping into the British music scene since before the 1950s. The close connection between jazz and blues meant that the jazz craze that gripped Britain during the War years contained the blues—often acoustic Delta blues played during breaks between traditional jazz sets. British musicians like Alexis Korner moved from jazz backgrounds to explore more traditional blues forms. Skiffle music combined jazz, blues, blue grass and folk elements—decidedly American influences—to become popular in the 1950s. Skiffle drew many aspiring musicians with its functionally egalitarian form—musical proficiency was not a prerequisite for Skiffle and it was indeed a starting point for many future music stars such as Van Morrison, John Lennon, members of the Rolling Stones, The Who and others. The commercial potential of this form and related musical forms became evident with the success of Lonnie Donegan's 1956 recording of the Leadbelly song "Rock Island Line" and this helped convince record companies to expand further into this genre. At the same time, American blues musicians such as Muddy Waters toured the United Kingdom turning all manner of musicians on to undiscovered blues musicians. These touring blues acts would often pick up British blues musicians to fill out their bands, which had been pared down for travel to the UK. It was not long before this influence began to show up in the homegrown British music of people like John Mayall and Long John Baldry. This music appealed to the Britain of the 1950s and early 1960s on a number of levels. Although not necessarily strictly played by the working class in Britain, it appealed to the lionizing of working class ideals that grew out of 1950s and gave rise to the concept of the "working-class hero". In the United States this music had grown out of resistance of an oppressed people and this found resonance with a generation in Britain constrained by the traditional class structure. On a purely demographic and commercial level there were more young people than ever before in Britain and they had a degree of purchasing power encouraging record companies to expand into this genre. The fact that this music came from the United States gave it a certain exotic currency for a generation that wanted to look beyond its own shores and the limitations of its welfare state and controlled, managed existence.

Much has been written, said, and imagined about the 1960s. It was indeed a period of drastic social change. But, as with most periods of history, there were also strong currents of continuity during this decade. The iconic band of British popular music and rock and roll of the 1960s was the Beatles and they were in part a product of the expanding music scene of the late 1950s with John Lennon and Paul McCartney coming together in 1957 and in this sense they were emblematic of the change in popular music, but there are elements

American Blues Musicians in the UK	
Musician	**Tour**
Muddy Waters	1958
Sonny Terry and Brownie McGhee	1958
Big Bill Broonzy	1952
Bo Diddley	1963
Howlin' Wolf	1964

of earlier popular music that finds its way into much of the Beatles early work and in that way they can be seen simultaneously as a force in music continuity. The song "A Taste of Honey" which appeared on their first album was a Broadway show tune and "Baby Its You" was co-written by popular song-writer Burt Bacharach. Robert Harris has demonstrated links between "Please, Please, Please Me" and the work of Bing Crosby, the Everly Brothers, and Scott Joplin. Another episode that illuminates traditionalist forces in music of the revolutionary 1960s Britain erupted when Bob Dylan took to the stage on his 1965 UK tour and began to play an electric guitar. Stony silence and eventually outright hostility greeted this artistic innovation.

Despite such elements of continuity there was much that was musically new during this decade. Rock and roll as such arrived in a packaged form in the mid fifties with tours of artists like Bill Haley and the Comets and Jerry Lee Lewis. British bands like the Rolling Stones took the music of Buddy Holly and Chuck Berry, mixed it with their experience of the blues and made it their own. Along with other bands such as The Beatles, Manfred Mann, The Troggs, and the Animals, the Rolling Stones led the so-called British Invasion of the American music scene in the mid 1960s and as the decade progressed rock and roll in North America and the United Kingdom cross-pollinated to create a very dynamic music scene. When the economic dislocation of the mid 1970s met some clever commercial promotion a British version of what was becoming known as punk rock developed in London. High unemployment and a generally bleak outlook gripped many urban youth in the 1970s and this led to a distinct anti-establishment, in some cases almost nihilistic philosophy, with an associated fashion and, of course, music. Punk rock was hard and fast. Its simple "arrangements" and propensity to use guitars more as percussion instruments than string instruments drew in all manner of would-be musicians—many of them decidedly middle class. The form itself was a rebellion against the musicianship of "elite" pop rock of bands like the Beatles. Prototypical UK bands such as the Sex Pistols, The Clash, and the Buzzcocks sought to shock audiences in an attempt to show their disdain for an establishment they saw as funnelling them into dead-end jobs—or no job at all— in the service of an elite that made the meaningful decisions in society. Punk rock offered no real alternative to the grim socio- economic situation, simply loud and increasingly violent protest. Musically, bands like The Clash became more sophisticated and began to combine reggae influences taken from an increasingly popular Caribbean genre that was making inroads on the back of immigration and a globalizing music culture. Despite the fact that in part its origins

Joe Strummer (1952–2002)

Born John Mellor in Ankara, Turkey, Strummer was the son of a British foreign officer. After attending boarding school in London he was admitted to art school but never finished. During his time in London he gained experience as a busker. He was influenced by British and American rock and roll as well as the folk music of Woody Guthrie. In 1976 Strummer met Mick Jones and Paul Simonon and they formed The Clash, eventually joined by Topper Headon behind the drums. Strummer was the singer and rhythm guitarist. The Clash wrote songs woven through with leftist politics that expressed the disaffection felt by many London youth. As time wore on they became more musically sophisticated, mixing reggae, ska, and other influences into their sound. In the early 1980s their success reached beyond the UK and American tours followed. After the Clash broke up in 1986, Strummer spent his time acting, writing soundtrack scores and playing with various bands such as The Pogues. At the time of his death he was performing with his new band the Mescaleros.

Activity:

The Age of Prosperity

Source A

From a speech to a rally of Conservative supporters by Prime Minister Harold MacMillan, in 1957.

> Indeed let us be frank about it–most of our people have never had it so good. Go around the country, go to the industrial towns, go to the farms and you will see a state of prosperity such as we have never had in my lifetime–nor indeed in the history of this country.

Source B

From "Mother's Little Helper" by the Rolling Stones (Jagger, Richards) 1965.

> "Things are different today"
> I hear ev'ry mother say
> Cooking fresh food for a husband's just a drag
> So she buys an instant cake and she burns her frozen steak
> And goes running for the shelter of a mother's little helper
> And two help her on her way, get her through her busy day
>
> Doctor please, some more of these
> Outside the door, she took four more
> What a drag it is getting old.

Source C

From "Lost in the Supermarket" by the Clash (Strummer, Jones) 1979.

> I'm all lost in the supermarket
> I can no longer shop happily
> I came in here for the special offer
> A guaranteed personality
>
> I wasn't born so much as I fell out
> Nobody seemed to notice me
> We had a hedge back home in the suburbs
> Over which I never could see
>
> I'm all tuned in I see all the programmes
> I save coupons from packets of tea
> I've got my giants hit discotheque album
> I empty a bottle I feel a bit free
>
> Kids in the halls and the pipes in the walls
> Making noises for company
> Long distance callers make long distance calls
> And the silence makes me lonely.

Questions

1 Explain the following references:

   a "a state of prosperity" (Source A)

   b a "mothers's little helper" (Source B)

2 Compare and contrast the views of Britain's consumer society expressed in Sources A and C.

3 Assess the origin, purpose, values and limitations of Sources A and C as historical sources.

4 Using these Sources and further research, evaluate the consumer economy as it developed in Britain in the years 1950 to 1980.

came from unemployed youth, the commercial potential of the punk movement became evident and some punk bands enjoyed great commercial success. By the end of the 1970s and into the 1980s punk music spawned other forms such as New Wave while reggae continued to grow in popularity.

Film, radio, and television

Going to the cinema as a pastime, had been growing in popularity since the introduction of motion-pictures during the inter-war period. For 30 years after 1946, however, attendance declined in part due to the growing popularity of television. In many ways, the film industry in Britain reflected broader societal concerns and issues. Class was an ever-present theme. Of the British Film Institute's top 100 films—94 of which come from the 1945–2000 period—over a third deal with class either directly—*Saturday and Sunday Morning* (1960) —or indirectly—*The Full Monty* (1997). Arthur Mawick has pointed to three ways in which this social commentary was expressed on the screen. Social satires such as *Nothing But the Best* (1966) used humour to skewer social conventions. Other films portrayed working-class life in all its rich and gritty reality. Films like *Kes* (Dir. Ken Loach, 1970) and *This Sporting Life* (Dir. Lindsay Anderson, 1967) used this approach. As the 1960s progressed more experimental films such as *If* (Dir. Lindsay Anderson, 1968) took an innovative approach to this old theme. As the period wore on, other themes such a race and sexuality welded themselves onto class relations in such movies as *My Beautiful Launderette* (Dir. Stephen Frears, screenplay by Hanif Kureishi, 1985), the *The Crying Game* (Dir. Neil Jordan, 1992) and *Secrets and Lies* (Dir. Mike Leigh, 1996).

The history of British broadcasting, both radio and television, has been dominated by the British Broadcasting Company (BBC). Operating from the early 1920s, the BBC enjoyed a state-mandated monopoly until 1954. It was funded by fees assessed on radio receivers and other public funds and operated by an arms-length board. This structure meant that although its origins lay long before the advent of the post-war welfare state, it fitted well into the nationalizing philosophy of the Labour government. While the structure may have suited Labour ideals, its governance had been far less egalitarian since its inception, with the governors over-representing the establishment elite. When the Conservatives came to power they introduced a level of competition to the growing technology of television, but left the essential structure of the BBC intact. After the war the BBC split its radio programme into three services: Light Programme, broadcasting what the governors believed to be light entertainments; the Home Service programmed more "serious" dramas and lectures; the Third Programme focusing on cultural programming. The BBC extended its reach beyond London with the development of BBC orchestras throughout the country. In the late part of the century this streaming of content was transformed into BBC Radio 1, 2, 3, and 4. The BBC expanded its television offerings by establishing a second channel, BBC2, in the 1960s. The BBC has been responsible for much of the significant Television programming of the period such as *Fawlty Towers* (BBC2, 1975, 1979) the *EastEnders*, (BBC1, 1985–) *Yes Minister* and *Yes Prime Minister* (BBC2, 1980–84, 1986–88) as well as comprehensive news coverage. The independent broadcaster ITV has also had success with programmes such as *The Naked Civil Servant* (ITV, 1975) and *Brideshead Revisited* (ITV, 1981). In 1982, a further public broadcaster, Channel 4, was established to break up the duopoly of the license-fee funded BBCs and ITV as the sole commercial broadcaster.

British films, 1945–2000		
Film	**Director**	**Year**
The Third Man	Carol Reed	1949
The Bridge on the River Kwai	David Lean	1957
Lawrence of Arabia	David Lean	1962
Alfie	Lewis Gilbert	1966
Kes	Ken Loach	1969
Don't Look Now	Nicolas Roeg	1973
Chariots of Fire	Hugh Hudson	1981
Caravaggio	Derek Jarman	1986
Withnail and I	Bruce Robinson	1987
The Crying Game	Neil Jordan	1992
Secrets and Lies	Mike Leigh	1993
Trainspotting	Danny Boyle	1996

British Television
Coronation Street (ITV, 1960)
I Claudius (BBC2, 1976)
Steptoe and Son (BBC1, 1962–5, 1970–4)
The Sweeney (ITV, 1975–8)
The Avengers (ITV, 1961–9)
GBH (Channel 4, 1991)
The Prisoner (ITV, 1967–8)
Dr Who (BBC1, 1963–89, 1996, 2005–) (ITV, 1967–8)
Till Death Us Do Part (BBC1, 1965–75)
Doctor in the House (ITV, 1967–70)

Discussion point: *Alfie* (1966)

You know what? When I look back on my little life and the birds I've known, and think of all the things they've done for me and the little I've done for them, you'd think I've had the best of it along the line. But what have I got out of it? I've got a bob or two, some decent clothes, a car, I've got me health back and I ain't attached. But I ain't got me peace of mind–and if you ain't got that, you ain't got nothing. I dunno. It seems to me if they ain't got you one way they've got you another. So what's the answer? That's what I keep asking myself–what's it all about? Know what I mean?

From *Alfie* (1966), directed by Lewis Gilbert and starring Michael Caine.

Michael Caine plays Alfie, a playboy from a working-class background. What is his essential critique of British society? How are his comments reflected in other films and plays of the period?

Pop culture and subculture

The music that grew out of the 1950s, 1960s, and 1970s was often associated with various subcultures complete with norms, ethos and fashion. The rock and roll of the 1950s helped spawn the Teddy Boys, elegant youth sporting Savile Row suits. While some were casually associated with the subculture, others formed into gangs that clashed with rivals. Teddy Boys played a conspicuous role in the Notting Hill race riots. Unemployed working-class Teddy Boys took the frustration of poverty out on equally poor immigrants from the Caribbean in a riot that lasted for five days in 1958. In the early 1960s two new subcultures developed. Rockers took their image from American motorbike gangs, donning leather jackets and blue jeans and listening to American rock and roll. Mods, on the other hand, affected a more sophisticated "modern" look, sporting tailored suits and riding European motor scooters. The Mods listened to pop, jazz, ska and reggae. With such contrasting styles it is not difficult to predict that there would be clashes, often violent, between gangs of Rockers and Mods. These clashes shocked the staid British society leading to the growing belief that British youth were out of control. Rather they were seeking meaning from a subculture that was theirs and not that of the older generation. The content of the sub culture, be it Teddy Boy, Rocker or Mod was in many ways irrelevant. What was important was that it was not the fashion, music, or beliefs of the older generation. These group identities were reinforced when they could be juxtaposed, often violently, with other subcultures. In the later 1960s the hippy subculture grew popular as it did in the United States and other countries. A similar pattern emerged in the 1970s with the Punk subculture. Unemployed London youth took a distinct fashion sense from Malcolm McLaren's clothing store called "Sex", featuring ground-breaking fashion designs by Vivienne Westwood.

> ### Vivienne Westwood (1941–)
>
>
>
> Born Vivienne Swire, Westwood was a fashion designer who originally studied at art school and later at the University of London. Starting out as a primary school teacher, she met Malcolm McLaren with whom she worked in pioneering what would become a distinctive punk fashion style through the McLaren's clothing shop "Sex." Her fashions gained notoriety when they were worn by the punk band The Sex Pistols who were managed by McLaren. In the following years she opened a number of fashion shops of her own and gained popularity in the fashion industry that has lasted into the 21st century. She has been awarded the Order of the British Empire and been named British Designer of the Year in 1990, 1991 and 2006.

Punk rock grew out of this scene. Punk fashion was designed to be as different as possible from the suit-wearing middle and upper class. Commitment to this anti-social ethos could be demonstrated by permanent and semi-permanent body modifications. Tattoos and piercing that could not be covered up showed a permanent contempt for society and discouraged those who were recreational punks, donning suits for work during the day and playing the punk scene at night. The skinhead subculture had developed in the 1960s enjoyed a revival in the later 1970s as, in some ways, a response to the punks—or at least the later punks who many believed were growing more commercial and thus more

 How can fashion reflect social views? What examples can you find in your own society?

Teddy Boys on a London Street. What does the fashion of Teddy Boys tell us about their sub-culture?

Malcolm McLaren and Vivienne Westwood, wearing one of her T-shirt designs in 1977.

mainstream. Skinheads affected a stylized working-class "uniform" —blue jeans, suspenders, work boots and close-cropped hair. As the Rockers and Mods before them, punks and skinheads fought pitched battles large and small. Tensions in the larger society often found expression in these youth subcultures. Issues like race and unemployment were central to their activities, although arguably, with the exception of later skinheads,

politics was not the core motivation for these groups. Rather they were associational, an expression of the contradictory impulses of youth—to belong and to be different at the same time.

> ### Discussion point: Subcultures
>
> **How have the subcultures that developed in the 1950s, 1960s, and 1970s carried forward into the 1990s?**
>
> What new subcultures have developed? What does this tell us about British society in the 1990s?
>
> ### Extended discussion
>
> 1 How did music reflected the economic and social reality of the 1990s?
> 2 What new themes have emerged in film, drama, and literature at the end of the century?
> 3 To what degree does the United Kingdom still "export" its culture? What cultural elements has the UK imported in the last decade of the century?

Immigration, emigration and race relations

Immigration has always played an important role in British history, but post-war immigration permeated all areas of British society. Just as Irish immigration had helped provide the labour force for 19th-century industrialization, it was recognized in the Royal Commission on Population in 1949 that if British industry was going to expand in the post-war period it would need immigrant workers. The British birth rate had begun to slump again after a brief post-war baby boom and the resultant deficiency in the labour force could only be alleviated by immigration. Reconstruction required a great deal of labour and the British government looked to traditional sources in Europe. As in the past, the Irish made up the bulk of this immigration, supplemented by those fleeing the spread of authoritarian communism in Eastern Europe. Other factors helped structure the wave of immigration that would come after the late 1940s. Decolonization, especially in the British Empire, coupled with the British Nationality Act of 1948, which expedited immigration from **Commonwealth** countries at a time when the United States was restricting immigration. The UK was an attractive alternative for immigrants from the West Indies. The newly independent Indian subcontinent was also an important source of immigration in the 1950s and 1960s. This immigration was as ethnically diverse as the subcontinent itself. Indian immigrants came from western India and the Punjab. They were Hindus, Sikhs and Muslims. Immigration from South Asia continued into the 1970s as family members that had established themselves in the 1950s provided a connection for later migrants.

> **Commonwealth** A loose association of independent countries that had once been part of the British Empire.

This immigration has changed the structure of the British population. The number of those born outside the UK as a proportion of the total population has increased in every decade since the end of the Second World War as have the absolute numbers, such that by the turn of the century over 8 per cent of the population was born outside the UK. Europe, especially Ireland, continued as the most common place of birth for these immigrants, but European immigrants as a proportion of the total immigrant population has decreased since the 1950s from a half to a third.

Relations between these immigrant communities and the wider British population have been tense at times during this period. During the 1950s this tension reached from the highest seats of government down to the streets of British cities. Officially, the government was committed to an "open door" policy when it came to immigrants from Commonwealth nations.

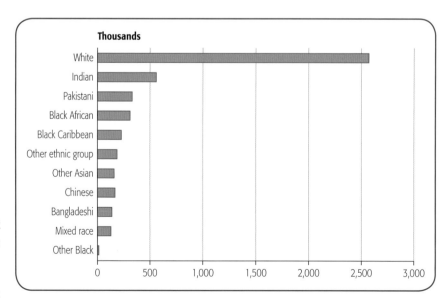

Foreign-born population: by ethnic group, April 2001, UK.

Source: UK Office of National Statistics, People and Migration. http://www.statistics.gov.uk.

Privately, however, the both Labour and Conservative governments sought to encourage white immigrants and discourage non-white immigrants and these sentiments found their way into law. From the 1960s, legislation has sought to sculpt both the nature and the size of the immigrant population by becoming increasingly restrictive, starting with the Commonwealth Immigration Act of 1962 that limited the right of entry from Commonwealth countries. In 1968 a new act set up quotas based on country—and thus indirectly on ethnicity. In this same year a Conservative Member of Parliament named Enoch Powell gave a speech known as the "Rivers of Blood Speech" in which he attacked the flow of non-white immigration. As late as 1993, the Asylum Act curtailed refugee immigration.

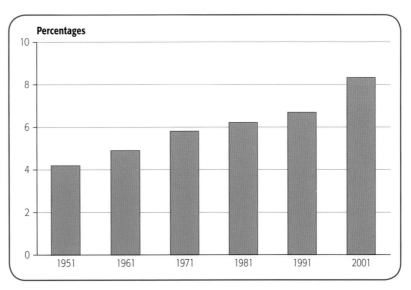

Foreign-born as a per centage of total UK population.

Source: UK Office of National Statistics, People and Migration. http://www.statistics.gov.uk.

These tensions erupted into violence on occasion. In 1958 a racially focused riot broke out against non-white immigrants in the Notting Hill suburb of London. Race was the focus of riots in other parts of Britain in the mid 1960s as well. As well as these large, racially motivated explosions of violence, there continued smaller attacks on visible minorities throughout the UK. Much of racial intolerance was parroted and promoted by extremist right-wing political parties that emerged in the 1950s and 1960s. Parties like the British National Front railed against the "swamping" of British identity and character by the waves of post-war immigration.

Against this backdrop of tension there was a contradictory tendency toward tolerance. In years following the Notting Hill riots the British government used a series of Race Relations Acts in 1965, 1968, and 1976 to work toward limiting racial discrimination in the workplace and other areas of British society. Because it is a Member of the European Union, Europeans are permitted unrestricted entry to the UK. In 1966 the Labour government set up the Race Relations Board whose job was to oversee the implementation of the 1966 and subsequent Acts.

Activity:

On immigration

The following is an excerpt from an interview given by Margaret Thatcher in the wake of a race riot in Wolverton in 1978. In this interview, given before she became Prime Minister, Thatcher uses democratic ideals to justify a position against immigration.

> … *if we went on as we are then by the end of the century there would be four million people of the new Commonwealth or Pakistan here. Now, that is an awful lot and I think it means that people are really rather afraid that this country might be rather swamped by people with a different culture and, you know, the British character has done so much for democracy, for law and done so much throughout the world that if there is any fear that it might be swamped people are going to react and be rather hostile to those coming in.*

Source: Margaret Thatcher, Leader of the Opposition, TV Interview for Granada World in Action, 27 January 1978. http://www.margaretthatcher.org.

 What are the strengths and weaknesses of this argument?

Draft a response to Thatcher and be prepared to defend your position.

Immigration and race relations in the post-war period have thus been characterized by contradictions. Legislation has both sought to encourage immigration in some instances while restricting it in others. Amid a democratic principle that values equality and tolerance, some politicians and citizens have spoken and acted against these principles.

> **Discussion point: Immigration and emigration**
>
> 1 How has immigration transformed the British economy? What occupations have attracted the most immigrants? Why? Do these patterns vary by country of origin?
>
> 2 To what extent has emigration affected British society in the post-war years? What is the social background of the population that has left the United Kingdom?
>
> 3 What are the requirements for British citizenship? What is the process by which immigrants become citizens? What rights do they have before they achieve full citizenship?

The economy and technology

The immediate post-war years were predictable characterized by economic recovery and reconstruction. The economy has a massive task on its hands. It had to rebuild a seriously damaged infrastructure as well as absorb the demobilized war-time army. It had to do this amid material shortages and while the government began to implement the welfare state and experiments in economic planning. The war had largely been financed on credit and this amounted to £3 billion. New loans had to be secured from the United States and Canada, but this was simply a stop-gap measure. The general weakness of the economy struck at its core—the pound, which grew weaker and weaker in the first years after the war. This situation led to one of the great paradoxes facing democratic socialist governments, that need for a welfare state is generally most pronounced at times when the means for implementing the welfare state are the scarcest. To complicate matters, the dangers of unemployment in a post-war economy lead to lower interest rates, which then exacerbated inflation. This bleak situation eased somewhat after 1947 by Marshall Aid and a devaluing of the pound which lowered the cost of British goods and thus increased exports. Britain limped into the 1950s, battered, but intact. In fact, a number of factors that emerged out of the war helped position Britain for a period of recovery and prosperity in the 1950s. A number of war-time factories were made available at favourable terms to industrialists. Nuclear technology developed during the war made its way into civilian use. Construction on the first of Britain's nuclear power plants was begun in 1946. Medical advances piloted on wounded soldiers were now widely used. The British aerospace industry flourished in the post-war era in part because the British invested more than any other European country on the development of transportation and communication technology in the decade after the Second World War.

In the early 1950s the UK bid farewell to war-time rationing and to the Labour government as well. What followed was a decade of economic prosperity. But it was not due to any cost Conservative cost-cutting or *laissez faire* ethos—the Conservatives maintained and in some ways expanded the welfare state. The British economy had largely been rebuilt—it had grown each year since

British Nobel Laureates in Chemistry, 1945–2000	
Scientist	**Year**
Robert Robinson	1947
Archer John Porter Martin & Richard Synge	1952
Cyril Hinshelwood	1956
Frederick Sanger	1958
John Kendrew	1962
Dorothy Hodgkin	1964
Ronald Norrish & George Porter	1967
Derek Barton	1969
Geoffrey Wilkinson	1973
Frederick Sanger	1980
Harold Kroto	1996
John Walker	1997

British Nobel Laureates in Physics, 1945–2000	
Scientist	**Year**
Martin Ryle	1946
Edward Appleton	1947
Patrick Blackett	1948
Cecil Powell	1950
John Cockcroft	1951
Brian Josephson	1973
Andrew Hewish	1974

the end of the war. The welfare state meant that the working class did not have to spend a large proportion of their income on such things as medical care. The major influence, however, was the expansion of the world economy as the United Kingdom was just one of a number of Western economies that had thrown off the Second World War and were now prospering. In any event, real wages increased during this period and with it the consumer economy. Technology played an important role in this expansion both in the UK and around the world. On the one hand, improved efficiency in manufacturing produced cheaper consumer goods, supported by a concurrent increase in real wages. Televisions, radios, refrigerators, washing machines found themselves into more and more homes such that by 1971 nearly 90 per cent of homes had a television and nearly two thirds of homes had a washing machine. These goods also formed an important part of British exports. On the other hand, technological progress was not limited to the explosion in consumer goods. Her traditional strength in heavy industry also benefited. Oil and its chemical offshoots expanded. But affluence also breeds inflation and this was the case in the mid 1960s, which hurt the value of the pound and British exports. The United Kingdom had worked its way into a prolonged period of affluence after the hard years of the Depression and the War.

If the 1950s and 1960s can be characterized as a period of growing affluence, then the 1970s and early 1980s provided a sharp corrective. The nagging problem of any growing economy is the spectre of inflation. As the 1960s came to a close, inflation was rising and this was biting into exports and the jobs that depended on them. As with the period of prosperity, the hard times of the 1970s were also linked to the global economic context. Political instability in the Middle East and the resulting energy crisis affected all industrialized economies. This crisis widened cracks in the industrial economy of the 1950s and 60s and unemployment began to increase. When the Conservatives took power again in 1970 they attacked this situation with spending cuts as well as tax cuts. Unemployment kept wages low, but inflation pushed prices higher. This led to a volatile labour market and unions tried to fight back. The Conservative government saw in the unions a major practical and ideological barrier to increased productivity and efficiency. By 1975 inflation was pushing 25 per cent. The outlook was bleak.

In retrospect, the mid 1970s was a low watermark in terms of inflation. At the time, however, the economic situation was turbulent. By 1978–9 strikes were once again sweeping across the economy—Ford Motor Company workers and Transport workers leading the way.

Superintendent John Nesbit arrests Arthur Scargill, NUM President at Orgreave during the 1984–5 miners strike in Orgreave, South Yorkshire.

Exports, nonetheless, increased, and inflation stabilized a little. It was in this situation that Margaret Thatcher began her tenure as Prime Minister in 1979. The economy again proved volatile—inflation rising and then the cycle completing itself with a decrease in that same inflation and a drastic increase in unemployment by 1982. Because unemployment increases the available supply of labour, unions are particularly vulnerable during these periods. The Thatcher government took aim—partially ideological, partially practical—at what it saw as a bloated union culture that was a cumbersome obstacle to economic efficiency. Her labour legislation compromised the position of organized labour at a time when it was weak both in bargaining power and public sympathy. Union membership halved. In 1984 Thatcher waged a protracted war with the miners' union led by Arthur Scargill. Massive numbers of police were pitted against striking miners, and after a year of bitter confrontation and hardship the miners lost out to the government.

In an effort to distance itself from the image of inefficient and obsolete socialism with which Margaret Thatcher had so skillfully branded it, the Labour party looked to Tony Blair and "New" Labour. Blair's centre-left economic policies sought to maintain a commitment to issues of equality and social justice with a modern economic philosophy that looked to new knowledge industries and a global economy. The end of the century saw the British economy flourish and with it Blair's popularity.

Activity:
Economic and social control

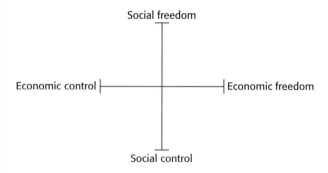

Clement Atlee's Labour Government, 1945–1951

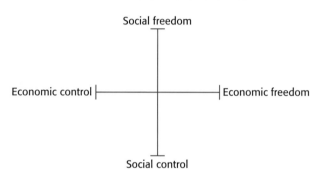

Margaret Thatcher's Conservative Government, 1979–90

Questions

1 **a** List the social and economic policies of Clement Atlee's Labour Government 1945–1951.

   b List the social and economic policies of Margaret Thatcher's Conservative Government 1979–90.

2 Determine to what degree their legislation and policies enhanced economic and social control or freedom. Use your conclusions to plot each government in one of the quadrants in the diagrams.

3 Make three generalizations about each government regarding the above information. Support these generalizations with evidence of their policies and/or outcomes.

Extended discussion point:

1 What evidence contradicts the characterization of the 1950s and 1960s as a period of prosperity and the 1970s as one of economic instability?

2 Much has been made of Margaret Thatcher's radical changes to the British society that had emerged out of the Second World War. To what extent did her policies maintain continuity?

3 How does the British economy of the late 1990s compare to the economy of the 1980s?

4 Tony Blair's approach to governing had been called the "Third Way"—an approach to governing that departs from older labels such as left-wing and right-wing. To what degree was Blair successful in this?

Why is public opinion so important to labour unions during strikes?

Case study: Iran, 1953–2000

From 1953 to 1979, the political system in Iran was shaped by the autocratic monarchy of Mohammad Reza Shah. The revolution of 1979 toppled his regime, after which the political forces around Ayatollah Khomeini took power, following a fierce and violent competition with secular nationalists and leftists. The Islamic Republic was a complex combination of elected and unelected institutions, combining both the features of a democracy and a dictatorship.

Economic development

An Englishman who visited Iran in the early twentieth century wrote: "There are no cities in Persia [Iran], and likewise no slums; no steam driven industries, and therefore none of the mechanical tyranny that deadens the brain, starves the heart, wearies bodies and mind with its monotony. There are no gas and no electricity, but is not the glow of oil-lamps pleasanter?" By the end of the century, he would have barely recognized the country that he had described somewhat nostalgically. The population of Iran had risen from an estimated nine million in 1900 to nearly 70 million in 2005. In the same period, the share of agriculture in the **GDP** dropped from 65 to 15 per cent, while the industrial output and the oil export grew rapidly. Oil-lamps became rare in even the most remote parts of the country. While in 1977 merely 16 per cent of the rural population had electricity, in 2004 that per centage had increased to 98 per cent. Considerable scientific and technological advances were made as well. Iran has become a regional leader in nanotechnology and one of the eleven countries that have launched their own satellite into orbit.

As these figures illustrate, the economy transformed dramatically in the 20th century, but not in a strictly linear fashion. The per capita income roughly doubled in the first half of the century and more than tripled in the second half. There were big setbacks and leaps forward; some sectors and regions modernized while others remained traditional. As we will see below, economic developments went through three distinctive phases: the autocratic modernization (1953–78), revolution and war (1979–88) and reconstruction and reform (1989–2006).

Autocratic modernization, 1953–78

There is a good reason to start our account in 1953. From that year onwards, oil income became the predominant source of financing industrialization, which had already started in the 1920s. Oil was discovered in commercial quantities in 1908 and a year later the Anglo-Persian Oil Company was established. From this moment to the early 1950s, around 800 million pounds of the total oil income ended up in Britain, while the Iranians received merely 105 million pounds. No wonder Winston Churchill, the British Prime Minister

TOK Link
Context and Perspective

The events, trends and developments discussed here are for the most part recent history with many of the participants still alive. How might this affect the objectivity of historians studying this period?

Discussion

1 Is the knowledge acquired through this study any more or less reliable than that acquired about a more distant period in history?

2 How does this affect the ways of knowing used in studying recent history in comparison to the study of earlier periods in history?

Gross Domestic Product (GDP)
The value of all final goods and services made within the borders of a country in a year.

403

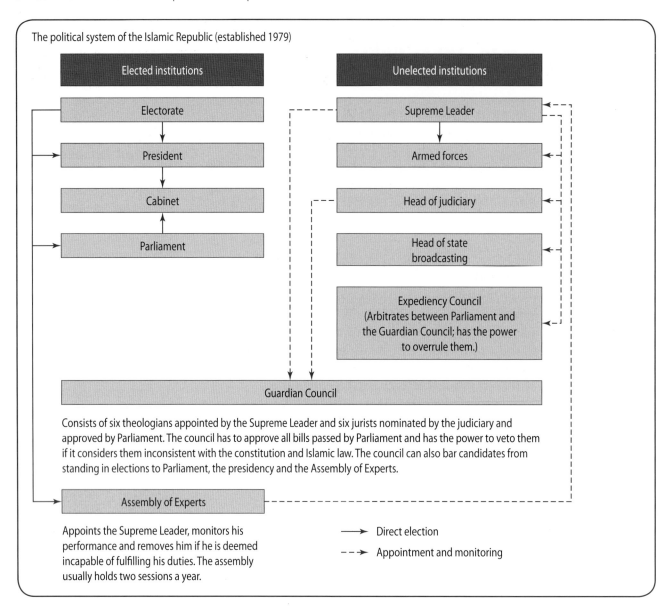

The political system of the Islamic Republic (established 1979)

Elected institutions	Unelected institutions

Electorate → President → Cabinet ← Parliament

Supreme Leader → Armed forces, Head of judiciary, Head of state broadcasting

Expediency Council
(Arbitrates between Parliament and the Guardian Council; has the power to overrule them.)

Guardian Council

Consists of six theologians appointed by the Supreme Leader and six jurists nominated by the judiciary and approved by Parliament. The council has to approve all bills passed by Parliament and has the power to veto them if it considers them inconsistent with the constitution and Islamic law. The council can also bar candidates from standing in elections to Parliament, the presidency and the Assembly of Experts.

Assembly of Experts

Appoints the Supreme Leader, monitors his performance and removes him if he is deemed incapable of fulfilling his duties. The assembly usually holds two sessions a year.

→ Direct election
--→ Appointment and monitoring

(1940–45 and 1951–5), called Iranian oil "a prize from fairyland beyond our wildest dreams". Many Iranians, however, regarded this as an unfair practice that represented the Imperialist domination of their country by United Kingdom from the 19th century. This sentiment was voiced by a nationalist lawyer, Mohammad Mossadegh, who was elected Prime Minister in 1951. When his government moved to nationalize the Iranian oil industry, the British and American secret services organized a coup against him. In this, they were assisted by the monarch, Mohammad Reza Shah, who resented Mossadegh's popularity and the growing power of his government and the Parliament. In turn, the US assisted the Shah financially and militarily to establish and consolidate an autocratic regime.

Ironically, the Shah benefited from the pressure that the nationalist movement had exerted on the foreign companies, which conceded to Iran a 50:50 profit-sharing agreement. He also benefited from foreign investment and cheap loans by aligning with the West. The Shah used a large part of this new-found income to rapidly industrialize the country from above. This meant that the state made investments in new industries, infrastructure and banks that lent money to private clients. In other words, oil became the fuel and the state the engine of industrialization. This pattern of economic development was very similar to that followed by other developing countries.

Iran's oil revenues rose from $34 million in 1954–5 to $20 billion in 1975–6. Oil earned Iran more than $55 billion in the course of this period. The Shah spent a large part of it to build the three pillars that held up his authoritarian state: the military, the bureaucracy and the royal court. Between 1954 and 1977, the military budget grew from $60 million to $5.5 billion. Employment in the military expanded from 127,000 to 410,000. The Shah became known for his weapon-purchasing frenzy. By 1975 he had the largest navy in the Persian Gulf, the largest air force in Western Asia, and the fifth largest army in the whole world. His arsenal included more than 1,000 modern tanks, 400 helicopters, 173 F4 fighter planes, 141 F5s and ten F14s. With the help of the American FBI and the Israeli Mossad the Shah established a new intelligence agency, the SAVAK, which became renowned for its cruel methods of intimidation and repression of dissidents.

The Shah also expanded the bureaucracy. By 1975, the state employed more than 304,000 civil servants and some one million workers in state-owned companies. This allowed the state to direct the economy and centralize the administration of the country. Some of the oil income flowed to the court and the close allies of the Shah. The possessions of the Shah and his 64 family members were managed by the Pahlavi Foundation, which at its height had assets worth $3 billion. In 1979, the *New York Times* reported that: "Behind the facade of charitable activities the foundation is apparently used in three ways: as a source of funds for the royal family, as a means of exerting control over the economy, and as a conduit for rewards to supporters of the regime."

Of course, the Shah did not spend all the oil income on the military, the bureaucracy and patronage. A large part was used to industrialize the economy. This was initiated in 1956 with an ambitious Seven Year Plan that gathered pace after 1963 when the Shah launched the White Revolution, supported by the Kennedy administration in the United States that was worried about the growth of communist and nationalist movements in the "Third World". The cornerstone of this reform program was the redistribution of agricultural land away from large landowners. The White Revolution had two main goals. These were the prevention of a revolt by poor peasants and the creation of the preconditions for capitalist development. In the context of the Cold War and the aftermath of the Cuban Revolution (1959), the USA and the Shah regarded land reform as a bulwark against the "communist menace".

As we will see later, the White Revolution had a contrary impact as it eventually destabilized the regime of the Shah. Economic growth between 1963 and 1977 was, however, impressive. The GDP per capita grew at unprecedented rates that averaged eight per cent a year. This made Iran one of the fastest-growing developing countries. The government's main economic strategy was based on import-substitution industrialization. It protected the domestic market from foreign competitors by imposing restrictions and tariffs on imported goods. At the same time it invested in industries that provided cheap loans and gave a favourable treatment to foreign capital. This policy favoured the large enterprises that used modern technologies and the rich Iranians and foreigners who owned them. This was justified by a "trickle down" economic theory according to which economic growth will eventually lead to a more even income distribution. In reality the gap between rich and poor continued growing during the economic expansion. As oil income increased, so did corruption in the court, the royal family and the elite.

Oil prices increased fourfold during the Arab–Israeli War in 1973, boosting the Shah's ambitions. He announced that Iran would become one of the world's top five powers in the 20th century. At this point the Shah pumped a significant part of the oil income into the economy, without realizing that it would lead to inflation, shortages and overheating of the economy. The situation was made worse by the increase in military expenditure. Many technically educated Iranians, for instance, were put to work in the armed forces and in building projects for military bases, equipments and infrastructure. At times there were shortages of cement and other building materials in the country because of heavy military demand. This resulted in housing shortages and a rise in home prices, aggravated by the willingness of American personnel, of which there were some tens of thousands, to pay high rents.

While the rising oil prices in the early 1970s raised expectations among ordinary Iranians, but for a tiny rich elite they remained unfulfilled. Rising inflation seriously harmed the living standards of the majority of the working and middle classes. The cost of living rose by 90 per cent between 1970 and 1976. The increase of the price of essential goods was even more dramatic. A report published by the *Economist* in 1976 estimated that rents in Tehran rose 300 per cent in five years, and that by 1975 a middle-class family could be spending as much as 50 per cent of its annual income on housing. Confronted with this problem, the Shah appointed a new prime minister in mid 1977 to fight the inflation. These draconian measures had two very negative consequences.

The government placed the blame of inflation squarely on the shoulders of the traditional business community, the *bazaaris* (merchants, shopkeepers and artisans), by starting an "anti-profiteering campaign" against them. The government imposed strict price controls and sent "inspectorate teams" to the bazaars to wage a "merciless crusade against profiteers, cheaters, hoarders, and unscrupulous capitalists". The bazaaris turned to their traditional allies, the Shi'a clergy, who already resented the Shah for his "Westernization" of Iran. This added to the public discontent around political repression and social inequality that fuelled the revolutionary movement which emerged from early 1977 and toppled the Shah in February 1979.

The second consequence of the government's anti-inflation measures was an economic recession. This was caused when the government cut back its investments, stopped wage increases and cancelled the bonuses to state employees. As a result, real wages started to fall and unemployment increased after 400,000 people lost their jobs. Adding insult to injury, the Shah warned workers saying: "Those who do not work, we shall take them by the tail and throw them out like mice. He who does not do his job properly is betraying not only his own conscience but also his patriotic duty ... I remember years ago a mason ... was prepared to work a whole day for a mere meal and he never had enough work. But today, in this period of transition, we are in need of more workers and have to beg them to work."

The Shah ended the interview by saying that people had to work harder, make more sacrifices and tighten their belts. The recession and the Shah's offensive policy towards labour sparked off a series of industrial strikes as the revolutionary movement was getting momentum in 1978. These strike actions, especially in the strategic oil sector, fatally injured the regime of the Shah, who fled the country on 16 January 1979. Ayatollah Khomeini, who had played a leading role in the opposition against the Shah, returned from exile in France and established the Islamic Republic of Iran.

Revolution and war, 1979–88

Following the revolution of 1979, the Iranian economy entered a period of rapid decline. At its trough in 1988, real GDP per capita had dropped to 54 per cent of its peak in 1976. This was the result of three factors: political instability, the war with Iraq and economic mismanagement. The revolution and its chaotic aftermath led to a huge capital flight when many business people, especially those connected to the old regime fled the country. They were followed by thousands of technicians and professionals, who were desperately needed to rebuild the economy. When Saddam Hussein invaded Iran in September 1980, matters got worse. Iran's oil installations, cities and infrastructure were targeted by the Iraqi military. The eight-year war with Iraq absorbed the economic resources that the country badly needed at a time when the population was growing very fast.

The new political elite had no clear economic policy at the beginning. Some of them, like the bazaar merchants and the traditional clergy, preferred a *laissez-faire* market economy. In politics, they were represented by the conservatives or the right faction. Others, many of them with a middle class background, wanted a strong state that would intervene in the economy to promote industrialization and serve the needs of the poor at the same time. They were represented by the radicals or the left.

The need to centralize the economy to win the war and mitigate the impact of the economic crisis on the

An Iraqi soldier watches as the Iranian Abadan refinery, located near the Iraqi border, burns in September 1980. The Abadan oil refinery was under constant fire from the Iraqi air force during the Iran–Iraq conflict.

population tilted the political balance towards the left faction in the 1980s. They used their control of the Parliament and government and the support of the Supreme Leader Khomeini, to create a statist economy. The basis for this was laid in the early days of the revolution, when the assets of Iran's 51 wealthiest families were confiscated. Hundreds of firms were nationalized in the following years. Parallel to an expanding state sector, a para-state sector was created with the establishments of *bonyads*, religious foundations. They received some of the confiscated lands, buildings and firms of the old elite. These foundations, which fall under the jurisdiction of the Supreme Leader, have charitable and economic functions. They combine the provision of social assistance to the poor with financial and productive activities. For instance, the Foundation of the Oppressed and Disabled was established in March 1979 and absorbed the possessions of the Pahlavi Foundation. It was estimated that by the mid 1990s it had at least 800 companies and employed 700,000 workers. Its companies produced 20 per cent of Iranian textile, 40 per cent of soft drinks and two thirds of the glass products. It can be rightly called a capitalist monopoly. The state sector and these *bonyads* control nearly 80 per cent of the economy.

In one important aspect, the economic policies of the 1980s represented a continuation of those under the Shah— Import Substitution Industrialization. The goal of this strategy was what Khomeini called *khodkafa'i* (self-sufficiency). The government tried to restrict the import of consumer goods by controlling foreign trade and stimulating the national industries. This policy was partly successful as imports declined and the non-oil exports increased from $400 million in 1985 to $1,300 million in 1990. Export was not confined to Iran's traditional products like pistachios and carpets, but also included industrial products. However, as the Iranian manufacturing sector grew, the import of intermediate and capital products that were necessary inputs also increased. Thus, while the Iranian economy had become more isolated from the world market than before the revolution, its dependence on it had not really decreased. This is even more obvious if we consider the importance of oil export for Iran's economy. New technologies were needed to increase the productivity of Iran's industry and oil sector. Because technological innovations take place on an international scale, often in the developed countries, Iran's relative isolation became a break on further economic development.

When oil prices nose-dived in 1986 and the war with Iraq was still continuing economic problems reached a boiling point. Those that blamed the state control over the economy became more vocal, pleading for economic liberalization. Although small steps were taken in this direction, like the opening of the Tehran Stock Exchange in 1988, real changes only emerged after 1989.

Reconstruction and reform
With the end of the war in August 1988 and the death of Ayatollah Khomeini in June 1989, the Islamic Republic of Iran ushered in a new period of economic development. The driving force behind this

process was a new political faction, known as "the modern right" or "the pragmatists", led by President Ali Akbar Hashemi Rafsanjani, who was in power 1989–97. He replaced the principle of *khodkafa'i* with *towse'eh* (development) and *islahat* (reform) and oriented the economy towards the free market. The reception of the World Bank/International Monetary Fund mission to Iran in June 1990 symbolized this turn. Rafsanjani's reforms very much followed these institutions' recipe for economic "restructuring": foreign trade liberalization; decontrolling prices and eliminating subsidies; privatization; deregulation; foreign borrowing; encouragement of foreign investment; establishment of free trade zones; stimulation of the Tehran stock exchange; and the reorganization of the banking and financial services.

At first, the economic restructuring was helped by the rising oil revenues which made possible bigger investments. The drop in the price of oil in 1993 halted this process. Moreover, deregulated markets created their own problems. Iran's foreign debt increased eight fold between 1990 and 1995, and inflation reached almost 50 per cent. Privatization and liberalization increased the gap between the rich and poor, adding to the growing discontent among the population. The government reacted by strengthening its grip on the economy.

Despite Rafsanjani's pro-market reforms, the role of the state in the economy remained dominant. The management of just 48 companies was transferred to shareholders. The whole process of privatization was accompanied by corruption and fraud as the enterprises were cheaply sold to people with government connections. Reminiscent of what has happened in other developing countries, privatization became what Nobel Prize-winning economist Joseph Stiglitz has called "briberization". For instance, Rafsanjani's administration created several hundred semi-public enterprises. "The procurement department of a given ministry would function as a company, selling supplies acquired with the ministry's funds to the ministry, for profit. The profits were then distributed among shareholders, who were mostly the same ministry's personnel". As we have already seen, many *bonyads* had developed economic activities, the profit from which partly disappeared in the pockets of the managers and their relatives. The brother of the director of the Foundation of the Oppressed and the Disabled was found guilty in 1995 of embezzling $450 million.

In 1997 Mohammad Khatami was elected President, promising to introduce political reforms that would give more freedom and rights to the population. He continued Rafsanjani's policy of economic liberalization by reducing the system of subsidies and social protection, and increasing the rate of privatization. According to the data provided by the Iranian Privatization Organization, privatization amounted to over $16 billion between 1991 and 2007. Almost 26 per cent of this amount was realized under Rafsanjani, 43 per cent under the presidency of Khatami's and 31 per cent during Ahmadinejad's presidency in 2005–06.

Like his predecessor, Khatami was confronted with the close connection between oil revenues and economic growth. The brief economic recovery of 1996 and 1997 was thwarted by the decline of oil revenues in 1998. Serious economic growth resumed after oil prices started to rise from 1999. In order to reduce the effect of the fluctuation in oil prices, Khatami created the Oil Stabilization Fund. In times of high oil prices the government would save money, which it could then withdraw from in less fortunate times.

To understand why this was a good idea, one has to consider the huge fluctuations in the Iranian economy. After the war, economic growth started with a high of 12 per cent in 1991, falling to zero in 1994, and again rising to over 7 per cent in 2002. The economic growth during these years averaged 3.4 per cent. Taking into account the increase of the population, the per capita growth rate averaged two per cent, which was not enough to provide jobs for the growing population and to eradicate poverty and inequality. As a result, the dismal state of the economy is an important source of discontent among the population of a country which has ten per cent of the world's oil and 14 per cent of its gas reserves.

Finally, when looking to Iran's economic performance, it is important to take into account the role of economic sanctions as well. The first sanctions by the United States against Iran were ordered in April 1980, following the occupation of the American embassy in Tehran by a group of militant Islamic students. They held 53 American embassy personnel hostage for 444 days from 4 November 1979 in protest against American attempts to undermine the revolution. The students also demanded that the US should send the Shah back to Iran and apologize for its meddling in the internal affairs of Iran and for the overthrow of Prime Minister Mossadegh in 1953. This episode created a crisis in the diplomatic relationship between Iran and the United States.

The Iran Khodro auto plant is the largest car producer in the Middle East. It made "Paykan", based on the British 1975 Hillman until the 1990s. Its recent cars are Samand, based on Peugeot 405, and Peugeot 206.

Activity:
The rentier state

Scholars often describe the oil-producing countries of the Middle East as "rentier states". This theory was first developed and popularized by the Iranian economist Hussein Mahdavy in relation to the developments in Iran in 1950–70.

Research the theory of the "rentier state" online and apply it to the case of Iran.

Discussion point:

Compare and contrast the economic policies before and after the 1979 revolution.

1 During the 1980s, a large part of economic transactions shifted to the "black market".

2 Discuss which factors could have accounted for the growth of the "black market" after the revolution.

3 Discuss some of the advantages and disadvantages of an oil-dependent economy like Iran.

Social transformations

The economic developments in the second half of the twentieth century, together with political events like the 1979 revolution caused profound social transformation in Iran.

Class structure is one of the most important factors that shape the relations among the members of any society. It is, however, as in the case study of the United Kingdom, also very difficult to define in the modern era and in application to the diverse social structures of nation states. Here, we will use the following definitions of the most important classes in Iran:

- *Capitalists* are the owners of the physical and financial means of economic activity and employ workers.
- *Petit bourgeoisie* (the lower-middle class) are self-employed persons who do not hire any paid workers but may rely on the work of unpaid family members.
- *The middle class* are employees in administrative-managerial and professional-technical positions.
- *The working class* are those workers who do not own the means of production and do not benefit from the authority and autonomy of those in the "middle class".
- **Political functionaries** are those employed in the political apparatus of the state. They are in an ambiguous class position, neither being included in the middle class nor in the working class.

> **Political functionaries** According to the social scientists Farhad Nomani and Sohrab Behdad political functionaries form a distinct social group in Iran that is neither middle class nor working class, but defined by their identity as state employees. This large group of people are employed in the political functions of the state, such as the administration of ministries, municipalities, the judiciary or the army.

Activity:

Class definitions

When social researchers observe and collect information about any topic X in the social world, they are confronted with two main questions:

1 What is meant by X?

2 How to measure X?

"Conceptualization" refers to the first question (i.e. specifying what is meant by a term). "Operationalization" addresses the second question (i.e. translating the concept into specific measures that enable us to collect data about it). The many controversies in the study of social classes stem from different conceptual and operational definitions of class.

The definition of class in this chapter is borrowed from a study by Farhad Nomani and Sohrab Behdad into the class structure in Iran in their book *Class and Labor in Iran: Did the Revolution Matter?* (2006).

Nomani and Behdad have distinguished four classes—capitalists, the middle class, the *petit-bourgeoisie* and workers. They define class relations through involvement in the economic activities of production and distribution. These relations have three dimensions:

1 Means of economic activity (owner or employee);

2 Authority in the organizational hierarchy (being able to hire employees or not);

3 Scarce skills (possessing expertise or lacking skills).

Different combinations of these dimensions make it possible to determine class categories in society. In order to operationalize social class in Iran, Nomani and Behdad use the employment data in the censuses that the Iranian government conducts every ten years. People are thus categorized in one of the social classes according to their employment status.

Complete the table below

In the left column are the four classes. The top row gives you the three dimensions of involvement in economic activities, production and distribution. According to Nomani and Behdad:

- the class position of capitalist, *petit-bourgeois* and worker is defined by two dimensions (the third dimension is not a necessary indicator). One of these is already indicated in the table by the sign +. Add another + in the rows for "capitalist", "*petit-bourgeoisie*" and "working class" under one of the relations which you think is necessary to make a person part of this class.

- the "middle class" is defined by only one dimension, the others can vary. Put an + under the dimension that best defines this class.

Relation to	the means of economic activity		authority in organizations		scarce skills	
Classes	Owner	Not owner (employee)	Hires labour	Does not hire labour	Possesses expertise	Semi-skilled or unskilled
Capitalists			+			
Middle class						
Petit-bourgeoisie	+					
Working class				+		

Activity:

Case studies

Following are personal examples of employment under Iran's current social structure. Can you match them to one of the four classes, defined by Nomani and Behdad?

1 Mr Ghassemi has a small shop in the bazaar of Isfahan where he sells carpets. One of his sons takes care of the transport of the carpets, while the other sells them in the shop. Their father manages the finances. His wife repairs carpets in their house.

2 Mrs Kianpour works as a taxi-driver for one of Tehran's private companies that were initiated to transport female passengers.

3 Mr Ardalan is employed in a small shop where he repairs electronics, but he does not earn enough to make ends meet. Some years ago he bought an ice-cream van and in the evenings and Fridays (Iranian weekend) he sells ice-cream in a park in the old city of Shiraz.

4 Ms Ehteshami works as a freelance journalist, writing on youth culture and its growing underground music scene.

? What makes the individual case studies ambiguous? Discuss with your group any difficulties you have in placing these case studies of employment within the categories given.

Changes to the class structure in Iran

For centuries the social structure of Iranian society was dominated by nomadic tribes. The modernization policies of Reza Shah (1921–41) weakened the position of tribal leaders by bringing them under the control of the central government. Modernization also created new social classes through the expansion of the industry and the education system. This process accelerated under Mohammad Reza Shah. The traditional dominant classes were further weakened as his land reform of the White Revolution marginalized the big landowners. The land reform stratified the countryside into some 1,300 commercial enterprises each owning 200 hectares; some 640,000 landlords owning between ten and 200 hectares; 1,200,000 families owning less than ten hectares; and some 700,000 labourers. Because in many regions ten hectares of land was not enough to make a living, many smallholders had to sell their land or join co-operatives which were controlled by the government and functioned as big corporations. The land reform created on the one hand big capitalist agricultural producers and an army of small landowners and landless labourers. Many of them left the countryside to find a job in the cities.

The land reform in the countryside and rapid industrialization in the urban areas created a complex class structure. At the apex was an upper class of families linked to the royal court. This included a capitalist class which owned more than 85 per cent of the large firms. In the middle there were two classes: the traditional *petit bourgeoisie* (the propertied middle class) and the modern middle class. The first group was composed of merchants, shopkeepers and workshop owners of the bazaar. Despite economic modernization, the bazaar continued to control half of the handicraft production and two-thirds of the retail trade in the 1970s. Through kinship and the historic links between the bazaar and the mosque the clergy was also part of the traditional *petit bourgeoisie*. The salaried, modern middle class was composed of white-collar employees and educated professionals like engineers, lawyers, doctors and journalists. It included 304,000 civil servants in the ministries; some 200,000 teachers and school administrators; and more than 60,000 managers and professionals.

The urban working class numbered 1,300,000 people, including 880,000 people employed in modern industries; more than 30,000 people working in the oil industry; 50,000 miners; 150,000 dock workers, railwaymen, truck drivers, and other transport workers; and 600,000 workers in small plants. These figures include the large number of shanty-town poor formed of migrants from rural villages. Many of them tried to make a living as construction workers or peddlers, but many were unemployed. The rural population consisted of three strata: prosperous farmers, smallholders and village labourers.

These social changes meant that the traditional social basis of the monarchy, the landlords class, was weakened, while the social classes that opposed the monarchy, the urban middle and working classes, increased in number. The land reform created an army of landless peasants that migrated to the cities, creating a pool of discontent. The *petit bourgeoisie* that suffered from modernization had the money to finance the opposition against the Shah. A multi-class coalition was born and subsequently revolted in 1978–79 against the monarchy.

The 1979 revolution had a significant impact on the class structure. The existing upper class almost entirely disappeared, as many of its members fled the country. The economic meltdown of the 1980s, followed by a relative recovery in the 1990s, and the social policies of the Islamic Republic re-shaped the class structure in important ways.

The capitalist class

At the onset of the 1979 revolution, the capitalist class in Iran was small and fragmented. In 1976, there were 182,000 capitalists, mostly owning small-to-medium-sized enterprises. Only a small number of very large enterprises were owned by a group of very successful capitalists who were directly or indirectly connected to the state or multinational corporations. The largest enterprises were owned by the state. This situation was exacerbated in the 1980s, due to two factors.

The **petit bourgeoisie** was defined by Karl Marx as a class situated between capitalists and workers. The group he had in mind, especially in France of the early 19th century, consisted primarily of small shopkeepers, self-employed artisans and landowning peasants. Professionals were also included.

With the increase of professionals in modern capitalism some people started to use the terms new or upper middle class to distinguish them from the *petit bourgeoisie*, which became known as the traditional or lower middle class. In countries like Iran, where the economy is characterized by a big informal sector and small-scale production, the *petit bourgeoisie* makes up a large part of the population.

Millionaire mullahs

The term "millionaire mullahs" was coined by the Russian investigative journalist Paul Klebnikov, who published his research about the Rafsanjanis and other members of the clerical and political elite in *Forbes Magazine* (July 2003).

The 1979 revolution transformed the Rafsanjani clan into commercial pashas. One brother headed the country's largest copper mine; another took control of the state-owned TV network; a brother in law became governor of Kerman province, while a cousin runs an outfit that dominates Iran's $400 million pistachio export business; a nephew and one of Rafsanjani's sons took key positions in the ministry of oil; another son heads the Tehran Metro construction project (an estimated $700 million spent so far). Today, operating through various foundations and front companies, the family is also believed to control one of Iran's biggest oil engineering companies, a plant assembling Daewoo automobiles, and Iran's best private airline … Rafsanjani's youngest son, Yaser, owns a 30-acre horse farm in the super-fashionable Lavasan neighbourhood of north Tehran, where land goes for over $4 million an acre.

Source: http://www.forbes.com/forbes/2003/0721/056.html

On the one hand, the number of agricultural capitalists increased under the Islamic Republic through the confiscation and redistribution of land. The number of capitalists engaged in small production increased as the economic crisis deepened. On the other hand, the large enterprises came into the hands of the state and the para-state foundations, the *bonyads*. These huge monopolies formed an obstacle for the growth of the private capitalist class. From the 1990s onwards, however, this class started to recover from the blows of the revolution and increased to more than half a million members in 1996. Overall, however, the vast majority of capitalists owned relatively small enterprises that employed less than ten workers. One significant development has been the emergence of the "millionaire mullahs", members of the political elite who have benefited from their privileges and have joined the ranks of the capitalists.

Petit bourgeoisie

The *petit bourgeoisie* grew from 32 per cent in 1976 to 40 per cent in 1986, becoming the biggest single class in Iran. This reflected the growth of small-commodity production. Land redistribution to peasants contributed significantly to this process. A new group of small-landholders working as self-employed workers (including family members) came into being. But the ranks of the *petit bourgeoisie* also swelled because those workers who could not find jobs tried to survive by selling merchandise on the streets, engaging in small-scale production or working as taxi drivers. Many of them combined this with temporary jobs in small manufacturing establishments or in the construction industry. With the start of economic liberalization in the 1990s, this sector shrank.

Traditionally, a large part of the urban *petit bourgeoisie* (both handicraft producers and retailers) was concentrated in the bazaar. Through their ties with the clerical establishment, some benefited from the 1979 revolution. They acquired high positions in the bureaucracy, or became managers of state-owned enterprises and the *bonyads*. Life was difficult for many members of the *petit bourgeoisie* as economic reforms diminished the black market and stimulated the growth of big capitalist firms and shopping malls—their main competitors.

Esfahan Bazaar, photographed in 2000.

The middle class

After the revolution, career opportunities for the middle class increased as the bureaucracy and employment in state-owned enterprises expanded. Those with Islamic credentials or links to the political elite climbed the social ladder and gained managerial and administrative positions. The share of the middle class in the workforce increased from

5.4 per cent in 1976 to 10.2 per cent in 1996. The vast majority of them are employed in the state sector. The growth of the middle class was caused by two factors. First, as the economy recovered in the 1990s it became more complex. This increased the managerial and administrative functions. Second, with the expansion of healthcare and education, the number of paramedical workers and teachers who are included in the middle class increased. As such, the middle class represents the fastest growing class in modern-day Iran.

The working class

In 1976 the working class in Iran numbered 3.5 million, or 40.2 per cent of the workforce. About 84 per cent of them were employed in the private sector, the other 16 per cent in the public sector. The largest part of the working class was active in production, construction being the largest single sector. While a large part of the working class was unskilled and widely dispersed in small capitalist enterprises, a significant proportion of the working class were skilled and concentrated in particular in the state sector.

Class structure of the workforce in Iran: 1976, 1986, 1996						
	1976		**1986**		**1996**	
	Total 1,000	%	Total 1,000	%	Total 1,000	%
Capitalists	182	2.1	341	3.1	528	3.6
Petit bourgeoisie (including family workers)	3,831	43.5	4,874	44.3	5,996	41.2
Middle class	477	12.8	774	7.0	1,493	10.2
Working class	3,535	40,2	2,702	24.6	4,474	30.7
Political functionaries	731	8.3	1,851	16.8	1,560	10.7
Unspecified	41	0.5	458	4.2	463	3.2
Total	8,799	10.0	11,000	100	14,573	100

Source: Nomani, Farhad & Behdad, Sohrab. 2006. *Class and Labor in Iran. Did the Revolution Matter?* Syracuse. USA. Syracuse University Press. p. 89

The economic crisis of the 1980s led to a process of deproletarianization. In absolute terms, the working class declined from three and half million in 1976 to two and half in 1986. In relative terms it declined from 40.2 to 24.6 per cent in the same period. Many workers joined the ranks of the *petit bourgeoisie*, becoming active in the informal economy, or combining their job with activity in this sector to make ends meet. The end of the war, economic liberalization and rising incomes from oil led to economic recovery in the 1990s. The share of the working class in the work-force increased from 24.6 per cent in 1986 to 1.1 per cent in 1996. Social scientists call this process proletarianization. Almost one third of the working class was engaged in the state sector in contrast to the 16 per cent in 1986.

Discussion point: Middle or working class?

At a protest of school teachers in Tehran in early 2009, one of them told the reporters: "Our pay is ridiculously low. A school teacher with a masters degree takes home less than $300 a month. In a city like Tehran, any family of four with an income less than $500 a month is living below the poverty line".

Do you think school teachers should be counted as part of the middle or the working class? Explain your criteria?

Gender

Relations among people are not only defined by class but also by gender. In this section we will examine how the socio-economic, cultural and political position of women changed in the second half of the twentieth century in Iran. The first steps towards the emancipation of Iranian women were taken in the early 20th century, when a small group of women entered the political scene to demand equal rights. In the following the decades, a growing women's movement, the expansion of education and women's entrance into factory work, teaching and nursing helped relax traditional restrictions on women's lives. During his reign Reza Shah (1921–41) took some measures to protect women in their family relations. However, his 1936 order to women to unveil and dress in Western-style clothing was problematic. Some women saw this as going out naked and refused to leave their homes, as the police sometimes tore chadors from women on streets. While this did not affect women from upper classes, it contributed to the marginalization of the majority of women. Reza Barahani, the Iranian novelist, recalled the crisis in his family when unveiling became a law:

> Since there were no showers in Iranian homes, women had to go to a public bath. The husband would put his wife in a large sack and carry her like a bale of cotton to the bath. I remember from my childhood, when my father would carry his mother in the sack, empty his load in the bath, and then come back for his wife. He once told me that Reza Shah's policeman had asked him what it was that he was carrying. He had improvised an answer: pistachio nuts. The policeman said, "let me have some," and started tickling Granny. First she laughed, and then she wiggled her way out of the sack and took to her heels. My father was arrested.

> **Source:** Barahani, R. 1977. *The Crowned Cannibals: Writings on Repression in Iran*. New York, USA. Vintage. p. 54.

Women's suffrage was introduced in 1963 as part of the White Revolution by Mohammad Reza Shah. Encouraged by the pressure from women's groups, the Shah introduces legal reforms in the Family Protection Law. This was passed in 1967 and amended in 1975. According to the new law, men could no longer unilaterally divorce their wives; they had to take their case to the court. Guardianship of children, which in Islamic law goes to the husband, was to be awarded by the judge. No man could marry an additional wife without the permission of the previous wife. Although the law had some important shortcomings and was far from introducing equality between men and women, it represented a step forwards. However, the Family Protection Law and other measures became associated with the increasingly unpopular dictatorship of the Shah and his pro-Western attitude.

This situation provided a fertile ground for the emergence of a counter-movement that based itself on a conservative interpretation of Islam and claimed that the unequal status and rights of women originated from nature and religion. After this movement managed to take power in 1979 under the leadership of Ayatollah Khomeini, it started to roll back the rights and social status that women had won during the revolution. Women had participated in their thousands in the demonstrations, strikes and political debates, but their newly won freedoms were gradually taken away. In 1980 Ayatollah Khomeini abolished the Family Protection Law and made the wearing of the veil obligatory. Women's rights in divorce and child custody were once again reduced. Gender segregation was introduced in schools, universities and public transport. Women were encouraged to stay home and devote themselves to motherhood, and they were excluded from some occupations.

The changes to the status of women after the revolution were, however, contradictory. The new state closed some doors but opened others. Many women from the lower class and religious families had not benefited from the changes under the Shah and some of them resented the forced changes of his regime. The changes under the Islamic Republic created a climate in which women could participate in social life more actively than before, although they soon confronted serious obstacles. Moreover, as the war with Iraq continued in the 1980s and engaged a large part of the male population, the government started to involve more women in public life and the labour market. The expansion of the education and health system and the introduction of family planning programmes enhanced the position of women. Between 1991 and 2007, the share of female students enrolled in public universities rose from 28 to 58 per cent. The number of women in the formal labour force increased as well, reaching its pre-1979 level of 13 per cent by the mid-1990s and has continued to rise. Political developments had an impact as well. The strict dress restrictions were also loosened by the turn of the century, but under President Mahmoud Ahmadinejad restrictions have once again been enforced.

Women have reacted in different ways to their exclusion and unequal status, showing great perseverance in remaining in the public sphere and participating in social, economic, political and cultural activities. As writers, novelists, journalists and film directors women have unveiled the mechanisms of gender discrimination. They have highlighted the legal and social problems of women and portrayed their courageous activities. Some women, secular and religious, created a movement for equal rights. They worked together in publishing women's magazines like *Zanan* (Women) to address women's issues, crossing political and ideological differences.

Under the presidency of Khatami, some women's rights activists tried to negotiate with the political and religious elite by promoting an egalitarian interpretation of Islam in place of the dominant conservative interpretations. This was mainly the strategy of "Islamic feminists", who were supported by secular feminists. Female Members of Parliament who were elected as part of the reformist faction attempted to change the discriminatory laws, but their attempts were stopped by the conservative Guardian

Shirin Ebadi (1947–)

Shirin Ebadi is from a family of academics and practicing Muslims. In March 1969, she became the first female judge in Iran. While serving as a judge, she continued her education and obtained a doctorate with honors in 1971. After 1979 the Islamic Republic dismissed her from her post with the argument that women were not fit to be judges. She started working as a lawyer in the 1990s and co-founded the Association for Support of Children's Rights in 1995 and the Human Rights Defense Centre in 2001. She won the Nobel Peace Prize in 2003 for her human rights activities.

Discussion point: Muslim women

In the early days of the revolution, Ayatollah Khomeini and his followers constructed an ideal image of Muslim womanhood on the model of the lives of Fatimah, daughter of the prophet Mohammad, and Zaynab, his granddaughter. Fatimah symbolized the perfect mother and wife in the domestic sphere, and Zaynab, who fought alongside her brothers in the battlefields but who returned in peace time to take up her responsibilities as a good wife and mother.

Why do you think the government used this image during the revolution, the war and the period of economic reconstruction?

Council. As the whole political reform project of President Khatami was derailed by conservative forces, the debate about strategy between "moderate" and "radical", "Islamic" and "secular" feminists intensified. Some argued for street demonstrations and other visible methods, while others preferred methods that would avoid repression and arrests. Despite these differences, women's rights activists have continued their campaigns. In 2006, for instance, Nobel Prize Laureate Shirin Ebadi and other activists launched the One Million Signatures Campaign to demand an end to discriminatory laws.

Welfare, poverty and social inequality

Like many developing countries, Iran has not developed a welfare state like that of most Western countries. However, it has put in place social policies to improve human welfare and, in particular, meet the needs for education, health care and to raise the standard of living for disadvantaged sectors of society. Iran entered the 20th century with a population of ten million and rather dismal social indicators: a high infant mortality; average life expectancy of less than thirty years; absence of any nationwide hygiene or health facilities; and a 95 per cent illiteracy rate. Although Reza Shah made some improvements, it was only in the second half of the century that social policies began to make a real difference.

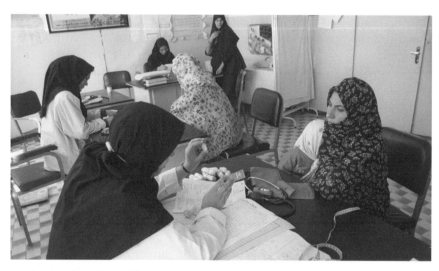

Family Planning Clinic. With family planning programs, including the distribution of condoms, the Islamic Republic brought down the birth rate from 3.2 per cent in 1986 to just 1.2 per cent in 2001.

Rising oil revenues and a constant high economic growth provided the Shah with the resources to invest in healthcare, education and other social welfare programmes. As part of the White Revolution, which was aimed at preventing a "red revolution", the Shah created a Literacy Corps to reduce illiteracy and a Health Corps to improve the health conditions in rural areas. His government created a Social Affairs category, which received 15 per cent of the total budget, equivalent to the average annual amount spent in the 1960s. This figure doesn't represent a big commitment to social welfare if we consider that the same amount was spent on defence in this period.

What was the impact of this expenditure on education and health of the population? The overall level of education as measured by literacy rates doubled from 15 per cent in the mid-1950s to thirty per cent in the mid-1960s. However, there was a huge difference between men and women and rural and urban areas. In the mid 1960s, the literacy rate for women (17 per cent) was less than half that for men (40 per cent).

Young boy in poor neighbourhood of Tehran in 1979.

In this period, 50 per cent of the urban population was literate compared with only 15 per cent of the rural population. In urban areas, 61 per cent of men and 39 per cent of women were literate, while in rural areas only 25 per cent of men and 4 per cent of women were literate. These differences would be even bigger in absolute terms because more than 60 per cent of the population was still living in rural areas in the 1960s. So, while there was some improvement in urban centres, there was much less investment in the rural areas.

The same pattern emerges when we look to the health indicators now. Life expectancy was estimated to be 49 years in 1960. By 1973, it had reached 55.1 for men and 56.3 for women. Here, too, there was a huge gap between rural and urban areas. For instance, in 1973 the population in cities lived 10 years longer on average than village populations. Despite this gap, there was an overall improvement in health conditions due to vaccination and anti-malaria campaigns in the 1960s and 1970s that brought down infant and child mortality rates.

After the quadrupling of the oil price in 1973, the absolute level of spending on education, health, and social welfare rose between fifteen and twenty times. Expenditure on Social Affairs increased in relative terms as well, reaching an average of 18 per cent per annum between 1973 and 1977, but expenditure on the military, at an annual average rate of 23 per cent, was still higher. What education and health indicators were there to reflect these increases? By 1976, literacy rates in urban areas had gone up to around 60 per cent for men and 35 per cent for women. Despite the literacy campaign that started in the early 1960s, with the promise of eradicating illiteracy in rural areas, by the mid 1970s more than half the male population and 80 per cent of rural women were still illiterate. Healthcare provisions remained very inadequate in this period. In the late 1970s, there were 1.5 hospital beds per thousand people in Iran. Only in Tehran did the ratio come down to 3:1, close to the international standard of four beds per thousand people.

Iran: Average annual urban household expenditure by deciles, 1959–74		
Deciles (poorest to riches)	**1959–60**	**1973–4**
First	1.7	1.3
Second	2.9	2.4
Third	4.0	3.4
Fourth	5.0	4.7
Fifth	6.1	5.0
Sixth	7.3	6.8
Seventh	8.9	9.3
Eighth	11.8	11.1
Ninth	16.4	17.5
Tenth	35.3	37.9

Source: Abrahamian, Ervand. 2008. *A History of Modern Iran*. Cambridge, UK. Cambridge University Press. p 41.

One important step that was taken in the 1970s in the field of social policy was further extension of the "Social Insurance Organization" and a broadening of its coverage to include retirement and unemployment benefits. Here, too, the geographical coverage was limited to urban areas, which is a common problem in most low- and middle-income countries. The reason behind this inequality was an ideology of development models that focused on industrial development and a commercialization of agriculture. The benefits were supposed to "trickle down" to the poor and rural sectors of the population.

Iran: Average annual growth rates of per capita expenditures by deciles, 1984–9						
Decile	**Iran**		**Urban**		**Rural**	
	1984–89	1990–94	1984–89	1990–94	1984–89	1990–94
1	−4.28	4.58	−9.27	4.71	−2.21	4.42
2	−4.01	4.18	−8.16	4.58	−2.16	3.71
3	−4.06	4.10	−7.94	4.56	−2.07	3.34
4	−4.52	4.18	−7.71	4.68	−2.16	3.14
5	−4.74	4.30	−7.43	4.71	−2.30	3.02
6	−5.12	4.35	−7.59	4.75	−2.42	3.02
7	−5.42	4.34	−7.79	4.68	−2.62	2.95
8	−5.96	4.35	−7.90	4.57	−2.81	2.68
9	−6.45	4.39	−7.95	4.63	−2.70	2.55
10	−7.19	4.46	−7.67	4.46	−3.47	2.64

Source: Salehi-Isfahani, D. 2006. "Revolution and redistribution in Iran: poverty and inequality 25 years later" http://www.filebox.vt.edu/users/salehi/Iran_poverty_trend.pdf. Data source: Statistical Center of Iran.

This model of economic development during the regime of the Shah inevitably widened the gap between the haves and the have-nots. As a result, in the 1970's Iran had one of the most unequal income distributions in the world. In 1973, the 20 per cent poorest part of the urban population accounted for only 3.7 per cent of expenditure, while the share of the richest 20 per cent was 55.4 per cent. The gap between rich and poor widened in the period between 1953 and 1978 (see table).

Iran: Distribution of government budget per selected expenditure by percentage, 1971–99						
Exenditures	**1971**	**1976**	**1986**	**1991**	**1996**	**1999**
Public Affairs	6.8	9.5	9.1	9.1	8.1	8.2
Defense	12.0	29	13.6	9.4	7.7	9.0
Social Affairs	11.7	19	43.8	49.5	44.3	46.7
Economic Affairs	22.3	23	17.2	21.7	20.1	19.4

Source: Messkoub, Mahmood. 2006. "Social policy in Iran in the twentieth century". *Iranian Studies*. vol. 39(2). pp. 227–52.

The huge gap between urban and rural areas and between the rich and poor was one of the most important reasons for the unpopularity of the Shah. Against this background, it is no surprise that the demands for equality, the eradication of poverty and the provision of welfare were central to the 1979 revolution. Ayatollah Khomeini and his allies tried to win popular support for their political movement by promising to deliver on these demands. Their Islamic ideology stressed the centrality of social justice and inequality. Khomeini declared: "We are for Islam, not for capitalism and feudalism, not for land-grabbers, but for the barefooted, for deprived classes. Islam originates from the masses, not from the rich. The martyrs of the Islamic Revolution were all members of the lower classes, peasants, industrial workers, and bazaar merchants and tradesmen." After the revolution, the Islamic Republic tried to build a base of support among the lower classes by providing social assistance, subsidies on essential products and welfare programmes, but without dismantling capitalism as an economic and social system.

Chapter three of the Constitution that was drafted in 1979 covers individual rights, including education and social welfare. Article 29 states that it is everybody's right to have social security regarding such matters as health, unemployment, and retirement that should be met through public finances as well as public and private co-operation. According to article 30, the state must provide free education up to and including the secondary level for everybody. However, these radical statements reflect the spirit of the revolution rather than actual practice under the Islamic Republic. Nonetheless, in the decades after the revolution there were very significant developments in welfare programmes, education, health and the reduction of social inequality and poverty.

After the revolution the share of Social Affairs in the total government budget increased and has remained the biggest

> ### Measuring inequality
>
> Social scientists use various indexes to measure the distribution of income, wealth or expenditures. One of them is the Gini-coefficient. Its value varies between 0 and 1. A value close to 0 indicates a more equal distribution
>
> Another regularly used method is to divide the population in ten even parts (deciles), with the poorest at the bottom and the richest at the top (10th), and measure their total income and expenditure.

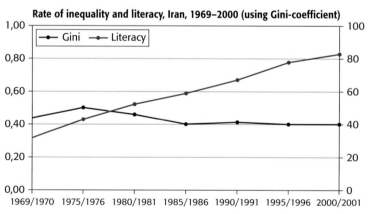

Rate of inequality and literacy, Iran, 1969–2000 (using Gini-coefficient)

Source: Central Bank of the Islamic Republic of Iran

Discussion point:

How do the different methods of interpreting data support the analysis of social trends?

component. It reached a high after the end of the war with Iraq and has hovered around 45 per cent since. Most of the Social Affairs budget was spent on education, health and social security. Because the total national income decreased and the population grew very fast after the revolution, social expenditure per capita was in fact lower than before the revolution. However, a much more equal distribution between both the rural and urban areas and social classes was achieved.

As the economy shrank in the 1980s, the government tried to limit the negative impact on the lower classes by providing subsidies and imposing price controls. Also one in every four Iranians, 12.4 million people, benefited from the social assistance of the Foundation of the Oppressed and Disabled, the Martyrs Foundation, the Imam Relief Committee and the 15 Khordad Foundation. Social insurance, including health, was expanded both in scope and coverage after the revolution. An important improvement was the introduction of a (limited) unemployment insurance. In 1995 the government passed the Universal Health Services law which offers health insurance to all, including for the first time those living in rural areas.

What was the impact of these policies on social inequality and the living conditions of the population? As the figures for the Gini-coefficient illustrate, inequality decreased after the revolution, but it has remained relatively stable at what is still a very high rate. A more impressive achievement was the reduction of poverty. Only about two to three per cent of the population lives below the international poverty line of one dollar a day, compared to 25 per cent in India. Measured by Iran's own poverty line of $2.4 per day per person in rural areas, $2.9 in urban areas, and $4 in Tehran, we find in 2002 poverty rates of 32 per cent in rural areas, ten per cent in urban areas and six per cent in Tehran. Poverty declined from the early 1990s, but still remains high despite the egalitarian promises of the government.

Iran has successfully reduced its infant mortality rate, which is a good indicator for the overall condition of healthcare, decreasing the rate by 54 per cent, from 52 per 1,000 live births in 1990 to 28 per 1,000 live births in 2000. The same pace of progress was visible in the field of education. The increase in the rate of literacy, from 47.5 per cent in 1976 to 84.6 per cent in 2006, is one important indicator.

The United Nations Development Programme has developed the Human Development Index which combines various indicators to measure the social conditions of societies. The Human Development Index of Iran has increased over time and now stands at a comparable level with Turkey. Not only has the access to healthcare and education improved, but more Iranians have also attained access to other essential services and household appliances. For instance, the percentage of urban households with a refrigerator increased from 36 per cent in 1977 to 98 per cent in 2004. The increase for rural households was even more dramatic, from 8 per cent to 92 per cent. In the same period, the portion of rural households with access to electricity rose from 16 per cent to 71 per cent.

Discussion point:

The social and economic policies of the Islam Republic are often referred to as populist. What does populism mean and why does it apply or not apply to Iran?

Table Human Development Index, 1980–2005	
Year	**HDI**
1980	0.559
1990	0.671
2000	0.735
2005	0.770

Source: http://hdrstats.undp.org/en/indicators/01.html.

Religious trends

The majority of Iranians, approximately 89 per cent, are Shi'a Muslims. Sunni Muslims make up eight per cent of the population; they are to be found among the Arab, Baluch, Turkmen and Kurdish minorities. The remaining three per cent of the population is made up of Zoroastrians, Christians, Jews and Baha'is. The Constitution of the Islamic Republic only recognizes Zoroastrians, Jews, and Christians as religious minorities who are guaranteed freedom to practice their religion. It has even guaranteed them political representation, reserving five of the 270 seats in Parliament for these religious minorities. However, members of religious minorities, in particular the Baha'is, have regularly reported discrimination, harassment and even imprisonment.

Because of its dominant influence in Iran society, we will focus here on the development of Shi'a thought in the last half of the 20th century. There has been indeed much development, change and variety in Shi'a thought, than is usually realized. For instance, the political rule of the clergy that was established after the revolution of 1979 is based on a relatively new interpretation of Islam, which was developed by Ayatollah Khomeini.

Until the 1960s, the Shi'a clergy in Iran followed what is called the "quietist" tradition. They believed that Ali and his 11 male descendants, known as the imams, were the rightful successor of Prophet Mohammad as the religious and political leaders of the Muslim community. The imams had resisted the caliphs as successors of the Prophet, whom they regarded as corrupt and oppressive rulers. However, their opposition was met by persecution and some of the imams died in battle. The sixth imam, Jafar al-Sadiq, then formulated the idea that the authority of the imams did not derive from political claims but from their descent from the Prophet and their "knowledge of the divine". He declared that the imams were the exclusive and infallible authoritative source in religious matters and divorced religious from political rule until such a time when God would decide otherwise. This separation was consolidated when clerics in 873 declared that the twelfth imam, Mahdi, had gone in to the Occultation, which meant that he was alive and present, yet hidden from view. He would return at the end of time "to fill the world with justice and equity as it is now filled with injustice and oppression". Until then, religious and political authority would be separated. In the meantime,

Discussion point: Clientelism

Clientelism refers to a form of social organization common in many developing countries, which is characterized by "patron–client" relationships. Relatively powerful and rich patrons promise to provide relatively powerless and poor clients with jobs, protection, infrastructure, and other benefits in exchange for votes and other forms of loyalty.

Does clientalism exists in Iran?

Sunni and Shi'a Muslims

Prophet Mohammad (570–632 CE) stood not only at the head of a religious community; he was also the leader of a political community. After his death, most of his adherents followed the rule of the first three caliphs, or successors, while a minority felt that succession belonged to Mohammad's cousin and son in law Ali. What started as a political disagreement developed into diverging religious ideas over time.

The group who recognized the caliphs without granting them religious powers beyond the protection and spreading of Islam came to be called Sunnis. The party ("Shi'a") of Ali believed that religious and political leadership should reside in the male descendants of Ali and developed various doctrines over time.

the highest Shi'a clerics who had studied jurisprudence would interpret the religious texts. Out of this idea emerged later the highest clerical position, *marja' e taqlid* (source of imitation). Every Shi'a Muslim is allowed to choose his/her *marja'e taqlid* and follow his interpretations and prescriptions in religious matters. In this dominant "quietist" tradition, the clerics would not aspire to political power, yet would have their say about this or that political decision.

For many centuries, the Shi'a clergy and the state lived in a peaceful symbiosis, legitimizing the authority of each other. The Shi'a clergy developed into a hierarchical structure, although it was often challenged by dissident currents that harked back to the oppositional tradition of Shi'asm. In the 1960s the conservative "quietist" tradition was seriously challenged by some clerics and lay Shi'a intellectuals who developed their own version of Islam as a political ideology.

In 1962 some prominent Shi'a clerics published a series of lectures that they had given on political and socio-economic issues. In the same year, Ayatollah Khomeini launched his opposition to the Shah and his White Revolution. Such an Islamic response was well-received because the repression of nationalists and leftists after the 1953 coup created a political vacuum while the regime of the Shah remained unpopular. Another significant development was the opening of a new Islamic centre in 1963, the Hosseiniyeh Ershad. It was here that the charismatic intellectual, Ali Shariati, held his lectures which blended Islam and socialism and criticized traditional clerics.

The new religious ideas that were developing in the 1960s were mainly a reaction to the dictatorship of the Shah, the foreign domination of Iran by the United States and the social desolation that was produced by modernization. Immigrants from the countryside that flooded big cities like Tehran felt socially and culturally uprooted. The lower classes, the traditional *bazaaris* and the clergy resented the increasing Westernization of Iran by the Shah, which they associated with politico-economic domination by the West. These grievances started to be increasingly voiced in religious rather than secular terms. This shift was symbolized by the writer Jalal Al-e Ahmad, who became the intellectual leader of a new generation of Iranian thinkers. Born in 1923 into a clerical family, he became a communist at twenty. Disappointed with the inability of the left to resist the Shah and imperialism, he turned to an interest in Islam when the clerics became leaders of opposition to the Shah in the early in 1960s. However, his motivation was political rather than religious. He coined the term *gharbzadegi*, "Westoxication" in a political booklet with the same title. He argued that Iranians had become alienated from their identity and therefore an easy prey for Western imperialism. By defining the causes of injustice in terms of culture rather than class, Jalal Al-e Ahmad paved the way for the popularity of political Islam among intellectuals.

The intellectual that developed and popularized a version of political Islam was the sociologist Ali Shariati. As a student in the early 1960s, he was inspired by the national liberation movement in Algeria and socialist ideas. On his return in Iran in 1964 he was arrested, but in the following years became immensely popular among students, intellectuals and professionals. Thousands visited his animated lectures at Hosseiniyeh Ershad or listened to the recordings which were widely distributed. He was eventually arrested, imprisoned and force to leave for England in 1977. Shortly after his arrival he died at the age of 44. His works had one main message: that the true essence of Shi'ism is revolution against all forms of oppression, be it feudalism, capitalism or imperialism. He also argued for a better treatment of women in society. The mission of Islam was not only to bring humanity closer to God, but also to create a classless society. He also criticized the conservative and apolitical ("quietist") clergy. He accused them of deceiving the masses and collaborating with the ruling class.

Shariati's works appealed to the educated youth, while Khomeini's message was much more directed to the clergy who passed it on to the masses that visited their mosques. Ruhollah Musavi Khomeini was born in 1902 into a religious family. He followed a theological study in the 1920's and early 1930's and attained the title of *marja' e taqild*. While he was critical of the monarchy, it seems that he adhered to the "quietist" tradition in the 1950's. His attitude started to change in the early 1960s, when the Shah launched the White Revolution. He denounced the reforms of the Shah, claiming that they spread *gharbzadegi* and turned Iran into a dumping ground for American products, favoured the cronies of the regime and failed to bring essential services to the villages. He accused the Shah of supporting the Israeli repression of the Palestinians. He was three times arrested in 1963. When a year later the Shah wanted to grant Americans immunity from Iranian law, Khomeini fiercely denounced him for selling the country to the United States. Khomeini's opposition to the Shah brought him national fame and a fearful Shah exiled him to Iraq in 1964.

Living in the holy city of Najaf, Khomeini continued his opposition to the Shah, distributing his message via cassette-tape recoordings. He also started to develop his own interpretation of Islam. He articulated his new ideas in a series of lectures to seminary students in 1970. These were published in his book *Velayat-e Faqih: Hokumat-e Islami* (The Jurist's Guardianship: Islamic Government). According to his new interpretation, the senior clerics who had specialized in interpreting Islamic law had the ultimate authority to rule the state. His novel reasoning ran along this line: God had sent the prophets and the imams to guide the community; they had left behind the Shari'a (Islamic law) to keep the community on the right path; in the absence of the twelfth imam, his deputies in the world, the senior clerics, became the guardians of the shari'a and responsible for its implementation. This interpretation had no precedence in the Koran or the teachings of the imams and in fact represented a break with orthodoxy.

Khomeini was aware of the fact that his doctrine of the *velayat-e faqih* was in fact controversial, not least among senior clerics. During the 1970s, he avoided mentioning this doctrine and instead tried to win popular support by attacking imperialism and social injustice. Being aware that he was competing with the left on this terrain, he used a different terminology to distinguish himself:

mostazafan (the oppressed), *taqut* (the ruling class), *estekbar-e jahani* (world arrogance, i.e. imperialism). It was only after the fall of the Shah that Khomeini pushed the principle of *velayat-e faqih* to the foreground and managed to enshrine it in the constitution of the Islamic Republic.

There were of course other voices among the clergy. Among the best-known ayatollahs playing a different role in the revolution and putting forward alternative ideas was Ayatollah Shariatmadari. He supported Khomeini against the Shah, but kept at a distance and remained faithful to his principle that the clergy should abstain from direct intervention in politics. After the revolution, he was pressured into silence and put under house arrest. There were also lay religious intellectuals and politicians who were critical about the rule of the clergy. One of them was Mehdi Bazargan, who became Prime Minister after the fall of the Shah. He represented the religious nationalists who wanted a liberal democracy in which religion would play an important role.

The opponents of *velyat-e faqigh* were driven out of politics in the early 1980's, but new religious ideas started to flourish in the 1990s. The most important development was the emergence of the "new religious thinkers". They had been adherents to political Islam themselves, but developed a critique in the 1990s that is either an outright rejection of the principle of *velayat-e faqih* or a strong modification. Probably the most influential thinker in the 1990s was the philosopher Abdolkarim Soroush. He has argued that religion can be interpreted according to time and place. He has also called for a "democratic religious government" in which the clergy do not have a privileged role. Some clerics have also gone in that direction, notably Mohammad Shabastari and Mohsen Kadivar. The former has argued that only general religious principles are eternal, while specific rules and practices must change. The latter has gone much further, criticizing the doctrine of *velayat-e faqih* itself.

Dissatisfaction with the official religious interpretation by conservative clerics has spread to the highest ranks of the clergy. One of the most important *marja' e taqlid*, Ayatollah Montazeri, has voiced his critique about the way *velayat-e faqih* functions. Another grand ayatollah, Yesef Sane'i, has issued relatively progressive religious decrees on women's rights, human rights and ethnic and sexual discrimination.

> *Velayat-e faqih* has no credible foundation in Islamic Jurisprudence … Refuting *velayat-e faqih* does not in any way undermine any of the Islamic teachings, requirements or obligations. … Democracy is a product of reason, and the fact that it has first been put to use in the West does not preclude its utility in other cultures—reason extends beyond geographic boundaries.
>
> Mohsen Kadivar, 2002

Abdolkarim Soroush (1945–)

Abdolkarim Soroush was born in Tehran in 1945. Having obtained a degree in chemistry, he continued his study in the fields of history and philosophy in London. After the 1979 revolution he returned to Iran and played a controversial role in "Islamizing" the universities. During the 1990s, Soroush gradually became more critical of the political role played by the clergy. He co-founded the monthly magazine Kiyan as a forum for religious intellectuals and espoused the ideas of pluralism, tolerance and democracy. In 1998 the government closed down Kiyan and Soroush lost his job at the Tehran University.

425

Religious ideas have not only changed among the clerics and intellectuals, but even more dramatically in the population at large. Secularization is the most salient development. A 1995 survey among Iranian youth showed the following results: over 85 per cent of young people spent their leisure time watching television, but only six per cent of them watched religious programmes; of the 58 per cent who read books, less than eight per cent were interested in religious literature. A staggering 80 per cent of Iranian youth were indifferent or opposed to the clergy, religious obligations and religious leadership, and 86 per cent of students refrained from saying their daily prayers. However, this did not mean that young people were abandoning Islam altogether. Most of them indicated to have strong "religious beliefs" and "religious feelings." What these figures show, is that the youth of Iran view religion increasingly as a private matter.

The arts: literature and cinema

The arts have always played a very central role in Iranian society, and have stood much closer to popular culture than is the case in most Western countries. There are few other countries in which poetry is so often and casually recited in daily life and classical music listened to in so many houses. As a result, social and political developments are not only very much reflected in the arts but they were themselves shaped and moulded by it. Resistance to tradition, the development of new forms and content, as well as a reaction to the contradictions of modernization, all play a role. Here the focus is on literature, film and music.

Literature

Modern Iranian literature developed at the turn of the 20th century around two main themes. There was a growing awareness among writers and intellectuals in general that their country was lagging behind in a rapidly changing world and that it was being dominated by foreign powers. They wanted to change the traditional social and political realities that held the population back and stifled its independence, seeing literature as a means of national awakening. This was bound with the second theme focused on the desire to make literature accessible to the masses, which revolutionized literary expression in both prose and poetry. Thus social and political engagement became a preoccupation of Iranian modern literature. The advocates of modernism were inspired by the changes and developments in Western literature, adapting aspects of it to their own cultural and social realities.

Nima Yoshij (1896–1960) started a new movement in Iranian literature that is referred to as "new poetry" , taking poetry out of the sterile rituals of the court and bringing it to the streets, using the

Discussion point: Fundamentalism

Arguing against traditionalists after the revolution, Ali Akbar Hashemi Rafsanjani—at that time a close collaborator of Khomeini—asked:

> *Where in Islamic history do you find parliament, president and cabinet ministers? In fact, 80 percent of what we now do has no precedent in Islamic history."*

 In what way does his statement contradict the view that political Islam in Iran is a form of "fundamentalism"?

Discussion point: Political Islam

1 Some have described political Islam as "nationalism in a religious disguise". Analyse the validity of this argument, using the Iranian experience.

2 Discuss the doctrine of *velayat-e faqih* and explain how it has been institutionalized, using the diagram of the political system in Iran on page 404.

natural speech of the people. After the 1940s, his ideas were adopted by a new generation of poets. Most notable among them were Ahmad Shamlou, Forough Farrokhzad, Mehdi Akhavan-e Sales and Nader Naderpour. With his mystical evocations of nature, Sohrab Sepehri occupies a special place among them.

Their works reflected their commitment to social change and the ebbs and flows of politics. Mehdi Akhavan-e Sales, for instance, became involved in the anti-government protests of the early 1950s and was briefly imprisoned after the fall of the nationalist government of Mossadegh.

Forrough Farrokhzad contributed to the development of a feminist literature, living the kind of free and varied life that was usually the privilege of men and dared to write about sexuality, to the shock of her contemporaries. The most famous contributor to the "new poem" was Ahmad Shamlou. Like many other writers of his generation, he inclined towards socialist politics and his poems were a testimony to his love of life and passion for justice. Like many other writers and intellectuals, he was confronted with harassment and censorship under the Shah and welcomed the 1979 revolution, but disillusionment was to follow.

> **Activity:**
> ## Poetic reflections
>
> Explain how the following poems reflect the conflict within modern Iranian society, and the mood of the times.
>
> ### It is Winter
>
> *They are not going to answer your greeting,*
> *their heads are in their jackets.*
> *Nobody is going to raise his head,*
> *to answer a question or to see a friend.*
> *The eyes cannot see beyond the feet,*
> *the road is dark and slick.*
> *If you stretch a friendly hand towards anybody,*
> *he hardly brings his hand out of his pocket,*
> *because the cold is so bitter.*
>
> Mehdi Akhavan-e Sales
>
> ### In this dead-end
>
> *They smell your mouth*
> *To find out if you have told someone:*
> *I love you!*
> *They smell your heart!*
> *Such a strange time it is, my dear …*
>
> Ahmad Shamlou, July 1979

Important changes occurred in prose as well, which was traditionally a less developed form. Important contributions in this field were made by Sadeq Hedayat, Jalal Al-e Ahmad and Bozorg Alavi, who had close ties to the communist Tudeh party. Alavi, one of the party founders, had a considerable influence on literature and literary criticism of the 1960s and 1970s. As with the work of Hedayat, Alavi's writings had a strong psychological perspective. The smothering atmosphere of *Her Eyes* (1952), for instance, depicts the social conditions under the dictatorship of Reza Shah and the personal agonies of leftist activists. Samad Behrangi was another influential writer. His encounters as a school teacher with rural life, poverty and Azeri folk culture very much shaped his writings until his mysterious death in 1968. Well known is also the social realism of Mahmoud Dawlatabadi who in 1978–84 wrote *Kalidar* in 10 parts, depicting the lives of nomads in the plains of his native region in north-eastern Iran.

From the 1960s onwards, many more women writers were active, including Simin Daneshvar, made famous by her novel *A Persian Requiem* (1969) about the disruption of traditional society by foreign occupation during the Second World War. Others landmarks included Shahrnoush Parsipour's novella *Women Without Men* (1989), using the narrative techniques of **magic realism**. In the aftermath of the 1979 revolution, poetry declined both in terms of volume and of reception. Politically committed leftist poets like Ahmad Shamlu and Mehdi Akhavan Sales, who had inspired social change among students and ordinary people prior

> **Magic realism** The narrative technique of magic realism was popular among Latin American authors such as Gabriel García Márquez.

to the revolution, lost their motivation. Others, such as Said Soltanpur, lost their lives or went into exile. Some, like the poet Simin Behbahani, remained very productive and developed new approaches. Qazaleh Alizadeh, Monirou Ravanipour, Fariba Vafi, Zoya Pirzad, Lili Farhadpour, Sepideh Shamlou, and Mahsa Moheb-Ali are among the many women novelists who started writing from the 1990s onward.

> **We are writers!**
>
> *We are writers. By this we mean that we write our feelings, imagination, thoughts and scholarship in various forms and publish them. It is our natural, social and civil right to see that our writing—be it poetry or fiction, drama or filmscript, research or criticism, or the translation of works written by other writers of the world-reach the public in a free and unhampered manner. It is not within the capacity of any person or organization to create obstacles for the publication of these works, under whatever pretext these may be.*
>
> Declaration of 134 writers, 1994

The last decade of the 20th century witnessed a rise in writing and interest in short stories, novels, and drama after the initial lull following the revolution. However, the new literary endeavors were seriously restricted by censorship and intimidation. These restrictions had the reverse effect of creating a new sense of social and political commitment among Iranian writers, reflected in the Declaration of 134 writers in1994.

Film

Iran's productive art-house cinema has gained international recognition, with many films winning awards at prestigious film festivals. This is mainly an achievement of the post-revolutionary decades. Like literature, cinema reflected Iran's social and political developments. The economic growth of the 1960s and 1970s was reflected in an outpouring of popular films, most of them B movies made to compete with Indian Bollywood. Some had a political undertone. *Qarun's Treasure* (Dir. Siamak Yasami, 1965), for instance, contained the message that the White Revolution had reconciled the Shah and the people, who had collided in 1953 and again in 1963. The mood changed as it became increasingly clear that the White Revolution did not deliver on its promises. Before the revolution, few critical films were produced that became popular among the educated population. *Cow* (Dir. Dariush Mehrjui, 1963) was based on a short story by the radical playwright Ghulam-Hussein Saedi. It depicted rural poverty. *Tangsir* (Dir. Amir Naderi, 1973) depicted the struggle of a dispossessed peasant against the local rulers, including clerics, money lenders and government officials.

During the revolutionary events of 1979–82, Iranian and foreign films were banned. After the ban was lifted, the government imposed strict limitations, giving no permits to films that were believed to violate Islamic ethics. Women were prohibited to play roles that were used to arouse sexual desire and had to be dressed "Islamically." Most films that were produced in the 1980s had a propagandist aim. They were often about the war with Iraq and the defence of the Islamic Republic against "external" and

Activity:
Film criticism

According to film critic Richard Tapper:

> *The treatment of women and children in Iranian films has drawn special attention for good but opposing reasons, both related to censorship. Women—veiled, commonly exoticised and subject to tight constraints on their behavior—have suffered restrictions both before and behind the camera, while boys and girls appear both as surrogate adults and in remarkably realistic roles of their own.*

Test out this viewpoint by writing a critical analysis of one of the following films:

Where Is My Friend's House? (Dir. Abbas Kiarostami, 1987)

The Apple (1998) (Dir. Samira Makhmalbaf, 1998)

"internal" enemies. The first movies that could be counted as art cinema were Naderi's *The Runner* (1986), Mehrjui's *The Tenants* (1986) and Bahram Beyza'i's *Bashu, The Little Stranger* (1988).

At this stage, Iranian films began to appear at international film festivals. Abbas Kiarostami's film became very popular among the general public and critics in the West. They include *Where Is the Friend's House?* (1987), *Through the Olive Trees* (1994) and *The Taste of Cherry* (1997). Also well-known is Mohsen Makhmalbaf, who started as a committed Islamist but later changed his views and made very successful films. These include: *The Cyclist* (1989) and *Gabbeh* (1995). Many Iranian movies fall into the category of new social criticism. Jafar Panahi's *Crimson Gold* (2003) for instance is an indictment of the class divide in Iranian society, despite the talk of social justice.

There are a number of successful women directors, including Tahmineh Milani, renowned for provocative films such as *Two Women* (1999), Marzieh Meshkini who directed the trilogy *The Day I Became a Woman*, set in the Persian Gulf island of Qeshm with its African-Iranian inhabitants, and Samira Makhmalbaf whose films include *The Apple* (1998) based on a true story of young girls who were literally never allowed outside the house, and *Blackboards* (1999) which won the jury prize at Cannes.

Iranian films, 1950–2000		
Film	**Director**	**Year**
Qarun's Treasure	Siamak Yasami	1965
Cow	Dariush Mehrjui	1969
Tangsir	Amir Naderi	1973
The Runner	Amir Naderi	1986
Bashu, The Little Stranger	Dariush Mehrju'i	1988
Through the Olive Trees	Abbas Kiarostami	1994
A Moment of Innocence	Mohsen Makhmalbaf	1995
The Apple	Samira Makhmalbaf	1998
Two Women	Tahmineh Milani	1999
The Day I Became a Woman	Marzieh Meshkini	2000

Migration and the Iranian diaspora

Because of its geographical position—the site of the famous Silk Road that once crossed it—Iran has always encountered flows of people and cultures. This is in fact reflected in the mosaic of different ethnic groups that make up its population (see chapter ?). Although emigration and immigration have always been part of the social reality in Iran, the events preceding and following the 1979 revolution created the biggest movement of people across Iranian borders for centuries. While millions of Iranians moved out of the country, creating a large diaspora and one of the biggest rates of **brain drain** in the world, millions of Afghani and Iraqi refugees settled in Iran, creating one of the biggest communities of refugees. Iran has also experienced a high rate of internal migration from rural to urban areas, resulting in one of the steepest urbanization rates in the world.

Brain drain The emigration of educated individuals with technical skills or knowledge. It is also called human capital flight, since emigrants take away with them the value of the educational training that the government provided.

Immigration

Although Iran is well-known for its emigration, it has frequently topped the list of refugee-hosting countries. In 1991, the refugee population exceeded four million, consisting of approximately three million Afghan refugees and 1.2 million Iraqis. Iranian officials estimated that there were some 2.57 million immigrants in Iran in

2002, of which more than 90 per cent (or 2.3 million) were Afghans. Iran also hosts some 30,000 refugees of various nationalities, including Tajiks, Bosnians, Azeris, Eritreans, Somalis, Bangladeshis, and Pakistanis.

The migration of Afghan workers, pilgrims and merchants in Iran has a long history, but in the 1980s Afghans fled their country in their millions after the Soviet invasion of 1979. In this period, Iran adopted an open policy towards Afghan refugees who were granted status. In theory, Afghan refugees were granted social benefits, such as access to free education, health services, adult literacy training, and subsidies on basic essentials. In addition, refugees were permitted to work in one of 16 designated, menial occupations. In reality most Afghan refugees lived in poverty and were often confronted with discrimination. The fact that Western countries refused to give assistance to Iran, which claimed that the number of refugees exceeded its own capabilities, worsened the situation. According to Iranian estimates, expenditures on all refugees totaled $20 billion from 1979 to 1995. After the withdrawal of Soviet troops in the early 1990s from Afghanistan, the Iranian government changed its policy in regards to the repatriation of Afghan refugees.

The other large group of refugees in Iran was made up of Iraqis who fled persecution under Saddam Hussein, they were mainly Shi'as or Kurds. Although the first Iraqi refugees arrived in the 1970s, after Saddam Hussein crushed a Kurdish rebellion, the largest number arrived in Iran in the 1980s. After Saddam Hussein attacked Halabja with chemical weapons in 1988, around 700,000 Iraqis fled to Iran. Another mass movement of 1.3 million Iraqis followed at the end of the 1991 Gulf War, when Saddam Hussein launched a crackdown on the Shi'a rebellion in southern Iraq. The vast majority of Iraqi refugees returned to their country over time. The UNHCR estimated that there were over 200,000 Iraqi refugees in Iran in 2003, composing over half of the entire Iraqi refugee population in the world.

Emigration

The pattern of Iranian emigration since the 1950s shows three waves, which have followed each other with some overlap. The first wave of emigration started in the 1950s and lasted until the 1979 revolution. The economic growth in this period allowed some middle and upper class families to send their children abroad for higher education. In the 1977–78 academic year, about 100,000 Iranians were studying abroad, more than a third of them in the United States; the rest were mainly in the United Kingdom, West Germany, France, Austria, and Italy. At that time, Iranian students formed the largest community of foreign students in the USA. Although some of them returned to Iran, many stayed abroad after the revolution and were joined by their relatives. On the outbreak of the revolution the close associates of the monarch such as government officials and military personnel left Iran. Also some members of religious minorities, especially Bahai's and Jews, fled the country.

The second wave of emigration started after the revolution in the early 1980s. Members and activists of socialist and liberal organizations fled Iran after Ayatollah Khomeini and supporters started a clampdown on the opposition. This group of refugees was joined by those who fled military service and the devastating consequences of the Iran–Iraq war as well as those who wanted to escape the suffocating social restrictions.

At this time the brain drain accelerated. This is illustrated by the dramatic decrease of the number of higher education professors, from 16,222 in 1980 to 9,042 two years later. It is estimated that one out of three physicians and dentists left the country, followed by many other professionals, like journalists, lawyers, engineers and managers.

The third wave of emigration started from the mid 1990s. Adding to the brain drain, a new generation of educated and skilled young people went abroad. Another group consisted of working class migrants who left Iran for economic reasons. In the year 2000 alone, more than 34,000 Iranians applied for refugee status, the highest rate since 1986. The countries hosting the largest populations of Iranian refugees are Germany, the United States, Iraq, the United Kingdom, the Netherlands and Canada.

The size of the Iranian diaspora is estimated to be between two to four million people. Like any other diaspora, it forms an extremely heterogeneous group with respect to ethnicity, language, religious and political affiliations, social status, and timing and motivation for departure. As an example of Iranian influence on host countries, according to official data from 2000, Americans of Iranian ancestry were among the most highly educated people in the United States. More than one in four Iranian Americans over the age of 25 hold a graduate degree or above, the highest rate among 67 ethnic groups, according to the Iranian Studies Group. In addition, their per capita average income is 50 per cent higher than that of the population overall. This mainly reflects the background of the Iranian immigrants who settled in the USA.

Members of the global diaspora include artists such as Sherin Neshat and Marjane Satrapi whose graphic novel and animated film, *Persepolis*
(Dir. Marjana Satrapi and Vincent Parronnaud, 2007), presents a touching and funny account of her adventures during the 1979 revolution and her subsequent emigration to France. In many ways it captures the collective experience of Iranians who fled their country after the revolution, and in particular the struggles faced by its young people.

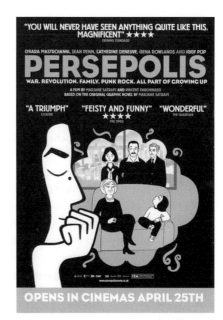

Allegiance with Wakefulness, 1994, photograph by Shirin Neshat.

Shirin Neshat (1957–)

Just before the revolution, Shirin Neshat left Iran for the US to study art. Although she has lived and worked in New York most of her adult life, her artwork explores the position of women in Iran and elaborates on the ideas of loss, meaning and memory. Her photographs and videos which have been exhibited in many major cities of the world have made her one of the most famous members of the Iranian diaspora.

Exam practice and further resources

Sample questions

1 Examine the extent of social change with regard to class since the Second World War.
2 How far would you agree that the role and importance of religion in society has declined since 1945?
3 "There has been a revolution in the film industry since the Second World War." Discuss in relationship to ONE country.
4 Assess the impact of urbanisation on any ONE country you have studied.
5 Analyse the consequences of industrial change in one 50-year period.

For this section, students should have a detailed knowledge of ONE country. It is perfectly legitimate to choose material from either the 19th or the 20th centuries.

Recommended further reading

United Kingdom:

Carnevali, Francesca and Strange, Julie-Marie.(eds). 2007. *20th Century Britain: Economic, Cultural and Social Change*. London, UK. Pearson Education.

Hebdige, Dick. 1979. *Subculture: The Meaning of Style*. London, UK. Methuen.

Marwick, Arthur. 1990. *British Society Since 1945*. London, UK. Penguin.

Thompson, F.M.L.(ed.). 1990. *The Cambridge Social History of Britain, 1750–1950*. vol. 3. Cambridge, UK. Cambridge University Press.

Iran:

Ervand, Abrahamian. 2008. *A History of Modern Iran*. Cambridge, UK. Cambridge University Press,

Axworthy, Michael. 2008. *Iran: Empire of the Mind*, London, UK. Penguin.

Keddie, Nikki, R. 2003. *Modern Iran. Roots and Results of the Revolution*. New Haven, USA; London, UK. Yale University Press.

Nomani, Farhad and Behdad, Sohrab. 2006. *Class and Labor in Iran. Did the Revolution Matter?* Syracuse, USA. Syracuse University Press.

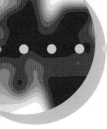

Index